THE MANUAL
OF BRITISH RURAL SPORTS

THE PURSUIT OF WILD ANIMALS FOR SPORT

COMPRISING

SHOOTING, HUNTING COURSING & FISHING

THE MANUAL
OF BRITISH RURAL SPORTS

THE PURSUIT OF WILD ANIMALS FOR SPORT

COMPRISING
SHOOTING, HUNTING
COURSING & FISHING

COMPILED BY
DR JOHN HENRY WALSH
FOREWORD BY
SIR JOHN SCOTT

The
History
Press

First published, 1856
This edition, 2008

The History Press Ltd
The Mill, Brimscombe Port
Stroud, Gloucestershire, GL5 2QG
www.thehistorypress.co.uk

British Library Cataloguing in Publication Data.
A catalogue record for this book is available from the British Library.

ISBN 978 0 7524 4761 2

Typesetting and origination by The History Press Ltd.
Printed in Great Britain

Contents

Book II – HUNTING

Book III – COURSING

Book IV – FISHIING

Foreword
by Sir John Scott

I am delighted to have been asked to write the foreword for the new edition of *The Pursuit of Wild Animals for Sport*. The author, Dr John Henry Walsh FRCS, was a luminary of the early Victorian sporting world and is one of my literary heroes.

Born in 1810, the year Tom Cribb beat Tom Molyneaux in a bare-knuckle prize fight lasting forty rounds, John Henry Walsh grew up in the tail end of an era that produced sportsmen such as Colonel Hawker, 'Mad Jack' Mytton, Squire Osbaldeston, Lord Henry Bentinck, Colonel Thornton, Peter Beckford, Hugo Meynell and the sporting authors Surtees and Apperley (Nimrod). Although Walsh qualified as a Fellow of the Royal College of Surgeons in 1844 and practiced for some years in Worcester, his first love was field sports. He hunted, kept greyhounds and entered them at match coursing meetings, broke his own pointing and setting dogs, and was a keen falconer and shot, despite having lost a considerable part of his left hand when the barrel of his shotgun burst at the fore end.

In 1852, he abandoned surgery to pursue a career as a sporting journalist, contributing articles to the magazine, *Bell's Life*, under the pseudonym 'Stonehenge'. He brought out his first book in 1853, *The Greyhound, on the Art of Breeding, Rearing and Training Greyhounds for Public Running, their Diseases and Treatment*. From 1857 until 1888, he was editor of *The Field* magazine and during that period instituted a series of gun trials which largely contributed to the development of the breech-loading shotgun, the modern rifle, nitro-compound cartridge manufacture and improvements to the Birmingham Proof House. He was a founder member of the National Coursing Club (1858) and the All England Lawn Tennis Club (1868). A committee member of the Kennel Club and as editor of *The Field*, actively involved in the initiation and promotion of gun dog field trials. He was a prolific author of books across the spectrum of field sports and conversely, on domestic management, housekeeping and health and fitness, as well as editing a number of cookery books. Dr Walsh died in 1888.

The Pursuit of Wild Animals for Sport, published in 1856, was the second book Dr Walsh wrote and was probably his most successful, running to sixteen editions up to 1886. It is a priceless and encyclopaedic record of every aspect of hunting, shooting, coursing and fishing at a transitional period in the long history of field sports, written in an enviably easy and readable style. The revised Game Laws, which allowed a landlord to let his sporting rights, and the expansion of the railways had made field sports more popular and available to a wide cross-section of society than at any other time. Advances in gun-making technology were about to revolutionise shooting and, prophetically, Walsh was already warning that the quality of sport should not be measured by the weight of the bag. Coursing and hunting were in the heyday of their popularity. The great game fish rivers, grouse moors and deer forests of Scotland were now reachable in hours where previously the same journey had taken days. Britain was relatively wealthy in the 1850s and communications made field sports of every kind accessible to all walks of life, from the wildfowler to the Meltonian, the game shot, fisherman or long dog enthusiast.

The Pursuit of Wild Animals for Sport is a fascinating book of enormous historical importance, which will be compulsive reading to anyone with an interest in natural history and the sporting heritage of Britain.

Introduction

The term 'Rural Sports' usually comprehends those outdoor amusements in which man either pursues wild animals for sport, or competes with an antagonist in racing, by means of the horse, the boat, or indulges in manly games of skill. The love of sport appears to be inherent in the breast of man, for since the earliest ages we have records of the chase; and whether in the forests of America, or the squalid streets of the manufacturing towns, the same taste is displayed, though, necessarily, shown in different ways. Thus while, in days of yore, the native American employed nearly his whole life in the pursuit of deer, the buffalo, or the bear the cotton-spinner of Manchester can only spare time for an occasional rabbit-course, or perhaps a boat race, or pedestrian march; nevertheless, the desire is equally implanted in each, and is peculiarly strong among the natives of the British Isles. Differing in all respects, as do the English, Scottish and Irish, they yet seem all to unite on this common ground, and to enjoy with equal zest the sports of the field. There is a bond of union nothing seems able to break, viz., and their mutual love of field sports.

No one can doubt for an instant the utility and importance of outdoor amusements in promoting health, and this alone ought to be sufficient to cause their encouragement. In an age like the present, when in the struggle for precedence in the senate, the bar, or the haunts of commerce, time is considered as of equal value with money, it can scarcely be wondered at, that many of the competitors in the race lose health, both of body and mind. Nothing enfeebles and lowers the bodily and mental tone more than an entire giving up of all the energies to one single pursuit; the overworked lawyer or merchant, however, has only to bestow an occasional day upon any one of the various sports within his reach, and he speedily recovers himself, and instead of losing way in the course which he is pursuing, he is enabled to do more than make up the lost time which his absence has occasioned, by the increased vigour that his change of scene and occupation have given him. This is so well understood in London, that many of our first merchants make a regular practice of devoting one or two days a week to some kind of outdoor amusement. Some take to hunting, others to shooting; others, again, to coursing, or to farming on the small scale; and all of these act upon the principle of unbending the bow to enable it to regain its spring, and all are attended with the same happy result in various degrees. But the health of the individual is not the only advantage aimed at and obtained by the promotion of field sports; and this has lately been exemplified in a very remarkable manner at Alma, Inkermann, Balaklava and Sevastopol. Where would our officers and men have been in those dreadful fields of carnage but for the habits of daring and endurance which the manly sports of Britain have instilled into their minds immemorial? To those who have seen the perils of the steeplechase, the hunting field, or, I may I say, the modern cricket field – ardently sought for and encountered by the youth of this country without flinching – it can be no wonder that they have excited the admiration of their foes as well as their friends in the Crimea. It may appear absurd to compare together such apparently widely different degrees of danger, but when the stimulus to each is taken into account the difference is not so great. We have all seen many bold but bad riders undertake to pilot a horse in a steeplechase with the almost certain risk of being ridden over during its course; and, again, when in cricket fast bowling was becoming the fashion, and before the various guards were introduced , how small was the chance of escaping serious injury in a long innings; for if bones were not broken, important organs were often seriously bruised and injured; and yet there was no flinching, until the repeated occurrence of permanent injuries necessitated the use of leg and body-pads. Thus it will be manifest that these amusements not only improve the health of the people individually, but collectively they enable them, by giving vigour, courage and power of endurance – or, in other words, 'pluck' – to withstand, as a nation, the encroachments of their neighbour. In fact they make good healthy subjects for peace or war.

But it has often been said that field sports injure the moral and religious habits of the people, and this is even more important to consider than the question regarding their effect upon the body. There is no doubt in my mind that however they may benefit the bodily and mental powers, yet if they can be clearly be shown to be opposed to religion and they are unworthy of the support of right-thinking man. Now, in considering this important subject, it is right to inquire – first whether they are opposed to the laws of God, or supported by them; secondly, whether they are likewise opposed to or supported by the laws of nature; and thirdly, whether, as far as we can judge by human reason, they do really aid or oppose the cause of law and order. With regard to the law of God, there can be no doubt, from many examples in the Old Testament, that the chase was permitted; and though we have no reason to conclude that it was for the purpose of sport, yet we are distinctly told that all beasts are given up to the use of man. It is clear, therefore, that if it can be established that field sports are not only pleasurable but also useful to the people indulging in them, then the purpose of the Almighty is fulfilled, and the life of the animal pursued has not been wantonly sacrificed. But in this view of the case it is all-important that the end and object should be a good one; there is a difference between 'cock-shying' (in which a poor cock is tied to a stake for the purpose of allowing a lot of lubberly boys to try their skill in throwing at him) and fox-hunting, in which two or three hundred men and horses and twenty-five couple of hounds are all fully engaged in foiling the artful dodges of that wily animal; and this only under certain recognised conditions, which give the fox a clear chance of escape. Still, all pursuit of game merely for sport has an element of cruelty attending it; and it should always be remembered that this stain must be subdued, and, if possible washed out by the many counterbalancing advantages. At all events, even though it may be granted that the pursuit of game as sport is not distinctly enjoined, or even mentioned, in Holy Writ, it may also be admitted that there is no command against it. In the early ages of mankind, as in the case of Esau, venison was sought for as food, and in that capacity it was ordered to be used; but in this country no game could or would be reared solely for food, except in very small quantities perhaps for the higher and luxurious classes of society. Few pheasants cost less than 30s a brace; and it is said, though I scarcely think with truth, that three hares eat as much as a sheep. Rabbits, we know, destroy three times as much as they eat; and the only harmless kind of game, in point of cost, is the partridge; for its congener, the grouse, is costly enough, from requiring extensive moors for its breeding and rearing, undisturbed by the presence of man to any great extent.

In the next place, let us examine into the question by the laws of nature, where the case is clearer, since all analogy tells us that we are right in preying upon our inferiors. The tiger and all the cat kind not only catch and eat their prey, but they play with it and torment it; I do not say that this justifies us in doing the like, but that nature has evidently implanted in them a love of sport, and of a most cruel order apparently. Again, many animals will only devour their prey while yet warm, and refuse to eat it when cold, or even when taken by another of their own kind. Nothing is more astonishing to the lover of nature, and the admirer of her laws, than the series of destructions and restorations which are constantly going on. The grass preys upon the ingredients of the soil, raising its materials from the inorganic condition of the mineral world to that much more complicated one of the vegetable kingdom. Next, the grass is seized by the graminivorous animal, and is digested in his complicated stomach, becoming converted into flesh; and this flesh again is torn and mangled by the carnivorous quadruped or bird, after hunting it down; or is devoured, if killed by other means, by some one of the many natural scavengers of creation in the shape of the vulture, the hyena, or the eel. But in either case the results of the digestion are again returned to the earth, to form the first step in the eternal round of assimilation, by again supplying food for some of the grasses. Thus, all nature teems with examples of one class or species preying upon a lower one; and even in many cases, as in that of parasites, an inferior class preying upon another much higher in the scale of creation.

The third inquiry, namely, whether, as far as we can judge by human reason, field sports do really aid or oppose the cause of law and order, is a much more complicated one, and for its correct elucidation the science of statistics must be carefully studied. On the one hand, by the indulgence of sport, we have the benefits afforded to the health of the people which we have seen that they give; we have also general contentment and happiness increased by a knowledge that the feelings and wishes of the masses are consulted by their lawgivers; and we have, in addition, the full persuasion that by preventing the indulgence in field sports resort would be had, in most cases, to the public house, for the purpose of relieving that careworn feeling which incessant work inevitably causes. The old adage, 'All work and no play makes Jack a dull boy,' is strictly true; and therefore it becomes a question what kind of play is best fitted to produce the good effect which is required. One thing is certain, that the field sports of Great Britain have been, and are still, the means of, and the cloak for, untold abuses; but, it may be answered, that this may be said of everything under the sun, however useful or beneficial it may really be; and therefore, to avoid this imputation, let us all take special care to purge away the foul abuses, and, as far as in us lies, to retain only what is true to nature, and to nature's God. If this purpose is rigidly adhered to, and the vicious grafts upon sport are carefully pruned away, then we may hope to obtain the full benefit of the scheme propounded to us by nature, unalloyed by the base additions made by the vice of man. There can be no reason why hunting or shooting should not be carried on without any drawback except the one to which I have already alluded, viz., the inherent cruelty attending upon them. Coursing, also, need have no alloy; and even racing, which, as now conducted, is perhaps more injurious to the morals than useful to the warlike purposes of the nation, may be purged of all its bad and vicious tendencies. Then, if this is possible, why should it not be done? Let our legislators look well to this, for much of our future well-being, as a people, depends upon this question. Man will have amusement of some kind, and for his bodily and mental health, in the present state of society, that amusement must be out of doors. Much has been done to destroy the evil agencies at work among us; 'the Betting-houses Act', the alteration of game laws, etc., have been useful in their several ways, but much yet remains to be done. Let it be remembered, that sport should be used and not abused, and let not the abuse of it be urged against its use. Then may we hope to see the full amount of good developed, of which this element in our social life is capable; and then may the sportsman, who is also the legislator, lie down after his day's sport with a full conviction that he has had a share in one of those institutions of his country, of which we may well be proud.

The Pursuit of Wild Animals of Sport comprehends shooting, hunting, coursing and fishing. In this enumeration, pugilism, cock-fighting, bull and badger-baiting are omitted, as being contrary to the laws of the land; and, as of 1861, nothing is inserted which can injure the morals, or destroy that gentlemanly feeling which it should be the object of every true sportsman to encourage, a prescient thought for the rural sports community in 2008.

MANUAL

OF

BRITISH RURAL SPORTS.

PART I.

THE PURSUIT OF WILD ANIMALS FOR SPORT.

BOOK I.—SHOOTING.

CHAP. I.

PRESERVATION OF GAME.

SECT. 1.—SELECTION OF PRESERVE.

1. In all the varieties of the chase, whether hunting, shooting, coursing, or fishing, the first thing to be provided is, that there shall be something to pursue. Mrs. Glasse's very sensible first precept for roasting a hare is, "first catch your hare;" and so all sportsmen should remember, that before they can have sport, they must have game in existence, though not in their larder. Nothing is so galling, even to the proverbially patient angler, as to be without a "nibble;" and the blank day to the fox-hunter is the *summum malum.* The former is comparatively well satisfied if he hooks a fish or two, although he may fail to land them; and the latter would much prefer to sit on his horse, and even hear the hounds find their fox, and go away without him on the other side of a large wood, rather than go home with the sad words, blank! blank!! blank!!! constantly in his ears. If the fish or fox is lost, it may be from accident or a bad scenting day, or some other mischance; but if not found, there is less hope for an improvement on the next occasion. But it is to the shooter that these observations more especially apply, since he is more particularly dependent upon the preservation of game for the quality of his sport. To walk all day, and see nothing, is still more disheartening than to whip the waters without a rise. A brace of hares, or a single fox, will serve for the amusement of a large field of fox-hunters or thistle-whippers; but the pheasant, grouse, or partridge-shooter, is more voracious, and the quality of his sport

is too often measured by the weight of the game-bag. I confess, that in my humble opinion, this thirst for blood, or, as the phrenologist would say, destructiveness, is destructive often of true sport. The bag is considered too much; and to get game (in a sportsman-like manner if possible, but at all events to get it) is too often the desire of the gentlemen in shooting costume; still, such is now the prevailing taste, and if you wish to gratify your friends with a day's shooting, your only certain plan of affording them that gratification is to show them plenty of game.

2. WHEN A CHOICE IS TO BE MADE OF A MOOR or enclosed manor, it is highly desirable that every pains should be taken to see that it is suited for the purpose for which it is to be rented. If the intending tenant is a young sportsman, he should be very careful not to be taken in, and he had better consult some more experienced friend, upon whose judgment he can rely. The frauds which are yearly committed upon the young sportsman on the moors, as well as in the stubbles and coverts of England, are enough to make him cautious before engaging a beat. There are only two seasons of the year in which it is possible to ascertain the amount of game which a preserve contains—first, during the shooting season, by actual experience; and secondly, during the pairing season, when dogs may be allowed to hunt the ground with impunity. During the former of these times many would think that the sportsman could scarcely be taken in, as he sees what is left after his sport, and can judge for himself; but this is a great mistake, as many have found to their cost. To guard against it, he should bargain, if he

B

agrees to take the ground, that it should be at *once* given up to him, for I have known a wonderful difference between the head of game, on an extensive beat, in the first, and that in the last week of September. Keepers, we all know, *can* poach if they like, and if they are not to be retained by their new masters, it is to be expected, that many of them will take advantage of the knowledge acquired during their previous term of office. Wherever, therefore, you have decided upon taking a manor, make up your mind either to retain the keeper, if you think him trustworthy, or to displace him at once, if otherwise, although you are certain even then of losing a considerable quantity of game. It is evident that a strange man cannot compete with one who knows all the haunts of the game; and, therefore, the old hand has the opportunity of robbing you if he likes,—or if he does not do so directly, he can indirectly, through some of those half-poachers, half-keepers, with whom so many are in league. But the best time to make choice of a moor or partridge manor, or, more particularly, of an extensive covert, is in the month of February or March. At this time you may, by a little perseverance, have ocular demonstration of nearly every head of winged game on the beat. By taking out a brace of strong and fast pointers or setters, you may easily beat over a couple of thousand acres of arable land, or double that quantity of moor land, and you will thereby find at least three-fourths of the birds. In this proceeding you must take care not to let the keeper palm off the same birds upon you two or three times over, which he may easily do, if you are not on your guard. To avoid this trick, observe the line which the birds that have been put up take, and instead of following that line, which the keeper will most probably try to induce you to do, just keep to the right or left of it. In beating, also, go straight a-head, if the manor is extensive, and do not follow the same plan as if you were shooting. Take one field after another in straight line; and though you will not thereby see so much game as you otherwise would, you will, at all events, avoid the mistake of fancying that there are 150 brace instead of 50. With regard to pheasants, you may always be shown these birds at feeding time, as the keepers know where to find them as well as barn-door fowl. If, therefore, they are not shown, depend upon it, *if it is the interest of the keeper to show them*, that they are not in existence. As to the number of hares and rabbits, you may generally make a pretty good guess at them by the state of the runs and meuses. If these are numerous and well used, there is sure to be plenty of fur; or at all events

there has been till very recently. The spring months are also the only ones in which vermin can be successfully trapped, and therefore you have every reason for taking your moor or manor at that time of the year.

3. In all CONTRACTS FOR TAKING MANORS, the agreement ought to be in writing, and properly executed on a stamped paper. The following form has been found to answer all the purposes required, and is more simple than most of those in general use:—MEMORANDUM of an agreement made this day between A. B. of ——, and C. D. of ——; the said A. B. agrees to let the said C. D. (without power of sub-letting or assigning) the whole of the game on the lands, farms, or moors in the parish of ——, from this present date to the —— of ——; that is to say, that he, the said C. D., shall have full power by himself, or others having his authority, to kill game over the above-named lands, during all lawful times and seasons. And in consideration of the same permission of A. B., the said C. D. agrees to pay the sum of —— on the 25th day of January in each year; but the first payment to be made at the signing of these presents. And the said C. D. further agrees that he will preserve the game in a fair and proper manner, and that he will not destroy, in the last year of his tenancy, more than he has done, or ought to have done, in the previous ones. And, in the event of any difference of opinion, it is further agreed by and between the parties to these presents, that the same shall be referred to the arbitration of some two parties, one to be chosen by each, with power to choose an umpire, if necessary, whose decision shall be final. In witness whereof we do hereby sign our names, in the presence of E. T., A. B., C. D. Dated this 25th day of March, 1855.

SECT. 2.—DUTIES OF GAMEKEEPER.

4. Gamekeepers, to be really useful, should be almost more than mortal; a perfect keeper should be handy, honest, clever, and brave; he should be civil, yet not too good-natured; and, above all, he should *be fond of his business*. Without this last qualification, it is hopeless to expect a good head of game; and, even if you do obtain this point, yet you will have your gun, or perhaps your dogs, spoiled from some mis-management on his part. When it is remembered that to do his duty a keeper must be out in all weathers, and at all hours—that he must run all risks in detecting the manœuvres of his opponents, and in opposing them when detected—and that, in addition, he has to be out early and late for the purpose of trapping and feeding—it will be seen that his task is no sinecure. A gamekeeper also

should have a good knowledge of the laws affecting game, or he will be constantly leading his master into scrapes. With regard to the numbers required, it is scarcely possible to give anything like a direction, since they must vary according to the nature of the ground, and the number of poachers infesting it. In some localities, one keeper can easily look over and preserve 1,000 acres of partridge-land and covert—whilst in others three or four would be required for the same extent of beat. Wherever foot-paths abound, keepers must be in proportion. Manors with these nuisances in abundance can scarcely be strictly preserved, as it is almost impossible to prevent the poacher from recovering the foot-path before he is caught or seen—that is, if he has his wits about him. It is seldom necessary to allow the keeper to use a gun, except in very extensive manors, when the head keeper should be allowed the privilege, for the purpose of shooting the hen-harrier, or other hawk. If for defence, the revolver is much better; and, in the hands of a steady man, who will not use it except in extreme cases, when his own life is attacked by numbers, it is a wonderfully useful weapon, and is equivalent to two or three assistants all armed with guns. All four-footed vermin should be trapped or poisoned.

Sect. 3.—Rearing of Game Naturally.

5. After the selection of the shooting-ground, supposing this to have been made in the month of February, or before that time, the duty of the keeper is to take such measures as that the game on the beat shall be allowed to breed undisturbed by any of the many nuisances to the game preserver which are so common. No dogs, other than the sheep-dog, should be allowed at liberty, and on no account should pointers or setters be broken after the end of February, or on the moors scarcely so late. Shepherds' dogs are a standing evil, but as they must be tolerated, the only remedy is to watch their evolutions as much as possible. Many of them destroy the eggs of the grouse, partridge, or pheasant, or find them for their masters' profit, who often realise five shillings for a nest. It is better, therefore, for the keeper to be on good terms with the shepherd, and to be allowed to give him an occasional gratuity, than to be always quarrelling with him for his dog's peccadillos. The affection of these men for their dogs is not astonishing, since they are their sole companions; and, consequently, any abuse bestowed upon their bosom friends is resented by all the means in their power. The poachers, also, are constantly on the look-out for eggs, and at the time of laying, they require nearly as much watching as in the commencement of the shooting season. It is a great pity that these men should be tempted as they are: for were there no market for eggs, they would have no object in taking them. Most of our great preservers, for the purposes of the battue, have recourse to purchasing eggs for artificial rearing, and often pay for those robbed from their own land. It should be made illegal, under a heavy penalty, and not as now only under a penalty of 5s., to buy or sell game eggs, since there can be no necessity for this traffic, and it leads to numberless crimes, and temptations to crime.

6. The keeper should also take care that his pheasants are well fed at all times, but especially at the pairing season, as they are very restless at that time, and are constantly quarrelling among themselves. The old hen of each hive or nide is always anxious, if alive, to retain her old nest, and to drive the young hens away from her neighbourhood. If, therefore, the keeper is not on his guard at this time, the hens stray far off his beat, and make their nests in some spot where they easily fall a prey to the poacher at the end of summer, and it is impossible to avoid this entirely; but if the keeper has his ears and eyes open, he can easily detect the nest of nearly every pheasant on his beat, and if they are likely to be taken, he may then, and then only, as soon as the hen has laid her full number, remove them and place them under a couple of bantam hens. Hen-pheasants will spread themselves abroad, and no art will keep them closer together than they like, but the above plan may be adopted to save a great many eggs. There are many other situations in which the nest should either be disturbed if found early enough, or the eggs taken if found too late—as, for instance, in situations likely to be flooded, as ditches or hollow waterways, or in clover fields, or vetches which will inevitably be mowed over before the time of hatching. There is no situation for the nest so good as the wheat or barley-field, especially the former.

Sect. 4.—Artificial Rearing of Game.

7. The artificial rearing of game is only to be had recourse to under the circumstances above mentioned; but in every large preserve, the keeper, if he knows his business, will always have to rear a very considerable number of pheasants as well as partridges by hand. The latter are the more difficult to bring up, and, luckily, do not require so often the care of the keeper, as they hatch nearly a month before the pheasant, and, consequently, are generally off before the mowing of the clover or the late vetches. In the early grass crop, however, many are mown over; and this is unavoidable, as the partridge's nest is much more difficult to

find than that of the pheasant. It is commonly supposed that to rear these birds by hand great experience and care are necessary, but I believe that by attending to the following directions, three-fourths of those hatched may be reared in good feather. The great difficulty is to *hatch* them, for eggs are so easily spoiled by being shaken, that even in the keeper's pocket they are liable, by an unexpected spring or fall, to be injured. This is especially the case in the early days of sitting—the embryo chick is then so delicate that a very slight blow or shock destroys its life, and the egg becomes addled. If a hen can be reckoned on, it is far better to wait till about five or six days from the time of hatching, as the eggs will bear removal very well at that time, if placed in a basket full of warm dry wool. In this way I have removed eggs more than twenty miles, and afterwards hatched nearly all under a common hen of moderate size. The larger the hen the better hatcher she is; but if very large, her legs are so strong, and her body so heavy, that she is sure to kick and trample most of her young charge to death. Hence, though no better as a sitter, yet, as a rearer, the bantam is far the best. After hatching, let the hen alone for at least twelve hours, then remove her carefully, and place her in a properly constructed coop, which should be made as follows :—Let a box be made three feet long, two feet wide, and two feet high in front, sloping off to one foot at the back, and having a boarded floor. This box should have a lath front, with intervals to allow the young birds to pass out. This is the coop for the hen, but the young birds ought to have a further space of about two yards square to run in, fenced off by some means. I have succeeded best in rearing young pheasants and partridges in a walled garden, as they are then more safe from the attacks of the weasel, stoat, or rat. If this cannot be procured, then be careful in selecting a good aspect, sheltered from the east and north, and open to the morning sun. It should not be exposed to the incursions of common poultry, especially the turkey-cock, who is a very troublesome gentleman among young game. For food, the best thing is the ant's egg, if it can be procured in sufficient quantities; or if not, then maggots may always be supplied by a few days' notice, but they should be scoured, by placing them in bran for twenty-four hours. Oatmeal and eggs should be mixed up together carefully, and after tying up in a cloth, they should be boiled till they are hard. Then breaking the mass into small pieces, it makes an excellent food, and one of which the young birds partake with avidity. After they are a fortnight or three

weeks old, soaked bread, or coarsely bruised and soaked barley, may be given; and soon after this, whole barley, in its natural state, may form the principal food; but scoured maggots or ants' eggs must still be given, and indeed they are necessary till the birds can be turned into the woods or standing corn, which they may be at about two months of age; after which they require watching, lest they should fall a prey to the poacher or to the fox. At first the young birds must be fed three times a day, but after the first fortnight, feeding twice a day only is required. In cold and wet weather the outer run of the coop should be covered over by a cloth, and at all times by a net, if exposed to the hawk or other bird of prey.

8. YOUNG PARTRIDGES AND PHEASANTS are very subject to the pip, or gapes, in which the bird seems to be gasping for breath. It is said that a daily pill, containing one grain of black pepper and half a grain of mustard, will relieve this disease, but I cannot speak from actual experience. Dry gravel mixed with ashes should be placed within reach, and in masses, so that the young birds may bather in it. The coops ought to be moved daily, as the stain of the birds is injurious to them. No water is to be given for the first three weeks; and afterwards, if diarrhœa comes on, give rice water instead, and boil some rice in alum water and give as food, mixed with their maggots or ants' eggs. In this way it may fairly be calculated that about one-half of the eggs brought home will be reared—one-quarter being addled, and one-third or quarter of those hatched generally dying of accident or disease.

SECT 5.—PRESERVATION FROM POACHERS.

9. In spite of every precaution in rearing game, unless equal or greater care is taken to preserve it from the poacher and the attacks of vermin, it is useless to expect a good head at the shooting season. With regard to the poacher, everything depends upon the labourers on the farms. If they like to countenance the poacher, or if they unfortunately are poachers themselves, all the efforts of a keeper will be of little avail. The best plan is to make all the labourers feel an interest in the preservation of the game. Let every man receive at Christmas a certain sum proportionate to the head of game killed during the season, and the outlay will be found to be well bestowed, since it will go much farther than the same sum laid out in extra watchers. I have known 650 acres of land preserved entirely, in the neighbourhood of a large town, without any regular keeper, and with an outlay in the shape of presents to labourers certainly not exceeding £20 a year. On this farm, hares were as thick as sheep, and partridges suf-

ficient to allow thirty brace to be killed in three or four hours. All parties were in earnest in keeping poachers away, and the result was as I have stated. This shows what labourers can do if they like, and what they will do if it is made their interest to do so. They are either a great evil or a great boon to the game preserver, and he must make up his mind either to have them as warm friends or bitter enemies. The regular and systematic poacher is a formidable fellow, opposed to all law, and making a living in the best way he can. After a time, nothing comes amiss to him; and though at first he has taken to his trade from a love of sport, it has ended in his adhering to it from necessity, since he cannot get work when his character is known, nor can any man, after poaching all night, be fit for work in the day also. The existence and career of the poacher is the great drawback to the sportsman; and it almost justifies the strong desire which so many hold to do away entirely with all game, in order to get rid also of the tendency to poach. This is a question, however, which I shall not enter upon, as it concerns the legislator more than the sportsman. At present, the law permits the preservation of game; and it is believed that the evils attending upon it are more than counterbalanced by its many advantages. As good subjects, therefore, we have only to avoid encouraging the poacher; and the plan I have proposed, of making it the labourer's interest to discourage the system, is the most humane, as well as the most successful. Of regular poachers, there are four chief varieties, viz.—1st, the systematic London poacher; 2nd, the poaching gent.; 3rd, the regular rural poacher; 4th, the poaching labourer.

10. THE LONDON POACHER is almost always one of a gang, and they conduct their operations in a variety of ways. Sometimes they scour the country in dog-carts drawn by a fast horse, by which they are enabled to shoot along the sides of a road, either in covert, or by catching the pheasants on their feed, or by beating the stubbles or turnips adjacent to the road, or even invading the moors; as soon as a keeper or other person approaches, they take to their heels, and on reaching the dog-cart are soon out of sight. It is against these men that the regular labourer may be made the most useful. Few farms in the shooting season are without a labourer within a field or two of every point likely to be invaded; let every one of these be provided with a railway whistle, and let him blow it loudly as soon as he sees a suspicious person in his vicinity. This may be heard for a mile or more, and the keeper may very soon be made aware of what is going on. Besides, the whistle itself alarms the poacher,

as it proves the existence of a good system of watching, and he prefers moving off to quieter quarters. These men generally travel in parties of five, of whom one remains with the horse, and the other four either together surround a small covert, and command every side, so that a dog put in is sure to drive out every thing to one or other of them, or else they take each side of the road, in the stubbles or turnips, &c. In this way a heavy load of game is often bagged by these rascals, by selecting a line of road studded with preserves, and suited to their purpose. By keeping within the number of five, they avoid the penalties under the 32nd section of the Game Laws, and only come under the 30th and 31st section, if they should be overtaken by the keeper, and can only be fined £2 each. They seldom indulge in night poaching, but are always ready to deal with the local poachers for the game which they may take in that way.

11. THE POACHING GENT. is generally a man who is ardently fond of shooting, and yet has not the opportunity of indulging his appetite for sport, from want of land to shoot over. He, therefore, is constantly trespassing upon the lands of his neighbours, and of course subjects himself to the penalty of two pounds on conviction for each offence. He is almost always, however, so good a shot, that the produce of his gun enables him to pay this sum, because he is so wary as to choose his opportunity, and often to escape detection for a considerable time. He knows where he is least likely to be caught, and the times which will suit him best, and acts accordingly. There is seldom much difficulty in dealing with these men, and the harm they do in well preserved districts is very trifling. It is only in half-preserved farms that they are to be dreaded, and there they often get the lion's share of the spoil. On the grouse-moors, an inferior grade of this class is very destructive to game—he is the sporting miner or blacksmith, or perhaps the denizen of some neighbouring small town, in which he *ought* to be standing behind the counter of a whisky shop, or very often he is a shoemaker or tailor. These men are not regular night poachers; but they are infected with a love of sport, to gratify which they brave all dangers, and encounter even the risk of the county-jail — they wait for days, till the keepers are engaged in some particular direction, and then, by keeping on the sides of particular hills, or other means suitable to the country, they are enabled to shoot an enormous quantity of grouse.

12. THE REGULAR RURAL POACHER is the chief bane to the sport; for, though the London hand is very successful occasionally, he does not often pay more than one or two visits

to the same preserve; whilst the rural one is always on the look-out. It requires nearly as many keepers or watchers as there are poachers, to be quite safe against their incursions; and even then, if a watch is put upon every known man in the neighbourhood, they will outwit you, by giving intelligence to some distant friends in the same trade. They pursue their operations partly by day and partly by night. If by day, their plan is to select a small covert which has just been visited by the keeper, for whose round the poacher has been long waiting in concealment, and then as soon as he is out of sight, the poacher sets his wires and nets in a very few minutes, and enters and disturbs the coppice, either with or without a dog taught to run mute. In five minutes more, every hare is caught, and quickly disposed of in some secret spot, often a labourer's cottage, till night-fall. In this way, also, a few pheasants are taken, but not so easily as the hares, as they do not run so easily as the latter, and if sufficiently roused to do this, some one or more are sure to give notice to the keepers in the distance, by flying off to another covert, which of itself is sufficient to arouse suspicion. At night, the tricks of the regular poacher are most ingenious, and are constantly varying in proportion to the discoveries of the keepers. In moonlight and wet windy nights, the poacher's harvest is made. He can then see his game, without being heard so distinctly as he would be on a quiet evening. He shoots the pheasants on their perches, either with the air-gun or fowling-piece, which is made to take to pieces easily, for the convenience of putting in the pocket. Grouse and partridges are chiefly netted; but the former may be more easily shot with the air-gun at night, since the net is much interfered with, in consequence of the heather preventing its acting; the poacher, however, has no difficulty with either, if he can only guess pretty nearly where they are, and this he takes care to do by watching them with a glass at the close of evening. After taking his bearings at that time, he is enabled to drop his net over the place without the trouble of using the stalking-horse or the wide drag-net. The only certain prevention against netting is to watch the birds at night, and disperse them; but this makes them so wild, as to spoil the subsequent shooting. Bushing the stubbles interferes with the drag-net, but not with the bag-net. It is a very good plan to go round every evening, just before the calling of the birds, and put a small bush, or even with a spade throw a lot of fresh earth, on the last night's place of rest, which is known by the droppings; this prevents their settling near the same

spot, which they otherwise would do, especially grouse, and of which fact the poacher takes advantage by marking their droppings by day, in order to find their settling place at night. Hares are taken by gate-nets in the fields, or by wires and bag-nets in the coverts. It is a very remarkable fact, that these cautious animals rarely use a hedge-meuse by night, preferring the gateways, apparently from a fear of being surprised by the stoat or fox—whilst by day, the reverse is the case; the poacher, therefore, cannot take them on the feed with the wire, except in going in or out of the covert, but has recourse to the gate-net, which he fixes to the gate between the feeding field (usually a piece of swedes or clover) and the covert; then sending a mute-running dog into the field, he waits the coming of the hare into the net, and takes them out as fast as they run into it. There is no certain way of avoiding this mode of poaching, excepting by careful watching; the chief guide is the scream of the hare when caught, which may be heard on quiet nights, but it is a practice very easily pursued by the poacher, with little fear of detection, if he is a clever and experienced hand. A practice has lately been introduced of setting wires in the runs made in the middle of feeding fields; it requires the wire to be very carefully set at a certain height, by means of a twig, and is very destructive. It is also very difficult to detect; but as the poachers cannot find them except in very open moonlight nights, the keeper knows when to have his eyes open.

13. Lastly comes the POACHING LABOURER, a perfect pest to the parish in which he resides. He is constantly committing a breach of trust, and does it at so little risk, as often to escape detection for a long time. These men have generally a little terrier, which is capable of being taught to do everything but speak, and assists in a wonderful degree in the capture of game. They have also an old gun which takes apart, and may easily be concealed under the smock frock. If a covey of birds is seen to collect near the cottage, a slight noise is made, and up go their heads, at which moment the gun goes off, and they are all dead at one swoop. The cottage is generally near a road, and some hedge-popping boy is made to bear the blame. Again, these men have generally small gardens, in which are parsley, pinks, &c.; these are a favourite food of the hare, she therefore is almost sure to visit them, and in her passage through the garden-fence of course makes a meuse, or at all events, she leaves her mark or prick in the soil; if she goes through a gate, this leads to her destruction the next night by wire, gin, or net; and no one can possibly prevent it, even with the eyes of an Argus. Pheasants, also, are sure to come

within their reach occasionally, and if they do, they are wired easily enough. A man, for instance, is put to hedging or draining, and is on the ground by six o'clock in the morning, a time when pheasants have not left their feed; he has only therefore to lay a few horsehair loops along the ditches, and by gently driving the pheasants into them, apparently in the course of his work, he captures, every now and then, the value of a day's work in a few minutes. Of course, he conceals the booty till night.

14. Such are the most common tricks of the poachers, but the most successful are those who invent plans of their own; the keeper has enough to do to outwit them, and his grand object should be to find out their plans, and circumvent them—it is diamond cut diamond. A reformed poacher, if really reformed, makes the best keeper, but, unfortunately for this purpose, their exposure to night air, and to wet and cold, and their habits of intemperance, have almost always destroyed their constitutions before they think of reforming. It is only when worn out as poachers, that they think of turning round and becoming keepers. When the head-keeper is really up to his business, the poachers stand a very poor chance, especially if the master is ready to support his servant with his influence and protection. In every case, whether on the open moors or in enclosed districts, the first thing to be done is to make out a list of all the poachers likely to visit your manor; then discover their habits and haunts, and the kind of game which they excel in taking. Next, get some steady, hardy, and useful watchers, if possible, strangers to the locality, and therefore not likely to be influenced by the ties of affinity or friendship. Let these men speedily make themselves conversant with the appearance of all the poachers on your manor, or your head-keeper can initiate them by degrees. They should all have glasses, and be made conversant with their use; for even in a comparatively small beat, it often happens that a poacher cannot be approached within many hundred yards, and yet it is quite impossible to speak with certainty to a man's identity at the distance of a quarter of a mile. When these men know their duties pretty well, each should have one or more poachers allotted to him, and should always be able to give an account of his or their whereabouts. He does this partly by his own powers of watching, but chiefly from information gained from other parties. By such a mode of proceeding, almost any gang of poachers may be outwitted; and they seldom show fight when they find themselves no match in brain, though in personal prowess they may be superior. Intel-

lect and pluck will always be served, even when mere brute force has totally failed.

SECT. 6.—PRESERVATION FROM VERMIN.

15. But, in addition to the attacks of the poachers, the keeper has also to ward off those of the great variety of vermin which attack game. Here, however, a good man is always rewarded; for, though he may be outwitted by the arts of a first-rate poacher, which are constantly varying, he has only himself to blame if he allows anything beneath his own level to circumvent him. Vermin are endowed with the same instincts now as they were thousands of years ago; and as these instincts are well known, he has only to take advantage of that knowledge, and destroy them. The following is a complete list of the various kinds infesting Great Britain; their habits should be well studied, and the different modes of taking them understood, by every man who sets up for a regular keeper. I shall therefore take each variety separately, and describe its appearance, its habits, its prey, and the best mode of capture.

16. THE CAT—(*Felis Domestica*).—It was formerly supposed that this was merely the wild cat tamed, but more recent investigations have led naturalists to conclude that they are two distinct species. The chief difference consists in the tail, which is long and taper in the house cat (*fig.* 1), but blunt and shorter in the wild cat (*fig.* 2).

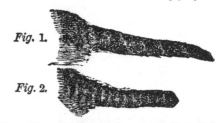

Fig. 1.

Fig. 2.

The wild cat is now no longer found in this country, and its ravages therefore among game are no longer to be feared. Its place, however, in this respect, has been taken by its substitute, the domestic cat, which, in her proper sphere, is of the greatest importance to mankind. Like most other blessings, she is liable to become a curse; and that is most assuredly the case when she takes it into her head to invade the game preserve. Here she is as different from her household character as it is possible to conceive. She is no longer ready to be noticed and fondled, but is wild and wayward, retreating to some secure place on the approach of man, and only venturing out at night. Her ravages are so extensive, that it is fortunate that she is easily taken by trap, which should be the ordinary steel trap, of middle size, between the fox-trap and that for the rat. The trap should be rubbed with the herb valerian, if easily procured, but it is seldom positively necessary, as the cat is almost always readily caught. The trap may be baited in the usual way with a small bird or young rabbit. If there is the slightest difficulty in taking the cat, it is only necessary to use three of these traps sunk in the earth, and surrounding a live bird tied to a stake, elevated about a foot from the ground, and she is sure to be caught. A more minute description will be given of this trap under the Fox. The gun may be used if necessary, but a cat will carry off an enormous quantity of shot; and even a bullet, if put into the cat anywhere but in the brain, is by no means sure of destroying her.

17. The Fox—(*Vulpes Vulgaris*).—This is, in some districts, one of the worst kinds of vermin, and carefully trapped—whilst in others it is as carefully preserved. In our present list it must appear as an enemy, although numerous and warm controversies have taken place as to its game-destroying powers. No doubt, the fox may be preserved in the same coverts with the pheasant; and, I believe, if supplied with rabbits, he will not often fall upon any other game, and certainly not upon the hare, to which the rabbit is always preferred; the scent of the fox is so strong, that most animals are aware of his proximity, and, therefore, they are able to keep clear of him, except on rare occasions, of which he does not hesitate to take advantage; the pheasant, for instance, seldom ventures within his reach; if disturbed, he has recourse to his wings, and does not often run into danger fast enough to be off his guard against the scent, though he will often run down an open ride, or in the fields, where he is secure from this insidious enemy. If, however, a pheasant is wounded, he is sure to fall a prey to vulpine attacks, and so is the wounded woodcock or snipe; but this is of very little consequence, and such a poor maimed creature as a wounded bird is better out of its misery. Keepers are great enemies to the fox, and aggravate his faults, for two reasons; firstly, because he interferes with their chief perquisites, the rabbits; and secondly, because he is the only legitimate scape-goat for their short-comings. If the complaint is made that there is no game, the answer is always ready, "why, sir, if you will preserve the foxes, you must not expect so much game." There is no other game-destroyer that a keeper can charge with the loss, without damaging his own character, since, in proportion to the scarcity or abundance of all other vermin, is his own character raised or depressed. The great misfortune is, that

the keeper is induced to play all sorts of tricks, in order to comply with the directions of his master, to preserve foxes as well as game, which he fancies are conflicting in themselves, since they, no doubt, are opposed to his own wishes and interests; but being compelled to do so, he proceeds on a plan which enables him to find foxes, though bad ones—thus keeping the order to the letter, but breaking it in spirit. Half of the foxes found in game preserves are only just turned down when the hounds are thrown into covert, or, when at large, have been fed daily with rabbits close to their earths, by which they are rendered so fat and lazy, that they cannot stand five minutes before a good pack of hounds. In districts where no hounds are kept, but where game abounds, as in the Highlands of Scotland, and in some parts of Wales, there can be no reason for the preservation of foxes, and there they should be killed down as closely as possible. They are not very difficult to trap with the gin of full size, four, five, or six of which should be set round a dead lamb or rabbit, with the inside exposed as a means of spreading the scent, and partly buried in the ground as if for a dog. Of course, the traps should be carefully fastened down with a short chain. The best way to set them, is to dig a piece of ground well over, about five or six feet square, then take out four, five, or six spades full of earth, each leaving a hole sufficient to contain a trap; in these lay the trap, and fix it by driving in the peg, concealing the chain and every part but the spring and the jaws and plates. The trap should then be set, propping up the plate with a bit of stick, to which a string is attached, in order to withdraw it; then cover all up with finely chopped grass or moss, and withdraw the stick by the string. If the fox is very wary, it is better to leave the traps unset for a night or two, and throw down, every night, a rabbit or pigeon on the ground at some little distance, but clear of the traps. When these have been taken freely for a couple of nights, a similar bait should be placed in the middle of the traps, without handling it, or treading on the newly-levelled earth, or the covering grass, which would at once raise the suspicions of the fox. If these precautions are taken, the most wary will generally fall. Chaff answers remarkably well to cover these traps with, but it has the serious evil of attracting the pheasants, who come and search for grain, and in that way sometimes are caught, instead of the fox or cat, for which it was set; the grass or moss ought to be very short and light, or it may catch in the trap, and prevent its acting. If the keeper has only one trap, it should not, as is often done, be set in a run, for fear of its catching the game, but an open space a short distance off the run should be thrown into it, by making a gap, if there is not already one, and in that gap the trap should be laid; the bait should be raised, in this case, on a stub or short stick driven into the earth, which should be about as tall as the animal to be taken can just reach with his nose, so that he will walk on his toes, and not crouch on his belly, in reaching it. In this way the leg is well seized, and not the toe only, or what is still worse, altogether lost by the body being first grasped, and then slipping out of the trap; thus, for a fox the bait should be twelve inches, for a cat eight inches, and for a weasel or polecat four inches above the level of the plate of the trap. The keeper should spring these traps every morning, and oil them or repair them, with the file and hammer when necessary to their perfect acting.

18. THE MARTEN—(*Martes Abiëtum et Foina*).—The marten, the polecat, the stoat, and the weasel all belong to the sub-family, *Mustelina*. There are two kinds of martens,—the pine and the beech marten, the former being more common in the north, and the latter in the southern parts of the island. The martens inhabit large woods, living in the hollow of trees, or in an old magpie's nest, or squirrel's. They have from three to four young. They feed on game and other birds, or mice, rats, and squirrels. In colour, they are of a reddish-brown, and are the largest of the mustelina or weasel-like family. This sub-family have all long bodies, short legs, long tails, small head, with powerful jaws, sharp teeth, an insatiable desire for blood, and great tenacity of life. They all prefer the blood and brains to the rest of the body, and do not eat the flesh except from necessity. Being all so much alike in their habits, I shall defer the description of their mode of capture till I have described them all.

19. THE POLECAT—(*Putorius Fœtidus*).— The polecat, fitchet, or foulmart, is very common in this country, and is the most destructive to game of all vermin, except, perhaps, the domestic cat, when become wild; it will even surprise the hare in her form, or the pheasant on her nest. They generally make a short burrow in the side of a sandy bank, which emits a tolerably strong scent of the animal, and is thereby easily known by the keeper, who proceeds at once to dig the animal out; this, however, he cannot always do, as the polecat is very fond of choosing the root of an old tree under which to make his burrow. Farmers are apt to suppose that this creature does them much good in destroying rats; but he is too bulky to follow them in their runs in the wheat ricks, and they are too wary to be caught napping out of them. The pole-

cat is smaller than the marten, and of a blacker colour, approaching to a dark tortoise-shell.

20. THE STOAT—(*Mustela Erminea*).—This is the next in size of the *Mustelina*, and is even more voracious and blood-thirsty, in proportion to its size, than the polecat. It is, in summer and in mild winters, of a reddish brown, with a black tip to its tail, but it becomes more or less white in winter, according to the degree of cold, always, however, retaining the black tip to the tail. It, like the polecat, burrows in the ground, making a smaller hole, and not being easily discovered in consequence, or by its scent, which is not nearly so strong as that of the polecat. It pursues all kinds of game, and destroys the eggs of pheasants and partridges with great perseverance. It should be diligently trapped and exterminated.

21. THE WEASEL—(*Mustela Vulgaris*).— The smallest of its tribe, never being more than seven inches in length from the nose to the tail. It resembles the stoat in most respects, but is less hairy, and its tail is shorter in proportion, and without the black brush at the extremity, which, in the stoat, forms that remarkable hairy tuft so conspicuous in the ermine-fur. The weasel makes longer jumps or bounds in its run than either of its congeners, that is, in proportion to its size. Its habits resemble those of the stoat and polecat, and it is quite as bold and voracious, but is not able to cope with the hare or pheasant, though it is said to fasten on the back of the hare, and suck its blood for miles, till the poor creature sinks from exhaustion.

22. MODE OF TRAPPING THE MUSTELINA OR WEASEL KIND.—They may all be taken in two kinds of traps—the gin or steel trap, and the box-trap. The gin should be of the small size suited for rats, or for the marten and polecat, a little larger. It should be set a little out of the run of the animal wherever that has been discovered, and should be buried as for the fox, and covered over with feathers, or fine moss or grass. The bait should be an egg impaled on a stick, and the contents, half escaped are then easily scented, or part of a pigeon or rabbit, especially the liver and entrails. By taking the precaution to set these traps a little out of the hare and rabbit runs, these latter animals will escape, especially if the entrails of the bait are rubbed against the sides of the opening which leads to the trap, as game have all a dislike to the smell of blood and garbage. In no case should the bait be placed upon the bridge of the trap. If the polecat or stoat has been carrying off the eggs from a nest as fast as they are laid, ascertain, if

possible, its track in reaching the nest, and there place your trap, with an egg impaled a little beyond it. It must not be too near the nest, or the parent-birds may be caught. Next to the gin, the box-trap is the most useful, and it has this advantage, that it never admits the hare or the pheasant, and if by chance the rabbit enters, it is not injured. It consists of a long box, about nine or ten inches square, with a slide at each end, which is held up by a long arm or lever proceeding to the centre of the box. Here the two are held down by a catch, which, when set, holds up a small stage at about half or three quarters of an inch from the floor of the box. Hence, any animal in passing through the box, is sure to tread on the stage, which, by the way, ought to be made so as to occupy the whole width of the interior. By placing the bait on both sides of the stage, at whichever end the animal enters, it is encouraged to proceed, because it first cautiously seizes and devours the one-half nearest to it, which should not be large enough to satisfy its hunger, and then proceeds over the stage to lay hold of the other portion, when, on placing its forefeet on the stage, the catch is released, and the slides at each end fall and enclose it. The slides should not be made to lift above three or four inches, for fear of the hare entering. When set, the box ought to be placed in a run or dry ditch, and the space at the sides of each end should be filled up and gradually assimilated to the run or ditch by means of stones, or rubbish, or earth, so as to compel the vermin to enter or turn back. All this should be done in as cunning a manner as possible, so as to escape the observation of these animals; but they are not nearly so difficult to deceive as the fox, the rat, or the magpie. They may also be poisoned by arsenic, but it is a dangerous plan, as the poisoned baits are liable to be devoured by dogs.

23. THE RAT—(*Mus Decumanus*).—This noxious animal is too well known to need description. It breeds so rapidly, as to overwhelm the farmer if not kept down, bringing forth twelve or fourteen young ones three or four times a-year. It is not very injurious to game, unless it is more than usually abundant, as it has generally the wheat-rick of the farmer, or his hen-roost or pigeon-cote to attack, in preference to game; still it sometimes happens that a more than commonly voracious rat attacks the eggs of the pheasant or partridge, and if so, he must be destroyed if possible. It is very difficult to trap them, and the best mode is to ferret out or poison them. Very often the rat takes up his abode on the banks of arti-

ficial water, which is generally near some game covert, and in that situation he is very destructive to waterfowl as well as young game. Here the following method of trapping will answer well:—Get a wooden frame, made of two cross pieces of wood, with a block in the middle; upon these set four common rat-traps, loosely let into the pieces, with the spring towards the outside, and weight the whole so that, when floated in the water, the traps will just sink an inch below the level of the water; then, by placing a bait on a short post, raised about six inches above the middle block, the rats, in swimming to it, or raising themselves to reach it, are almost sure to strike one of the traps with a hind or fore leg, and as the traps are only placed loosely on the cross bar, and fall off suspended by a string, the rat is drowned at once, and does not prevent others from incurring the same fate. This is the only certain mode of trapping rats; and though the poisoning of them is easy enough, it has many disadvantages—firstly, it is dangerous to children and dogs; secondly, the dead rats are apt to cause foul smells in any neighbouring house when they die. To effect this object, arsenic should be mixed up with malt-dust, or wheat-flour, in the proportion of half a pound of flour to an ounce of arsenic; then with water make into a paste, and drop a few drops of oil of aniseed in, of which rats are very fond. The mass should be broken up into small pieces, of all sizes and shapes, not round like pills, but just as they happen to break by chance; then taking one or two of these in a spoon, and carefully avoiding the contact of the hand, which the rat easily detects, drop them into such places frequented by rats as are too narrow for dogs or children to reach. By dropping them thus, as it were accidentally, one or two in a place, the suspicions of the rat are lulled, and he generally eats them greedily. If eaten, death is pretty certain; but sometimes they cause vomiting, and the rat escapes.

24. THE HEDGEHOG—(*Erinaceus Europæus*).—The hedgehog is only destructive to the eggs of game, never eating the living animal. It ought, however, to be destroyed; but it is not nearly so dangerous as any of those which I have already described. It is easily found by the terrier, and may then be destroyed by the keeper.

25. THE OTTER — (*Lutra Vulgaris*).— This creature is a kind of water-polecat, and is as destructive to fish as that fierce little animal is to game. In general form it also somewhat resembles it, but its head is more blunt, its fur shorter and thicker, and its feet are webbed. It is amphibious in its habits, and is soon drowned, if kept

under water more than a few minutes at a time. It measures usually, from the nose to the tail, nearly two feet, and the tail itself is often sixteen inches in length. The eyes both look upwards, and it is thus enabled to watch the fish while lying below them on the bed of the river, and, therefore, unseen by them. The footmark, or *seal* of the otter, is easily recognised by a round depression corresponding to the ball of its foot. Its burrow is always entered under water, and it admits air only by a small hole worked from the inside, and not readily found. In some districts the otter is hunted, and affords good sport, and when that is the case, it should not be interfered with; when, however, no otter hounds are within reach, the otter may be trapped in the same way as I have recommended for the rat in the water. Of course, the whole apparatus must be larger, and the traps should be of the full size for a fox; the bait should be a fish, raised about a foot from the water, and the traps should be sunk three inches. It is a more certain trap for the otter than even for the rat, as the former is not so sagacious an animal. If the apparatus is thought too troublesome, by watching for the *seal*, the haunts may be discovered, and a single trap may be baited in the same way as for a polecat, using a fish for bait, and suspending it nine or ten inches before and above the trap; but the water-trap is far more successful, and will soon clear a river of these rapacious poachers of fish.

26. In the various parts of Great Britain we find a long list of birds of prey, all of which are more or less injurious to game, from the eagle to the merlin. But there are few districts in which all are found; the larger kinds are chiefly to be met with in the inaccessible parts of Scotland and the Hebrides, as well as in some parts of Ireland, whilst the smaller varieties are very troublesome in the woodlands of the south. At the head of the list stands

27. THE GOLDEN EAGLE—*(Aquila Chrysaëtos)*.—This beautiful bird is now seldom found in Great Britain, and is very rare, except in the most remote districts of the North. It can only be confounded with the osprey in this country, since there is no other bird of prey at all near these birds in size, which is about that of an ordinary turkey. The golden eagle is a rich golden brown colour, with powerful hooked beak, and strong talons, and destroys large game to a fearful extent, as well as young lambs. The flight of the eagle is very beautiful, and they generally hunt in pairs. The hen lays two eggs of a creamy-white ground, with brownish spots; the nest is very rudely constructed, in some very inaccessible crag or rock, and is merely a heap of sticks and grass.

28. THE OSPREY—*(Pandion Haliaëtus)*.—Is only found on the sea-coast, or very near it. It is of the same size as the golden eagle, but differs in colour and in food, which is composed entirely of fish. In the salmon fisheries it sometimes is a sad depredator, especially at the salmon leaps, when they happen to be near the sea. Here it will seize the fish as they are struggling up the fall, and if once it takes to this dainty, it is sure to return to it; it is less wary than the golden eagle, and may generally be approached with care while fishing. Both these eagles must be shot, as they are very difficult to trap, and their nests are generally fixed in such an inaccessible crag, as to be almost beyond the reach of man.

29. THE KITE — *(Milvus Regalis)*. — The kite, or gled, is very common in the wild districts of England, and is a game-destroyer, though not to any great extent. It may always be recognised by its long, forked tail. Its length is more than two feet. The legs are yellow.

30. THE BUZZARD — *(Buteo Vulgaris)*. — Is considerably less than the golden eagle, being about twenty-two inches from tip to tail, and is very different in general aspect and habits. When seeking for food, it sits at the top of some high tree, and generally on a dead branch, keenly watching for the appearance of some young rabbit or hare, or for a brood of grouse or pheasants. As soon as these come in sight, it darts down and picks up its prey, without alighting, and is sure to seek the same branch with the purpose of devouring it. The buzzard builds in trees; its eggs are generally four, of a whitish colour, with pale brown spots.

31. THE PEREGRINE FALCON—*(Falco Peregrinus)*.—The blue or peregrine falcon is very destructive to all game, but it has been almost exterminated in this country. It is one of those best suited to falconry, which has been one reason of their scarcity. They build in the most inaccessible parts of the mountains, and can rarely be trapped. The hen is very beautiful. Back of head, dark slate colour; outside of wings and back lighter slate; under part of neck and throat white; breast of a buff ground, with dark brown oblong spots or streaks. Length, from point to point of wings, forty inches; from tip to tail seventeen inches.

32. THE HOBBY—*(Hypotriorchis Subbuteo)*.—Is a bird of passage, and only a summer visitor; it can therefore scarcely be considered a dangerous game destroyer, nor can it easily be taken at that season.

33. THE MERLIN — *(Hypotriorchis Æsalon)*.—This spirited little hawk is, among the falcons, very much like the weasel among the *Mustelina*, being as bold as a gamecock, as voracious as a shark, and as nimble

as an eel. It is said to attack the grouse, and sometimes to succeed in capturing them by the force of the blow. It is a very fast bird for its size. The male and female are nearer of a size than in the others of its family. It is of a bluish brown on the upper parts, with a deep buff ground for the breast, studded with dark streaks. Its entire length is only thirteen inches. It seldom weighs quite eight ounces. These three species of the falcons are all used in falconry, and are all difficult to trap.

34. THE HEN-HARRIER—(*Circus Cyaneus*). — The plumage of the male and female varies so much, that for a long time they were regarded as two different species. The former is of a light blue, while the latter is brown. Both have white rings on the tail, and a black mark on the ends of the wing feathers. They are about forty inches across the wings, when extended. In length they are about seventeen inches. They are dreadful destroyers of the grouse, and beat their ground in the most regular way, crossing it like the pointer or setter, and flying close to the surface, and swooping on the unhappy grouse or partridge the moment their eyes catch sight. They build their nests on the ground, in heather or thick bushes. These should be diligently sought for, as the young birds, once found, are a sure mode of trapping the old ones.

35. THE SPARROW-HAWK—(*Accipiter Nisus*).—Considerably smaller than the last, never being more than fifteen inches in length, and the male seldom more than nine. It is chiefly injurious to the game preserve, from taking off the very young partridges and pheasants, upon which it delights to pounce. It builds upon high trees, laying four or five eggs, of a white ground, with variable reddish marblings.

36. THE KESTREL OR WINDHOVER—(*Tinnunculus Alaudarius*). — It is commonly supposed that this bird is a very bold destroyer of game, but I am quite satisfied this is a great mistake—it will always prefer the mouse to any bird, and I believe rarely attacks any other prey than the mouse or the frog. It will not attack the young of the game birds, and its only fault is, that it will sometimes take the very young leveret. As, however, these little things are seldom visible, and as the kestrel hunts solely by sight, it is very seldom that this accident happens. This bird may fairly be allowed to benefit the farmer, without injury to the game preserver. It is a very ornamental bird in its flight and general appearance, and when young is more like the owl than any of the hawks.

37. MODE OF TRAPPING WINGED VERMIN. —Nearly all these birds may be taken with the steel trap, which should be variously set, according to the habits of the particular bird. The buzzard is not very difficult to trap though it does not alight to take its prey, and it may also be shot while perched on its bough. A circular trap has lately been invented, and is sold at all the gunmakers, which requires no bait, and is simply to be placed on those boughs which are frequented by these birds. It requires, however, far more watching to detect their haunts than to get near them with the gun. If the attempt is made to shoot this bird, it generally requires the rifle for its destruction, as it is usually seated out of the distance suited to an ordinary fowling-piece. The harrier is somewhat difficult to trap, but it may be taken, and so may the buzzard, by means of a dead grouse or partridge set up on a little mound of earth, and studded with large fish-hooks. Both of these birds make a swoop at their prey, and in that way they may often be caught with the hooks, which should have their points directed towards the tail of the bait, and should project about half an inch above the feathers. One should be firmly on the back, one on the head, and one on the shoulder of each wing. The hook on the head is the most likely one to catch, and it should have a firm attachment by means of a line a few inches long. The hooks will not hold the hawk long; but by placing four concealed rat-traps around the bird, the hawk, in its struggles to free itself, is sure to strike one, and is then securely held; but the taking the young of these birds is by far the most easy way of destroying them. It is very much less trouble to watch the bird to her nest, than to trap them, or to shoot them even. When the nest is discovered, and while the hen is sitting, a ball may often be sent through the old bird, and the eggs will not then require to be reached, as they will of course be addled. As soon as the young birds are laid hold of, it may fairly be concluded that the old ones are in your power; for by fastening them down alive in the middle of three or four concealed traps, the old birds are soon tempted into their jaws. Each young bird should be fixed in the centre of a circle of traps at such a distance apart, that both old birds may be caught.

38. It is often said by keepers that they can dispense with the GUN in destroying these birds of prey; and many masters strongly object to the use of it, from the fear of its being abused; but in districts where the hen-harrier, or the buzzard, or the peregrine falcon abound, the gun *must be used*, or a sad loss of game will be the result. The nest cannot always be found or reached; and sometimes it is on another property altogether, in which case it cannot of course be taken without the consent of the adjoin-

ing keeper, who is as jealous of his rights and distinctions as a Turk.

39. THE BARN OWL—(*Strix Flammea*)— Is generally considered very destructive to game, but I believe erroneously so. Like the kestrel, it lives almost entirely on mice and rats; it will, however, when it has its young to provide for, attack the leveret or the rabbit, and perhaps the young pheasant; but, on inspecting the casts of these birds, I have never seen any quantity of feathers or fur, which would inevitably occur if they fed to any extent upon game. The nest may be easily taken, or the owl trapped or shot. A great parade is generally made by the keepers of the owl, as it is a bird which makes a great show among the list of killed, and yet is not very difficult to destroy.

40. THE RAVEN—(*Corvus Corax*)—Is not very common in this country, and is principally met with in wild districts, like the New Forest, or Dartmoor. The raven is very voracious, and nothing comes amiss to him, from carrion to eggs or fish. It breeds in the holes of high rocks, or on very high trees, and the nest is very difficult to take on that account. The eggs are four, of a dusky green. It is a very destructive bird to game, and should not be suffered to live, as it has no good qualities like the owl and kestrel. It is a very wary bird, and difficult to shoot or trap.

41. THE CROW—(*Corvus Corone*)—Is a smaller edition of the raven, which it resembles in every respect but size. It is too well known to need description.

42. THE JACKDAW—(*Corvus Monedula*)— Is also very much of the same habits as regards game, but is only obnoxious to the eggs. Its nest is seldom within the keeper's reach, being almost invariably in some old tower or church steeple.

43. THE MAGPIE—(*Pica Caudata*).—This pretty, lively bird is one of the most persevering destroyers of the eggs of the game birds. It ought to receive no mercy, but it is a very shy and cunning bird. Its nest may almost always be found, and the young taken and used as decoys, as I have already described. It builds in the tops of trees, high and low. The nest is domed, and built of a mass of sticks curiously interlaid.

44. THE JAY—(*Garrulus Glandarius*).— This beautiful bird resembles the magpie in its thirst for eggs, but is not quite so voracious.

45. THE HERON—(*Ardea Cinerea*).—The heron is only injurious among fish, which form its sole food. It is often preserved with great care, on account of its association with baronial sports. It is now, however, seldom used for hawking purposes, and, wherever the fisheries are preserved with care, herons are diligently destroyed.

It may be shot, or hooked, or trapped under water by the floating trap, as used for the otter, placing the bait in the same way, but fixing it in the shallows.

46. THE POISONING OF WINGED VERMIN. —I have already alluded to the different modes of trapping the winged varieties of vermin. It remains for me only to speak of the modes of poisoning them which are sometimes adopted. For the eagles, hawks, buzzards, and kites, arsenic is the best; but there is great danger in using it, lest some dog should feed on the poisoned bait; the liver is the best part in which to insert the arsenic, as it is generally the choice morsel first selected by them all, or the brain, as is the case more particularly in the falcons and the sparrow-hawk. For the raven, crow, magpie, and jay, strichnine acts well, and they will take it with great facility. These poisons should never be trusted to any one but a person of good character for care and integrity, as they are equally destructive to man. They may best be used in the egg, by making a small hole, then inserting five grains of either, and closing the hole again with a piece of paper and a little collodion. In this way, there is less chance of any dog or child getting to it, as the egg may be placed in the fork of a tree, out of sight from below.

SECT. 7.—NEW GAME LAWS.

47. Having provided for the procuring and preserving game necessary to the sport we are considering, it is next desirable that this should be conducted agreeably to law. The following Abstracts of the various Acts are therefore given; but it will be requisite, before proceeding to any legal prosecution, to obtain the act itself, or the assistance of a professor of the law. The abstracts, however, will be sufficient for the sportsman's guide in ordinary cases.

ABSTRACT OF GAME LAWS.

1 & 2 *William IV.*, c. 32.—*Oct.* 5, 1831.

Sec. 1.—Repeals old statutes, excepting the following, viz.:—Those relating to tame pigeons and birds; forms of deputations and notices; actions for trespass; and the act 9 Geo. IV., c. 69, relating to persons found at night armed with intent to kill game, and further extended by the 7 and 8 Vict., c. 29; also those relating to game shooting certificates, 6 and 7 Will. IV., c. 65. By these acts, persons taking or destroying game by night, viz., from an hour after sunset till an hour before sunrise, shall be committed, for the first offence, for three months; second offence, six months to hard labour, and find sureties afterwards; for third offence, be liable to be transported. Owners and occupiers, lords of manor, or their servants, may apprehend, and if violent resistance is made, it shall be a misdemeanour, and may be punished with transportation for seven years, or two years' imprisonment. Limitation of proceeding, one year. *Three* persons entering land *armed* for the purpose of taking game, shall be guilty of misdemeanour, and punishable by transportation or imprisonment. The act 7 and 8 Vict., c. 29, makes this act extend to the unlawfully taking any game or rabbits by night, *on any public road, highway, or path, or the sides thereof, or at the openings, outlets, or gates* from any such land into any such public road, highway, or path.

Sec. 2.—" Game" to include hares, pheasants, partridges, grouse, heath or moorgame, black game, and bustards.

Sec. 3.—Any person killing or taking game, or using a gun, dog, net, or other engine for that purpose, on a Sunday or Christmas day, is subject, on conviction by two justices, *to a penalty* not exceeding 5*l*. and costs. Limits the taking of game as follows:—

Partridges not to be taken from . . } Feb. 1 to Sep. 1.

Pheasants, ditto . . Feb. 1 to Oct. 1.

Black game, in Somerset, Devon & New Forest } Dec. 10 to Sep. 1.

Black game elsewhere . Dec. 10 to Aug. 20.

Grouse . . . . Dec. 10 to Aug. 12.

Bustard . . . . March 1 to Sep. 1.

Penalty not exceeding 1*l*. for every head of game so taken.

Any person poisoning game, to be fined not exceeding 10*l*., with costs.

Sec. 4.—Persons licensed to deal in game, who shall buy or sell, or have in their possession, any bird of game after ten days (one inclusive and the other exclusive), from the days above fixed; and persons unlicensed, who shall buy or sell any bird of game after such ten days, or shall have in their possession any bird of game (except such as are kept in a mew or breedingplace), after forty days, shall be subject, on conviction before two justices, to a penalty not exceeding 1*l*. for every head of game.

Sec. 5.—Act not to affect the law relating to game certificates (now raised to 4*l*. 0s. 10d. by the addition of 10 per cent.)

Sec. 6.—Game certificates to qualify to take game (subject to trespass). Gamekeepers' licences not to extend beyond the limits of their appointment.

Sec. 7.—Makes game the property of the landlord.

Sec. 8, 9, 10.—Act not to affect rights of manor, forest, chase, or warren, or any royal forest rights. Lords of the manor still to have game on waste lands; and also right of deputation.

Sec. 11.—Landlords may authorize any person or persons to shoot who have certificates.

Sec. 12.—When landlord reserves right of game, tenant shall not kill or take it, or cause it to be killed or taken, under a penalty not exceeding 2*l*.; and for every head of game, not exceeding 1*l*., with costs.

Sec. 13, 14.—Lords of manor may appoint gamekeepers, and authorize them to seize all dogs, &c., used within the manor by uncertified persons. Lords of manor may also grant deputations.

Sec. 15.—Persons seized in fee, or for life, of lands in WALES, of the clear annual value of 500*l*., and not within any manor, lordship, or royalty, or enfranchised or alienated therefrom, may appoint gamekeepers.

Sec. 16.—Gamekeepers to be registered with the Clerk of the Peace.

Sec. 17.—Certificated persons may sell game to licensed dealers. Gamekeepers not to sell game except on account of master.

Sec. 18.—Justices may grant licences in July, to any householder or keeper of a shop or stall, not being an innkeeper or victualler, or licensed to sell beer by retail, or the owner, guard, or driver of any mail coach, stage coach, stage waggon, van, or other public conveyance, or a carrier or higgler, or in the employ of any such person, to buy game of any person who may *lawfully* sell it; such parties to have their names in full, together with the words "licensed to deal in game," on a board in front of stall.

Sec. 19.—All parties obtaining a licence shall also obtain a certificate on payment of 2*l*. duty, in the same way as game certificate; penalty for non-compliance, 20*l*.

Sec. 20.—List of such persons to be made out by collector of assessed taxes.

Sec. 21.—One licence only necessary for two or more partners.

Sec. 22.—A conviction under game act to forfeit licence.

Sec. 23.—Persons killing or taking game, or using any gun, dog, &c., for the purpose of searching for game, without game certificate, are subject to a penalty not exceeding 5*l*., as well as the penalty under game certificate act.

Sec. 24.—Any persons not having right of killing game on land, or permission from the person having such right, who shall wilfully take or destroy, on such land, the eggs of any bird of game, or the eggs of any swan, wild duck, teal, or widgeon, or shall knowingly have in his possession any eggs so taken, shall pay a sum not exceeding 5*s*. for every egg, with costs.

Sec. 25.—Persons selling game unlawfully, to be fined not exceeding 2*l*. for every head so sold, or offered for sale.

Sec. 26.—Allows innkeepers to sell game

to customers, such having been procured from a person licensed to sell game.

Sec. 27.—Persons not licensed to deal in game buying game from *unlicensed* persons, subject to a penalty not exceeding 5*l.*, with costs.

Sec. 28.—Penalty for licensed persons not complying with provisions of the act, £10, with costs.

Sec. 29.—Servants of licensed persons may sell game.

Sec. 30.—Persons trespassing in the day-time in search of game, woodcocks, snipes, quails, landrails, or conies, may, on conviction by one justice, be fined not exceeding 2*l.*, with costs ; or if to the number of five, £5 *each*, with costs ; and the lease of the occupier, if not entitled to the game, shall not be a sufficient defence against the land-lord.

Sec. 31.—Trespassers may be required to quit, and to tell their names and abode ; and in case of refusal, may be arrested, and on conviction before one justice, may be fined not exceeding 5*l.* But the party arrested must be discharged, unless brought before a justice within twelve hours, though he may even thereby be afterwards summoned.

Sec. 32 & 34.—In case five or more enter upon land, (as in Sec. 31,) and shall, by violence or menace, endeavour to prevent any authorised person from approaching for the purpose of requiring them to quit, or tell their names, or places of abode, *each* person shall be fined not exceeding 5*l.*, with costs.

Sec. 35.—Penalties, as to trespassers, not to extend to persons hunting or coursing, and being in fresh pursuit of any deer, hare, or fox, already started.

Sec. 36.—Game may be taken from tres-passers who shall refuse to deliver up the same.

Sec. 37.—Penalties to be paid to overseers of the parish, one-half to go to the use of the county, and the other to the informer.

Sec. 38.—Imprisonment in case of non-payment.

Sec. 39.—Gives form of conviction.

Sec. 40.—Justices to have power to summon witnesses.

Sec. 41.—Prosecutions to be commenced within three calendar months of offence.

Sec. 42.—Prosecutor not obliged to ne-gative by evidence any certificate, licence, &c., but party adducing it bound to prove it.

Sec. 43 & 44.—Convictions to be returned to Sessions. Persons convicted entitled to appeal to the same.

Sec. 45.—No conviction to be quashed from informality.

Sec. 46.—Permits the prosecutor to pro-ceed by the old action for trespass.

Sec. 47.—Limits the bounds of action against magistrates and others for exceeding their powers.

Sec. 48.—This act only to extend to Eng-land and Wales.

ABSTRACT OF LAW ENFORCING SHOOTING CERTIFICATE.

Act 6 & 7 Will. IV., c. 65.

Penalty for shooting without certificate, 20*l.*, which is to be added to that in Sec. 23 of the preceding act—in all 25*l.* : and also to the surcharge or double certificate—in all, 33*l.* 1*s.* 8*d.* Annual certificate, with 10 per cent. added, 4*l.* 0*s.* 10*d.* For gamekeeper, 1*l.* 8*s.* 6*d.*

For refusing to produce certificate to any assessor, collector, landowner, commis-sioner, inspector, surveyor, or occupier of land, or to any gamekeeper, or other per-son (provided the two last produce their certificates previous to requiring yours), penalty, 20*l.*

Gamekeepers, with the reduced certificate, are liable to the full penalties, if off their manors ; or with the full certificate, to the old action for trespass, or the new penalties under game law.

A certificate is required for killing game, described as such under the New Game Law ; and also for killing snipes, woodcocks, quails, landrails, or rabbits, except under the following conditions :—

Exception 1. — Taking woodcocks and snipes with nets and springes, which are permitted.

Exception 2.—Taking or destroying rab-bits in warrens or any inclosed ground ; or by any person on land in his occupation, either by himself, or by his directions.

Certificates expire on the 5th July in each year.

ABSTRACT OF LAW PERMITTING THE KILLING OF HARES.

11 & 12 Vict., c. 29.

Sec. 1.—Permits any person in the actual occupation of any inclosed lands, or for any owner thereof, who has the right of killing game thereon, by himself, or by any person authorised by him in writing, according to the form of the schedule thereto annexed, or to the like effect so to do, to take, kill, or destroy hares being upon such land, without duty or certificate.

Sec. 2.—No owner or occupier to have power to grant permission to more than one person at the same time in each parish ; such authority, or a copy thereof, to be de-livered to the clerk of the magistrates.

Sec. 3.—No person authorised to kill any hare as aforesaid, unless otherwise charge-able, to be liable to gamekeeper's duties.

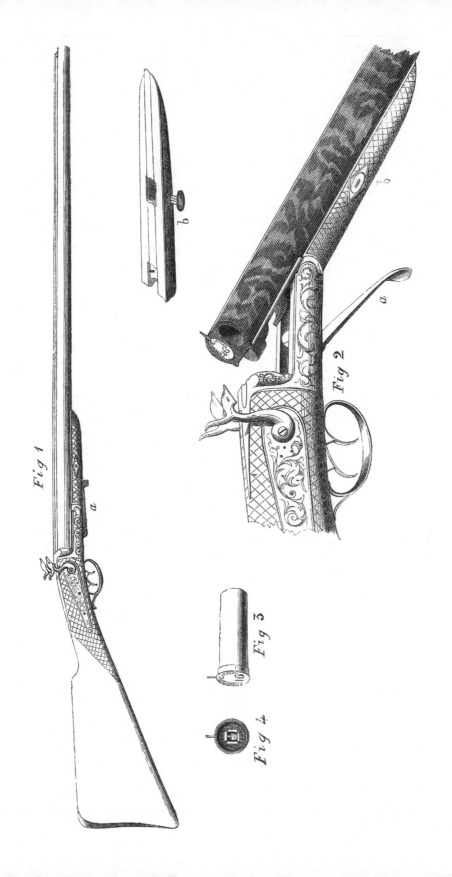

Fig 1

Fig 2

Fig 3

Fig 4

Sec. 4.—Permits coursing without certificate.

Sec. 5.—Debars poisoning game, and the use of guns by night.

Sec. 6.—This act not to affect old agreements relative to game.

SCHEDULE.

I, A. B., do authorise C. D. to kill hares on my lands (or the lands occupied by me, as the case may be), on ——, within the —— of ——, (here insert name of parish or place.)

Dated this —— of ——.

Witness,   A. B.

ACT FOR THE FURTHER PREVENTION OF THE OFFENCE OF DOG-STEALING.

Act 8 & 9 Vict., c. 47.

Sec. 1.—Repeals 7 & 8 Geo. IV., as far as relates to dogs.

Sec. 2.—Enacts that the stealing of dogs shall be a misdemeanour, punishable by imprisonment, with hard labour, for any term not exceeding six calendar months, or with a fine not exceeding 20l. above the value of the dog stolen. For a second offence, the imprisonment may be extended to eighteen months.

Sec. 3.—Provides that if any dog, or the skin thereof, shall be found in the possession of any person, knowing it to have been stolen, the justices may restore such dog to the rightful owner, and convict as above.

Sec. 4.—Provides a penalty of 25l. for the advertising of rewards for the recovery of stolen dogs.

Sec. 5.—Justices may grant search-warrants; and parties found committing any offence under this act, may be apprehended without warrant. Persons to whom dogs are offered for sale, if they have reasonable ground of suspicion, may apprehend the party offering them.

Sec. 6.—Provides that any persons corruptly taking money, under pretence of aiding in the recovery of a dog stolen, shall be guilty of a misdemeanour.

Sec. 7.—Justices may remand persons accused.

Sec. 8.—In case of summary conviction, justices may commit, in default of payment of fine, for any term not exceeding two calendar months, if the fine is 5l.; or four months, if the fine is 10l.; or six months, if more.

SECT. 8.—OLD LAWS NOT REPEALED.

48. THE OLD ACTION FOR TRESPASS is still in force, but notice must be given prior to the trespass, unless the judge certify that it was wilful and malicious. Owners or huntsmen may follow fox-hounds, harriers, or greyhounds, while in hot pursuit of their game, without penalty under game-law, and also clear of the old action for trespass, unless notice has been served upon them.

NOTICES must be served either verbally or in writing, and should come from the tenant of the particular parcel of land on which the trespass is committed. Gamekeepers, or other persons, may serve notice, if deputed by occupiers or by lords of manors; but they must expressly name the occupier, &c., as giving them orders to warn off.

If, after receiving notice, a person, instead of going on lands himself, sends his dogs upon them, he is liable to an action for trespass as much as if he himself went.

FORM OF NOTICE.

To A. B., residing at ——, in the parish of ——, in the county of ——.

——, I do hereby give you notice not to come into or upon any of the lands or woods occupied by me in the parish of ——, county of ——, and commonly known as the farms or woods of ——; and in case of your so doing, I shall proceed against you as a wilful trespasser.

Witness my hand, this — day of —, 18—

C. D.

N.B.—In case the lands are in more than one parish or county, or both, it must be specified in the notice. If the notice is to warn off *rivers or waters*, then insert such words, instead of *lands or woods*. In case of a joint occupancy, the notice must commence *We*, and for *me* and *I* in the body of it, *us* and *we* must be substituted. It must be signed by all the tenants. Newspaper notices are not legal services.

DOGS TRESPASSING.—If kept and used for sporting purposes, may be seized and destroyed by lords of the manor, or their keepers.

WILDFOWL may be shot anywhere without certificate, but the shooter will always be liable to an action for trespass if found upon land which is private property.

RABBITS IN WARRENS, AND WILDFOWL IN DECOYS, are private property, and a person sporting with them is liable to an action for damages, without notice.

TAME PIGEONS.—For shooting these without leave, penalty 20s., unless they are shot while injuring corn, when they must not be removed from where they are killed.

PERSONS FOUND ARMED AT NIGHT.—This act has already been alluded to in the first section of the Abstract of the Game Laws, at page 13.

CHAP. II.
THE GUN, AND THE MODE OF USING IT.

SEC. 1.—DESCRIPTION OF THE GUN.

49. GENERAL REMARKS ON DETONATORS AS OPPOSED TO FLINT GUNS.—The first half of the nineteenth century will always be remarkable in the history of guns and gunnery, as being the time of the invention of the "detonator." This lock has now so completely superseded the old flint and steel, in every department of gunnery, that it is scarcely necessary for me to do more than allude to the old plan in the most cursory way. It is universally admitted, that percussion-guns shoot much more rapidly than the flint, that they are much less liable to hang fire, and that they are also less affected by wet or damp—which formerly used to cause the sportsman much vexation, from his gun missing fire, and generally, as it appeared to him, at the most inopportune moment; they should, therefore, for these advantages, be universally chosen, since they combine all the requisites of a good ordinary gun. It is very true, that a good shot may, and does, bring down his birds with any gun which he may happen to pick up; but what the sportsman desires, is to be placed in the best possible situation for the prosecution of his sport, and not simply to be enabled to carry on the war in an "any-how" manner. Emulation is one great essential to the enjoyment of sport; and the good shot who goes out with the idea that his companion has a better gun, or better dogs, than himself, is already deprived of a considerable share of the pleasure which he would otherwise enjoy. Besides this point of view, another must be taken—guns not only shoot with different degrees of force and accuracy, but also with *very varying degrees of safety.* A cast-steel gun of the most ordinary metal would, probably, shoot as well as any other, if carefully bored and finished; but in point of safety, it would be highly dangerous, even if by accident it stood the proof-charge. It is well known that cast metals assume different forms of crystallization long after they are cool, and that after a considerable period has elapsed they often become much more brittle than at first; hence there would be great risk in using this material. And this is not the only one which should be avoided; but the controversies on the subject are so warm, and the evidence so conflicting, that it is difficult to arrive at the truth. Some contend that steel barrels are the most safe, as well as the best shooters; others, that they can never be made safe: but, at all events, there can be no doubt that different barrels shoot with very different degrees of safety. I shall, there-fore, consider the choice of a gun—first, on the score of safety; and secondly, on the score of efficiency.

50. THE COMPONENT PARTS OF THE GUN are—1st, the barrel; 2nd, the breech; 3rd, the nipple; 4th, the lock; 5th, the stock; 6th, the ramrod.

51. THE BARREL must vary in gauge, in length, and in weight, according to the work for which it is required. It is quite out of the sportsman's province to understand all the delicate points in the manufacture of this article; a little knowledge is here highly dangerous, for it will lead him to fancy himself a sufficient judge to enable him to dispense with that requisite, without which he ought never to feel safe—I allude to the guarantee afforded by a respectable maker. Without this, he will never be free from danger; and with it, he can comfort himself, in case of accident, with the reflection that it is not his fault, since he took care to go to a respectable house, whom he thought he could trust. Gun-makers themselves are often deceived; and, therefore, it is reasonable to suppose that no inspection which an amateur can make, will detect the defect in the quality of the iron or workmanship. No one should buy a cheap gun who values his life or limbs; at all events, he should be careful to have the recommendation of some one who really understands his business before he trusts to one. Gun-barrels are made of iron in some of its multifarious forms, it being the metal which combines toughness, strength, hardness, and cheapness in the highest degree. Many are now made of steel, which is procured for this purpose from old coach-springs, as it is found that steel which has been in vibration for a long time without breaking, is improved in quality; or, at all events, being old, it shows that it is strong—that it has not broken in work; hence it may be trusted in preference to newly-made steel. They are also made from this metal, mixed with varying quantities of the Wednesbury iron, which has now nearly entirely superseded the old stub-iron, in consequence of the bad quality of the stub-nails in common use, and it is what is now commonly termed stub-iron in the trade. Whichever of the materials is used, it is forged into a long tape-like bar, thicker towards one end than the other, and is then wound spirally round a mandril, and welded into a hollow tube by means of the furnace and hammer. In this stage, it presents a rough tube, thicker at one end than the other, with an irregular cavity running its whole length, and much smaller than the intended bore.

C

After this, by means of drills and files, which are worked backwards and forwards while the barrel is kept revolving, the interior and exterior are finished off to the requisite form. In boring the barrel, in order to cause the shot to scatter, and yet shoot with as much strength as possible, it is necessary to avoid making it a perfect cylinder. This is effected by various modes adapted to different lengths. The old flint gun and the modern detonator require very different boring, and hence the altered guns are seldom good ones for any purpose. In the old guns, it was the practice to bore the first six or eight inches "opened;" that is, increasing in size towards the breech, by which means the powder was detained and obstructed in its explosion, and the charge was sent out with great force. But it is found that in the percussion-guns the explosion is so rapid, that the same amount of opening causes more recoil, which, in a long day, is found to be very unpleasant to the shoulder. It is, therefore, now the practice, for ordinary fowling-pieces, to bore a perfect cylinder for three-fourths of the barrel from the breech, and then to "relieve" the remaining fourth more or less, according to the degree of scattering required. In long and heavy guns, even though detonators, a slight "opening" behind may be made, but it must be very carefully done, or the powder will escape by the side of the wadding. For a duck-gun, the barrel should be more and more tight, down to within six inches of the breech, when it may be slightly "opened" down to the breech, increasing the length of the opening in proportion to the length and strength of the gun. The object of the former is to ease the shot out, and yet, by the latter, to give sufficient impetus by the early confinement of the explosion in the first six inches. There are so many points to consider in fixing upon the precise length, bore, and strength of a barrel, that a gunmaker ought to have every particular before he attempts to suit his customer. But whenever such a maker as Purday, Lancaster, Lang, or Moore, who now take the front rank in London, receives full instructions, he is enabled at once to select a pair of barrels which only want putting straight, to give full satisfaction. These particulars are— first, the range—whether for long or short shots — that is, whether chiefly for the end or beginning of the season; and secondly, the degree of ease in shooting required, which depends upon the loading, rather than the boring, if the gun is properly turned out of hand. Barrels are now made from 2 feet 6 inches, for covert and early partridge-shooting, to 2 feet 8 inches for partridges and grouse later in the year, or 2 feet 10 inches for single guns.

52. BREECHING.—When the barrel is thus forged and bored, being still only a cylinder, it requires the large and stout end to be completed by means of the addition of the breech. This is a strong chamber forged for the purpose, out of the best iron, and screwed into the open and thick end of the barrel. The breech has a shoulder to the screw, which renders it of the same size as the barrel, when the two are accurately fitted to one another by the skill of the workman. The breech contains within itself a chamber for the powder, variously formed by different makers, being a mere cup, communicating by a small tube with the touch-hole or nipple, in the Manton-breech; whilst in Wilkynson's, the tube leading to the nipple is expanded into an oval chamber, having a contraction near its distal extremity. This is said to facilitate combustion, by detaining the powder; but I much doubt its practical utility, since I am assured, and believe, that the form of the chamber has little or nothing to do with the firing. In the breech of most of the best guns a plug of platina is introduced, containing a very fine hole—the vent-hole. This allows a portion of air to escape in loading, and also in the firing, both of which are thought to be beneficial.

53. PROVING.—In this stage—that is, as soon as the breech is fitted into the barrel, a small hole is bored, to which a train of powder is laid by the men employed, and it is proved at the "proving house,"—a process which all barrels are required to go through according to law. This is effected by firing certain charges of powder, with a ball rammed down in the usual way, and the charge varies from 11 oz. for a No. 1 gauge, down to 5½ drachms for a 50 gauge. It should be known that the numbers of these gauges correspond with the weight of ball which each will carry; thus, No. 1 carries a ball of 1 lb. weight; No. 2 carries a ½ lb. ball; No. 14 carries a ball weighing one-fourteenth of a lb., and so on; and, consequently, No. 16 carries an ounce ball, and No. 32, a half-ounce one. The marks of the various proving houses are given in the annexed wood-cut.

54. THE NIPPLE completes this part of the gun, and is merely a short piece of tubing, which is tapped into the breech, more or less perpendicularly, or at right angles, with the axis of the barrel. The bore of this tube enlarges towards the inner extremity, and receives a part of the powder, which is forced into it from the breech-cavity by the pressure of the ramrod. Its exterior should be round for about three-eighths of an inch, then square, to facilitate its removal, and afterwards tapped, for the purpose of fixing.

55. THE LOCK comes next under examination. Its principle is simple enough, being merely a mode of exploding the cap on the nipple, by giving it a sharp blow. It is, therefore, only in delicacy of mechanism that its beauty consists, for any bungler can make a lock which will discharge a cap. An artist, however, will make one which shall discharge it with certainty, and with its *full force exerted* at the end of its stroke, so that it confines the gas resulting from the explosion of the powder within the barrel, and does not allow it to escape, as many weak and badly-made locks do. He will also take care that the trigger acts with delicacy, and yet that the cock is quite safe at half-cock. The spring, also, should not be so strong as to overpower the thumb, as in cocking carelessly it may explode, and do serious damage. The various parts of the lock are—1st, the cock, or striker; 2nd, the lock-plate; 3rd, the main-spring; 4th, the tumbler, upon which the spring acts by means of the swivel, and in unison with which, on the outside of the lock-plate, the cock rises or falls; 5th, the tumbler-screw, which fastens the tumbler and cock together; 6th, the scear, which catches the tumbler at half or whole cock; 7th, the scear-spring, which holds the last in its place; 8th, the bridle, which caps the tumbler, and receives the scear-screw; 9th, the side nail, which fastens the lock to the stock. Locks are now sometimes made "back-actioned;" that is to say, the main-spring and lock-plate are thrown back, for the purpose of keeping them out of the way of the wet and also of the corrosive power of the cap. This weakens the stock, but not to any great degree, and many of our best makers still retain the forward action.

56. THE STOCK is generally made of walnut, and should be bent to the most convenient angle to suit the party intending to use it. It should also vary in length, according to the length of arm, the average being fourteen and a half inches, from the butt-end to the trigger. It should be as much reduced at the gripe, or handle, as the strength of the wood will allow; and the butt-end is always capped with iron, hollowed out from above downwards, to fit the shoulder, and slightly rounded from side to side. The stock extends up the barrel, which it is hollowed out to receive, and which is attached to it by means of the loops or eyes, confined in their places by sliding-bolts. Into the part of the stock which receives the breech, a piece of iron called the false breech is screwed; and into that part beneath the lock, the trigger-plate, and guard containing the trigger, are firmly and neatly inserted. The length and bend have been already alluded to, but another point in the stock must be attended to, namely, the *casting-off*, which is a slight lateral bend inclining the aim inwards, and of great importance in a perfect stock. The loading also should be remembered. This is merely a piece of lead inserted under the butt-plate, and as near the lower part as possible; it is solely intended to balance the weight of the barrel, but a good artist now avoids this unnecessary weight by lightening the barrels forward. It is in this part of the gun that the London makers so greatly excel; it is there generally sent out without polish, but if any is used, I know no composition so good as the following; it equals the French polish in beauty, and stands heat or water to any extent; it should be used *with the locks and barrels removed:*—Butter of antimony, ½ oz.; spirits of wine, 1 oz.; vinegar, 1 oz.; linseed oil, ¾ to 1 pint: mix and shake well together. Enough oil should be added till the whole is of the consistence of cream; rub on with plenty of elbow-grease, using a piece of flannel.

57. THE GRAVITATING STOP, OR SAFETY-GUARD, is a very important feature in the manufacture of guns, since upon it mainly depends the safety of the shooter. Nothing is more annoying than to find a lock refuse to act, from some irregularity in the stop, or from its not being properly released at the right time; and for these reasons many good shots have, until lately, discarded its use. At the same time, it cannot be disputed that without it loading is *always* attended with some degree of danger, and that a cocked-gun, carried over the shoulder, is at all times liable to go off, from a fall on the part of the sportsman carrying it. I have examined a very simple and good stop, used by Mr. Lang himself, and many of his customers, which has been in use for many years, and which seems simple and incapable of getting out of order. It has the great advantage of requiring no thought to put it into action, but it is moved solely by the weight of the gun on the right hand at the grip. It is a simplification and improvement upon the stop of the late Joseph Manton.

58. THE RAMROD completes the gun. It is, as its name implies, a rod for loading, and

lies in the circular eyes attached to the lower part of the barrel, but many of the great *battue* men now-a-days dispense with this, and carry it separate from the gun. It has a copper, or, what is better, a copper-gilt head, and a worm for drawing the charge, covered with a cap, at the smaller end. Such is a description of the single gun; the double one differs only in having two complete barrels, with their necessary appendages, the locks and triggers

59. DOUBLE BARRELS.—No good plan has yet been discovered for dispensing with the second barrel of the fowling-piece, by means of a revolving chamber, as in the pistol and rifle; and the reason is, that it is exceedingly difficult to confine the powder and shot so as to avoid the risk of their falling out during the first discharges. To those, also, like Col. Hawker, and most fast shots, who habitually keep both their locks at full cock, the inconvenience of having to cock in the interval between the discharges, would be greater than that of loading every second charge. However, the attempt has not yet succeeded, nor do I think it likely to be carried out for the above reasons; and Mr. Lang's breech-loading gun, to be presently described, does away with all necessity for it. In placing and soldering the two barrels side by side, it must be remembered that the two lines forming the axis of each barrel should not be exactly parallel; but as the breech-end of each barrel is so much thicker than the muzzle, the two former would be separated by a piece of metal equal to double the thickness of the breech, less that of the two muzzles. This would be too great a difference, and consequently a portion of the two thick ends is filed away so as to bring them closer together, without weakening them, because they support each other. The reason for avoiding an exact parallelism is, that in double barrels each barrel shoots a little away from its neighbour's axis, in consequence of the greater support which it receives on that side. To the lower side of the metal, between the barrels, are attached the ramrod-eyes and the stock-eyes; and on the upper surface, the sight is fixed at the muzzle, which is merely a stud of silver, and of very little use, except for a sitting-shot or dead-mark.

60. THE ELEVATED RIB is intended to be a means of adjusting the sight, so that when the eye appears to be directing the gun to a given object, it is really aiming considerably higher. It was introduced by the late Joseph Manton, but is now almost entirely dispensed with, by decreasing the bend of the stock about the eighth of an inch. It is manifest that in all guns, the breech-end being thicker than the muzzle, the line of sight is not parallel with the axis of the bore—and, consequently, in all cases the barrel really points to a spot higher than the eye does.

61. THE BREECH-LOADING GUN.—A gun of this description was introduced some years ago by a French maker, but which was little known in this country until recently taken up by an English gunmaker, Mr. Lang, of Cockspur-street, London, who has succeeded in improving upon the principle to such an extent as to produce a really useful gun, which can be discharged four times while a common fowling-piece can be loaded and discharged once. The principle is exceedingly simple and beautiful, but it requires good workmanship to carry it out; and certainly in that respect Mr. Lang has done full justice to the original idea. The following is a description of this most ingenious invention, which will be better understood by a reference to the engraving:—The barrels are united to the stock by a strong hinge, which is set at liberty by moving the lever (*a*, fig. 1), a quarter turn to the right, as shown in fig. 2. This turn releases a bolt which connects the barrels firmly to the stock when ready for firing, as shown in fig. 1. After turning the lever, the barrels may be raised from the stock, as shown in fig. 2, and are then ready for loading, for which purpose a cartridge is used, containing within itself all the requisites for the gun's discharge. These cartridges, which will be presently described, are carried loosely in the pocket of the shooting-coat, or in a properly-made belt, and supersede the necessity for powder-flask, shot-pouch, cap-holder, wadding, &c., &c. In loading, the shooter turns the lever, the barrels then raise themselves by their own weight, and he places into each the cartridge, turns back the lever, and the gun is ready for use, the whole operation being only an affair of a few seconds. On reloading, it is necessary to draw out the discharged cartridge before inserting a fresh one; but the time required for this is scarcely more than that consumed in removing the exploded cap before putting on the fresh one in an ordinary gun. In Mr. Lang's gun, the old breech-chamber is entirely done away with, and the barrels merely drop down against the flat surface of the false-breech, just as in the revolving pistol. They are bored larger at the breech-end to admit the cartridge, the calibre of which should exactly correspond with that of the rest of the barrel, and thus form with it a continuous tube; the barrel, therefore, has a shoulder at the part where the cartridge ends. THE CARTRIDGE itself is composed of a thick brown paper-cylinder two inches long, and varying in bore according to that of the gun; one end is open to

receive the charge, which is the same as in the ordinary gun, the other is closed by a brass capsule, which overlaps the paper nearly a quarter of an inch, forming a strong joint. In the middle of the inner surface of this capsule, is a small brass chamber, firmly supported in its place, and containing the small cap which fires the charge. A brass pin eight-tenths of an inch in length, and about a line in diameter, passes through the capsule and one side of the small chamber, and receives the cap on its point in the same way as the ordinary nipple. The other end of the pin projects beyond the cartridge about one-fourth of an inch, and lies in a notch between the barrel and the false-breech, beyond which it stands up to receive the blow of the striker. All this will be more readily understood by a reference to the engraving (figs. 3 and 4). The cartridge-case is sold with the cap, all ready for receiving the powder and shot; and this is the best plan of using it, because then dry powder may always be obtained, and they are as easy to charge as an ordinary gun. Their price is a penny a-piece, containing a cap; and this additional cost is the only drawback to the use of the breech-loader with which I am acquainted. The advantages of this gun are manifest, and to all those who value rapid and safe loading as highly as it deserves, I should strongly recommend a trial of it, since it appears to me to supply a great desideratum, and if as good in practice as it appears to me to be theoretically perfect, its invention will be almost as great an era in gun-making as that of the detonator itself. Time, however, and time alone, must decide its merits.

62. WEIGHT AND LENGTH OF GUNS.—The usual weight of a double-barrelled gun is now from 5½ to 7½ lbs. The former *may* be safe, but is scarcely to be recommended, especially if not made by a perfect artist. The smaller the bore the lighter the gun may be, and consequently the sportsman must make up his mind, if he wants a light gun to suit his powers of carrying it, to be content with a small bore and diminished charge of shot. A bore less than eighteen is scarcely useful for killing game, since it will not put a sufficient number of shots into a moderate circle to ensure the certainty of killing. With a fourteen or sixteen-gauge, the barrels should be from thirty to thirty-two inches in length. Single-barrelled guns should weigh from five to seven pounds, for general use, and the barrel should be from thirty-four to thirty-six inches in length. For covert-shooting, a difference should be made of about four inches. It should be remembered, however, that it will not always answer to cut this length off a thirty-six inch barrel, as the forward relief is thereby removed, and the barrel is left a perfect cylinder throughout.

63. THE RANGE of guns varies so much, that it is scarcely possible to give any definite idea, further than to assign the average of the certain killing power of a thirty-inch barrel of a fourteen gauge, and seven pounds weight, at about forty yards. Beyond this many birds are killed, but the best shot will occasionally, and, indeed, often miss, because the shot beyond this distance spread so much as to leave vacant spaces as large as the object aimed at. A heavier gun, with an extraordinary charge, will often kill with great certainty at ten yards greater distance; but the above is certainly the full average, in my opinion. I am not now speaking of picked, but average guns, by first-rate makers.

SECT. 2.—CHOICE OF A GUN.

64. TRIAL OF THE GUN.—The maker having received his orders, will produce one or more guns for inspection and trial, and the following is the mode in which that trial should be effected. Every gun, if made to order, should be carefully examined before it is engraved, as in that state the slightest flaw may be detected; but now-a-days gunmakers have, generally, no difficulty in fitting their customers with ready-made guns, and then the whole dependence must be placed on the character of the maker, as far as safety is concerned. It is very easy for the experienced eye to detect, in a moment, whether or not a gun has been highly finished, but few have had that amount of experience which will be serviceable to them here. The worst guns are now filed smoothly enough, and even in them no eye can detect the bumps and lumps which Colonel Hawker speaks of as distinguishing the bad from the good barrel. It is not in this point that the inferior gun is deficient, for all of these being worked by machinery, the surface is easily made true; but it is in the quality of the metal, and its forging, that the chief difference lies, as well as in the superior filing of the London barrels, and the delicacy and accuracy of the locks, and other fittings, which are very important to safety, and also to correct shooting. To try the gun, it is only necessary to fire it at some mark which will show the result, such as a quire of thick brown paper, or any similar material; or at an iron-plate, covered with whitewash after each shot, and which shows the strength of the shooting, as well as its closeness and regularity At forty yards, an ordinary fowling-piece ought to deliver its shot regularly over a thirty-inch circle, leaving no space of the size of a partridge

without a shot in it. If a choice is to be made between certain guns, and that choice depends upon their relative driving powers, it is very easy to test them, by trying the number of sheets of paper into which each will drive a given quantity of shot; but due regard should always be had to the regularity of the delivery in a given number of discharges. Some guns vary much in that point, sometimes scattering their shot much more than at others.

SECT. 3.—CLEANING THE GUN.

65. THE CLEANING OF GUNS should be conducted as follows :—Get a bucket half-full of cold water, then place the barrels upright in the water, and insert the cleaning-rod armed with a piece of sponge, or cloth, or tow. Work this well up and down. Then change the barrels to a jug, or other vessel of clean hot water, and remove the lead attached to the barrels by the wire-brush. Now take them out of the water, and wipe all clean inside and out; then pass an oiled *rag*, not tow, down the inside, and rub over the outside with the same. All the iron-work should be slightly rubbed over with fine salad oil.

SECT. 4.—ACCESSORIES TO THE GUN.

66. GUN-CASES AND THEIR CONTENTS.—All the *additamenta* should be contained in every gun-case, which is made either of wood or leather; the latter being, I think, the most convenient on account of its greater portability. The appurtenances to the gun are comprehended under three heads—1st, the shooting materials, including powder-flask, shot-belt or pouch, cap-holder, and wadding-punch, with wadding; 2nd, the cleaning materials, including cleaning-rod, complete with tow, cloth, linen, oil, &c.; nipple-wrench and turn-screw; 3rd, spare articles, a spare ramrod, nippers, a Macin-tosh cover, spare powder, shot, and caps, with patent wadding when used; also, Eley's cartridges.

67. THE COPPER-CAP is now universally employed for general purposes, but for punt-guns, where much wet is often experienced a different mode of ignition is employed; this we shall explain under the head of wild-fowl shooting. In purchasing caps, be careful that they are of the kind called anti-corrosive. Eley's waterproof caps are made with a layer of India-rubber, and answer the purpose well; indeed, I believe they may supersede the necessity for the side-primer in punt-guns.

68. THE POWDER-FLASK AND SHOT-POUCH are too simple and too well known to need description. The improved flask, made with the sloping charger, is much quicker in loading, and also much more safe; and the careful shooter will attend to this point, as upon it his safety will, in a great measure, depend. The common sorts are liable to explosion from various causes.

69. GUNPOWDER should always be perfectly dry, and is generally in that condition when uncorked from the canister; if, however, it is allowed to get damp in the flask, or after the canister is opened, the only safe way to dry it, is to get some plates which have been heated in an oven, or before the fire, and pour the powder backwards and forwards from one to the other; as soon as the two plates are cooled, fresh ones must be supplied; but the object is generally soon attained with a moderate quantity of powder. A safer plan, recommended to me by Mr. Lang, is to place the flask, full of powder, in a basin of boiling-water, which will raise the strength, as proved by the *epreuvette*, a couple of degrees. The drying should be effected at a distance from any fire. Messrs. Pigou, Laurence, and Curtis, have the reputation of producing the best powder for sporting purposes; but it is very easy to try the strength by a little instrument called the *epreuvette*, which is like a small pistol, without a barrel, and having its breech-chamber closed by a flat plate, kept in its position by a spring, and fixed on a centre. On exploding the powder, the plate is driven back, according to the strength of the powder, and is retained, in its extreme state of propulsion, by a ratchet-wheel. Hence it marks, with great accuracy, the force of the explosion, and is an useful and ingenious little instrument. Powder, generally called No. 2, which is not over-fine, is the cleanest and the best, being fine enough to enter the nipple, without being so fine as to foul the gun. The coarser grain cannot enter the tube of the nipple, so as to ensure certain firing. For heavy charges, such as are used in punt-guns, coarse powder is much more desirable. Gunpowder is invariably composed of nitre, sulphur, and charcoal; but the proportions and mode of manufacture vary in some degree. The nitre should be very pure, and especially free from common salt, which, by attracting moisture from the atmosphere, prevents the proper ignition of the powder. The sulphur ought also to be purified, and the charcoal should be carefully prepared from alder, dogwood, or willow. These woods are charred in iron cylinders, and the charcoal is afterwards ground, and, like the two first ingredients, it is passed through a proper sieve. The three are then mixed, and spread upon the grinding-stones, which are calcareous, to prevent the risk of ignition by flint; the composition is moistened so as to make a dry cake; and, after some time, it is sent to the corning-house, where it is first pressed

into a hard mass, and then broken up into lumps, which are again reduced into various sized grains, by rotation, on a disk of hard wood, in a sieve of parchment, perforated with holes varying according to the size of grain desired. The corned powder is then hardened, and polished by being made to revolve rapidly in a cylinder; after this the operation is completed by drying, which is effected by steam.

70. SHOT.—The different kinds and sizes of shot are as follows, according to the list issued by Messrs. Walker and Parker, who are generally considered the first makers of the day:—

MOULD SHOT.

L. G. contains in the oz. -		$5\frac{1}{2}$	pellets.
M. G.	„	„	-	$8\frac{1}{2}$	„
S. G.	„	„	-	11	„
S. S. G.	„	„	-	15	„
S. S. S. G.	„	„	-	17	„

PATENT DROP SHOT.

A. A. contains in the oz. -		40	pellets.
A.	„	„	-	50	„
B. B.	„	„	-	58	„
B.	„	„	-	75	„
1	„	„	-	82	„
2	„	„	-	112	„
3	„	„	-	135	„
4	„	„	-	177	„
5	„	„	-	218	„
6	„	„	-	280	„
7	„	„	-	341	„
8	„	„	-	600	„
9	„	„	-	984	„
10	„	„	- 1,726	„

Dust shot variable.

For general purposes, No. 6 is that usually preferred, and as an average shot, it will suit well throughout the season; but let it always be remembered that, *cæteris paribus,* small bores take smaller shot than larger ones. Later in the season, No. 5 may be introduced into use. Some shoot with No. 4, and others again consider No. 7 or 8 not too small; but every sportsman has his own fancy, and much depends upon the distance at which he generally shoots. Some men prefer dropping their game as soon as they are on the wing, and for them a scattering gun and small shot will answer the purpose better than a close-shooting gun with larger shot. Others, on the contrary, wait to cock their guns in the most deliberate way, and always allow their birds to get forty yards off before they fire; for these a larger shot must be used, or their game would almost always escape. Many men use mixed shot; but I believe this plan is essentially bad, producing an irregularity in the delivery which constantly leads to disappointment. Sometimes, also, it is oiled, but this also appears to be perfectly useless—though no doubt it is harmless, which cannot always be affirmed of useless inventions.

71. ELEY'S CARTRIDGE.—This invention is only of use towards the end of the season, when game of all kinds becomes wild and difficult to approach. They are now much improved upon the original plan, and really deserve the encouragement of the sportsman. The best plan is to keep one barrel loaded with the cartridge, and the other with ordinary shot. There is no doubt that they will kill at a greater distance than the ordinary charge of shot, and at short distances they act like a ball, and can be used in the same way. Many believe that they wear out the gun very rapidly, by increased friction, caused by bone-dust used in their composition.

72. WADDING.—Almost all sportsmen now use, for common purposes, punched wadding, made either from pasteboard or felt prepared with various oily matters, or of metal. The latter seems to prevent leading, but in spite of it some guns will acquire a lining of this metal. The wadding acts by impeding the explosion of the powder, and interposing between the shot and it, thus converting the shot into a kind of bullet till it leaves the barrel. Colonel Hawker advises a thinner wadding to be placed above the shot than that which lies under it, but few sportsmen will like to be bothered with two kinds at the same time, nor does it really answer the purpose he proposes.

SECT. 5.—LOADING.

73. The old plan of loading, by filling a measure with powder, and then re-filling the same with shot, is now almost entirely given up, except by the remnants of the last century. The spring powder-flask is, however, not free from danger, as in using it the charge may be ignited in the barrel, from a piece of burning tow or cork being left in it after the last discharge, and a communication being kept up with the powder in the flask, a very serious explosion has sometimes taken place; but by taking care to allow the spring to drive the slide of the flask well home before the charge is poured into the barrel, even if it is fired, then no further damage would be so likely to take place. Most guns require about as much powder as shot, *by measure;* that is, about one-seventh by weight, since shot generally weighs from seven to eight times as heavy as powder. For most guns, the following proportions will be the best, viz., from $2\frac{3}{4}$ to 3 drachms of powder, with from $1\frac{1}{8}$ to $1\frac{1}{4}$ ounce of shot. This is a smaller proportion of shot than was formerly directed; but I am persuaded that guns are more frequently overloaded with shot than the reverse. Before pouring the

powder into the barrel, the strikers or cocks should be let down on the nipples. After using the powder-flask, and returning it to the pocket, drive down each barrel, with the ramrod, a single piece of wadding. Give this two or three smart taps when home, by which the powder is driven well up into the nipple; then pour in the charge of shot, drive down another wad, return the ramrod, and take up the gun to put on the caps. These may be either carried loosely in the pocket, or in a charger, which latter has the advantage that it can be well used with the glove on, whilst the caps are too small for the fingers covered with leather. Before putting the cap on, examine if the powder makes its appearance at the nipple; and if not, give the gun two or three smart blows with the hand. No gun can be considered certain of discharging without this precaution, unless in very perfect order. After this, place the caps on, and push them well down with the thumb, not with the cock or striker. The gun is now ready for use. As guns vary much in their shooting, it is well to try various charges of powder and shot with the one which you are about to use, and to select the proportion of each which seems to suit your piece the best; but this is better left entirely to the gunmaker. The old shot-belt is now superseded by the shot-pouch, which performs its part wonderfully well, being everything which can be wanted, and safe in every way.

The following rules should be carefully remembered and followed, in order to prevent accidents during loading:—

Rule 1.—Always uncock the loaded barrel of your gun after discharging the other. The loaded one should be left at half-cock, and the other with the striker down on the nipple.

Rule 2.—In loading the last-discharged barrel, always keep the loaded one farthest from the hand.

Rule 3.—Never put the caps on before loading—the cock may slip, even with the best lock. Moreover, the powder is prevented from reaching the end of the nipple.

Rule 4.—After the caps are on and pushed home, never leave the cock down on them, as in this position a blow on the cock, or even on the butt, may occasion an explosion.

Rule 5.—Never point the gun, or allow it to be pointed at, or passed by, either yourself or any living object, except the game you are in pursuit of. This rule is especially necessary during cocking and uncocking, when the cock is very apt to slip from the hand of a cold or awkward person.

SECT. 6.—PRICE OF GUNS.

74. The price of the ordinary percussion-gun varies more than that of most articles—ranging from £2 to 50 guineas for a double-barrelled gun, without its complement of powder-flask, &c. The first is out of the question with the sportsman, and the guns sold at that price *must* be made to sell, rather than for use. Nevertheless, thousands are sent abroad every year, and are used where accidental explosions are of little consequence—that is to say, where life and limb are estimated at a lower rate than a few pounds will balance. The first London makers charge high for their work, but they also pay high wages for first-rate workmen, and turn out nothing but safe and good articles. With these makers, from 50 to 60 guineas is the ordinary price for a highly-finished double-barrelled gun, complete in case, with all its appurtenances. This, certainly, seems a large sum, considering that in Birmingham a gun, which the tyro would scarcely know from the London make, is to be had, in case complete, for from £10 to £30. But, while a first-class London gun may be obtained for less than £40, *cash*, it seems absurd to give 50 per cent. more; and certainly it will be admitted that, for all the essentials desired by the crack-shot, Mr. Lang's gun may lay claim to as high a standard as those of any of his rivals. His prices are as under:—

For a best double-rifle, complete in case . . . }	48 guineas.
For a best double-gun, in case, complete . . . }	38 "
For a best double-gun, to load at the breech . . }	40 "

If with patent safety-guard, 2 guineas extra. Single-barrelled guns rather more than half the above prices.

The description of the Rifle and Duck-gun will be found under the chapters on Deer-stalking and Wild-fowl Shooting.

SEC. 7.—SHOOTING DRESS.

75. THE DRESS OF THE SHOOTER will vary according to the season and the kind of sport which he is engaged in; I shall, therefore, leave its consideration to each particular department.

SECT. 8.—MANAGEMENT OF THE GUN.

76. Before attempting to use the loaded gun, the shooter, whether young or old, should always make himself thoroughly master of it. Many of the accidents which so constantly occur, arise solely from a neglect of this precaution; but if the sportsman is early drilled with the notion that he has a dangerous yet useful weapon in his hand, he will seldom forget the importance of the precept. One or two points should be diligently impressed, the most important one being—*never to point the gun at any time, by design or otherwise, at anything but the mark intended to be shot at.* It is

astonishing how often this is neglected. Guns are often pointed in play at females with a desire to frighten them, or at dogs, cows, or other objects, in mere wantonness; or, again, whilst carrying the gun, its muzzle is held so as to point to every part of the visible horizon. All this is unsportsman-like, unsafe, and worse than useless. There can be but three directions at which the gun should ever be pointed :—firstly, while held with the trigger-guard on the fore-arm, the point should be directed to the earth; se-condly, on the shoulder, the point should be directed to the heavens; and thirdly, to the mark, wherever that may be. With this provi-so kept steadily in view, even the gun at full cock is perfectly safe, except from bursting.

Sect. 9.—Learning to Shoot.

77. Let the embryo-shooter commence by practising, for an hour at least, with a cop-per-cap only, and no powder; this will ac-custom his nerves to the explosion, trifling as it is, and will also teach the use of the trigger. It may be best carried out as fol-lows:—Provide gun-caps, &c., in a good-sized room at night; then get a tallow-candle, and place it at about two yards' dis-tance, on an ordinary table. Raise the gun to the shoulder, take deliberate aim, and pull the trigger. If the aim is good, and the bore of the gun about 16, at that distance the candle will be put out, or its flame will be seen to be affected. Persevere in this practice, and try how often the above feat can be accomplished, and as it becomes more and more easy, bring the gun up more and more quickly. In doing this trick, the gun may be held with the left hand tolerably forward; but in after-shooting, the nearer the fingers are brought to the trigger-guard, the greater the amount of safety; though even with this precaution they are not posi-tively safe, as I can speak from painful ex-perience. When the mastery has been so far gained, that the candle can be extinguished with tolerable certainty at two yards, and the gun feels pretty handy, the next lesson may be taken with powder, out of doors. It is better to do this a few times, than to proceed at once to the use of the full charge. Nothing spoils the nerve of a young shooter like the giving him a kicking gun with a full charge at first.

78. The Cocking and Uncocking should be diligently practised with the gun un-loaded, as it is of vast importance as regards safety to obtain full command over the lock; but in the above candle-snuffing lesson, the pupil has accustomed himself to cock and uncock the gun; and the only difference be-tween the firing with the cap alone, and with powder also, is the increased noise and smoke accompanying the latter.

79. Shooting Sitting.—After this lesson, put in a moderate charge of shot, say one ounce, and try your aim at any object, such as the stump of a tree, or a particu-lar stone or brick in a wall, or any such mark, which will not readily tell tales if you miss. Do not at first care much about hitting, but fire away until your nerves be-come quite steady; then try to hit a card or a sheet of paper, avoiding doors, which only lead to accidents, as the pupil is sure to pull the trigger after aiming at a door, even if it has been opened, and a man, woman, or child has made his or her appearance at it. When the card can be readily hit, proceed to take aim at any small birds, &c., which may be seen, or come within shot; and when all these still objects can be mastered, the first part of your education may be said to have been satisfactorily accomplished. In taking aim, it is better to keep both eyes open, though many first-rate shots always close the left eye.

80. Shooting Flying.—This is the grand object of the shooter's ambition, and one which the detonator enables him to accom-plish with great certainty, if his nerves are good, and he has only ordinary quickness and tact, improved by practice. The best way of learning to shoot flying is, to begin by tossing up a penny-piece, and then shooting at it while it is falling. Nothing is more easy than to hit this while at its highest point, since it is then almost stationary; but the object should be to hit the penny while descending. A small turnip, also, or an apple, afford very good lessons. Then begin by shooting at any small birds which may cross your path on the wing, in which they will afford good practice as to the ne-cessity for shooting well in front of every flying shot which crosses the gun. The de-tonator has made this less necessary than it used to be with the old flint, but it must still be done, or the bag will return home empty. According to the speed of flight, must be the advance of your aim; but, on an average, one foot is not too much for most birds, and is scarcely enough for the snipe when making a shoot; still, if that allow-ance is made as a rule, it will soon be varied a little by the experienced shot, and scarcely any need be made with the central-firing plan used in the needle-gun, or in that already described as the breech-loading gun of Mr. Lang. Next get some spar-rows, or other small birds, and going to an open field, let them fly one at a time, shooting at them, when at about twenty yards off, with dust-shot. If these birds are so scarce as not to be easily obtained in any number, the better plan is to be-gin by putting a collar of paper round the necks of the first, by which their flight is

impeded. As these birds always go straight from you, the gun should be aimed well at them, a little over their backs, and not before them, as in cross-shots. After this, the next lesson may be at any small birds which happen to come in your way, such as blackbirds, or thrushes, or sparrows, chaffinches, &c. These afford very good marks, and will do everything but get rid of the nervousness which the sudden rise of partridges or grouse always occasions at first.

81. HEDGE-POPPING, as this small-bird shooting is called, is very good practice, and should be diligently followed by the young shooter. Its successful prosecution gives great confidence, and it ensures quickness, and a knowledge of the range or distance at which your game must be killed. There is a sport which is often indulged in extensively by crack shots, which, however, only requires knack and quickness—I allude to

82. PIGEON TRAP-SHOOTING.—The pigeon is placed in a box at twenty-one yards distance from the shooter, who, either by himself or deputy, pulls the lid open, and releases the bird. A condition is, that the gun shall be held below the elbow at the time of pulling the string, and the bird must drop within 100 yards, to be counted as a dead bird. This sport was formerly very fashionable in the neighbourhood of London; and a celebrated locality—the Red House, at Battersea—has witnessed many well-contested matches. The house, however, is now no more, and the sport is going out of repute. It has little to recommend it, except that any one who could command a few shillings might indulge in it, and it has long been found that it is a bad introduction to grouse or partridge-shooting. The pigeon is always taken before it gets to its full speed; and good pigeon-shots find that the habit they have acquired, of killing their birds the moment they are out of the trap, is very prejudicial to good shooting on the moor or stubbles, though many good pigeon-shots are also good shots in the field. Sparrows are also shot from the trap in the same way, and are even more readily killed.

83. SWALLOW SHOOTING is another sport which many indulge in, with a view to improve their hands for future shooting at game. It differs, however, so much from most other kinds, that it is of little use. The swallow-shooter generally selects the moment when the bird is balancing herself, in her hawking for flies, when she is in fact almost stationary. If the shooter can kill his swallow when at full swing, and making her shoots, he is perhaps very likely to command a snipe or woodcock, especially the former, whose queer gyrations are something like those of the swallow when avoiding the gun. But swallow-shooters seldom attempt this, and content themselves with killing at the most favourable time. It is, on the whole, a sport not to be recommended, being useless as an improvement to the shooter, and destructive to a very harmless and, indeed, useful bird.

84. ROOK-SHOOTING is of very little use as an introduction to other species of shooting, because it is generally practised with a small pea-rifle, or with an air-gun. No one dreams of shooting these birds sitting, with shot, because they present such easy marks, as to make it butchery rather than sport. The pea-rifle is only a small rifle, carrying a very small bullet, and therefore adapted for the size of these birds, and the distance at which they are generally killed. It is generally now made on the breech-loading plan, either of Mr. Lang, or that of the ordinary needle-gun. This last principle is very simple, being merely a cock which plays against a breech, withdrawn by a lever. The cock is armed with a long needle, which perforates the breech, and discharges a cap placed at the bottom of a cartridge. It is so arranged that, after cocking the gun, the breech can be unscrewed and withdrawn, and then the cartridge is inserted, and the gun is fit for use.

85. LARK SHOOTING may generally be obtained, as there are few localities where there are not many unpreserved farms, over which the young shooter may roam in pursuit of these birds. It is a capital introduction to larger game, and is deserving of the attention even of more advanced sportsmen than those for whose benefit I am now advising its prosecution. The shooter will find these birds in great numbers on vetches or seed-clover, or lucern, or, in fact, any green-crop which has afforded a cover for their nests. Here the young have been reared, and towards August they remain there in great numbers. By walking over these fields, enough shooting may be obtained to gratify any young sportsman, and by the end of August he may have attained great excellence in the art. The only drawback to improvement for the purpose of partridge-shooting is, that the larks seldom cross the shooter as partridges and grouse do, but go straight away from him, or rise into the air. In the latter case, they are always out of shot before they begin to hover and sing, or they would tempt their fate sadly, as they would then afford an extremely easy mark. The shooter must aim well over the backs of the larks, as they always rise more or less. With these instructions, the shooter may proceed to the indulgence of his passion, either by grouse or partridge-shooting, or wild-fowl or covert-shooting; a description of each of which will be found under the proper heading.

DOG-BREAKING FOR OPEN SHOOTING.

SECT. 1.—DIFFERENT MODES OF FINDING GAME.

86.—In shooting, as carried on in this country, the game is found by the sportsman in three different modes—first, on the open moors, stubbles, and marshes, by means of the powers of the pointer or setter; secondly, in coverts, by the aid of spaniels and beaters; and, thirdly, in stalking deer on the hills, or wild-fowl in the lochs, by the eye of man, aided by the telescope. The present subject comprises the mode of teaching the dog to find game on the open moors, stubbles, and in the marshes. It is one which interests the lover of nature and of sport in as high a degree as any which is followed in this land of sports. It is true, that it is unattended with danger, except from the bursting of the gun, or from unpardonable carelessness, and it cannot compete in this respect with the tiger or elephant-hunts of India or Africa; but it displays the instincts of the dog, and man's power over him, in a way to which no other sport can approach. Who that has seen a brace of dogs doing their work in gallant style, and setting and backing with that beautiful and excited attitude, which even Landseer would fail in fully conveying to the canvas, can refuse his meed of praise and admiration to the efforts of their breaker? Here is no unnecessary cruelty; the poor animal sought for is not pursued till utterly unable to raise a gallop, but, unaware of its impending fate, it is killed dead (or it ought to be), and at once put out of its misery. For myself, fond though I am of coursing and hunting, yet neither can, in my opinion, compare in beauty with grouse or partridge-shooting, especially the former. The season is so exhilarating, the country so wild, the air so fresh and healthful, and the constant excitement kept up by the working of the dogs is so pleasing, as to combine in making the sport to me the most captivating in the world. Hunting is, no doubt, like the fine burst of a full orchestra, though often with a long and dreary green curtain to commence, which even sometimes remains down all day. Coursing may be compared to a series of pretty little airs, interrupted by constant dull and heavy intervals, during which there is no amusement whatever; but shooting is one long and delightful song, only interrupted by the mid-day lunch. The drawback to this sport is its enormous expense. No one can enjoy *good* grouse-shooting under £200 or £250 per gun per annum, and this sum is generally far within the expense of the best moors. Partridge-

shooting is not so expensive; but even this sport will entail an expenditure to each gun of from £50 to £150 per annum—that is, if preserving is carried on to any extent. Wild partridge-shooting, of course, may often be had at the cost only of a little gratitude, but seldom sufficiently good to remunerate the shooter for his trouble, excepting in the first week or ten days of September. Snipe-shooting, it is true, may often be met with, at little expense, but it has not the same charms for me which partridge or grouse-shooting presents. The dogs cannot range in the same bold and dashing manner, for the body of the bird is too small to give out scent enough to be felt at any distance by the pointer; hence, it requires an old, steady, and somewhat pottering dog for this sport. The first requisites for shooting are the birds themselves, and they would naturally first occupy our attention; but as the two principal varieties of open-shooting are only very slightly different from one another, I shall first describe the general principles in which the two agree, and then proceed to describe the peculiar characteristics of each. Open-shooting, then, is the pursuit of grouse, partridges, or snipe, by means of the pointer or setter, aided by the gun, and by markers, to enable the shooter to follow up his birds.

SECT. 2. — CHARACTERISTICS OF GROUND BIRDS.

87. The gun has been already described; and the markers are only specimens of the genus *homo*. In this chapter, therefore, I shall give a general description of the game pursued in open-shooting, and of the dogs by which they are found. A great variety of birds are confined to the ground, and are found only, or chiefly, in the open, as, for instance, larks, quail, landrail, plover, &c.; and in some of their more prominent features they resemble one another. Both grouse and partridges are ground-birds—that is, they do not perch on trees, but habitually frequent the ground, and, until driven there, do not enter woods or covert. They both lie, or squat, when alarmed by the approach of the sportsman or his dog; and, unless very wild, they allow the shooter to get within range before they rise, and they both often run before the dog, especially the grouse. Both give out two kinds of scent— the body-scent, which is wafted by the wind to some considerable distance, and the foot or ground-scent, which they leave behind them, attached to the surface of the soil. Both keep together in broods until the pairing-time—the nest of partridges being called a covey, and that of grouse a

pack. Both are short-winged birds, and yet fly with astonishing velocity for a short distance, affording a fair mark for the sportsman, and trying his skill. Each, as well as the snipe, will be more minutely described under the chapter devoted to an account of their separate pursuits.—(See Grouse, Partridge, and Snipe shooting.)

Sect. 3.—Dogs used in Open-Shooting.

88. In order to enable the sportsman to find his birds in the open, it is necessary that he shall avail himself of the powers of the dog, in some shape or other. Without his assistance, in the early part of the season, he would walk over many miles of ground before he would put up a covey or pack, because they then lie so close as to elude his observation; and towards the end of the season he would be unable to circumvent them, because he would not know, by his own unaided powers, to what point to direct his attention and cunning, till too late to profit by them. At first, the spaniel was taught to hunt the birds within a given distance of his master, and showed his proximity to his game by working his tail and giving tongue. This last sign being inconvenient, in consequence of its alarming the birds, mute spaniels were employed, and also a large smooth dog, the pointer, resembling the spaniel in delicacy of nose and mode of working. These dogs were taught to work with great caution, and were at last broken so carefully, that when they caught the body-scent, instead of rushing in and putting up the birds, they were so excited, yet so afraid of incurring their master's displeasure, that they became stiffened from fear, yet still anxiously desiring to rush upon their prey. This has been cultivated and improved; till at last we possess in the pointer and setter the three essentials which combine to make the most extraordinary specimen of subserviency to man's purposes which any domestic animal affords. There is still the hunting power of the spaniel, its delicacy of nose, its power of standing work, and its lashing of the tail; but the tongue is mute, and the stop from fear has been developed and naturalized into a dead halt, which is really a true cataleptic condition, and which is often shown, without the slightest fear of man, in the young puppy pointing in the fowl-yard. The two varieties used, are the pointer, which is smooth, and the setter, a rough dog, more nearly resembling the spaniel. The pointer, again, is either the old Spanish or the modern English pointer; and the setter is either the Irish, Russian, or English. All these several varieties are given and fully described in the chapter treating of the natural history of the dog, in which they form the most prominent feature of the first division, comprehending "those dogs which find his game for man, leaving him to kill it." They all have the same family characteristics; all beat their ground in a regular and systematic way, when well broken; all ought to stand and back; and their education ought to be the same, whatever may be the variety of breed, or game, to find which they may be devoted.

Sect. 4.—Breaking of Pointers and Setters.

89. In the present chapter, then, I shall take up the consideration of the "setting-dog," as applied to the finding of game in the open, and shall examine into the best mode of fitting him for the task which he has to perform—this task is, the finding of ground-game in the open without springing it, and the showing that find by the dead stop or point. Now, it will be manifest, that to perform this task well, there is required, 1st, extraordinary acuteness of scent, for without this a dog cannot find his birds in the dry hot days of August and September; 2ndly, great powers of endurance, in order to enable the dog to beat over a sufficient extent of ground; 3rdly, steadiness of point, so that the sportsman may have time to come up and get within range before the birds are sprung; and, 4thly, implicit obedience—active as well as passive, so that the dog shall not only abstain from doing wrong, but shall also do whatever his master orders him. I shall now proceed to consider the best means of teaching the dog all those several points which depend upon education, supposing, of course, that he has, by natural good breeding, those which are inherent in the animal himself—viz., the two first good qualities enumerated. Many sportsmen may think it great drudgery to break their own dogs; and to some people no doubt it is so, and, in fact, by many it is an art wholly unattainable. It requires great patience, coupled with firmness and consistency, and also an amount of tact and love for the animal, which every one does not possess. But those who have these qualities, I should strongly recommend to exert themselves in breaking their own dogs; for there can be no doubt that dogs will never work for others as they do for those who have educated them. Either, therefore, your own keeper should break and work your dogs; or if you hunt them yourself, you should also break them. To me, it is the most interesting part connected with shooting; but as all do not think alike, I offer this advice to those who prefer entrusting the breaking department to their keepers.

90. BREAKING DIVIDED INTO THREE EPOCHS.—Every dog's education should consist of three distinct parts: First, the preparatory; secondly, the intermediate; and thirdly, the complete. The first should be confined to the house, the road, and the field, without game. The second should not go beyond the finding of game, without killing it; whilst the third should extend to finding, killing, and retrieving it, even though the two last are not effected by him.

SECT. 5.—PREPARATORY BREAKING.

91. WITH regard to this first department, many sportsmen think it wholly time thrown away, and that their dogs may be suffered to run wild till the commencement of breaking to game. Now, I am ready to admit that there is some truth in this, for I have seen more dogs spoiled by too early breaking than too late. In this, however, much depends upon the breed and temper of the particular dog. If he is very high couraged, and well bred, he can hardly be too soon attacked; but if shy, and not well bred, it is better to leave his education alone for a while. It is much easier to take the courage out of the very boldest animal, than to put it into a timid one; but I am quite sure, that the first part of the education of the pointer can hardly be too soon commenced, whatever difference of opinion may exist as to the second. Young dogs *must* be taken out to exercise, and *must* be taught to follow; they *must* be prevented from killing poultry and cats, and from stealing whatever is presented to their noses or appetites. While at exercise, they should be taught to come back instantly when called, either by the word "Heel," or "Come to heel," and should be compelled to remain there till allowed to run on, when, by the word being given, "Hold up," they may again range forward, and should be made to do so. Every order should be firmly carried out, and care should be taken that its full execution can be compelled, if it is resisted. Next, give lessons in lying down when ordered, and do not suffer the dog to leave his position till " Hie on " is uttered. With the right hand, and whip if necessary, force the dog to the ground, crying "Down," in a sonorous voice all the time, and at the same moment hold up the left hand, to enforce obedience by sign. As soon as the dog is perfect in dropping at the word "Down," or at the hand being held up, begin to try the plan at a yard or two's distance, and if he does not at once drop, walk up to him and make him; then leave him by degrees, and make him lie exactly where you left him, for any indefinite time, rewarding h m by a piece of meat for obedience, and punishing him by a blow, or a pull of the ear, if not complying with your orders. Next, take him into his feeding-place, and put down his usual food; then, when he approaches it, cry "Toho, Toho," in a stern voice, and keep him from touching his food, either by a sharp tug of a check-collar, which you may use on him, or, if his courage is not too high, by the voice alone. If the puppy is under good command in all other respects, he will generally be easily stopped in going to his food, and will eye it eagerly and wistfully, but without attempting to take it. Whenever the dog is taken into the fields, which should only be allowed where there is no game, he should be called back at every fence, or stile, if he attempts to pass or "break" it. If he does, he should be immediately called back, with the rate "Warefence," and made to understand that he is never to leave the field in which his master is. This is easily done by checking him *the moment he passes the fence;* not by waiting till five minutes afterwards, as is often done, and then scolding him for a fault the nature of which he does not understand. If he chases any thing, rate him with "Warechase," and even chastise him, if this rate is not enough. During the walk, the sportsman should take out a pocket-pistol, and, without noticing the dog, occasionally let it off; but beware of letting it off designedly to attract his notice; this is a very bad plan, and often occasions the very mischief it is intended to obviate. If, however, the discharge is made without reference to the dog, he soon disregards it, and afterwards will not be affected by a similar noise in the field. Beyond this, I would never attempt to educate the young pointer or setter till he is at least ten months old, if a dog, or if a bitch, till nine months of age; but all the above points should be repeated, day after day, and ground into the young dog, till he is as obedient, as a machine. Two or three lessons will often *appear* to do all that is required; but it will be found that they are soon forgotten, if not kept up; and that after a month, all will have to be done over again. From the commencement of the first part, therefore, till the time of beginning the second, the dog should be taken out nearly every day; and at least three times a-week he should be drilled regularly in these simple first principles, which are useful, as inculcating habits of implicit obedience, and also as the foundation of his future more complicated drilling.

SECT. 6.—INTERMEDIATE EDUCATION.

92. THIS should always commence at a time when birds will lie well, which is only at the pairing-season, or in the end of August or beginning of September. We have, in the preparatory drill, arrived at a stage in which the dog is taught to come back when called, to go on when ordered, to lie down, to stop from gratifying his appetite at the word "Toho," to avoid breaking fence, and chasing cats, pigeons, &c. The several words of command being, "Heel," "Hold up," or "Hie on," "Down," "Toho," "Ware-fence," and "Ware-chase." All this may be taught to any dog, whether greyhound, pointer, spaniel, or house-dog; and there can be no excuse for neglecting this part of the education; but in the following divisions, good or bad breed makes all the difference in the amount of trouble required, and in the degree of success which may be obtained. Some dogs may be broken in one day to a greater extent than others can in a month; but, generally speaking, in proportion to the courage will be the difficulty of high breaking. A high-couraged dog will often begin to point as soon as he goes into the field; but the difficulty is to complete his drilling, so as to break him from chasing fur, or from running to his bird when dropped to the gun.

93. TIME TO BEGIN BREAKING.—The most important point in the intermediate education, is to teach the young dog to range and beat his ground regularly and systematically. The time for this is, without doubt, in my opinion, the months of February and March, when any amount of time may be spared; and with most dogs it is no little which will suffice. Colonel Hutchinson, however, who is certainly by far the best authority extant, contends that the pointer should never be thus broken, but that his education in ranging and pointing should be deferred till his birds can be killed to him. On this point I must beg to differ from him, though I do so most reluctantly, as the greatest part of his instructions are calculated to teach the correct mode of doing that which he wishes to inculcate; but here, I am confident he is wrong, and for the following weighty reasons:—It must be remembered, that the Colonel is writing for the sportsman's use, and not for the gamekeeper. Now, if it is considered that the best part of the season for grouse-shooting and partridge-shooting lasts respectively very little more than a month, it will be seen that a great part of that month's shooting will be spoiled in breaking your dogs. If the whole sport consists in breaking dogs, then I can understand the propriety of devoting and sacrificing your best shooting-days to the operation; but as most men break in order to shoot, and do not shoot in order to break, it will be readily conceded that, if possible, that time should be avoided. Besides this, it will at once be admitted, that the age of

four months is too young, and sixteen months too old, to begin to break; and yet that will, in nine cases out of ten, be his age in the September of the first and second years of a pointer's existence. No one would dispute the Colonel's reasoning, if his premises were good; that is to say, if it could be shown that a dog *cannot* be well broken at pairing-time; but when it is notorious, and when I know, from my own experience in numberless instances, that the thing may be done, I cannot admit the truth and correctness of the data upon which he reasons. I have seen pointers go out, and stand, and back, the first day they ever saw game, but they were never made good dogs; nor did I ever see a dog, which finally was of a first-rate class, made perfectly steady in one day, or even in a week. Two grand points are required—good finding, and good working-powers. With good finding-powers, a well-bred dog often becomes steady at the first or second point; but if his powers of endurance are good, his courage is generally so high, that at first he will be sure to chase his game when his eye catches sight, or to run to it when it falls. These errors (for errors they are as regards the sport, though venial in the puppy), require time to correct; and the act of correction generally spoils your shooting, by frightening your birds, and irritating your own nerves. My advice, therefore, is to do all which can be done without the gun at the pairing-time, and to carry on to a second stage the lessons already begun. At this time, the dog should be taught the following further lessons:—First, to range; second, to point; third, to back; fourth, to down charge: and the whole of the lessons inculcated in the first stage may be still further drilled into the dog, especially as to breaking-fence and chasing. In fact, his education may be thoroughly completed, and he may be taught everything which will be required in September, unless it is wished that he should retrieve, which I believe to be in all cases very injurious to the pointer and setter—but of this hereafter. Let it, however, be remembered, that however steady you may get a dog in the pairing-season, and without the gun, yet in August or September, when he sees the birds tumbling about his ears; and, moreover, when, instead of single birds before him, he scents and sees, perhaps, fifteen or a score, he will at first be maddened by excitement, and will require a little correction. This is, however, very different to entire breaking, and will seldom take many hours, as the dog is only to be corrected, and not taught. I have already remarked upon the difference between putting courage into a dog and taking it out; and the same may be said of the difference between putting sense into his head and taking it out. When once you have made him understand what he ought to do, half the battle is over, and you may correct him to any extent, without fear of injury; but beware of punishment without his knowing why. I have had more than one dog which would, from excessive high courage, occasionally chase hares, or even birds, and would refuse to hunt till he had come to me to receive a flogging; immediately after which he would jump off, and work and point better than ever. These dogs did wrong knowingly, and I had no scruple in using the whip, and indeed without it they were never worth a farthing. Again, I have had others which would never do wrong knowingly, but would, in their extreme anxiety to find, be constantly making false points. Here, the whip would be worse than useless, and the only remedy is the grave—that is to say, if it is a confirmed failing. Well, then, having settled this knotty point, at least to my own satisfaction, I shall proceed to point out how the young pointer may be broken at pairing-time, intending the word pointer to apply to setters also.

94. THE RANGE should be carefully taught, and in teaching it the pointing instinct is sure to be developed. Take out your young pointer at first with a wide-ranging dog, not too old, but perfectly under command. "Hold up" both, and take no notice at first of the young dog till he clearly understands what the sport is; this will not always be apparent to him till the other dog has found a bird or two; but when the young one sees the other stand, he is sure to be attracted to him, and he goes up in a wondering and curious manner, and begins, as it were, saying to him, What in the world do you look so stiff for? The puppy then sniffs about, and finally puts up the birds, upon which he expresses great delight, and chases them a few yards, or, if of high courage, as far as he can. I always like to see this; if well bred and healthy, there is no fear of his pointing steadily, and the desire to chase is an indication of courage. After this, the young dog begins to range on his own account, and as soon as he will do so freely, I should dispense with the services of the old dog, for various reasons, not the least of which is, that he will derive no benefit himself from seeing the bad performances of his young and raw companion. Then, taking the young dog out by himself, begin at once to make him range to hand; make him work to the right by waving the hand in that direction, and to the left by doing the same to the left. Work him towards you, by waving the hand to you; and from you, by casting the hand under, as in bowling.

In doing this, if the dog does not readily comply with your orders, proceed to him, and, by your own example, induce him to follow your instructions, leaving no stone unturned to render him perfect in this all-important lesson. High-couraged dogs will readily take to their work, and will gallop at a very great pace for many hours together; by all means encourage this, and do not begin to rate them till they clearly understand what you want; never mind their flushing a few birds, this they are almost sure to do; but their instinct tells them that they have a more sure way of getting game than by chasing it, and after a few hours' work they begin to point. During this lesson, the breaker should give the dog every advantage of wind, and should endeavour to hunt him exactly as he will hereafter do when using the gun, going steadily upwind, and working always in that direction, whether in the fields of enclosed countries, or on the open moors. If in the stubbles or young wheats, this cannot always be effected; then keep the young dog at heel till you have reached the leeward side, when he may be "hied on," and turned to the right or left. By no means should he be suffered to make his own selection; and if he goes off without orders, bring him back, and start him off in the contrary direction. When he has proceeded about from 60 to 100 yards, right or left (which, in an enclosed country, generally brings him to the hedge), whistle to him, and when you have caught his attention, wave him forward; then, after he has gained 30 or 40 yards in the forward direction, wave him towards you. He will, in following your last order, cross immediately in front of you, because you have been walking forwards gently during his progress, and as he will gallop about four times as fast as you walk, while you are walking forty yards forward he will have reached the hedge, run up thirty yards, and reached your front again; that is, 65 yards + 30 yards + 65 yards = 160 yards, or four times 40 yards. Repeat this operation in the opposite direction, waving him on as he passes in front of you, till he reaches the same distance to the right or left, then take him forward, and wave him to you again. In this way he will learn to beat the whole ground, by taking a breadth at a time, and will receive the scent of any birds which may lie within thirty or forty yards of his line of beat. It is a very difficult lesson to teach, and requires great perseverance and tact to carry out with strictness and full success. Many days must be spent, and the dog will be steady enough to his "point" before he will have learnt it. It should always be taught single-handed, since the young dog is very apt to acquire the habit of following an older one, and hunting with him, a trick which it is very difficult to break him of, and one which is unsightly and worse than useless, from exciting jealousy in the leader. Besides, most old partridge-dogs get a trick of running up the side of the hedge, and pottering there for game, generally rabbits, which they are very fond of making out. Now, this is a habit especially to be avoided, and yet it is the one which young dogs soonest acquire from others. They are some time learning it themselves; but the presence of hedges seems attractive to all dogs, and from the first they should be carefully watched when near them. The moment they dwell there, without birds are before them, call them off with the whistle, and send them forward, or to the right or left. Do not suppose that the gun is required to develop the desire to range; if a dog is well-bred, and of high courage, as soon as he gets the first puff of the body-scent, he is sufficiently excited by it to induce him to hunt for many weeks together without hearing a shot fired. If a dog will not work with this stimulus in the spring sufficiently to learn his trade, depend upon it, when the hot days of August arrive, and the ground is like iron, he will soon leave his master in the lurch, and refuse to work for him. I would not own a dog of this character, and I care not how he may be broken; but with a good and well-bred dog, the plan I have advocated is, I am sure, the correct one. When the range, single-handed, is completely taught, it will not yet do to commence working double; but I shall omit all reference to this, as nothing is so easy as to put two good single dogs to work together, as far as range is concerned, if they work to hand, which a compliance with the above lesson will always enforce. Besides the usual quartering of the ground, there is another kind of range which must be taught, viz., that in which the pointer is lifted to the end of your beat, and made to work to you, as in a field for partridges, or with grouse, at the edge of a beat, when the wind is from that edge. In such a case, the sportsman should remain on the edge, and send his dog to beat to him; but it is very difficult to teach. It can only be done by degrees; but by patience, most dogs may be taught. The dog must be sent on by the hand, then stopped by the whistle, and made to turn to the right or left; then, when he has beat a sufficient distance, whistle, and catch his eye, beckon him to you, and after he has come forward, wave him to the opposite side, and repeat the instruction till he is quite under command. It is very useful towards the end of the season, as partridges and grouse will often lie, with the dog beyond them, when they would run, or get up wild if he pointed on your side. Its full perfection shows a very highly-broken dog.

95. POINTING, SETTING, OR STANDING.— These three appellations are given to the stiff cataleptic condition which the pointer or setter assumes when near his game. I have already remarked, that it comes on without teaching in the well-bred young dog, though there can be no doubt that, originally, it was an acquired habit, and that in the present day it may be taught even to the greyhound, or the lady's lap-dog. It only requires a good nose, which even the greyhound possesses in a greater degree than he usually gets credit for, and which I have succeeded in developing in him, for curiosity's sake, to the full extent of pointing. By working the young dog in teaching him to range, in all probability several birds will be sprung; at first the dog stands astonished, then he runs cautiously forward, working his stern, and inhaling the foot-scent left on the ground; while doing this, the breaker should walk up to him quietly, crying "Toho! toho! toho!" in a prolonged and base voice, but not in a scolding tone. It is now that the breaker, if a bad one, produces a fault which can only be acquired from bad breaking— this is "blinking." It proceeds from a want of discernment in the breaker, who chastises the young dog for not pointing, whereas he should never do so until the point has become confirmed. When once this takes place, and the dog leaves his point to run up birds, the whip may be used, but very cautiously, unless the courage is very great. "Blinking" arises from a dog being disgusted with his business; and, as the presence of birds is associated with the whip, he naturally leaves them, from a dislike to that unpleasant alternative. The whip will never produce the true point, though it will steady it when once produced, and there is then less fear of disgusting the dog, already too much excited to care about it. When he gets to the dog, he should pat and encourage him, still crying "Toho," and letting him lie on the foot-scent for a few seconds while thus patted; then, not letting him dwell any longer, cry "Hold up!" and proceed with the range. The next time the pointer comes near birds, the chances are that he scents them, and makes a slight stop, as if astonished; he then draws quickly forward, and puts up his game, which this time he generally chases. If the breaker is near enough, he should "Toho" the dog as soon as he feels his game, which will tend to make him dwell longer on the point, but not often to make him yet stiff and steady. Each successive

find makes him more and more stiff, and by repeating the "Toho!" and increasing the encouragement in proportion to the increased length of stand, the dog becomes hourly improved, especially if he beats a considerable quantity of ground, and thereby tires himself. If the dog, after the first five or six finds, continues to chase the birds, he should be brought back with the already-taught rate, "Ware-chase;" but I have always found that, at first, it is better to avoid all rates if possible. Reward is the first essential to success; and when the system of encouragement has produced the zest, and it begins to lead to an overflow of spirits, the repressing hand of man may be exercised, but always with due caution. Whenever it is necessary to use the whip, let each stroke be followed by a caution in reference to the particular offence. Thus, if for chasing, "Ware-chase" must be repeated again and again, followed each time by the stroke of the whip, which bites in the words used. There is one most important particular to be invariably observed in using any correction—never let the dog leave you till he has made friends with you; do not hit, and let him escape without forgiveness, but keep hold of his collar (which every pointer and setter should wear), until you have done the scolding part; then gradually alter your tone, and appear to forgive him, by changing your manner; finally, pat him, cry "Good dog, then," and let him start afresh. Some breeds will scarcely bear the whip at all, whilst others are no use without it; and this latter condition is especially seen in the setter and the pointer crossed with the fox-hound. This cross is very valuable, when well kept in hand, but he is a most unruly dog by nature; he can hardly be over-punished, and never owns a master, till he has exercised his authority by using the whip. When the point is once steadily made, so as to allow the breaker to walk up to his dog before the birds are sprung, he should pat and encourage the dog for some minutes, if possible, using the "Toho" in a low, cautious, yet pleased tone. This at once gratifies the dog, yet teaches him to exercise his caution; and the breaker should take care to crouch all the time, as if anxious to avoid springing the birds. All these little points are soon caught by the dog, who is a very highly imitative animal. Now, still patting the animal, crouchingly walk forwards, leaving him standing, and put up the birds; upon which he will attempt to come up, and perhaps chase, but he must now be made to drop, by crying "Down," raising the hand at the same time, to enforce obedience. Keep him down for a few minutes, then pat him, and encourage him,

and "Hold up," as before. This lesson must be repeated till the dog is perfectly steady at his point, refuses to chase, and is "Down" the moment the birds are sprung. If the point is a false one—that is, if the birds are gone, cry out to the dog, "Gone away, gone away;" and make him understand that it is so, by kicking the grass or stubble, which shows him that they are really gone. Some dogs are very difficult to convince, especially if bred in-and-in, by which their cataleptic tendency is developed, and their reasoning powers made subservient to it. It is unnecessary to enter upon the mode of teaching dogs, other than true-bred pointers or setters, to point. It is a tiresome task, and requires some degree of cruelty, by means of the check-collar and whip. As I said before, *any dog* may be taught, but few will be serviceable in the field; and, as the true breed are so easily obtained, it is quite unsportsmanlike to attempt the use of any other.

96. BACKING.—The young dog has now been brought to perfection, as far as he can be, for single-handed work, without the gun. The next lesson must be devoted to the instruction necessary for teaching him to "back," and to beat his ground, in conjunction with his fellow. It must be remembered, that all this time the breaker has been cultivating the dog's love of approbation, which in this breed is peculiarly strong; he must now take care that it is not carried so far as to produce jealousy; this feeling is the bane of the shooter, and should be put down when manifest, *vi et armis*. Most young dogs will try to get nearer to the birds than the one which first found them, and in doing so, will generally put them up. For this, they should be brought back to a place a full yard behind the first finder, and then made to stand, and well rated in a scolding voice by "Toho;" and, after a repetition of the offence, by even a smart blow or two, according to the courage of the dog, and the nature and degree of the offence. When put to hunt together, dogs almost always watch one another, and the moment one finds and stands, the other catches sight of him, and at first is sure to run on and put up the game; or, if steady single-handed, and he has an equally good nose, he also points either a little before or behind the first finder. Some very high-bred dogs, the first time they see another point, are rendered stiff, as if by sympathy, and "back" at once; but generally it requires the following process to be gone through:—As soon as the auxiliary, which should be a very steady dog, has pointed, and the young dog has caught sight, the breaker should call out his name, and add to it the word

D

"Toho," repeating it in a scolding and cautioning tone, thus, "Bacchus! toho! toho! toho!" This use of the dog's name should not be carried into the shooting-field, but in breaking is very important. Dogs are very sly, and ready to make any excuse to themselves for not obeying their orders; but if their names are actually used, they dare not disobey—at all events they feel sure of the consequences if they do. On hearing this order, and knowing that it means them to stop, they do so; but knowing also that game is afoot, by the attitude of the other dog, they become, to a certain extent, stiffened into a semi-cataleptic condition, which is called "backing;" any dog may be made to "back," whether he has a nose or not; but none can be rendered semi-cataleptic except the true breed. It is the same in "pointing;" here, as I before remarked, any dog with a good nose may be taught to point his game, if stopping, and abstaining from flushing it, can be so called; but the only "point" and "back" which can be depended upon, is the one in which this cataleptic, or semi-cataleptic, condition of the nervous system is developed. It is exactly similar to the effect in the human being, produced by the mesmerist. He can raise the arm of his subject, and, by a few passes, render it as stiff and rigid as the pointer's tail; and this is only the result of the counteracting powers of excitement and repression exerted at the same time. Just so the pointer is excited and repressed at the same moment, until, being of a highly nervous temperament, he is reduced to the rigid condition which is desired. Wherever the second dog is, however, far from the pointing dog, he should at once stop and "back," and the breaker's whole care should be bestowed upon him. The other, as I before remarked, being steady, will demand no attention; but the young dog should be anxiously watched, and stopped the moment he catches sight of the "point." When he has stopped, and is steadily "backing," walk up to him, and praise him, saying, "Good dog—toho! Good dog—toho." Then, if the birds rise, make him drop, by "Down! good dog," in an encouraging yet firm voice. Walk a little way towards the other dog, still keeping both down; and if the young dog offers to stir, rate him severely; after a minute or two, "Hie on" both. Be very particular that your auxiliary dog does not run jealous, and that he "backs" steadily, in case the young dog finds. This is very important, for many old dogs refuse to "back" a young one, till they have once or twice satisfied themselves that their "point" is correct. But such jealous and crafty dogs are not fit to help to break others to "back;" since their

declining to "back" the young dog, encourages him to return the compliment, and they mutually increase each other's jealousy. If the birds lie very steadily to the old dog's "point," first encourage the young dog, then leave him, and walk up to the old one, and put up the birds, making both drop on their own ground. This lesson is rather difficult, as the "backing" dog naturally runs up to his master, and if he will not stop and drop to the hand, and "down," a cord and stake must be fastened to a spike-collar, which he must wear, and the stake driven into the ground, before leaving him, or an assistant must go up and put up the birds; but I prefer doing everything without any looker-on, as the dog has then his attention wholly directed to your own movements. Some very high-couraged dogs are very difficult to make "back;" and, indeed, I have known many highly-bred ones in which the cataleptic condition was never fully developed. They were made to stop, but not to "back;" that is to say, they were not influenced by any condition but fear. I once had a very extraordinary young pointer, the fastest and best-nosed single-handed dog I ever saw, which took many months to teach this accomplishment. He was "steady before," when I bought him, at twelve months of age, at the end of the pairing-season. I had him with me all the summer, and got him under beautiful command on the road. He was a very small and delicate-looking dog, but the most untiring animal I ever had; no day was too hot or too long for him, and, with anything like a scent, he would beat any dog I ever saw. When I began, about the eighteenth of August, he was steady enough singly, but the moment I put him down with another dog, he would neither "point" nor "back," his whole attention being devoted to the taking the other dog's point. I thought I would tire him down, and I worked him for one whole week by myself or servant, for at least six or eight hours a-day, going as fast as a foxhound in view, or nearly so. But at the end of that time he was as fresh as ever; and, though he had settled down to a steady point himself, he would never abstain from running up and taking his fellow's. Very fortunately, he staked himself in chasing a hare, by which he lost a good deal of blood, and lamed himself, and in this state I began the season; and on three legs, weakened from loss of blood, he was glad to obey my voice, and stopped, though he never "backed." By the end of the partridge-season he was steady enough in all points but "Down charge," as he *would* go to his bird if he saw it drop, and no punishment stopped him. This fault lasted even to his eighth year, though constantly shot over by a very good man, after I sold him. This dog, however, next pairing-time, was as bad as ever behind another dog, and never could be depended on, in this respect, till his third season. Even then his "back" was an apology for the real thing; and while his "point" was perfection in beauty and rigidity, the "back" was totally the reverse. He was crossed with the greyhound; which cross, I believe, is far superior to the fox-hound, for the purpose of giving courage and speed; and though increasing the pointer's tendency to chase hares, is not here worse than the fox-hound. I have known one very perfect specimen in the first cross, which was almost as fast as the greyhound which got her, and yet "pointed" and "backed" as steadily as I ever saw; but this bitch, when put to a thorough-bred, old-fashioned pointer, threw a lot of puppies which never could be thoroughly broken, and resembled the greyhound much more than the mother did. Such is the uncertainty of cross-breeding.

SECT. 7.—MECHANICAL REMEDIES FOR FAULTS.

94. These are, first, the puzzle-peg; and, secondly, the check-collar. The former is unduly neglected, in my opinion, by Col. Hutchinson, as it really is a very useful means of correcting a very troublesome fault. I confess that, on this point, I think the Colonel is wrong, as I do not believe that his mode of teaching the pointer to raise his head will answer in the field. Still, I am open to the conviction of experience; but I never found that any thing taught in the closet, as it were, is useful in the field, except when it is connected with the fear of punishment. However you may have inculcated the raising of the head at the word of command, which he uses, viz., "Up;" yet, when there is the temptation afforded by the foot-scent, the dog, if naturally inclined to hunt foot, will lower his nose, and dwell on the scent. It is the breed which is in fault, and nothing but compulsion will remedy it; besides, when a dog is 100 yards off, how can the word "up" be heard? A whistle here is hardly to be conveyed to him; and yet it is under a hedge at this distance that the dog generally foots his bird, and dwells on it to the extent usually called "pottering." The puzzle-peg is merely a piece of wood, about a foot in length, pointed at one end, and flattened towards the other; an ordinary leather collar is nailed to the flat end, and about four inches from this a leather strap, or piece of cord, is nailed to the two sides, leaving just sufficient space for the dog's lower jaw to be inserted, with the strap lying between the canine teeth and the molars.

PUZZLE-PEG.

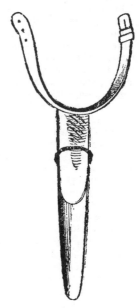

By the constant use of this puzzle-peg, which does not interfere with the dog's ranging, and only prevents his lapping water in shallow ponds or rivers, which will not allow him to bury the "puzzle-peg" in them, the dog loses, by habit, the tendency to stoop, and I have known a natural "potterer" become converted into a fine, handsome, and bold ranger; the chances, however, are much against this fortunate result, and I would never speculate upon it; it is the worst defect, next to refusing to range altogether, which is absolutely incurable. The CHECK-CORD is intended to apply to those dogs which range too wide, or refuse to "back," or to "point," even, when very troublesome to break. It is merely a line of various degrees of size and length, according to the strength and courage of the dog; it may be generally of the length of 20 yards, and of good stout cord, well twisted, yet not too heavy. The object is not always to tire the dog, but to gain absolute command over his motions, in bringing him back to you, or in stopping him from chasing. Of course, the longer and heavier the cord, the more it tires the dog: but some animals are so delicate, that they refuse to range with it, and yet are difficult to stop; altogether, however, it is an exceedingly useful mode of bringing dogs under command; but it is not so necessary for the pointer as for the spaniel, or even the setter, which is a bolder, hardier, and more headstrong dog than the pointer.

94. I have not said one word of this part of the education of the pointer, because I am strongly of opinion that the true sportsman should always have a separate dog for this purpose. Whether in partridge or grouse-shooting, the same kind of nose, and style of hunting, will rarely serve the purpose of finding live and dead or wounded birds. For partridge and grouse-shooting, I am quite sure that far more game will be killed, if the pointers are never suffered to touch a feather, than if used as retrievers as well as in their ordinary capacities. The best dog for this purpose is, I think, a little rough terrier, expressly broken to retrieve, and kept for this alone. He has a wonderful nose, is perfectly under command, much more so than the spaniel, and will retrieve any game, from the snipe to the pheasant. Such dogs I have seen do wonders, and follow the shooters all day, "backing" the pointers in the most steady manner, and *making no fuss* when called upon to retrieve, so that they will often fetch a wounded bird, if permitted, from the middle of a scattered covey, without flushing one; whereas, the pointer must either be taken from his point, or the other birds must be put up and shot at before the wounded bird is retrieved. They should be taught to be completely under command, and the pointers should be made to be perfectly free from jealousy, which they soon become *when the retriever is small*, but refuse with an ordinary-sized one. I shall give the mode of education of these little useful dogs here, since it will complete the lessons necessary for open-shooting. Of course, the same instruction will apply to the pointer, when he is required to retrieve; but I am quite confident that the extra keep of this little retriever will be well bestowed, and he will be doubly useful in covert-shooting. All retrievers should be taught early; begin at two or three months old, by teaching them to lay hold of any soft substance, and drag it from you; this developes the instinct which they have, of appropriating to their master's use whatever he wishes: the stick, the glove, or the ball, have no allurement for the puppy naturally; but you must give him the zest for it, by playing with him. All young dogs have an irritable mouth while teething, and at this time they like to have any soft substance drawn from their teeth. By taking advantage of this period, they may be made to appropriate to themselves the glove or the stick held to them; then, when they become fond of it, throw it a yard or two, and, if likely to become retrievers, they soon run to it, lay hold of it, and bring it to you, for the purpose of having a second and third edition of the same kind of play.

After giving them only a few of these lessons daily, and not nauseating them, they are, as they grow older, accustomed to fetch anything which is thrown, and often may be made to pick up whatever they are told to lift, by the words "Fetch it," pointing to the particular article. In throwing the glove for them to fetch, occasionally throw it into high grass, or in the garden, into carrots or potatoes, then cry "Seek, seek," and encourage the dog to look for it, by appearing to look for it yourself. After six months of age, the puppy may be taught to find and bring young rabbits, purposely concealed in grass, &c.; but should never be allowed to hunt rats, since they, by their bite, raise the terrier's ire, and cause him to retaliate, and consequently to become hard-mouthed with his game. When the retriever has learnt to find and bring young rabbits without injury, and is under very good command, he may safely be taken out with pointers, but at first should be led by a servant, and only suffered to go loose when a bird is killed. He will then at once proceed to find it, and bring it to you; during all which time the pointers must be still "down," let the search be ever so long and distant. After a short time, when the retriever has been thoroughly accustomed to the work he has to do, he may be allowed to go at large, keeping him always at the heel of the shooter, and only suffering him to retrieve at the words "Seek seek," if the birds are wounded, or "Fetch it," if dead. The retriever should always be made to bring the game to the actual foot, or even the hand, of the shooter, and not lay it down at a distance, as he may choose sometimes to leave it on the wrong side of a fence or river. In teaching these dogs to take water, it is only necessary to begin in the summer, and to avoid throwing them in. They will always, at that season, readily enter the water, and fetch anything floating out of it. Nothing is so easy as to teach a retriever to do his work, but the difficulty is to keep him at heel till ordered off; but by firmness, and a little system of rewards and punishments, this may always be effected. I shall go more at length into the system of teaching retrievers under the head of Water-fowl Retrievers, but the lessons I have here described are quite sufficient for land-retrieving; some further mention, however, will be made of this retriever, under the heads of Grouse and Partridge Shooting, where the actual working of the pointer, setter, and retriever, will be more fully gone into. Hitherto, I have described the preparation only of the gun and the dog for this sport; in the next chapter, I shall treat of the sport itself.

GROUSE-SHOOTING.

SECT. 1.—VARIETIES AND HABITS OF GROUSE.

95. VARIETIES OF GROUSE.—In the consideration of this fascinating sport, I shall first treat of the varieties and habits of grouse; next, of the dress and general accoutrements of the shooter; then of the varieties, selection, and management of the dog for finding them; and, lastly, of the address required in the sportsman.

The sub-family usually called grouse, or, in the language of the naturalist, *Tetraoninæ*, is composed, as far as the British Isles are concerned, of four species,—1st, the *Tetrao Urogallus*, CAPERCAILLIE, or COCK OF THE WOOD; 2nd, *Tetrao Tetrix*, BLACK-GAME; 3rd, *Lagopus Scoticus*, or RED GROUSE; and 4th, *Lagopus Albus*, the PTARMIGAN.

96. All these are now to be found in Great Britain, except the CAPERCAILLIE, which has become so rare as to be only seen where it can scarcely be called wild; for though the attempt was made, in 1837, by Mr. Buxton, to reintroduce this splendid bird on the estate of the Marquis of Breadalbane, yet it has signally failed; and I am afraid the capercaillie must be now considered as one of the extinct varieties of animals formerly found in Great Britain, though almost every year eggs are imported into different parts of the North, and hatched under the grey-hen. They can scarcely, therefore, be included with propriety in our present subject. It was once common in Ireland and Scotland, and is now often imported into Leadenhall market, from Sweden, in the dead state, and during the cold weather. The male is nearly as large as the turkey, but the female is much less than the hen of that bird. The "play" of the capercaillie is very remarkable; it is confined to the males, who indulge in it in order to astonish and excite the hens, just as the turkey-cock does in our farm-yards, but more resembling that bird, when his ire is aroused by a scarlet cloak. The nest is made on the ground, and the number of eggs is about 8 to 12.

97. THE BLACK-COCK and GREY-HEN are spread over England, Ireland, and Scotland, being, however, confined to wild and secluded forests. In England, it is found in the New Forest, and on the Quantock Hills, in Somersetshire, as well as in some parts of Dartmoor. Besides these localities, it is thinly scattered in Surrey, Staffordshire, and Dorsetshire, with some few birds on the northern moors of Yorkshire, Cumberland, and Northumberland. The male bird is very handsome, and weighs often nearly four pounds. The whole body is black, with a beautiful glossy blue over the neck and back; the wing-coverts are brownish, with the greater coverts white, forming a white spot on the shoulder, when the wing is closed; the tail is black, and much forked; the legs and thighs are covered with mottled feathers; toes are toothed; the eye has a red spot above, and a white one below it. The grey-hen is only half the weight of the cock; she is barred with dusky-red and black above, and dusky-red and white below; the tail is slightly forked; the nest is made on the ground, with an average of eight eggs, which are of a yellowish-white ground, marked with blotches of reddish specks. The young birds keep together till the spring, when a battle takes place among the cocks, for that supremacy in war, which leads to the same degree of success in love. This arises from their polygamous habit, by which the hens are seized upon by one cock, the boldest in the hatch, whilst the remainder, being defeated in the battle, remain in a state of compulsory celibacy. At the beginning of the season, black-game are very tame, and easily shot. They may then generally be found in rushy places, where they feed upon the rush seeds, and lie very close in this cover. On the moors, they feed also on cranberries and whortleberries, as well as on other seeds; in default of these, and when driven by hunger to the enclosures, picking up wheat, oats, or barley. As the season advances, they are compelled to have recourse to this farmer's food; but they then become very wild, and difficult to get near; it is only by "stalking" them, or lying in wait for them when they come to feed, that many shots can be obtained. In Scotland, as the harvest is often late, they attack the corn in the sheaves, and, by hiding in one of the "stooks," or bundles of sheaves, you may generally depend upon getting a shot; but this is tiresome work, and not worthy to be called grouse-shooting. In winter, they feed upon the tops of the juniper, birch, and alder, and may generally be found in the woods which are composed of these trees; they then afford much less sport than in the autumn, and your success will depend much upon the nature of the ground where they are found. If near high mountains, they are sure to leave the woods or moors the moment you approach, and it is then impossible to get at them, except by very careful "stalking." If, however, they are found in a tolerably level country, with a series of small coverts, there is a reasonable chance of getting a good day's sport. In the early part of the season, when on the

open moors, they will be found either in the rushy places above alluded to, or in the brushwood, near the oat-fields, and they lie so close, that, with a steady dog, you may put up each bird singly. Great care and quiet must be observed in hunting your dogs, and your gun must be a good hard-shooting one, as the black-cock takes off a very heavy charge. No. 3 is the best size for this bird, except in the early part of the season, when No. 6 may suffice.

98. The Red-Grouse, or Grouse, as they are generally called *par excellence*, is the shooter's delight, and affords more sport than all the other birds of Great Britain put together. It is exclusively a British bird, never being found elsewhere. In weight, it is not much over 1 lb., though sometimes coming up to 1½ lb. Its peculiar mottled brown colour is so well known as to require no description. Red-grouse pair like the partridge, and lay about ten or twelve eggs on the ground. Both of the old birds contribute to the cares of their young family, but after the young are able to shift for themselves, the cock does not keep so much with them as the hen. Grouse are found only on the moors, never being met with far from the heather, which composes the principal part of their daily food. They also form a strong attachment to the particular spot in which they were hatched, especially if slightly undulating, as it generally is. On the level plains, at the foot of the hills, they will seldom long remain, even though hatched there, but make for the upper grounds as soon as disturbed; but if found on the side of a hill, they will often drop just over the brow, or fly around its base, alighting out of view of the shooter. In the middle of the day, grouse lie very close under the side of a large rock, or some other secluded spot; but in the winter season, the hours which divide their two feeding times are very few. In sultry weather they lie very close, and not having stirred perhaps for hours, the dogs will pass over them, or within a yard or two, without winding them. In long rains they collect under the side of a ravine, or beneath a rock or strong heather, and at this time good sport can scarcely be expected. It is then utterly useless to attempt to get near them, as they rise on the wing far out of shot. In boisterous winds, also, they are always wild, even in the first part of the season. It is at these times that all the artifices of the sportsman are required, and he should take advantage of every inequality of the ground, walking up the beds of rivulets, at the bottom of ravines, &c., and avoiding bright colours in his dress. Grouse vary very much in colour and size in different localities. In Argyleshire, they are larger and brighter in colour than else-where, except in the western part of the Highlands, where they are still redder and larger. In Perthshire, on the contrary, they are very small and dark. This arises from the fact, that on the west coast there is so much wet, as to addle the eggs and reduce the numbers, and, consequently, to allow those that remain to grow to a good size. This will generally be the result of a bad hatching season, because, wherever food is scarce from over-stocking, the animals feeding on it will diminish in size; and the reverse takes place in diminished numbers; but this is not the cause of the alteration of colour, which is rather to be attributed to the change which occurs in the covert or heath frequented by them. It is a wonderful provision of nature, that all ground-birds, as well as other animals, soon assimilate in colour to the soil which they frequent. The ptarmigan and ermine, in winter, become white as the snow itself, as do the white hare, and numerous other animals. The grouse, consequently, when bred in heath of a bright colour, partakes of the same rich bright red; whereas, when they are found on bare moors or on stubbles, as in Yorkshire and the Lowlands of Scotland, they are of a much lighter brown, scarcely richer than the skylark in colour. Towards the end of winter, grouse feed more freely in the evening than in the morning, since the interval which they will have to pass without food is much longer, in consequence of the increased length of night. At this time, the afternoon-shooting is by far the best, as grouse, unlike partridges, are best approached when on the feed. Grouse feed almost entirely on the tops of the heather, rarely taking any other food, except a few grass-seeds. They do not lie so close together at night as the partridge, but collect within a short distance of one another—not in one solid mass, like that bird. These peculiarities should be known and appreciated by the grouse-shooter, as upon his knowledge of them depends his success in finding and bringing them to bag.

99. Ptarmigan are chiefly found in the most inaccessible mountains, such as Ben Lomond, and the other Bens. They afford no sport, being tame and dull of wing; they are, therefore, seldom sought after by the sportsman, unless he fails in procuring good sport with wilder and more wary birds. Like the red-grouse in their habits of breeding and pairing, and in packing also, they differ in being dull and stupid. Their legs and feet are feathered down to the claws, and in size they come very nearly up to the red variety. In summer, the colour of these birds is of a mottled-grey, not nearly so red as the red-grouse, but barred and marked in the same way; in winter this becomes of a

pure white, with an occasional spot of grey remaining; but the more northerly the *habitat*, the whiter the plumage. The nest is exactly like that of the red-grouse; and in general air and manner, when undisturbed, this bird resembles its more prized congener. There is one remarkable point of difference between these birds, which again contrasts in a singular way with their varied habits—this is, that, though the ptarmigan is a heavy and dull bird, as compared with the red-grouse, yet it can never be tamed, while the red-grouse is exceedingly easily domesticated. The ptarmigan feeds on rock-plants and berries. Its plumage changes in October, and the feathers not only become white, but thicker than before; by which provision of nature it is rendered capable of resisting the most severe colds. Indeed, Scotland does not seem sufficiently north for this bird, which prefers the inhospitable shores of Sweden and Norway. There it abounds, and is trapped or shot for the natives, as well as for the London market. The flavour of a good fleshy bird is very agreeable, though strongly impregnated with the plants upon which it feeds.

SECT. 2. DRESS AND GENERAL ACCOUTREMENTS.

100. DRESS.—For the purpose of grouse-shooting, with any prospect of a successful issue, the dress of the shooter is of great importance. None of the game birds in this country are so wary and so difficult to approach as the grouse; and an old cock-bird will often defy the efforts of half-a-dozen sportsmen for many successive weeks, finally escaping, to be the father of a future generation of clever ones. The colour of the clothes, therefore, must be attended to: but the most essential point is their suitability for preserving the health of the sportsman. In almost all cases, grouse frequent bleak and exposed moors, which are always cool, even in August, during windy and wet weather. Mists and storms are constantly to be guarded against, and for these various reasons, the material of the shooter's dress, throughout, should be of woollen; the more hardy may perhaps venture to put on a linen jacket in the very bright and sunshiny days which often usher in the shooting-season; but those who are subject to rheumatism, or colds, or, in fact, all those who are not very hardy and healthful, should carefully adopt the precaution of adhering to wool. It may be woven into thin fabrics; but, however light, it is still a very different material, in its capacity of resisting wet and cold, from linen or cotton. Flannel, also, should be worn next the skin, as a precaution against the chill so often felt when, on reaching the mountain-top, the skin, reeking with the perspiration poured out in its ascent, is suddenly submitted to the searching powers of the wind prevailing there. I should, therefore, strongly advise flannel waistcoats and drawers, however fine they may be, and, above all, worsted stockings; these last are not only necessary, for the purpose of avoiding a chill to the feet, but they also are by far the best for walking purposes. Cotton and thread, or even silk, are too hard for the skin, and will blister most feet in a very disagreeable manner. If the skin is very irritable, so as to render the woollen unpleasant to the sensations, a pair of silk socks may be worn under them; but the soft pad of the woollen material is necessary, to enable the shooter to wear the strong heavy shoe which is required, without suffering from it. For the feet, there is nothing like the laced boot, for those who are accustomed to have their ankles confined; but I have sometimes known those who have worn "Wellingtons" all their lives quite unable to bear with impunity any other form; in that case, the "Wellington" must be made stout in proportion, and the sole studded with nails; the heel, also, ought to be low, and resemble the ordinary walking shoe. All shooting-boots should be waterproof, as the dews or rains often compel the sportsman to submit his feet to a worse ordeal than a pail of water. In ordering shooting-boots, it is never desirable to procure them from a maker accustomed to consult appearances chiefly; on the contrary, a respectable cobbler is often the best man; but the leather is of more importance than any other point, and should be strong *cow-calf*. It is a remarkable fact, that the skin of the female calf is much more soft and yielding, and yet more durable and waterproof, than that of the male. The *cow*-calf-skin can only be recognised, when entire, by the remnant of the teat, which is always left in skinning, and which a good maker will select with care, for his sporting customers. Durability is not here a mere matter of £ s. d., for no money can supply the place of a pair of shoes to which the feet are accustomed. Every one knows the misery of walking in a new pair of boots, even when the distance is not great; but when many hours a-day must be devoted to a pursuit like grouse-shooting, it is all-important to provide against the discomfort attending upon a sore heel, or a blistered toe; let the shooter, therefore, some months before the season, provide himself with what will fit him, and let him wear them a little every day, till they have taken the form of the feet; then let him put them carefully away, after having them dressed with a composition, made of—boiled linseed

oil, one pint; bees' wax and resin, of each four ounces, melted together, and stirred till cold. It will ensure their future fit, if the boots are wetted by walking into water, before they are dressed; and in hot summer weather they may be suffered to dry on the feet, taking care to keep moving during that time, and to dry them thoroughly before dressing them. All sporting boots should have large-headed nails in the sole and heel, as, both in greasy fallows and on bare rocks, the foot, without them, slips about in a disagreeable and even dangerous manner. If the feet are very tender, and liable to excoriate, the best way is to soak them at night in strong hot alum and water, and in the morning to rub a little neats'-foot oil over them, before putting on the stocking. I have already said that the dress should be woollen; and any of the plain Scotch tweeds will answer the purpose, using the same material for trousers, waistcoat, and shoot-ing-coat. The heather-pattern is strongly recommended, from its resemblance to the general covert of the birds; but I believe that any plain and sombre colour will do, if neither too dark nor too light. Black and white alike strike the eye, by their contrast with the surrounding objects; but black and white *check* is as good a colour as any. The coat should have a strong patch of leather on each shoulder, for the gun to rest upon, and should be provided with an outside pocket on the left side, for the shot-pouch, and a similar one on the right side, for the powder-flask and wadding; a small pocket on each side, above these, will contain the cap-holder on the right side, and the nipple-wrench on the left. You will not require any game-pocket, because, at the grouse-season, no game will bear the heat of the body, without becoming speedily tainted.

101. THE GUN should be of the kind already described as suitable to every variety of open-shooting, but should be a hard hitter, and the shot used No. 6. If the BREECH-LOADING GUN, described at para-graph 61, succeeds as well as I expect, it will be found even more serviceable for open-shooting than for the *battue*. This will be evident to those who have experienced the annoyance of waiting to load, while a scattered pack of grouse, or covey of birds, are rising one after another, too fast to allow of more than two or three shots at them, and yet all within range. The other ACCESSORIES are for your own person,—the powder-flask, shot-pouch, cap-holder, wadding, dog-whistle, nipple-wrench, with spare nipples in it, knife, and dog-whip; and for your "gillie," as he is called in the North, a game-bag, dog-couples, spare powder and shot, caps, and wadding, Eley's cartridges, gun-cover, and Mackintosh coat.

SECT. 3. VARIETIES, SELECTION, AND MANAGEMENT OF THE DOG.

102. POINTER *v.* SETTER.—Having now described the habits of the game to be found, and having already prepared the dogs for the task which they have to perform; having also prescribed the best gun, and the most appropriate dress, I shall proceed to the investigation of the best mode of com-bining all these several elements, until they assume the form in which the cook or the Flemish school of painters especially de-light, viz., Dead Game. I have already given instructions in the general manage-ment of the gun; and it is to be supposed that its possessor, before he ventures upon the moors for the first time in his life, has made himself as perfect as he can, by assas-sinating all the cock-sparrows and larks which he can come near. If the moor has been judiciously chosen and well-preserved, it is fair to conclude that there are plenty of grouse upon it; and the only thing necessary is to find them, by means of the nose, saga-city, and steadiness of your dogs. But now comes the question which has been so often discussed—are pointers or setters best for this purpose? The arguments on both sides would fill up many a page, if carried on in the loose rambling way which sportsmen so often indulge in; but it will be much simplified by ascertaining what we are going to compare. A man goes to the moors, and takes a lot of heavy lumbering pointers, yet with good noses, and he complains that they find him no game, and knock up in a couple of hours—and it is perfectly true that they do. The old Spanish pointer, or any dog with much of his blood in his veins, has not courage sufficient to carry him over the wide extent of ground which must be beaten, in order to find these birds in any numbers. In partridge-shooting, the experienced eye will always, at each period of the day, inform the sportsman where he ought to look for his birds, and, therefore, although his beat may include two thousand acres, yet at no one time does he wish to go over more than two or three hundred. The reason of this is, that at certain hours partridges are on their feed; at others, they are in the turnips, or the grass, or under the hedges; in dry days they are on the fallows, and in wet they are not in turnips, and so on. But the grouse-shooter cannot thus make his selection, but must go steadily on, and his whole lot of grouse are spread, perhaps, pretty regularly over the full extent of his moor, as far as he knows, at all events. A good-ranging dog, then, is a *sine quâ non*; and a steady old pointer is, by himself, a useless animal. The consequence of all this is, that, since pointers include many heavy

brutes in their ranks, the whole tribe must bear the blame. Again, another man proceeds to his allotted ground with a team of setters, rivalling the whole world in beauty and apparent power of doing what is required; but they are as wild as hawks, and though occasionally setting and backing, they flush ten times more game than they find. These also, being setters, contribute to damage the reputation of their breed, and their owner gets rid of them, in the belief that "the pointer, after all, is the dog for the moors." But, yet, there can be no doubt that the pointer may be obtained capable of sustaining as much work, and of ranging as widely and as fast, as the setter. On the other hand, there can, also, be no doubt that the setter can be met with fast, and yet steady, and with a nose equal to any emergency. Now, let us consider what is the essential to good sport, without which no great amount of game can be bagged. The answer will be, steadiness and nose. Which breed is the most generally steady, and which has the best nose? I should unhesitatingly reply, the pointer. I have known some steady setters, and some with most excellent noses; but for one steady setter, I have known twenty steady pointers. Then if this, which is the *essential* point, is more readily gained in the pointer than the setter, I should certainly select him, if it is possible to meet with him of sufficient range and courage. Here, I think, is the real solution—is this possible? My answer is—certainly, it is possible, but not very easy. I have known a vast number of pointers, but I never saw half-a-dozen which could compare, in these points, with scores of setters which I have seen; but, at the same time, there ought to be no reason why they should not. Many suppose that the pointer's foot is too free from hair, to stand the battering and friction of the ground; and that his skin is too delicate for the rough work he has to do. This, however, is all a myth. The hair of the foot is no protection to the pad; and the coat of the pointer is as rough as that of the fox-hound, which has to encounter, and which is quite regardless of, the briars and thorns of the strong coverts in which he has to find his game. Depend upon it, the pointer's foot ought to stand his work as well as the setter's, and will do so, if properly managed. But there is one cogent reason why it does not, and why the pointer is so often knocked up. Every one knows that setters are more difficult to break, and more uncertain, than pointers, and consequently, before the 12th of August, the keeper or servant is instructed to give them plenty of work, to make them *steady*. But in doing this, he hardens the foot, and improves the wind, and, by a

natural consequence, he enables them to go through their work in a handsome manner, without betraying fatigue. The poor pointer, on the contrary, suffers from his well-known stanchness, and is allowed to remain in his kennel till he is placed on the train, for the purpose of reaching the scene of his future labours; and truly laborious they are to the fat, unexercised, and thick-winded animal; and this not only affects the individual, but his descendants. Wherever hares are coursed they run well, because those bred there must be the sons and daughters of hares stout and fast enough to save their lives on former seasons: so it is with all animals, if bred from bad-winded or soft sires and dams, they will exhibit the same peculiarities. But get a good, healthy pointer-bitch, keep her in health and condition by constant exercise; put her to a similarly-treated dog, and treat the offspring in the same way, and you will have no reason to complain of their want of range or stoutness, unless the breed itself was radically bad. If I wished to increase the ranging powers and courage of a breed of pointers, I should certainly select a good greyhound as the most likely to improve these faculties; and, having seen it answer on two occasions in particular, I can confidently recommend its adoption. No dogs amalgamate better; but in choosing the greyhound, care should be taken to select one of a stout and courageous breed. Some greyhounds are as defective in these respects as the old Spanish pointer; but a good stout breed, with a dash of the bull-dog, is that which will suit the best for our purpose. The cross hunt with their heads very high, and are very handsome in the field, being almost too fast for the average of days. It is a great mistake to suppose that the greyhound has a bad nose—the contrary is the case, and has been so remarked by that keen observer, "Scrutator," who offered, some time ago, to kill a fox, in the usual way, with a pack of true-bred greyhounds. The difficulty is, to prevent them from using their noses; as, if care is not taken, they will get into a covert, and hunt till they are fairly tired out. I have had many which would run for miles to a covert, the moment they caught sight of the trees, and that with all the constant supervision which I could give them; and once coming across a scent, they ever after dwell upon one, and would hunt it, if permitted. By this cross, the tendency to stoop and "hunt foot," so common in the foxhound cross, is not developed, and you get an increased degree of speed and stoutness, without loss of nose or tendency to stoop. Thus far I have written on the improvement of the pointer, and on his suitability to go through the work on the moors; but having asked, is it possible to obtain the requisites for grouse-shooting in the pointer, I must now make the same inquiry as to the setter. My answer would be, that you may breed some few setters better than any pointers for the moors, but that to obtain two good ones, you must breed at least twenty; and you cannot tell, until twelve months old, whether they are likely to be good or not. In the pointer, if you have a good form in the puppy, with good back and legs, and a power of holding himself together in the gallop, you may generally prognosticate that he will be steady, and of good nose; but not so with the setter—he is never to be fully fathomed till well and thoroughly broken, and is seldom to be depended upon till his third season. Many setters have I seen apparently well broken, and steady "before and behind," yet a week's or month's rest has rendered them so wild, that it will be some hours, and take some whip-cord, to restore them to a wholesome degree of discipline. They have the advantage of bearing that discipline better than the pointer; and if a shooter is in the habit of venting his ill humour, when he fails in his shot, upon his dog, the setter is the breed which he should select. They are hardy and good-humoured in the highest degree, and will work after punishment even more readily than before.

103. VARIETIES OF POINTERS AND SETTERS.—The selection of dogs, then, is to be made from the following: first, the old Spanish pointer; second, the modern pointer; third, the setter; fourth, the Russian setter. I have said that the old Spanish is too slow, lumbering, and pottering for grouse, and that the modern dog may be procured of good lasting and ranging powers, yet with good nose. The setter, I have also remarked, may be obtained sometimes with all the desirable points in perfection, but I have said nothing of the Russian setter. This variety is much more woolly in its coat than the English or Irish, and the quality of the hair is very like that of the Skye terrier. He has, generally, a very good nose, is very hardy, but bears heat badly, and constantly wants water. I have, however, known some exceedingly good dogs of this breed. They are very apt to get disease of the skin, and if they do they are very difficult to cure, on account of the matting of their hair. Altogether, therefore, I prefer a well-bred pointer; but I should select one strong and bony in frame, with good loins, and with feet round and *hard*. This last point is very essential; no matter what the shape, if the horny matter on the pad is thin, they will soon wear sore; the toes, also, should not spread apart, or the skin between will become sore, whether hairy or not. The head should be broad, with well-developed nose, and the secretions of that part should make the end moist and soft. But, it may be said, if the pointer and setter each possesses what the other wants, why not combine the two in one perfect cross? This theory has, however, been carried out with a want of success which too often attends upon that tempting bait—theoretical reasoning. Man's theory is, indeed, so often upset by actual results, that it seems as if his pride must require humbling; and, possibly, this may be the cause of its frequency. At all events, it is strange that the result of this cross should be exactly the reverse of what was expected. No dog is, generally, so bad as the cross between these two, and they do not even improve one another in any respect, but fall off in all. Why this should be so I know not, but so it is; and I would strongly caution every sportsman against trying this experiment, which has invariably failed, except in some few instances in the first cross, when they take after sire or dam, and do not resemble both.

104.—THE NUMBER OF DOGS REQUIRED for the moors, for each party of shooters, is not less than three brace. If one, two, or three guns work together, they will of course not require more than one gun. Few dogs will work more than six hours, but a good one should be able to do that; the average, however, will not come up to that mark; and therefore hunting twelve hours a-day, you will require the assistance of a third brace. No good will be done with more than a brace at a time, if good rangers; but if you have a pottering dog, which will not go far from you, he may as well be at large, and allowed to do what little he can; in my eye, however, he spoils the beauty of the work, as I cannot bear to see one dog faster than another. The perfection of grouse-shooting, to me, lies in the quartering, and exact working, of the dogs; yet if you have a steady old dog in the middle, and working between your two fast and wide rangers, they will not cross one another, but will and ought to refuse to encroach upon his beat, and turn upon their own ground when they come up to his. Most grouse-shooters calculate upon a kennel of at least six brace of dogs, which is about the average team. This number will not be too many if they are of the usual run of pointers; but if more carefully selected or bred, or if of a good breed of setters, the number I have named will be more likely to answer your purpose; still, it is better to have too many than too few: a cut foot, or any attack of disease, may deprive you of the services of one or two, and you may be left with perhaps one good one, or not even that. If, therefore, you have the means, and cannot fully depend from experience upon all your team, take at least an extra brace, or even two. It must not be forgotten, that some dogs which have appeared very good indeed, when tried without the gun, and worked by their breaker, will not turn out quite as well as you expected from their performances, and the characters given by their sellers. Some are not steady enough, others are too steady, &c. An amusing instance is told by Mr. Colquhoun, in his valuable contribution to our knowledge of Highland sports. "A gentleman, walking out with a high-broke pointer, suddenly missed him, when he presently espied him soberly and submissively following the heels of an old guinea-fowl, whose reiterated cry of 'Come back! come back!' he had thought it his duty to obey." If I had seen a dog following a guinea-fowl, I should certainly rather have suspected him of being fowl-mouthed, than of being too highly broke; but, as a story, it tells remarkably well.

Sect. 4.—Breaking to the Gun.

105. It will be borne in mind, that the education of the pointer, or setter, has only been carried up to the point at which it was compelled to stop, for want of the gun; and that there are some few essentials in regard to which it requires finish. The "Down-charge" is dependent upon the rising of the birds, and can better be taught at pairing-time than now; but, however well inculcated, it is too apt to be forgotten, and to be lost sight of, in the anxiety to bag the game. It will be remembered, that I have strongly recommended that the pointer or setter should not be used as a retriever, but that another dog should be specially set apart for that purpose. If this is not the case, the chances are ten to one that the young dog is allowed to go to his bird, if a runner, without waiting for his master's order; and if this is done once or twice, the habit soon increases, till at length both dogs rush in and tear their bird, in their anxiety to retrieve it. I should always advise that the "gillie" has charge of the dogs at this critical moment, and that he, *as quietly as possible*, but somehow or other, keeps them steadily down; this is all he has to do at that moment, though he may well do that, and mark at the same time. He may also lead the retriever, till he is steady enough to walk at your heel; but his grand use is to keep the dogs down when the birds rise, and this he should do under all circumstances. Dogs do not require to mouth their game as an encouragement; they are quite satisfied if they see it fall, and will continue the work as long as their strength

will allow, without touching a feather. By adhering strictly to this plan, all danger of their acquiring this inexcusable fault is done away. The ranging and quartering, of course, have been acquired in the mode I have advised; and they have been accustomed to the sound of a gun. If any one of them is wanting in self-confidence, be particularly careful in following him up, pay great attention to his point, and take great care to shoot his bird, if possible, or, at all events, to shoot at it. In this way, he finds that you estimate him higher than he thought, and he learns to depend upon his own powers, instead of following another dog, and always looking out for "points." In grouse-shooting, there is not the annoyance of the constant hedges, which are so detrimental to the pointer in the pursuit of the partridge; but there is a much greater chance of the dog pottering over a foot-scent, because the grouse runs so much more than the partridge, and being feathered down the leg, his foot-scent is so much more strong. It is here that a good setter shows his superiority, as he generally makes out a foot-scent better than a pointer; though I am bound to say, that I have seen one or two pointers that would make out anything. The very highly-bred pointer often has no notion of this; he points as stiff as a Chinese idol the moment he comes upon scent of any kind, and nothing will move him as long as that scent continues. Such dogs are useless on the moors, when you not only want to know that there is game somewhere, but also where it is. The essential feature of a good dog is, that he shall stop the moment he feels the scent, and satisfy himself that game is before him. As soon as he is quite sure of this, he should wait till you are within distance; on being assured of which, he should draw upon his birds, if they are running, taking care to stand quite steady, if he hears the faintest "Toho" from his master. This is sometimes necessary, if the grouse are strong runners, as the shooter must often head them before they will rise, though, for my own part, I should much prefer walking rapidly up to them, and putting them up, as they will seldom, till they are become very wild, get far enough before you to rise out of shot. Some dogs learn to leave their first point, and go round and circumvent their game; but this is only a rare accomplishment, and is scarcely to be desired; it is much better to send your man well on before them, ordering him to drop to the ground the moment they rise. Thus much for the management of the dogs. We will now consider how the intellect of the man may assist the instinct, and superior olfactory power, of the lower animal.

106. In this particular, the address of man is conspicuous. It is often said that a good dog knows where to find his game without looking for it; but I have invariably found that, though occasionally successful, such dogs are the worst animals for a whole day, and leave more game behind than they find; the same may be said of many sportsmen, who pick their ground in grouse-shooting. In partridge-shooting, as well as in coursing, much game is left behind by the man who is constantly saying, "Oh! we shall do no good here." The best plan, in the long run, is to get good-ranging dogs, with good noses, and beat all before you, taking care to have the wind in your face, unless it is very high, and you are on the edge of your ground, as then your birds will be sure to fly down-wind in spite of your teeth, and you will lose them, as they seldom return the same day. If there is a high south wind, begin at the south-east or south-west corner, and work up the south side, by which means your dogs will have a side-wind, and your birds will fly into the centre of your beat. If, on the contrary, the wind is from the north, begin in like manner at the north-east or north-west corner, and work up the north side. Under all circumstances, when you come upon game, you should *follow up that pack till you have either killed all, or lost them.* In pursuing this course, I do not mean that you should take your dogs up while going to the pack first shot at; but, in doing what I advise, hunt the intervening ground, and if you meet with fresh game, you may bag it if you can, as a matter of course. If the second pack should be marked nearer than the first, follow that up in preference; but, as a rule, if both are equally comeatable, stick to your first love. The object of this is twofold: in the first place, you scatter your game, by perseveringly following them up, and thereby have a much better chance of getting single shots; and, in the second, you make your whole lot of birds less wild, because you kill off those which are shot at, and leave the undisturbed ones for a future day. It is not the report of the gun alone which frightens birds, but the finding them, and putting them up, and then firing at them, which has that effect. By shooting once a-day at every pack, you would get, perhaps, on the average, 1½ birds out of each; say thirty brace a-day for three or four days, and twenty brace, or even less, afterwards. This plan would require you to disturb and alarm forty packs, to enable you to bag 1½ out of each; but thirty brace may be obtained from five or six packs, if they are followed up, and exterminated,

leaving thirty-four packs for the second day, twenty-eight for the third, and twenty-two for the fourth; all of which that are left would be as readily come at on the fifth, sixth, and seventh days, as on the first. This is very important, in a sport which is generally pursued unintermittingly for a week or ten days at least; for most Englishmen, when they hire a moor, are limited in their time, and have nothing else to do to fill up the intermediate days. I need not here observe, that, after a time, the flight of the grouse is often to so great a distance, as to forbid the sportsman from following them; but I am, of course, supposing that the thing is practicable, as it generally is in the early part of the season. Many men advise that the shooter should begin by driving all the birds to one part of the moor, towards the centre, because, by this plan, they are kept away from the adjoining moors, where, of course, they may fall a prey to the guns belonging to it. But this is difficult of accomplishment; grouse will not be driven like sheep, and make their point, let it be where it may. In making the attempt, therefore, you are just as likely, or nearly so, to drive them off your beat, as farther on, and, by so doing, spoil your sport, instead of improving it; if, however, you leave thirty-two packs out of forty quiet, they are safe from your neighbours, even though they beat to within a hundred yards of the place where your undisturbed grouse are. The shooter should, of course, always begin on the edge of his moor, selecting the lee side, and then working his way towards the centre, and following up his birds in such a way, if possible, as to keep them on his own ground. This plan, however, will not answer if the wind is very high, as already mentioned—in which case he must begin on the windward side: he will thus do less harm, in point of making them wild, and get more shots, than in any other way. If they approach the boundary, they must either be left alone, or the shooter must drive them back, trusting to his dogs to get the wind in their work; this they will do readily, because, as they cross the wind, it is of very little consequence to them in the greater part of their range. In beating the side of a circular mound, such as you so constantly see on the moors in Yorkshire, you may almost always reckon upon the pack you shoot at keeping to the sides of that hill; they will fly round and round, dropping always on the other side to you, and, by following them up, you may break them, and frequently bag every one. When on the feed, grouse seldom rise altogether, but generally leave one, two, or more behind; these should be diligently sought for, and brought to bag. There are many parts of even the best moors which are not "lucky for grouse," as the shepherds say; that is, the heather is not just of the kind they like as to growth. Their most certain finds are those parts which are patchy, with the heather leaving the turf peeping through here and there. It is not in the very thick, unbroken heather that they delight, but in those spots where they can sun themselves, or use their legs in running in the grass; but the best plan is to make yourself acquainted with their haunts, or to take some man with you who has that knowledge; though, after all, it is a lottery, the ground which they most frequent one year, being deserted by them the next. If the shepherds are made friendly, by a proper *douceur*, without which it is useless to expect their co-operation, they will always enlighten you as to the best spots for grouse. Let not the grouse-shooter hope to do without these gentry; they have everything in their power, and can make or mar his sport as they please. On every account, therefore, keep the blind side of them; and even if they quarrel with your keepers, take care they do not quarrel with you. Fresh-burnt heather it is no use beating; though this is the only rule which can be laid down, as in every other situation they are occasionally found. If the season is very dry, the near proximity to water is sure to afford a good chance of finding game; and, on the contrary, if wet, the hill-side, or even the top, is the only likely place. In grouse-shooting, more is to be done by early work than in partridge-shooting; but even here, since nature has her limits, it is better to wait till 8 o'clock. At this time of the year, the evenings are quite light till 8 o'clock, and twelve hours a-day are surely enough for the greatest glutton that ever shot. By "throwing off," therefore, at 8, and getting a good breakfast before starting, there will only be luncheon to provide on the moor; consequently, eleven hours at the least may be devoted to the sport, and the strength is reserved for the best part of the day, viz., the evening, when the birds are coming off the feed, gorged and lazy. The young and inexperienced hand should be on his guard against the "dodges" of the old birds, especially the cock; he will often endeavour to lead both dog and master away from the rest of the pack; but both, after a time, become initiated into his artful manœuvres, and leave him alone, unless the chance occurs of bagging him, which should be seized with avidity. Towards the end of September, the young birds have learnt to run as well as the old ones, and will often be seen to run out of shot, and then get up perhaps three hundred yards a-head. If they are seen running, the "gillie" may generally get beyond them, and stop them. At this time, a long and heavy single gun is the only one likely to do execution, and No. 2 or 3 shot, or Eley's cartridges, may be used with advantage; indeed, after the first week, the second barrel of your ordinary gun should always be loaded with one of these useful inventions.

SECT. 6.—GROUSE-DRIVING AND STALKING.

107. When grouse become very wild, two modes are sometimes adopted of getting shots, which are pursued chiefly in the most hilly moors. The first consists in driving, by means of the gillies, the grouse over or within shot of certain spots where the shooters are concealed. In those moors where walls are met with, one of these places of concealment is selected, and the sportsmen kneel down behind, at intervals of sixty yards from one another, and in such likely situations as it is supposed the grouse will fly over, when disturbed on the opposite hill. The gillies then take some good-ranging dogs, and having found the packs, they get beyond them, and drive them up in such a manner as to ensure, as much as possible, their taking the direction of the concealed sportsmen. This is sometimes, towards the end of the season, the only mode of filling the bag, but it is a tedious kind of sport, and more befitting the keepers than their masters; indeed, were I given my choice, I should far prefer the work allotted to the men, to that chosen by their masters. This will be considered want of taste on my part, I am afraid; but perhaps my destructiveness is not large; or perhaps, again, it will be said, that my success in dog-breaking is greater than that to what I have arrived in shooting. The last is perhaps the true solution.

108. STALKING is practised by the shooter himself, by means of the telescope, and is a very laborious pursuit, compared with the outlay of time and labour, especially if these are increased by the weight of the game-bag. It is conducted on the same principles exactly as deer-stalking, though on a smaller scale; and the reader may consult the chapter on that kind of sport, for the details of the various plans and manœuvres which are then called into operation, and which will be equally successful in stalking grouse.

SECT. 7.—THE RETRIEVER.

109. Upon the point of using a separate retriever, or allowing one of your pointers to retrieve, there is a great difference of opinion among sportsmen. I have already given my own opinion, that the use of a separate one is the better plan by far; and I have given my reasons for this opinion,

and also for selecting a small dog, in preference to a large one. In this opinion, I am supported by that good sportsman, Mr. Colquhoun, though he does not restrict the sportsman as to size or breed. On the other hand, Colonel Hutchinson says, "We have all our prejudices—every Englishman has a right to many: one of mine is, to think a *regular* retriever positively not worth his keep for general shooting, *if one of your setting-dogs will retrieve well.* However, if you shoot much in cover, I admit that a regular retriever, which can be worked in perfect silence, never refusing to come in when he is merely signalled to, or if out of sight, softly whistled to, is very useful, particularly where you employ beaters; but even then he should not be the idle rascal that one generally sees; he should be broken in to hunt close to you, and give you the same service as a mute spaniel. I grant this is somewhat difficult to accomplish, but it can be effected; I have seen it, and, being practicable, it is at least worth trying; for if you succeed, you make one dog perform the work of two, and if he accompany you in your every-day shooting, you will thus obtain, in the course of a season, many a shot which your other dogs, especially in hot weather, would pass over. If, too, the retriever hunts quite close to you, he can in no way annoy his companions, or interfere with them; for, I take it for granted, he will be so obedient as to come into heel the instant he gets your signal."—*p.* 266. This opinion, on the face of the passage, certainly would appear to be prejudiced; for I can scarcely understand how a dog, which he admits is very useful, can be "not worth his keep." I am fully aware that pointers and setters may be made to be steady to "Down charge," and yet retrieve; but I know from experience, that in nine cases out of ten, those which are unaccompanied by a retriever are so unsteady, that I am convinced few men are fit to exercise this controlling power. If only once or twice in a day a bird is winged, and the setter is enjoined or even permitted to retrieve, before the gun is reloaded, there is an end to all "Down charge," and every time a bird is shot, it is retrieved almost before it touches the ground. If, however, the shooter *and his friends* can command themselves, when "the bag" is endangered, one of the setters or pointers may be entrusted with the office; but in grouse-shooting, it must be remembered that three brace of dogs are required, and consequently you must have at least three out of the six broken to retrieve. It results from this that, in the first place, you must pay about £5 a brace more for the retrieving-setters than you would for the same breed and quality of

dog not broken to retrieve; occasioning altogether, besides the extra difficulty in the selection, an outlay of £15. For this sum, two good retrievers may be purchased, whereas only one is required; and by constant use, he soon becomes three times as perfect as the setters, which would only perform a third of his work, for nothing requires so much practice as retrieving. Not only a good nose, but a good "knowledge-box" is necessary, and experience in addition. It is quite wonderful to see the "dodges" which a wounded grouse will resort to—running, perhaps, a quarter of a mile in the most twisting directions, and at last thrusting himself so deeply into a tussock of grass, or a clump of heather, as to defy the nose of anything but an experienced dog. However, it matters little, as to our present subject, what is the variety of dog to be used, or whether setter, pointer, or separate dog. The sportsman is generally recommended to select either a St. John's Newfoundland, or a cross with that dog and the setter, which is the usual land-retriever *par excellence.* The latter has a better nose than the former, and is more easily broken also; it makes a very good dog for the purpose, but is expensive to keep, and not so useful in threading the small runs of a hedge, or of heather, as the little terrier. The sort I have used is, I fancy, a cross of the regular Scotch terrier and the old English beagle, showing a good deal of the latter about the ears and tail. They are quite mute, and *very quiet in their movements,* and can readily be made to back the pointer. The nose is so good as to indicate the beagle descent, even if the head, ears, and tail did not proclaim it. They are about 8 or 10 lbs. in weight, and can barely lift a full-sized hare. I have seen these dogs do more than any other retriever, but they do not display the same readiness in carrying sticks, gloves, &c., as the ordinary land-retriever. This, however, is not wanted by the sportsman, and is only to be exhibited for the purpose of display. Whatever the dog, the education *with the gun* is very simple, and is only to be taught by giving them practice. When first taken out they should be led, but soon become quite steady at large, and will, as Colonel Hutchinson suggests, often find single birds near the shooter, which the wide-ranging dogs would pass over. In that case, they ought to wait a moment before putting them up; and though they never positively stand firm, they readily learn to wait till they see the sportsman ready to fire. They should always be under perfect command; and, as they are not very high-couraged dogs, they are readily kept so; whereas the pointer and setter, being required to range far, and for many hours, must be of such courage as to require ten times the strictness which would suit the mild temper of any retriever-proper. I have already indicated the mode of commencing the breaking of this auxiliary, and have only now to allude to some of the methods which must be adopted for remedying his faults. The command is seldom difficult to acquire, and they may then be suffered to run to their bird as soon as it falls; they will not be like the pointer, wild with excitement, and make fuss enough to put up twenty others, if there, but they go gently forwards, and seldom miss the object of their pursuit, from marking the spot with the eye. If used to this, they soon learn to distinguish a wounded or towering bird; and I have recovered a partridge which towered three large fields off, by the little fellow going straight on the line, guided only by his sight, and while I was following other birds. This, of course, was an extreme case; but in wounded pheasants, the distance they are marked in this way is often nearly as great. I am now alluding to pheasants wounded in the open, and yet able to get away with a half-broken wing. When the retriever is thus allowed to run in at first, he gets near the bird, and on its line, and then is able to retain the direction very readily. Of course, there are circumstances where it is necessary to stop the dog, but the least sign suffices, or he is not properly broken. As retrievers do all their work by "roading" or "footing," they require that peculiar kind of nose, and not the high-winding nose which the pointer and setter display in such a marked and beautiful manner. Sometimes the retriever is "hard-mouthed;" but this is more often the case with the retrieving-setter than with the retriever-proper. The latter, however, is so sometimes, and many remedies have been suggested for this fault. One is, to give him a ball stuck full of needles to fetch; but I do not much believe in the plan. If a retriever has, naturally, or by bad usage, a hard mouth, he should be rejected, for it is a fault very difficult to eradicate, and shows a degree of impetuosity, and a bloody-mindedness, unfitting him for his vocation. I need not say, that all retrievers should be strictly kept from vermin-killing; the mildest dog will turn upon a rat, if caught by the lip; and the bite of the polecat or stoat is still more severe. Nothing is more clear than the propriety of keeping each kind of dog to his proper sphere of action. Each requires different tempers and faculties; and the brain and nose, which are adapted for the retriever, would be thoroughly out of place in the greyhound; but by making use of these several powers in their proper places, man is enabled to obtain a helpmate in all his sporting propensities—though not the same animal for all purposes—in the highest degree. Division of labour is known to favour high excellence in man; and the same rule applies to his assistant—the dog.

SECT. 8.—SHOOTING-PONY.

110. For grouse-shooting, the pony is only required (except for the lazy and infirm) to take the shooter to the moor; once there, he can scarcely avail himself of his assistance, without sacrificing his sport. During the time in which a man is dismounting, the grouse are getting on the run, and the interval, short as it is, will very often enable them to rise out of shot. Few active men try the experiment, but I fancy if they did, they would find that they could kill more birds with than without a pony. With his aid, you may get up to the birds much more quickly; and I do not think that the noise made by the canter of the pony occasions any disturbance to them. No doubt, the increased height is a disadvantage; but, to balance this, is the increased speed in getting to your dog's point. How often do we see the pointer stand at 150 or 200 yards off, and what a time it takes to get up to him, especially if against the steep side of a hill; on the other hand, many parts of the moors are not rideable. In making the comparison, it is generally the case that the shooter on foot is an active young man, and the pony-man an old and infirm one, who takes five minutes to get off, and perhaps rides up as slowly as the other walks. Still, I should never advise any good walker to adopt the use of the pony; but, at the same time, on *most* moors, I fully believe an active, wary man may, if he likes, use one with advantage, and especially when birds are running much. The pony only requires to be broken to stand the gun; to leap in hand, or follow over a fence; and to be handy, and used to stand without holding. This is so easily taught, that it is unnecessary to allude to it here.

SECT. 9.—EXPENSES OF MOORS, OR SHOOTINGS.

111. The following estimate of the expense attending upon the sport, is, I believe, about the average. In some cases, shootings are let at so much per gun, varying from £10 to £50 per month. It is seldom, however, that good shooting can be procured in this way; for, as the letters have all the expense of preserving, &c., they seldom perform their part of the contract fully. It is better, therefore, for one party to undertake the whole moor, and to divide the expense of the place with one or more companions.

EXPENSE OF GROUSE-SHOOTING ONE MONTH.

	£	s.	d.
Rent of Moor, per year	150	0	0
Two keepers, one 24s., one 12s.	93	12	0
Douceurs to shepherds	8	0	0
Keep of 7 dogs, at 12s. per week (These are also available for partridge.)	31	4	0
Fare to moor and back of two guns and one man, with dogs, taking the centre of England as a starting-place, and the centre of the moors to go to—about	15	0	0
	£302	16	0

Living at moors not charged.

I have calculated this for two guns; but more frequently the moor is divided among three or four. Such a one as would let for £150 will scarcely supply game enough for more than two guns, if pretty good shots, and ardent in pursuit of sport. Some few shillings a-week may be saved in the wages of the keeper; but I am persuaded that economy here is badly invested. A *really good* keeper is worth the sum I have named, in the Scotch or Yorkshire market; and he is so difficult to get, that I would rather give less for the moor and more for the man than adopt the other alternative.

Between a good man and a middling one there is a difference of at least 50 per cent. in the quantity of game; and, in mere money-value, this will make up five times the difference between a pound a-week and 24s. My advice, therefore, is to get a first-rate gamekeeper at any price; as good a moor as can be procured at your own price; and as good dogs as you can breed or purchase, breaking them carefully yourself—so shall the sportsman enjoy all the pleasures and delights which this exhilarating sport is capable of affording.

SECT. 10.—DOG-CART.

The following engraving of a railway-travelling dog-cart is introduced as likely to be useful to the grouse-shooter. It consists of a moveable box in front (A) to hold two brace of dogs, 4 feet 6 inches by 2 feet 3 inches high, and 1 foot 6 inches wide. Behind is a smaller box (B), to hold three dogs, and another or two may be placed under (A) where the driver's feet and legs are; (C) is slightly hollowed out, to receive the axletree, which crosses *above* it and *behind* the knees of the driver. The wheels may be packed behind (A), and after removing the shafts, it may be sent by an ordinary luggage-train at a great diminution of expense; and it may be made to suit the small Highland ponies, in point of size.

RAILWAY-TRAVELLING DOG-CART.

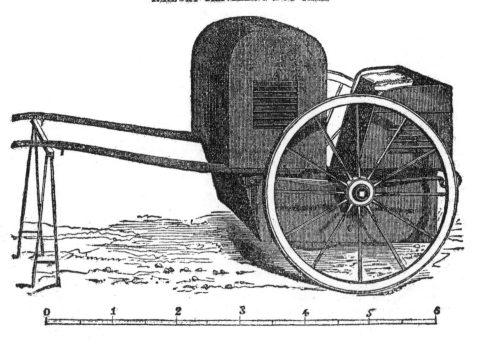

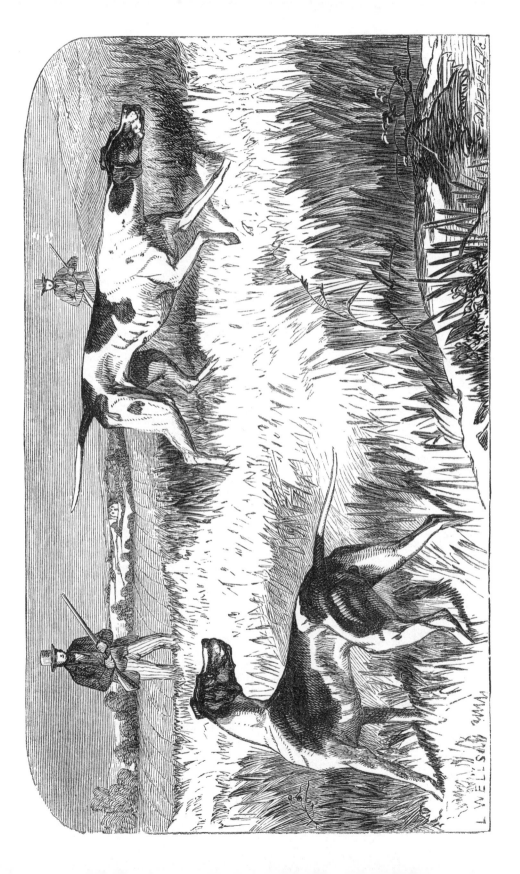

PARTRIDGE-SHOOTING.

SECT. 1.—VARIETIES OF THE PARTRIDGE.

112. This sport, though it closely resembles grouse-shooting, in its general features, especially in wild and unpreserved districts, yet differs in many particulars, which will be presently described.

THE COMMON PARTRIDGE (*Perdix Cinerea*), is the prevalent species, though the red-legged variety (*Caccabis Rufa*) is even now occasionally met with in England; the latter is, however, so destructive to all sport, from its tendency to run before the dogs, and also so dry and insipid in flavour, that it is purposely eradicated, wherever this can be effected.

113. THE COMMON PARTRIDGE is too well known by appearance to need description. It is found nearly all over England, and in Scotland and Ireland, wherever there is enclosed land. In some counties, as, for instance, in Norfolk and Suffolk, it is so generally preserved, as to be quite the pride of the locality, a good day's shooting being there considered the *beau ideal* of country pleasure. Nevertheless, I never could see this beauty in Norfolk shooting; the birds are so tame and so plentiful, that nothing is required but the very moderate use of the legs, and a good command over the gun. Dogs are altogether at a discount, and are scarcely thought necessary to the sport, except for retrieving and driving the stubbles. In my opinion, the expectation of true sport in partridge-shooting is now for ever defeated, in consequence of the improved system of agriculture almost everywhere adopted. Formerly, in every farm, during the month of September, nearly one quarter was left with good (*foul*) stubbles, at least eight or ten inches high. Here there was as good cover as in turnips, or nearly so, and with the advantage, that dogs were capable of finding their game without risk of running them up. Another very considerable proportion was left in rough fallow, undisturbed by the scuffle; and still another useful cover was met with in the shape of rough grass; but *nous avons changé tout cela.* The stubbles are all now bagged, or mown as bare as the back of your hand; the old stale fallow is no more; and the farm is so well stocked, that in September no old feg containing grass-seeds is to be met with. Thus, however desirous we may be of finding our birds on the stubbles or fallows, we cannot succeed, for want of cover in the one, and from the non-existence of the other. Besides, the science of farming is now carried to such a pitch, that no sooner is the corn off the ground, than the plough is set to work; and, therefore, we often find our best stubbles, at the time of partridge-shooting, disturbed by three or four teams of horses, with their attendant men. No wonder, therefore, that the sportsman leaves the South, and betakes himself to a country equally full of game of even a superior quality to the partridge, and allowing the full beauties of the pointer and setter to be developed. There is, however, no more difficulty in preserving a good head of partridges now than there used to be; the increase of turnips, and other green crops, has more than counterbalanced the loss of the stubbles, if the mere facility of rearing and killing game only is considered; but to kill any number of partridges in the old style, with a brace of dogs finding them, is now out of the question. We hear of more than 100 brace falling to one gun in one day; but how was this done? By using a lot of men to drive all the stubbles, and thus collecting the birds on a given number of acres of turnips or seed-clover, or some other green crop affording good lying for them. This is similar to the *battue* in principle, and, I think, more worthy of the butcher than the true sportsman. It is, in fact, the same spirit which leads to the use of the bagged fox or the trapped hare, though not, perhaps, quite so bad as those unmitigated Cockney tricks. It appears, to my limited capacity, that pigeon trap-shooting is quite as good a sport as this turnip-butchery, and it may be had much more easily, and at less expense; but, as Colonel Hutchinson says, "every Englishman must have his prejudices;" and whether this of mine is founded in truth or not, it is scarcely for me to say.

114. THE RED-LEGGED PARTRIDGE, which is now considered to be of a different genus to the common partridge, is considerably larger than that bird; the bill, iris, and legs are of a bright vermilion; the back and top of the head are of a reddish-brown, approaching to a slate colour on the forehead and sides of the body; and of a pale ash colour on the breast and belly; the chin and throat are white, mottled with black; and there is a band of white over the eye. Various bars occur on the quill-feathers, of brown and grey, giving the bird a very party-coloured appearance. It is not so thick and plump as the partridge, and differs much in its habits. It is very common throughout the temperate zone, and great part of the torrid. This bird is more inclined to run than fly, and for that reason is a pest to the shooter, giving rise to unsteadiness in the dogs, and rarely leading to a good day's sport. It also often, by associating with the common partridge, teaches that bird its own bad

E

manners. Unlike the common partridge, it perches on hedges and trees, but not so commonly as the pheasant, and always roosts on the ground. It was largely introduced into England some years ago, on account of its hardihood, and tendency to increase; but it is now, fortunately, almost unknown, except in some few districts.

SECT. 2. — BEST KIND OF DOGS FOR PARTRIDGE-SHOOTING.

115. In grouse-shooting, I have remarked that a wide range is essential to success; but it is generally supposed that the opposite to this is the case in partridge-shooting. There can be no doubt that, where they are very plentiful, you only want a very steady old pointer—indeed, a mute spaniel, which will not range more than twenty yards from the gun, is often preferred, because, from the delicacy of his nose, he will leave nothing behind; but, in wild, open districts, where you have to beat 100 acres before you see a feather, these pottering pointers will no more avail than on the moors. Here a grouse-dog is serviceable, but *he must not draw on his birds till ordered*, as partridges will seldom lie if the dog is not a perfect automaton; at the same time, a good dog ought to draw on his game when ordered to "Hold up," or "Hie on," or you may often be misled as to their exact locality. I know nothing more provoking than to walk up to a point, and, in spite of all encouragement to the dog, to be unable to make out where your game is. I have often seen this with very high-bred dogs; they seem to be unable to move a muscle, but stand as if carved in marble; and just when you have taken a circle, in the hope of finding the object of your search, the covey gets up fifty yards to the left or right of you. It is in this that the setter displays a marked superiority, as that dog almost always stands with his head to his game, and "draws" with great certainty, either by "foot" or "body" scent. This point, with me, covers a multitude of sins; and I would always reject a dog which stood in the idiotic way above mentioned. But, as many pointers are capable of drawing, I would by no means charge the whole breed with this sin; and, for partridge-shooting, on the whole, I much prefer them to their more handsome rivals.

SECT. 3.—NUMBER OF DOGS REQUIRED.

116. In this respect, partridge-shooting contrasts very favourably with grouse-shooting, in which I have shown that three brace of dogs at least must be provided; here, however, half the number will suffice,

and, indeed, one good dog will serve very well for the use of many people. Let it be remembered, that this sport is seldom followed for days together, as is the case on the moors. Those who indulge in it are generally near at home, and carry the gun perhaps only once or twice a-week, which is quite as often as the birds will allow, without becoming wild; the man, therefore, who has a large kennel, can scarcely keep them steady, and is not nearly so well off as he is who contents himself with a brace of staunch pointers or setters. This is especially true of the latter dog, which must be kept constantly at work, to be serviceable; but for the man who hunts one dog only, or even a brace, if he uses them three or four times a-week, the setter is very useful, as he is so much more hardy than the pointer, and a better feeder also; the great mistake is the want of work before and after the season begins—the former, to get the dogs steady, yet fit to work; the latter, to keep them so.

SECT. 4.—RETRIEVING, DRESS, &c.

117. RETRIEVING partridges is to be conducted exactly the same as for grouse.

118. DRESS.—This also should be the same as for grouse-shooting.

SECT. 5.—MANAGEMENT OF THE BEAT.

119. Col. Hawker was, I think, the first writer who drew attention to the great disadvantage of beginning to search for partridges before the dew is off the ground; it is, however, so important a caution, that I am much surprised it was not before his time generally acted upon, and also, that even now many experienced shots dispute the opinion; these, however, are the exceptions, as the Colonel's suggestion is now generally followed. His rules are so concise, and, at the same time, so sound, that I shall make an extract from them, being the summary of the requisites for successful partridge-shooting, viz.:—"*First*, to have good markers, judiciously placed, and *then* to disperse the birds; the best way to do which, is to head the birds, by making an extensive *circle*. The second is, to make no more noise than what cannot absolutely be avoided, by doing as *much by signal* and whistling, and as little by *hallooing*, as possible. Thirdly, go on the hills to find, and drive down from them, the birds; and then in vales, to kill them. Fourthly, when distressed for partridges, in a scarce country at the end of the season, take a horse, and gallop from one *turnip-field* to another, instead of regularly slaving after inaccessible coveys."—*p.* 165, *7th edition*. He also

adds, in a note, the following advice as to marking:—"Always be sure to tell a young marker that he must *carry his eye well forward*, when a covey of birds begin to skim in their flight; and consider that, as they may continue doing so for a field or two, he cannot safely say that he *has marked them down*, till he has seen them stop, and *flap their wings*, which all game must do before they can alight on the ground."—*Idem.* His advice as to the double-mounting of markers may be good; but it is so against all our notions of what is due to the dignity of the master by the man, that I can scarcely expect to hear of its being followed.

120. PRESERVED TURNIP-LAND.—I shall now proceed to describe the usual mode of conducting the sport in the highly-preserved turnip-districts. At nine o'clock in the morning—for if begun earlier, the birds will return to their feed—the whole of the stubbles are beaten by men and spaniels, in such a direction as to drive all the birds into certain large fields of turnips, clover, mangold-wurzel, or potatoes; all of which afford good cover. Two or three ponies are very serviceable, since they may be rapidly ridden over the ground, and they may serve to prevent the birds from taking a wrong direction; besides, as the whole ground must be beaten between nine and half-past ten or eleven o'clock, it requires the speed of the horse, or else a great number of beaters, to go over it. By the time last-mentioned, we will suppose all the birds driven into the largest fields affording the above cover for them; then the party of shooters form a line at one side of the field, and having a man at the end of every ten yards, and the guns at intervals of forty, they proceed to "walk the turnips." Being accompanied by the keepers, and a retriever or two, any wounded bird is expected to be retrieved; but many escape, since the scent of the turnips is so very prejudicial to the perfect use of the dog's nose. In walking straight across the field, it is divided by imaginary lines, which commence midway between each two guns, and run forward at right angles to the line; each shooter, therefore, is allowed to shoot only at those birds which are actually within the lines on each side of himself; and all birds killed in that space are said to fall to his gun, even if really killed by an adjoining one. This rule is laid down to prevent two or more shooting at the same bird; and also to set at rest the conflicting claims which any one or more may set up to a superiority in shooting. It is a very useful rule, and should in all cases be rigidly adhered to, not only with partridges, but also in grouse-shooting. It is only when both barrels have been discharged, unsuccessfully, that a

man's next neighbour has the privilege of "wiping his eye," if he can. From the immense numbers of birds which are often driven into turnips, the shooting is "fast and furious," and requires one or two spare guns to each shooter. It is no uncommon occurrence to find from 70 to 100 brace in one large field; and, early in the season, three-fourths of these may be shot at, since they lie like stones, and get up singly, or two or three at a time only; which, among a party of four or five, are soon disposed of. At every shot, the whole line wait either till the shooter has reloaded or changed his gun—which his servant, in the latter case, loads for him, ready for the next shot. In this way, the whole of the turnips, clover, &c., is closely beaten, and sometimes a second time over, with as good success as the first; for, as dogs are not often used, and the birds lie close, it is usually the case that one-half of them are not put up the first time. Those which escape the formidable line are carefully marked down, and followed up afterwards, when the numbers are reduced elsewhere. In this kind of shooting, however, it is scarcely desirable to follow up broken covies, since they all lie very well in the good cover which green crops afford; and the birds are so numerous, as to keep the guns constantly going for four or five hours, which is the usual term of this sport, for the birds leave the shelter of the turnips in the afternoon, and go on the feed again, where they are not to be slaughtered without more trouble than the Norfolk sportsman thinks they deserve. Such is the fashionable and modern style of partridge-shooting. It has many variations, of course, which depend upon the quantity of birds, and the size of the fields of turnips, &c.; and it is chiefly to be met with in perfection in those districts where turnip-husbandry is fully carried out; and these being generally of a light sandy soil, are peculiarly suited to the habits of the partridge.

121. THE WHEAT-LANDS. — Until very lately, exceedingly good partridge-shooting was often met with in the wheat-districts, even on the strong clays; but the wheat is now so very generally bagged, that the lying for them is gone, and, consequently, by the second or third week in September, the birds are off the moment the shooter enters each field. It is here that judgment is required, and that good dogs are so serviceable; for it is a singular fact, that birds will often lie after they are found by a steady dog, although without him they would get up at 200 yards' distance from the gun. In the early part of the season, in these bare stubbles, the birds may be found, when in any numbers, by one steady dog,

which should beat only about forty yards to the right and left of the gun. After the second week, however, it is generally necessary to permit a wider range; because, by that time, the game has become more scarce and wild, and, to find any number, the sportsman's legs would be too severely taxed for the powers of most people. If a very steady brace of tolerably fast and wide-ranging dogs are now used, the sport may be enjoyed to great perfection; but the dogs must be very well broken; must never be inclined to "foot" or "road" the birds till ordered, and must be very steady behind. The plan is to send them off into the far end of the field, ordering each off up the hedge side, and then letting them beat back towards you; or otherwise sending them round *outside* the hedge, with a marker, and letting him loose them at the other end. This is the better plan of the two, as the passage of the dogs under the hedge alarms the birds often, so as to prevent their lying. In well-broken dogs, accustomed to beat towards the gun, as well as from it, the whole field is then systematically hunted, the sportsman remaining where he first entered, and having his back to the wind. When either dog finds, the other, of course, backs, and they both remain firm on their "point" and "back." The shooter readily detects the "pointing dog," and walks straight up to him, or, rather, to his birds—and it will be found that in many cases very wild birds will allow him to come up and get "a right and left." This arises from their being inclined to lie close, with their heads down, as soon as the dog approaches on their scent. If the dog holds his head high, and stops steadily the moment he catches the body-scent, it is highly probable that they will neither run nor rise, but, watching the dog intently, will allow the sportsman himself to come up in the opposite direction. In this way, in a wild and bare country, I have often obtained shots which would have been wholly impracticable under the usual plan.

122. MIXED FARMS. — Hitherto, we have been considering the two extremes of partridge-shooting, viz., the turnip-shooting without stubbles, and the stubbles without turnips; but there is also a mixed country, consisting of the great majority of farming districts, and composed of stubbles and green-crops intermixed, but without the large fields of turnips found in the light soils of Norfolk, Suffolk, &c. Here we have, perhaps, four or five hundred acres in wheat and barley stubbles, with a few acres, here and there, of turnips or potatoes, and now and then a field of good feggy grass, &c. If, in such a district as this, the birds are pretty well preserved, and are not continu-ally being persecuted, good shooting may still be obtained. The following precautions will, perhaps, enable any sportsman, who has the privilege of shooting over one or two thousand acres of this mixed land, to proceed in such a way as to obtain good sport. In the first place, he should carefully abstain from shooting till all the corn on his own beat is cut, and also that on adjacent beats, if he thinks the owners of them likely to leave them quiet. Standing corn is such a harbour for birds, that you can do nothing with your own but frighten them away; and if your neighbours blaze away at their's, they will only contribute to fill your fields with game. Wait, then, till all your own is cut, and then begin throwing off some fine morning, as soon as *the dew is off*. First, beat for birds in the stubbles, taking care to have very steady dogs, and to give them the wind. As soon as a covey is found, endeavour to drive them up, by walking to them from a quarter at right angles with your dog's point, so that they shall not go straight away from you, but pass you, if possible, and give you a chance to fire both barrels, which you will do, if possible, at the *two first birds which get up*, they being generally the old ones; then, either yourself, or by your marker, mark down the remaining birds, and proceed at once to hunt for them wherever they may be, if not more than half-a-mile distant, which is not likely, so early in the season. If they have dropped in turnips, take up one of your dogs, unless both are very steady, and proceed to beat for them carefully. When found, they will often get up singly, but if not, then proceed as in the stubbles, and mark again; the third time they are almost sure to be scattered, and you may then secure all the remaining birds, if you have good luck, and a good steady dog. When this first covey is disposed of, but not till then, proceed to search for another, and, as the day wears on, try for them on the fallows, if dry, or in the turnips, where they collect in the middle of the day, even if not driven there on purpose; or you may often find them in the grass which is generally left by the side of a brook, especially if search is made, in the middle of a hot September day. Here they are almost always scattered, and require a good-nosed dog to make them out, and they lie very close. When, in the middle of the day, during the latter end of December, birds are not to be found, and there are open spaces of grass in any neighbouring covert, there is the most likely place to find them. They are exceedingly fond of such places, when they have been much driven about; but they seldom are found in thick underwood.

123. Hire of manor, which may be cal-
culated at £5 per 100 acres £50 0 0
One keeper, at 18s. per week 46 16 0
Gratuities to labourers . . 5 0 0
Travelling expenses *nil.*

£101 16 0

Or about one-third of the expense of
grouse-shooting.

SECT. 7.—QUAIL AND LANDRAIL-SHOOTING.

124. THE QUAIL (*Coturnix Communis*),
and the LANDRAIL (*Ortygometra Crex*), are
often met with in partridge-shooting. They
are nearly of the same size, but fly very
differently. Both are migratory birds, and
arrive in this country in the latter end of
summer, seldom remaining after the middle
of October, and generally not quite so late.
A *bevy* of quail, as the brood is called, is
seldom seen in Great Britain, but occasionally one or two turn up in a covey of partridges—they fly in the same way, and dogs
generally stand to them. Landrail are never
found in greater number than two together,
except by accident. Their flight is exceedingly soft and bat-like, though slow: they
can scarcely escape the gun when put up,
but run so much, as to be very difficult to
spring. They do much harm to the dogs, by
this propensity to run, and pointers and
setters should not be encouraged to hunt
them; they are oily for the table, and are
only fit for the sport and amusement of
school-boys. These young gentlemen may
amuse themselves, by calling them with a
notched piece of copper, drawn over a piece
of bone, which imitates their note, and
brings them close to the gun, when they
may be routed out with a terrier or cocker.
They are eminently adapted to school-boy
sport, because they generally frequent places
unoccupied by game, and near villages, &c.,
such as vetches, willow-beds, and market-
gardens.

125. THE GREAT PLOVER (*Œdicnemus Cre-
pitans*), is often met with in September, by
the Norfolk, Suffolk, and Sussex partridge-
shooter; and, indeed, over all the sandy
soils in the south-eastern parts of England.
They frequent open sheep-downs, and large
fallow-fields, and are rather difficult of approach, so as seldom to allow the dogs to
point, but getting up wildly and out of shot.
By great caution, and keeping up wind,
they may sometimes be shot. Their food is
composed of snails, slugs, worms, and insects; and they are also said to devour
frogs and mice. In length, this bird is fully
17 inches. The iris is golden-yellow; base
of bill greenish-yellow, point black. The
back is of a pale-brown, each feather having
a dark-brown stripe down its middle; wing
primaries very dark brown, the two first
having a white patch at the end. Tail-
feathers tipped with black, then a broad bar
of white, and the remainder of a mottled-
brown. The breast, belly, and vent are
almost white; legs and toes, yellow; claws
black.

126. THE GOLDEN PLOVER (*Charadrius Plu-
vialis*), belongs to the true plovers. It is
found, during summer and early autumn,
on the high breeding-grounds of the grouse
and partridge, in Scotland and the north of
England. They associate in large flocks, as
soon as the breeding-season has terminated.
A remarkable peculiarity connected with
this bird, in common with some other plovers, is, that it changes its plumage in the
spring, and retains that change till the
autumnal moult. This change is common
to both sexes, and consists, in the golden
plover, of an alteration from a greyish-
white colour to black, on all the under parts
of the body. The old feathers actually receive the black pigment in the spring, and
new ones, in addition, show themselves. The
spring moult, therefore, is an addition, not
a change; and the quill-feathers are not lost
or altered. The golden plover lays four
eggs, of a stone-coloured ground, blotched
with dark brown. These are large in proportion to the size of the bird, which is 11
inches long. These birds feed on worms,
snails, &c.; they have a shrill, whistling
note, which may be easily imitated, and in
this way they are often decoyed. They are
excellent eating, and fetch a good price in
the London market.

127. THE DOTTEREL (*Charadrius Morinel-
lus*), approaches very closely to the golden
plover in habits, and is found on the same
kind of ground, though reaching somewhat
farther inland. In the downs of Wiltshire
and Berkshire, small flocks, or trips, as they
are called, are often found in the spring and
autumn, as well as on the chalk-hills of
Hertfordshire and Cambridgeshire; here,
however, they are only met with on their
passage to their breeding-grounds, which
are further north, on the high moorlands of
Scotland and the North of England. The
plumage of this bird is very rich: beak
black; iris brown; back of head and neck,
dark brown; back ash-brown — feathers
edged with buff; tail greyish-brown, tipped
with white; breast rich fawn-colour, with a
band of white extending from shoulder to
shoulder, and edged with a dark line; belly
black; legs and toes greenish-yellow.

128. THE GREY PLOVER (*Squatarola Hel-
vetica*), is like the golden plover in most of its
habits; but, from the presence of a hind
toe, it is not included among them. It

is only a winter visitor, breeding in high northern latitudes. The beak is black; iris very dark-brown; top of head white; back black and white; chin, breast, and belly, black; vent and under tail coverts, white; legs, toes, and claws, black; length of bird, twelve inches. In winter, the grey feathers become paler, and the belly is grey instead of black.

129. THE PEEWIT, OR LAPWING (*Vanellus Cristatus*), is so well known, as scarcely to require description. It is found on all poor, waste-lands, where the fields are large; but it is so wary, as rarely to come within gun-shot. Its eggs are sought after as a great dainty.

130. THE BUSTARDS, great and little, are now so exceedingly rare, as to be scarcely worth noticing in any treatise on Shooting. The last great bustard shot in this country was killed in 1831, and a little bustard, also, was bagged in 1839; since which time I am not aware that any bird of this genus has been seen in England.

SECT. 8.—SHOOTING HARES AND RABBITS IN THE OPEN.

131. THE HARE (*Lepus Timidus*), and the RABBIT (*Lepus Cuniculus*), are, in most countries, the object of the shooter in those situations only where the former is not capable of being coursed, and where the latter is found lying out, as among turnips, or in hedge-rows, &c. Both require the aim to be carried well forward; and if the former is going straight away, the tips of the ears, if erect, are the best situation to point the gun to. In coursing districts, it is considered as great a crime to shoot a hare, as in fox-hunting districts to shoot or trap a fox; but in thickly-enclosed countries, the hare affords even less sport to the courser than to the shooter, and there she may well be knocked over with a charge of shot. Pointers and setters will stand both hares and rabbits, if they are shot to them; but if this is never done, they soon learn to disregard the scent altogether, unless, by the way, they are allowed to chase. It is at those animals that the badly-broken dog so often tries the temper of his master, because

he not only, in chasing them, runs the risk of putting birds up, but he also very often chases the hare so far, as to be lost to sight for a considerable time. The whistle is used till the cheeks ache; and it only requires the presence of a Frenchman, and his constant "Sacré nom," &c., to complete the picture of impotent fury. It is no use thrashing the dog, the only result being, that he will refuse to come back next time, and will hang about at the distance of a field, completely upsetting all the plans of his master, who is set at defiance by his slave. For these rascals, the only remedy is the spiked-collar, which may be had at the gun-maker's, of varying degrees of severity; the pointer's thin skin requiring a less sharp one than the setter's hairy coat. By working the dog with a cord of about twelve or fourteen feet in length, he is capable of being stopped with great severity, if he chases when the hare starts from his point; or, if the hare goes off her form without his finding her, the cord generally brings him up at some hedge, or in cover. It is a cruel remedy, but the only one for a badly-broken and unruly dog, and is certainly preferable to a charge of shot, which is the alternative. Col. Hawker has given a drawing in his book of a collar, consisting of two side-pieces of iron, connected by a screw-piece at the top, and united at the bottom by a triangle running through open eyes in their extremities. This, he says, by attaching the cord to the triangle, is made very severe, the two side-pieces being pressed very strongly against the dog's neck. But as there can be no doubt of the *efficiency* of the spiked-collar, and as *both* depend upon the pain they give for their utility, I can see no object in substituting a cumbrous and expensive machine for a light and cheap one. Neither will stop a dog, except by the pain they give him, and therefore they are both objectionable, if they can be avoided; and if one of them must be used, which I believe it must in troublesome cases, I should certainly give the preference to the old and long-tried mode, over the plan proposed by Col. Hawker, high as his authority stands as a sportsman.

MARSH AND FEN-SHOOTING.

Sect 1.—The Birds met with.

132. SNIPE-SHOOTING is the most important and interesting of the various kinds of shooting included under the above head; but many other birds are met with in the fens of Cambridgeshire, Norfolk, Lincoln, and Essex, on the eastern coast; and on those of Lancashire, Cheshire, &c., on the western side of England, which are exceedingly good for the table. In Ireland, especially, this kind of shooting is very good; and in some of the bogs, forty or fifty couple of snipes may be easily bagged in the day. The following birds may all be included under this head; though some, as the plovers, for instance, are generally more abundant upon high and dry land. All, however, are found in the same manner as the grouse and partridge—by the aid of the pointer or setter—and, therefore, they can scarcely be included under Wildfowl-shooting. At the head of the list stand the snipes, as affording the best sport of any.

133. THE GREAT or SOLITARY SNIPE (*Gallinago Major*), is not very common in this country, but is occasionally met with in the fens of Essex and Norfolk, which it visits only in the autumn. In length, it is about 12 inches; and it weighs from 7 to 9 ounces; female larger than the male—which latter is lighter in colour than the female. The bill is of a pale yellow-brown, becoming darker towards the tip; iris, dark-brown—a dark line extends from the eye to the base of bill; top of head, rich dark-brown, with a longitudinal stripe of paler feathers. The whole of the breast, and the scapulars and interscapulars, of a rich dark-brown. Tail-feathers, 16, of which the eight outside ones are nearly all white—middle eight tipped with white, next to which is a bar of black, then a chestnut bar, and the bodies of the feathers composed of a brownish-black. Chin, pale yellow-brown; breast and sides covered with semicircular patches of dark-brown or pale ground; belly and vent, dirty-white; legs and toes, greenish-brown.

134. COMMON SNIPE, SNITE, or HEATHER-BLEATER (*Gallinago Media*), is an indigenous British bird; though many, also, arrive from beyond the seas in the autumn, and leave in spring. It breeds in considerable numbers in the heaths and moors of the northern counties; and often disappoints the grouse-shooter, by rising before his dog's point, when he anticipates a more desirable shot. When descending from its flight, it makes a peculiar noise with its wings, which is compared to the bleating of a goat; and, as it chiefly makes this noise when descending to its mate, after its rising to a great height in the air, it is supposed to be a manifestation of pleasure or excitement. Its food, like that of all its tribe, consists of worms and insects, small snails, and seeds; which last, probably, are only accidentally swallowed with the worms and other insects. The whole length of the common snipe is from 10 to 11 inches; beak 2¼; female larger than male. The plumage is much the same as the solitary snipe, with the exception of the tail, which has only fourteen feathers, of which the anterior two-thirds are of a dull black, edged with brown; beyond this they have a patch of chestnut, then a dusky-brown band, and, finally, tipped with chestnut. It lays five or six eggs, of a pale olive colour, irregularly blotched with dusky-brown.

135. THE JACK SNIPE, JUDCOCK, or GID (*Gallinago Gallinula vel Minima*), rarely breeds in Great Britain, which it visits in the winter only. It is more solitary than the common snipe, and is a very sluggish bird, being often difficult to put up; so much so, as sometimes to allow the dog to catch it on the ground. Unlike the common snipe, it utters no scream on rising, and is remarkable for confining itself to peculiar localities, which it almost invariably visits at the same period of the year. It is very rarely known to breed here; and the eggs which have sometimes been shown as those of the jack snipe, are pronounced, by Mr. Yarrell, to be those of the purre. In length, it does not exceed 8½ inches; beak 1½. The plumage, in winter, is more of an ash-grey than the reddish-brown which it bears in autumn and spring. The old birds may be known by the brilliant irridescence of their feathers. The plumage differs from the two above described, in the following particulars, viz.:—It has no light longitudinal mark on the top of the head; tail-feathers, twelve, all greyish-black; breast, belly, and vent all white.

136. Besides these three species, there are also found, occasionally, though very rarely, the BROWN SNIPE, and SABINE'S SNIPE, the description of which it is unnecessary to give.

137. IN ADDITION TO THE SNIPES, on most of our fens, great quantities of birds peculiar to these localities are to be met with and shot, if approached with quiet and caution. The sport they afford is not, certainly, equal to those kinds I have previously described; but, as it does not require a certificate to shoot any of these birds, with the exception of the snipe, and as in many of the fens permission to shoot is easily obtained, it is well calculated for the young beginner. In the fens of Cambridge-

shire, near the University, there is seldom much of this kind of sport, because the Cantabs are continually driving the birds away by their persecutions; still it is of service to them in affording exercise, and the hope of sport, if not the reality. At some distance, and towards the coast, plenty of birds may be found, and a great variety also. The following are the principal varieties, and their usual haunts :—

138. THE BITTERN (*Botaurus Stellaris*), is not now so common as it formerly was; it is, however, still found occasionally, and it may then be known by its "booming," when on the wing of an evening. This sepulchral sound is not unlike the deep bellowing of a bull. It was one of the birds which was the object of the falconer's art, and would often injure his hawks with its powerful bill. The plumage is of a rich reddish-yellow ground, variegated in a beautiful manner with dark-brown and black marks, especially on the back of the neck. It is from 28 to 30 inches in length; legs and feet, grass-green. It feeds on fish and reptiles. Its nest is built on any slight mound out of flood's way, and it lays four or five greenish-blue eggs. The bittern is a slow and heavy bird in its ordinary flight, though sometimes it shoots at a good rate, and is then more difficult to kill. It is a very shy bird, and difficult to approach within shot.

139. THE HERON (*Ardea Cinerea*), is a bird renowned in falconry, and has been immortalised in the work of Dame Juliana Berners on that subject. It is a gregarious bird, breeding, like the rook, in what is called a heronry. It feeds almost entirely on fish, which it watches for with great patience. In colour, it is of a pale slate over all the upper parts; and of a creamy-white, with dark spots on the breast and belly. The accompanying description will fully answer the sportsman's purpose, as far as the gun is concerned. As it is no longer preserved for hawking purposes, it is seldom met with. There are still more than thirty heronries in England, and from them a stray bird often escapes into the fens, and is there picked up by the sportsman, who should be very careful in approaching it, if only winged, as its bill is strong and sharp, and will inflict a severe wound. Colonel Hawker advises that they should be galloped at on the leeward side, using a fast horse, and shooting from his back; but, as their ground is generally fenny, I should not like to attempt the feat.

140. THE RUFF, female REEVE (*Philomachus Pugnax*), is celebrated, as its name implies, for its pugnacious habits. The plumage also changes in a very remarkable manner at certain periods of the year. At the breeding-season, a beautiful frill of feathers appears round the neck, which is also variable in colour. Each male, or *ruff*, has his own little walk, which he defends from all intruders, *vi et armis*. The females, or *reeves*, however, are gladly welcomed; and on their arrival a regular pitched-battle takes place, in which the grass is strewed with feathers. The nest is formed in a hollow of the grass, and in it three or four eggs are deposited, of a greenish-white, blotched with brown. The ruff is easily shot, when it can be approached; but it is taken in springes with still greater facility; or, by means of stuffed decoy-birds, which entice the ruff, through his propensity to fight, they may be allured into the net. When taken, they are fattened for the table, and are then considered a great delicacy. The food used is bread and milk, with hemp-seed bruised, and mixed with it. They leave Great Britain in the winter.

141. THE KNOT (*Tringa Canutus*), is very like the ruff in its habits, and somewhat resembles that bird in all respects but the frill. It is shot or taken in the same way, by means of springes or nets. On first arriving in this country it is stupid and dull, but soon becomes wary, and difficult of approach. It feeds on aquatic insects and worms, and swims with great ease. Its length is 10 inches; its general colour is a reddish-brown, with black or dark-brown markings. Wing and tail-feathers, greyish-brown; chin, neck, breast, and belly, of a rich chestnut; legs, toes, and claws, bluish-black.

142. THE GODWITS, BAR-TAILED and BLACK-TAILED, (*Limosa, Lapponica et Ægocephala*), are not so common as formerly, when they used to be fattened in large quantities for the London market. The chief distinction between the two species consists in the tail-feathers, which are black in the latter species, and barred in the former. The length of the whole bird is 17 inches, and of the beak alone, 4 inches. The plumage varies much in the winter and summer. In winter, the back is ash-brown; primary quills dusky-black, with a bar at the base of each, visible on the entire wing; tail-feathers black at the outer two-thirds; chin, breast, and belly, light-ash; vent white; legs and toes dusky-brown. In summer, the back changes to dark-brown, each feather becoming almost black at the base; the breast also becomes of a white ground, with bars of red-brown and amber.

143. Among the plovers, the males are larger than the females; but the reverse is the case with the snipes and godwits. The great plover, golden plover, grey plover, and dotterel, are found also among the fens and marshes, but they are more frequently

found on high and dry ground; and I have, therefore, included them in the chapter treating of that species of shooting. All these birds are migratory, and some are only occasional visitors to Great Britain. To the sportsman, the most interesting are the snipes, the bulk of which arrive in the autumn, on the east coast, where they only stay a short time, and then pass on to the interior, and to Ireland. They return in the spring, taking the reverse course, and are again found on the eastern coast in February and March. The whole of the low coast, on the eastern side of this island, is the resort of these birds in the autumn and spring; but during the severe winter months, they prefer the warmer bogs of Ireland, and the west coast of England and Scotland. Snipes almost invariably fly up-wind, and, when the gun is pointed at them, they dart and twist in a wonderfully rapid manner, at which time they are very difficult to hit; but by catching them either the moment they rise, or when they have done twisting, they may be readily bagged with No. 8 shot. They are not capable of carrying off much shot; and, if a larger size is used, the intervals between the shot with an ordinary gun will be greater than the size of the snipe's body, and, consequently, frequent misses will occur.

SECT. 2.—THE DOGS USED IN SNIPE-SHOOTING.

144. Snipe-shooters prefer the setter, because he is more capable of sustaining with impunity the wet and cold of the marshes, in which this bird is found, than the smooth-skinned pointer; he should, however, be a very steady dog, and accustomed to work to hand, and to keep to heel when ordered. A pointer will do the work well for a time, but is almost sure to suffer from rheumatism, or the yellows, before he has done a week's work. Every snipe-shooter, when he means business, should provide himself with one or two good setters, and a retriever, though the latter is not so necessary as in partridge-shooting; for, as the setter is generally used for snipe single-handed, and as he must learn to foot the snipe, and to potter a good deal, he will scarcely get much harm from retrieving, if made steady to "down charge."

SECT. 3.—SNIPE-SHOOTING.

145. When starting in search of snipe, choose, if possible, a mild day, after rain, but with the surface just becoming dry; for if very wet, the snipe refuse to lie, as do most birds, in fact. Walk up-wind to the end of your beat, with your dog, or dogs, at your heel, and you will pick up a few shots, but not many; when arrived at the end, cast off your dog, and let him steadily beat every inch of ground, taking it in a zig-zag direction, but always keeping your face more or less down-wind. This will give your dog the chance of using his nose, and yet enable you to get between the snipe and the wind, which they always try to face, and, in doing so, are very apt to make a circle round you, thereby offering a very favourable shot. When your dog stands, keep well to windward of him, always going up to him on that side; be very careful not to hurry yourself or your dog, and do not shoot till the snipe has done his twistings, unless he first rises at more than twenty yards from you, when have him down at once. If your dog finds a snipe to windward of him, and you are behind, your only chance, unless you are a crack shot, is to head your dog well, and prevent the snipe going off in the wind's eye away from you, in which case his vagaries are so eccentric as to baffle most eyes and hands; but as snipe generally lie well, you need not make so great a circle as for partridge or grouse, under similar circumstances. Setters generally take to snipe soon; and only require a few to be killed to them, to make them as fond of the sport as of grouse or partridge-shooting.

SECT. 4.—DRESS.

146. Recollect, that in snipe-shooting there is a constant risk of getting into water, up to the hips, or nearly so. Long and waterproof boots should be worn, with plenty of warm hose, drawers, and flannel-waistcoats. It is seldom, in spite of these precautions, that the snipe-shooter passes the day without getting wet, as he is almost sure to get into water while shooting. Nothing is so treacherous as boggy and marshy land, and therefore he ought to walk slowly and cautiously the whole day; if, however, the sportsman takes care to keep his boots waterproof, by the following composition, he will only require to keep his upper works dry, by avoiding severe rain, and absolute duckings.

RECEIPT FOR WATERPROOF BOOTS.
Boiled Linseed Oil . . . . . . 1¼ lbs.
Yellow Wax . . . . 3 ozs.
Canada Balsam . . . . 1 oz.
Mix over a slow fire. This is to be rubbed in alternately with neat's-foot oil.

But the snipe-shooter may persevere with impunity, through any amount of wet, if he takes care to keep moving, not to drink any quantity of ardent spirits, and to change his clothes the moment he gets home. He should also, as soon as he can after a wetting, soak his feet and legs in strong hot salt and water, and then clothe warmly.

The two great promoters of disease are spirits, and sitting in wet clothes; and both may easily be avoided, without loss of sport. The coat, waistcoat, and trowsers should be of woollen, but varying in thickness, according to the weather. Velveteen is very cold when wet; and all the Mackintosh inventions retain the perspiration too much, to be safe for those who indulge in active pedestrian exercise.

SECT. 5.—THE GUN, AND ACCESSORIES.

147. These may be the same as for partridge-shooting, but the shot should never be larger than No. 7; some use No. 9, but it is not heavy enough to bring them down with certainty; and it is more humane to allow them to escape the shot, than to send them off with two or three wounds in their bodies, containing each a pellet of No. 9, which may cause them to die a lingering death.

SECT. 6.—EXPENSES.

148. The expenses of snipe-shooting are so variable, as to make it quite impossible to form an estimate which could be at all serviceable. Many English and Irish marshes may be shot over without difficulty, not being preserved at all, or with very little strictness. The French marshes are also celebrated for this sport, especially the neighbourhood of Abbeville; but as this book is restricted to British sports, I shall not venture into a consideration of them.

CHAP. VII.

COVERT-SHOOTING.

SECT. 1.—HABITS OF THE PHEASANT.

149. Pheasants, woodcocks, hares, and rabbits, are all found and shot in the woods of Great Britain; but the PHEASANT (Phasianus Colchicus) is the grand foundation, the pièce de resistance, of the covert-shooting in this country. Cock-shooting is said, by Colonel Hawker, to be comparable to fox-hunting; but it is only attainable at certain periods, soon passing away, and is confined, even then, to favoured localities. Pheasants, however, may be reared in any part of England, Ireland, or Scotland, where there is dry, healthy covert for them. They are esteemed as the greatest delicacy, being of a flavour commensurate with their size, and form a most important item in a basket of game sent as a present. For this reason they are carefully preserved, and most probably will continue to be so, by those who have purses long enough to be able to pay for such an expensive luxury; for, though they may be bought at about 7s. per brace, they generally cost more nearly £1 1s., than that lower sum. But, while they are so easily poached, and sold by the poacher, this will always happen, because the game-preserver rears three times as many as he bags; and, therefore, he must always calculate each bird to cost him three times as much as it would do, if no poaching was carried on. It is quite unnecessary to describe the form of this bird, which is familiar to all. It is not indigenous to this country, but was introduced from Georgia originally; it has now, however, become naturalized, though its high price in the market would soon render it as scarce as the bustard, if not strictly preserved. It can be tamed to a certain extent, but, even if brought up with poultry, it retains a certain degree of wildness, so that the least alarm occasions it to retreat in terror to some protection afforded by an adjacent shrubbery or plantation. The pheasant roosts in trees, and is very fond of the fir, and other horizontal-limbed evergreens, which afford good shelter from the rain, and also a substantial perch. Spruce-firs they are very partial to, and in these trees they are not readily picked off their roosts by the midnight poacher. Pheasants have a strong propensity to use their legs in preference to their wings, when disturbed; and this must be considered well by the sportsman in pursuit, as well as the keeper in defence, of his game. The latter I have already directed how to manage his department, in the chapter devoted to the preservation of game; the former I will endeavour to assist in the present one.

SECT. 2.—BEST DOGS FOR PHEASANT-SHOOTING.

150. For the purpose of hunting the pheasant, so as to compel him to rise before the shooter in covert, the spaniel or cocker is, no doubt, the best kind of dog. Pointers or setters which are broken to run in when ordered, may do in open spring-falls, and there they afford excellent sport, but they are too large for thick covert, and recourse must be had to a team of small spaniels, either regular springers or cockers, including King

Charles's and Blenheim spaniels. These generally give tongue, varying in note with the kind of game before them; but they are sometimes mute, in which case they require each a bell attached to a collar. Terriers, also, are occasionally used; but they have seldom sufficiently good noses for the purpose, and they are difficult to break from vermin. The springer is a larger dog than the cocker, has a longer nose, a smaller eye, and greater strength and hardihood. He gives tongue sooner and louder on a scent, and is much more impetuous by nature, requiring strong coercion. The cocker, on the contrary, has a most delicate nose, and a keen perception of the shades of scent; giving a slight whimper on first touching upon it, and changing to a merry note only when quite hot upon his game. These last are exceedingly pretty workers; and if they only had equal powers of endurance with the springer, would be ten times as valuable; they are, however, delicate; and their full eyes are so liable to be bruised and torn, that a very few hours' work will knock them up. Many sportsmen prefer the setter or pointer for covert-shooting; and if there is much spring-fall, so that the setter can be seen, he is, I think, quite as good as the very best spaniel, and much better than a bad team; in thick coverts, however, he is of no use, as his size prevents his getting through the runs, and he would leave great quantities of game unfound. If used, he ought to break his point at command, and is often even better than any spaniel at a body-scent, provided he has as good a nose; still, it seldom happens that he can hunt a foot-scent like these dogs, or that he can distinguish between a true and a "heel" scent, which spaniels soon learn to do. It is very wonderful to see pointers and setters go into covert, and break their points continually, and then come out and stand for an hour in the open; yet such is constantly seen in old, steady dogs; but such animals are seldom of much use out of covert, as they are constantly poking along the hedge-rows, and leaving the regular line of beat untouched. My preference, therefore, would be given, for pheasant-shooting, to a good, useful team of the Sussex spaniels, which have plenty of courage and hardihood, but require, also, lots of work to bring them down to steady hunting. Once broken, they are exceedingly good dogs, and their noses are as tender as that of the best cocker that ever hunted.

151. NUMBER OF DOGS REQUIRED.—Of the large springers, a couple and a-half, or two couples, are enough for any covert, and one couple will suffice for most purposes. Of the smaller sorts, double the number will be none too many.

SECT. 3.—BREAKING AND USING THE SPANIEL.

152. The BREAKING the SPANIEL should be commenced very early, especially with the larger and stronger sorts. They are naturally very impetuous, and yet must be restrained in their range to thirty yards from the gun, at the most. They should be taken out, first of all, in small coverts and hedge-rows, and imbued with the desire to hunt, which they acquire readily enough, and at six or eight months old are generally quite ready for any sport they may be entered to. Previously to this, they should be accustomed to come to heel, and keep there as long as they are ordered; and they should be used to hunt to the wave of the hand, and not to break fence till permission is given them. Great care should be taken that they are not allowed to amuse themselves by "self-hunting," which they are very apt to indulge in when first entered to game. When spaniels are intended exclusively for pheasant or cock-shooting, or both, they should be kept carefully to those birds, and should be stopped, and rated soundly, whenever they "speak to fur;" but the great point is to get them to keep close to the gun, and not to press their game until they are assured that the sportsman is near enough to take advantage of their efforts. Few spaniels are really worth having till they are nearly worn-out, for their struggles in wet covert, with briers and thorns, soon spoil their looks, and their constitutions too. When too riotous, there are three methods of steadying them: first, to put one fore-leg into the collar, compelling the dog to hunt on three legs; second, to hang a shot-collar round the neck; and, third, to confine one hind-leg by a strap, buckled tightly round the leg, above the hock. The strap must be changed repeatedly from leg to leg, as it soon cramps the muscles so much as to render them useless. If the fore-leg is put in the collar, this leg also should be occasionally changed. There is very little choice in these modes; either will answer the purpose of subduing the courage and pace of the dog; the shot-collar is, perhaps, the least discouraging, but it scarcely acts sufficiently with most dogs; and, if a heavy fall is sustained, the neck may be broken by the shock. If the puppy is not inclined to hunt, let him be put on the scent of pheasants when just off the feed, and let him rout them about well for a few minutes; this is not often to be done without injury to the preserve, but it may be occasionally ventured on after the young birds are able to fly, as the dog soon causes them to get into the trees, leaving a strong scent behind. Spaniels should be made to

drop to the gun and to the hand very strictly, and this may be taught by the pistol; but it must be enforced on all occasions when game is before them. A retriever is very useful, as it is very difficult to prevent the whole train of spaniels from bringing game, if any one is allowed to do so; but they soon learn to "down charge" strictly, and then the retriever goes to the dead bird, and retrieves it for his master. In first entering young spaniels to hunting the hedge-rows, if the breaker is out alone, they should not be allowed to go through to the other side, but should be kept carefully on the same side as the shooter; afterwards, however, when they are accustomed to the range, and keep watchfully eyeing the sportsman, to see that he is within reach, they may be sent to the other side, and put to hunt everything out on the same side as the gun, which is always the most effectual mode with a single shooter. When the young spaniel is first put into a large wood, and is beyond the supervision of his master, he often ranges the entire covert, and does immense mischief to the sport, driving everything out of shot. He should be well loaded with shot, or one of his legs taken up, and put to hunt with two couple of steady old dogs, even if he is so confined as to do nothing. He will soon learn to imitate his fellows, when he sees them pay all attention to the gun, and when he finds that game falls to their hunting, whereas he has never yet succeeded in obtaining such a result. After a time, his leg may be set at liberty, and he may probably take to his work kindly enough, and refuse to leave the other dogs far. He will not probably do much good, as this work requires great experience, but he will do little harm. It cannot be expected that the spaniel will learn his business in one season, and he is seldom perfect in two; but he will help to do the looking-on part, and will animate the old, stale, but steady and clever dogs, to increased exertions. Many sportsmen are constantly animating their spaniels, by cries of "Have at 'em!" "Cock! cock! cock!" &c. &c.; but this is perfectly useless, the slightest whistle being sufficient to indicate the whereabouts of the gun, and, more than this, interfering with the sport, because it shows the game what they have to avoid, and when to avoid it. If the spaniel is fond of his master, and accustomed to work for him, he is as much occupied in watching his motions as in seeking for game. These dogs have a very strong love of approbation; and very fortunately this is so, because they are so much more beyond the master's control than the pointer or setter.

153. MODE OF USING SPANIELS IN LARGE COVERTS.—Unlike grouse and partridge-shooting, the early morning is as good a time as any for pheasant-shooting; and most ardent sportsmen of the old school select that time, especially if they mean to beat the hedge-rows, which they can do as the birds are returning from their feed, after which they should follow them into covert, and, with a wave of the hand, order in the spaniels, with "Have at"—pronounced "Haave aat"—which should only be used just at first, by way of encouragement. After this—keeping them carefully near him—the shooter should watch for a whimper, and press rapidly forward to that dog; as soon as he gets to him, the little creature is sure to push on, and will, if of a good nose, soon either undeceive him by silence, or drive up a pheasant or cock. The great point is to rush well forward, as far as possible in front of the dog throwing his tongue, wherever he may be, and being regardless of thorns or brambles. Nothing can be effected without this rush, as pheasants will run for many yards before dogs, if not rapidly pushed, and will generally get up far out of shot, or so protected by the trees, as to be defended by them from your gun. Little, light men have, consequently, a worse chance at this sport than strong and tall ones, who are able to raise their arms and guns above the underwood, and carry all before them. It is seldom that a pheasant can be marked into another part of the same covert; and, indeed, if it is so, the bird seldom remains near where he alighted, but runs a long distance, and then lies quietly in the thickest and most impenetrable part. If this sport is to be followed with much success, the spaniels must be broken from "fur," both in the form of hares and rabbits, as they will, otherwise, neglect the pheasants, and take to the four-footed game. This can only be done with spaniels whose breed is very pure, and free from the stain of the beagle, which so many of our old spaniels are crossed with. The Clumber breed, when pure, is said to disregard hares and rabbits, until thoroughly entered to them, and always to prefer "feather" to "fur." This, however, I never saw; nor did I ever witness the hunting of a thoroughly-broken team of any spaniels. I have seen a few good ones in my life, but never a perfect team at work. For this reason, perhaps, I never saw so much to admire in covert-shooting as in partridge or grouse-shooting.

SECT. 4.—VARIOUS KINDS OF PHEASANT-SHOOTING.

154. In hedge-rows and spinnies, as pheasants have a strong scent, both body and ground, they may readily be found by the

setter or pointer; but they are so carefully driven by the keeper every night and morning into the coverts after feeding, that it is, generally, out of the question attempting to shoot them anywhere but in these secure retreats. In former days, good sport was often afforded by spaniels in hedge-rows, or by a steady old pointer; and even now, in certain situations, near preserves, where the keepers have not the right of driving them, *and where this right is carefully watched*, a good hour's sport may often be obtained. The shooter should begin near their covert, as soon as the pheasants are running back to it, which they generally do up the dry ditches, or under the hedges, if the former are wet or absent, immediately after feeding. By thus intercepting them, they are obliged to rise, if the dogs are worked down the hedge-rows away from covert, and there is a gun on each side the hedge. It often happens that there is a brook or river intervening between the corn-fields and the covert; here the pheasants *must* rise to return; and if they are in the habit of crossing it to their feed, the shooter should station himself near the brook, and send his spaniels to beat in at the other end of the fence, and drive towards him. The pheasants are sure to run till they know they must rise, which they do about 30 or 40 yards from the edge of the brook, in order to get well over it; and at this point they may be met and knocked over, taking care to have a good water-retriever, in case they fall into the brook. In many situations, also, there is a chain of small plantations, where the pheasants breed in preference to large woods, and which the keepers soon drive them from, if permitted to do so. Here they may be shot readily in the early part of October, by sending in the spaniels, and posting two guns on each side of the end towards which they are to be driven, and two others walking on each side the plantation parallel with the dogs. A man or two, however, should accompany the dogs, and beat steadily through the whole length of the plantation, to prevent the pheasants running back. This kind of sport is generally met with on farms where the game belongs to the tenant, and where the pheasants are preserved with some little care, from the end of hatching to the middle of October; by which time they are all either shot, or driven to the neighbouring strictly-preserved large woods, from whence the old hens originally came. It must be remembered, that pheasants are polygamous birds, and the hen only is concerned in the care of the young. She is ready enough to remain with the rest of her sex in the harem of her lord and master, till she is obliged to prepare her nest, at which time she is looking out for solitude, and prefers a quiet little spinney or plantation all to herself, even though in the midst of cultivated land, to sharing the secluded wood with her rivals, of whose jealousy she is afraid for her brood, though not for herself.

155. WILD PHEASANT-SHOOTING.—Again, in large woodlands, which are either wholly unpreserved, or not carefully preserved, an occasional pheasant may be met with in the course of a day's cock-shooting; but these are exceptions now-a-days, and cannot often be calculated upon with sufficient certainty to warrant a man in going out for pheasants alone.

156. THE BATTUE.—It is for the purpose of the *battue* that pheasants are now reserved and preserved with all the formidable retinue of head-keepers, under-keepers, day-watchers, and night-watchers. None but men of large means, and in possession of extensive coverts, can indulge in this amusement, except by the invitation of those who have at their command these pleasant auxiliaries to sport; but in this instance power has been abused, and instead of promoting sport, it has totally destroyed it. No one can deny the fitness of the pheasant for affording gratification to the good sportsman, if the bird is fairly found, put up, and shot; but as well might "mobbing" a fox be called fox-hunting, as a *battue* be considered genuine pheasant-shooting; and this I will endeavour to show in the following description of this amusement:—In the *battue*, nothing short of hundreds, or, if possible, thousands, of killed, to say nothing of wounded, will constitute a successful day. The pseudo-sportsman, who should be tempted from his fireside and his "Times" after breakfast by anything short of five brace an-hour to his gun, would be strongly inclined to complain, and would think, if he did not say, that his presence had been obtained under false pretences. The mode usually adopted is as follows:— First, gather together eight or ten crack shots, who may, many of them, be in wheeled-chairs, or on shooting-ponies, but should be capable of killing, without spoiling, this beautiful bird; then, having breakfasted the party, proceed to post them at certain stations where the game must cross a piece of open ground commanded by the shooters' guns. Thus, in wide coverts, the guns are arranged along the edges of the open springs, at about 40 or 50 yards apart, so as to command every head of game which passes, whether pheasant or hare, or sometimes rabbits, &c., each shooter having two or three guns, and a man to load them. As soon as these are posted, the beaters are sent to the other end of the portion of wood which is to be driven, and they proceed to

drive the game through it, often with the aid of a steady dog or two, but as often without any such assistance. For some time, nothing is heard but the men calling to each other to keep the line, or their taps on the trees, &c., which may be distinguished at a long distance; presently a hare canters quietly out of the edge of the covert, and, putting up her head to observe what is going on, is knocked over—as easy a shot as a farm-yard cock tied to a tree. Next, perhaps, a rabbit shares the same fate; she, however, seldom waits to look about her, but goes at a flying pace, and is a fair mark for a good shot. By and by, another and another shot is heard, with the squeal of a hare or two following them; then the beaters may be distinguished approaching, and their blows and cries are very loud and audible. Expectation is on tiptoe, every moment being the one at which the slaughter is supposed to be about to begin; suddenly a loud "whirr-r-r" is heard, followed by the peculiar "cock-cock-cock-cockle" of the cock-pheasant, of which some one, two, or three rise from the edge of the high wood, to be as certainly brought down; as fast as one falls, another shares his fate, and in ten minutes, or less, the ground is covered with the slain. In many instances, low nets are fixed along the edge of the old wood, which compel the pheasants to get off their legs and rise, as they are so very tame, and so much inclined to run, as to escape in that way without the nets. In this manner, the whole of the pheasants in a portion of wood, or a great part of them, that is, all those which have neither doubled back nor escaped the guns, are brought to bag, and the keeper's retrievers are set to work, to recover those which are not artistically disposed of. As soon as this part of the work is accomplished, another portion of wood is driven in a similar way; and this is again repeated, till the whole of the preserves are exhausted, or till the sporting (!) propensities of the guests are fully gratified. Now, it will be observed, that in this description nothing has been said of finding the game, or of the use of the instinct of the dog, or of the gratification of the desire for exercise, or even of the benefits derived from it; on the contrary, the admirers of this sport are generally wholly ignorant of the art of finding game, or of the hunting of the dogs, or unwilling or incapable of using their legs; they only long for blood—which may really be said to form the positive, comparative, and superlative degrees of their ideas on the subject. There may be some excuse for the boy feeling gratification and pride in obtaining the mastery over a fine pheasant by this kind of butchery; but I never could see the grounds for these feelings in a full-grown man, with all his faculties about him. For a gouty valetudinarian also, who still clings to his old associations, I can find some excuse; but these form only a small proportion of those who habitually delight in the *battue*; however, we have no right to complain of the taste of others, especially when the gratification of that taste is not within our reach on every occasion. The appetite for money no doubt increases by its gratification, and I suppose the same must take place in the votaries of the *battue*, as nothing else will account for the extraordinary lengths to which it is carried. When the covert is of such a nature as to prevent the posting of the shooters in the spring-falls, portions of it are divided off by long nets, and the game is driven towards the open fields, in the same way as I have before described; but here every bird that escapes is liable to be lost, as it flies clear away, and if it has no secure retreat within the same preserve, is almost certain to fall a victim to some expectant gun; good shots are therefore at a premium in such a kind of wood, and few bad ones find themselves included in the invitations. It sometimes happens that the nets are evaded, by the birds hopping over them; but these are exceptions, and the great majority never attempt to pass them, after finding themselves stopped from running by them. A net a yard high is quite sufficient; but even if they have run the gauntlet of half-a-dozen nets, they get caught at last in the final corner, where they are surrounded on all sides by the beaters, and compelled to face the redoubtable phalanx awaiting them. I have been repeatedly tempted to partake of this amusement, but I never felt otherwise than ashamed of myself during its continuance; and I would desire nothing more than to stir up the same feeling in the breasts of others, before they have been tempted to try its effect upon themselves.

157. EXCUSE FOR THE BATTUE.—The excuse made for this abuse of sport is, that where pheasants are thick, no one gun, or even two or three, can pursue them in the old sportsmanlike way without losing a great many, which are driven off into an enemy's country. Now, this I admit fully. It *is* impossible to enter a covert abounding with pheasants, and hunt them with spaniels, without nine-tenths of the birds running off out of shot, and escaping to a distance; and if pheasants are wanted for the table, and must be killed for it, and, by consequence, must also be reared and preserved for it, then kill them in this way; but let paid hands do the butchery, and do not gloat over your victims, and dignify their slaughter with the name of sport. Domestic

poultry must be reared, and killed; but who would admit the pleasure of wringing their necks, or cutting their throats? Yet where lies the difference? The pheasant is not even a difficult shot. On first rising from covert, his flight is slow and hurried, though when in full swing, it is often fast enough; but the shots presented in a *battue* are almost always easy ones, and the practice afforded is so great, that those who indulge in them are almost sure of their mark. The only excuse I could ever make for myself or others who have partaken of the *battue*, is, that as it is a rare and expensive amusement, people are apt to value it by the general estimate—namely, its cost. Every one knows that pheasant-preserving causes a most extravagant outlay, and he also knows that he cannot indulge in the sport many times a-year. This may perhaps account for the high rate at which it is estimated, but is only a lame apology at the best.

Sect. 5.—Dress and Gun.

158. The sportsman should be well protected with velveteen or fustian jacket and trowsers; and he should have a strong cap, with a good projecting peak or poke to it, which will save his eyes from the thorns and brambles. His gun, also, should be a short double-barrelled one, not exceeding twenty-eight inches in length of barrel; and, in fact, two inches less, if a good one of that length can be procured.

Sect. 6.—The Woodcock.

159. The Woodcock (*Scolopax Rusticola*) is a native of the north of Europe and Asia. It is rarely known to breed in Great Britain, but visits this country in the winter, arriving in the beginning of October, and leaving in March or April. After its first arrival, it is always confined to the thickest and most impenetrable covers by day; but at night, and very early in the morning, it visits the swamps and meadows, in search of the worms upon which it feeds. When it breeds here, its nest consists of a loose mass of leaves and grass, placed in some sheltered bank far from the prying eyes of children. It lays three or four eggs, of a yellowish-brown, blotched with brown of a darker colour, and mixed with grey. In length, it is about 14 inches, and 25 from tip to tip. Its weight is about 12 to 13 ounces; the head is of an obtusely-triangular shape, and the eyes are placed very near the top of the ears. The upper mandible measures about 3 inches in length, and is furrowed nearly the whole length. Its tip projects beyond the under one, which it overlaps, forming a kind of knob, and this is endowed with an extreme degree of sensitiveness, by which the bird is enabled to discover the insects it is in search of in the mud. The woodcock is essentially a nocturnal bird, and its eyes, like all of that class, are large, full, and dark. While other birds are alive and doing, these are asleep under some bush, concealed by thorns or evergreens; and it is only when aroused by the dogs that they fly up and endeavour to reach a more secure place of concealment. Several varieties of this bird visit our shores, and this most probably arises from their migrating to us from such an extensive range of country. Dr. Latham makes out three distinct varieties; but as one of his has a white head, it is most probable that it was only an accidental pye colour, and not a distinct and continued variety. It may, however, be asserted pretty generally, that the first comers are fuller, fatter, and duller than the November cocks, which are nimble and active, easily rising high above the underwood, and being, consequently, difficult to kill. The male is scarcely distinguishable from the female by the feathers or form, the only distinction being, according to Pennant, a narrow stripe of white on the exterior web of the feather in the female, which same part is spotted with black and white in the male. Every epicure is familiar with the flavour of the woodcock, and with its mode of dressing without being drawn.

160. Principal Localities of the Woodcock.—These birds are never, or very rarely, seen to arrive on the coast; which is not so much to be wondered at, since they are, in other respects, nocturnal. They generally come over with a light easterly or south-easterly breeze, but are often caught in their passage by an adverse current, and are then much exhausted, so as to be almost unable to rise for some time after landing. At this time they may be found in the ditches near the shore, and will submit almost to be killed with a stick or a stone. They soon pass inland, and even cross over to Ireland in great numbers, though a great many also reach that country direct from France and Spain. Large quantities of woodcocks are taken by traps and nets, chiefly on the coasts of Devonshire, Dorsetshire, Hampshire, and Sussex, from which counties they are sent up in great numbers to the London markets, and to the great provincial towns. In Wales and Scotland—particularly its western coast—they are also taken in the same way, to a great extent, and these supply the Bath and Bristol, and the Edinburgh and Glasgow markets. Indeed, it is seldom that a shot woodcock is sold in the shops, for the bird is so easily torn and disfigured by the gun, that the netted one is vastly preferred, and therefore the poacher commands the market.

Sect. 7.—Dogs used for Cock-Shooting.

161. These are the same as those recommended for finding the pheasant; but the setter is here wholly useless, as the haunts of the cock are inaccessible to so large a dog. The Sussex spaniel is the best I have ever seen, being hardy, and capable of bearing wet with impunity. His nose is also wonderfully good, which its full development, in point of size, would lead one to expect. They are bred so much for hunting cocks that they own the scent very easily, and seem to delight and revel in it, giving generally a very joyous note on touching upon their trail. The true Sussex may easily be kept strictly to feather, and though they will readily hunt fur when nothing else is to be had, they do not prefer it, as most other dogs do.

162. Number of Dogs used in this sport should be at least 2½ or 3 couple, as the coverts are generally large and very thick; but I should always prefer hunting two couple at a time, and giving the other couple an hour's rest—thus, always having one couple fresh and one tired at work together.

Sect. 8.—Cock-Shooting.

163. The Mode of using these Dogs in Cock-Shooting is very similar to that adopted in *wild* pheasant-shooting, except that different localities are visited by the two kinds of birds—the pheasants keeping as much as possible to the dry and sound parts, and to those which are tolerably open, whilst the cocks select the neighbourhood of moist low ground, though they do not choose the actual swamp for roosting. For this purpose they prefer the shelter of thick bushes, and low evergreens when they can find them; for, though they frequent wet and marshy ground for feeding, they are particularly addicted to protected roosting-places, such as holly and juniper bushes, or even laurel or lauristinus, when planted in the midst of water, as in ornamental islands, &c. During long frosts the inland springs are frozen, and the cocks are compelled to leave them and seek the salt marshes, where the springs are seldom quite hard; but in very severe winters even here their food is sometimes frost-bound, and great numbers of woodcocks are starved to death, as in the winter of 1838-9, and in this present one of 1854-5. Woodcocks, generally, take the same line of flight in going to feed as is the case with nearly all migratory birds; and in flying, even from one covert to another, they may always be seen to take the same ride or break in the trees. In beating large coverts this is very conspicuous, as there are always certain spots where cocks are shot, if any are to be met with. Knowing old

hands take advantage of this, and station themselves there to await their crossing. Beaters are very useful to assist the dogs in this kind of shooting; but the grand requisite is a set of good markers, because the cocks can seldom be shot the first time they are put up, and do not run like the pheasant after they alight. Many good sportsmen place two or three *good* markers in the highest trees, on the opposite side of a large covert to that which is to be first entered; then, going in themselves, they get what shots they can, by pushing up rapidly to the dogs, as in pheasant-shooting; and as soon as they reach the other side, they are guided to the points where all the disturbed cocks have dropped, which a good marker can point out by the trees which he has marked and knows. Here they will always be found by careful hunting, and may then, generally, be flushed and shot at, if not bagged. In high bare-stemmed larch or fir coverts, these birds are more easily shot as they rise above the low underwood, and before they reach the branches of the trees; but, in lower oak or beech woods, they must be watched for in the openings, and snapped at in a moment, or all chance is lost. Woodcocks, when disturbed by the dogs, often settle just outside the coverts, which the markers can readily see, and here they can easily be got at and shot with facility. They generally go straight away from the gun till they near the bushes, when they shoot and twist in a manner which makes them very difficult to kill at that moment. Each successive time they are disturbed they lie closer than before, but when put up their flight is more rapid and snipe-like, in proportion to the frequency of their disturbances. If, therefore, the middling shot misses a good opening the first or second time, he seldom replenishes his bag, in the subsequent ones, at the same bird; and, in this way, I have known six or seven shots fired at one cock on the same day, without ultimate success, though afterwards another bird has immediately fallen to the same gun.

This variety and uncertainty give great interest to the sport; and it certainly deserves all the encomiums which have been passed upon it. The irregular flight of the bird; his mode of flapping his wings, peculiar to himself; the way in which he shoots right or left, after a slow and smooth flight—changing from that of a tame owl to the velocity of the hawk—all conspire to give interest to his pursuit. Sometimes you may hear him and see him with facility; at others you hear him, but cannot catch even a glimpse of the bird; whilst again you hear and see him for a moment, then lose sight, and finally obtain such a view as to be able to account for him to your own satisfaction, if not his. But it is chiefly in wild, rocky districts that this bird can be pursued with every advantage; in fact, in those only where open spaces alternate with thick clumps of low bushes. Here he may generally be hunted with spaniels to great advantage, and, indeed, their presence is essential to the sport, as no man can penetrate the thick clumps of holly and juniper which abound in some parts of Wales and Scotland. No bird is so often missed, because every one who can get a shot is sure to snap at him with the chance of a stray shot telling; whereas, in the pursuit of partridge, grouse, or pheasant, the shooter does not put his gun up without a fair chance, knowing that, if he does not get a shot at them to-day, he will, or may, next week. The woodcock, also, is so very deceiving in his flight—beginning often so heavily, and then, again, all at once shooting off at a tangent—that it is no wonder that good shots even miss him. No one likes to maul a woodcock to pieces, by firing at a few yards' distance, which might often be done when he first gets up; the shooter, therefore, in great anxiety to obtain the prize, waits till he is at a fair distance, and then is suddenly surprised to see him begin to shoot round some shrubs, which he fancied too low to interfere. His much-coveted prize is this time secure; but he follows him up, and, after much trouble, gets a good shot, and perhaps drops upon another or two in finding this one. Such are the glorious uncertainties of woodcock-shooting. No bird lies closer than a cock, and in some situations, when they are not much disturbed, the spaniels will actually rout them out with their noses, and chop them even occasionally; but this is not often the case, as the bird is very nimble in evading the jaws of his enemy. In order to hunt them well in thick coverts, the spaniels ought to have their master with them, as they require every encouragement to make them penetrate the tangled masses of underwood frequented by the cocks; if, therefore, the keeper is accustomed to them, by all means let him hunt them; but if not, the master must undertake that duty, even if he loses a few shots by so doing. I have said that, in all cases, if a spaniel is on the trail of a cock, the shooter should get to him as quickly as possible; but if he is hunting with the wind, and *there is enough of it* to be plainly felt in covert, the bird is almost sure to come up wind into the shooter's face; and he had therefore better remain quiet in as open a spot as he can pick, and catch his bird as he comes. Woodcocks killed dead sometimes fall at some distance, and are very difficult to find, as few retrievers can hit off the body-scent of a dead

cock, which has not run at all. In this kind of retrieving, the sagacity of the Newfoundland comes into advantageous play, as they seem to mark the spot where the bird fell with great accuracy, and find it by eye rather than by nose.

SECT. 9.—THE DRESS AND GUN.

164. The shooting habiliments should be the same as in pheasant-shooting, except that, as the ground is generally more or less swampy in places, the boots should be carefully dressed with the waterproof composition. Snipe-boots would soon be destroyed by the thorns and briers, and are, therefore, out of the question, besides being too cumbrous for this active exercise. The gun is exactly the same as for the pheasant.

SECT. 10.—HARE AND RABBIT-SHOOTING.

165. THE HARE (*Lepus Timidus*) is usually shot in covert, except when preserved for coursing; but it is poor sport, as, while in covert, she never goes faster than a canter, and may be killed with certainty by any tyro. It can only be for the pot, or for the purpose of increasing the list of the slain, that this game is shot. Besides, the killing hares when using spaniels spoils them for pheasant or cock-shooting, as they always own the scent of game which is killed to them.

166. RABBIT-SHOOTING is a different affair altogether from shooting hares, and affords, in my opinion, the very best sport in covert of all, excepting only wild pheasant and woodcock-shooting. This, of course, has reference to the hunting them with dogs, and the shooting while going at their best pace, which is undoubtedly a racing one. Rabbits breed in warrens, in hedge-rows, and in covert, and multiply very fast indeed. There are said to be several distinct varieties; but I believe there is no truth in the assertion, the kind of food only causing a *temporary* difference, and not permanently causing a distinct variety. Warren-rabbits removed to a covert, and there allowed to breed, soon attain the same character as the prior denizens of the same locality. The sport of shooting rabbits is never carried on in the warrens, because the warrener does not wish his property wasted, and prefers trapping them, for obvious reasons—one being, that the wounded rabbits often escape into the holes and die out of reach. In hedge-rows, they may be hunted with spaniels or terriers, and shot as they come out; but they generally have holes in the banks, and then soon reach them in safety. When driven to their fastnesses, the ferret is the only resource; and these animals, after being muzzled, soon drive them either to the gun or into bag-nets placed over the

F

holes. But it is to the covert-shooting of rabbits that I wish to draw attention, that being the only kind of rabbit-shooting which is to be considered worthy the attention of the true sportsman, and which, I have already remarked, is really worth it. Rabbits are now much encouraged in large pheasant-preserves, partly for the sake of the keepers, whose perquisite they are, but chiefly because they afford food for the foxes preserved for fox-hunting, which would otherwise prey upon the pheasants. The keeper feeds his foxes when young regularly upon rabbits wounded and left near their earths; and, consequently, these rabbit-fed animals keep to the same fare, and are thus prevented from interfering with the pleasures of the *battue*. The keeper continues to shoot a few outlying rabbits round the covert, and those which are thus wounded suffice to keep up the supply for the foxes, in addition to those which the keeper may purposely leave for him, or the fox may himself succeed in laying hold of. When the pheasant-season is over, and the foxes also have been thinned, it will be found that the rabbits must be kept down on account of the young crops, which they begin to bite off most cruelly. In February and March, therefore, good sport is usually afforded by this thinning of the rabbits, several hundred couple being often killed in a single preserve. At this time a great number of rabbits lie above ground, preparing for their young, or driven to seek the pleasures of love, or from other causes, of which we, in our ignorance of their language, have not yet fathomed the motive. However, there they are; and in the spring-falls of a large wood they may be found lying in tussocks of grass, or in little bushes. For these the vermin-terriers of the keepers are the best dogs, as they hunt them very quietly, yet strongly, and your regular springers or cockers would be utterly spoilt for pheasant or cock if allowed to hunt rabbit. By sending the keeper and his terriers into the wood, the rabbits are driven across the drives, where the guns should be posted at 60 yards' distance from one another; or, if the spring-falls are quite open, they may walk then in line. As the rabbits are put up, they cut in and out of the rides or runs, and require great quickness of eye to catch them before they are lost to sight. The guns must be carried on the shoulder, full-cocked; and great care must be taken not to shoot the terriers as they are hunting close upon the scent of the rabbit. I once shot a very valuable dog in this way, with the rabbit actually in his mouth. This was as the rabbit was coming out of a bush, and the dog so close upon her, that, as she sprang through, the terrier did the same, and received my charge in her breast, killing both dog and rabbit. It is needful to shoot well before the rabbit, as they run so quickly by you, that if you do not take this precaution you are sure to shoot behind them. The knack is easily acquired by a quick ye and hand, but a slow man had better not attempt what he will be certain to fail in. In shooting rabbits, Colonel Hawker advises the sportsman to get into a tree, but this can scarcely be called sport, though something of a-piece with some kinds of wild-fowl-shooting. I should only advise pot-hunters or boys to resort to such an unfair advantage. If, however, they are to be *destroyed* as injurious to the farmer, the plan is, no doubt, a good one; but for this purpose the use of the ferret is far the best resource.

SECT. 11.—EXPENSES OF COVERT-SHOOTING.

167. The cost of rearing and preserving pheasants is enormous, usually reaching from half-a-guinea to a guinea a-head for each bird bagged. Woodcocks, being birds of passage, are not capable of being preserved, except during their short stay, when they require intruders to be prevented shooting or trapping them. Hares also require strong watching, and are even more liable to the attacks of poachers than pheasants; but as they are generally preserved with those birds, and are considered subsidiary to them, their extra cost is seldom brought into the calculation.

RIVER AND POND-SHOOTING.

168. Here we have little opportunity for the skill of the sportsman to display itself, and the pretensions of this kind of sport are not such as to meet with the approbation of such a glutton at the gun as Col. Hawker. Still, many sportsmen prefer it to the punt-shooting so much lauded by that ardent admirer of its peculiar advantages. I shall first enumerate the birds which are met with, and then detail the best modes of shooting them on the rivers, ponds, and small lakes of this country. Some of them, as the ducks, teal, and wigeon, are also shot from the punt; but as they are to be met with in large quantities in rivers and ponds, I shall include them under both kinds of sport. At the head of this list stands

169. THE MALLARD, or WILD-DUCK (*Anas Boschas*).—This is said to be the parent of our domestic duck, one variety of which it resembles in colour, though somewhat less in size, and having dark legs and toes. Some few ducks breed in this country, but the vast flocks which frequent our coasts and internal waters are migratory birds, and are only here in the winter season. When breeding in Britain, they make their nest in some quiet hedge-row, or high bank, near the river or brook, and lay 15 to 18 eggs of a greenish colour. The young wild-ducks are diligently sought for just when they are becoming fledged, and are scarcely able to make use of their wings, in which stage they are called "flappers."

170. WIGEON (*Mareca Penelope*), are next in size to the wild-duck. They seldom are found far inland, therefore they afford better sport to the puntsman than to the river-shooter; they are, however, very good eating, and will reward the sportsman for his trouble if they are shot on the internal waters. In the adult male, the length is about 18 inches; bill, brown-black; iris, brown; top of the head, white; cheeks and back of the head, chestnut-red; back, greyish-white, with irregular lines of black; tail pointed, and nearly black; wing-coverts, white, tipped with black; a green speculum, edged with black, on the outer webs of the secondary wing-feathers; chin and front of neck, black; lower part of neck, pale reddish-brown; breast, belly, and vent, white; legs and feet, dark-brown. The old male birds, to a great extent, assume the feathers of the female in July, and continue so till the autumnal moult. In the female, the length is about 16½ inches, and the following points of difference occur: head and neck,

reddish-brown, speckled with darker brown; back, of two shades of brown in each feather. The young male birds resemble the females.

171. THE PINTAILED DUCK (*Dafila Acuta*), is also occasionally found on our internal waters, and is one of the first taken in the decoys in October. Its flight is very rapid. No duck is better for the table, the flavour being excellent. In July the male assumes the same plumage as the female, but recovers his masculine colours in the autumnal moult. The length of tail will always serve to distinguish this duck from the wigeon, whose plumage it resembles in other respects.

172. THE POCHARD or DUNBIRD (*Nyroca Ferina*), receives its second name from the peculiar colour of the eye. It is a winter visitor to this country, appearing in October, and leaving in the spring. It resorts to inland waters as well as the sea-shore, and is a very shy and wary bird. It is of a very good flavour, and highly esteemed for the table, resembling the famous canvas-backed duck of the United States, though but a humble imitation, in my opinion. The length of this duck is 19½ inches. The male has a pale-blue bill, with a black point and base; iris, red; head and upper part of neck, rich chestnut; lower part of neck and upper part of breast, deep black; back, of a freckled-grey; rump and upper tail coverts, black; tail, greyish-brown; lower breast and belly, grey; legs and toes, blueish-grey. The female has the bill all black; iris, brown; head and neck, dusky-brown; lower part of neck and breast, dark-brown.

173. THE TEAL (*Querquedula Crecca*), is the smallest of our ducks, and one of the richest in flavour; it is, therefore, much sought after by the sportsman who regards his stomach, or those of his friends. It frequently breeds in Great Britain, especially among the lakes of Westmoreland. Its flight is very rapid, and it affords an excellent mark to the skilful shot. From this circumstance it is still better suited to single shots than to the large punt-gun. Like all the duck tribe, it feeds by night. The female lays only seven or eight eggs, of a whitish colour. In the adult male, the length is 14½ inches; the bill is black; eyes, hazel; forehead, and band extending backwards, chestnut-brown; a narrow line of buff from the gape to the occiput, over the eye, and also from under the eye to the lower part of ear coverts—between these two lines a spot of rich green; cheeks, and remainder of the side of the neck, chestnut; back of neck and back transversely lined with black and

white; wings, brown, in various shades—a speculum on the secondaries, of velvety-black, green and purple, tipped with white; tail, pointed, dark-brown; chin, black; front of neck, chestnut above, with spots of black on a white ground below; legs and toes, brownish-grey. Like the wigeon, the male birds lose their distinguishing feathers in July. The female has the whole of the head speckled with dark-brown; back, dark-brown, mixed on each feather with lighter brown; wing, like the male; chin, pale-brown; lower part of neck has crescentic brown marks, instead of spots of black; sides and belly, dull white, spotted with dark-brown.

174. THE BALD COOT (*Fulica Atra*), is a bird well known throughout England, being a permanent resident in the ponds of the ornamental grounds of our aristocracy. It weighs about 28 ounces. In colour, it is a deep black, excepting the outer edges of the wings, and a spot under each eye, which are white; under parts of a dirty lead-colour. The nest is a huge mass of rushes, &c., quite on the water's edge; and it lays eight or nine greenish-white eggs.

THE GREATER COOT is only a larger variety of the preceding, which it resembles in all other respects. The coots are often shot on our ponds, and by some are preserved expressly for that purpose. Colonel Hawker maintains, that they are not to be considered as worth powder and shot in fresh water, because they cannot then be slaughtered in sufficient numbers; but I confess I cannot see the force of his reasoning, though he has obtained such an undisputed empire over this species of sport, that it requires some courage to throw doubt on his dictum. Still, it appears to me, that there is quite as much sport in killing one bird with an ounce of shot, as in killing 20 with 20 ounces. Nothing surprises me more than the inconsistencies of sport. In one kind (as, for instance, partridge and grouse-shooting), it is considered as the highest degree of pot-hunting, to shoot into the middle of a covey or pack; whilst in another (the shooting of wild-fowl), the sportsman is told that one bird is not worth his notice, and that he must wait quietly till he can catch a whole lot of them within the deadly circle of his fire. How is the young sportsman to reconcile these incongruities? The only answer is like that so often given by English grammarians—" there is no invariable rule, but each kind is governed by its own laws." What is right at Poole or Southampton, is entirely wrong on the stubbles of Norfolk or the moors of Scotland. The coot is a very difficult bird to flush, as it keeps among the reeds and rushes, diving at the approach of the dog. By following these birds up with a good dog, they may sometimes be made to rise, and then afford an easy shot.

175. THE MOORHEN, or GALLINULE (*Gallinula Chloropus*), is very commonly met with in our rivers and ponds. Here it swims gracefully, searching for aquatic insects, and nodding its head at every instant. It dives remarkably well and quickly, and remains in the reeds with only its beak above the water. On account of its diving so rapidly, it is rarely bagged without the aid of a dog, as it does not rise to the surface if death takes place after the dive. On land it runs rapidly, cocking up the feathers of its tail, which are white beneath, and seeking the secure retreats afforded by the water as rapidly as possible. Its nest is built among the sedge, and it lays seven or eight eggs, of a yellow colour, with brown spots. The young birds appear only like a brownish-black mass of fur or down, and swim about in the most lively manner. In the male, the beak is yellowish-green, with a red base; on the forehead is a naked patch of red; iris, hazel; back, wings, rump, and tail, dark olive-brown; head, neck, breast, and sides, dark-slate; belly and vent, greyish-white; above tarsus, a ring of red; legs and toes, green.

176. THE WATER-RAIL (*Rallus Aquaticus*), resembles the moorhen in general figure, though differing in colour, which is more like the land-rail. The back is spotted or speckled-brown; cheeks, chin, sides, and front of neck and breast, lead-grey; vent, buff-colour; legs and toes, brownish-red; length, 11½ inches.

177. THE GREBES (*Podiceps Cristatus, P. Auritus,* and *P. Minor,* are like the moorhens in diving powers, and resemble them much in habits. All the grebes feed upon fish and water-insects. The lesser grebe is also called the *Dabchick.* It is a very timid bird, and disappears by diving on the slightest alarm. It is easily domesticated on our ornamental waters, and dives and comes up again, over and over again, as if for the amusement of the spectators.

Three varieties of the sandpiper frequent our rivers, of which the summer snipe, or common sandpiper, is the most familiar. They are—

178. THE GREEN SANDPIPER (*Totanus Ochropus*), of whose habits very little is known. They are very common in spring and autumn, and frequent the banks of brooks and inland rivers. They feed on worms and insects; and they have a shrill note, of a whistling character. Beak, greenish-black; iris, hazel—as in the snipes, a line from it to the eye; white mark over the eye; back parts of head, neck, and body, dusky-green; primaries, dusky-black; tail-coverts and feathers, white. The outside tail-feather

has one dark spot on the outer web; the next, two spots; and the third and fourth, two black bands; the others also have several bars. Under parts of the body white; throat, streaked with dusky lines; legs and toes, greenish-black. Length, 9½ inches.

179. THE WOOD SANDPIPER (*Totanus Glareola*), resembles the preceding in habits and general appearance, but differs in being somewhat smaller, the length being only 9 inches. Iris, dusky-brown; tail-feathers with six or more narrow transverse white bars, on a ground of greenish black; legs and toes, olive-green.

180. THE SUMMER SNIPE, or COMMON SANDPIPER (*Tringoïdes Hypoleuca*), is found very generally on all our rivers, lakes, and canals, where it breeds on the banks. It is mostly seen running along the gravelly edges in search of its food, which is composed of insects and worms. It utters a peculiarly sharp note when disturbed. Beak, dark-brown, with a yellowish base; iris, dark-brown; dark streak from beak to the eye; upper part of body greenish-brown; four middle tail-feathers greenish-brown, with a blackish stripe across the centre, and all barred with black—four outer ones tipped with white; primaries almost black, with a greyish patch on all but the first; all the under parts of a pure white; legs and toes, dark-green.

Such is a list of the birds chiefly frequenting our ponds and rivers. Occasionally, others are met with, but those I have enumerated form the bulk of the number.

SECT. 2.—BEST DOG FOR RIVER-SHOOTING.

181. THE BEST DOG for hunting these birds in the brooks is the old English water-spaniel; but a good rough fox-terrier will answer very nearly as well. The former will be found under the general description of the dog; but his specific education had better be here introduced.

182. BREAKING THE WATER-SPANIEL OR RETRIEVER.—As these dogs are required for punt-shooting, as well as river-hunting, and as their education is better commenced on the river-side than in the punt, it will be well to enter in detail into their education here. Nothing answers better for this purpose than the shooting of "flappers," which usually comes on in July and August. The water being then warm, and the young birds awkward, and not very good divers, great encouragement to persevere is afforded to the dog, and he may be easily induced to swim more or less for hours, and to hunt the side of a brook in the most ardent manner. There is very little difficulty in entering these dogs to wildfowl, as they seem to have a natural bias that way; but they should be carefully broken from rats, which abound on the banks of rivers and ponds. The only art consists in confining their range, by making them beat to hand, and in persuading them to retrieve wounded or dead birds. The range is much more easily taught the water-spaniel than the land variety, because he is almost always in sight of the shooter, and always within the sound of his voice. If, therefore, the puppy has been taught to come in at the word "Back," and to turn to the right and left on land, in obedience to the hand, as in ordinary spaniel-breaking, he will be sure to obey in the water, where he seems to ask for the directions of his master. The eye of the swimming dog is only able to command a small circle, being very little raised above the level of the water, and therefore it cannot see far from its nose; but by watching the hand of its master—for the voice should not be used more than necessary—it is often directed to the right spot, and afterwards is glad to claim the assistance which is found to be so useful. The water-retriever should be taught on land, like the land-retriever, to seek for gloves and young rabbits, &c., and to bring them, uninjured, to his master. After a time, he may be taught to bring a ball or glove from the water, which he does more readily even than on land, but is very apt at first to deposit it on the shore, as soon as he reaches it, in order that he may shake himself clear of the water hanging to his coat. This should not be permitted, but the dog should always lay his burden actually at his master's feet, because sometimes, if not checked, he leaves it in such a situation as to cause great difficulty in reaching it. The *desiderata* in a water-dog are—a liver colour, without white—black and white being alike conspicuous; an extraordinary nose, to make out water-fowl, whose scent is not remarkably strong; a strong woolly and oily coat, to resist the water. Here there is a very great difference, some dogs being able to remain in that element for hours, while others are rapidly exhausted, and this arises mainly from the cause above alluded to. He should bear cold as well as wet; and be thoroughly amenable to command, so that he will lie for any indefinite time without the slightest movement, waiting his master's order to hunt or retrieve. He should also be mute, as his tongue is never required, and would often disturb distant waterfowl. All these qualities are scarce, and should be highly prized when they are united in one, which they seldom are. The fault of the old liver-coloured water-spaniel is, that he is too often headstrong and impetuous; while the Newfoundland is too

bulky, and tires rather sooner than is desirable. His colour, also, is not so good as the spaniel's.

SECT. 3.—DUCK-GUNS AND ACCESSORIES.

183. THE DUCK-GUN is a totally different tool from the ordinary fowlingpiece, though for flappers, and some of the common sorts, the latter may suffice; but for the wilder varieties a more deadly weapon is required—and such is the long tube called a duck-gun. Colonel Hawker has established so thorough a control over the opinions of all sportsmen on the subject of wildfowl-shooting, that I shall make no further apology for quoting from him on most occasions. No other amateur has had such a long experience in these matters, and it is only in those open to the common sense of every sportsman that I shall venture to differ from him. On land I think there are many whose opinions deserve as much weight as his; but on water he is undoubtedly the king of this species of sport. He strongly recommends a country maker in preference to a London one, and specifies Westley Richards at Birmingham, Burnett of Southampton, and Clayton of Lymington, as the most likely to produce a good article in this particular line. Mr. Clayton seems to be the one to whom the wildfowl-shooter may most readily entrust his order, having worked for the Colonel, and under his eye, for some years past. The Colonel advises the following kind of implement :— It should weigh from 12 to 20 lbs.; should have a substantial stock, such as a fancy workman would be ashamed of; it should be made so large at the breech, that neat gun-makers would laugh at it; the stock should rise well up to the eye, because you have not the power to lower your head when holding out a heavy weight; and, above all, the barrel should *lie level*, and *well up to the eye*, instead of being let down into the stock so as to pitch under the mark in quick firing. A duck-gun should have either no heel-plate at all, or one of a metal which will not rust from loading in a wet place. The advantage of a duck-gun is, that it will carry large shot more compactly, and may be fired with double or treble the charge for a piece of the ordinary size. You are, therefore, enabled to use large shot with the same advantage that No. 7 may be fired from a double gun; by which means, at a large object, you may kill considerably farther, and, in a flock, many more birds at a shot. The recoil of a duck-gun can only be checked by weight of metal; and there are two ways to dispose of it : the one, by immense thickness, whereby the gun may be short, portable, and easily managed; and the other, by increasing the length, by which

you may kill farther, and take more accurate aim. The former was the plan of Mr. Joseph Manton, the latter that of the late Mr. D. Egg; and, in order to partake a little of both advantages, I should steer between the two, and have barrels never less than 3 feet 8 inches, nor more than 4 feet 4 inches, unless I used a rest. For pond and river-shooting, these guns may be from 12 to 16 lbs.; but more than that greatly fatigues the arm; and with a gun of this weight a good charge is carried a very considerable distance. A broad butt lessens the recoil, and a piece of sponge adapted to it will still further diminish that unpleasant feeling.

Colonel Hawker lays down a rule for the length of duck-guns, which is founded upon the length of the fowlingpiece to which the individual intending to use one is accustomed. It is as follow : —Measure the diameter and the length of the ordinary gun; then find how many times the former will go into the latter—and order the duck-gun to be four or six diameters more than it. Thus, supposing the gun to be 44 times the diameter, viz., 2 feet 8 inches, let the duck-gun of 7 gauge and 13 lbs. weight be from 3 feet 6 to 3 feet 8 inches, or even 4 feet in length. He also recommends the addition of a pistol-grip for the right hand, which takes off a little of the jar from the shoulder; and that this part should be bound round with twine like a cricket-bat. In loading a duck-gun, the farther you wish it to carry, the more powder and the less shot you must put in; this rule applies to all guns, but more especially to the duck-gun. (See Fig. 1.)

184. SPECIES OF PRIMER.—Duck-guns, of all sizes, are peculiarly liable to wet, and often to the spray from the sea. It is found that, under these circumstances, the ordinary copper cap will often miss fire, from becoming damp, or allowing the powder in the nipple to do so. Mr. Westley Richards, however, has invented a primer, which acts remarkably well for all sizes of duck and punt-guns; and the brass cylinder containing the percussion powder is perfectly waterproof; they may be applied to any percussion or flint-gun. But for single guns, these, as well as the percussion caps, are somewhat in the way of the sight,—at least Colonel Hawker says they are, which, to many, is the same thing; and he has invented a side primer, which consists of a flat anvil, on which a tube is placed, which also passes through a touchhole, similar to the old flint-guns. The striker explodes this tube, just as the flint set fire to the powder in the pan of the old flint-gun; and, as coarse powder can be used instead of fine, many advantages attend its use—one, that it is perfectly waterproof; a second, that coarse powder may be used; and a

third, that the gun rarely misses fire, because the tube reaches straight to the powder in the chamber of the breech.

185. DUCK-SHOT.—No. 1 or 2 is the shot for a 7 gauge, and A or B for a 5 gauge, or inch-bore.

186. WADDING.— Wilkinson's felt wadding is the best for this species of gun.

187. DRESS.—A strong *woollen* shooting-coat should be worn, as the cotton fabrics do not resist cold and wet sufficiently for this sport. Caps should always replace hats, making a considerable difference in the height of the individual; they should also not be too dark, but of a neutral colour. The trowsers should be of some strong woollen fabric, and woollen stockings, drawers, and waistcoat should be invariably worn. In situations where there is much wading, the long water-boot should be put on over two pairs of woollen stockings. Mr. Short, of East Yarmouth, is said to make these boots well. They should be well dressed with the linseed oil composition, or, *if time can be given them to dry*, with neats'-foot oil. Nothing keeps water out so well as this last; but it must be thoroughly soaked in the leather, and takes many months to dry, so as to be safe in point of health. I have put on boots thus treated, which felt exactly as if thoroughly wet, and would give cold as easily as if they were really so.

SECT. 4.—WILD-DUCK-SHOOTING IN RIVERS, &c.

188. WILD-DUCKS.— When the shooter seeks the wild-duck in the shape of flappers, he should go to the brook, or pond, where they are supposed to be in July, and send his dog into the rushes, woods, &c., along the banks; in process of time he will spring the old duck, and this will encourage him in the search for her brood. By and by a young bird is seen to rush about among the reeds, and makes perhaps an attempt at flight, in which she most probably falls a victim to your shooting propensities. The whole brood should be diligently followed when found, as those which are left will not remain to stand another hunt. In the month of August the young birds are able to fly to the corn-fields; and towards evening, and very early in the morning, they may be caught sight of and shot in their flight backward and forward to the water; or, after they are in that element, they may be hunted for in the banks and shot. This is very pretty summer shooting, and affords very good practice for both dog and gunner. In many large ponds, or ornamental waters, these birds are found in large numbers, but will seldom suffer the approach of the shooter, except in their morning and even-

ing flights at this season to the corn-fields. But when small brooks fall into these waters a few stray young ducks may generally be met with and shot.

189. SHOOTING TEAL.—Of all the varieties of river-shooting, that of teal affords the best sport, as they do not fly far when found, but alight again on the same brook, or pond. They are less cunning than the common wild-duck, and are, consequently, more easily approached; and, being of such a good flavour for the table, they are eagerly sought after. They fly very fast and strong, but not far; and will sometimes take half-a-dozen shots before they are killed, if the shooter is a young hand at the business. In marking a teal on a brook, be very careful to cast the eye well forwards, as he is very apt to appear to settle long before he really does, and in this way deceives the sportsman; or he will drop, and then swim away most diligently, without any attempt at concealment in the banks or rushes. The plan, therefore, is to send a man down below him to head him, and prevent his adopting these tricks.

190. IN SHOOTING COOTS AND WATERHENS, the object is to get them on the wing, as they dive at the flash so rapidly, that they can rarely be killed while in the water, or if killed, they die below the surface, and are thus lost. The best plan is to conceal yourself on the windward side of the pond, where you will not be heard or smelt by these birds; and get an assistant to go and put them up with stones on the other side, catching them, if possible, away from the bank; or he may fire at them a long shot, and thus make them rise: but, after all, they are an unmanageable species of bird with the gun.

191. THE GREBES are worse than the coots in diving at the flash; and are really scarcely worth the trouble of shooting.

SECT. 5.—DECOY-DUCK-SHOOTING IN THE HUT.

192. DESCRIPTION OF THE DECOY-DUCK.—This sport was originally practised in France, but is now being gradually introduced into this country. It requires, in the first place, the aid of six or eight tame and pinioned wild-ducks, and these should be of the French variety or breed, which, like their masters, are vivacious and talkative in the highest degree. Besides these, the shooter provides himself with one or two good duck-guns, and then proceeds to make his hut. In France, the shooters are generally of the peasant order, and follow the shooting of ducks as a trade, which is commendable enough, and the exercise of ingenuity in thus providing for the market, and for the wants of their wives and families,

is worthy of admiration and respect. In this country, however, this species of sport, as far as I know, has only been followed by gentlemen-sportsmen, who build huts, and use decoy-ducks, for their own amusement. Now, I have nothing to say against this, for the sport is fully equal, in my opinion, to any other shooting in ambush; and, perhaps, since it displays a little more ingenuity than usual, it may stand at the head of that class of sports. It can only be carried on with advantage in the neighbourhood of those spots which are frequented by the ducks in large numbers, because it is entirely dependent upon the power of "calling" down the wild-ducks which the decoy-birds possess. It is well known that all gregarious birds are induced to drop where a good "call-bird" is placed; and this is the case, without exception, through the whole tribe. The Frenchman, therefore, takes advantage of this knowledge, and fastens several decoy-ducks on the water in such situations as shall be within call of the ducks as they fly to and from their evening meal. Then, as they drop to the invitation of the decoy-ducks, they are shot by the ambushed-shooter, and retrieved by his dog. Sometimes these huts are fixed at a very short distance from the sea, and at others at some miles from it, but always under the regular line of flight which these birds take. The shooter having taken measures to procure his tame-ducks (which he does by taking either the eggs, or the nestling-birds while quite young, and rearing them with other and older birds), proceeds to build his hut in the summer season, in the following manner :—

193. BUILDING THE HUT.—He first selects a sound piece of ground, either a small island surrounded by shallow water, or a promontory of the same kind partly surrounded by such a shallow. Deep water does not suit his purpose so well, because it compels him to employ his dog in retrieving the wounded or dead birds; and also necessitates the use of a boat in going to and from his retreat. The hut is thus made: a trench is first dug all round the intended site, in order to drain off the water, and leave the bottom dry for the feet of the shooter; next, a space is cut, deep and large enough for the feet and legs of two men, so that they sit down comfortably on the turf itself forming the surface of the island. After this the top covering is put on, which is made of a semicircular form, of willows bent from side to side, and covered at the top with growing turf. A hole is left sufficient for the entrance of the shooters, and this likewise is closed with a turf or grass-covered door. The sides are made up with green twigs, sods, &c., so as to imitate the surrounding objects, and holes are left to admit the passing out of the barrels of the gun or guns in various directions, commanding the places where the ducks are expected to alight.

194. THE AMBUSH.—When complete, the hut is left till the winter; as soon as that season arrives, the shooter proceeds to his hut just before the flights of ducks are expected, and fixes his decoy-ducks quietly on the water, tying their legs to stakes driven into the ground, if the water is shallow, or to ropes stretched across, if it is too deep for this. Three, five, or seven ducks are thus fastened, with the sexes alternating; but always having a preponderance of ducks over mallards. The decoy-ducks keep up an incessant quacking and chattering; and if they become quiet, are started off again by one or other of the following expedients. The first is, to rouse them by pulling the cord attached to them; the other, to pinch, or otherwise annoy, a spare duck kept in the hut for the purpose. As the flights pass over, they drop some of their numbers to these call-birds, which are shot by the ambushed-shooter, who has retired to his hut as soon as he has fastened his decoys. He generally waits as long as he thinks it prudent, before he fires his gun, in the hope of collecting a great number of birds on one spot, so as to sweep as many as he can; but sometimes, by waiting too long, he loses all; and the great art is to take advantage of the last moment, without waiting too long. When a shot is made, he has only to pick up the dead, and retire to rest as well as he can, or return to his house till a little before daybreak, for no more business will be done till then. At that time the ducks are returning to the sea, and may then be caught napping, as before. Wild-ducks and teal are thus shot in large numbers, but wigeon, dunbirds, &c., refuse to be charmed by the voice of their pretended friends, and cannot be taken in this way. The old English plan of sinking an oil-cask in the ground, and covering it over, would, I think, be an improvement upon the mere earth excavation, as it would enable the roof to be kept much lower, and would also keep the feet and legs more dry. These huts are warm enough, in consequence of their small size, but they are necessarily damp; and, to those who pass the night in them, they often give serious colds, followed by rheumatism or fever; and it is a task rather than a sport, in my humble opinion.

195. DRESS.—The only thing which need be noticed under this head is, that long waterproof boots are required to wade to the hut, to fix the ducks, and retrieve the wounded and dead wildfowl.

SALT-WATER WILDFOWL-SHOOTING.

SECT. 1.—MARINE WILDFOWL.

196. The three following kinds of wild-fowl-shooting are practised on the internal fresh and salt-water lakes and estuaries of Great Britain and Ireland, such as the various lochs of Scotland, and the mouths of the different rivers which empty themselves on the south and east coasts of England; among which Southampton Water and Pool harbour are perhaps the most conspicuous. All kinds of wildfowl are shot indiscriminately with the punt-gun; but with the shoulder-gun the wild-duck, teal, wigeon, golden eye, &c., are chiefly thought worth the shooter's notice. I shall, as before, give the various kinds of birds which usually are taken, and then the punts, guns, &c., used in taking them. At the head of the list stands—

197. THE WILD-SWAN, or HOOPER (*Cygnus Ferus*).—Of this bird there are several varieties—the common wild-swan, Bewick's swan, the Polish swan, and two small sub-varieties of the Bewick swan. This last swan resembles the common wild-swan in the colour of the base of the upper mandible; but the Polish swan has this part of a pale-yellow, instead of the bright orange. The internal structure of the three is shown to differ by Mr. Yarrell, and, therefore, though the external difference is so slight, there can be little doubt that they are different varieties of this bird. The adult swan is of a pure white; but the young birds, like those of the tame, or mute swan, are grey in plumage. They breed in the Arctic ocean, and only visit these shores, in the winter season, when the colds of their summer residence are too severe for them. They are easily shot, till rendered wild and cunning by incessant firing at them. A charge of shot from an ordinary gun, if directed against the head, or under the wing, will often kill them; but not even swan-shot will penetrate the feathers of the back and upper surface of the wings. They weigh from 12 to 20 lbs., and strike with such force of wing as to break the arm of a careless or ignorant person.

198. THE COMMON WILD-GOOSE (*Anser Ferus*), generally called the grey lag, is more an inland bird than one frequenting the coast; but as it can scarcely ever be shot on the feed—which is its only reason for seeking the interior,—it may perhaps be kept with its congeners, although seldom taken with the shot of the punt-gun. In Scotland, however, it is often stalked among the lochs, which are accessible to the shooter from their bold and partially-wooded shores. It is the ancestor of the tame-goose.

199. THE BRENT GOOSE (*Bernicla Brenta*), the BERNICLE GOOSE (*Bernicla Leucopsis*), the BEAN GOOSE (*Anser Segetum*), the EGYPTIAN GOOSE (*Chenalopex Ægyptiaca*), and the WHITE-FRONTED or LAUGHING GOOSE (*Anser Erythropus*), are all closely allied to the grey lag in habits and general appearance. None are equal to the tame variety for the table, being fishy and strong in flavour; but the Brent goose is by some considered a dainty dish, when it happens to be fat and well-conditioned. Wild-geese generally average about 10 pounds, and measure 2 feet 9 inches in length, and 5 feet from tip to tip of extended wings.

200. The wild-duck, teal, and pintailed-duck, the wigeon and the pochard have been already alluded to at page 67. They form the staple of the punt-shooter's sport. They arrive in great numbers late in the autumn, the females coming by themselves first, and leaving in the spring—the same order being observed as in coming.

Besides the five ducks already noticed, the following are met with on the coast, and afford sport to the puntsman:—

201. THE SHELDRAKE, or BURROUGH-DUCK (*Tadorna Vulpanser*), and the RUDDY SHELDRAKE (*Casarka Rutila*).

202. THE BLACK SCOTER (*Oidemia Nigra*) and the VELVET SCOTER (*Oidemia Fusca*).

203. THE SHOVELLER (*Spatula Clypeata*).

204. THE EIDER DUCK (*Somateria Mollissima*).

205. LONG-TAILED DUCK (*Harelda Glacialis*).

206. THE GADWALL (*Chaulelasmus Strepera*).

207. THE GOLDEN EYE (*Clangula Glaucion*), of which the young is the MORILLON.

208. THE HARLEQUIN DUCK (*Clangula Histrionica*).

209. THE SCAUP DUCK (*Fuligula Marila*).

210. THE TUFTED DUCK (*Fuligula Cristata*).

211. THE GARGANEY, or SUMMER TEAL (*Pterocyanea Circia*).

212. THE DIVERS (*Colymbus Glacialis, C. Arcticus* and *C. Septentrionalis*).

213. THE CURLEW and WHIMBREL (*Numemius Arquata* and *N. Phæopus*).

214. To these, which form the bulk of the puntsman's objects of sport, may be added—the Ringed Plover; Turnstone Sanderling; Oyster-Catcher; Redshank, common and spotted; Little Stint; Dunlin, or Purre and Purple Sandpiper; the Oxbird, and the Dotterel; also, the Cormorant, Gannet, and Gulls. The Rockbirds, including the Guillemots, Auks, Puffins, and Razorbills, also afford objects for the shooter's power, rather than skill, to be displayed; though some of

the first-mentioned are difficult to reach, from shyness, and are only to be bagged by shooting from the punt, as I shall presently describe. The ducks, swans, geese, &c., including all of the duck tribe enumerated above, together with the Curlew and Whimbrel, and, also, the Divers, are those which, principally, may be considered wildfowl, and which the wildfowl-shooter sweeps down with his heavy duck-gun, or his still heavier punt-gun. I shall divide the subject into the three following heads: first, stalking wildfowl on land; secondly, ordinary shoulder-gun punt-shooting; and, thirdly, stancheon-gun punt-shooting.

SECT. 2.—STALKING WILDFOWL.

215. THE STALKING OF WATERFOWL can only be practised in situations where cover is afforded to the stalker, either by shrubs, trees, or rocks, and particularly where he can take the birds in rear, after discovering them in front—as in lakes or lochs, &c. In these he can first see them on the opposite shore, and then go round and attack them on the same side as that on which they are feeding. There are two ways of carrying out this mode of getting at wildfowl; one, by taking advantage of every *natural* shelter afforded by rocks, trees, &c., and keeping them between the body of the stalker and the eye of the birds sought; the other, by employing the inventive genius of man, and using the moveable stalking-machine invented by Colonel Hawker, or the stalking-horse of the old fowlers; but the Colonel's invention is by far the most successful, and, in my opinion, affords the very best kind of shooting which concealment or ambush is capable of. Mr. Colquhoun, in his admirable work on the "Moor and the Loch," describes wildfowl-stalking in the most glowing terms; and, to man in high health, fearless and regardless of cold and wet, it is, no doubt, as attractive as deer-stalking. I shall quote largely from his pages, if not in his words, yet using his descriptions as my text for an account of a sport which I never had an opportunity of witnessing in the localities which he assumes as the basis of his operations.

216. THE REQUISITES for this sport are—first, a hardy frame, great activity of body, and some degree of quickness of thought and fertility of invention, in order to take advantage of all the features presented by the rocks, shrubs, &c., as protections against the sight of the wildfowl; secondly, a good *double* duck-gun, of about 14 lbs. to 18 lbs. weight; thirdly, a retriever perfectly under command, and accustomed to hunt when needed; and, fourthly, a good telescope. For the retriever, Mr. Colquhoun prefers a cross of the water-spaniel or Newfoundland with the Scottish terrier; imagining that the latter will give *nose* to the former, which is quite in opposition to the general impression; though, I confess, it is in conformity with my own experience, as I have seen as many tender-nosed terriers as spaniels, and many more than I have seen among Newfoundland dogs. He advises all waterproof boots and coats to be discarded, as impeding the snake-like crawlings and stoopings which this sport requires; and seems to laugh at the wettings which the absence of waterproof leggings or boots must occasion. Few, however, can suffer this exposure to cold and wet with impunity; and I should advise great caution in venturing upon it, since there are not many who would escape scot-free.

217. GENERAL PRINCIPLES OF STALKING WILDFOWL.—Provided with his gun and retriever, and with glass in hand, the stalker looks out for his game in the distance, taking care to avoid showing himself, by keeping behind some projecting rock. To effect this purpose, he must creep cautiously towards the shore, and sweep the surface of the loch with his glass, resting it upon some large stone or rock, and concealing his whole person behind this object. As soon as he sees what he is looking out for, he should take the bearings of some two high trees on the same shore as the fowl, and as close as possible to them; one of these should be near the shore, the other further inland. Next, let him leave the shore of the loch, and make a detour to the other side, at a few yards' distance from the water, and carefully out of sight of the wildfowl. He must, while proceeding on this path, avoid any noise whatever; not even venturing to speak to his retriever, and taking great care of all rotten branches on the ground, or in his way, as the ears of all wildfowl are peculiarly sensitive. As soon as he has neared the more inland or his two marked trees, he must order his retriever to its root, and command him, by signs, to lie down, and remain there till summoned by the gun, which he should be taught to attend to. Relieved of the anxiety attending upon the movements of his four-footed assistant, he now steals cautiously forwards towards the mark nearest the water, and by the bearings he has taken he knows exactly where the fowl are; but he must endeavour, if possible, to approach them unseen, in order that he may seize the favourable moment, when several are congregated, for a shot while sitting in the water, or feeding in its shallows or on its shores. To do this great caution is required, as the act of raising the gun to fire will often cause the wildfowl to take the alarm,

and to dive or fly off. He, therefore, looks for a thin bush to fire *through;* or, if this cannot be gained unseen, then he must raise his gun *by the side* of one, or by a rock or stone. After the first shot, the fowl will often rise in a cloud from the water, and that is the time for the use of the second barrel. Mr. Colquhoun is strongly of opinion, that wildfowl do not possess that keen sense of smell which is generally assigned to them; and particularly by Colonel Hawker. He attributes their uneasiness, when to leeward of the shooter, to the acuteness of their ears, not of their nasal organs, and supports his opinion by some strong cases. For want of opportunity, I must leave the difference between these sportsmen to the judgment of those of my readers who may themselves be more calculated than I am to decide between them.

218. SOME FURTHER HINTS FOR PARTICULAR CASES are added by Mr. Colquhoun. If he is in pursuit of the divers, including the golden-eye, and the morillon (which latter, he thinks, cannot be the young of the former, because its flavour is so different), he proceeds, as before, till he gets as near the part of the lake where they are as he can without discovery; then, when he sees two or three dive together, he rushes to the shore, and awaits their coming up with his gun at his shoulder, being able to trace their whereabouts by the line of bubbles they send up to the surface. As soon as they come up and take wing, he directs you to shoot well forward, and you have a good chance of bagging a great delicacy, if the golden eye is the bird you have been stalking. When the flock is large, an unpractised stalker is puzzled to know what time to allow for his final run, because, as he is watching them, he does not know which particular bird comes up and goes down, as they are continually appearing and disappearing. The only way is to watch some detached bird, and that one may serve as a guide to the rest. Very shallow water is not favourable to this kind of stalking, because the disappearance of the rest of the flock is at once detected by the diving pair of birds, and they rise to the surface and are off before the shooter has completed his approach. Dunbirds, he says, may, in Scotland, be managed with the greatest ease, as, from not being much shot at, they are comparatively tame, and, from keeping together, afford a good shot to the heavy duck-gun. They may be easily manœuvred from one side to the other, by an assistant throwing bits of stick, &c., into the water without showing himself, and thus driving them into the part of the loch which the ambushed-stalker commands. Good sport can scarcely be had in large lochs, or where the shore is too closely wooded; as it is impossible, in the former case, to get round to the other side, and, in the latter, to approach near enough to the water without noise. The higher the banks the better, if the stalker is protected by irregularities of the ground, &c. "The wildfowl-shooter," says Mr. Colquhoun, "must never forget that the true proof of his skill consists in obtaining *sitting* shots, and stopping a number of fowl at one discharge; and, unless with divers, must not think of a flying right and left." Such is wildfowl law.

219. COLONEL HAWKER'S INVISIBLE APPROACH.—The second kind of stalking to which I have alluded, and which is carried on by means of a moveable cover, is well adapted for such lochs as are deprived of the natural ambush which I have been alluding to, as described by Mr. Colquhoun. It has been tried by Colonel Hawker, the inventor, and found to answer the purpose; though I should certainly have fancied that the approach of so bulky a machine on a *bare shore* would give the alarm to wary birds like the wildfowl. The machine is simply a long wheelbarrow, with a cover which opens to admit the stalker, and which cover and the wheels—which are also concealed with painted canvass—are dressed with boughs, so as to imitate a bush. The gun is protruded through an opening in the front, and is concealed, as far as possible, by overhanging boughs. The idea may, of course, be differently carried out, but this will depend upon the ingenuity of each person using the invention. In approaching birds by this machine, it would, of course, be wheeled as far as possible in the ordinary way; then, when all natural concealment must be given up, the lid must be cautiously opened behind, and the body of the shooter must enter, closing it after him. In Colonel Hawker's plate of the machine, the body is made to recline upon a canvass bottom; but how the shooter is to *progress* in this way I know not. If the machine were made with a perforated canvas bottom, it might be gradually moved forward by the legs and hands of the shooter, and the recoil of the common duck-gun could do him no more harm than in an ordinary discharge; but if a stancheon-gun is used, it is very important that the shooter should be a part and parcel of the machine, and be carried back with it in the recoil; he must, therefore, have a canvass bottom to rest on. A disregard of this caution would lead to serious consequences, but this will be more fully alluded to in describing the large stancheon-gun. Colonel Hawker says that this machine answered admirably well at some very wild leverets; and it is worth trying, certainly, in bare and difficult situations.

220. Here a new aid to the shooter is enlisted, and he has not only his dog and

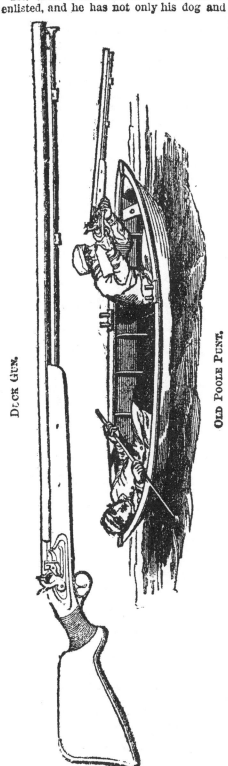

DICK GUN.

OLD POOLE PUNT.

his shoulder-gun of single or double-barrel, but he likewise has a punt to enable him to get up to his game on the water. The dog and gun are similar to those which I have already described, except that the latter is considerably heavier and longer; and its size being no longer limited to the capacity of the human arms to carry it, but only by the endurance of the shoulder in bearing its recoil, it may be unrestricted in absolute weight.

221. THE OLD POOLE PUNT (see *fig.*) is a very clumsy kind of expedient for this purpose, inasmuch as it is wholly exposed to the effects of rough water, and is consequently unfitted for any but smooth and calm weather. It has been in use for many years in the harbour of Poole, and also on Southampton-water, and other sheltered spots in that part of the southern coast; but it is now entirely superseded by

222. THE DECKED-PUNT, first introduced by Colonel Hawker, and since his time in common use wherever waterfowl are to be met with on the coast. In the old punt accidents were continually occurring, but in the decked-punt a tolerably heavy sea may be borne with impunity. The modern punt is usually about 15 feet long from stem to stern, and nearly 4 feet wide at the middle, gradually tapering towards the bows and stern. This will be better understood by a reference to the plan given in the opposite page, in which the shooter is protected from the sea by the deck over his legs; and between the shooter and the puntsman a canvas, which is there shown folded up, can be drawn tightly across so as still further to protect both of them. A considerable quantity of water is of course sometimes shipped, but not enough to swamp the punt; and by care and skill it may be used in any ordinary sea. In making all these light punts, the bottoms should be rounded a little, in order to give them life—if too much so, they are unsteady;— for a shoulder-gun only, the planks of white deal need not be more than one-third of an inch thick, and of one piece, as in the ordinary London outrigger. The seams should be well caulked, and the inside coated with resin softened with a little oil; the outside of the bottom painted with red lead; the sides and top of a light brown or fawn colour. This punt may be easily carried by two persons, and pushed anywhere before one of them over the mud, &c., for which purpose it has a square stern and two handles. (See *fig.*) It has a deck like the outrigger skulling-boats used on the Thames, &c.; which, however, cannot be made into a water-tight compartment, because the room is wanted for stowing away the gun, ammunition, &c., and also

for the legs of the shooter. By means of a land-carriage—which may be very easily constructed, either for the hand, like an ordinary truck, or for a horse, on four wheels—it may be conveyed to any creek, then launched over the mud, and used while the sea is too rough outside to admit of its being brought there by water. Any rough boat-builder or common carpenter can make this punt; but a regular boat-

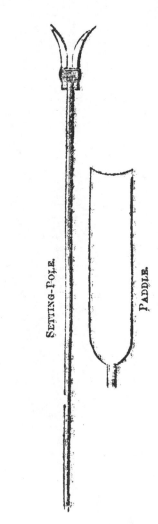

DECKED-PUNT.

SETTING-POLE.

PADDLE.

one of such general interest as to require their admittance here; nor ought any one who is about to lay out 20 or 30 guineas in building a boat, to grudge an extra sovereign in a book.

223. PUNTING ACCESSORIES.—To use this punt, either oars muffled with leather are employed, or a paddle or paddles, with a short handle for one hand, and tied to the gunwale by a short cord, so that they may be dropped without noise or the necessity for shipping them. (See *fig.*) A long and loaded forked stick is also required, to move

builder will of course turn out the most ship-shape article. No one will venture to think of building one without referring to Colonel Hawker's book, in which full directions are given, with the measurements necessary for the purpose. The subject is not

the punt on or off the mud-banks, and to pin down wounded birds with (see *fig.*); and in addition, a pair of mud-boards, from 12 to 16 inches square, which are securely fastened to the ankles, when wanted, as follows:—Put the foot between the two loops, with the heel against the loose line that is attached to both; then cross that line over the instep, and pass it under the loop, on each side, when bring it up to the instep again and tie. (See *fig.*)

MUD-BOARD.

224. MANAGEMENT OF THE PUNT AND GUN.—With these accessories the shooter proceeds, generally by night, with an assistant in the punt, both using the oars, paddle, or forked-stick, till nearing the wildfowl, when the shooter must sit with his legs under the deck in front; and the assistant, crouching behind, paddles or poles him to his game. Some go out alone, and proceed with the paddle in hand, and the gun lying by the side ready for use, till they see or hear the fowl on the mud. A shot is then made, first springing the fowl by tapping lightly on the bottom of the punt; those who are attended by a puntsman cause him to give the birds the alarm, and take advantage of it exactly at the right moment. The amount of success will be announced by the wounded birds beating on the mud. The puntsman then puts on his mud-boards, takes the setting-pole, and, together with the retriever, proceeds to pick up the dead and dying; but one-half of the wounded generally escape, if the shot has been made as it generally is by night. Flying shots are always refused by puntsmen, as not killing sufficient numbers.

225. THE FOLLOWING TERMS ARE IN USE AMONG WILDFOWL-SHOOTERS :—A flock of wigeon is termed "a company;" of swans, cranes, and curlews, "a herd;" of teal, "a spring;" of geese, "a gaggle;" of ducks, "a badelynge;" of mallards, "a sord;" of coots, "a covert;" of sheldrakes, "a dopping."

226. THE DRESS, &c., necessary for punt-shooting will be fully described under the next and more important section.

SECT. 4.—STANCHEON-GUN PUNT-SHOOTING.

227. In process of time, from continual shooting at waterfowl wherever they appeared, it became very difficult to approach them within 60 or 80 yards, the extreme limits of the *killing* range of the shoulder-gun. The invention however of the shooters soon met this difficulty, by contriving a larger and heavier gun, fixed upon a rest in the punt, and stayed from recoiling by ropes carried to the bows. These guns were at first very rudely constructed, and single-barrelled. They carried from a pound to a pound-and-a-half of shot, and were fired by a *flint* lock, for various powerful reasons. However, it is unnecessary for me to enter upon the *history* of the stancheon-gun and punt, as the old ones are now entirely superseded by Colonel Hawker's most recent invention, which certainly is a most ingenious one, and which by itself would suffice to make the reputation of an ordinary man. I confess, that but for this, I should be surprised at the reputation which he has achieved, since I can see nothing else which the long experience of any man of ordinary capacity should not have led him to devise; but this gun is not the result of any ordinary thought, but it is the effort of a genius devoted to one pursuit, and showing itself in one of the most happy combinations of mechanical ingenuity which it ever has been my lot to see. It must be remembered, that the object of the gunner is not to discharge a large *circle* of shot, as in shooting at objects in the air, but rather to fill an *oval* with his deadly little messengers. The reason of this is, that the fowl are lying on the water, and consequently do not form a circular target, but an oblong one, often extended to a great length. The gunner being on a level with them, or nearly so, has them almost on a line with the axis of his gun, and could perhaps dispense with still more of the upper and lower shot than is now effected by the double-barrel of Colonel Hawker. But not only is this oval instead of circular discharge of shot effected, but by using two kinds of priming—namely, the detonating powder of the side-primer for the one barrel, and the flint for the other, the two are discharged one after the other, and the recoil is thereby very much diminished, so that a much greater and more powerful shot may be made with the two differently-primed barrels, than could be permitted in two detonators, or even in two flints, and much more than in a single-barrel, even with a flint lock; moreover, there is this advantage attending it—there is the quickness of the detonator for the birds lying on the water-line, and then at a second's interval, just as the remaining birds are rising, comes the slower discharge from the flint. This gun, therefore, would be adopted by every wildfowl-shooter who indulges himself in punting, but for the expense; but as this is considerable, I shall first give a short account of the Colonel's single-gun and punt, and then of his finished

invention—the double stancheon-gun, and punt to carry it.

228. THE SINGLE-GUN should be in length of barrel from 7 to 9 feet; bore from 1¼ to 1½ inch; and weight from 70 to 80 lbs., including the patent plug. The smaller the bore, the farther you can shoot; but this size does not carry so large a charge of shot, and, consequently, will not take in so many birds within its circle. The barrel should be substantial in every part, and not filed away for any purpose. If the above weight be adopted, the flint-lock must be used, because this strength and size will not be safe with the detonator, on account of the recoil. If, therefore, the gunner wishes the detonating lock, the weight must be increased to 128 lbs., which, however, requires the aid of another pair of hands to ship and unship from the punt. The former size may be used with a rope-breeching, which is attached to the bows of the punt, in order to prevent the recoil; the latter would not be safe without Colonel Hawker's spring swivel. (See paragraph 231.)

229. THE ABOVE GUN is mounted in a punt built expressly for it, the weight being carried on the bottom or floor, which is the only part built of strong and substantial materials.

230. COLONEL HAWKER'S PLAN FOR FIRING A FULL DISCHARGE OF SHOT IN AN OVAL, WITH DIMINISHED RECOIL.—This invention is intended to supply entirely the above *desiderata*, and it appears to have fully answered the purpose. In the old plan, it was found that more than a pound of shot produced such a recoil as to endanger the safety of both punt and puntsman, and many accidents occurred to both. A pound-and-a-half to two pounds were often fired without extra precaution; but the recoil was tremendous. Nevertheless, as it was considered desirable to use this quantity of shot, the following is the Colonel's method of combining the use of even two-and-a-half pounds with safety and diminished recoil. In the first place, instead of discharging this enormous load of shot from one large barrel, he divides it into two, which are put together so as to fire two circles, each one partly encroaching upon or eclipsed by the other, by which an oval, instead of a circle, is included in the fire. Next, he fires one barrel with a detonating primer, the other with a flint, so that there is a trifling difference in the times of the ignition sufficient to cause an immense diminution of the recoil. To do this, the two barrels are put together so that their cylinders are perfectly parallel, the outsides being close at the breech, and wide apart at the muzzles. Such is this most ingenious instrument for doing what is wanted by wildfowl-shooters.

231. SPRING SWIVEL.—The recoil is lessened in the following manner:—A long loop is worked on, between, and under the barrels; in this loop runs a slider, which is attached to the swivel-pin that is raised or depressed in order to fire the gun. The two are connected by a strong pin, which also keeps the slider in its place. Before the slider, and kept in its place by a longitudinal pin, is a spiral spring, and this spring takes the shock of the recoil, and breaks it in a wonderful manner. The most important matter is the fixing of the loop, which should be carefully welded, not soldered on; because if this should tear away, the gun would fly back, and do most probably fatal injury to the gunner. Altogether, it is a very efficient, yet simple, means of taking off the recoil; it is supported upon a block fixed in the floor of the punt, and the danger of the slide breaking away from the barrels is diminished by the use of a spare rope-breeching from the gun to this block.

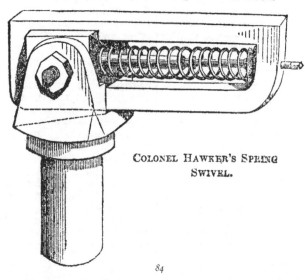

COLONEL HAWKER'S SPRING SWIVEL.

232. The Punt for this Double-Stan-cheon Gun is of the following dimensions and make:—It must be large enough to carry two men and gear, with dog and gun, weighing at least 600 lbs.; it must be decked, leaving only room for the gunner to take aim, and the man to work to the birds. It is desirable, also, that the man should be able to work his paddles without showing his hand above deck; and, consequently, a part of the deck must be made to ship and unship for that purpose. The whole must be made very light—the deck being covered with canvas, for the increase of its strength, and tightness from water. The deck must be supported in front where the man stands in loading, and in the places where the copper thowls are fixed for the oars. The inner edge of the deck, surrounding the open part, must be protected by bulwarks, or wash-boards, which are four inches high forward, and have the opening for the barrels of the gun stopped by an extra piece, when the sea is so high as to require it. The punt may be rowed stem-forwards by two pair of skulls, when the gun is raised by means of a block devised for the purpose; or, it may also be rowed stern-forwards by two pair, or by one pair in the stern; or it may be paddled. There is a cover for the open space when the boat is laid up in harbour. This punt sails or rows, and when the sail is used the birds are even more easily approached than when she is rowed, as the wildfowl become accustomed to the sight of sailing-boats, and their suspicions are lulled. By the use of the sliding-swivel the recoil is taken direct from the barrels, and the old large and cumbrous stock is now done away with. Of course, this slide may be adapted to either single or double-guns; and, if properly welded on, is much more safe than the rope-breeching. The detonator used by the Colonel is the brass-primer. Instead of a mere fork to rest the muzzle of the gun, Colonel Hawker uses a slide for that part. For the dimensions, and full particulars necessary to make these punts, and other apparatus used with them, the reader is referred to Colonel Hawker's book. He is the sole authority on the subject, and it would not be right to rob him of what he has taken so much pains to bring to perfection.

233. Various Requisites for the Gun.—Having described the single and double stancheon-guns, it remains that I should also give a description of the apparatus for loading, &c., which is the same for both guns. Among the old gunners, the only mode of loading the gun was to unship it; but there is now the following invention, by which this awkward process is avoided.

234. The Loading-Spoon (see *fig.* A) is merely a wooden rod, flat on the side corresponding with the spoon, which is of brass, and attached to the one end—the other being tapered-off and armed with a worm (B) protected by (c), which screws on.

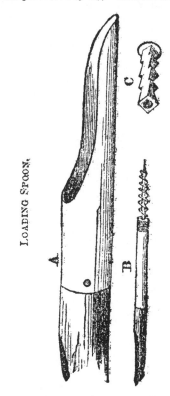

LOADING SPOON.

235. Loading.—The spoon should hold as large a *measure* of powder as the shot; and in loading it should be filled with powder, then gently introduced into the gun, still in a horizontal position, as far as it will go; as soon as it has reached this point the flat side is to be turned downwards, when the powder falls out, on giving the rod a gentle shake. It should be well-worked into the central hole with the small end (c); and if that hole wants clearing-out, or the cartridge is to be drawn, the worm (B) is capable of effecting that purpose. Great care must be taken that the powder is well worked into the central hole, as without this precaution the gun is apt to miss fire, or to shoot slow. After this, the wadding is to be driven down, and then the shot.

236. Eley's Cartridges are made of all sizes for large guns, and answer admirably.

237. The Powder should be coarse-grained, of the kind called "sea-gun," by Messrs. Curtis and Harvey, who manufacture it purposely for punt-guns

238. The Shot for Punt-Guns should be as follows :—

For shoulder punt-guns { No. 1 for fair shots. A for long shots.
For stancheon punt-guns . . . . . { No. 3 for starlight. No. 1 for fair shots.
Packed in cartridges . S.S.G., or L.G.
For Geese . . . . . A., or A.A.
Ditto, if very tame, S.S.G.

239. The Dress of the Gunner should be of such a nature as to resist cold and wet, and yet of a colour to be as far as possible invisible to the waterfowl. Without the last precaution, the birds will be frightened away; and without the two first, you will soon be unable to get to them, in consequence of the cramps and stiffness occasioned by damp and cold. Every part of the body but the feet should be clothed in flannel, wearing a Flushing-frock under a waistcoat of Bath-coating or shag; above the waistcoat, a short jacket of woollen cloth or swanskin. The cap may be of cloth, or of any waterproof material, with any extra warmth which may be required. The legs should be encased in very large and loose long boots, covering two pair of long and warm hose; and over these a pair of canvas or Flushing-coating trowsers, according to the weather. The hands should be protected with warm muffatees, and also warm gloves. But in very cold weather swanskin cuffs must be used in addition; and they may be drawn off in an instant when the gun is to be used. As to colour, all depends upon the light. If sun or moon is visible, light drab should be the outside colour; but in starlight a snow-white is far the best; and for this purpose a clean linen frock may be put over all. The waterproof which you may have required must be removed when you begin to work up to birds. When the punts are to be pushed over mud—and, indeed, in almost all cases—it is prudent to put a large canvas frock over all, as the mud, blood, feathers, and powder will soon spoil everything worn which is not capable of being washed. Colonel Hawker also recommends a large canvas umbrella, which may be used as a defence against rain, and also as a mizen sail. Hats are especially to be avoided.

240. Management of the Stancheon-Gun, and Mode of Shooting.—Having now described both the single and double stancheon-guns, with or without the spring-swivel, I must now proceed to the mode of using them. Many may fancy that they can easily use this wonderfully-destructive weapon, but experience will show them that it is not so easy to manœuvre as it looks. When it is considered that the gun is floating on an unstable element like the sea, and that even there one must sometimes attempt a flying-shot, it will at once be manifest that this kind of sporting requires more tact than the knocking down of a partridge or a grouse. When a flock of wildfowl is descried by the glass, the master and his man must set to work and either skull or sail as closely as they dare, without fear of disturbing them; then shipping the skulls, the gunner lies down to his gun, while the man paddles up to the birds, or, in punting language, "sets up to them." During this last operation both should keep as much as possible out of sight, the master only requiring the top of his head to be so much raised as to take aim, which he does by raising or depressing the pin of the swivel, and the man requiring only his hand and arm over the gunwale, in order to use the paddle. In this way the approach is made; and the following remarks will enable the gunner to reach and fire at each description of his game.

241. For Hoopers or Geese, he will generally have notice from the birds when it is the best time to fire, as they draw close together before taking wing, and raise their heads, which is the favourable moment for the discharge of the gun with effect. He may, therefore, persevere at night till within 40 yards, if they do not give this signal. If they still allow his further approach, previously to firing he should make some little noise, in order to draw them together.

242. Brent Geese are always wild, except in severe weather, or when it blows very fresh, when they keep in harbour all day, though they generally go out at night. If, therefore, there is sufficient water in harbour in the daytime, they may often be "set up to." In mild weather, prefer a small flock to a large one. In pursuit of wounded birds, it should always be recollected that they make for the heaviest sea they can reach, and the attendant boat should therefore intercept them, if possible. A blow from an oar across the neck will kill these birds, which will take a severe blow on the body with impunity.

243. The various Divers generally give notice like the geese; the ducks and wigeon not so well; and teal give no notice at all, but spring at once on the wing. In setting up to birds, it must be borne in mind, that distance on the sea is very deceptive; and that what looks like 50 yards, is more likely to be double that distance. When *curres*, or divers of any kind, are wounded, they must be shot with common detonators, as they duck at the flash very rapidly.

244. A Cripple-Net on the same principle as a landing-net for fish, but about two feet in diameter, is very useful in landing the wounded birds.

G

245. These punts have been chiefly used in the south, as in Poole Harbour and Southampton Water, but they are now being introduced into the saltwater lochs on the west coast of Scotland, where large flocks of wigeon, teal, and geese are often met with; and where they afford even better sport than in the south, because they are not rendered so wild by continually popping at them. This coast is very flat, and the punt is the only means of approach, stalking being out of the question; but, with the aid of Colonel Hawker's various inventions, such sport as wildfowl-shooting is capable of affording will be met with in full measure. The advocates of this amusement are enamoured of it to an extent which those who have not tried it can hardly imagine; but, just as in all cases of dispute which imply a difference of opinion, it may here be affirmed that *de gustibus non est disputandum.*

CHAP. X.

DEER-STALKING.

SECT. 1.—THE RED DEER AND ROEBUCK.

246. THE STAG, OR RED DEER (*Cervus Elaphus*), is the largest of the British deer, of which three varieties are known—viz., the red deer, the fallow deer, and the roebuck. The first is considerably the largest; and the following dimensions—given by Mr. Scrope in his interesting work on deer-stalking—will afford some idea of his enormous size:—

	ft.	in.
Height at shoulder	3	11¼
Girth at shoulder	4	7
Height from top of head to fore-foot	5	6
Length of antler	2	6
From top of antler to ground	7	10

Gross weight, 308 lbs.

In colour, the stag is usually of a reddish-brown, with blackish muzzle, and mane mingled with grey; the inside of the thighs and flank being lighter, and approaching to a fawn colour.

247. NOMENCLATURE, ACCORDING TO THE DEVONSHIRE HUNT.—Deer under one year are called *Calves;* till three, the male a *Brocket,* and the female a *Hearst;* at three, the male a *Spire,* and the female a *Hind;* at four, a *Staggart;* at five, a *Stag;* at six, a *Warrantable Stag;* and after this, a *Hart.* The female does not breed till three years old, and has only one calf.

248. HORNS.—The male is known from the female by having a pair of horns, which are shed yearly, and change in form with every succeeding year. Each fully-developed horn has a *brow, bay,* and *tray* antler, and *two points* also on the top. The three first are termed the *rights;* the two points, the *crockets;* the horn itself, the *beam;* the width, the *span;* and the rough part at the junction with the skull, the *pearls.*

249. AGE KNOWN BY THE HORNS.—The BROCKET has only small projections, called *knobbers,* with small *brow antlers;* the SPIRE a *brow antler,* and half-developed *beam,* called *uprights;* a STAGGART, brow, tray, and uprights; a STAG, brow, bay, and tray, with one horn crocketted and the other single; a WARRANTABLE STAG has brow, bay, and tray antlers, with crockets on both horns. After this no rule can be given, as the horns constantly vary in all points; but if they have three points, the harts are called royal.

250. AGE KNOWN BY THE SLOT.—This is the proper name, according to the laws of *venerie,* for the tread of the deer, which, in the hind, is much narrower and longer than that of the stag, especially at the toe. In the warrantable stag, the heel measures fully two inches; if more than this, and deeply indented into the ground, he is a large heavy old hart; and such usually bring up their hind-feet to the impression made by their fore-feet.

251. OTHER TERMS USED IN VENERIE.—The deer's haunt is called *his lair;* where he lies, *his harbour;* where he rolls, his *soiling-pool;* where he breaks through a fence, *his rack;* if he goes to water, he *takes soil;* if headed back, he is *blanched;* if he lies down in water, he is said to be *sinking himself;* an unwounded deer is called a *cold hart.*

252. HABITS OF THE RED DEER.—He is rather a delicate animal, and bites close like a sheep; requiring an enormous range of pasturage to afford him such a choice and change as shall keep him in health. The hart ruts about the end of September, or beginning of October; and this period is exceedingly short, as compared with the sheep and goat, only lasting a single week. They show the change by a peculiar swelling of the neck, where they throw out a ruff of long hair; and at this time their flanks are tucked up, from their refusing food and their tendency to fret. While rutting, they are very restless, and roll constantly in the

Fig. 1

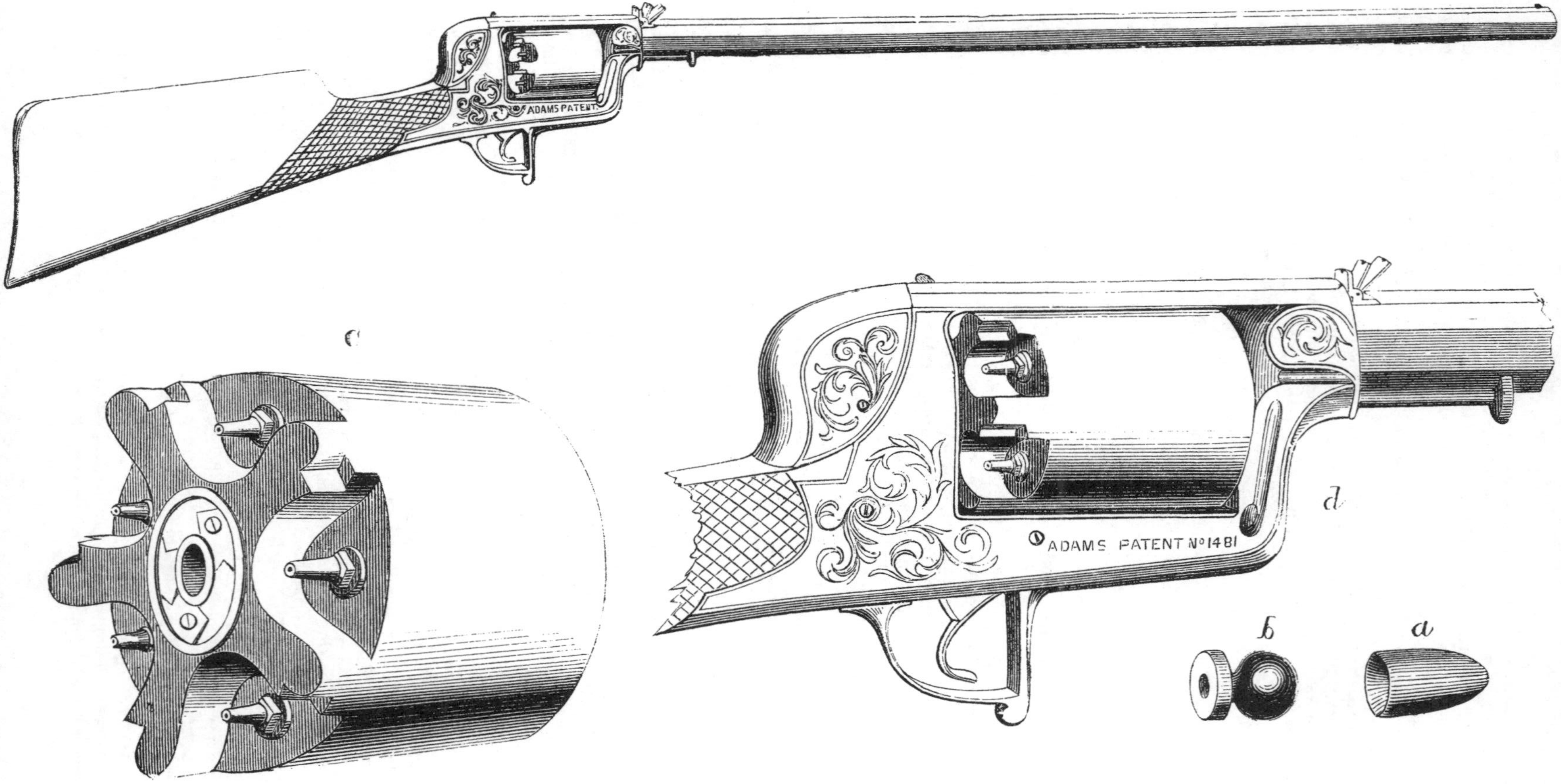

ADAMS PATENT Nº 14 BI

peat-mosses, becoming often perfectly black with the soil that adheres to them. They are now wholly unfit for human food, and are never sought after by the sportsman, who selects, in preference, the more backward harts and the hinds, which are then just coming into season, but seldom yet fat and of good flavour. The rutting-harts are exceedingly pugnacious, and terrible battles are constantly taking place for the possession of the females, a whole harem of which are the spoil of the conqueror. These battles are often fatal to one or both combatants; and many cases have even been known of two stags being so firmly locked together by their horns, as to be worried to death; an instance of which is commemorated by Landseer's celebrated pictures, "Night" and "Morning," in the first of which the harts are fighting fiercely, and in the second they are seen lying dead, with their horns locked together, so as to be perfectly inseparable.

253. THE PERIOD OF GESTATION in the hind is eight months; the fawn is left during the day concealed in the heather, and is only suckled at night. The suckling-hind is poor and tasteless, and should be allowed to escape from the rifle-ball. Hinds which do not breed are called yeld-hinds.

254. THE DIRECTION OF THE DEER'S FLIGHT is almost always up-wind, in order to be forewarned, by their acute sense of smell, of any approaching danger. There is great difficulty in changing this instinctive course, but it may be done under certain circumstances. The hinds are always the most vigilant, and are set to give notice to the harts. The hinds are also always put first in the run, except in cases of great danger, when the master-hart comes forward and boldly faces it.

255. THE TIMIDITY OF THE RED DEER is very remarkable, and he can scarcely, except by compulsion, be induced to remain near the haunts of man. Every movement alarms him, from the cry of the plover to the flight of the hill-fox. He is more especially timid when he cannot make out the exact nature of the danger which threatens him; while, if he sees his great enemy, man, even comparatively close to him, he is much more composed, though still wary, and never confused or flurried.

256. THE STAG, WHEN PRESSED, STANDS AT BAY, and in this position is a very dangerous antagonist for both dog and man, as he will defend himself with horns and hoof till the last extremity. By choice, he selects water, if pursued by dogs, as his instinct tells him that in this element his superior size and length of leg will give him a great advantage. Here few dogs can pull him down, and when they attempt to reach

him by swimming, they soon fall victims to the sharp points of his formidable horns.

257. THE AGE OF THE RED DEER is said to be three times that of man; and there is strong evidence for believing that this popular belief has some foundation in fact, as many very old men have known particular deer all their lifetime, and have had the same knowledge handed down to them from their fathers, and even their grandfathers. No rule can be drawn with perfect accuracy from the period of gestation, which was considered by the old naturalists to indicate the exact duration of life in all animals, because we know so many exceptions as to falsify it altogether. Thus the horse and the ass go with young the same time, and even breed together, yet the ass is nearly twice as long-lived as the horse. Again, the camel lives twice as long as the horse, and yet goes with young one month less. There is, therefore, no reason why the deer may not live to the age usually allotted to him by the foresters, though nothing is more difficult than to get at reliable facts bearing upon this subject.

258. IN DRIVING DEER, they always follow in single file, like the Red Indians of America, and only break this rule when hard pressed by the dog, or by other causes. When fat, they are soon blown, and cannot go any pace up hill whilst in that unwieldy state, which only lasts till the approach of the rutting season. They seldom attack man, unless they are surrounded and hard pressed; but in the rutting-season instances have occurred where savage and disappointed stags have attacked intruders upon their domains.

259. THE HAUNTS OF THE RED DEER in Great Britain are confined to the most retired and inaccessible parts of the Highlands of Scotland, to the Quantock Hills of Somersetshire, to some of the adjacent ranges of Devonshire, and to the New Forest; but, in addition to these, may be mentioned the deer confined in certain parks, as Richmond Park, &c.; but these can only be considered as deer in confinement. In Scotland only are they stalked, being reserved for hunting in the west of England and in the New Forest.

260. THE ROEBUCK (Capreolus Capræa), is also an inhabitant of some of the Scotch deer forests, but it is chiefly confined to the wooded parts, not choosing the mountainous and open situations like the red deer. In size, it is not to be compared to its larger congener, being only 24 inches in height. As, however, it is rarely stalked for its own sake, and as it is more calculated for showing sport before a pack of dwarf harriers, I shall include it among the objects of hunting rather than of shooting.

261. THE DEER FORESTS are confined to Scotland; and are only to be obtained by those whose purses are long enough to pay large sums for them. Indeed it is seldom that any are in the market, as the fashion of the day has made this sport more eagerly sought after than any other. The deer forests are—

262. First, those of Sutherland, the chief of which are the Dirrie-Chatt and Dirrie-Moss; the former being fifty miles long by an average of twenty miles wide, and the latter being about thirty miles by twenty. But, besides these, three smaller and detached forests are comprehended within this district—viz., the Parph, the Clibreck, and the Dirrie-Meanach. It is supposed, that about 1,500 red deer are at large in Sutherland.

263. Secondly, those comprised within Ross-shire are the Forests of Applecross and Gairloch, most of which are only adapted for the red deer, and are too wild and rugged even for sheep. Balnagown Forest is partly devoted to sheep, but red deer also are found here, and in Loch-Broom, Castle-Leod, Novar, and Tulloch. The estate of Foulis is peculiarly adapted for the red deer, but is now too much frequented by the shepherd. Coigach, the property of Mr. Hay Mackenzie, is strictly preserved; and, in addition, the islands of Harris and Lewis are sure haunts of this noble specimen of the deer kind. At Coul, the property of Sir George Stuart Mackenzie, the red deer are very numerous, though it is only of late years that they have become so. Applecross is a celebrated forest, and contains large numbers of deer within its secure and sheltered corries and on its hill sides.

264. Thirdly, Inverness-shire contains the celebrated Glengarry Forest, which, from east to west, is about seven miles in extent; also, Glenfeshie, containing 13,704 Scotch acres, but now used as a sheep-walk. Gaick, consisting of 10,777 acres, strictly preserved by Sir Jos. Radcliffe; Drumauchtar, comprehending 5,782 acres, now used as a deer forest by the Marquis of Abercorn; Glenavon, containing 22,086 acres, and held by the Duke of Richmond as a deer forest, in connexion with Glenbuily and Glenfiddich, the former in the same shire, and containing 3,396 acres, the latter in Banff, and making up 5,522 acres: these all formerly belonged to the Duke of Gordon.

265. Fourthly, Aberdeenshire has within its limits Invercauld, 18 miles in length by about three miles in width, and containing an enormous number of deer, though these fluctuate so much as to be difficult to calculate. They are generally very fine and large, mainly owing to the excellence of the feed in this district, and the strictness with which they are maintained in an undisturbed condition. The Forest of Mar is also in Aberdeen, closely butting upon Invercauld, and consists of the four following glens, viz — Glenquoich, Glenluie, Glendee, and Glenguildy. Its length is about 15 miles, and its breadth eight; and it is supposed to hold 3,000 deer. It is the property of the Earl of Fife.

266. Fifthly, Argyleshire contains the Forest of Corrichibah, in the district of Glenorchy, the property of the Marquis of Breadalbane, and holding at least 1,500 deer. It extends over 35,000 acres, and the nature of the ground is such as to render it one of the best deer-forests in Scotland.

267. Sixthly, Perth has also its Forest of Glenartney, the property of Lord Willoughby d'Eresby, and containing 2,800 acres, with from 700 to 1,000 deer; but its crowning glory, as far as sport is concerned, may be considered to reside in the Forest of Athol, in which 51,708 imperial acres are devoted exclusively to the red deer, with the exception only of Glen Tilt, where sheep are sometimes admitted; 7,000 deer are now supposed to be at large in Athol, but, at the lowest computation, there must be from 4,000 to 6,000. This noble property is strictly preserved by the Duke of Athol, and deer-stalking is here carried to that degree of perfection which has been so well described by Mr. Scrope.

268. And, seventhly, in the Hebrides, also, red deer are found, and chiefly in the islands of Jura, Mull, and Sky; but they are here in much less numbers than on the mainland: yet in Jura alone there are said to be 500, and in Sky about half that number.

Sect. 3.—The Telescope.

269. Every deerstalker, whether a principal or an assistant, should be provided with a good telescope; and I believe, by general consent, Dollond in St. Paul's Churchyard is considered the best maker. He is, however, rather expensive, and good glasses by other makers may be obtained for half the price. But it is really astonishing to see what a difference there is between a first-rate glass and an inferior one. With the former the eye takes in every thing as distinctly as if close at hand, whilst with the latter there is often a haze, which leaves it in doubt whether certain objects are red deer or rocks, or perhaps only heather in oddly-shaped masses. If therefore money is no object, Dollond would be the maker I should advise; and I am quite sure that in every other respect he will give perfect satisfaction. The telescope should be worn in a case slung round the right shoulder,

and should be carefully kept from scratches by drawing the slide well over the glass after using it.

SECT. 4.—THE GILLIES OR HILLMEN.

270. Nothing leads more to success in deer-stalking than the having two or three thoroughly good and experienced hillmen to aid and assist in the work. In most cases the whole management is confided to them, because they, from long experience, are better able to know the exact currents of air in the confined vallies, and also can foretell the precise effect of all their stratagems. Each man should be born a forester, and should have imbibed his knowledge of his trade with his mother's milk. He should be patient, sober, and hardy—civil and obliging, anxious to show sport, and at the same time should be jealous of his master's prowess and interests. Such men are scarce, and should be valued accordingly.

SECT. 5.—THE RIFLE.

271. IN THE CHOICE OF THE RIFLE much consideration should now be given; for the recent improvements introduced in France, England, and America, have effected quite a revolution in its form and powers. Under the old *regime*, a rifle was considered first-rate which would in a calm day kill at 150 or 200 yards; and a chance-made shot at 300 yards was a feat to be never forgotten. But by Mr. Lancaster's invention the windage of the ball is greatly reduced, while it is carried much further in consequence of its increased weight, and the ingenious discovery and adaptation of the principle, that the axis of its rotation should be in the same line with the axis of its flight, and not at right angles to it, as formerly. The theory of this is clear enough, and is very beautifully acted upon by Mr. Lancaster. It is quite manifest that if a circular ball is rapidly revolving round its axis at right angles to its course, the friction must be enormously increased, and as a consequence its flight must be retarded in proportion. To obviate this defect, Mr. Lancaster calculated that all the revolution which is necessary for straight shooting is about once in eleven feet, and that all beyond that should be avoided. He therefore made his barrels one-quarter of that length, or two feet nine inches, exclusive of the chamber in the breech, being two feet ten inches in all. This length is worked so that the rifle groove shall describe one-quarter of a revolution, or, in other words, so that each groove shall commence at the breech on one side, and end at the muzzle on the top or bottom,—that is to say, the side next to where it began. Consequently, this forma-tion communicates such a slow-revolving tendency to the ball, that on leaving the

muzzle it goes on with the same kind and velocity of revolution, working its way like a corkscrew through the air, but like one with a very open and long worm. The barrel, being thus formed, the ball is also made to suit it, being at the least one ounce in weight, and cylindrical in form, with a sharp cone at the one end and a segment of a circle at the other—sometimes as in the Minié rifle, forming a deep cup with a thin edge, which expands and fills up the groove, and thus increases the force and accuracy of its flight, without requiring any great pres-sure of the ramrod. (See *fig.* 1, *a.*) It is true, that theory and practice do not always agree, but in this instance they appear to harmonise in a remarkable manner, for, on trial, it is found that Mr. Lancaster's rifle will carry, point-blank, from one-half as far again to twice as far as the old ones; and will also carry, with the proper allowances, four or five times as far. I should therefore unhesitatingly select a rifle on his principle, with the common conical ball, or that of the Minié rifle. Double-barrelled rifles are much in use, and may be made of 8, 10, or 12 lbs. weight; but the new revolving principle introduced by Colonel Colt, and improved upon by Messrs. Dean and Adams, is now being applied to the rifle, and threatens to supersede all necessity for second barrels or second rifles for many purposes. These rifles will discharge five balls as rapidly as the trigger can be pulled, and with great power and accuracy; though, certainly, in this last particular they do not come up to the single rifle on the ordinary plan. At short ranges—as, for instance, at 100 yards—they may be tolerably accurate, but beyond this they are not so much to be depended upon; and the rapidity of their discharge is their greatest recommendation. They are, also, more noisy than the ordinary rifle, so much so as to require cotton in the ear to make them endurable. In the annexed engraving will be seen an exact representa-tion of Messrs. Dean and Adams's revolving rifle, which is made on the same plan as his pistol. It is usually constructed for a small charge of powder (about 1 1-8th to 1 drachm), and will drive a bullet with great force for several hundred yards. I have only seen it tried at 100 yards, and there it performed well; nevertheless, not, in my opinion, to be compared with the ordinary rifle. If, however, the herd of deer pass within 100 or 150 yards, and the stalker is provided with a revolver or two, he may almost annihilate the whole drive of deer as they pass—if his eye and hand are accurate enough; and the only necessity for holding the hand will be the limitation of men and deerhounds to retrieve the wounded. Every day, however, some new improvement is taking place, and, therefore, it will behove every rifle-shot to look well about him before making his selection. Nothing answers better than the common percussion-principle for the locks of these rifles, as they seldom are exposed to such weather as to cause the cap to fail.

272. But, besides the revolver, several breech-loading rifles have been introduced, including the original needle-gun, and those of Mr. Needham and Mr. Holland, which are attempted improvements upon Mr. Lang's French gun, already described at paragraph 61. All of these rifles require a cartridge; and, with the exception of Mr. Lang's, they are all open to many objections, in my opinion. In all the needle-guns there is great risk of breaking the needle, by closing the chamber before it is withdrawn; and when this accident happens, the gun is useless till repaired by the gunsmith. The choice, therefore, at present lies between the ordinary rifle, that of Mr. Lang, and the revolver; and their respective merits may be summed up as follows:— First, the single-barrelled rifle is the best and most accurate for long distances and single shots; secondly, the double-barrelled rifle comes next; thirdly, Mr. Lang's breech-loading rifle I believe to possess all the advantages of these, with the addition of rapid loading; and, fourthly, Messrs. Dean and Adams's revolver shoots five balls rapidly after each other, but not with quite the same strength and accuracy of the ordinary rifle, and with a great increase of noise. The bullets now used are either conical, or if globular they have a leaden tail rivetted to the wadding. (See *fig.* 1, in which *a* is the conical, *b* the globular, *c* the chamber of the revolver, and *d* the whole complete.)

SECT. 6.—THE DEERHOUND.

273. The last accessory to deer-stalking which I have to describe is the DEERHOUND, which is used to retrieve the deer after they are wounded by the rifle; for it often happens that, though fatally wounded, they do not fall at once, but run some distance, and, finally, even stand at bay, with a ball in some vital part. A dog, therefore, is wanted possessed of great speed, power, and courage, and capable of holding the deer by the ear or throat, if once he can get firm hold of either of those parts.

274. THE OLD SCOTCH DEERHOUND possessed all these requisites in perfection, and his feats have been handed down to us in song and prose. I have taken some pains to ascertain the exact breed of these dogs; and the only conclusion that I can arrive at is, that they are identical with the rough Scotch greyhound; *but, having been kept for a particular purpose, they differ in their mode of running from those dogs.* No one can say, by looking at the two breeds, which is the greyhound, and which is the deerhound; but the moment they are slipped, either at the hare or deer, a remarkable difference in the style of going is apparent, which detects the courser of the hare from that of the deer. They are equally fast, but the deerhound gallops with his head in the air, and his body raised off the ground, ready for a spring at the throat or ear, or even the thigh of his prey; while the greyhound, with his head close to the ground, lies down *ventre à terre;* and he is also prepared to pick up his game, not to pull it down. This difference is so remarkable, that I am assured by Mr. A. Graham, the highest authority on the subject of rough greyhounds, that in their ordinary play you may at once detect the two varieties, though in kennel it would be utterly impossible. Now, although such a difference as this is quite sufficient to incapacitate each dog for the purposes to which the other is applied, still, it is only of such a character as would be gained or lost in a few generations. There is not the slightest doubt that greyhounds, even smooth ones, might be bred with all the requisites for the sport in the highest degree; but the rough coat is desirable to resist the cold and wet which would cripple a smooth dog, while waiting for his master's shot. Mr. Scrope is of opinion that ordinary greyhounds have not courage enough for the purpose; but his experience of these dogs must have been very limited, or he would have known that many of them will pin a bull, and have nearly as much courage as the thorough-bred bulldog. Mr. Scrope gives the following dimensions as those of Buskar, a celebrated deerhound belonging to Captain M'Neill, of Colonsay:—Height, 28 inches; girth, 32 inches; running weight, 85 lbs.—of a black-muzzled red, or fawn-colour. He ascribes to him the following attributes, in the highest degree, viz.:—speed, strength, size, endurance, courage, perseverance, sagacity, docility, elegance, and dignity. He was used solely, or chiefly, for coursing the deer; but those of the same breed which are in existence have tender noses, and run either by view or scent. These dogs, however, are so scarce, that it is almost impossible to procure one of the true old breed, and the deer-stalker, therefore, has no resource but to breed for himself, using such crosses as will be most likely to suit his purpose.

275. MR. SCROPE'S BREED OF DEERHOUND is thus described by that gentleman:— "Not being in possession of any of the celebrated race of the original Scotch greyhound, which are now, indeed, very rare,

and finding that all the dogs in the forest of Athol were miserably degenerate, I bred some litters from a foxhound and a greyhound—the foxhound being the father. This cross answered perfectly; indeed, I was previously advised that it would do so, by Mr. John Crerar, who, after having tried various crosses for sixty years, found this incomparably the best. Neither of these animals themselves would have answered; for the greyhound cannot stand the weather, and wants courage to that degree, that most of them will turn from a fox when they come up to him, and see his grin, and feel his sharp teeth; they will scarcely go through a hedge in pursuit of a hare till after some practice. Besides, they have no nose, and run entirely by sight, so that when the hart dashes into a deep moss or ravine the chase is over, and the dog stops and stares about him like a born-idiot, as he is. The foxhound is equally objectionable: he has not sufficient speed, gives tongue, and hunts too much by scent; in this way he spreads alarm through the forest; and if you turn him loose he will amuse himself all day long, and you will, probably, see him no more till he comes home at night to his kennel. All these objections are obviated by the cross between the two. You get the speed of the greyhound, with just enough of the nose of the foxhound to answer your purpose. Courage you have in perfection, for most dogs so bred will face anything; neither craggy precipices nor rapid streams will check their course; they run mute, and when they are put upon the scent of the hart, they will follow it till they come up to him; and, again, when he is out of view, they will carry on the scent, recover him, and beat the best greyhound to fits—I mean, of course, on forest ground. The present Marquis of Breadalbane had two dogs of this description, Percy and Douglas, which were bred by me. As they were my very best upon scent, I gave the late Duke of Athol the use of them every season, to bring cold harts to bay, in which they were wonderfully successful; for, if they were fairly laid on, no hart could escape them. They are now (in 1838) nine or ten years old, and his Lordship informs me they are still able to bring the stoutest hart in his forest to bay, and are altogether perfect. These dogs, in point of shape, resemble the greyhound; but they are larger in the bone and shorter in the leg. Some of them, when in slow action, carry the tail over the back like the pure foxhound; their dash, in making a cast, is most beautiful; and they stand all sorts of rough weather. As the above is, I think, the best cross which can possibly be obtained for the modern method of deer-stalking, so it should be strictly adhered to—I mean, that when you wish to add to your kennel, you must take the cross in its originality, and not continue to breed from the produce first obtained; for, if you do this, you will soon see such monsters staring around you, as the warlike Daunia never nourished in her woods and thickets, or as cannot even be surpassed by the sculptured ones at the Villa of Prince Palagonia, near the shores of Palermo. The late celebrated sportsman, Glengarry, crossed occasionally with the bloodhound, instead of the foxhound; his famous dog Hector was, probably, bred in this way; and I believe Maida, the dog he presented to Sir Walter Scott, had also a distant cross of the bloodhound in him. Two of these small bloodhounds he generously gave to me, though he was chary of the breed; but they ran away from my kennel, and were unfortunately lost. A cross with the bulldog was once tried in the Forest of Athol, to give courage, but the produce was slow, as might have been expected, and the thing was overdone, for they were all killed by attacking the deer in front. High-couraged dogs of every breed, indeed, are subject to accidents; they get wounded, and even killed, by the harts; are maimed for life, or meet their death by falling over precipices in their reckless pursuit, particularly in rounding a corner."—*Scrope*, p. 314.

276. DISCUSSION OF THE MERITS OF THIS CROSS.—I do not, of course, dispute the result of Mr. Scrope's experimental breeding. Doubtless, his dogs were good, and served the purpose to which they were applied; but, at the same time, I am strongly of opinion that a pure greyhound would answer the purpose much better. I have said that Mr. Scrope could have had little experience with greyhounds, or he would not have accused them of want of courage, want of nose, and idiotcy. No dogs fight more savagely; and the greatest annoyance in the greyhound-kennel is the constant occurrence of lameness, owing to this cause. Muzzles are needful on many breeds, or there would be nothing left when the dogs are wanted for coursing. I recollect, on one occasion, watching two puppies of my own, only five months old, which fought for two hours, and held one another at the end of that time so tightly, that they were obliged to be choked off. These same puppies afterwards would face anything, from a cat to a bull, and were certainly bold enough to run into any deer which ever ran. Many others I have known as bold as these; but, nevertheless, I admit that the generality of modern greyhounds are of a more mild and pacific turn; still, the breeder would have no difficulty in selecting a strain which would give him

plenty of courage of the kind he wants. Next, as to want of nose—greyhounds are always debarred from using the power which nature has given them, in common with all dogs, of running by scent as well as by sight; the consequence is, that they do not exercise that power, and, to a certain extent, it is in abeyance; but, if they are allowed to use it, they soon acquire a delicate and acute sense of smell, and can work out a scent as well as the foxhound. Mr. A. Graham tells me, that he formerly used to run his greyhounds a good deal with blinkers on, by which they were prevented from doing more than just rushing at their hares, and instantly losing them. These dogs, he says, soon acquired the most perfect use of their noses, and would hunt a hare as well as a beagle; or even wind her while in her seat, and then, guessing at the spot which they were unable to see, they would pounce upon their victim, and seize her in their relentless jaws. Such evidence is conclusive as to the nose of these dogs; for if they can do these things while discouraged in every possible way, what might they not be expected to do if properly entered to their game, and allowed the eight or nine years' practice which Mr. Scrope's Percy and Douglas were indulged with. I have often had puppies drag their leader across a field in pursuit of a hare by scent, keeping their noses to her trail, and following it exactly, some time after she had run out of sight. In the young greyhound the sense is much stronger than in the old kennelled-dog, as might naturally be expected; and I am quite certain that a young dog may be entered to hare, fox, or deer, and taught to hunt either, as well as any foxhound. In this respect there is a great difference in different breeds, but I should, of course, select that which would suit my purpose, only confining myself to the pure-bred greyhound, with only a slight cross of the bulldog, which so many good breeds already have. The last charge, of idiotcy, is still more cruel than that of want of nose; for we really have too much ability and cleverness, rather than too little. In spite of all our precautions, dogs *will* run cunning, and yet Mr. Scrope accuses them of being born-idiots. If they are allowed to associate with man and to use their faculties, they speedily become clever in the extreme; and many a poacher's dog is as well-bred a greyhound as any in the world, though from his exposure to hardship he is, perhaps, rough-coated and dirty, or perhaps deprived of his tail. The cleverest poacher's dog I ever saw was one of this kind; he would work to his master's orders like any pointer, and brought his hares when killed for miles, refusing to allow any one to relieve him of his burden. This dog, if put upon the scent of a hare, would be certain to return with her, even if she took him through half-a-dozen coverts; but his master seldom dared to try his powers in this way, for fear of his being seized or shot by the keepers. I have seen plenty of dogs which would do this, but few so accomplished as this one. No one, however, who knows much of the habits of the greyhound, would refuse to admit that he has sufficient intellect, if permitted to use it. He has, certainly, a deficiency in that love of approbation which makes the poodle, the Newfoundland, and the spaniel so anxious to please, that they exhaust all their powers of invention in finding out their master's wishes; but he has quite sufficient of this faculty or quality to induce him to try to please, and to exert his faculties in every way for that purpose. The courser, however, discourages all this, and wishes only to develop the tendency to run hares under certain laws, leaving all other faculties in abeyance, because if cultivated they lead the dog to husband his powers in such a cunning way, as to interfere with those laws under which he is running. Thus, I have shown that the greyhound has plenty of courage, nose, and intellect, producing sagacity and docility; and that he has endurance, speed, perseverance, and size, cannot be denied; or that he has elegance and dignity. Many of our modern smooth dogs are equal in height, girth, and weight to the measurement of Buskar, recorded at page 86; indeed, one of the best dogs now out (Mr. Borron's Bluelight), is at least 27 or 28 inches high, with a girth of 32 inches. His weight, if in such running condition as to fit him for deer-stalking, certainly would be over 75 lbs. I could name many more of the same weight, though latterly the best dogs have not often been of such majestic proportions.

277. PROPOSED BREED FOR DEER-STALKING.—Believing that speed is too much sacrificed by the foxhound cross, I should certainly advise the selection of a good greyhound strain, crossed six or seven generations back with the bulldog. Mr. Scrope is mistaken in supposing that this cross causes a reduction of speed, and indeed many, with the late Mr. Thacker, fancy that it gives an increase to that valuable quality. There is, however, one inestimable point in deer-stalking which it affords,—viz., the retaining the hold when once taken. This is very important, for a dog gets terribly mangled if he is constantly rushing in and grappling with the deer, and then as rapidly losing his hold. The bulldog-cross, however, ensures his firm and tenacious grasp; and

this peculiarity is remarkably developed in some greyhounds, which are obliged to be choked-off their hares. The qualities to be looked for are, as stated by Mr. Scrope, size, strength, speed, courage, endurance, perseverance, nose, docility, sagacity, and beauty. Now if Mr. Scrope, or any other deer-stalker, will get hold of any of Mr. A. Graham's old rough breed of greyhounds, and cross them with such a smooth and large dog as Mr. Laurence's Lopez, or Captain Besant's Black Prince, or Sir James Boswell's Puzzle'em, or Mr. Wilson's Jamie Forest, he will find that the produce, if *well reared*, will have all the qualities above-mentioned in a higher degree than the cross he has so highly vaunted. But to ensure success, they must be well reared, and should have plenty of milk till three or four months old, and afterwards be fed with a liberal quantity of flesh and meal. They should also be accustomed to be taken out, and allowed to use their noses without restraint, always, of course, taking care to keep them under control when necessary. They will run anything, from a lark to an elephant, if they meet with such rare game; and the only thing necessary is to enter them to deer and keep them strictly to it. If this is tried, I fully believe that a breed of dogs will be obtained quite equal to the old Scotch deerhound, and much faster and bolder than the foxhound-cross, with as good, or perhaps even a superior nose. The elements are in existence, and only require to be educated and developed to the full extent of which they are capable. Such, at least, is my belief, founded upon a very full acquaintance with the qualities of this noble animal.

SECT. 7.—QUALITIES NECESSARY IN THE DEER-STALKER.

278. It may readily be supposed, that for the pursuit of deer-stalking a hardy frame and plenty of pluck in the stalker are required. These qualities are indispensably necessary; but in all other points he may vary as much as the average of men are seen to do. The *model* deer-stalker, however, should be of good proportions, moderately tall, narrow-hipped to give speed, and with powerful loins and well developed chest for giving endurance and wind. No amount of fat should be allowed; indeed, the deer-stalker ought to be in as good training as the racehorse or greyhound. The foot should be sure, and the eye keen and long-seeing, as the telescope cannot always be applied to that all-important organ. He should be practised in running stooping, in crawling on his belly or on his back, by means of his elbows and heels; and should care neither for business, nor cold, nor wet.

The nerves should be good, for the excitement produced by this sport is such as to render unsteady the hand of all but those who are of the phlegmatic temperament. "Dutch courage" is not desirable, but "Dutch phlegm" will here serve in good stead. The bodily powers are not the only ones which should be well-developed, for the brain should be as active and energetic as the body itself. The red deer is as cunning an animal as any alive, and to circumvent him, all the resources of the mind of man must be called into play. The stalker must be full of plans and resources, yet cautious in putting them into execution, for many a well-matured scheme has been frustrated by some thoughtless act on the part of the schemer. Great control over the feelings is absolutely essential; for the giving way to the exultation of hope, or the depression produced by the fear of losing a shot, will generally cause that which is most to be apprehended. Above all, temperance must be practised—no shaking hand or flinching eye will serve the purpose of the stalker; nor will the parched throat or the perspiring skin avail him when rushing up the hill side or through the winding valley. In fact, strict training, in all its details, is required; and the more it is carried out, the more complete will be the success of the practiser of its disagreeable duties.

279. THE DRESS OF THE DEER-STALKER should be light and elastic, yet tolerably warm. For these purposes, the Scotch twilled-plaid is the best for the coat and vest, while the lower garments may be of somewhat stronger texture, yet still of wool. The head should be covered with a close-fitting cap, and the shoes should be studded with strong nails, to enable the foot to take secure hold of the slippery stones found in the burns and among the heather. A pair of leather gaiters should be worn also, as a protection against injury, and may either be put on under a pair of trowsers, or worn with knee-breeches, according to the taste of the sportsman. The colour of all should be sober and neutral; grey, or a mixture of black and white, being as good as any, since it accords well with the granite rocks which are so common in the haunts of the deer.

SECT. 8.—THE THREE MODES OF STALKING.

280. Thus, provided with glasses, rifles, gillies, and deerhounds, the stalker now has to commence operations on the red deer, which may be shot in three different modes,—1st, by quiet stalking; 2nd, by stalking in quick time; and 3rd, by driving.

281. QUIET STALKING.—The following is the mode of conducting this species or

stalking, as described by Mr. Scrope :—One or two stalkers getting on their horses, proceed to the edge of the deer forest, where they leave them, and are joined by two or three gillies, and a brace of deerhounds in slips. The first point is to ascend the most likely mountain to its top, and that will be the one which commands the glens and hillsides upon which the deer are most likely to be at that particular time. Having reached its summit, the stalker, or one of his men, should cautiously raise his telescope over its brow, and, applying his eye, should sweep the whole range presented to his view with deliberate caution. As soon as the deer is discovered, an attempt must be made to approach him, without being scented, seen, or heard; and this is well described in the following scene, which is extracted from Mr. Scrope's book, with some few abbreviations and omissions. The hart is just descried, and Tortoise (Mr. Scrope) thus speaks to his friend and pupil, Lightfoot :—" A noble fellow he is, Maclaren; I can just see his horns, and the point of his shoulders. It is a glorious chance, for once in the burn, we can get within a hundred yards of him, and that is near enough, in all conscience. Here, Lightfoot, look at the fine fellow; pull off your cap, and rest the glass on the stone." "Not the semblance of a deer can I see; but I'll take your word for it, I daresay he is there, since you say so. And now explain to me how you mean to get at him; communicate, my good fellow; for it seems, by all your caution, that even at this distance you dare not show a hair of your head." " Creep back there behind the hill, whilst I mark the very spot in the burn which is opposite his lair. Well, now, I will tell you: we must go all round by the east, behind yon hill, and then come up at the notch behind yon two hills, which will bring us into the bog; we can then come forward up the burn, under cover of its bank, and pass from thence into the bog again by a side-wind, when we may take his broadside—and thus have at him; so let us make the best of our way. It would be quite easy to get at the hart, if it were not for the hinds on the top of the hill; but if we start them, and they go on belling, the hart will follow them whether he sees us or not. Get your wind; he cannot. Maclaren, you will remain here, and watch the deer when I have fired. Sandy, follow you at a proper distance with the dogs; and come you along with us, Peter, and take the rifles. And now, my lads, be canny." The party then advanced, sometimes on their hands and knees, through the deep seams of the bog, and again right up the middle of the burn, winding their cautious course according to the inequalities of the ground. Occasionally the seams led in an adverse direction, and then they were obliged to retrace their steps. This stealthy progress continued some time, till at length they came to some greensward, where the ground was not so favourable. Here was a great difficulty; it seemed barely possible to pass this small piece of ground without discovery. Fraser, aware of this, crept back, and explored the bog in a parallel direction, working his way like a mole, while the others remained prostrate. Returning, all wet and bemired, his long, serious face indicated a failure. This dangerous passage, then, was to be attempted, since there was no better means of approach. Tortoise, in low whispers, again entreated the strictest caution. " Raise not a foot or a hand; let not a hair of your head be seen; but, as you value sport, imitate my motions precisely; everything depends upon this movement; this spot once passed successfully, we are safe from the hinds." He then made a signal for Sandy to lie down with the dogs, and, placing himself flat on his stomach, began to worm his way close under the low ridge of the bog; imitated most correctly and beautifully by the rest of the party. The burn now came sheer up to intercept the passage, and formed a pool under the bank, running deep and drumly; the leader then turned his head round slightly, and, passing his hand along the grass as a signal for Lightfoot to wreath himself alongside of him, said, " Now, my good fellow, no remedy—if you do not like a ducking, stay here; but if you do remain, pray lie like a flounder till the shot is fired. Have no curiosity, I beg and beseech you; and speak as I do, in a low whisper." " Pshaw! I can follow wherever you go, and in the same position too." " Bravo! here goes, then; but if you love sport, do not make a splash in the water, but go in as quiet as a fish, and keep under the high bank, although it is deeper there—there is a great nicety in going in properly; that is the difficult point. I believe it must be head foremost; but we must take care to keep our heels down as we slide in, and not to wet the rifles. Hist! Peter, here, lay the rifles on the bank, and give them to me when I am in the burn." Tortoise then worked half his body over the bank, and, stooping low, brought his hands upon a large granite stone in the burn, with his breast to the water, and drew the rest of his body after him as straight as he possibly could. He was then half immersed, and, getting close under the bank, took the rifles; the rest followed admirably; in fact, the water was not so deep as it appeared to be, being scarcely over the hips. They proceeded in this manner about 20 yards, when, the ground being more favourable, they were enabled to get on dry land. "Do you think it will do?" "Hush! hush! he has not seen us yet; and yonder is my mark; the deer lies opposite it to the south—he is almost within gunshot even now." A sign was given to Fraser to come alongside, for they were arrived at the spot from which it was necessary to diverge into the moss. In breathless expectation they now turned to the eastward, and crept forward through the bog, to enable them to come in upon the flank of the hart, who was lying with his head up-wind, and would thus present his broadside to the rifle when he started; whereas, if they had gone in straight behind him, his haunches would have been the only mark, and the shot would have been a disgraceful one. Now came the anxious moment. Everything hitherto had succeeded; much valuable time had been spent; they had gone forward in every possible position: their hands and knees buried in bogs, wreathing on their stomachs through the mire, or wading up the burns; and all this one brief moment might render futile, either by means of a single throb of the pulse in the act of firing, or a sudden rush of the deer which would take him instantly out of sight. Tortoise raised his head slowly, but saw not the quarry. By degrees he raised himself an inch higher, but Peter plucked him suddenly by the arm and pointed. The tips of his horns alone were to be seen above the hole in the bog— no more. Fraser looked anxious; for well he knew that the first spring would take the deer out of sight. A moment's pause, when the sportsman held up his rifle steadily above the position of the hart's body; then making a slight ticking noise, up sprang the deer—as instantly the shot was fired, and crash went the ball right against his ribs, as he was making his rush. Sandy now ran forward with the dogs, but still as well concealed by the ground as he could manage. "We must louse a dog, sir, or he will gang forrat to the hill." "Let go both of them; it will be a fine chance for the young dog; but get on a little first and put him on the scent, the deer is so low in the bog that he cannot see him." Fraser now went on with the hounds in the leash, sinking and recovering himself, and springing from the moss-bogs, till the dogs caught sight, and they were slipped; but the fine fellow was soon out of the bog, and went over the top of the Mealown. On following over the hill, the voice of the hounds broke full upon the stalkers, and they saw the magnificent creature standing on a narrow projecting ledge of rock within the cleft, and

in the mid course of a mountain cataract; the upper fall plunged down behind him, and the water coursing through his legs, dashed the spray and mist around him, and then, at one leap, went plump down to the abyss below; the rocks closed in upon his flanks, and there he stood, bidding defiance in his own mountain hold. Just at the edge of the precipice, and, as it seemed, on the very brink of eternity, the dogs were baying him furiously—one rush of the stag would have sent them down into the chasm; and, in their fury, they seemed wholly unconscious of their danger. All drew in their breath, and shuddered at the fatal chance that seemed momentarily about to take place. Of the two dogs at bay, Derig was the most fierce and persevering; the younger one had seen but little sport, and waited, at first, upon the motions of the older, nay, the better soldier. But his spirit being at length thoroughly roused, he fought at last fearlessly and independently. Whenever the deer turned his antlers aside to gore Tarff, Derig seized the moment to fly at his throat; but the motions of the hart were so rapid, that the hound was even compelled to draw back, which retrograde motion brought him frequently to the very verge of the precipice; and it was probable that, as he always fronted the enemy, he knew not, or, in the heat of the combat had forgotten, the danger of his situation. At this stage it was necessary to act speedily; and Tortoise having at length gained a spot which commanded a view of the stag, prepared to pour in a final shot. Three times the rifle was raised, but each time the aim was abandoned from fear of wounding the dog, or missing the deadly spot. At length an opening; the crack was heard faintly in the din of the waterfall—the ball passed through the back of the deer's head, and down he dropped on the spot without a struggle. The dogs now rushed forward and seized him by the throat, and were obliged to be choked-off. The men came cautiously on, and began to lift the huge animal out of the water, two at his fore and the same number at his hindquarters. At last they laid him on the grass, then plunging the long knife into his throat, and opening him for the purpose of gralloching him, his head was bent back on his shoulders, a black flag was tied to his horns to scare away the ravens, a little gunpowder was shaken over him, and he was left to be sent for on the next day with the aid of the forester's pony. Such is the account of stalking this animal in quiet style, let us now see the nature of the second mode adopted.

282. STALKING IN DOUBLE-QUICK TIME.— This is practised upon a somewhat different

principle to quiet-stalking, and is intermediate between that species of sport and the driving of the deer, which is only practised on rare occasions, and for high and mighty personages. Both these latter plans disturb the deer so much that they would, if often adopted, scare them, and drive them all off to other forests; and, therefore, the quiet-stalking is that usually preferred. It is practised by sending one, two, or three gillies, after the discovery of the deer by means of the glass, as before, to such points as shall induce them to move off towards the sportsman, who, when forewarned of their approach by the signal of the hillmen, rushes upon them as they pass a certain point most favourable for the purpose, and fires his rifles, furnished to him one after another by the attendant. Two or three points are here of great importance: first, that the gillies sent on should only allow the wind to convey their scent to the deer, and should not actually show themselves to their sight; secondly, that the leading hinds should always be suffered to pass before the rush is made, because, otherwise, the herd would stop short and return the way they came, or up some side ravine, instead of passing by the expectant stalkers. Great experience and tact are necessary in the gillies; and, after all, upon them more than upon the principal depends the success or failure of the attempt. It is all very well to fancy that they are acting under orders, but, even according to Mr. Scrope's own showing, they are obliged to use their own wits, and to have recourse to fresh expedients on every change of direction taken by the deer. No signalling can be carried on, because they are out of sight of the party and of one another; and all must act independently, though still in combination, for a specific object—viz., the *gentle* compulsion of the deer towards a spot near which the stalkers are lying in wait. Mr. Scrope's description of a scene in which this mode was adopted, is quite as characteristic as that which I have already extracted. Its great length, however, must prevent my doing more than to give a part of the narrative. The gillie, Maclaren, has been sent off about half-an-hour, and Tortoise and Lightfoot are waiting behind a projecting rock, with the deerhounds and rifles attended by Peter. Lightfoot *loquitur*:—"What beautiful creatures! They are all standing up, and gazing at the summit of the hill. How stately the stags look, with their jutting necks and towering antlers! Are you sure they are not elks? By Hercules, I think they are. Now they are moving forward to the hind in advance, which you seemed to have such an antipathy to. What in the world makes them shift their quarters?" "Why, Maclaren is nearly opposite to them, but at a great distance above, behind the swell of the hill; and, doubtless, has just shown the top of his bonnet over the sky-line; but they are all going wrong, and do not seem inclined to accommodate us." "They are not much alarmed, I think; for now they are standing still, and the hind has walked back a few paces, and is gazing up the hill again; the others seem to watch her motions, and to be guided by her judgment, whilst the harts appear to give themselves very little trouble about the matter." "No, the lazy rascals! but we may rouse them yet. Yes, they are alarmed, or, more properly speaking, suspicious. They have that sort of discretion which makes them run away in cases of danger; but you can never frighten them out of their wits with so small a force as ours. They are deliberately trying to make out what is going on, before they decide upon the direction of their retreat, and are too proud to fly without evident cause. But, just keep your eye upon them; Maclaren will not let them off thus: he will make a push for it at any rate." And so it seems he did, for in a few minutes they turned aside, and came a little way down the hill, gazing more towards the south. "By Jove, they are turning! Capital! Well done Maclaren!" "Doubtless, when he saw the deer going southwards, he slipped back behind the hill, ran like an antelope, and then came in again over the sky-line, and showed himself partially more in front of them. I may as well tell you, that if the hillman had come down right upon them in the first or second instance, and endeavoured to drive them as one drives sheep, they would immediately have raced away straight south, right up the wind, and have soon been out of our cast." Peter now pressed his master's arm, and pointed: "Did you no see yon parcel of hinds—these towards the shank of our hill? They canna choose but join them; and they will come, but it will be low doun." And now the gillie, who had a clear view of all these things, began to set to work in earnest. He passed forward rapidly, still out of sight of both parcels of deer, till at length, when he came sufficiently forward, he dashed down the hill in full view, shouting, hallooing, and hurling stones down the mountain with all his might—going to and fro as the deer shifted—slipping, clambering, and tumbling in such perilous places as would have endangered the life of a mountain-goat. The hinds last-mentioned, which were opposite them on Ben-y-venie, collected and whirled about, much admiring what all these strange noises might portend. Now had the decisive moment arrived, when the thing must terminate either one way or the other. Whilst this was doing, the stalkers were preparing for their work. Tortoise pressed his friend's arm—"Now then, or never! Creep back quickly, and prepare for action; for, by Herne the hunter, they are coming;—low, low, for your life! We must get on to that large stone, and they will all come into our very mouths. Now, then, forward! Take this rifle, and hold well at the best antlers when time shall serve; be steady, and fire well forward, taking care not to drop the gun when you pull the trigger." The clatter of hoofs was heard, as they were picking their way obliquely along the rocky ridge; but how uncertain are all the chances of the chase—instead of coming on, they turn away. "Come along, your best pace, Harry, for the hinds are startled, and our parcel is racing up to them; keep you above me, which will save you ground; and, Peter, do you stalk the deer, and I will stalk you, which will give me a pull also. We will make a push for it yet." In pursuance of this arrangement, Fraser peered down at the deers' horns, over the ribs of the hill side, ducking, skipping, and running, so as to keep out of their sight, and nearly alongside of them; the riflemen above keeping parallel to him, and dressing according to his motions. The deer, however, were steady to their tactics; for they were resolved not to come over the steep part of the hill, when, by losing the wind, they might come unawares on an enemy; thus they come, rapidly advancing towards the point of the hill where the slope was so open and gradual, that they could see a long way in advance, and, consequently, could not be suddenly surprised. Tortoise now changed his tactics, and turned suddenly to the right, going rapidly over the hill in a new direction; for as the herd had never seen him, nor any of his party, he judged they would remain, for some time at least, on the round swell of the hill below, which they were now approaching. Here Lightfoot was obliged to give up, and remain behind; but his absence was not noticed by Tortoise in the heat of the advance; after a short time, however, he again followed behind. And now Tortoise and Peter had reached the crags on the opposite side of the hill towards the west. Here was an absolute precipice, and large, angular stones were lying down it with their edges uppermost. Happy was the foot that did not slide down on their sharp ridges, and charmed was the leg that was not either cut or broken by them. Tortoise had forgotten his companion, so completely was he absorbed in his occupation. The struggle now was to get under the hill, on the side opposite to that where the deer were crossing, so as to arrive there in time to take them as they passed over the boll of it, still preserving the wind. Arrived at length at this desired spot, breathless, flushed, and covered with perspiration, they crept forward, and wound themselves through the heather, till, from behind a small knoll, they saw the deer feeding forward very leisurely, but still restless, and with their sentinels looking back towards the east. Tortoise now thought of Lightfoot left behind. "Here is a glorious chance," said he, "and I would not have him lose it on any account." At this moment he was descried approaching along a very precipitous and difficult path. Davy was sent back to assist him, and at length succeeded in bringing him up. Fraser, who had been peeping, from time to time, through a bunch of heather, now pressed Tortoise's arm, and whispered, "Be ready—they are coming." Both were lying flat on the heather, with the rifles on the ground, on one of which Tortoise had his hand; but as yet he did not raise it. They lay still as death, till some hinds passed within an easy shot; next came a four-year old hart, which was suffered to pass also; the better harts were following him in the same direction, and the points of their horns were just coming in sight when, lo! Lightfoot, who had that moment come into the ground, fired at the small hart, which was galloping away gaily, and gaily did he still continue to gallop. This injudicious shot struck woe and dismay into the soul of Tortoise. Up he sprang, and dashed forward, but it was only to see an antler or two vanishing out of sight under the swell of the ground; still he went on as fleetly as ever he ran in his life, cutting off to the point where he expected the deer would reappear in crossing the bottom. Here he stopped short, and, taking a deliberate aim, the peculiar swash was heard which tells that the bolt has struck its mark. The whole party now lay quietly down, and Fraser was set to examine the herd as they passed up the opposite heights, and to keep his eye on the wounded hart. This is the surest way of recovering him; for, if you press him, and he is not hit deadly, he will get forward into the middle of the herd whilst his wound is fresh, and run with the other deer in such a manner as will, most probably, occasion you to lose him; but if thus managed, his wounded part has time to stiffen, he slackens his pace, and generally falls out from the rest of the herd, if badly wounded; whilst, if only slightly wounded, you must lose him at any rate. "Now tell me, my wayworn and much-injured friend, what made you shoot at that little deer?" said Tortoise, as soon as he had time to cool. "A little deer!

a little deer! *Haud credo,* I thought he was an enormous monster." "I must reply as Master Dull did to the erudite Holofernes—'Twas not a *haud credo,* 'twas a pricket. Extremely juvenile he is, but you will soon learn to distinguish better." A dog was now slipped, and the deer finally retrieved, much as in the last described chase. Here again, the chief part is performed by the gillies;—Tortoise and Lightfoot play the subordinate part, except in being permitted to use the rifle, which is only another species of genteel butchery. However, this must be said *sotto voce,* because, while deer-stalking is so fashionable, it will always be prized, for such is invariably the case in all societies.

283. DRIVING DEER.—There is very little difference between the principles on which this sport is conducted, and those adopted in the quick-stalking. The chief points in which they are unlike is in the number of hill-men employed, the number of deer driven, and the number of stalkers placed in ambush. In all these respects deer-driving has the advantage of a considerable superiority—that is to say, if sport is to be measured by the number of its victims, as is the case in most instances. The pheasant-shooter and the wildfowl-shooter are both discontented with a small bag; and by a like desire for blood the deer-stalker is stimulated when he hopes for the death of tens, twenties, or hundreds, instead of single victims to his skill. In deer-driving on the large scale a great number of men are sent out, and by commencing at the extreme boundary of the forest, at stated distances apart, and gradually approaching the pass up which the deer are to be driven, all those within this circle are pressed on till they arrive at the point desired. In this progress the men have become much closer together, and in proportion as the deer accumulate, and the difficulty of pressing them on has increased, so has the number of men, in proportion to the ground covered, increased also; thus, supposing the semicircle first included was 10 miles in diameter, then the semicircle itself would be 15 miles in extent, and would require 120 men in order to give one to each furlong. But when the pass to which they are to be driven is only half-a-mile across, the semicircle would be reduced to three-quarters of a mile, giving one man to every 11 yards; and, if only a quarter of a mile, one man to every $5\frac{1}{2}$ yards. Such a *cordon* would be difficult to break, one would think; but, nevertheless, the deer, when alarmed in front, often wheel round and charge the drivers. Such an accident is well described in Sir Walter Scott's "Waverley," and the scene given in Cooper's "Smuggler" is also a good representation of one of those grand affairs. To these novels and to Mr. Scrope, I must however refer the reader who wishes to follow out this sport. It is one only adapted for princes; and those who are admitted to its pleasures should peruse the spirited descriptions presented by the above novelists, and by that practical sportsman Mr. Scrope. Most of us would, I have no doubt, enjoy the diversion, valuing it the more for its rarity; but for any other attraction, I confess I look in vain; excepting always the wild and picturesque scenery which its prosecution presents to the eye.

PART I.

THE PURSUIT OF WILD ANIMALS FOR SPORT.

BOOK II.—HUNTING.

CHAP. I.

MATERIÉL NECESSARY FOR HUNTING IN GENERAL.

SECT. 1.—THE GAME TO BE HUNTED.

284. Hunting may be defined to be the pursuit of certain wild animals, by means of a pack of hounds, following by scent. The animals hunted are—first, the red deer; second, the fallow deer; third, the roebuck; fourth, the fox; fifth, the hare; and sixth, the otter. The badger and marten are also hunted in some districts, but never, as far as I know, by a regular pack of hounds; and their pursuit will not, therefore, come under the above definition.

285. THE RED DEER (*Cervus Elaphus*), has been already fully described at page 87, under the chapter on Deerstalking. It is hunted in certain parts of England in a wild state, and is also sometimes turned out before a pack of staghounds, after being deprived of his horns, if a male, and taken to the meet in a deer-cart.

286. THE FALLOW DEER (*Dama Vulgaris*), is usually met with in our parks, where large herds are generally congregated, and form those pleasing groups which add so much to the effect of the beautiful scenery peculiar to Great Britain. It differs from the stag in size, being less, and in the form of the horns, which also are smaller, and flat instead of being round; they are also broader, palmated at the ends, and better garnished with antlers. The red and fallow deer never mingle together, even when confined in the same park avoiding one another most carefully, and never breeding together. The rutting season also in the latter is a fortnight or three weeks later; and the males at that time are not nearly so furious and excited; hence they are better suited for our parks, and the neighbourhood of man. They breed at two years, and bring forth one, two, or three fawns. They come to maturity at three years, and their average age does not exceed twenty. Fallow deer are easily tamed, and may be readily induced to follow their keeper into any crowd, which they speedily get accustomed to. At the rutting season, however, they are sometimes troublesome, and should then be carefully confined, or they may injure children or infirm persons, more especially those who show a fear of their horns. In England there are two varieties of the fallow deer—the spotted deer, said to be of Bengal origin, and similar to the AXIS or CHEETUL (*Axis Maculata*), and the dark, self-coloured brown, which is supposed to have been introduced from Norway by James I., who was devoted to the chase, and especially to stag-hunting. Fallow deer, when hunted, are always turned out of a cart; and their horns are generally removed when the buck is the object of pursuit.

287. THE ROEBUCK (*Capreolus Capræa*), was formerly common throughout England, but is now chiefly met with in Scotland, north of the Forth, though it is occasionally found still in Dorset and Devon. Its extinction in the southern parts of this island is owing to its dislike of confinement, not bearing even the walls of our parks. It will not admit of being tamed, and is very savage and morose when in close confinement. It is much less than the fallow deer, being only 24 inches in height; and it is even more elegant in its shape and movements. It is not gregarious, but lives singly, or in pairs, and drives off its young at nine or ten months of age. The horns are short and small, divided into three small branches, not palmated, and they are seldom more than a foot in length. This deer is seldom hunted; unlike the stag which is found on the bare mountains, it prefers the thick underwood of large forests; and it is only on rare occasions that it can be driven into the open lowlands and hunted with a pack of hounds. The rutting season is at the same time of the year as in the stag, but it continues as long as in the fallow deer. The female goes with young five months and a-half, and brings forth two or three fawns. The term of life is not more than 15 years.

288. THE FOX (*Vulpes Vulgaris*), has been already described as a species of vermin; in which capacity its destruction has been permitted, and even enjoined. Here, however, he reappears as the cherished object of the sportsman's care; and no animal is so jealously watched and tended as is Mr. Wiley, in the best fox-hunting districts. Coverts are made on purpose, often at great

expense, and kept undisturbed solely for his use. His ravages in the pheasant-preserve and hen-roost are overlooked, and the man who injures him is considered to have wounded the feelings of the whole hunt, and sullied his own honour. Nothing but this universal *esprit de corps* could have saved the fox from annihilation. Like the wolf, but for this protection, he would long since have been among the things that were; and the glorious sport he gives us would be impossible, for want of the necessary animal to hunt. Foxes are found of two or three varieties in the hunting districts, besides the hill-fox of Scotland, which is well calculated for showing sport before hounds, if the country would admit of *horses*. These varieties are—the grey-hound-fox, a large, tall, and fast animal, of a greyish-red; the bulldog fox, thicker, and darker-coloured, with a heavy head; and the smaller, redder, and more compact fox, which has been, and still is, imported from France or Germany. All these several foxes have the end of the tail black when young, and becoming white in after years. I have already enlarged upon the preservation of foxes, and the means by which the keeper may satisfy both the pheasant-shooting and fox-hunting tendencies of his master. The fox burrows underground, in what is called his "earth;" and the vixen produces from four to six cubs at a birth, once a-year—generally in April or May. When cubs are turned down in the summer, they require regular feeding and looking after for some time, as they are unable to get their own food, from a want of parental teaching. In process of time, however, instinct prompts them, and they gradually learn to provide for themselves. A want of this precaution has caused the loss of many litters of cubs, procured at great expense and trouble.

289. THE HARE (*Lepus Timidus*), is too well known to need a full description. For hunting purposes she is well suited, because her instincts are so remarkably well developed in showing her how to foil the pursuit of her enemies. She doubles and returns upon her trail in a way which seems to prove the existence of reason; and sometimes even swims down a river to escape her pursuers when hard pressed.

There is a variety peculiar to Scotland, the SCOTCH HARE (*Lepus Variabilis*), and also an IRISH HARE (*Lepus Hibernicus*). The former is somewhat, and the latter much, less than the English hare; they are both, however, fast and stout; but the mountain-hare of Scotland, which is the one alluded to above, is not well calculated for hunting or coursing, having instincts very different from the ordinary Scotch or English hare.

290. THE OTTER (*Lutra Vulgaris*), has already been described at page 10.

SECT. 2.—HOUNDS, AND THEIR MANAGEMENT.

291. THE VARIOUS KINDS OF HOUND were formerly much more distinct than at present. Nothing can be much more unlike the old southern hound or bloodhound, than the diminutive beagle; and almost the only point of resemblance is the exquisite power of scent which both possess. At present, hounds may be divided into—first, bloodhounds; second, staghounds; third, foxhounds; fourth, harriers; fifth, beagles; and sixth, otter-hounds.

292. THE BLOODHOUND, SOUTHERN HOUND, or TALBOT (See *Art.* "DOG"), is still met with in England, but it is entirely superseded by the foxhound or harrier for all the purposes of the chase. In parks, however, it is still used for singling out certain deer, and running them down, when they are to be taken for the purpose of hunting or for stall-fattening, or for removal. Here great caution is required, as the bloodhound is a dog which cannot be kept under command; and no whip or rating will prevent his gratifying his desire for blood when he has the opportunity. His nose, however, is so perfect, and he has so completely the power and the instinctive desire to keep to the hunted deer, that he will follow it through the whole herd, and pass them by regardless of their attractions. He has been also, and still is, used for hunting sheep-stealers and thieves of all kinds, and must then be muzzled. Besides his intractability, he is also comparatively slow, and the fox or stag-hunter of the present day would not require his thoroughbred horse to keep pace with his movements, but would vote him "a potterer," and would be more inclined to ride a steeplechase home than to watch his slow hunting. In size, he is the largest of the hounds, being about 27 or 28 inches high at the shoulders, and often weighing 80 lbs. The colour is generally black and tan, with a great preponderance of the red—which is, moreover, more yellow than red; but in the Talbot and sleuth-hound the yellow and black-pie was the usual colour. The head is very handsome; ears large, soft, and pendulous; jowl square, and lips well developed; nose broad, soft, and moist; and eyes lustrous and beautifully soft when in an unexcited state. This dog is nearly identical with the Talbot, and old southern or sleuth-hound, of which we now have no pure representative; but they may be said to be one variety, and to be the stock from which the staghound, foxhound, harrier, beagle, and otter-hound have been all bred.

293. THE STAGHOUND AND FOXHOUND may be considered as the same, the former

being only a larger variety of the latter; but though originally descended alike, they are not now bred from the same strains indiscriminately. As with the old deerhound and greyhound, so with these hounds, although their organisation and appearance are identical, yet from being entered and kept for many generations to different game, they are to be readily distinguished by their style of hunting. Nevertheless, no one could say where the line which divides them passes, and it would be impossible even for Mr. Davis to distinguish a large spiry foxhound from one of the smallest and lightest of her Majesty's beautiful pack. The staghound, therefore, may be considered as a large foxhound, or the foxhound as a small staghound; the one devoted to the hunting of deer, the other to that of the fox.

294. THE ORIGINAL STOCK of these two varieties of the hound is undoubtedly the southern hound, bloodhound or Talbot. But in process of time, when the country was cleared from forest, and more speed was required, and when the horse could be used in order to keep pace with that increased speed, a faster hound was sought for, and the old-fashioned, deep-toned, and careful hound was bred, which has been immortalised by the verse of Somerville and the prose of Beckford. These were faster than the southern hound, but still slow compared with the modern foxhound. In those days the cold scent of the morning drag was hit off by the hound, and the fox was hunted up to his retreat in the woodlands before he had time to digest his nocturnal meal, or to sleep off his fatigue in procuring it. Hence, nose was all in all; and the fox being full of food, could not go the pace which he now does at 11 or 12 o'clock, eight or ten hours after his belly was filled with the fat capon or the wary old "rooster," as our transatlantic friends denominate the dunghill cock. It is not fully known by what crosses this increase of speed was obtained; the subject was formerly enveloped in much mystery; and masters of hounds were embued with a very different spirit to that which prevails among them in the present century. But there is strong reason for believing that the greyhound, and, most probably, the old Scotch deerhound, were had recourse to, either directly or through the northern hound, which was a decided cross of the southern hound with the deerhound. In her Majesty's pack most of the hounds are fully 26 inches in height, and the bitches at least 24; they have broad short heads, with straight hind legs, well furnished thighs, and sterns more feathered than is often seen in the ordinary foxhound. They have very delicate noses, can hunt a cold scent, and yet with a blazing one they run breast high, but not quite so fast as some of our packs of foxhounds when the scent is good. The deer's foot-scent is not good; but he leaves a strong body-scent, which falls to a certain height, according to the state of the air, and is readily owned by the staghound. The endurance of this dog is great, but not perhaps equal to the foxhound, as is to be expected from his greater size and weight. Few packs of staghounds could bear the road-work which most foxhounds undergo besides their runs, which are sometimes two or three in the day; they also escape altogether the work in covert, which is most trying to the lesser hound. Even where wild deer are hunted they are "unharboured" by slow hounds of the old breed. Consequently, the actual chase is all that is committed to the staghound, together with the road-work to the meet— generally pretty near the kennel; and the homeward journey, which, however, is often a long and dreary one, but not, as in the foxhound's case, prolonged into the night.

295. THE MODERN FOXHOUND is a most extraordinary animal; fast almost to the same degree as a slow greyhound, he has extraordinary stoutness and power of endurance, with a hardy constitution. To these invaluable qualities he adds a good nose, not quite equal, however, to a cold scent; with great docility, when considered in conjunction with his courage and dash. With regard to his origin, there is strong reason for believing, as with the staghound, that he is the old southern hound crossed with the greyhound, with perhaps a dash of the bulldog; but here, again, all is conjecture, and we can only guess at his origin from his form and peculiarities. Beckford describes the model hound as follows :— "Let his legs be straight as arrows; his feet round, and not too large; his shoulders back; his breast rather wide than narrow; his chest deep; his back broad; his head small; his neck thin; his tail thick and bushy—if he carry it well so much the better . . . a small head, however, as relative to *beauty* only; for, as to *goodness*, I believe large-headed hounds are in nowise inferior . . . The colour I think of little moment, and am of opinion with our friend Foote, that a good dog cannot be of a bad colour." —p. 52. To this must be added a point of great importance, which has been insisted on by Nimrod—namely, the length of the back-ribs, which, as in the horse, should be well developed, and firmly fixed to the hips by strong muscles. Nimrod also very properly insists upon length of thigh, and good strong stifles, without which speed cannot be long

H

maintained. This description will avail equally well in the present day, although written more than 50 years ago. He also recommends a middle-sized hound, neither too large nor too small; but, like many other writers on sporting subjects, he does not further define what he means by giving the middle height of the foxhound, or even the extreme ranges to which they go. I think that 24 inches for dogs, and 22 for bitches, will be found to be about the outside height which will be desirable for fast and open countries; while in strong woodlands, with much work in covert, an inch less will be desirable, because the large hound has more difficulty in following out the runs traversed by briars, &c., than the dog a size smaller. The quickest pack I ever saw, and that which worked in covert the best, was Lord Redesdale's hunting the Heythrop country, which were not more than 23 inches, dogs, and 22 inches, bitches. This pack, however, went like birds, and flew the stone walls as well as a greyhound. Indeed, the contrast with Earl Fitzhardinge's larger hounds hunting the same district during part of their season, was, I think, much in favour of the little ones. They were, certainly, the most beautiful pack, to my taste, which I ever saw; and so unusually " suity," as to please the eye in that particular in a way which no larger hounds could be expected to do. It is always easier to draft large hounds than small ones down to a certain size; and, consequently, a small-sized pack can be kept much more level than a larger one; and the difference also between the sexes being less marked, they look better when the dogs and bitches are hunted together.

296. THE HARRIER AND BEAGLE may be taken together, since they are now bred one with the other so much that it is difficult to say what are harriers and what beagles. The latter is the more specific breed, and may therefore with advantage be first examined. It should be remembered that the hare, unlike the fox, is constantly " doubling," that is, returning upon her track, and thus endeavouring to foil her pursuers; for this reason, an exquisite nose is required, with great patience, and considerable cunning, to meet artifice by artifice. Hence, the hare-hound must differ from the fox-hound, in possessing an acuter sense of smell, a slower pace, less dash, and more patience; he must also be able to distinguish a "heel-scent," as he may otherwise return upon the hunted line, fancying he is following a "double" of the hare. One other point, also, is of vast importance—he must "pack closely;" for as the hare so often doubles back, if the hounds are all over the field the chance of foiling the "double" by their own scent is

increased when they spread widely. The beagle, as embodying all these points in perfection, is, therefore, the model hare-hound of the old school; and has also lately been re-introduced in high quarters, being a great favourite at Windsor. In size the beagle measures from 10 inches, or even less, to 15. In shape they resemble the old southern hound in miniature, but with more neatness and beauty; and they also resemble that hound in style of hunting. No scent is too cold for them, and they can work out, in all its windings and foils, that of the most cunning old hare, if allowed time to do it. Nothing is more beautiful than to watch the working of these diminutive hounds; and I trace my first fondness for hunting and the sports of the field to the occasional sight of a pack of them belonging to the father of a schoolfellow of mine, Mr. Harding, living near Dorchester. The extraordinary style of these little beagles I have never seen surpassed; but I fancy there was more in the mode of hunting, than in the hounds themselves. They were never lifted, and rarely cast, but left to work out their scent in their own way; and, consequently, their brains were thrown upon their own resources, and very rich those stores certainly were. Often have I seen them apparently consult, and then, without the slightest *external* cause, hit off the scent as if by mutual inspiration, and carry it on without a check for a mile or two. Slow they were, at least so slow that we could keep up on foot by cutting corners, &c.; but at times, with a blazing scent, they would race away from us. I would that I could now catch a view of their graceful forms. The head and ears of the beagle are much broader, and the ears longer, than the fox-hound—very nearly approaching to the bloodhound in development; the legs shorter, and the body bigger and stouter. He is a very hardy little dog, and will stand an immense deal of work. At the two extremes of the beagle subdivision stand the dwarf beagle—a little smooth lapdog, with very long ears, and almost pug nose; and the fox-beagle, resembling the foxhound in all but size and dash. The essence of the beagle is the freedom from this quality, and it should never, on any account, be permitted to be displayed. Patience, co-operation, freedom from jealousy, goodness of nose, and Lilliputian dimensions, are, in fact, the essential qualities of the beagle. There is an air about them which the sportsman recognizes, but which is very difficult to describe; nevertheless, there it is, and a comparison will soon show it. Besides these, there is the rough beagle, a cross with the rough Scotch terrier, and partaking of his tongue rather than of the old mellow tone of the southern hound. We may, therefore, sum up the varieties of this little hound as — first, the medium beagle, which may be either heavy and southern-like, or light and northern-like; second, the dwarf or lapdog beagle; third, the fox beagle; and fourth, the rough or terrier beagle.

297. THE HARRIER is now a mongrel animal, bred in all sorts of ways, and varying from 21 inches down to 15 or 16. In looks more like the foxhound than the beagle, he has some remnants of his old breed in the longer ears, wider head, and stouter body which he possesses. He should, however, have a most delicate nose, even more so than the beagle; for as his increased size carries him faster over the ground, so is he more likely to overrun the scent, and foil it so that he cannot recover it. Some of these hounds, however, have a wonderful power of carrying a scent at full speed, and will race into a hare in such a time as to finish her up almost as soon as found; this, however, spoils sport in great measure, as, by their speed, they prevent all those artifices on the part of the hare which give zest to this otherwise slow amusement. For this reason it is that harriers appear to have as good noses as beagles, though they really have not; for by depriving the hare of scope to double back, by pressing so closely upon her scut, they give themselves much less to do, and have only to work out a straightforward scent. Many huntsmen of harriers now cast forward as if hunting a fox, and with reason too; for as the hare *cannot* double back, she tries all her wiles in a forward or side-direction—hence the alteration in the principles called for by the alteration in the speed of hounds. It is, however, in my opinion, an alteration for the worse; and I hope that as hare-hunting becomes more common, as will most probably be the case, that beagles, rather than harriers, will be the hounds selected. From an hour to one hour and a-quarter is the proper average time to kill a hare in; she then has a quarter of a mile law all through, and stops and pricks up her ears, and considers, and then doubles and doubles again, and resorts to all sorts of expedients, which try the powers of the little animals behind. The pack, which is shown in the cut hereafter given with the chapter on Hare Hunting, is a cross of the beagle and foxhound; they are from 16 to 17 inches in height, can go quite fast enough to keep horses galloping, and can give a good account of 19 hares out of 20, having, indeed, killed 51 in the season of 1854-5. They are of Lord Sefton's blood, and such hounds I should like to see

throughout England, kept at little expense, and affording amusement to hundreds on horseback and on foot.

298. OTTER-HOUNDS are nothing more than the old southern hound crossed with the Scotch terrier and water-spaniel, and kept for generations to the hunting of the otter.

SECT. 3.—CONSTRUCTION OF KENNELS.

299. THE KENNELS form a most important item in the management of a pack of hounds; and much controversy has arisen on the subject; the chief points of difference in opinion consist—first, in the soil upon which they are built; secondly, on their aspect; and, thirdly, on their formation and ventilation.

300. THE SOIL FOR KENNELS should certainly not be a porous one. Sand is the very worst possible stratum for the purpose, since it absorbs and retains all the excrementitious particles which the dogs must pass whenever they leave their kennels, either in their yards or grass-courts. A cold clay is perhaps too much in the other extreme, since it is always accompanied by a raw and damp atmosphere; and is on that account prejudicial to health. Of the two extremes, however, it is, I think, the better; and I should build on clay in preference to gravel. Marl is the best stratum for the purpose, or chalk, which does not absorb to the same degree as gravel. Either of the two last is well suited to the purpose, and one or the other may be procured in most districts.

301. THE ASPECT is all-important; sun is necessary to the health of all animals, and is doubly so to the dog, yet an afternoon-sun is too hot, and causes the sleeping-room to be uncomfortably warm in the height of summer. A south-eastern aspect, therefore, should be chosen, well sheltered from the east and north by plantations or hills, but not so much so towards the former direction as to shut out the morning-sun. The gently sloping side of a hill, therefore, which looks to the south-east may be selected, and the kennel built facing in that direction, by which means the drainage will all be carried off out of the way of the yards and sleeping-rooms; and the yards themselves may easily be levelled and drained laterally so as not to interfere with the kennel. This will be better understood by the annexed diagram, in which the dotted line *a b* indicates the old level, and *c d* that of the yards and kennel, with a good trapped-drain at *e e*, into which both yards and lodging-rooms are washed and drained. By this arrangement the internal parts are kept high and dry, and are cut off from all damp by the drain between them and the open yards. The morning

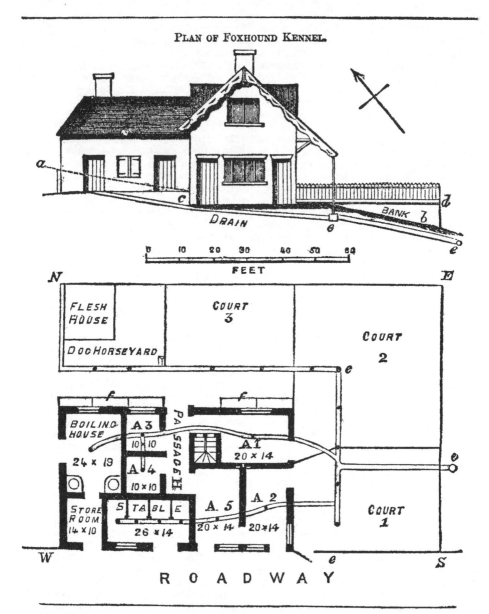

sun has full power, and gives health suffi-cient for all purposes, whilst in the heat of the afternoon the doors may be thrown open, and the interior is all in shade as well as great part of the yard.

302. IN THE CONSTRUCTION OF THE KEN-NEL, one grand point is to select materials which will not absorb either the moisture or noxious effluvium emanating from the hound. They should be, therefore, either hard stone or flints, or well-burnt and hard bricks. Sandy and porous bricks make the very worst walls for kennels possible, and should carefully be avoided. Next, as to size and shape:—the former must depend upon the number of hounds; but, as it is easier to build a large kennel originally than to increase it when once built, it is as well to calculate upon one which will hold 40 couple of hounds, the number which will suffice for stag or fox-hunting three or four days a-week. For such a pack, the dimen-sions given in the annexed plan are suffi-cient. The essentials as to accommodation are very simple, and consist of—first, the lodging-rooms; secondly, the feeding-room; thirdly, the boiling-house; fourthly, the men's rooms; fifthly, the men's stables; and sixthly, the courts. The lodging-rooms should consist of five rooms—three large, and two small—A1, A2, A3, A4, A5. A1 is for the regular pack; A2 for the pack

drafted for hunting next day; A 3 for invalid dogs; A 4 for bitches in season; and A 5 for those whose room is drying after being washed down. Where a dog and bitch pack are kept separately, one other room, at least, must be set apart for the bitches. These houses should all have benches, raised about 20 inches from the floor, and about 80 inches wide. These should surround three sides of the room, and should have open lattice-work bottoms, with a front-edge to them about four inches deep, of stout timber, well rounded off. They should also be lined with board, towards the walls, at least eight inches from the top of the bench. The size of the rooms is indicated in the plan annexed. All should be paved with *glazed* tiles, sloping to the centre, which should have a trapped-drain; and they should be on a foundation of concrete, composed of large cinders or broken bricks, with lime and gravel. When expense is of little importance, all kennels should be built on brick arches, which, after all, are not very expensive, a single brick arch being quite sufficient. These rooms should be from 12 to 14 feet high, and ventilated by means of three or four trap-windows, similar in principle to those in church windows. The traps should, however, be capable of being entirely removed in the heats of summer. One large feeding-room is all that is necessary, but I have not given it in the plan, as I should much prefer an open verandah, running the whole length of the kennel, for this purpose. Here the troughs may be placed, and in the summer time the food cools more rapidly, while, after feeding, and indeed at all other times, the verandah allows the hounds to enjoy the shade from the sun, or protection from the rain. The troughs *f f* are made, with perforated covers; and when these are shut down, they form a seat for the men, or a bench for dogs to lie upon, high and dry. The boiling-house may be placed at the end of the building, or at some greater distance, if desirable; but it should be tolerably near, on account of the increased labour of carrying the pudding, broth, &c., from a distance. It should be a room *open to the roof*, to admit of the escape of the steam; and containing two large cast-iron boilers, set in proper brickwork. These boilers should hold from 50 to 60 gallons, and should be kept, one for meal, the other for flesh. In the boiling-house, also, there should be two or three coolers, eight feet by five feet, and one foot deep, in which the pudding or broth may be allowed to cool. This room should also be floored with tiles or bricks; no concrete is necessary, but a drain must be added, to allow of the blood, &c., from the flesh, being washed away.

Over one of the three lodging-rooms (A 1) are the rooms of the kennel-huntsman, or feeder, who should always be at hand at night, prepared to put down the first symptoms of quarrelling by the voice, or, if necessary, the whip. Opposite the junction of the inner wall of A 1 with that dividing A 2 from A 5, there should be in the feeder's room a small stove, or fireplace, fed with air from three air-drains, one of which commences at the bottom of each of the three lodging-rooms. By this plan, when his fire is lighted, a draught is maintained from the lodging-rooms, and the air kept pure thereby, compelling the entrance of fresh air from the windows. Over the room A 2 is a meal-room, and over A 5 a hay-loft, for the stable adjoining. At the end of the passage, at H, is a foot-bath for the hounds after hunting; it should be made of Roman cement on brickwork, about four or five inches deep, and filled with warm broth; a plug easily allows of the escape of the broth after use. As the hounds pass backwards and forwards to the feeding-trough, they bathe their feet in the warm broth, which they afterwards lick off, the tongue finishing the good work begun by the warm broth. A bucket of hot broth mixed with an equal quantity of cold water is sufficient for this purpose. Three courts are in the plan, as follows, viz. :—I., for the hunting-hounds; II., for the general pack; and III., for any others, or for feeding. The posts of the verandah stand in these courts; and there should be a trap at the foot of each, leading to the drain, for a purpose which every person conversant with the dog will readily understand. There should also be a grass-court or paddock adjacent. The stabling is calculated for four horses, which is quite as many as should be at the kennel at one time—the change-horses being better at the regular hunt-stable; but these three or four horses being done by the kennel-men, are better at the kennel; and in the summer-time the stable is required for the cub-hunting horses, which are seldom more than screws adapted for that purpose. Good hunters would be sacrificed at this time, owing to the hardness of the ground, and the great amount of covert-work. Kennels of these dimensions and construction ought to be put up without much ornamental work, but in a thoroughly substantial manner, for from £200 to £250, according to locality and expense of materials.

SECT. 4.—THE MASTER AND HIS MEN.

303. THE MASTER of a pack of foxhounds, staghounds, or even of harriers, ought to possess the qualities which would fit him for the command of an army in the field,

together with that particular knowledge which is essential to hunting. He should be able to keep in good order—first, a pack of high-couraged hounds; secondly, a set of opinionated men, in the shape of Huntsman & Co.; and, thirdly, a disorderly field of sportsmen. If, fortunately for him, he is master of his own pack, without the aid of subscriptions, his task is comparatively light; but even then he is often considered to be the property of those who hunt with him; and, if things go wrong, he is pulled to pieces as much as if he were the servant of his followers, instead of their being immeasurably obliged to him for enduring the trouble, and undertaking the expense, of his establishment. There can be no doubt that a man who undertakes to hunt a country, even at his own expense, is bound to carry out his engagements, because one part of the arrangement is the giving up the country to him; and, while he is in possession, no other master has a right to it. Sometimes nearly the whole of a fox-hunting country belongs to the master—that is to say, the whole of the large fox-coverts; but this is seldom the case, and generally he is dependent upon the permission to draw them, granted as a part of his district. This permission is given on the implied understanding that sport shall be shown, for no man wishes fox-hunting to be conducted in a slow or unsportsmanlike manner; and hence those owners of coverts who have granted leave to draw, have clearly a right of interference; but they are seldom the grumblers, the actual malcontents being generally the sporting butchers, &c., who indulge the field with their presence. If this grumbling happens with the master who keeps his own hounds, how much more likely is it with the master of a subscription pack. He has unfortunately a hundred subscribers, or sometimes more, each of whom fancies himself justified in calling him to account, or in refusing to obey orders, if he has been transgressing the limits which are compatible with the enjoyment of sport. Yet a field *must* be kept in order; the how? is the problem to be solved, and its solution has puzzled the brains and exhausted the energies of many a high-spirited and well-intentioned sportsman. The master should possess the iron nerves of the "Iron Duke," and yet with these should be joined the polished courtesy of the Earl of Chesterfield. Oaths and imprecations *may* succeed with the self-supporting master, but even then they are better left at home; but these tactics are misapplied with the subscription pack. Nothing but firmness, united with gentlemanly language, has a chance in these days; and their union, when combined with a knowledge of the noble science and good riding, will be sure to succeed anywhere and everywhere; the combination, however, is rare; and there are few men who possess it in full force who will not soon give up their office in the full knowledge that the same talents applied in a different way, will lead to success in the legislature, or in some collateral pursuit. Every master, however, should have a good knowledge of the theory and practice of hunting; and though he may be inferior, in some respects, to his huntsman, who has made it the business of his whole life to study hounds and hunting, yet he ought to know enough to be able to judge whether he is doing right or wrong. If this is not the case, the man will too often exult over the ignorance of the master, if he attempts to interfere; and if he does not in any way take the management, he is the slave of a despot rather than the master of a good servant. However, in all cases the master must undertake to keep the field from overriding the hounds, and from surrounding a covert, and thereby heading a fox back, and causing him to be "chopped," from an incapacity to break, in face of a lot of chattering cigar-smokers and scandal-mongers, who care little about hunting, and only want to have the pleasure of exhibiting their persons in pink before the young dressmakers of their town or village. These gentlemen must be ranged in their places, or the efforts of the best pack of hounds and the most clever and persevering huntsman will be rendered abortive, whenever there is a light scent. With a blazing scent, after once hounds are away, no care is required; but in nine days out of ten, unless the master uses his "Hold hard! gentlemen," pretty unceremoniously, the sport is spoilt, or, at all events, greatly interfered with. Such are the duties of the master in the field, which every man, noble or gentle, who undertakes to hunt a pack of foxhounds, takes upon his shoulders. With his kennel duties, if self-supporting, no one whatever has a right to interfere; but if supported by subscriptions, his subscribers have a right to expect that he shall see that their money is properly expended in the use of the meal, &c., for the hounds, and in all other ways. There is a very great difference in different packs in the money spent, amounting to about 50 per cent.; and this can only be accounted for by the management being good or bad on the part of the master.

304. THE HUNTSMAN next comes before us, and he, like the master, should be a general out of place; but his duties are not so multifarious, as he has nothing to do with the field, while the master should have the

knowledge of a huntsman, and also be able to keep his unruly friends in order. In all cases, whether the master hunts his hounds himself or not, he should have a steady man to act as huntsman during the exercise, and in cub-hunting, &c.; also in his absence, from business or ill health. But the regular servant must possess the following qualities: temperance, judgment, hound-knowledge, knowledge of hunting, including the ways of all foxes, knowledge of country generally, and of the particular country hunted; good horsemanship—by which is meant anything but random riding, nevertheless, a huntsman ought, in nine cases out of ten, to be able to get to his hounds; *sometimes* a park-wall, or a river, or canal may interfere, but these exceptions do not often occur. A good voice is also essential, and the more peculiar the better, as the less hounds answer to strange voices the more successfully the sport will proceed; and, in particular, he should have the faculty of making hounds fond of him. With these requisites, added to a quiet, civil deportment, and a natural liking for the science, a man will always command sport; and in proportion to his success there, will be the respect paid him by the field. For a pack of harriers or beagles the huntsman requires much less dash and hard-riding, and should be quieter, more steady, and less interfering. His field is generally smaller; the farmers take care that their wheat, &c., are less ridden over, and the hounds have full chance to do their work without being interfered with. An older man is therefore more suited to this place, as he is more required in the kennel than the field; for if he gets command of his hounds in the former, he will easily manage them in the latter. Indeed, a word from a huntsman is enough with harriers; they turn like lightning, and are, or ought to be, as handy as kittens.

305. UNLIKE THE HUNTSMAN, IN EVERY RESPECT, SHOULD BE THE WHIPPERS-IN, both first and second; they should both be good horsemen, and, may be, perhaps, a little more dashing at times in their riding than their superior officer—that is to say, that it may be permitted to them to risk a drowning or a broken neck when certain things are to be effected, which risks the huntsman seldom has occasion to incur. If a hard-run fox is heading for certain earths which are open, woe to the whip who does not risk the breaking of his own neck and his horse's heart in getting to them in time. If hounds are changing their fox, and the hunted one is close before a single hound, or a couple or so, then, at all hazards, the other hounds must be stopped, and the whip's riding must be daring enough to effect his object. He, however, should not think exactly for himself, but should work in a subordinate capacity to the huntsman. There may often be two courses to be pursued, and it is not for him to consider which is the best, but that which the huntsman will consider the best, and that is the one for him to work to. He should always be on the look-out for "riot," and careful to check it in the bud; using a rate, if that will act, and if not, then getting to the rebellious hound directly and "serving him out." No plan is so bad as that of constantly flicking and cutting at hounds; if they do wrong in spite of a rate, then punish them severely; but in all cases try the gentler means first, and if they fail, use the whip with power, but at the same time with care and caution, *as the dog's eye is very easily cut out.* The first whip's duty is chiefly to restrain any wildness in the leading hounds, to stop them, or to check riot; while that of the second whip is to bring up the tail hounds, to drive on those hanging in coverts, and generally to keep the slow hounds up with the pack. The duties of the second whip are very subordinate, and require nothing but a strict attention to plain orders. Nevertheless, he may do harm by over-using his whip, or by a want of activity; but most second whips are ready enough in acting; and, as they are generally selected for their good horsemanship, their task is performed with ease and satisfaction to themselves.

306. THE FEEDER is a Jack-of-all-trades, in a subscription pack especially. He has first to look out for and kill the dog-horses, and should be able to know what to accept and what reject. Some over-drugged and diseased horses are absolutely injurious to the kennel, and the hounds had much better live on their pudding alone, than be poisoned with unwholesome food. Besides this duty, he has to wash out all the lodging-rooms, and mop them dry; to boil the flesh, and make the pudding and broth, and to get the food ready for them, either when returning from exercise or from hunting. It is usual for the feeder to undertake the grooming, &c., of one or more of the men's horses, generally the huntsman's; but sometimes a helper is allowed. In almost all cases the whips do their own horses, and there can be no reason why they should not; then, if there is only one horse kept at the kennels for the huntsman, the feeder may well undertake him, as his duties are over when the hounds come in, and he has nothing to do but attend to this horse; whereas the huntsman should himself feed the hounds, and attend to any wounds, &c., which they may have incurred in their day's work. This will take him nearly two

hours, including a short interval for his own stomach. The feeder ought to be a thoroughly trustworthy man, civil and obliging, and also fond of hounds. A good deal must be trusted to him; lame and sick hounds must be left in his charge, and if he does not carry out his instructions, many hounds will die or be ruined. If, also, he is not careful in drying the sleeping-rooms before the hounds are returned to them, or if he leaves doors or windows open in bitterly cold days, from thoughtlessness or carelessness, kennel-lameness, or some other form of rheumatism, is sure to show itself.

307. Lastly comes the EARTH-STOPPER, a very important functionary to a pack of foxhounds, though only wanted there, and sometimes superseded by the keepers, who engage to stop, on notice being given them; but in all well-appointed establishments he is still a regularly paid official. His office is, to proceed at night when the foxes are all out feeding and stop the earths, wherever they are likely to be run to on the following day. If he is a man who knows his business, it is only needful to tell him what coverts will be drawn; but although this is all that is necessary for him to know, yet he should in all cases tell the first whip what earths are stopped, in order that, if the run is by chance different to what was expected, he may know whether it will be needful for him to get forward and head the fox before entering the open earths. After hunting, the earth-stopper should also carefully unstop the earths, and leave as little trace as possible of his midnight work. If the keepers are to be trusted to do this, they of course easily can; but it is so important to hunting to see well to this part of the arrangements, and disappointment so often follows the reliance upon men whose hearts are more often set upon the gun than the hound, that it is much better for the earth-stopper himself to see to this part of his duty. I have certainly seen many runs spoilt from a dependence upon the aid of the keeper.

308. THE HORSES OF THE MEN should be good useful hunters, especially those for the huntsman, who ought to be the best-mounted man in the field. It is all very well to say they may be blemished, but so may any hunter. Who cares for blemishes in the hunting-field? Many of our best and highest-priced hunters have had badly broken knees, and with these drawbacks, or with scored-hocks, have fetched £400 or £500. If a man is not well mounted he cannot get to his hounds, and should not be blamed for failing in effecting an impossibility. The whips may be put on half-made horses, because, in case of accident,

their places may be more readily supplied; but the better horses they have, the better they can perform their duties. In hunting three days a-week, the huntsman and whips require a fresh horse generally every other meet; and in fast countries the huntsman usually has two out in the same day.

SECT. 5.—KENNEL MANAGEMENT.

309. THE FEEDING AND KENNEL MANAGEMENT of all hounds is nearly the same, making due allowance for size. Cleanliness is the great virtue to be practised, and without it no hound can be preserved in health, and in perfection of nose. It will be remembered that, for the purposes of the general pack, their lodging-rooms are devoted according to the plan of kennel at page 100. One of these (A 5) has been empty all night, and should have been washed out and have had time to dry by morning. Into this the general pack should be turned the first thing in the morning, after giving them an airing in the grass-yard, if dry, or under the verandah, if in wet weather. The feeder should then sweep out their lodging-room (A 1), and after doing so he should mop it out well, leaving it quite sweet and clean, taking care afterwards to dry it as much as possible. This will be ready for the hounds again by eleven o'clock, when, in the usual way, they may be returned to it, after feeding and exercise. A 5 may then be roughly swept, but not washed; and then, after just walking them into the yard, the hunting pack may be turned into it while their lodging-room (A 2) is being swept and washed out. They will remain there an hour or two, and then should be taken out for half-an-hour or an hour, according to the work they are doing, when they may be brought home, fed, and returned to their regular lodging-room (A 2). This again leaves A 5 empty, and it may be thoroughly cleansed at any time when the feeder has leisure. Thus, the hounds are never turned into wet kennels, and consequently are not subjected to the chances of rheumatism. With regard to the hour of feeding, it should, as a general rule, be about eleven o'clock for the general pack, and from one to two for the hunting pack, according to the time of meeting and the distance they have to travel. By giving two hours between the feeding times of the two packs, the duties of the feeder are lightened, and he has time to exercise and feed the former on hunting days without help. In many kennels it is the practice to give a little broth or thin gruel to hounds at night; but even in the case of delicate hounds I do not think it of much use. Some certainly are so delicate that they can scarcely be fed too often; but these

are exceptions, and they should be treated as such. Water should always be within reach, and raised above the height of the belly of the dogs, or it will be soiled by their urine. It is best in iron troughs, one of which should be in each sleeping-room and court-yard. In summer the doors and windows of all the rooms may be left open, and access to the yards admitted night and day; but in severe weather the doors must be shut, and ventilation only carried on by the tops of the windows, and by the air-flue communicating with the chimney of the feeder's room. The food should be principally of flesh and meal, with an occasional mixture of vegetables. The flesh is always that of the horse, to save expense, and should be boiled for hours in one of the iron boilers till it is ready to leave the bone. A great saving of expense is made in the long-run, by having digesters instead of open boilers; they cost about three to four pounds a-piece *untinned*, and will save the difference in prime cost in a single season. This difference is not only in the extra goodness of broth obtained from the meat and bones, which is, however, at least 15 or 20 per cent., but also in the fire, which need not be above half what is required for the open boiler. If the digester is used, it should be set like a boiler; and it is a very good plan to screw a pipe in it near the top, which can be led into the drain adjoining, by which means all the disagreeable smell given off from the stale flesh in boiling is carried into the bowels of the earth. This benefits all parties—hounds, horses, master, and men; for all are nauseated by the hot, greasy, and sickening smell of boiling stale meat. The flesh having been thoroughly boiled, may be withdrawn by a pitchfork, and set to cool under the shed of the flesh-house, or in the boiling-house, if the weather is not too warm; then taking out one-third, or thereabouts, of the broth, pour it into the other boiler, and fill up with water till nearly half-full, in which condition the other is left. Both may then be thickened with meal, which should be oatmeal chiefly, but mixed with coarse wheaten-flour, or Indian-meal, or barley-meal, according to the fancy of the master. The first I believe to be the best and strongest for giving the power of standing work; the second very nearly, or quite as good; and the third only fit to fill hounds' bellies, without benefitting them in any other way. Indian-meal and barley-meal are usually about the same price; but the former is ten times as good, and has the valuable property of bearing a much greater amount of boiling than the oatmeal, which is not the case either with wheaten-flour or barley-meal. Wheaten-flour requires about half-an-hour to boil; barley-flour, one quarter; Indian-meal, two hours; and oatmeal, about one hour, or nearly so. Hounds will generally thrive best, if hard-worked, upon equal quantities of oatmeal and wheaten or Indian-meal; one pound of the mixture being sufficient for each hound. Enough only for two days should be boiled at once; and one-half being made with better broth, the other will serve for the more delicate light-fleshed hounds. Each boiler holding, when half-full, about 80 quarts of broth, there will be required the same number of pounds of meal, which will serve 40 couple of hounds two days; if more or less, the quantities must be regulated accordingly. In many kennels, as soon as the thickened broth, or stirabout, has boiled sufficiently, the fire is drawn, and the pudding is allowed to cool in the boilers; but by far the best plan is to draw the fire, and then ladle out the stirabout into the coolers, which have been already described in the boiling-house department. Here the meal sets much more rapidly, and has not time to get sour, as it soon does in the summer. I am quite satisfied that, cooled in this way, it forms a much more wholesome, and even a more palatable food, than when suffered to grow cool in the boilers. After cooling, it forms what is called "the puddings," and is thick enough to be cut out with a spade. It may always be reduced with thin or thick broth to any quality desired for bitches, invalids, &c.; but for working-hounds it should be pretty solid. When they are to be fed, this should be broken up with the spade, and carried into the feeding-troughs, and the meat, after being thoroughly cut up small, should be incorporated with it. By some it is said, that the meat is more easily picked out of thick than thin "puddings," but this is a mistake. If they are thick enough, it is ten times more difficult for the dainty hound to pick out the bits, and he is obliged to eat all as it comes, or none. In feeding, every hound should be called by his name, commencing with the light feeders, and giving them the best "puddings" in a separate trough. The huntsman—except the general pack on hunting days—should always feed, as he is the best judge of the wants and powers of each hound. Throwing open the door of the room or court where they are, he keeps all in expectation, but not daring to cross the threshold; then, with a decided, yet encouraging tone, he calls out the name of each hound intended to share the first trough, thus: "Wanton! Racer! Wasteful!" &c., &c.; generally drawing, at first, six or seven couple. When these have filled themselves, he calls two or three couple more by name, and allows them also to get their fill with the first lot; thus often encouraging the first to take a little extra food through jealousy of the second. When these have also fed they are all sent back, and the third lot, consisting of all the remainder of the hunting hounds, except a few very gross feeders, are admitted. These are allowed to fill themselves as far as the huntsman thinks proper, ordering each off as he has had what his feeder thinks right. Then, lastly, the same kind of process is repeated with the general pack of lame and non-hunting hounds, and the gross feeders, which are admitted either in lots of eight or ten couple, or altogether, according to the fancy of the huntsman; but all called by name, and ordered off in the same way. This last feature is of great importance, as it uses hounds to attend when their names are called in the field, and the slightest word then serves to call their attention to their master's rate. Once a-week in the winter, usually on Sundays, some greens, potatoes, or turnips, are boiled and mixed up with the food, and serve to keep the hounds cool and in good general health. In the hunting season, about from a quarter to half-a-pound of flesh per hound per day is sufficient, and many use even less; this is the average, but some take more, some less. The oatmeal should be at least one year old; and the Scotch meal is much better and goes farther than the English. Wheaten and Indian meal need not be so old. In summer the feeding may be conducted on a very different plan, and the hounds are better divided into a dog and bitch pack, whether such is the hunting division or not. One of the best and most

cooling kinds of food is, then, the lowest stomach or paunch of the cow, full of grass half-digested. These should be thrown on the grass raw, and the hounds soon tear them to rags and devour them. Properly, each paunch should be given to about six couple of hounds by themselves, but few huntsmen care to take this trouble. This food will suffice for three days a-week, given in the morning; and on the same evening, which is the best time for feeding, some cabbages, or turnips, or potatoes should be given boiled in broth. On the intermediate days thin porridge, not "puddings," may be given, being weak broth thickened with Indian-meal, as the cheapest, or oatmeal, or a mixture of each. Little or no flesh should now be allowed, as the hounds have nothing but walking exercise, and do not gallop about like greyhounds. They should be fed so as to look healthy and bright, but still not so as to be round and fat to the extent of concealing their ribs. I know no food which keeps hounds so bright and healthy as the butcher's paunches; and they may be obtained at a very low rate in the neighbourhood of a town of any size. The half-digested grass is a capital alterative, and there is also considerable nourishment in it. Hounds are very fond of it, and prefer it to any food you can give them; and nature seems to point it out to them in the summer, for they are then always looking out for grass and garbage. Very little physic is required, as a rule, but a dose of Epsom salts or castor-oil now and then does no harm. If worms are present, or other disease, treat according to directions given under the chapters on the Diseases of Dogs.

CHAP. II

STAG-HUNTING.

SECT. 1.—HUNTING THE CARTED-DEER.

310. Stag-hunting may be divided into two grand sections—1st, hunting the carted-deer; and 2nd, hunting the deer in its wild state. The former is confined to the red deer and the fallow deer; the latter to the red deer and roebuck. In describing stag-hunting, I shall assume that the pack is a perfect one, because there are no rules for making it so, and I have no personal knowledge on the subject; besides, it is so rare a sport, that few of my readers are likely to want this knowledge.

311. IN HUNTING THE CARTED-DEER, besides the pack of staghounds already sufficiently described, and usually consisting of from 18 to 20 couple, and, besides the master, huntsman, and whips, there is also employed a cart or small caravan, to convey the deer to the meet. This is drawn by one or two horses, and it is accompanied by two or three yeomen-prickers, or, as they are called in some hunts, "verderers." One of these drives, and the others release the deer and prick him on, and when taken, hobble him and replace him in the cart. It often happens that the same deer is hunted from twelve to twenty times in the season, and at last becomes so used to the gallop as to show little fear of the hounds. One peculiarity of the staghound is his great tractability, in which he far excels the foxhound and bloodhound, and is, in fact, selected, in great measure, for this virtue; for if the whips are unable to stop the hounds when the deer is at bay, the

animal's life is sacrificed, and much future sport, if sport it can be called, is put an end to. All these officials, with the deer, being assembled at the spot appointed for the meet, which is generally a common, in order to allow the deer to get well on his feet before he arrives at the enclosed country, the deer is uncarted, and, with a great parade of whip-smacking and horn-blowing, is turned off into the open country.

312. THE DEER, which ought to be, and usually is the red deer, male or female, has been some time before deprived of his horns, if a male, and also trained by compelling him to gallop round his enclosure for a considerable time each day. In most hunts three or four, or sometimes five or six brace of these deer are turned into a large paddock, surrounded by a high fence, and they are daily driven round and round at a moderate pace by men on horseback, or muzzled hounds, or sometimes by hounds trained like sheep-collies, to bark without biting. Without this training they would be wholly unable to stand ten minutes before the hounds, but would be blown at once, because they are highly fed in order to get them into good condition, and would become internally fat, if this food was allowed to be converted into that material so unsuited to produce good wind. Any hounds will hunt deer naturally, and are peculiarly fond of the scent; and therefore it is only when carted-deer are to be turned out and preserved from the fangs of their assailants, that the highly-broken stag-hound is so necessary. Sometimes the hind is used, and many of this sex have afforded as good sport as their lords and masters. In this case there are no horns to be removed; but in the latter part of the season they are so much disposed to lay on fat, that they require a great deal of work to keep them in good training. The cart accompanies the progress of the hunt as nearly as may be, and the yeomen-prickers ought to be in attendance at the place where the deer is at bay, to hobble him. The hobbles are leather straps, which are buckled round the hind fetlocks, and are then drawn up on each side of his shoulders to a loop of rope thrown over the neck, and so secured. When the fallow deer is used as a substitute for the red deer, his horns also are removed, and he is trained in the same way; but this species has neither the boldness nor the speed of the red deer, and does not consequently afford anything like the same amount of sport. Formerly, hounds were kept to hunt the fallow deer, called buckhounds—a smaller kind of staghound, but they are now wholly out of fashion, and I am not aware that any such pack is maintained in Great Britain at this present time.

313. AFTER THE ENLARGEMENT OF THE DEER, FROM FIVE TO TEN MINUTES' LAW is usually allowed before the hounds are laid on; during this time the deer has been driven away, selecting, as far as possible, the desired direction, and arousing his fears by whip-smacking, hallooing, and horn-blowing. Sometimes great difficulty is experienced in getting the deer to go straight away, and he runs the roads, instead of taking to the open country. It is always the best plan to send one or two mounted-men to start him off, and these, in the Royal Hunt, are termed yeomen-prickers. Occasionally, however, a good and bold deer takes a line, and goes straight away without dwelling a moment; and such deer have even escaped into the forest, and been lost for some time. Often they will stand before the staghounds, fast as they are, for two hours, or even two hours and-a-half; and instances have been known of runs lasting three hours without a check. This long period of time would require at least 40 or 50 miles to be traversed, and such a distance has really been accomplished on some memorable occasions; one of which is recorded by Johnson, in his "Sportsman's Dictionary," as having taken place in 1796. The stratagems of the stag are sometimes very curious; he has been known to enter the bed of a rivulet, and run for some considerable distance *up the stream;* then, leaving its banks, he has again pursued his way, and as the scent has been carried by the water many yards below the point where he left the banks, it does not correspond with the actual line of the stag. This is a very puzzling affair, as a cast is necessitated, and nothing but great experience in the ways of deer will enable the huntsman to make it in the right direction. When hounds, therefore, suddenly throw up at a brook, and cannot carry the scent beyond it, the huntsman at once guesses either that the deer has "taken soil," or that the above manœuvre has been practised. If, however, the former is not found to be the case, which the eye soon detects by examining the brook, he has only to cast widely enough forwards, remembering that the deer is almost certain to take up stream, and he, most probably, hits off the scent. Deer are also very fond of running through sheep, and nothing foils the hounds so much as a flock of these animals. Here, again, a cast is required, and the huntsman's experienced eye must enable him, if possible, to guess in which direction to make it; but as the deer has been reared in a pack, and has no knowledge of the country he is traversing, this is often a matter of pure speculation.

314. CASTS ARE EFFECTED AS FOLLOWS :— When the huntsman perceives that the hounds are at fault, and have thrown up their heads, being unable to hit off the scent, he gives a note or two on his horn, by which the hounds are gathered at his heels, and "lifts them" clear of the sheep, brook, or small covert, or whatever else may be the cause of "the check." Then, making up his mind what is the most likely direction for the hunted deer to have taken, he trots off with his hounds so as to cross that line at some hundred yards off from the original scene of the check. Here, if his surmise is correct, the hounds at once hit off the scent; and if they fail to do so, he proceeds to cast his hounds in another direction, only giving up all hope when he has tried every possible plan of proceeding, and has failed in all.

315. THE TAKE OF THE STAG is the wind-up of the royal sport, and is effected wherever the animal is standing at bay before the hounds. He usually "takes soil," that is, enters a pond or river, and there, with his back against a high bank, or some similar defensive position, he awaits his assailants. It is always necessary in stag-hunting that the huntsman or whipper-in should be with the hounds, because, though from long custom they are so polite as to waive their title to a slice of the haunch, yet nature will prevail sometimes over education, and the deer, unprotected as he is by the defensive armour which his horns would be to him if not removed, must not be left undefended also by his former assailants—but now guardians—the huntsman and whips. These officials immediately whip off the hounds, and await the arrival of the verderers or yeomen-prickers, whose task it is to hobble the deer. The hounds are thus never blooded, which may account for their tractability, and their refraining from fastening upon the stag when first running into him at bay. The chief packs are at this time (1855)—Her Majesty's, the Cheltenham, Baron Rothschild's, and Mr. Petre's, in England; and the Ward Union in Ireland.

316. THE EXPENSES OF A PACK OF STAG-HOUNDS vary immensely, from the enormous outlay of the Queen's Pack to that bestowed upon the Cheltenham Staghounds, which have been at times supported upon little more than £900 a-year. Few staghounds meet more than twice a-week, and consequently one pack and a double set of horses are all that are required. Setting aside, therefore, the master's personal expenses in horses, &c., the necessary outlay will be as follows, calculated on the most economical scale :—

EXPENSES OF STAGHOUNDS, PER ANNUM.

	£ s.	£
Huntsman and clothes. . . .	100 0	
First whip, ditto	70 0	
Second ditto ditto	55 0	
Feeder and verderer in one . .	30 0	
Taxes on servants	4 0	
		259
Feeding 25 couple of hounds, at 1s. 6d. a-week each	195 0	
Medicines, dressings, &c. . . .	5 0	
Tax on ditto	30 0	
		230
Six horses, for six months, at 15s. per week	108 0	
Ditto ditto summering, at 7s. .	54 12	
Shoeing	16 0	
Veterinary surgeon	6 0	
Saddler	15 0	
Tax on horses	6 0	
Helper in stable, at 12s. per week, for six months . . .	14 8	
		220
Allowance for keep of deer, accidents, &c.		91
Total		£800

SECT. 2.—HUNTING THE WILD RED DEER, OR ROEBUCK.

317. This is a very different affair from the pursuit of the carted-stag, but it is now almost unknown as a regular sport. Her Majesty's staghounds still hunt the wild deer, for a week or ten days, in the New Forest; and, until very recently, the Devon and Somerset staghounds had usually some good days on the Quantock Hills in Somersetshire, and in the Forests of Exmoor and Dartmoor. Now, however, I believe they are obliged to abandon their much-prized sport for want of the deer, which have become gradually exterminated by the encroachments of cultivation and the aid of poachers. Killarney, in Ireland, still boasts of her occasional days of sport, the gaps being filled up by the hunting of the carted-deer. It is useless to describe the hunting of the roebuck, because, as far as I know, no established pack is used for the pursuit of this wild and beautiful little variety of the deer. Whenever it is hunted, it is when it has been seen or heard of in the neighbourhood of any of the Scotch packs of harriers, and then it affords often a very good day's sport. No particular laws or rules can be laid down, as its being hunted is only an exceptional case.

318. THE FINDING THE WILD DEER is the point of difference between the two modes of stag-hunting; for here the animal is "harboured" in some secure retreat, instead of in his cart. Certain men, called "harbourers," with hounds trained for the

purpose, called "tufters," undertake the task, and proceed into the forest for the purpose, the regular pack being held at hand by the huntsman and whips, ready to be laid on when the hart or hind is "unharboured." The harbourers being always in the forest, know the haunts of the deer, and can generally tell pretty nearly where to find them. By walking round any coppice supposed to harbour a hart or hind, they ascertain by the "slot," or tread, and by the "fewment," or dung, whether the animal is in season, and of a proper age for hunting; that is to say, whether his age is such as to make him "warrantable,"—a term already explained at page 87, as meaning six years of age. The hounds also, by their tongues, indicate the sex and the presence, if any, of a calf with the hind; and if so, they refuse to hunt, knowing, by previous experience, that these are unsuited to their master's purpose.

319. CERTAIN PERIODS ARE FIXED for hunting wild red deer; being, for the warrantable hart, from the 20th of August to the 31st of September, both inclusive; after which he is so weak from rutting, as to be unfit for sport. The hind is then hunted for a short season; and in the spring again, from the 10th of April to the 20th of May, old barren hinds, warrantable as such, are hunted, and afford good sport. Thus, wild stag-hunting has a very short season, and three months out of the twelve is the utmost extent to which it can be strained. It is, therefore, no wonder even if wild deer could be found, that the park-fed and trained-deer should be used to fill up this gap; and these are almost always hinds,

the stags being out of season after their rutting; though sometimes they keep their condition in the paddock, and are able to stand a run as well, or even better, than in their autumnal state.

320. THESE WILD DEER ARE HUNTED exactly in the same way as the carteddeer, but the hounds getting blood, they run much more fiercely, and with more resemblance to the dash of foxhounds. The huntsman must still keep well with his hounds; not as before, to save the deer, but rather to assist the hounds when the deer is at bay, and to save them from his horns, which are dangerous weapons of defence. Sometimes, however, a deer is saved from the hounds, because of their scarcity; but the rule is for the huntsman to go in as soon as he can, or dare, and cut the deer's throat with his knife while he is engaged with the baying of the hounds; the latter are allowed to lap his blood, which they do eagerly, and then he is "gralloched," and his entrails distributed to them. After this the carcase becomes venison, and is carried home on the harbourer's pony, to be treasured as a special dainty.

321. THE EXPENSES OF THIS KIND OF SPORT do not much vary from those given at par. 316, as applying to the carted-deer; the varying margin being that devoted to fees to harbourers, &c., &c., which cannot be estimated. I have, however, heard that the Devon and Somerset hounds were kept, all expenses included, for about from £1,000 to £1,200; which, considering that they rarely had a dozen days' sport in the year, is indeed paying dear in proportion to its amount.

CHAP. III.

FOX-HUNTING.

SECT. 1.—GENERAL REMARKS.

322. THE NOBLE SCIENCE, as fox-hunting is called by its votaries, is, by common consent, allowed to be the perfection of hunting. The animal hunted is just fast enough for the purpose, and is also full of all kinds of devices for misleading his pursuers. He leaves a good scent, is very stout, and is found in sufficient abundance to afford a reasonable chance of sport. It would, therefore, be consistent with the importance and dignity of fox-hunting to have placed it above stag-hunting, in the consideration of the varieties of hunting; but in order to avoid disconnecting staghunting from deer-stalking, the former has

been placed in a more prominent situation than it deserves, unless the size of the animal hunted is to be taken as a guide to the value and importance of the hunt. In this point of view it would certainly rank much higher than fox-hunting; but in every other it sinks immeasurably lower. Still there are certain advantages attendant upon the one which the other does not enjoy; for example, the followers of the stag may allege that they can always be sure of a gallop within certain hours, and can therefore calculate on being in their places, either of business or pleasure, by a certain hour. Thus, members of either the House of Lords or Commons may hunt with Her

Majesty's staghounds, and yet be in town in time for their duties at the palace of Westminster. These considerations, and these alone, appear to keep up the expensive establishment at Ascot Heath.

SECT. 2.—LAWS OF FOX-HUNTING.

323. These laws are very difficult to get at, because they are not recorded in any written code of rules, but are retained in the traditional records belonging to the families of the various masters of foxhounds. Certain countries have long been held by certain families, from father to son, and any attempt to encroach upon them would be resisted by all parties concerned, with as much force as if the title-deeds to their estates were themselves endangered. Long disputes and violent controversies have estranged the masters of neighbouring packs from each other; but, nevertheless, no step has been taken to avoid a recurrence of these unpleasant fracas, by the framing of written rules, to which an appeal could be made. Objections are doubtless easily produced at the onset to any such course; for it would be rather a dangerous proceeding, perhaps, to admit *on paper* that A has a right to draw B's coverts whenever it suits him. It may be all very well to *suffer* it as a habit or custom between gentlemen; but to admit it as the preliminary section of an established law would do away with the liberty of the subject. At present A has the right (recognised among gentlemen) of drawing B's coverts during the time not objected to by him; but more than that would be conceded, if B admitted the force of a law by which he would allow to A the right of entering for the purpose of drawing any of his coverts. If A conducted himself ever so obnoxiously towards B or others, there would be no means of getting rid of his presence, and he would really be more the master of the property, for sporting purposes, than B himself. B, therefore, virtually says—"As long as you continue to hunt this country to the satisfaction of the hunt, including myself, you may draw my coverts, and, at all events, until I give you notice to the contrary." And such is really the understanding everywhere, though much more strong in self-supporting hunts than in subscription ones. The law of the land says, that before a trespass with hounds can be committed, due notice must be given of the action which will in that case be brought; and this notice can at any time be served upon the master of hounds who is obnoxious to any owner of a covert. But if a law relative to drawing had been signed by this land-owner, the power of giving notice would have been suffered to lapse, and the master would be entitled to enter and draw in spite of the real owner. This would no doubt be an evil, and is, I think, a sufficient reason for leaving fox-hunting laws as they now exist—only in the breasts of gentlemen; for while all conduct themselves as such there is not likely to be a dispute, and the presumption is, that if such a dispute has arisen, some one has outraged those other laws which gentlemen hold sacred among themselves, and which are independent of the code peculiar to fox-hunters. All land-owners, therefore, individually, can spoil sport; and many cases of such selfish proceedings do occur, though not so often as might be expected from the feeling which game-preservers have that fox-hunting is injurious to their interests. In spite of this feeling, such is the general impression in favour of fox-hunting, that even the coverts most strictly preserved for the purpose of the *battue* are open to the foxhounds whenever the master pleases. No one can dispute that the disturbance of the game is then very great, and that many pheasants are driven by the noise, &c., out of bounds and lost for ever to the owner of that preserve; but, nevertheless, all is borne with good temper, and the interests of the select few are made to bow to those of the many who compose the hunt. A more unselfish and praiseworthy act can scarcely be quoted, than that of the pheasant-shooter giving up his most cherished preserve to the use of a sport in which neither he nor any of his perhaps partakes. Fox-hunters are certainly rather *exigeant* in their demands when they require this concession as a public right, but custom has sanctioned it, and the refusal is now considered the act of a churl. But though this permission is a great boon, a greater one still is generally practised by the very same individuals—namely, the actual preservation, or rather the breeding and rearing of foxes for the express purpose of affording sport to others, but annoyance to themselves; and this also fox-hunters seem to claim as a right, and complain if it is not acted up to; but if the reverse is the case, if not only is there no permission to hunt, and no preservation of foxes, but in addition, if a stray fox is trapped, then maledictions are heaped upon the head of the offender in language more strong than elegant; and no punishment which could be devised would be thought too strong. But is this in conformity with the fair spirit of gentlemanly feeling which ought to exist? I can hardly think so; I honour most highly the fox-preserving pheasant-shooter, but I confess that I absolve from actual blame him who *openly* professes to forbid his presence on his property. The

man of all others, however, who is to be despised and discountenanced is that one—too common, to my knowledge—who professes to preserve, and is always ready and pressing with his invitations to the master, and yet only disappoints him with a tame fox or a bagman; the former being fed up to his throat with rabbits and poultry, and the latter just shaken out before the hounds. These covert-owners, therefore, must be allowed to have the power of doing what they like with their own, by the law of the land as well as the law of fox-hunting; but, by the universal consent of gentlemen, it is settled that while they have this *negative* right of withholding their coverts from the master of the hunt in which their property is situated, they have no *positive* power of inviting a strange master to enter and draw. This is a very wholesome rule, because it prevents one gentleman from annoying his neighbour by bringing an extra pack of hounds into the district, and thus being an extra source of damage as well as of rival-claims. This rule, however, is only in operation as to coverts which have been habitually drawn, and are included within the limits of hunting countries actually in existence; and it is admitted, that if a covert is not drawn by a pack of hounds for a certain number of years, which is variously stated to be five and seven, that the proprietor has a right to hand it over to another and adjacent hunt. If this be done, and no reclamation takes place immediately, supposing that no draw has been made during the last seven years, then the covert becomes definitively attached to the new hunt, and no law of fox-hunting allows its disseverance. These are the only really recognised laws among fox-hunters; for all mutual agreements between neighbouring hunt-clubs or masters are not laws, but simply temporary agreements, revocable at will. I know of no law which can be considered as such, other than those I have already stated. The agreements are as to stopping each other's adjacent earths, in case of drawing coverts on the borders of the respective countries; and these being mutually beneficial, are acted upon on all occasions; because, otherwise, every border-fox would escape by running to the nearest earths in the next country, and, consequently, all coverts but the central ones would be quite useless. No one disputes the law, which is universally acted on, that a hunted fox may be followed into another hunt; and it is better for the hounds to do so than to whip off while the scent is good, and there is any probable chance of blood; but if the scent is bad, no sportsman would think of risking unpleasant reflections by casting his hounds, or otherwise assisting

them. This would lead to an imputation of an attempt to find a fresh fox, and should be cautiously avoided. Such are the laws and customs relating to this noble sport; and nothing shows the general high estimation in which it is held more than the universal concession of private convenience to its purposes.

324. THE FOLLOWING IMPORTANT DECISION has lately been given, by two of our highest authorities on the laws of fox-hunting countries. It referred to a dispute which had existed for a long time between the Essex and Herts Hunts, with respect to the right to draw a particular covert, viz., Takeley Forest. A committee was formed to collect evidence, and conduct the case before the arbitrators, Lords Yarborough and Redesdale, who have given the following award, which is a lucid and searching exposition of the merits of the respective claims, and deserves to be placed amongst the archives of fox-hunting law, as establishing clear and fundamental principles with regard to the difficult subject of neutral coverts:— "1. Immemorial usage is the common title to a fox-hunting country. When the date of the commencement of such usage is known, the right to it will depend on the manner in which it commenced. 2. In the case referred to us, satisfactory proof is given that the forest has been drawn by both hunts as long as any living man can remember. The evidence of the Calvert family, as to its belonging exclusively to the Herts Hunt, can only be received as a record of their opinion. At the time when the statement was made the Essex were drawing it, as well as before and since; and in making the statement, Mr. Calvert does not say that they did so by permission asked and granted, or give the date and particulars of any agreement on the subject. 3. There is a wide difference between permission and sufferance, as regards a title to a fox-hunting country. No term of years will bar an original right of the liberty to draw, commenced on permission granted conditionally, with a power to resume. An encroachment may be neglected for a time, and, nevertheless, afterwards properly and successfully resisted, if satisfactory proof can be given that it was an encroachment and an innovation on former practice between the hunts. But a practice claimed as a right by one hunt, and suffered to be exercised by the other for a period of sixty years and more, when all evidence as to the time and manner in which it originally commenced is lost, must be held to establish that right, or a door would be opened for endless disputes as to boundaries. 4. The fact of the forest having been drawn by the Essex

is admitted, and a reason assigned for its never having been formally objected to—viz., that it was a great nursery and preserve of foxes, and then so strong and impracticable a woodland, that there was no getting a fox away, and no chance of a run from it; and that, as it was necessary for the sport of both counties that it should be routed as much as possible, 'the Herts were glad to see the Essex go there, and do the disagreeable work, and therefore no objection was taken to their doing so.' This is a very important admission. It is seldom that so clear a reason can be assigned in the origin of a neutral draw, as the case of a woodland, to which no one was very anxious to go, but which it was the interest of both hunts to have regularly disturbed. 5. The neutral districts so established between the hunts, extended beyond the forest, and disputes arose. In 1812, an arrangement was come to between the masters of the hunts, which the Herts rely on as establishing their exclusive right to the forest, because it is not mentioned among the neutral coverts. The answer of the Essex is, that it is not mentioned because there never was a doubt as to its neutrality, and that the dispute was only as to certain woods outside. In support of this they prove that the forest was regularly drawn by them afterwards. The Herts reply that this was done because Mr. Houblon, the chief proprietor there, became joint-master of the Essex, and asked permission to draw it from Mr. Hanbury, the master of the Herts; and a copy of a letter from Mr. Hanbury to Mr. Houblon is produced, in which he says that he understands that the latter wishes to draw 'some more coverts' as neutral, and that though he was not himself an advocate for a neutral country, he and Mr. Calvert had every wish, on Mr. Houblon's account, to accommodate him, and would meet him and ascertain his wishes. What these were is not known—the words 'some more coverts' could hardly apply to the forest, nor is there any proof given that they did apply, or that any extension of the neutral country then took place. On the contrary, from the care Mr. Hanbury and Mr. Calvert bestowed on these matters, it is hardly possible that, if anything was done, no written memorandum should have been kept; and the probability is that, on discussing the matter, the objections of Mr. Hanbury to extend the neutral country were found insurmountable, notwithstanding his desire to accommodate Mr. Houblon. 6. The forest continued to be drawn by the Essex till 1832, when Lord Petre took the Herts hounds, and 'claimed an exclusive right to the forest and the other coverts, and asked for a reference.' A meeting took place, and the result was that there was no reference, and that Mr. Conyers was not dispossessed. Again, in 1838, Mr. Houblon, the owner of the forest, became master of the same hounds, and desired 'to have the forest drawn on certain defined conditions, or a reference;' but Mr. Conyers still kept his old ground. It is clear that if Mr. Houblon's father had only got leave to draw the forest conditionally from Mr. Hanbury, in 1812, there must have been positive evidence of that fact in 1832, as it must have been known to many. It is asserted, that in 1832 the claim was only waived during Mr. Conyer's life, but, as in 1838, the owner of the forest, then master of the Herts hounds, asked to have the arrangements respecting that draw 'defined, or a reference,' it is clear that no abandonment of the Essex claim of right took place in 1832; while Mr. Houblon's demand negatives the idea of any agreement having been then entered into by the Herts to abstain from making a claim only during Mr. Conyer's life. 7. The reference asked for on these two occasions has now been brought before us, and, after having given our best consideration to the subject, we are of opinion that, according to fox-hunting laws, the forest does not belong exclusively to either hunt, but must be considered neutral, for the reason assigned in the third and fourth paragraphs.—YARBOROUGH, REDESDALE.—*Nov.* 19, 1854."

SECT. 3.—FOX-HUNTING COUNTRIES.

325. The different fox-hunting countries are classed under two heads—crack countries and provincials. This is a curious line to draw, as if either were a metropolis, as opposed to a province. It is true that the grass-countries of Leicestershire, with parts of Nottinghamshire and Lincolnshire, are, as it were, one centre of hunting, and, even geographically speaking, of England; but, nevertheless, for one province to call others provincial, is like the Chinese calling all other nations barbarians. One thing is clear, that the grass-countries have a great advantage over all others in holding a scent, and enabling hounds to go their best pace with a middling one, as they often do. Any hounds can race with a blazing scent in any country, but for one good scenting-run in an arable country there are six over grass. Horses also can live through a much longer and faster burst on sound turf than on arable land, however well drained; and the ridges and furrows alone, without the extra depth and stickiness of soil, will make all the difference. Many horses can carry weight

above ground which would die away at once in dirt, and, consequently it is as easy to be carried up to fast hounds in Leicestershire, as up to slow ones in deep arable countries. Good fences are required in grass-countries, because the grazing of cattle always necessitates a strong fence; and that which will keep an ox in his pasture, requires a good made-hunter to get over it; but as the taking off is sound and springy, the horse has a better chance of doing his jump well, and clearing the fence without touching it; and this is a very important feature in grass-countries. Again, as the land in these districts is very valuable, it is seldom planted to any greater extent than for game-preserving purposes; and the only coverts where foxes can hang are those narrow belts which are formed for the *battue*, or the spinnies, and gorse-coverts, expressly made for his own convenience. Hence, the obstructions which large woodlands present are not offered in the crack countries, at least not in the crack portions of them, and hounds can have fair scope for their powers. No wonder, therefore, that they often burst a fox in twenty or thirty minutes; and that a run lasting more than an hour gets the reputation either of being after a wonderful fox, or of being wonderfully slow in itself. The excitement in these "bursts" is very extraordinary; men are as jealous of success in getting forward here as in the army, the forum, or the bar; and perhaps, as the blood of its votaries is generally younger, the contest is to the same extent hotter and more ungovernable. Neither accident nor illness will cause a man to remain with his friend, and "*sauve qui peut*" is the order of the day. It is truly a glorious sight to see two or three hundred of England's best men mounted on her still unrivalled horses, and racing for the lead. Glorious is the view of this the most beautiful cavalry in the world, while waiting at the covert-side; but far more glorious is the first swoop made in charging the fence which presents itself after the word is given, and "hounds are gone away," as well as the fox. Crash goes everything if not easily cleared, and horses and men make light of ox-fences, brooks, or gates, in the first frenzy of their charge. On the other hand, in arable countries the scent in the first place is comparatively bad, from the nature of the soil, varying much according to its precise kind, and the mode of its cultivation; next, the depth of the soil is too great for horses, and to a certain extent interferes with hounds; and lastly, there are almost always large woodland tracts which come even into the heart of the country, and cause checks at every few miles. Besides

these obstacles, every plough at work affects, more or less, the line of the fox, and therefore straight runs are the exceptions; while the short, sharp, and decisive bursts of twenty or thirty minutes' duration are almost unknown. Much lifting and quick casting are here constantly required, if a fox is to be killed in the modern and fashionable style; and if a hound has nose enough to work out a scent through all the intricacies of small and large coverts, constantly-repeated small flocks of sheep, chasing of sheep-dogs, &c., he will be so slow as to be ridden over by the field, in their impatience. Either, therefore, the modern system requires, and must receive, attention, or the arable (provincial) countries must be gradually extinguished. From this there is no appeal, and one horn, or other of the dilemma must be encountered. It is no wonder, therefore, that the crack grass-countries look down with contempt upon the worst arable ones; but there are some, not included in the grazing countries, which afford as good runs as can be met with anywhere. Such are some parts of the Beaufort hunt; great part of the Oxfordshire country, some part of which is grazing Land, it is true; the Heythrop, including the beautiful slopes of the Cotswold Hills; Mr. Farquharson's, in Dorsetshire; the York and Ainsty and the Holderness, in Yorkshire; and the Vale of White Horse, now hunted by Lord Gifford. Still, if a good sportsman *had his choice*, he would settle himself in one of the crack countries; and, as he would then be able to command several packs, he would enjoy hunting in all its glory. This, however, requires a good stable of horses, because to be badly mounted there argues and necessitates the loss of a good place in the field. If all are equally badly off, good horsemanship may shove a bad horse into a good place; but when in a large field, every position is filled by a good man on a good horse, it is idle for even a good workman to appear on a sorry and inferior hunter; he had far better be contented with a slower country, and settle himself where an occasional check will give him the chance of seeing the hounds between the find and the worry. Less than this is not *hunting*; for mere riding to hounds I hold to be anything but that amusement. If the working of hounds is not seen and watched, and admired when good, or blamed and criticised when defective, no one can really be said to participate in the sport of hunting the fox. He may ride as well as a rough-rider, and as boldly as the Light Division at Balaclava, but he knows nothing of hunting as a science, and should not flatter himself that he is anything more than a good horseman, with, perhaps, a good eye for country.

I

Sect. 4.—The Preservation of Foxes.

326. This being the primary and most essential part of fox-hunting, is necessarily the first thing for a master to attend to. Hounds may be bought even at a month's notice; horses may soon be got together if a cheque is only written for their value (real or supposed); but foxes *must* be bred, if sport is to be shown. Any number may be turned down in the autumn, but they will either be shot or trapped if the keepers are not otherwise ordered; or, if allowed by them to escape, and living till they are found by the hounds, being in a strange district, instead of making good their point they will be running circles like hares. The general and, if possible, the ready consent of the owners of coverts being obtained, they should all be requested to see that their keepers do their duty; but the keepers themselves should also be engaged in the cause by certain promises of reward for every *good* find. They should specially be informed that wild foxes only will be paid for, and that if the evidence is strong of the fox found being a bagman, they will be mulcted of their *honorarium.* An additional present for a good run will never be thrown away, as these gentlemen have more in their power than is generally known. These arrangements in subscription-packs are usually left to the committee, and perhaps properly so, because the disputes with keepers are better kept out of the master's hands. Whenever the foxes are short in numbers, cubs must be obtained in the summer, or vixens turned down in the spring. There are in a great many hunts certain localities unfitted for this sport, and yet in which foxes are very apt to breed. Here the cubs may with propriety be dug out and turned down in some more favoured spot, as, for instance, in a gorse-covert in the middle of a good open country. Great numbers of French foxes and cubs are introduced every year into this country, but they are unfitted for hunting, and the best by far are the Scotch foxes from non-hunting districts, if these can with certainty be obtained. Of course every fox-dealer will account for the possession of his cubs, if requested to do so; but too often no questions are asked or answers given, and the fox or cubs are thankfully paid for from whatever quarter they have been obtained. Bad as this system is, it is so general that one act neutralizes another, and the fox-stealer only takes the trouble off the hands of the whips or earth-stoppers, who would have to look out for woodland cubs, if they were not taken possession of for the purpose of sale in another and perhaps adjacent country. The cubs, when turned down, require careful feeding for some time, and seldom can take care of themselves until the end of September or the beginning of October. No master can calculate upon more than one half of his cubs turning up at the beginning of the season, the others not escaping the chances of death and imprisonment which the fox-dealer, the small farmer, and the badly instructed keeper are constantly endeavouring to compass.

Sect. 5.—The Number of Packs kept.

327. At this time nearly 100 packs of fox-hounds are kept in England and Wales, exclusive of a considerable number in Scotland and Ireland. Each of these packs costs, on an average, about £1,500 a-year, some being three times as costly, and others again not costing half that sum. In England, therefore, a yearly expenditure of at least £150,000 may be calculated on as the cost of the establishments alone, while, if to this is added the additional cost of hunters to mount "the field" attending each hunt, the whole outlay cannot be less than five or six hundred thousand pounds. In a national point of view, therefore, as supporting the breed of horses calculated for war purposes, this sport should be encouraged; and not only as keeping up a good supply of these useful animals, but also as keeping up to a high standard of health, the courage or pluck, and bodily constitutions of the men who ride them. Many obstacles are now interfering with these establishments—low rents of landlords, bad times for farmers (latterly never pleaded), the increase of railways, and the yearly progress of the plough—all combine against fox-hunting, which is becoming in some districts less popular than hare-hunting. How much of this is due to its own change of management we shall, perhaps, hereafter explain; but that it is so, the lists of the two kinds of hounds sufficiently show. For my own part I care not, as far as the country is concerned, which sport is triumphant; but one or the other certainly ought to be encouraged for the sake of that country's welfare. Some countries are totally unfitted for fox-hunting, and are yet pretty well adapted for the pursuit of the hare, which takes a smaller range, and can often be well hunted on a few hundred acres. Let these, then, be reserved for her pursuit; but let the establishment be of such a character as to reflect credit upon its subscribers. Expense is not the criterion I mean; but let the hounds only be well hunted and well fed—which last is not a very expensive proceeding—and I am quite sure the number and quality of the horses kept for the purpose

of following them will be quite equal to those which would be used with an inferior pack of foxhounds, hunting a country unfitted for the display of their peculiar powers.

SECT. 6.—EXPENSES OF FOX-HUNTING.

328. Nothing varies more than the bills of various packs of foxhounds. I have seen a pack, costing little more than £700 a-year, show more sport in the same country than another subsequently established, and costing £1,400 per annum. The following may be considered as the cost of two packs—one for three days, the other for five days a-week :—

ESTIMATE FOR A PACK OF FOXHOUNDS HUNTING THREE DAYS A-WEEK.

	£	s.	£
Huntsman	100	0	
First whip	70	0	
Second whip	55	0	
Feeder	30	0	
Earthstopper, or fees to keepers	25	0	
Taxes on servants	4	0	
			284
Feeding 30 couple of hounds at 1s. 6d. per week each	234	0	
Medicines, dressings, &c.	6	0	
Taxes on ditto	36	0	
Expenses of walk, for 20 couple of young hounds	65	0	
			341
Six horses, for six months, at 15s. per week each	108	0	
Ditto ditto summering, at 7s.	54	12	
Shoeing	16	0	
Veterinary surgeon	6	0	
Saddler	15	0	
Tax on horses	6	0	
Helper in stable, at 12s. per week, for six months	14	8	
			220
Total			£845

ESTIMATE FOR A PACK OF FOXHOUNDS, HUNTING FIVE OR SIX DAYS A-WEEK.

	£	s.	£	s.
Men, as before, with the addition of second horse-man for huntsman, at £30 per annum, and extra tax on ditto			315	0
Feeding 55 couple of hounds at the same rate	429	0		
Medicines, dressings, &c.	10	0		
Taxes on ditto	66	0		
Expenses of walk, for 30 couple of young hounds	100	0		
			605	0
Carried forward,			£920	0

	£	s.	£	s.
Brought forward,			920	0
12 horses, for six months, at 15s. per week each	216	0		
Ditto ditto, summering, at 7s. a-week	109	4		
Shoeing	30	0		
Veterinary surgeon	12	0		
Saddler	20	0		
Tax on horses	12	0		
Three helpers in stable, one at 15s. and two at 12s. per week	102	18		
			502	2
Total			£1,422	2

These estimates are both exclusive of all fees to keepers and rents of coverts, &c., which vary in different countries so much, as to make it impossible to form any correct idea as to their amount.

SECT. 7.—DIFFERENT STYLES OF FOX-HUNTING.

329. Foxhunting in the eighteenth, and foxhunting in the nineteenth centuries are somewhat different pursuits; the former was truly hunting, from the time when the drag was hit off up to the end of the run, which generally lasted more than two hours. Contrast this with the speedy burst in the neighbourhood of Melton Mowbray in the present day, and one would scarcely recognise the two as being included under one head. In order that modern fox-hunters may be able to compare the old style with the modern, I will here quote Beckford's imaginary run, given in his celebrated letters; reminding my readers that this was written little more than seventy years ago, when already the old slow southern hound was being replaced by the cross with the northern hound and the greyhound. Beckford begins by recommending the *hour of sunrise* as that for the meet. How would this suit the men of the present day I wonder?

330. BECKFORD'S DESCRIPTION OF A RUN. —"Now, let your huntsman throw in his hounds as quietly as he can, and let the two whippers-in keep wide of him on either hand, so that a single hound may not escape them; let them be attentive to his halloo, and be ready to encourage or rate as that directs. He will, of course, draw up-wind, for reasons which I shall give in another place. Now, if you can keep your brother sportsmen in order, and put any discretion into them, you are in luck; they more frequently do harm than good; and, if it be possible, persuade those who wish to halloo the fox off to stand quiet under the covert-side, and on no account to halloo

him too soon; if they do, he most certainly will turn back again. Could you entice them all into the covert, your sport, in all probability, would not be the worse for it. How well the hounds spread the coverts! The huntsman is quite deserted; and his horse, who so lately had a crowd at his heels, has now not one attendant left. How steadily they draw; you hear not a single hound, yet none are idle. Is not this better than to be subject to continual disappointment, from the eternal babbling of unsteady hounds?

"‘ See! how they range
Dispersed; how busily this way and that
They cross, examining with curious nose
Each likely haunt. Hark! on the drag I hear
Their doubtful notes preluding to a cry,
More nobly full and swelled with every mouth.'
SOMERVILLE.

How musical their tongues! and as they get nearer to him how the chorus fills! Hark! he is found! Now, where are all your sorrows and your cares, ye gloomy souls? or where your pains and aches, ye complaining ones? one halloo has dispelled them all! What a crash they make! and echo seemingly takes pleasure to repeat the sound. The astonished traveller forsakes the road, lured by its melody; the listening ploughman now stops his plough, and every distant shepherd neglects his flock, and runs to see him break. What joy, what eagerness in every face! Mark how he runs the covert's utmost limits, yet dares not venture forth—the hounds are still too near! That check is lucky. Now, if our friends head him not, he will soon be off. Hark! they halloo; by G—— he's gone! Now, huntsman, get on with the head hounds; the whipper-in will bring on the others after you; keep an attentive eye on the leading hounds, that, should the scent fail them, you may know at least how far they brought it. Mind Galloper, how he leads them! It is difficult to distinguish which is first, they run in such a style; yet, he is the foremost hound; the goodness of his nose is not less excellent than his speed. How he carries the scent! and when he loses it, see how eagerly he flings to recover it again! There, now! he's at head again! See how they top the hedge! Now, how they mount the hill! Observe what a head they carry, and show me, if thou canst, one shuffler or skirter amongst them all. Are they not like a parcel of brave fellows, who, when they engage in an undertaking, determine to share its fatigues and its dangers equally among them? It was, then, the fox I saw as we came down the hill; those crows directed me which way to look, and the sheep ran from him as he passed along. The hounds are now on the very spot, yet the sheep stop them not, for the dash beyond them. Now, see with what eagerness they cross the plain! Galloper no longer keeps his place—Brusher takes it; see how he flings for the scent, and how impetuously he runs! How eagerly he took the lead, and how he strives to keep it! yet, Victor comes up a-pace; he reaches him! Observe what an excellent run it is between them; it is doubtful which will reach the covert first. How equally they run! how eagerly they strain! Now Victor! Victor! Ah, Brusher! thou art beaten, Victor first tops the hedge! See there, see how they all take it in their strokes! The hedge cracks with their weight, so many jump at once. Now hastes the whipper-in to the other side of the covert,—he is right, unless he head the fox——Listen! the hounds have turned; they are now in two parts—the fox has been headed back, and we have changed. Now, my lad, mind the huntsman's halloo, and stop to those hounds which he encourages. He is right—that, doubtless, is the hunted fox! Now, they are off again. Ha! a check. Now, for a moment's patience. We press too close upon the hounds. Huntsman, stand still; as yet they want you not. How admirably they spread! How wide they cast! Is there a single hound that does not try? If there be, never shall he hunt again. There, Trueman is on the scent: he feathers, yet still is doubtful. 'Tis right; how readily they join him! See those wide-casting hounds, how they fly forward to recover the ground they have lost! Mind Lightning, how she dashes; and Mungo, how he works! Old Frantic, too, now pushes forward; she knows as well as we the fox is sinking. Huntsman! at fault at last? How far did you bring the scent? Have the hounds made their own cast? Now make yours. You see that sheep-dog has coursed the fox. Get forward with your hounds, and make a wide cast. Hark! that halloo is indeed a lucky one. If we can hold him on, we may yet recover him; for a fox so much distressed must stop at last. We shall now see if they will hunt as well as run; for there is but little scent, and the impending cloud still makes that little less. How they enjoy the scent! See how busy they all are, and how each in his turn prevails! Huntsman, be quiet! Whilst the scent was good you pressed on your hounds: it was well done; when they came to a check you stood still, and interrupted them not. They were afterwards at fault; you made your cast with judgment, and lost no time. You now must let them hunt. With such a cold scent as this you can do no good: they must do it all themselves. Lift them now, and not a hound will stoop again.

Ha! a high-road at such a time as this, when the tenderest-nosed hound can hardly own the scent! Another fault! That man at work, there, has headed-back the fox. Huntsman, cast not your hounds now! You see they have overrun the scent: have a little patience, and let them for once try back. We must now give them time. See where they bend towards yonder furze-brake. I wish he may have stopped there. Mind that old hound how he dashed over the furze: I think he winds him! Now for a fresh *entapis!* Hark! they halloo. Aye, there he goes! It is nearly over with him; had the hounds caught view, he must have died. He will hardly reach the covert. See how they gain on him at every stroke. It is an admirable race; yet the covert saves him. Now be quiet, and he cannot escape us; we have the wind of the hounds, and cannot be better placed. How short he runs! He is now in the very strongest part of the covert. What a crash! Every hound is in, and every hound is running for him. That was a quick turn! Again another! He is put to his last shifts. Now Mischief is at his heels, and death is not far off. Ha! they all stop at once—all silent, and yet no earth is open. Listen! now they are at him again. Did you hear that hound catch view? They overran the scent, and the fox had lain down behind them. Now, Reynard, look to yourself. How quick they all give their tongues! Little Dreadnought, how he works him! The terriers, too, they now are squeaking at him. How close Vengeance pursues! how terribly she presses! It is just up with him! Gods! what a crash they make! The whole wood resounds! That turn was very short! There! now—aye, how they have him! Who—hoop!" This glowing description, except in the time fixed for the meet, is a beautiful account of what a run should be in the present day; but there is one remarkable proof contained in it, that the speed was in those days very different to what it is now. Suppose, for instance, a moderately-fast run in a grass country, and a terrier by chance started with the hounds, where would the little rascal be at the kill? Yet Beckford expressly mentions *the* terriers as squeaking at him before the kill while the hounds are running in the last covert. Now the terriers here alluded to can only be those belonging to the pack, which were formerly, indeed, part of the establishment, and which must have started with them when the fox was found. This speaks volumes its to comparative speed. I am quite sure that even in provincial countries a terrier cannot live with foxhounds of modern blood and speed; if he could, a pack of terriers would be better than foxhounds, for they can generally hunt lower than fast foxhounds. The remarkable patience and want of interference on the huntsman's part, in this account, would strike any one who is now in the habit of seeing the hounds perpetually lifted and capped to halloos,—whips sent on to points to view him, and to halloo if viewed, and all those *human* artifices rather than *canine* by which time is saved, and the fox so quickly killed. But all these artifices and pressing forward, it may be said, are now necessary, in order to get out of the way of the impatient field. Well, they may be so, and are, no doubt; but then, why should the field be allowed to be so unruly? This is the fault of the master, though of fashion also; for if this latter all-powerful motive power were to say that order in the field must be kept, no doubt the master's voice would be scarcely needed. As it is, the horsemen are vieing with each other for a good place, and are utterly regardless of the proceedings of the hounds, or of the necessity for giving them fair play.

331. THE DISADVANTAGES OF THE MODERN SCHOOL are, that hounds being so constantly taken hold of and lifted on every possible chance of doing so, they cease to persevere when in difficulties, and look to their huntsman for aid rather than to themselves and the delicacy of their noses. Hence, the evils react upon one another—first, the horsemen press upon the hounds, and, as a consequence, the hounds are obliged to be got forward out of their way; secondly, the hounds, in being thus constantly lifted for the above reason, are injured in hunting power, and cease to afford those beautiful specimens of the old-fashioned style of hunting, which will induce men, if anything will, to watch their proceedings with interest and caution, lest they should be disturbed. Nothing affords so strong an argument in favour of the old style of hunting as this double reaction of the errors of the present day; and the cautious riding of the "thistle-whippers," as they are deridingly called by the fox-hunter, is a clear proof that hunting, when carried to perfection, will always be watched with attention. Observe the same men with foxhounds and harriers: with the former, they are all alive for galloping and getting a good place—jealousy of their friends is the predominant feeling, and the hunting of the hounds is not seen, or, if seen, is not regarded; but next day the same parties attend a "thistle-whipping concern," and there they are all attention to the beautiful self-casts of the harriers or beagles, and admire as much as anybody their brilliant powers. I believe, even now, in spite of fashion, if a

master would only be firm, and, after breeding his foxhounds with a little more hunt in them, would rigidly abstain, through his huntsman, from assisting them except in extreme cases, that, in a very short time, the field would pay that attention to their efforts which they now bestow upon their horses and themselves. At all events it is worth trying the experiment in enclosed and arable countries, where it is impossible to vie with the grass countries in *pace*; but where in hunting a cold scent the hounds may display such powers as to attract attention and command respect. But even here discouragement meets the provincial master, for with the most delicate-nosed hounds he can scarcely expect that a scent will be made as much of over his fallows, as would be shown in Leicestershire by hounds not nearly such good natural hunters. None but a practical and experienced man can be a judge of these points, and such men are rare indeed in the hunting field. Nevertheless, I should much like to see the trial made, and in course of time, I cannot help fancying, that the system, if well carried out, would induce many to admire the genuine hunting of the fox under difficulties, as much, or perhaps more than the comparatively easy task of bursting one in the grass-lands of the crack countries.

CHAPTER IV.

FOX-HUNTING (*Continued*).

Sect. 1.—Pack to be Obtained at once by Purchase.

332. No one now-a-days would dream of getting together a pack of foxhounds by breeding them himself from a bitch or two, without any considerable outlay. Such a plan is impracticable, because several important elements of success must co-operate at the same time, and will not wait for one another in idleness, as—first, the country cannot lie open and unused; secondly, the huntsman, whips, &c., would have nothing to do, and yet are required for a small pack as well as a large one; and thirdly, patience will seldom last long enough, even if the other elements were so accommodating as to allow of this mode of business. All these several items must, however combine; and all *might* be kept dangling on but "the country," which will not wait; and which alone will put a stop to all dallying with such a fickle mistress. The moment, therefore, a master undertakes the important duty of "hunting a country," he must put his best leg foremost, and set about getting a pack of foxhounds in earnest. The country and the fox-preserving I have already dilated upon, and it now remains to consider how the procuring of the hounds is to be compassed in the quickest time, in the best manner, and at the most economical rate. These three items will form my guide in considering the subject in the following pages; being really those which ought to guide every prudent master throughout his career.

333. The Best Mode of Getting Together a Pack of Foxhounds, is to purchase a lot of draft-hounds from those kennels which your fancy leads you to select. In my own opinion, there is little choice in this respect; all hounds are well enough bred, and you may always succeed in getting together a good pack in a few years, from drafts obtained from any of our best kennels, if only you are careful in your subsequent breeding, kennel management, *and hunting*. I am quite satisfied, in hunting all depends upon the huntsman; and that a good man will always be able to make good tools, provided that he is not stinted in horses, meal, and whips; and has a good country with plenty of foxes. With these advantages he will readily make a good pack, but not always a good-looking one. It sometimes happens that too much attention is paid to looks, and good hounds are drafted from having coarse heads or throats, necks, &c., while neat but useless animals are prized and carefully retained. Draft-hounds may always be bought at three guineas a-couple; and one-quarter, or a third of them, will generally be serviceable for one or two seasons. The remaining two-thirds, or three-quarters, will, on trial, be consigned to a speedy death; and the result will be, that for thirty couple of tolerably useful hounds, from 200 to 250 guineas must be paid; and if this result could only be calculated on with certainty, it would be a cheap way of getting such a pack of hounds together. Unfortunately, however, it will be found that this number will be more than the average, though, with luck and some little judgment in going to work, the above has been accomplished on more than one occasion. Sometimes a good pack is to be sold; and if steady, well bred, and well-hunted, it is cheaper to give £500 for an

entire pack of forty or fifty couple, young and old, than to buy drafts at three guineas a-couple. One, two, and even three thousand guineas have been given for packs of foxhounds; but 500 guineas is the usual and average price, and more than that is only a fancy one. But supposing a draft pack is determined on, and the country is a "three days a-week" one, then you should purchase about from 80 to 100 couple, according to your luck in the first drafts you buy; but, at all events, you must persevere in your purchases until you can reckon on fifty couple of *serviceable looking* hounds—that is, hounds which have no apparent bodily defect, such as lameness, blindness, &c. For it must be remembered that in drafts there must be no picking and choosing, but the lots offered must be either taken entire or refused. Such is the custom; and as they are the huntsman's perquisite, there is great reason for this liberal mode of dealing. Well, then, having at length got together fifty couple of useful looking hounds, they must be kept on till the month of August, when cub-hunting will soon show you which can be retained, and which must be discarded as useless, from their babbling, skirting, or slack-running propensities. The head and tail must also be drafted at this time—that is, the very fast and the very slow hounds, because the beauty of a pack and their efficiency also are marred by one, two, or three leading away from all the rest, or by the same thing happening at the tail, but in an opposite direction.

Sect. 2.—Breeding.

334. This pack thus got together then, must be kept up by Breeding; and if some brood-bitches are procured in February or March, something may be done in this way during the first summer. The best months, however, are March or April for this purpose, which would require the bitch to have been put to the dog nine weeks earlier. Of course at this time the young master of hounds must be dependent upon his longer-established fellows for the sires of his whelps; but he will seldom have much difficulty here, unless he is very particular, or has a very limited hunting acquaintance. In subsequent seasons he must breed from twenty to thirty couple of whelps, if he wishes to attain anything like excellence in his pack; for out of these he will not choose to send out to walk more than half that number; or if sent, he will speedily weed them down to about from twelve to fifteen couple, which should be the young entry every year. If the bitches whelp very early, they should be allowed to have a warm place, such as a loose box or

stall in a stable which is warm enough to preserve the whelps from the effects of cold; and the young puppies should not be sent out to walk before the end of April or the beginning of May, unless the person who is to rear them is one who will take care their growth is not checked by cold.

335. The Best Blood of the Present Day is to be found in the kennels of Lord Fitzwilliam, the Duke of Beaufort, Earl Fitzhardinge, Lord Yarborough, Lord Southampton, and Mr. Drake; however, these hounds are very much of the same blood, and have been bred one with the other to a great extent. No kennel could long be maintained in all its excellence without an occasional infusion of fresh blood; and though I believe in-and-in-breeding may be practised to a certain extent with advantage, yet if persisted in without occasional fresh infusions, it will ruin the constitution of either horse or dog.

336. The Working Excellencies of the foxhound, and for which he should be selected, are—first and foremost, the dash peculiar to his breed; secondly, a good nose; thirdly, a tendency to cast forwards, and never back like the harrier; fourthly, great power of endurance of fatigue, cold, and wet; fifthly, sufficient tractability, without having too much softness; and sixthly, perfection in drawing and hunting.

337. The Defects which should especially be avoided are—first, the throwing the tongue too freely, commonly called "babbling;" secondly, mute running; thirdly, skirting, or a tendency to leave the rest of the pack, and not, as the foxhound should do, "scoring to tongue"—this is that excess of jealousy which should be avoided in the foxhound as much as it should be encouraged in the greyhound; fourthly, pottering and dwelling on the scent; fifthly, hanging in covert when hounds are gone away; sixthly, running riot; which means that the particular game which is being hunted should be adhered to, and all other considered as "riot;" thus, the fox and hare are "riot" to the staghound, while deer and hare are in the same category as regards the foxhound, and the deer and fox to the harrier. Some of these faults are easily broken by means of the whip, if necessary, or a severe rate in milder cases; and the three last only require the aid of the whipper-in, but "babbling," "mute running," and "skirting," are dependent upon a defect in breeding, which nothing will eradicate; and they also generally increase with age, so that little hope of amendment is afforded, and the rope or the river must be resorted to at once.

338. The Selection of the Individual Bitch should be very carefully made. Her

pedigree, above all, should be such as to lead you to expect good performances in the field. I should never, certainly, breed from a foxhound or harrier-bitch, however well formed, which had not shown good hunting qualities during at least two seasons; but even this recommendation would not suffice without good blood, and, in addition, shapes suited to her office. Exceptional cases of good hunting are common enough, even with mongrels; but though good in themselves, such bitches will not throw good puppies. In crossing her, due care will be taken to select such a dog as shall improve her good qualities, and eradicate bad ones. Thus, if she is too small, she should be put to a dog of good size, or *vice versâ*; again, if light in the body, a dog of full proportions in that department must be given her; or, if she is thin and weak in the feet, her mate must be remarkable for good understandings. On these principles the cross must be selected, and every pains must be taken to get what is the *desideratum* for her. After lining, the bitch may hunt for about three or four weeks; but from that time she must not be taken out for fear of injury to her burden, which then begins to show, so as to make her also unwieldy and short of wind. She should, however, be allowed her liberty, if possible; or should, if confined, be regularly exercised, since her health, and consequently the health of her litter, will suffer by entire want of this advantage. When near her whelping-time, she should be allowed to choose her bed in some quiet corner of an outhouse or loose box, or in that part of the kennel which ought to be especially set apart for breeding. She should not be allowed to get too fat; but still she should be maintained in good condition. The former is bad, as leading to difficulty in whelping, whilst the latter is necessary, because she will have to sustain great drains upon her constitution. When pupping, great quiet is desirable, as many bitches are so nervous as to destroy or devour their whelps if alarmed. The usual attendant, whether feeder or kennel-huntsman, should be the only person who should go near her; and he should always speak before opening her door. It is necessary, however, that he should occasionally visit her; because

bitches are sometimes so long in labour as to demand assistance; and they also often require a little stimulating and supporting food, in the shape of broth, or even caudle. When the whelps are brought forth, the mother should have some gruel with the chill taken off, and after 12 or 14 hours, a little warm broth or milk. After this, she should be well fed upon milk, or broth with a little flesh mixed in it. For other particulars, see the general management of bitch and whelps, under the article Dog.

Sect. 3.—Rearing the Whelps.

339. The Young Hounds will require to be Rounded, which is an operation for the removal of a portion of their ears, so as to prevent their being torn by the briars and thorns of the woods they traverse. Removing the ear entirely does great harm, and the cropped terrier is almost useless in covert, from the water getting into the ear, and from the want of protection to the delicate outside skin. But there is the happy medium to be preserved, and this is effected by rounding off the tips of the ears, and leaving only enough to guard the interior. It is a very easy operation, and requires only a steady hand and care to avoid cutting the two edges unequally long. The two layers of skin should be held firmly, and without allowing them to roll upon one another; and should then be cut through with a pair of sharp scissors. This should be done at about three or four months; for earlier than that it is very difficult to cut off exactly the right quantity, as some ears grow very differently to others at various ages. The dew-claws often require removal, if not sitting very close to the leg; and in all cases the claw itself should be drawn out by the teeth or nippers. If the claw is very prominent, the whole had better be removed at the end of the first week. At this time, also, it is usual to remove a small portion of the tail; but fashion now has reduced that portion to an infinitesimal dose. Before sending them out to their walks they should be branded, and duly entered in the list kept for the purpose. Now, also, the name should be given, selecting from the following list, which is equally applicable to the staghound, harrier, or beagle :—

DOG-HOUNDS.

A	Arrogant	Baffler	Boisterous	Brutal	Carver
Acton	Arsenic	Barbarous	Bonnyface	Burster	Castor
Adamant	Artful	Bedlamite	Bouncer	Bustler	Castwell
Adjutant	Artist	Bellman	Bowler		Catcher
Agent	Atlas	Blaster	Bravo	C	Catchpole
Aimwell	Auditor	Bluecap	Bragger	Caitiff	Caviller
Amorous	Awful	Blueman	Brawler	Caliban	Catkiller
Antic		Blueboy	Brazenface	Capital	Cerberus
Anxious	B	Bluster	Brilliant	Captain	Challenger
Arbiter	Bachelor	Boaster	Brusher	Captor	Champion

Charon
Chaser
Chanter
Chieftain
Chimer
Chirper
Choleric
Claimant
Clamorous
Clangour
Clasher
Clinker
Combat
Combatant
Comforter
Comrade
Comus
Conflict
Conqueror
Conquest
Constant
Contest
Coroner
Cottager
Counsellor
Countryman
Courteous
Coxcomb
Craftsman
Crasher
Critic
Critical
Crowner
Cruiser
Crusty
Curfew
Currier

D
Damper
Danger
Dangerous
Dapper
Dapster
Darter
Dasher
Dashwood
Daunter
Dexterous
Disputant
Downright
Dragon
Dreadnought
Driver
Dustman
Dulcimer

E
Eager
Earnest
Effort
Elegant
Eminent
Envious
Envoy
Errant
Excellent

F
Factor
Factious
Fatalist
Fearnought
Ferryman
Fervent
Finder
Firebrand

Flagrant
Flasher
Fleece'em
Flinger
Flippant
Flourisher
Flyer
Foamer
Foiler
Foreman
Foremost
Foresight
Forester
Forward
Fulminant
Furrier

G
Gainer
Gallant
Galliard
Galloper
Gameboy
Gamester
Garrulous
Gazer
General
Genius
Gimcrack
Giant
Glancer
Glider
Glorious
Goblin
Governor
Grappler
Grasper
Griper
Growler
Grumbler
Guardian
Guider

H
Hannibal
Harbinger
Hardman
Hardy
Harlequin
Harasser
Hazard
Headstrong
Hearty
Hector
Heedful
Hercules
Hero
Highflyer
Hopeful
Hotspur
Humble
Hurtful

I & J
Jerker
Jingler
Impetus
Jockey
Jolly
Jollyboy
Jostler
Jovial
Judgment
Juniper

L
Labourer
Lasher

Laster
Lanker
Leader
Leveler
Liberal
Libertine
Lictor
Lifter
Lightfoot
Linguist
Listener
Lounger
Lucifer
Lunatic
Lunger
Lurker
Lusty

M
Manager
Manful
Mariner
Marshall
Marksman
Marplot
Marvellous
Match'em
Maxim
Maximus
Meanwell
Meddler
Menacer
Mendall
Mender
Mentor
Mercury
Merlin
Merryboy
Merryman
Methodist
Messmate
Mighty
Militant
Minikin
Miscreant
Mittimus
Monarch
Monitor
Motley
Mounter
Mover
Mungo
Musical
Mutinous
Mutterer
Myrmidon

N
Nervous
Nestor
Newsman
Nimrod
Noble
Nonsuch
Novel
Noxious

P
Pageant
Paragon
Paramount
Partner
Partyman
Pealer
Penetrate
Perfect

Perilous
Pertinent
Petulant
Phœbus
Piercer
Pilgrim
Pillager
Pilot
Pincher
Piper
Playful
Plodder
Plunder
Politic
Potent
Prater
Prattler
Premier
President
Prevalent
Primate
Principal
Prodigal
Prompter
Prophet
Prosperous
Prosper
Prowler

R
Racer
Rallywood
Rambler
Rampant
Rancour
Random
Ranger
Ransack
Rantaway
Ranter
Rapper
Rattler
Ravager
Ravenous
Ravisher
Reacher
Reasoner
Rector
Regent
Resonant
Restive
Reveller
Rifler
Rigid
Rigour
Ringwood
Rioter
Risker
Rockwood
Romper
Rouser
Router
Rover
Rudesby
Ruffian
Ruffler
Rummager
Rumbler
Rumour
Runner
Rural
Rusher
Rustic

S
Salient

Sampler
Sampson
Sanction
Sapient
Saucebox
Saunter
Scalper
Scamper
Schemer
Scourer
Scrambler
Screamer
Screecher
Scuffler
Searcher
Settler
Sharper
Shifter
Signal
Singer
Singwell
Skirmish
Smoker
Social
Solomon
Solon
Songster
Soundwell
Spanker
Special
Specimen
Speedwell
Spinner
Splendour
Splenetic
Spoiler
Spokesman
Sportsman
Squabbler
Squeaker
Statesman
Steady
Stickler
Stinger
Stormer
Stranger
Stripling
Striver
Strivewell
Stroker
Stroller
Struggler
Sturdy
Subtle
Succour
Supple
Surly
Swaggerer
Sylvan

T
Tackler
Talisman
Tamar
Tangent
Tartar
Tattler
Taunter
Teazer
Terror
Thrasher
Threatener
Thumper
Thunderer
Thwacker
Thwarter

Tickler
Tomboy
Topmost
Topper
Torment
Torrent
Torturer
Tosser
Touchstone
Tracer
Tragic
Trampler
Transit
Transport
Traveller
Trimbush
Trimmer
Triumph
Trojan
Trouncer
Truant
Trueboy
Trueman
Trudger
Trusty
Trial
Tryer
Trywell
Tuner
Turbulent
Twanger
Twig'em
Tyrant

V
Vagabond
Vagrant
Valiant
Valid
Valorous
Valour
Vaulter
Vaunter
Venturer
Venturous
Vermin
Vexer
Victor
Vigilant
Vigorous
Vigour
Villager
Viper
Volant
Voucher

W
Wanderer
Warbler
Warning
Warrior
Warwhoop
Wayward
Wellbred
Whipster
Whynot
Wildair
Wildman
Wilful
Wisdom
Woodman
Worker
Workman
Worthy
Wrangler
Wrestler

BITCHES.

A	Credible	Furious	Lively	Rampish	Toilsome
Accurate	Credulous	Fury	Lofty	Rantipole	Tractable
Active	Crony		Lovely	Rapid	Tragedy
Actress	Cruel	**G**	Luckylass	Rapine	Trespass
Affable	Curious	Gainful	Lunacy	Rapture	Trifle
Agile	Current	Galleyslave		Rarity	Trivial
Airy		Gambol	**M**	Rashness	Trollop
Aunty	**D**	Gamesome	Madcap	Rattle	Troublesome
Angry	Dainty	Gamestress	Madrigal	Ravish	Trueless
Animate	Daphne	Gaiety	Magic	Reptile	Truemaid
Artifice	Darling	Gaily	Maggotty	Resolute	Tunable
Audible	Dashaway	Gaylass	Matchless	Restless	Tuneful
	Dauntless	Ghastly	Melody	Rhapsody	
B	Delicate	Giddy	Merrylass	Riddance	**V**
Baneful	Desperate	Gladness	Merriment	Riot	Vanquish
Bashful	Destiny	Gladsome	Mindful	Rival	Vehemence
Bauble	Diana	Governess	Minion	Roguish	Vehement
Beauteous	Diligent	Graceful	Miriam	Ruin	Vengeance
Beauty	Docile	Graceless	Mischief	Rummage	Vengeful
Beldam	Document	Gracious	Modish	Ruthless	Venomous
Bellmaid	Doubtful	Grateful	Monody		Venturesome
Blameless	Doubtless	Gravity	Music	**S**	Venus
Blithsome	Dreadful	Guilesome		Sanguine	Verify
Blowsy	Dulcet	Guilty	**N**	Sappho	Vicious
Bluebell		Guiltless	Narrative	Science	Victory
Bluemaid	**E**		Neatness	Scrupulous	Victrix
Bonny	Easy	**H**	Needful	Shrewdness	Vigilance
Bonnybell	Echo	Hasty	Negative	Skilful	Violent
Bonnylass	Ecstasy	Handsome	Nicety	Songstress	Viperous
Boundless	Endless	Harlot	Nimble	Specious	Virulent
Bravery	Energy	Harmony	Noisy	Speedy	Vitiate
Brevity	Enmity	Hazardous	Notable	Spiteful	Vivid
Brimstone	Essay	Heedless	Notice	Spitfire	Vixen
Busy		Helen	Notion	Sportful	Vocal
Buxom	**F**	Heroine	Novelty	Sportive	Volatile
	Faithful	Hideous	Novice	Sportly	Voluble
C	Fairmaid	Honesty		Sprightly	
Capable	Fairplay	Hostile	**P**	Stately	**W**
Captious	Famous		Passion	Stoutness	Waggery
Careless	Fanciful	**I & J**	Pastime	Strenuous	Waggish
Careful	Fashion	Jealousy	Patience	Strumpet	Wagtail
Carnage	Favourite	Industry	Phœnix	Suity	Wanton
Caution	Fearless	Jollity	Phrenzy	Sybil	Warfare
Cautious	Festive	Joyful	Placid	Symphony	Warlike
Charmer	Fickle	Joyous	Playful	Syncope	Waspish
Chantress	Fidget		Playsome	Syren	Wasteful
Cheerful	Fiery	**L**	Pleasant		Watchful
Chirruper	Fireaway	Lacerate	Pliant	**T**	Welcome
Chorus	Firetail	Laudable	Position	Tattle	Welldone
Circe	Flighty	Lavish	Precious	Telltale	Whimsey
Clarionet	Flourish	Lawless	Prettylass	Tempest	Whirligig
Clio	Flurry	Lenity	Previous	Temptation	Wildfire
Comely	Forcible	Levity	Priestess	Termagant	Willingmaid
Comfort	Fretful	Liberty	Probity	Terrible	Wishful
Comical	Friendly	Lightning	Prudence	Testy	Wonderful
Concord	Frisky	Lightsome		Thankful	Worry
Courtesy	Frolic	Likely	**R**	Thoughtful	Wrathful
Crafty	Frolicsome	Lissome	Racket	Tidings	Wreakful
Crazy	Funnylass	Litigate	Rally		

It is the custom to name all the whelps of a litter after the initials of sire or dam; but it should always be the endeavour of the person who chooses the names to select those as much unlike one another as possible, in order that the puppies may distinguish them with more ease.

340. THE WALKS FOR THE YOUNG HOUNDS should be chosen in such situations as that they shall be accustomed to all sorts of company, from children to horses, and shall not consequently be shy and retiring. Boldness in the foxhound is an essential point, and a shy one utterly useless; he will not pass through a town, nor even face a cow feeding, but is constantly incurring the wrath of the second whip, from his lagging propensities. If a walk at a farmhouse can be procured so much the better, or at a butcher's, or village innkeeper's. Wherever they are reared they should be well done, and not starved into the rickety

frames which one often sees. Here they remain till after the hunting season is over, when they are brought back to the kennel, and at once are submitted to its discipline.

341. WHEN FIRST RETURNED TO KENNEL, the young hound is generally sulky at losing his liberty, and often refuses his food for some days; this does no harm, and no notice need be taken of him, when, in all probability, in the course of a few days he will recover his appetite and spirits. For some little time a low diet, with an occasional dose of castor-oil, should be adhered to, because the change is considerable, from the free roving life of "the walk" to the close confinement of the kennel. Little or no flesh is required at this time, and the free use of vegetables should be encouraged. For some little time these young hounds will often refuse to notice their new master, but by kind words and feeding them, they learn to attach themselves afresh, and may then be treated like any other member of this great family.

342. BREAKING FROM RIOT should be commenced from the very first day that the young hounds are taken out to exercise. This should be regularly carried on every day during the summer months, both with young and old; and all the young and unsteady hounds should be in couples; always putting together a young and an old hound, and dogs with bitches. In this way they may at first be taken out along the adjacent roads, choosing the more private ones in preference, till the young hounds know their names and attend to a rate pretty quickly. At first, until they are accustomed to their new huntsman, only 8 or 10 couple should be aired at a time; and for a day or two they should only be walked out in the paddock in couples, and caressed and fed by the huntsman. As soon as they seem to be pretty ready to own his voice, and to follow him at heel, he may take them into the roads, and after a time, varying according to circumstances, he may gradually increase his numbers, till he can venture to take out all the pack, unless a very large one. When quite tractable on the road, they should be walked through sheep and deer, beginning again with small numbers at first, and gradually, as before, increasing them. With sheep and deer, at first *all* should be in couples; and, after a time, a few at a time should be released; and when found to take no notice, they may be coupled again, and others set at liberty, till all have had the chance of showing their propensities without restraint. In this way, during the summer, the huntsman, by his kennel-management, already described, and by exercise as here detailed, teaches his pack obedience, and breaks

them from riot of the above description— viz., from sheep and deer, which may almost always be met with in some park adjacent. Deer must especially be guarded against, because the scent is so tempting to all hounds, and seldom a week passes in the hunting season without the run leading through a deer-park. Very often, too, they may be broken from hare and rabbit-riot, during the summer, to a certain extent; but too much must not here be attempted, as the young hounds are easily made shy of hunting altogether if they are continually being rated, and never encouraged. Until, therefore, hounds are entered to their particular game, they must not be too much rated and broken from "riot;" but sheep and deer being of great value, must at once be protected; and on no account should cub-hunting be commenced till all the hounds are quite steady from them. A neglect of this precaution has led to great expense and annoyance, for, as while exercise only is the motive, couples may be kept on, so while hunting itself is going on they cannot be confined, and the hounds having no mechanical restraint are much less manageable; and if they begin to run a flock of sheep or a herd of deer, they generally end by pulling down one or more victims. When once this blood has been tasted, there is no saying when and where the passion may return, and the hound, apparently cured by the whip, is never safe from a repetition of his frolic. Stop the tendency therefore thoroughly, early in the summer, and never mind the fear of making shy the young entry. If they are well-bred, they will soon find out that something is meant when they are thrown into covert, and they will readily join in with their fellows, when their game is afoot, though perhaps at first shy for fear of the lash.

343. THE AMOUNT OF DAILY EXERCISE during the summer months should be very considerable, since the hounds are only walked out, and seldom trotted. The huntsman should take them out early in the morning on the road, for a couple of hours, and may also do the same in the evening, in the paddocks, or on any grass hill, of which he can command the use. Nothing but the time of the men ought to limit this essentially healthy part of the management of the pack; and as foxhounds are a very high-couraged set of animals, unless their energies are suffered to expend themselves in this way, they will, in the first place, be always fighting in kennel; in the second place, they will be under very little command; and in the third, they will be out of health. In the morning road-work the men should be on their horses, but in the evening on foot. In all cases

when out with hounds, they should have their hunting-coats on.

SECT. 4.—ENTERING YOUNG HOUNDS.

344. In grass-countries, by the month of August, in arable-countries, as soon as the corn is cut, and in the large woodlands, even before, the young hounds should be entered to fox. If the pack is altogether new, it will be prudent to take the old hounds out first, without any of the young entry, since many of them are sure to be altogether useless—some from incurable tendency to "riot," others from "babbling" propensities, and others again from hanging in covert, skirting, or slack hunting. There will, therefore, be quite enough to do for some days, to get the old hounds handy, and to decide upon what are so incurably bad as to be wholly useless, and even injurious to the young hounds. Some of these vices certainly do not show themselves plainly in the early cub-hunting; but the experienced huntsman may make a very good guess even on the first day a fox is found. He must not expect too much, but must be contented if he can get from fifteen to twenty couple of hounds, tolerably steady from riot, and with hunting enough in them to drive a fox pretty hard in the woodlands. He need not yet care about the hounds "packing" well, nor can he yet judge of their powers in this respect; all that he has to do is, to get them to hunt steadily and perseveringly their own game, to avoid "skirting," and to turn to his horn quickly and readily. The hunting tendency is partly dependent upon breeding; but much must be owing to previous education. It is generally too late with draft-hounds to instil hunting into them; but if they are slack for want of blood only, by perseverance, even with a bad pack of draft-hounds, early in the season, a few cubs can be run into, and chopped, somehow or other. This will often, with a persevering and encouraging man, totally alter the disposition of a hound; for nothing is so infectious as the *manner* of the men. If they are slow and careless in cub-hunting, so will the hounds be, while if they are bustling and energetic, these qualities are rapidly imbibed, and the whole aspect of the pack is changed. I have seen this effected in a very short time when a slack pack has changed hands, partly from higher feeding, but chiefly from the determined energy of the men; they have become lively and full of dash, instead of looking dull, and hunting like slow harriers. The old hounds must at once be well flogged, if not free from riot, and the incurably bad ones must be drafted at once before the young hounds are entered.

345. WHENEVER THE OLD HOUNDS ARE TOLERABLY STEADY AND HANDY, but not till then, begin to think of entering your young ones; taking out five or six couple of them along with the steadiest and best hunters of your old pack, and remembering that *your chance of good sport through this season and the next* depends more upon your young entry than upon the old draft-hounds. No huntsman makes the mistake of parting with old hounds, unless they are either infirm from age, or are bad hunters in some form; but many men draft young hounds from their looks not pleasing the eye, or from their being too high or too low, or not being "suity," as it is called, and yet in doing so perhaps give you the best blood of their kennels, and a hound which will do you as good service as if picked out of ten thousand. Cherish, therefore, this young entry, and sacrifice time, cubs, and old hounds to make them perfect. On the first appearance of the young hounds, it is very desirable to find a cub as quickly as possible, for as they are sure to run something or other, if they have any sort in them, they will be likely to run "riot" if nothing else turns up; and the whip is a poor introduction to their first day's sport. Some even go so far as to wait till the old hounds have found before they give the young ones liberty, keeping them in couples outside the covert till the cub is on foot. This, I believe, to be a very good plan, but as it is a troublesome one, it may not suit the notions of all. When once the old hounds are running a cub hard, and the scent is strong, the young ones rapidly chime in, and there is very little more trouble in urging them on. Hallooing, however, should be indulged in to any extent; encouragement is the order of the day, and too much devil can now hardly be infused. The sound of the huntsman's voice, if with his pack, also keeps them together, and prevents the young ones from losing themselves, which they might otherwise easily do. It should be understood that this cub-hunting begins at three or four o'clock in the morning, when, even in the summer, the air is cool and refreshing and scent lies pretty well—though the ground being generally dry, it is not so good as in the autumn. After the cub is killed let the huntsman lay hold of him, and take him into the first open space he can find, then, before the blood of either fox or hounds has had time to cool, let him excite the hounds by a few cheers—not too long continued however, and throw him to them. After this first-blooding it is better, if the morning is not far advanced, to draw for a fresh fox; choosing, if possible, an unsoiled part of the woodland, and proceeding to this chiefly in order to have an

opportunity of rating the young ones for speaking to "riot," while under the fresh recollections of the encouragement which they have received in their entry to their own particular game. Much punishment should be avoided; a severe rate or two generally suffices; and, if possible, the whip should not be used so soon as this. If, however, a young hound chops a hare or rabbit, and will not drop it, let him have a taste of the whip, and be compelled to leave his dainty meal undevoured. If another cub is soon found, let him be killed also, if possible, or else marked to ground, and the hounds well encouraged after doing so; but do not by any means tire out the energies of the young entry, rather letting them leave off while still feeling a zest for their new sport. This is a very important consideration, as all means should be taken to inculcate a desire for the peculiar kind of game to which they have just been introduced.

Sect. 5.—Regular Cub-Hunting.

346. This should now be entered upon in earnest; and should, in September and October, be followed two or three times a-week, or, with a very large entry, still oftener. Upon it depends the sport to be obtained during the coming season, not only as regards the hounds, but also in reference to the foxes. It should be known that cub-hunting and regular fox-hunting have two entirely different objects; the former being to prepare for future sport, the latter to afford present amusement to the field of sportsmen attending the meet. Cub-hunting is, therefore, merely a kind of breaking-in of the hounds and men to their respective places; and yet some sportsmen are particularly fond of this business—for sport it is not intended to be. I can easily understand this, when they are interested in the future success or failure of the pack, but cub-hunting *per se*, without any reference to the future, is, to my taste, a most tiresome affair. First of all, it requires a strong temptation to induce me to leave my bed at one or two o'clock in the morning, in order to reach a woodland-meet 10 or 15 miles off; secondly, there is little pleasure in crashing through thick tangled underwood, which at this time and season is heavy with dew on the leaves; and thirdly, the ground is so hard that a gallop is out of the question, and anything like a leap destructive to the joints of the horse. Few, therefore, would willingly undertake the task; but, nevertheless, it must be perseveringly conducted as often as I have stated, in order to effect two principal objects; first, the dispersion of the foxes; and secondly, the blooding and entering of the hounds.

347. The Dispersion of the Foxes is one of the most important features in cub-hunting, and one which is perhaps too often neglected. Foxes naturally prefer large woods, and especially those which so often are connected with others of a similar character. There are many districts where the soil is so unfit for grass, or to bear cereal crops, and is yet so well calculated for timber trees, that it is, and has been, long devoted to that purpose. These extensive woodlands are generally on the outskirts of the hunting country, and are often far removed from any populous neighbourhood; hence, they are chosen by the foxes; and these animals are often to be found in great numbers in these secure fastnesses, at a time when they are scarce enough in the best coverts. Now, if these large woods are never thoroughly routed during cub-hunting, there is seldom much chance of doing this afterwards, because they are always unpopular meets, and are only had recourse to for want of foxes in coverts likely to afford good runs. The huntsman, too, often likes an early good run from a good covert, in preference to a tiresome and hard morning's work in the thick underwood; and if his heart is not in his work, or if he is not compelled to do so by his master, he will avoid trouble, and instead of doing good for the future, and driving out the foxes into the small coverts, he actually drives them back again into the large woods. This I have often known done, and especially by young masters themselves, who often like to go out cub-hunting, and have a quiet little spin to amuse themselves with; but such masters will seldom show good after-sport, and only eat bad pudding in September, instead of getting it good in November or December; for no run early in the season can be compared to a winter one, when the ground is cool, the scent good, the turf soft and elastic, and the fences may be taken by the hunter without fear of injury. Let, therefore, all masters, as well as men, bottle up their impatience till the proper season, and take care to avoid cub-hunting for pleasure. They should never enter, on any consideration, a favourite spinney or small covert, in the middle of a good hunting country, but should always stick to those woodlands where foxes are sure to breed, and where they may be killed in great numbers without injury to future sport; whence, also, they should be systematically driven. These large woodlands are almost always on the boundaries between two countries, and sometimes are hunted by two packs. In such a case every master will endeavour to drive out the foxes into his own country, and for this purpose

will draw towards it, not entering them on his own side, but commencing to draw them as far as possible from it, and driving all out towards his own dominions. Much, perhaps, cannot be effected in this way; but it should be tried nevertheless, for without a trial nothing can ever be done.

348. THE NECESSITY FOR BLOODING THE HOUNDS is the second and most immediate object of cub-hunting. Without blood even the pack in regular work soon becomes slack, and the hounds hang back, instead of getting forward with the true foxhound dash. Beckford relates a case in point, in a modest note, to the following effect :—" A pack of hounds which had been a month without registering a kill, at last ran a fox to ground, which the men dug out and threw to them. After this, their spirits were so renovated, that they killed seven days in succession." Now this *might* have been a run of luck, but most probably the marked change in their success was due to the cause to which he assigns it. However, all practical men are agreed that blood must be had even during the season; then, how much more necessary must it be before hounds are made to know their business, to give them blood.

349. AS SOON AS THE YOUNG HOUNDS ARE DULY ENTERED, and have had a fair share of blood, the pack may be hunted exactly as in the season, due reference being had to the remarks already made on the early hour necessary, on the propriety of drawing only the large woodlands, and on the imperative want of blood, almost daily,

which must be had, somehow or other, either by marking to ground and digging out, or by chopping, or some other means. At this time, even bag-foxes are justifiable; for it is not until hounds are rendered fastidious by success, that they turn up their noses at bagmen with disdain. These animals cause disgust, because their scent, instead of possessing the due amount of fox-flavour suited to the hound's nose, has become rank by confinement and fear, coupled with constant irritation. The fox, in common with the polecat, cat, and all others of his kind, has a reservoir of offensive scent under the root of the tail, where it is secreted by certain glands for the purpose. When these animals are annoyed, as they are in confinement, this scent is found in large quantities, of a rank nature, and the consequence is that they smell, or rather, in common English, they stink most abominably. But when young hounds are first entered, they *can* hunt this strong scent better even than that of a wild fox, and they do so because they have not yet learnt to know better. If, therefore, wild cubs cannot be found, a bagman or two must be obtained, and turned down before the hounds, and they will afterwards work with redoubled zest. The bagged fox should be turned into some small covert free from wild foxes, as the hounds will be thereby encouraged to draw, which is one of their most disagreeable duties. The management of hounds in drawing, &c., will be considered under the chapter devoted to regular hunting.

CHAP. V.

FOX-HUNTING (*Continued*).

SECT. 1.—PREPARATIONS FOR HUNTING.

350. SEVERAL DUTIES DEVOLVE UPON THE MASTER preparatory to a hunting-day :— First, he should have previously given the usual notice of the meet; and it is advisable that this meet should be so fixed as to suit two or more coverts if possible, so that every attendant shall be obliged to appear at the place appointed, foot-people included. If this is not done, a great number will assemble at the covert to be drawn, rather than at the meet, and often they surround it so that no fox can break; but by this precaution, on taking the hounds on to draw the covert, the foot-people cannot anticipate them, and a fox has time to make his point before he is headed. Secondly, the hunting-pack must be drafted on the

previous day, fed, early or late, according to the distance they have to travel, and separately shut up for the night. When drafting the hounds for the morrows' hunting, a list should be entered in the huntsman's book; and he should take a copy of this with him in hunting—so should the master, if he at all interferes in these matters. In making this draft it is usual for the huntsman to select the hounds which are the best suited to the particular country which is to be drawn, if he has sufficient numbers for that purpose; and also to proportion his pack to the strength and extent of the coverts. Thus, for an open country with nothing but small spinnies, eighteen or twenty couple are amply sufficient, while for large woodlands twenty-four couple will not be too many. Thirdly, the earth-stopper and keepers should have their orders what earths to stop, and whether to stop at night or in the morning, according to the season, for if in the spring, they must not be stopped too long, or the cubs may be starved, if there are any. All these preliminary duties should be carefully attended to, since a failure in any will affect the chance of sport on the morrow.

Sect. 2.—Going to Covert.

351. According to the distance from the meet must the start be made from the kennel. About six or seven miles an hour is the pace at which hounds generally travel on the road, except in very wet days, when eight miles an hour will better serve to keep hounds and horses from feeling any ill effects from this disagreeable attendant upon hunting. The hounds seem to know the hunting days, and are as impatient as the most ardent tyro. They are all life and animation on first bursting out of kennel, and are the better for a turn in the paddock to empty themselves before getting on the road. The men should then mount and proceed on their way, the first whip leading, with the huntsman in the middle of his hounds, and the second whip bringing up the rear. This order is maintained until their arrival at the meet. It is always advisable to avoid the crowded streets of towns as far as possible for fear of accidents; as it is not always that the hounds can be safe from the careless driving of carts or carriages, whose charioteers will not always pull up for them to pass. When arrived at the meet the men may tighten their girths, &c., but the hounds should be kept moving on the grass and not allowed to lie about, except it be in the very warm and dry weather which is sometimes experienced at the beginning or end of the season. Hounds in going to covert are very apt to pick up bones, and will sometimes in their greediness for these unwonted dainties, swallow large ones. This should be prevented by the second whip, as their possession only leads to delay and quarrelling; and if of large size, and they are swallowed, they do not improve the wind.

Sect. 3.—Drawing.

352. No part of a huntsman's duties is so often performed in a slovenly manner, and yet none is of more consequence than the drawing of coverts. It is so unpleasant to all, that it is no wonder that it is shirked; but, nevertheless, it is like business with regard to pleasure, it should come first in importance, as in precedence. One of the most beautiful sights in fox-hunting, is the perfect drawing of a pack of hounds. I have rarely seen it to perfection, because it

is seldom that the eye can command the covert so as to get a bird's-eye view. But in the Heythrop country some of the best coverts are merely willow-beds under the sides of the hills; and there I have seen the hounds, when under Lord Redesdale's mastership, drawing in a style which elicited my admiration, as well as that of all the field. Every square yard of covert seemed to have its allotted hound, and they drew from one to the other, and back again, so as to leave no single patch of ground untried. No hound could be seen following another, but, apparently, each cautiously avoided this common defect. It happened on one occasion that this was conspicuous, through a long series of blank-draws, on the same day, and still, even to the last, these persevering hounds spread out and drew their ground as closely as ever. It was, I recollect, a great disappointment to me to meet with a blank-day, after travelling more than forty miles to the meet, especially as, from the rare occurrence of such an event, I did not expect it; but the gratification afforded by the perfection of the drawing, quite made up for the loss of the expected run. The first thing the huntsman does is to send the pack into covert with a wave of the hand, which is all the signal that ought to be required; then, entering himself, he takes the line which he wishes his hounds to follow, keeping a little behind the body of his hounds, but well with them. Much will depend on the size of the covert as to the proceedings from this time. If large, the draw is made up-wind, and the first whip is sent on to the point where the fox is most likely to break, in order to view him away, and save time by hallooing, which signal is of course at once acted on by the huntsman. If the woods are very large, it is no use for the first whip to go to any *one* point outside— he must rather select some ride or break, which the fox must cross at some distance a-head of the body of the hounds, and, as they approach, quietly slip off to a second and more distant one. He will thus have a good chance of viewing the fox as he crosses, and at last may post himself at the outside, at the point where foxes usually break from that particular covert. I need not say that, while engaged in this occupation, strict silence should be kept, and no one should approach the whip for any purpose, much less enter into conversation with him. Some masters, when drawing large coverts, station five or six men in different parts, and give them a separate signal. This is of great use, and is certainly carrying out Beckford's rule to the fullest extent. In this case, also, much noise is to be avoided, as it is not desirable to drive the fox out of his kennel far before the hounds; the second whip should be a little in the rear of the huntsman, and should urge forward the lagging hounds. It is most important that the huntsman should himself penetrate the thickest parts of the covert; it is here that the fox will most probably be lying; and many a one has been drawn over unfound, from the dislike of the huntsman to set the example to his hounds. They will go anywhere with encouragement; but a slack huntsman is soon imitated, and if he leaves untried the thick part of the underwood, so will his pack. The field seldom can judge of these things, because they seldom are where they should be, in covert, but are talking, laughing, and cigar-smoking, often where the fox is most wanted, or, most likely, to break. If they would all enter and assist the huntsman inside, they would be as useful as they now too often are the reverse, As soon as the first challenge is given, the first whip should be all attention to his duty, and carefully watch, by eye and ear, for his charge's appearance. If he sees him, no notice should be taken till he has reached the first fence from the covert; but as soon as this has been gained, he should screech and halloo in such a way as to bring every hound, with the huntsman, to the spot in less than no time. Thus is a fox well found, which is the first item towards killing him. If, however, the covert is small, it is not necessary to take all these precautions; but, the huntsman entering with his hounds, the whips may each take the skirts outside the fence, so as to see the fox break before them, driving every hound which appears outside into covert; and thus, with as much noise as they like, the spinney or gorse may be threaded. Here the fox seldom gets away far enough before the hounds to require caution; and the moment the scent is owned, they settle to it, and are away.

But it often happens that foxes in large coverts when first found, instead of breaking at once, run ring after ring inside, and at last break down wind, at the point where the hounds entered. These are generally foxes which have been unkennelled just before the hounds, and perhaps headed by the whip, or by some other person who is trying to be over-clever. Sometimes these rings are repeated so often, that the whole covert is foiled by the hounds so constantly running over the same ground, and the consequence is that they cannot hunt a yard. This is a most annoying affair, and tries the temper of all parties more even than a blank-draw. Whenever it happens, and the hounds begin to throw up, and really *cannot* hunt, it is better to take them

away to some other covert than to persevere in this hopeless pursuit.

SECT. 4.—THE RUN.

353. "GONE AWAY! GONE AWAY!!" resounds through the covert, and every nerve is strained by master, men, hounds, and field to fill their respective stations with due credit. The first whip now is a gentleman at large, in comparison with his previous duties; and need only ride so as to be at hand in a moment, in case of difficulty. He should now carefully husband the powers of his horse. The second whip should bring up the tail hounds, and see that none are hanging in covert, using his whip and tongue pretty freely to compel all to get "forrard," which is constantly now to be in his mouth. Thus they stream over hill and dale. After leaving the covert the huntsman gives a few notes on his horn, and a cheer or two, then places himself by the side of his hounds; carefully watching them, and taking advantage of every bend in the leading hounds to cut corners and thus be with them. He thus sees when and where the scent fails in case of a check, and is able to notice any facts which may assist him in his cast, if necessary; as, for instance, the presence of sheep, or deer, or a plough at work, or a sheep-dog, or the scent ceasing at a road or river, or fifty other such occurrences. Upon these facts, trifling as they appear to unlearned eyes, the skilful huntsman founds his calculations, and acts according to them. At this time the master should be in the rear of his huntsman, and ready to restrain the field from pressing upon the hounds, if necessary. Presently a check occurs, and, "Hold hard, gentlemen!" should be the order from the master before mischief is done. The hounds now, if used to cast themselves, will do so without a moment's loss of time, and spread right and left, or wheel in a body, in order to recover the scent. It is extraordinary how clever some hounds are in this self-casting; and how, if left to themselves, they try every stratagem likely to occur to a dog's imagination. But there are many facts which they do not grasp, and of these the huntsman takes advantage; nevertheless, I believe, that if left to themselves, hounds would in the long run kill more foxes than if interfered with too much. Here, as in every other pursuit, moderation is the great virtue, and the huntsman who interferes at the right time, and then only, is the man who is to be applauded. But though hounds when left to themselves will kill their foxes, yet they do not kill them *secundum artem*, because the hunting of the fox is now considered to be a compound operation, partly canine, but partly human; and therefore if the

biped is ignored by the quadruped, and the latter can do without him, the only party who can use his tongue in intelligible language is sure to throw it pretty freely.

354. THE FIRST CHECK is the trial of both hounds and huntsmen. Time is now precious, for the fox is travelling; but "most haste is often worst speed;" if, therefore, nothing very evident presents itself to the huntsman as the cause of the check, by all means let the canine instinct have fair play—for a very short time at all events—and then cast them in favour of some reasonable proceeding which the huntsman's brain may have devised, as that which the fox has employed in his defence. Now the scent is either hit off, or fails altogether; and, in the latter case, what is to be done? Either wait for a "halloo," or at once lift the hounds to the point which the fox is most likely to make, and this is generally the nearest covert. Halloos are ticklish affairs, and the man who attends to them indiscriminately, when he does not know by whom they are given, is sure to mislead himself and his followers, in nine cases out of ten. As long as the scent is owned it is better to work it out, unless a halloo which is to be depended on is heard, and then it should certainly be attended to; but if hounds are lifted from the scent and disappointed, they soon become slack, and lose that confidence in their huntsman which is the strong link between him and them.

355. But a common accident occurs perhaps in the run—the hunted fox is CHANGED for a fresh one. It happens, unfortunately for foxhounds, that the fox, unlike the deer, loses scent as he goes on; the deer, as he warms, sweats and emits a very strong scent with it, which falls on the ground, and increases mile by mile; on the other hand the fox, like the dog, its congener, never sweats, and what scent it emits is gradually lost during the progress of the chase, becoming fainter and fainter, though generally lasting for the length of a run. Hence, while the deerhound sticks to the hunted deer, by preference for its scent, the foxhound is tempted by the fine fresh scent of a newly-roused fox to take after him, in preference to the sinking animal before him. Hence the difficulty in which the huntsman is placed, for the natural powers of the dog would here mislead him, and it is in this predicament that foxhounds most want his aid. For this also he must always be on the look-out, especially in covert, when running his fox through. During this time it is very important that he should be with them, and that his first whip should be on the other side of it, in order to view any fox which breaks, and

decide whether he is the hunted one or not, whilst, at the same time, he may be able to halloo forward the huntsman and hounds, if all is right. But there are some signs which may indicate the hunted fox, as, for instance, the following:—Supposing the hounds divide, then the huntsman should be able to know in which lot are the leading hounds at the time of the division; to these he should stick, regardless of those who were skirting at the time; and the whipper-in should stop the others, if possible, and bring them to him. During a division the second whip should wait anxiously for orders, and be ready to act in a moment when he sees to which side the huntsman is leading. Now all goes on again, and the hounds are running breast-high: soon they press still more eagerly forward, and the huntsman can perceive the fox hard pressed only a field before him; at this time he fancies that his prize is won, and halloos and screams to encourage his hounds, which then certainly do not want it. Alas! his hopes are damped, for, after carrying on to the middle of the next field of turnips, they throw up their heads, and cannot own the scent. What can have happened! The fox *must* have lain down in the hedge-row, or run down the ditch; but the horsemen are so forward that all idea of hunting back for him is out of the question, and the hounds must be lifted to the hedge. Here, after a careful cast, he is hit off, and at last run into only a hundred yards or so from the line, being fairly blown, and lying in the ditch.

SECT. 5.—THE KILL.

356. It is usual, when hounds have killed their fox, for the huntsman to dismount, and get in among them, for the purpose of laying hold of the fox and removing it, in order to "worry it." This done—in order that the hounds may recover their wind, and that the tail-hounds shall be encouraged as well as the leaders—the fox is held aloft, and the huntsman or whip gets into a tree, or on a high bank, holding the fox towards the hounds. The cheers and noise are then redoubled, and the baying of the hounds in addition, constitute a chorus most gratifying to the sportsman's ear. Presently the fox is thrown among the hounds, and soon torn limb from limb, and eaten. Such is the finale of this exciting sport, in which the energies of so many have been long engaged.

SECT. 6.—RUNNING TO GROUND.

357. This happens sometimes as a finale to a run, instead of a kill or losing the fox, and is certainly a better finish than this last conclusion, the most unsatisfactory of

K

all to the good sportsman. When hounds have marked their fox well, and there is no doubt about his having gone to ground, they may, after some few minutes, be taken off to some fresh "draw," or home, if the day is too far gone. Sometimes, however, it is desirable to dig out or bolt the fox, when hounds have been short of blood; and then, a terrier having been procured, he is put in, and soon pins the fox in some corner where he is heard baying him. Over this point the spades should be used, and soon come down upon him in the ordinary way. Sometimes, however, though rarely, the fox is bolted by the terrier, and may even run the gauntlet of the hounds, and escape, as has happened on some occasions. The use of the terrier is to mark the exact situation of the fox, and to prevent his digging on further, which he will often do in sandy soils. Sometimes in shallow spouts or drains a terrier may be made to lay hold of the fox, and, by withdrawing him, the fox will be brought out. If he can be reached, a whip-thong should be first introduced, in the hope of taking off the fox's attention from the dog, who has then a better chance of escaping his teeth.

Sect. 7.—On Scent.

858. No single subject connected with hunting has received so much attention as this, and for this simple reason, that none is so difficult to settle, from an ignorance of the laws which govern it. But not only do we know nothing of its laws, but we also are at sea with regard to facts, for of these we have none upon which certain dependance can be placed. One party asserts that different foxes have different scents; and consequently, that scent varies with the individual fox; but, says another, "scent varies in a few minutes with the same fox—then how is the individual the cause of the variation?" There can be no doubt that this often happens. We have all often seen on the advent of a hail-cloud, scent melt away as if by magic; although over the same country it was previously a good one. But what is there that we have not seen? that is the question in reference to scent. One thing may be said—viz., that we have seen no one fact with regard to scent which could be considered so constant as to form the basis of a rule. Is even "the southerly wind and the cloudy sky" a certain prelude to scent? I trow not; and I should be sorry to depend upon it. Living for many years in a bad scenting country, I have been saluted on all occasions with prophecies as to scent; but never did I find the man whose foretellings were worth a farthing. Scent must be either good or

bad, or indifferent, on any given day; and therefore it is an even chance that any opinion given beforehand will be right, because the indifferent scent will do for either, and will be claimed by both parties. Yet I never knew any man receive general credit for knowing anything on the subject, practically. I believe, however, that scent really does depend upon the individual fox, and, moreover, that this scent is constantly varying with his hopes and fears. My impression is, that it is only partially dependant upon his skin, and that when that only emits the scent hounds have a difficult task. Did any of my readers ever catch a cat in a trap set in a room? If so, they will surely remember the rank scent which pervaded that room; and which was not produced by the skin of the cat, but by its anal glands. So with the fox. When first disturbed he emits a considerable quantity of this scent, and if hard pressed at first, it is produced in great quantities, and to such an extent as to enable hounds to hunt breast-high; hence the advantage of pressing him early, for the more he is pressed the better scent he gives; but if this scent is gradually and slowly emitted, as it is when he is suffered to go his own pace without fear, the result is that the hounds are less and less able to own it, and he has a fair chance of escaping. Again, supposing a change of atmosphere from a cloud, or whatever other cause may produce it, these glands suddenly cease to emit their scent, and the change is as rapidly transmitted to the hunting of the hounds. The soil and air have much to do with the "bad scent" and with the skin-scent, but with this glandular-scent his fears and anxieties are the chief agents; or, in the state of repose, his hopes and desires. This theory will, I think, explain some of the anomalies of scent, but that it will do away with all difficulties is beyond my fondest fancy. When we know all the intricate laws connected with and governing the electrical condition of the air—that called ozone and the laws of storms—we may hope to improve our knowledge of scent; but, perhaps, then it may elude our grasp. If, however, attention is paid to nature it will, I think, be found that however useless in practice, the above is the true theory of scent as regards the fox. At all events it explains some of the facts which before were at variance with each other; but it will only explain the strong variations in scent, and will not affect the ordinary rules which Beckford gives, and which every one re-echoes, though not exactly believing in them. Such, however, as they are they should be known, and are given by him as follows:—"It depends chiefly on two things—*the condition the ground is in, and the temperature of the air;* both of which should be moist without being wet. When both are in this condition the scent is then perfect, and, *vice versâ*, when the ground is hard and the air dry, there seldom will be any scent. It scarcely ever lies with a north or an east wind; a southerly wind without rain, and a westerly wind that is not rough, are the most favourable. Storms in the air are great enemies to scent, and seldom fail to take it entirely away. A fine sunshiny day is not often a good hunting-day; but what the French call *jour des dames*, warm without sun, is generally a perfect one—there are not many such in a whole season. In some fogs I have known the scent lie high, in others not all; depending, I believe, on the quarter the wind is then in. I have known it lie very high in a mist, when not too wet, but if the wet should hang upon the bushes, it will fall on the scent and deaden it. When the dogs roll, the scent, I have frequently observed, seldom lies—for what reason I know not; but, with permission, if they smell strong when they first come out of kennel, the proverb is in their favour, and that smell is a prognostic of good luck. When cobwebs hang on the bushes there is seldom much scent; during a white frost the scent lies high, as it also does when the frost is quite gone. At the time of its going off scent never lies; it is a critical minute for hounds, in which their game is frequently lost. In a great dew the scent is the same; in heathy countries, where the game brushes as it goes along, scent seldom fails; when the ground carries, scent is bad, for a very evident reason, which hare-hunters, who pursue their game over greasy fallows and through dirty roads, have great reason to complain of. A wet night frequently produces good chases, as then the game neither like to use the covert nor the roads. It has been often remarked that scent lies best in the richest soils, and countries which are favourable to horses are seldom so to hounds. I have also observed that in some particular places, let the temperature of the air be as it may, scent never lies." Beyond this nothing, as far as I know, has been added to our knowledge of the laws of scent.

Sect. 8.—On Drafting Hounds for Faults.

359. The characteristic of the foxhound is "dash." As the harrier can scarcely be too cautious, so the foxhound can hardly be too fast, *if only his nose is good.* The combination, therefore, of these two points should be encouraged, and all old and slow hounds, however good they once were, must be drafted. Few hounds retain their

dash after five or six seasons; and though they can hunt a cold scent then perhaps better than ever, they will dwell too long upon a good one, and will thereby only do harm to the younger hounds. Let not any feeling of favouritism keep these oversteady old hounds in the hunting-pack, but discard them at once whenever their places can be supplied by younger and more vigorous hunters. Inveterate skirters, also, and conceited babblers, by all means hang—they are not worth keeping a day, and deserve no mercy. Hounds should carry a good head, and not follow one another like a flock of geese; and each should seem to struggle for an opening. It is remarkable how various are the powers of different hounds: some seem to hunt best in covert; some can pick out a cold "pad scent;" whilst others again, though not otherwise faster, can rattle away with a breast-high scent, and beat their rivals at that particular point, though, with the fox in view, they might again be overmatched. But the various classes of hounds seem themselves aware of these variations, and depend upon one another for assistance—Rattler, Rainbow, and Admiral giving way to Jowler, Concord, and Beauty at certain conjunctures, and again appearing to resume their positions by sufferance, whenever that conjuncture has passed by. Nothing does so much harm to hounds as leaving them in covert to hunt "riot" unchecked. The second whip ought, therefore, to be careful in getting all away; and he had better be out of the run altogether than leave four or five couple behind him; they learn all sorts of bad tricks, and if some are left every day, almost any pack is speedily ruined. Nothing is more wonderful than the power which hounds have of threading their way through horsemen, and reaching the body of the pack. With a Leicestershire field this is truly marvellous; and when the pace is considered, it will be admitted that it is difficult to account for the way in which tail hounds get forward; but if they do not, they are useless, and they also should be drafted.

Sect. 9.—The Duties of the Men.

360. THE HUNTSMAN.—The general duties fo the men have been already alluded to in the preliminary chapter; but I shall now say a few words on those which are peculiar to the hunting of foxhounds. In the first place, the huntsman must be a man in the prime of life, a good and bold horseman, and able to be with his hounds wherever a horse can live. Beckford was of opinion that the huntsman's office is not so important as that of the first whip; and in his days, when hounds were a good deal

less interfered with than now, perhaps such was the case. But now-a-days a huntsman must be a very superior man; for he must interfere a good deal, or lose his character for "fastness;" and yet, when he interferes, he must really do something or other in a way superior to that which the hounds themselves would have followed. His casts, consequently, must not be general casts, which the hounds themselves would have managed as well as he; but they must be with some particular object in view, and that object ought to be really founded on observation and experience. Beckford says, "I am very well satisfied if my huntsman be acquainted with his country and his hounds; if he ride well up to them; and if he have some knowledge of the nature of the animal which he is in pursuit of; but so far am I from wishing him to be famous, that I hope he will still continue to think his hounds know best how to hunt a fox." In the present day, however, if a huntsman is not "famous," his hounds will have a poor character, and the sport will not be considered as good as it should be. A huntsman's temper should be good, both for the sake of his hounds and for that of the field; and he should revel with delight in his business, not following it solely for a livelihood, but enjoying it with as much zest as the youngest of his followers. His language to his hounds should be good, and his manner to them of an animated character, whether encouraging them or repressing their ardour. The dog-language chiefly used by the huntsman is—"Hark! hark! to Governor!" when Governor speaks, and is deserving attention; or, when encouraging all to draw, he cries, "Yooicks! yooicks! there, have at him! Rout him out! Push him up! At him, again, boys!" These are his chief words of encouragement. The horn brings hounds to his heel in casting or lifting, or in leaving covert, and is always a signal for the second whip to bring on tail-hounds. The great misfortune is, that the huntsman of a pack of foxhounds requires an old head on young shoulders, which is seldom met with; in fact, Hector and Ulysses in one would not be a more improbable combination than that desirable in the model-huntsman. I can conceive no situation more trying than that of a huntsman when things *will* go wrong; a bad scent, a short-running fox, an impatient field, and an easy-tempered master, are enough to try a Job in pigskin. Some excuse, therefore, should be made for such trying circumstances; but when ill success lasts all through a season, or perhaps two, no man should be astonished at grumblings on the part of the attendant

"field." Success will generally in the long-run be commanded if it is deserved; and if a man has a good head, a good seat, a good eye, and, above all, a fox-hunter's heart, he will generally both deserve and command success. "Scrutator," who has lately written a series of interesting letters on hunting and hounds, appears to lean to the system of non-interference, and thinks, with many others, that the modern system of lifting over fallows, and all kinds of halloos, is a bad one. This opinion, coming from a gentleman-huntsman, is a very valuable one, because these are generally the men who delight most in exercising their own talents in preference to those of their hounds. But, after all, it is a question of taste, and it is not to be decided by the number of foxes killed in each way, which is not a decisive test, but rather by the general opinion as to which way is most consonant with the preconceived idea of sport. If the number of kills is to be received as decisive in all cases, shooting birds sitting, or shooting into "the ruck" of a covey, ought to be praised; but the reverse being the case, is an example of the rule not applying in all cases. While, therefore, the present fashion lasts, the huntsman must interfere whenever he thinks (*and is right in thinking*) that he can do so with a prospect of advantage—not waiting till the hounds cannot hunt, but always lifting or casting when he is satisfied that his doing so will gain time in pursuing his fox. Such I believe to be the modern rule, and if so, it requires, as I before remarked, a better head than does the office of first whip, although his duties are by no means light and easy. In remarking on the duties of the huntsman of a pack of foxhounds, I have passed over his kennel-duties, and those which refer to entering his young hounds, because they are pretty much the same with all hounds and huntsmen, and have already been sufficiently insisted upon in the preliminary chapter on Hunting. The following twelve rules may be useful to the young huntsman:—

Rule 1.—Avoid extremes in interfering with hounds, for though too much assistance will destroy their hunting powers and make them slack, too little will make them tie on the scent, and hunt *heel*.

Rule 2.—Always cast on the most likely ground first—taking a hedge, for instance, in preference to the open field; and casting rapidly or slowly in proportion to the goodness of the scent.

Rule 3.—Be careful not to mislead hounds, let them always know what is the precise nature of the work to be done.

Rule 4.—Always make good the cast in

each direction before trying another, and do not have to go over the same ground twice. In returning from a bad cast over soiled ground, trot as quickly as possible, as the hounds then are not to suppose themselves doing anything.

Rule 5.—When it is *probable* that the fox is headed back, if a forward cast is first decided on, let it be a very short and quick one, and do not lose more time than necessary in that direction.

Rule 6.—When hounds are running in covert, if the fox is seen *in* a ride, and not *over* it, no attempt should be made to interfere with the hounds, as they must hunt very carefully to avoid over-running the scent.

Rule 7.—Although the horsemen are better in the covert than out, yet they should not be riding all over the wood, or they will foil the scent.

Rule 8.—When a fox is hunted up to a farm-yard or village, great care should be taken not to leave him behind. The hounds are very apt to overrun the scent for half-a-mile or more, when there is the hallooing of the farmer and his men, or of the villagers, and the fox may escape by taking refuge in any outhouse.

Rule 9.—The heel-scent is sometimes stronger than the right-scent, in consequence of the wind favouring it.

Rule 10.—When a fox runs his foil in covert, the tail hounds may be lifted and thrown in at head (Beckford).

Rule 11.—When hounds are seen to be perfectly unable or unwilling to cast themselves, and are apparently bewildered, the chances are that the fox is headed back.

Rule 12.—If many foxes are a-foot, it is better to let the hounds divide and hunt all of them at once, as by these means all are equally distressed, and one is sure to break; when the remaining hounds may soon be got up to the hunted fox by the efforts of the whips.

361. THE FIRST WHIPPER-IN is truly a Jack-of-all-trades; he is expected to rate hounds, and stop them from riot on all occasions, as well as the second whip; yet, in case of the huntsman's absence from the field, from any cause, he must be able to hunt them as well as he does. Now, every one knows that half of the power of the huntsman over his hounds is vested in their personal attachment to him, and that *cæteris paribus*, the man who best succeeds in making his hounds fond of him, in the summer and in kennel, will do most with them in the hunting field. Yet the first whip, who is always to be rating and using his whip, is at once to step into the huntsman's shoes, and show sport as well as if every hound was accustomed to fly to him,

instead of from him. Next, the first whip must be able to foretel the exact point of the fox in breaking covert, and ought to be there to see him; or, if in a larger covert, he ought to be *wherever he is wanted*, which is rather a large space to cover. Then, if the fox unexpectedly takes a line which leads to open earths, the first whip must get there before him, let the pace be what it may, or the maledictions on his head will be many and loud. Such are his greatest difficulties, often so great as to be insuperable; but the regular duties he may fulfil in a satisfactory manner, and they are chiefly the following; and even in these he may easily exhibit extraordinary talent:— He must, of course, be a good horseman, and should be a tolerably light weight; the more under 11 stone the better, and never over that weight. In stopping hounds, never let the whip begin to rate them before heading them, but gallop well before them, and *then* begin to smack his whip and rate them. This is particularly necessary when in the open, but it should also be attended to in covert. While the hounds are running many slight offences may be passed over; which, however, should be treasured up, and considered in aggravation of punishment on the next similar offence. When not running no offence should be passed over, and if the rate and whip are not attended to, the hound should be taken up and well flogged. When hounds are very riotous, it has been the custom to introduce the subject of their riot to the kennel, and flog them well in its presence, rating them the while; but this is certainly a bad plan, and quite unnecessary, if due care is taken in the summer to accustom hounds to riot, two or three couple at a time. When these means have been taken in the summer, and the whip sufficiently used then, the rate "Ware-hare," or "Have a care," or "Ware-sheep," will generally nip such offences in the bud; and that is the time when they are the most easily prevented. Besides these rates, the first whip should chiefly use the halloo on viewing the fox, and should be able to give it artistically; thus—"Taally ho! taaally ho!! taaally ho!!! Go-n-e away! go-n-e away!! go-o-n-e aw-a-y!!!" followed by the peculiar scream which no words will convey. If, however, the fox is headed back, he alters his note to "Tally ho! back! Tally ho! back!!" and, with a smack of his whip, sends the hounds into covert again as fast as they appear. In assisting the huntsman to get hounds out, not by the whip, he uses the words, "Elup! eluppe!! eluppe!!!" One thing a first whip should especially guard against, and that is, the giving the huntsman any cause for jealousy. This feeling is always sufficiently near the surface, and if encouraged, adieu to all hopes of co-operation on the part of two men whose duties are as much connected as is the right hand with the left. If, however, the huntsman fancies that the whipper-in is trying to show off at his expense, or to supplant him in the estimation of the hunt, he is sure to endeavour to lower him, and in so doing he interferes with sport; and the same is the case with the whip himself. They can do as much harm by opposing one another, as good by co-operation. Many think that a good whipper-in makes a good huntsman, but the two offices are so very distinct that it rarely is the case. The one has a limited field of operations, and has confined himself for many years to that field in which he has been activity itself, and has rivalled " the varmint" himself in skill and daring. The other has a much larger field, and requires to know not only the habits of the fox, but those of the hound as well; also, the natural history of everything upon which his eye falls in the hunting-field: the habits of the crow, whose flight often indicates the line of the fox; the habits of sheep, who often in the distance may be seen to indicate the fox's presence among them; the peculiar style of hunting of each hound, who each often tell him something of what is going on; and lastly, the general features of the part of the country which he is hunting, upon which much depends in his casts and lifts.

362. THE SECOND WHIP has a much more easy place, as far as head-work is concerned, but his hands will find full occupation, even if he had a dozen pair. He must look out for riot in covert, and stop it quickly and decidedly; he must be ready to bring up the tail-hounds, and on all occasions work to the huntsman whenever he is getting his hounds forward, and lifting them either in covert or out. "Forrard, forrard," is his everlasting cry, and the acting up to it his chief duty. If he does this well, and takes care to leave no hound behind him, he will fulfil his duties to everybody's satisfaction.

SECT. 10.—POINTS OF DIFFERENCE FROM STAG-HUNTING.

363. STAG-HUNTING being a sport in which the game is to be saved, hounds must necessarily be easily stopped; they must therefore be very tractable, which, to a certain extent, is desirable with foxhounds, but still not so much so as with staghounds. Nothing perhaps would be more difficult than to save a fox close before a pack of foxhounds, and many a vixen in the spring pays the penalty of this excessive desire for blood. Without it the dash of the foxhound

would be lost, and the chief beauty of the sport marred; it would indeed sink into tameness, and the high price at which it is purchased would be totally thrown away.

SECT. 11.—POINTS OF DIFFERENCE FROM HARE-HUNTING.

364. HARE-HUNTING, as we shall presently see, is a sport totally different from fox-hunting; and requires different men, different horses, different hounds, and a very different field. Harriers should certainly never be interfered with, and should be able to carry on their hunting under every difficulty. It must be remembered that the hare is always above ground, and that the hounds ought to be able to pick out her scent through every disadvantage; consequently, time is of no consequence, and the end must always come if only the hounds can continue to hunt. Patience, therefore, may have full play; and the huntsman has little to do but to watch his beauties, and admire their wonderful efforts to out-manœuvre the turns and doubles of the hare. As Beckford observes, fox-hunting without its spirit would be no longer fox-hunting; it would be as stale small-beer to champagne. The harrier or beagle is always at work, but is content to do that work "slowly and surely;" he should never be hurried; while the foxhound's dash leads him to try forward and get on as rapidly as his nose will allow him to do. With a strong bold fox this quality is very necessary, and no true harriers or beagles would reach him; but with a short-running and bad one, the case is different; and then the latter hound would perhaps succeed better than the high-bred foxhound. But when foxes take a straight line, hounds must race as well as hunt; and it is their great peculiarity that they are capable of doing this. Beckford distinguishes hunting the fox from fox-hunting; and, to illustrate his position, shows that a hackney, though he runs a race, is not therefore a race-horse. The foxhound therefore ought to be kept to his own game, and not be used for the hare, whose style of running he is not suited for. If hares are to be raced into, greyhounds are the appointed dogs; and it is a poor kind of coursing when the hounds occasionally stoop to the scent, and at other times run their hare in view. Fox-hunting in its very essence implies courage, impetuosity, pace, and dash in all engaged; whilst hare-hunting is inseparably connected with cool, cautious, old-gentlemanly discretion and wile. Towards the end of a run the difference is very remarkable. The foxhound *vires acquirit eundo*, is more and more full of dash, and as he catches view is literally frantic with excitement; but

throughout the hare-hunt the same steady and beautiful, but calm kind of hunting goes on; and even at the kill the hounds seem scarcely to enjoy their bloodless victory. Beagles cannot possibly be too tender-nosed, provided they are all alike and pack well; but the foxhound may easily be so, if he is thereby tempted to tie on a scent and potter, whereby time is lost, and the fox escapes to his earth. FOX-HUNTING IS THE SPORT OF YOUTH AND EARLY MANHOOD, and is rarely enjoyed to the fullest extent after that period of life is gone. Few men after forty-five can get up the steam sufficiently to enter into it with all the zest which it is capable of inspiring; and though many who have passed their grand climacteric join in its pleasures, it is generally without also partaking of its perils. A perfect hunter and a little riding to points will generally suffice for the prevention of accidents, but the sport is not then enjoyed as it was at thirty; nor is it really partaken of in all its glories and perfections. How seldom do we see any man above the age I have specified at all near the hounds! Certainly there are some brilliant exceptions, and especially with some of our most prominent huntsmen of late years, whose grey hairs seem no impediment to daring horsemanship, and proper and efficient assistance to hounds. I have heard of some men who prefer a tough beefsteak to one cut from a tender London rump, because the former lasted longer than the latter; and with them perhaps a four or five hours' fox-chase is the perfection of the sport; but though I like to see hounds left to themselves a good deal, I confess it is only that they may get on the faster, not dwell the longer on a scent. All hounds go fast enough with a good scent, but no hound can go the pace which a foxhound can with a bad one; and in this is another point of difference between the two hounds. It must be remembered that during every minute lost, the fox is nearing his point of safety by some hundreds of yards; whilst in the case of the hare she is only crouching close to you in all probability. For all these reasons foxhounds should always be above their work, in order to retain that dash which is so highly prized; while harriers can scarcely be too much worked, as thereby they are rendered sufficiently steady and ready to stoop.

SECT. 12.—BAG-FOXES.

365. Whenever bag-foxes are to be used, they should be hunted solely for the purpose of giving blood; and if it is intended to depend upon them entirely, a pack of harriers will serve the purpose much better than foxhounds. They run much more like hares than wild foxes, and, not knowing where to look for earths, they do not take a line; and consequently are soon run into by foxhounds which will condescend to hunt them. Old hounds which have tasted good, sweet, and healthy wild foxes, will scorn such carrion; and the fact of a bag-fox being shaken out before hounds by the keeper, is often clearly indicated by the best hounds refusing to take their usual leading places at the head of the pack. Harriers, however, will hunt bagmen with great alacrity; and the sport is very similar to a run with the hare; and, as displaying all the excellencies of the beagle, is not to be despised. I should much prefer such a sport with a good pack of full-sized beagles, to the slow sport which is afforded by bad foxhounds in a bad country, where foxes are perpetually lost, or changed, or chopped; and where a good run is a rare exception.

SECT. 13.—CONSEQUENCES OF A SEVERE RUN.

366. When hounds have had a very severe run, they require some time to recruit; and the same pack should not be again taken out for three, four, or five days, if it is possible to avoid it. In all cases, the hardest working hounds suffer the most, and they must have rest, while those which have husbanded their powers, must make up the pack with the hounds which were left at home on the occasion of the hard day. When hounds have been very severely tested, they often take a week to come round, and should have it at all costs, as these are the treasures of the pack, and if they are over-worked, will sadly injure its brilliancy. Hard-worked hounds should have a little extra flesh; but this will not entirely do away with the necessity for rest, and, carried to extremes, will only make them mangy, and full of humours. Lame hounds, also, ought to have full time to recover, and should never leave the kennel till quite recovered; it is a stupid and cruel plan to take out lame hounds in order to make up the numbers. They must lag behind, and only occupy the time of the second whip, in getting them taken care of at some keeper's house or labourer's cottage. It is far better to start with short numbers of useful hounds, than to cheat the eyes of the uninitiated, by taking out a lot of cripples to the meet—a practice which every sportsman soon condemns in the hearing of the whole field.

SECT. 14.—NECESSITY FOR BLOOD.

367. It is commonly, and indeed almost invariably, said that foxhounds must have blood; and, since the time of Beckford, the saying is constantly paraded. But though

some blood is necessary, yet it by no means follows that it is well for the hounds to kill every fox they find. Even were it possible, it would not, I think, increase their dash, or add to their hunting; for an occasional disappointment is more likely to give zest to success, than if the constant termination by a kill was the goal to which all hounds look forward without a doubt or fear. Observe how differently an old greyhound runs when he thinks there is a chance of losing his hare; he then puts on the steam, and is a different animal to what he was when he thought ultimate success as certain as fate. And so with the foxhound;

if he finds blood always reward his exertions, he will not try nearly so hard as he would do if he was doubtful of success. Hence, how often we see, after a week's bad scent, a good pack go off with a fair scent, and run as they never ran before. Such dash! such a head! as never was seen. They have been disappointed day after day, and are savage *for want of blood*. But this must not be carried too far; if they are hopeless of success, they will become slack, and in time this is always the result of bad management. Hounds soon learn to know if they are well hunted; and, like race-horses, they do not half answer to bad handling.

CHAP. VI.

HARE-HUNTING.

SECT. 1.—HARE-HOUNDS—AND HOW TO PROCURE THEM.

368. The varieties of hounds for hunting the hare have been already mentioned at page 98, under the heads of Harriers, Medium-Beagles, Dwarf-Beagles, Fox-Beagles, and Terrier-Beagles. I shall, therefore, now proceed to describe, as in fox-hunting, the best mode of obtaining a pack. It will be evident that here time is no object, for a man may spend half-a-dozen years in procuring a pack if he likes; and I am inclined to think he would succeed the best by so doing. A pack of hounds to the exact taste of the intended sportsmen is seldom in the market, and the first thing a purchaser does is to set to work to get rid of certain peculiarities inherent in his bargain. Thus, they are too high or too low, or too fast or too slow, or too flashy or too low hunters; or some other fault will be found which destroys his pleasure in hunting them. There is such a vast difference between the two extremes, and so many shades to be met with, that few men can exactly please themselves with any but bantlings of their own breeding. Besides, a man can easily breed six or eight couple of hounds in one season, and these, with a few old and steady hounds, will serve very well for him to begin with. He will also, if he hunts them himself, be better able to manage a small pack, and may teach himself and them at the same time. I should, therefore, advise intended masters of hare-hounds, unless they meet with a pack *exactly* to their minds, to set to work and breed, rather than to buy an indifferent pack. Three or four bitches should be selected of the exact

size, blood, and symmetry which is desired, and any price given for them. Let no moderate sum be considered too high to procure this nucleus of the future "little terribles;" for upon them all depends, since, whatever they are, such will be your young hounds, subject always to the change produced by the cross with the intended sire. Now, it will be seen at page 94, that I have recommended the beagle-blood to be selected in preference to the foxhound for hare-hunting, because in them is developed to the highest extent the hunting powers of the old tender-nosed hound, with sufficient pace only to allow the hare to exhibit all those wiles which serve to display the hunting of the hound. Unlike the fox, the hare cannot save herself but by her doubles; and the beagle has full time to follow her in all her mazes and wanderings. The hare-hunting foxhound, on the contrary, presses her too much, prevents her running in her natural style, and races into her in a most bastard and unnatural manner, comprehending the bad features of both kinds of hunting without their good ones. By all means, therefore, I should steer clear of that cross, except in a very remote degree, or in very small hounds which bear the foxhound cross without injury, because, with all their dash, they cannot press the hare sufficiently to prevent her display of doublings.

If the purpose, however, is to get together a pack of average-sized harriers, say of about 18 to 20 inches, the less foxhound-blood they have the better. Of course it may be easy to err in the opposite extreme, and to get hounds which will sit down on their seats of honour (if they have any), and throw their tongues in the most melodious manner without stirring their legs. Such animals are absurdly slow, and will please no one, I should imagine; nor indeed would they be easy to procure in the present fast age. But plenty of tender-nosed harriers can be procured, with more or less foxhound blood in them; and the brood-bitches should be selected according to taste from these hounds. These bitches will also serve to enter the young pack, for, as the dash and speed of the foxhound are not wanted in hare-hunting, their age and caution will be exceedingly useful in picking out the scent when the young hounds are in difficulties. The full-sized and naturally fast modern harrier is particularly adapted for running trapped hares, when a gallop of twenty minutes is all that is desired, or that can be expected. These hares run as straight as a fox, and in very much the same style; often topping the low fences like a dog, if hard pressed. They do not try the hunting powers of the hound, because, in the first place, their scent is strong; and in the second, their ignorance of the country they are in seems to prevent all attempt at safety by artifice, and they run straight till picked up by their followers. Small and comparatively slow hounds are here out of place; displaying neither the pace which may be obtained with the trapped hare, nor the beautiful hunting met with in the wild one. The small drafted foxhound is very little different from those modern harriers, but not having been so long confined to the hunting the hare, is not so well suited to the hare-hunter's purpose; and I should prefer breeding from such a pack as the Blackmore Vale Hounds, which are true foxhounds in blood, though long used to hunt hares. These hounds are very fast, and burst their hares generally within half-an-hour; they have also excellent noses, but they are too fast, in my humble opinion, for the sport of hare-hunting. Occasionally a quick hare, or one of the down hares, may stand before these hounds for miles, and show as straight running as a fox often displays; but if such is desired, why not hunt the fox at once? in which you will get such runs constantly, and not as exceptional cases. If harriers are to be used as a means of giving a gallop, trapped hares are by far the best, and for them these dwarf foxhounds are fully adapted; but if for showing true and close hunting, without reference to pace, we must go further back towards the old southern hound to procure a hound suited for the purpose. Nevertheless, as all may not think alike, it is well that every one should know how to procure that which will produce exactly what he wants. This I have endeavoured to show, and also to point out how the pack may be bred exactly to suit the taste of the master; but if that plan is considered too slow and long of accomplishment, two or three packs are generally sold every season, at a price varying from 60 or 80 guineas to 300 guineas; the latter being a very high price for harriers, though £700 is said to have been once given for a celebrated pack. From these one may be selected, and if it does not answer the purpose, it is no fault of mine.

SECT. 2.—BREEDING.

369. When the choice is made of a particular kind of hound, it is necessary in the pack of harriers, far more than in foxhounds, that all should be bred to that standard. This is not only desirable on account of looks, but also on the score of efficiency; for, if hounds are not of the same size and form, they are much less likely to pack well than if all are cast in the same mould. Let the bitches, therefore, be all as much as possible alike and of the same blood; though, for after-convenience of breeding, not too nearly related. Then put them all to the same dog, or to similar ones, for if they are put to dogs of various sizes and blood, the progeny will vary also in externals as well as in style of hunting. It is well known that breeding in-and-in will not do if carried too far, but with harriers it may be carried to a great extent, and thrice in to once out will keep up in a pack a sufficient amount of strength of constitution. Supposing, therefore, two couple of bitches have been bred from, they will, in all probability, throw from 12 to 15 couple of whelps; and with a little aid from other bitches, for which purpose many may generally be obtained at the right time, that number may be reared. These must be sent out to walk at two or three months' old, and, with good luck, 10 couple of young hounds will come in towards the beginning of January, and may be at once subjected to kennel-discipline, and in a month's time may be entered to hare; which, however, they should never run for more than an hour or so in the day during their puppyhood. These hounds, however, may be entered much earlier than foxhounds, but the larger dog-puppies should be kept until the autumn. The management in kennel is the same as already described under the first chapter on Hunting, and the breaking from riot also; remembering that for them hare is not riot, but the contrary. Much time is gained, and great advantage in every way results, from entering harriers to their game at this early age; and I am sure that the development of the taste for the sport is in a ratio with its early instilment; besides, as these hounds

have not the courage of the foxhound, so they are less calculated to bear any loss of this quality; and yet, during the next summer, they must be constantly exercised, with the whip and rate perpetually going, though the less these are used the better. But if they have been entered, their natural propensity to hunt has been encouraged and gratified, and they will afterwards bear some degree of rating during the summer. During this first entering and the next season, it will not be possible to be very strict in drafting hounds, because there is little choice, and the master must make up his mind to rub through this time with what he has, looking forward with pleasure to the future as the time of perfection. By again breeding the same number of whelps, at the end of the first season he may begin to draft, as he finds there is a probability of supplying their places with more efficient and elegant substitutes; and by the beginning of the second season he may take the field with a good-looking pack of perhaps 18 or 20 couple of hounds, which, if not quite up to all the dodges of the hare, are at all events soon likely to be—that is, if properly managed, and not too much interfered with. This plan will produce a pack in two or three years, at only a few pound's expense, for walking and keep of hounds, over and above the original price of the brood-bitches. It will also afford the master the pleasure of feeling that he has bred his pack to his own model of perfection; and if he has not fully succeeded, he will be sure to console himself by the belief that he has approached it as nearly as possible. We are all prone to hug ourselves in this way, and a great happiness it is to most that human nature is so constituted. Every man's goose is a swan in his own eyes, however manifest its anserine properties are to all the rest of the world.

Sect. 3.—Peculiarities proper to the Men.

370. The Huntsman, who is also with hare-hounds generally the master, should be a very different person to the huntsman of a pack of foxhounds. Sometimes a young man succeeds in this task; but more frequently he fails from want of temper and patience; and the age which is best suited for the sport is that at which man usually has arrived at some degree of control over his natural impulses. Still there are some exceptions to this rule, and I have seen harriers exceedingly well hunted by very young men. But, whatever the age of the huntsman, he should be quiet, persevering, cautious, and free from meddling, and should trust to the noses of his hounds

in preference to his own head. Beckford recommends that the huntsman of a pack of harriers should be bred from a female of the family of the "quiet gentleman" in the "Spectator," crossed with a knowing huntsman; and probably this cross would suit; but, as with the poet so with the huntsman, *nascitur non fit.* He must be taken as he is framed by the Almighty; and few are so framed as to fit them for the management of harriers till they have sown a crop of wild oats in other and more exciting amusements. The chief art of the huntsman here is in breeding his hounds, and in drafting them, so that they shall be "suity," and pack well; for when once they are in the field, little or no interference is necessary. They should be as handy as kittens, and should scarcely require a whipper-in; and indeed some of the best packs I have ever seen have been without that appendage. By constantly taking out hounds in summer, and breaking them from riot, and by feeding them after drawing each by name, and otherwise getting control over the hounds in the summer season, it is seldom that any occasion occurs for the office of the whip. If the huntsman rides well to them, he is always near enough to them to interfere when this is wanted; and the hounds are not cowed by the needless display of power, which, if placed in the hands of a whip, is sure to be exercised. But the critical eye of the master is always employed, though he may otherwise be idle, in watching the actions of each hound, and noting his hunting and his pace, also in detecting skirting and babbling, and in deciding upon all the various qualities which will lead him to draft certain hounds, or to breed from others. This is interest sufficient for any man; and to a real lover of hunting it is a most delightful amusement. A comparison may here be drawn between getting a perfect pack of beagles together, and putting four horses in harness so as to exhibit a perfect team. In both cases any one can manage them when broken; but the artist is shown in getting them all to pull together, and to be exact repetitions, the one of the other. In a four-in-hand team, one horse ought not only to be like the others in size, colour, and shape, but his action should be the same, his carriage the same, and he should do exactly his own share of work, and no more. This is the perfection of four-in-hand driving, and a very difficult task to accomplish satisfactorily; and so it is with harriers or beagles—they may easily be handled when well-matched; but it is in the matching that the huntsman's power is shown. He therefore requires a great knowledge of individual character in the hounds, so as to select those only, which exhibit what he wants in great perfection, to breed from, and to cross with those which will develope still further those good qualities, or suppress the bad ones.

371. THE WHIPPER-IN should be a mere groom, solely intended as a second pair of hands to those of the master; and he should never be allowed to use them without orders. With a gentleman hunting his own pack, such an assistant is very desirable, for holding gates open, turning hounds, keeping them from tieing on the scent, and from riot, &c., all which are tiresome tasks, but may be easily performed by one pair of hands, if the owner of them does not mind the trouble.

SECT. 4.—PREPARATIONS FOR HUNTING.

372. The pack intended to hunt on the following day should be drafted and fed at about twelve or one o'clock, and then shut up. From twelve to fifteen couple are quite sufficient for hare-hunting; and the hounds ought to be all equally free from lameness, and very level in condition. Beyond this nothing is requisite, as there is no earth-stopping to be attended to, or public notice of the meets; but the privileged few should have their information in good time, which is arranged in different ways, according to the different circumstances of the pack. Sometimes harriers are publicly announced to meet two or three times a-week, but the injury done to the crops and fences by the field, if numerous, is so great, that there will always be great objections to this. Hares almost always take a ring, and often the same fields are run over several times; and, consequently, much greater damage is done than in a straight run, as with foxhounds. It is only, therefore, where hounds have a great reputation that farmers will allow their land to be thus sacrificed; but in some neighbourhoods the sporting tendency is so strong as to overpower the love of gold, and with them the result is, that a well-behaved field of horsemen is always welcome. There is never any excuse for wantonly riding over turnips, or young wheat, or seeds, with harriers, because the pace and direction are seldom such as to compel the maintenance of a straight line, and a slight detour to avoid such crops will never much interfere with the enjoyment of sport. Some excuse may be made for the field of fox-hunters riding over any crop, let it be what it may, in the ardour of pursuit; but even then some little care should be taken to avoid doing injury to one's neighbours; but in the pursuit of the hare, the man who does such a thing deserves to be well-rated by the master, as well as the sufferer, for his thoughtlessness.

SECT. 5.—HARE-FINDING.

373. THE FORM OF THE HARE, or, as it is sometimes called, her SEAT, is very easily seen by some men, and with as much difficulty by others. This does not seem to depend upon quickness of sight only, for I have known many who could see long distances, and were very quick-sighted, who never could find a hare in her form. Others, again, of comparatively weak sight and slow habits, were sure to find her if she was within view; so that it may be considered as a knack or gift, a good deal dependent upon the powers of observation. Much depends upon the observance of colour, for it appears to me that this is the chief guide. I have generally observed that quick hare-finders have corrected a mistaken "See, ho!" by the remark, "No, that is too red for a hare;" or, "That is too green." Never, "That is not the right *shape*," but always the difference being referred to colour. It is probable, therefore, that good hare-finders have a very delicate perception of the shades of colour, and by that faculty are able to find the hare in her seat. Hares sit in different situations, according to the weather, and should be looked for accordingly. Thus, in windy weather they get out of its way, and sit on hill-sides under the lee of the wind, or under the protection of a hedgerow, and not far from it. In dry weather they affect damp and marshy grass-bottoms, and in wet weather will only be found on high and sandy banks. They seldom sit on their feeding-ground, though this rule is not an invariable one. Fallows are a very favourite and chosen seat for hares, and when there they generally choose their forms near the top of the ridge. Fallows newly ploughed are never used by the hare for much less than a fortnight, and very stale ones are also rejected. It is difficult to account for this last rejection, because we cannot understand why a stale fallow should be disliked by the hare; but so it is, and the fact is well known to the hare-finder. Some fields, also, are much liked, year after year, by hares, and others as much rejected; but, here again, no one can assign a reason, since their food has nothing to do with the choice, and we know nothing of their other *penchants*. In hare-hunting, it is very desirable to find the hare sitting, because she may otherwise sit so close as to be "chopped" before she gets away, a consummation to be carefully avoided; and, at the present usual hour of meeting, the trail up to the form can seldom be hit off, in consequence of the hare having too long been in form to have left any scent on her road to it; though in this way hares are much

more easily found than foxes, the scent of whose drag is much more faint than that given out by the trail of the hare. The hare-finder therefore, if possible, finds the hare for the master, who brings up his hounds to within a reasonable distance, and then the hare is put up out of view; immediately after this the hounds are laid on the scent, and the run begins. If this cannot be managed, and no hare is found by man, the hounds proceed to draw for puss on the most likely ground; and as the hour of meeting is, as I before remarked, generally too late for the trail, they spread themselves over the land, in the hope of finding her in her form. The objection to this is that the hare always gets up in view, and is frequently chopped; but if she escapes this early death, the view makes the hounds flashy and unsteady, and prevents them settling down to the scent as they would have done if not excited by the view. Much, however, depends upon the hounds and upon the hares, also upon the kind of hunting preferred; for if the fox-hound style is preferred, this flashy kind of hunting will not be rejected. If a hedge is to be beaten, a man or two should advance a few yards before the leading hounds and beat it well, or otherwise the hare in jumping out is sure to be chopped. In any case the drawing of the hounds is a very beautiful sight, and the careful trying and even-spreading of the little symmetrical animals is one of the prettiest parts of the sport. Hounds, when thus accustomed to find their hares, take a great delight in looking for them, and go on from tussock to tussock, and from one likely spot to another, in the most lively yet knowing way—reminding one of the peering ways of the magpie, by their sharp and quick, yet quiet style of trying every likely spot. This part of hare-hunting has always appeared to me the one in which they may assume a superiority over fox-hunting; for here the eye finds an opportunity of dwelling with admiration in the minutes of expectation, whilst in drawing for a fox, it is but seldom that the expectant and impatient fox-hunter can find any amusement or occupation, except in his cigar or the gossip of the covert-side. Next in beauty to the working of a brace of pointers or setters, I should place the drawing of a pack of "suity" beagles or harriers; it is, to my taste, not far behind that beautiful picture, though the find certainly does not come up to the "set and back" of the shooter's grand assistants.

SECT. 6.—THE RUN.

874. The artifices of the hare are truly wonderful, and beat those of Mr. Wiley hollow. Why the fox should have obtained this name in preference to the hare, is very unaccountable; for every man conversant with hunting is aware that the hare is ten times more cunning than the fox in her doubles and running devices. If she is watched before the hounds, she will be seen to go straight away while in view, and then to commence a series of doubles, which certainly must require a degree of reasoning power for their development. She returns on her track, perhaps, then makes three or four enormous jumps, and starts off again at a right angle with her former course; she will then, if in a wall-country, jump on to the top of a wall, and run some yards along the top; then, descending with a long jump, she will perhaps squat till she ascertains the success of her manœuvres. After this, if unsuccessful, she will try others, such as running through sheep, or through a covert and back again, coming out at the same meuse, and running up the ditch, and off again on a fresh circle. Often she will pass by a furze or thorn-bush, at the distance of a couple of yards, then, returning, she will carefully follow her former course, and from it throw herself into the bush, where she calmly remains while the hounds hunt by her. Again, she will perhaps take water, and endeavour to foil the hounds in that way, often swimming a tolerably-wide river in effecting her purpose, and generally without perhaps intending it, being carried down the stream, while the hounds are sure to cross straight over, or as nearly so as possible. Such are a few of her artifices, and the hounds should be able, and also be permitted, to follow out all these various devices without assistance; the huntsman knowing that time will always bring her to bag, if they can only hold on with any scent at all. Hunting is here the perfection of the sport, and no one should care for the gallop. Plenty of fencing may be had, if it is desired, or the hare-hunter may otherwise avoid it in most cases, by availing himself of gates and gaps. If, however, a huntsman is to be in his proper place, he must take all before him just as with foxhounds; though this is not necessary for the present day's sport, but rather for that of the future; for unless he sees all the working of the hounds, he cannot possibly distinguish the good from the bad, for the purpose of drafting or breeding. Hare-hounds seldom or never require a cheer; they are only too apt to overrun the scent without it; and, *as a pack*, they should be left to their own devices on all occasions but the following—first, when they come to a check, and cannot recover the scent; secondly, when they change hares; and

thirdly, when they divide. Individual faults must of course be rated by the huntsman himself, or through him, by the whip.

375. THE CHECK is the great criterion of the harehound's powers, for while the good pack spreads and tries every yard of ground with the greatest care, persevering even beyond all apparent hope of success, the bad one soon gives up, and the hounds stand idly and listlessly about, expecting the hare to jump into their mouths. In hare-hunting the check generally arises either from the stain of sheep, or from the hare having practised some unusually clever double, or from her passing through a covert stained with the scent of rabbits or other hares. When the check is in the open, and from sheep, the hounds having tried their cast and failed, the huntsman should try round the whole field, taking the hedge carefully, and not allowing the hounds to follow at his horse's heels, but encouraging them to try all the way. If the scent cannot be hit off, and the hounds are good, the probability is that the hare has squatted in the middle of the field, which she often does; and if there is any covert, as in turnips for instance, every yard of it should be tried. During this second cast in the field, it often happens, if a good look-out is not kept, that the hare steals away without being seen, and in that case may be missed; though if the ground is carefully beaten she will be sure to be hit off by some of the hounds. If, nevertheless, no hound can scent her, the huntsman must extend his cast and try the hedgerows next beyond, taking them in the order of their probability; and remembering that hares have always a tendency, *unless they have a decided home*, to return to the place where they were found. If, however, they have a home, he should try forward towards that home; and in that direction will generally succeed in recovering the scent. Most hares now-a-days are bred in covert, and return to it whenever disturbed; and these will generally be easily recovered by a cast in the direction of their home. Where the check arises from a double, the huntsman should have previously observed the nature of the doubles which have already been followed out, because these will afford some clue to the one now interfering with the sport; for this reason, that the same hare generally adopts the same *kind of* double throughout her run. Thus, if she has been returning on her line, then taking a jump and on again, she will most probably repeat this over and over again, but under different circumstances—as, in or near a hedge, or in or near a brook, &c.; and the huntsman must expect these variations of the same artifice. Again, if she has been making a

small ring and hunting the hounds once, she will be sure to try it again; and when most at fault, the hounds may just have passed over her in her secure retreat, where her scent is completely overpowered by that of the hounds.

376. IN CASE OF THE CHANGE OF HARE, the hounds should be stopped from the fresh hare, and the old scent recovered if possible. Nothing disturbs hare-hunting so much as the over-abundance of hares; and where they are thickly preserved it is quite out of the question to attempt this kind of sport. In many preserves a change would occur every five minutes, from a fresh hare jumping up before the hounds; and, therefore, the sport is totally unfitted for such countries. The hunted hare may almost always be known by her changed colour, and wet and dirty appearance, while the fresh one is clean and dry. Hares long hunted become very dark indeed, and almost of a dark slate colour.

377. WHEN HOUNDS DIVIDE, the huntsman, if both hares are fresh, may choose which he shall follow, and send his whip to stop the hounds from the other, and bring them up to him. If one is the hunted hare and the other a fresh one, no one will hesitate a moment in selecting the former, and stopping the hounds from the latter.

SECT. 7.—THE KILL.

378. THE KILL is generally, with harriers, the most painful part of the whole business; because, in the first place, the cries of the hare are often piercing and piteous in the extreme, resembling those of a child in agony; and the hounds not being always allowed to have her, the whip is obliged to be used at a time when they least deserve it. It is true that some packs are so highly broken that they will not tear the skin of the hare even; but few have arrived at such a pitch of perfection without losing their hunting powers, and it is not, I think, to be attempted by the amateur-master. Ordinary hounds will occasionally gratify their desire for blood, and should be indulged with a hare once a-week at the least; indeed, many huntsmen like their hounds to have the last hare they kill on each day; but this is perhaps more than necessary. If the huntsman is a good horseman, and is well up with his hounds, he may generally pick the hare up without using the whip, as the hounds will not break her while he is so close; but if at a distance at the time, they will take advantage of his absence, and when once the blood is tasted, the whip must be used, to stop them in time. No one but the huntsman should attempt to pick up the hare without the whip, as the hounds will only

tear her from his hands. I confess that I should at all times be unwilling to interfere, as I would much rather see the hounds enjoy their dainty morsel, than see it reserved for the stomachs of less deserving bipeds, who have not earned even the currant jelly with which it is served up.

SECT. 8.—THE EXPENSES OF HARRIERS.

379. Compared with fox-hunting, the expenses of hare-hunting are very trifling, and they may be calculated as follows. It must be also recollected that the first outlay is much less.

	£ s.	£ s.
24 couple of hounds, at 1s. 6d. per week per head	187 4	
Tax on ditto	28 16	
Medicines, &c.	4 0	
Carry forward,		220 0

	£ s.	£ s.
Brought forward,		220 0
3 horses for 7 months, at 15s. per week	63 0	
Ditto ditto 5 months, at 7s.	21 0	
Tax on ditto	3 0	
Veterinary surgeon	3 0	
Shoeing	7 10	
Saddling	12 0	
		109 10
Helper and whip, at 12s. per week each	62 0	
Tax on ditto	2 0	
		64 0
Total		£393 10

By great economy, and the dispensing with the Whip, and using one horse only, with twenty couple of hounds, only about half this sum will suffice, especially with beagles.

CHAP. VII.

OTTER-HUNTING.

SECT. 1.—THE OTTER, AND ITS HAUNTS.

380. At page 11, the otter has been already partially described, but for hunting purposes his habits and peculiarities must be more carefully studied. He is an amphibious animal, living entirely upon fish, and seizing them by swimming under them, and thus taking them when they least expect it. His scent is very strong, so that hounds can hunt it for some hours even after the otter has passed. He is very tenacious of life, and a very hard biter, and will easily break the leg of a dog if he gets good hold. The otter does not confine himself to the water, but travels up the side of the river or brook for some distance, and leaves his foot-mark, called his *seal*, which may be easily recognised by the round ball or cup-like depression, and the marks of the webs, which are visible in the well-marked *seal*. The hounds can, therefore, generally hunt the otter up the banks of the brooks which he frequents; but the *seal* will afford the best signs for tracking him to his burrow, the entrance to which is like the water-rat's, always under the water, while a small and invisible hole supplies it with air. This burrow is called his *couch;* and his coming to the surface to breathe, which he is obliged to do every few minutes, is called his *vent;* his dung is also called his *spraints.*

SECT. 2.—OTTER-HUNTING IMPLEMENTS.

381. Otter-spears are the chief requisites for this sport, and are of great assistance to the otter-hunter, not only in killing the otter, but in enabling the sportsmen to leap over brooks, &c. They consist of two portions, the pole and the head. The pole is an ashen staff, about 12 feet long, and strong in proportion to the strength of the party using it, but stout enough to bear his weight as a leaping-pole. It should have an iron head, either fixed on or screwed into a socket fixed on the pole, but the permanent head answers all the purposes required, and is very much cheaper. It can also be made by the village blacksmith, and, if lost in the ardour of the chase, may be easily and cheaply replaced. If the head is made to screw on and off, it is usual to have a concealed barb, which comes out of a mortice, on the animal being transfixed, and thus holds him firmly fixed on the spear; but the slightly-barbed spear-head is quite sufficient to secure him firmly if fairly through him, and even the concealed barb will not do this unless it also pierces the body of the animal. Each sportsman

should have a spear, and one or two spare ones should be carried by an attendant, in case of accident.

SECT. 3.—THE OTTER-HOUNDS.

382. The otter-hound has been also partially described as a descendant of the old southern hound crossed with the wire-haired Scotch terrier, and probably with the water-spaniel. He is the nearest approach of all to the southern hound, and has the length of ear, the full pendent lip, the dewlap and throaty frill, which are so characteristic of that hound. His nose is very good, which is required to track the cold scent of the otter, and to follow him in the water, where the otter-hound often speaks to the scent in a wonderful manner. The pure foxhound has been successfully used by Mr. Grantley Berkeley for the otter, and will hunt him no doubt, as indeed he will hunt whatever he is entered to; but he is quite out of place here, being too fast on land, and not a sufficiently good swimmer in the water, nor capable of bearing that element for so long a period as the webbed otter-hound, whose greasy and woolly coat is impenetrable to wet. These last two peculiarities he obtains from the water-spaniel. The deep-toned note of the otter-hound is another remnant of the old southerner, and he may be often seen to throw his tongue on the scent, without the power of moving his legs, so great is his pleasure and excitement. This, however, is too much of the old school, and should be got rid of in the perfect hound; and generally is, if the terrier and spaniel cross is sufficiently introduced. Both these dogs have no disposition to tie on the scent, but if too much of their blood is introduced, the hound will suffer in delicacy of nose, and will want perseverance in hunting. Otter-hounds are very savage animals, and will fight to the death, which is a common result of their quarrels. If not savage, they will scarcely cope with the otter without flinching, as his bites are exceedingly severe. The otter-hound may be obtained without much difficulty in Wales, Devonshire, or Scotland, where packs of them are still kept up, and hunted wherever the otter is heard of. The great drawback to the sport is the scarcity of the otter in any given spot, so that to obtain sport a large district must be ransacked, and the hounds taken long distances, often to seductive promises of sport which are without real foundation. Nothing is more disheartening than to find, after travelling 20 or 30 miles to a river where otters are promised to be shown, that no *seal* is visible along the whole course of the banks. This mark is always to be met with, either fresh or stale, and the experienced otter-hunter knows that if it is entirely absent, he has been deceived by false representations. Otter-hounds are generally bred about 24 inches in height, the bitches being less, as usual with hounds. There is a smooth otter-hound, but the rough one is that generally in use.

SECT. 4.—THE MEN.

383. A huntsman is required for this sport as well as for all others where a pack of hounds is engaged; for no pack can be properly managed except by a man who is always in the habit of taking them under his control. Unless, therefore, the master of the hounds undertakes the task himself, he had much better entrust the entire management to his man; because they will seldom work so savagely and courageously for any one else as they will do for their regular feeder and attendant. Otter-hounds are no use unless they try most perseveringly every inch of the bank; and they must stand the water, or at least continue to be wet for hours together. This, even in the summer-season, is a very cold business in the early mornings; and they soon begin to be slack, unless animated by a person to whom they are strongly attached. For this reason, therefore, I should prefer the regular huntsman to any other person. The only other paid servant necessary for this sport is an attendant to carry a spare pole or two.

SECT. 5.—THE HUNT.

384. When an otter has been heard of as having been seen in any neighbouring stream, or when his presence is suspected there from his "spraints," or "seal," or from the half-eaten remnants of the fish which he has caught, the hounds are started off very early on a summer's morning—that is, by dawn of day. No other season but the summer will suit this sport, because the cold water of early spring, winter, or autumn, will chill and cramp hounds and men to a dangerous degree. But while the warmth of summer is necessary to heat the water sufficiently, the rays of the mid-day sun are inimical to the scent; and, therefore, the hunting must be over by nine or ten o'clock. The meet should take place by five at the latest, which will give four or five hours' hunting. When the river is gained, the sportsmen should divide into two parties, one-half taking each bank, and anxiously looking for the "seal" of the otter. The hounds at the same time should try every likely place; and when used to their work they do this most systematically; scenting and trying every inch of ground, and especially those which, by experience, are likely to contain the

"couch." The roots of old trees are especially likely, and those still pools which are just below a point in the river are the usual places where the otter chooses his " couch." At this hour in the morning the otter has not long retired from his nocturnal foray, and his trail may then generally be hunted even when his seal is not visible from the hardness of the ground, or its being covered with grass. There is no reason why otter-hunting should not be commenced as soon as the water is warm enough in some rivers where the meadows are grazed on each side; but where there is mowing-grass it must be postponed till that is cut, because the men and dogs do great injury to that valuable crop. After some search, perhaps a "challenge" is at last given, and one of the most tender-nosed hounds hits off the scent, with a note which informs his master, 'in the most unmistakable manner, that his game is at hand. Now every sportsman must take his place and perform his allotted task. Some one or two should pass upwards to the next ford, and carefully watch that point; another pair should take the same post at the ford below; while the remainder must watch every intervening yard for his "ventings." Meanwhile, the hunt proceeds, and the hounds are following the "challenger's" steps, and endeavouring to make out the whereabouts of their game. At last, the scent becomes stronger and stronger, and the couch is reached with a grand chorus of music from the whole pack. At this moment, from the ford above, a halloo is given, and he attempts to pass it, but is turned by the spears of the hunters posted there. The otter, knowing full well that his couch is not secure, generally leaves it before the hounds arrive there; and it is from that cause that he has tried the stream. He next tries the ford below, and here again he is turned; then, seeking the pools of the intermediate space, he is obliged to " vent," and is met with the spear of the hunter, or the fangs of the hound. If, now, the hunters appointed to watch the fords will only keep well their ground, his death is almost certain; but too often they are watching the progress of the sport above or below, and while doing this, neglect their own allotted office, and suffer the otherwise doomed animal to pass their watch. A lull ensues; no vent is seen, no tongue is heard, and disappointment is marked on every face. Every inch of water is tried, and still without success; for the otter has broken through the ford, and is perhaps a mile off at the time when the first pool is finally pronounced untenanted. The next step is to decide upon his having run up or down stream, which is always a lottery; for when hunted, he will be as likely to run up as down; and *vice versâ.* One or the other, however, must be tried; and the hounds will here soon pronounce whether the selection has been a good one or not. If, therefore, after trying in one direction for a quarter or half-a-mile, no challenge is heard, by all means try in the opposite direction. As soon as any certain indication is afforded of his having chosen either course, it will be desirable at once to halt, and to send a party of three or four of the best runners down to the next ford, at least half-a-mile below. Here they should diligently keep a look-out while the hounds hunt up or down to them; and if this pool is blank, then let them run on to the next. When once the otter is again pounded, he must be again hunted as at first, a party being placed to interrupt him above and below, and the remainder, with the hounds, hunting him in the pool. This is the only way to kill an otter with any certainty; for if he is regularly followed, he will assuredly tire out any pack of hounds, since he swims with ten times the ease with which a dog can follow him, in deep or shallow water. But by pounding him at the fords, and confining him within given bounds, he tires himself in his efforts to swim from one to the other, and to avoid the spears and hounds; and yet is obliged to come up and "vent" for want of air. In doing this, he is sure to fall a victim sooner or later; and as his "vents" become more and more frequent in his increasing exhaustion, he is at length impaled upon the spear of one of the hunters, and borne aloft in triumph. Sometimes a hound seizes him; but it takes a very bold and strong one to hold him, for his bite is exceedingly severe, and his strength in the water is very great; many dogs have been drowned in their efforts, and sometimes both otter and hound have been killed under water. The spear should be used with caution when hounds and otter are closely mixed in the *melée,* or a valuable hound may suffer from the care-less thrust of some impetuous hunter. Upon these general principles all otters should be hunted; but in deep streams without fords it is quite impossible to hunt him with any chance of success. In these situations he takes off at once, and unless the hunters are in sufficient numbers to watch the stream for miles, for his " vent," he will probably never be seen again. But if such were practicable, it would scarcely be hunting; for the hounds can take no part in the sport, and the spear must do all the work, if done at all.

385. The Annexed Description of a Run with Mr. Oswald's hounds, in Ayrshire, will afford a good indication of the way in which

this sport is now conducted:—"Exactly at half-past eight, at a signal from the master, John's cheery, 'Ho, wind him, ho!' rang through the clear morning air, and opening in full chorus, the pack dashed for the river. No sooner, however, had they rushed to the water, than every hound settled to his work, and not a stone or root escaped their notice. I may here mention for the information of such of your readers as may not be acquainted with the locality, that the river Ayr is broad, though not deep, with rocky and rugged banks, in many places wooded to the water's edge. The coverts are well-stocked with game and roe-deer; and it is, therefore, necessary to have hounds steady and free from riot; and, from the nature of the banks and the number of roots and natural 'hovers,' it is of the utmost importance that hounds should work slowly and carefully, even with a good scent. We had drawn on for rather more than a mile without a whimper, when Rattler, who had swum to a large stone in the middle of the stream, opened, and a 'true bill' was speedily returned by Old Comely, Nailer, and Dazzler, whilst the rest of the pack struggled to gain the rock, where Old Comely had sat down to discourse sweet music. From this point we had a cold drag for about two miles; but on reaching a celebrated stream, where the largest trout are to be found, 'a change came o'er the spirit of our dream.' Lambton, always the last hound to own a scent, began to cast anxiously from side to side—now trying the water, and now springing from rock to rock, his stern erect and his hackles rising. At last, on a small tuft of grass, he hit it off; his clear loud note rang through the cliffs, and brought every hound to his side; for well they know that when *he* speaks the chase has begun in earnest. In a moment the rocks and woods rang with the cry of the whole pack, as they carefully followed the zigzag track of the otter, who, contrary to the usual custom, it was evident had fished up stream. I never remember to have seen anything more beautiful. You might, in reality, have covered the hounds with a small sheet, the very puppies entered this season took it up. Forward was still the cry, till he reached the holm below Barskimming House, where there is a large and deep pool; at the lower end is a shallow ford, on the right hand side a high rocky face, and on the left a steep earth embankment, on which stands a row of old plane trees. On arriving at this pool the hounds were at first a little at fault; it was evident the 'fishmonger' had entered the water by the ford at the bottom. John pushed through the water; with a single twang on his horn every hound was with him; and,

making for the top of the pool, he cheered them on with a 'Ho, cast for him, good hounds.' We were not kept long in suspense: Old Rally, who devotes her attention almost entirely to roots, opened loudly at the foot of a large plane tree, and was instantly joined by Ringwood; with a dash the rest of the hounds made for the spot, and we were left in little doubt that the varmint was at home. Pincher and Charlie were now brought into requisition, and disappeared through the open net-work of roots laid bare by the late heavy floods; they had not been in above a minute, when a large otter bolted almost through the middle of the pack, and made one long dive, rising in the centre of the pool to see where his pursuers were; but finding them in his wake, he disappeared. It would be tedious to recount to you (though to us, at the time, highly exciting) the various dodges he tried to elude his pursuers; now diving under one root, again lying resting in the still pool, with nothing but his nose above water, and then endeavouring to run the lower ford (this we had manned, leaving him free access to the upper waters). For full two hours he afforded us incessant work; and we were beginning to doubt if the hounds could stand the cold any longer, when he suddenly disappeared, 'leaving not a trace behind.' John, however, had been too long at his work to be done in that way, and, leaving us to watch the pool, he made a cast forward about 500 yards, when the whole pack opened with a burst of music that sent us after them in double-quick time. When we reached the spot, we found all hands busy at a hole, where a severe fight was going on, the voices of Pincher and Charlie were both clearly distinguishable above the deep ring of the hounds as they bayed at the mouth of the hover, from which they were tearing huge mouthfuls of earth and roots, and in the centre of them stood John, up to his middle in water, now swearing at a hound to 'keep quiet,' and now digging with his hands like the best of them. What took place 'in the hole' we could not exactly see, but the earth seemed to give way before the united efforts of John and his hounds, and in a minute or two he appeared with a large otter grasped tightly by the fore-legs, with Pincher, Billy, and Charlie hanging to his mouth like so many leeches. He had just time to change his grip to the tail, when the pack were upon him. But John is not the man to let go; he held on till, by the united efforts of three men, he and his hounds were pulled on to the green grass, and then, with a 'Hi, worry-worry,' that made the echoes ring, he threw him to them. I never remember to have seen an otter fight so long; he drew

L

blood from almost every hound in the pack, and nearly cut the terriers to pieces. He was a large dog otter, and weighed exactly 22¾ lb. We found the drag about half-past nine or ten o'clock, and killed him at three o'clock in the afternoon."

Sect 6.—Dress for Otter-Hunting.

386. It may readily be supposed that, if possible, waterproofs would be used in this sport, but they are inadmissible for many reasons. First, they are too cumbersome for the active exertions which must be made. This is not like fly-fishing, where the fisherman stands for some time in one spot, but the legs are constantly called into play, and sometimes at a very rapid rate; and, consequently, the height and bulk of long waterproof-boots would be beyond measure annoying. Besides this, it must be remembered that, unlike snipe-shooting, the season is a warm one, and if the water was kept from penetrating from the outside, the interior would be damp, and even wet, from the sweat produced by exertion and excitement. From all these causes, there-fore, india-rubber is tabooed. Flannel is the article in request, and should be worn all over the body. No linen should touch the skin, but fine Jerseys should be worn over the upper half of the body, covered by open but soft clothing in the shape of a Tweed shooting-coat, or some similar material; whilst plain white flannel trousers are the best investments for the lower half of the body. Strong shooting-shoes, well nailed, are the best covering for the feet, and good woollen socks should be worn under them. With this clothing, although the wet easily penetrates, it is as easily dried, and no chill takes place from the absence of confinement or of wet linen next the skin. It is only necessary to keep moving till the whole dress is dry, and no ill effects will be likely to follow.

Sect. 7.—Expenses.

387. The cost of otter-hounds may easily be estimated at 3s. per couple per week for the hounds, and 14s. to 18s. per week for the huntsman; beyond this no other expense need be incurred.

PART I.

THE PURSUIT OF WILD ANIMALS FOR SPORT.

BOOK III.—COURSING.

CHAP. I.
PRIVATE COURSING.

SECT. 1.—THE HARE.

388.—The hare has already been described at page 69, under the head of Shooting; and again, at page 102 in the Section describing " The Game to be Hunted." For coursing-purposes, however, it may be still further remarked, that several varieties exist which test the properties of the greyhound very differently, but which varieties are only dependent upon the situation and soil of the localities upon which they are bred. Thus, there are in England down-hares, enclosure-hares, covert-hares, and homeless-hares; and besides these there are, in Ireland and Scotland, the Irish hare and the Scotch mountain-hare. The down-hare is a very fast, yet rather small variety, exceedingly stout and bold, sometimes going away without a turn from a brace of good greyhounds. Some of these little hares have a wonderful knack of throwing out the greyhounds, without appearing to be very fast, but just contriving to elude their pursuer by a hair's breadth. They do not stretch far away between their turns, but make them as soon as they are pressed, and, with one eye forward and the other behind, they always manage to escape any but a more clever killer than usual. These hares are found upon all the open and hilly grounds of Wiltshire, Berkshire, Yorkshire, and part of Lincolnshire, and afford better sport in coursing than other hares, because they are so stout, and yet not often fast enough to get clear away without a turn. It is no uncommon thing to see a course of three or four miles with them in which there are more than a hundred turns; but, generally speaking, if the hare lives long enough to elude thirty or forty efforts of the dogs, she is able to get away to her home. It is seldom, now-a-days, that hares are found on the downs, except in the vicinity of coverts in which they are bred; and I know of no locality, where they are met with in any numbers, at such a distance from any home as to be considered down-bred. Formerly, however, this was the case in many neighbourhoods; but the poachers take good care that it shall not be so now. Wherever therefore, on the downs, hares are not preserved they are extirpated; and if preserved, they are provided with a home in which they may breed, and where they may be more easily watched and protected. For coursing-purposes, also, this plan answers very well, as the hares can at any time be driven to make their forms in the open, either by fixing a net round the covert when the hares are on the feed—which is the best plan—or by driving them out at sunrise with dogs, when they do not return that day, but sit out at once. The enclosure-hare, a variety found in the thickly-enclosed farms of the midland counties, is generally a large and fast hare, fond of threading the hedgerows, and too often spoiling the course by so doing. These hares are also generally bred in woods or plantations, but sometimes they breed in the open fields or thick hedges. In any case, as soon as the corn is cut they retire to the nearest covert, and remain there, except for feeding, until the leaves drop off in November. Whether the dislike to these places of retreat at this time is caused by the noise of the falling leaf, or from any other reason, I do not know, but the fact is clear, that as the leaf falls they begin to sit in the open fields, and not till then in any numbers. Much, I fancy, depends upon the coverts being disturbed for pheasant-shooting at this time; and, probably, this has as much to do with the change of seat as the fall of the leaf, or perhaps more; but still it is undoubted that till that time it is of no use looking for hares out of covert when such a retreat is near. These hares will often stand a long time before greyhounds, but mainly from their trying their fencing powers to so great an extent, because the hare does little at the fence, whilst the greyhound has to make an extraordinary effort either to fly over it or through it. Nevertheless, I have often seen enclosure-hares run as stout and as fast as any down or marsh-hare, independently of the fences, and in large enclosures of 50 or 100 acres each. Nothing is perhaps more beautiful than the fine fencing of a greyhound, but it can so seldom be seen, that the beauty is wasted for want of witnesses. Wherever the fences are strong enough to try the powers of the greyhound, they are too strong for an ordinary horse in cool blood, nor do the farmers generally approve of riding over such land. The spectator on foot, therefore, must content himself with the view of the course up to and over the first fence, and imagine the remainder, unless he happens to be posted on a high hill which commands the view of the whole course in the distance. The homeless-hare is one which is bred on highly-preserved land at a distance from any covert, and is now chiefly found on the reclaimed marshes of Essex, Bedfordshire, Lancashire, and Lincolnshire. These hares, when good, are wonderfully strong and fast, and test the merits of greyhounds to their fullest extent; but there is this objection to these hares, that they never go straight away home, but keep running circles, large or small according to their boldness, and thus always favouring one dog more than the other. I have seen these hares make ten or a dozen circles round a ring of a few yards' diameter only, and then break away, and beat their antagonists hollow, which is a feat never tried by hares that own some place of safety as a home. They seldom make the strong short wrenches of the down-hare, but turn more or less at a right angle, and are careless of being brought round. From the different style of running of these various hares, a dog used to one sort will often find some difficulty at first in running another, and therefore it is well to accustom him to the kind of hare he is to course before his merits are fairly put to the test. The Irish hare is, I believe, a very small, fast, and quick hare, but never having seen her performances, I cannot speak from personal observation of them.

SECT. 2.—THE GREYHOUND.

389. For private coursing, a different dog is required to that which will suit the purpose of the public courser; the latter *must* have that dog which will win him the stake for which he competes, even if his dog only lasts for a few months—as indeed is generally the case; but the private courser will not like this constant necessity for change, and requires his favourites to continue fit for use at least three or four seasons. Hence, he sacrifices some essentials to this lasting condition; and is content if he can produce a tolerably fast, stout, and *honest* dog, that will also last honest for three or four seasons. In enclosed districts he must also fence well; and, in addition, he must be hardy in constitution to stand the exposure to weather without clothing, to which he is generally open. All these requisites may easily be obtained, and many private kennels have them in great perfection, and produce greyhounds which, in

private trials with one another, appear to do as much as any public greyhounds; but when actually put to the test are found somewhat too slow, and not *quite* quick enough at their turns. But to all private coursers I would offer this advice—viz., to avoid most carefully the blood which is found to be successful in public, especially that of the most winning puppies. These greyhounds will not do for the private courser, because he will find that after thirty or forty courses they begin to run cunning or slack, and are then useless to him; whilst his own will run some hundreds of hares before they show the same amount of lurching propensity. The drawback is a serious one to the public courser; but as he breeds for a specific purpose, and can only succeed by selecting that blood which is most successful, he must put up with the inconveniences and do the best he can with them. Unless, therefore, the private courser will make up his mind to breed a fresh team every year, he must stick to private blood, or to some of the most true and honest strains which appear in public. The reason of all this is very clear: if the intellect of the dog is sufficiently developed to make him take to his business very quickly and well, he will also be quick enough to learn more than that; and he soon finds out that if he husbands his resources he will obtain his end much better than if he exerted himself too much at first. Hence he is of early maturity (mentally) but early decay. If the private courser is a pot-hunter, these dogs are often the best killers; but as I am assuming that he pursues coursing as an amusement, for the purpose of competing with his neighbours in a friendly way, and not solely to kill hares, I do not for a moment look at his wishes from that point of view. The man who habitually takes a brace of cunning greyhounds out solely to kill hares is no sportsman, though any one may sometimes do so when he wants a hare; and, as I write for sportsmen, I will not insult them by supposing such a thing. The greyhound for private coursing may be obtained from any of the districts where this amusement is carried on; but some of the best breeds are very difficult to get at. Indeed, I believe, some private greyhound-owners would not allow their dogs to be used on any consideration whatever. This may appear very absurd, but I do not look upon it in that light; because, though they may be easily beaten by many greyhounds, they would not so easily succumb if the match was to be run on three occasions—that is, once during three successive seasons. Having decided upon the blood which will suit him, let the intended greyhound-owner get a brace of whelps if he can, or a brood-bitch, and put her to a dog of a similar strain of blood. For private coursing, there can be no doubt that the best mode of rearing those whelps is to send them out to walk until they are about ten or twelve months old, when they should be brought home and regularly exercised for the rest of their days till done with. If the brood-bitch is obtained, and is bred from, she may be treated in the same way as any other brood-bitch, which will be fully described under the article Dog. No one in private coursing will take all the trouble, and go to the expense, requisite to ensure success in the public coursing-field, and therefore all that need be done is to treat her in the same way as pointers, setters, &c., which will there be found at full length. For private coursing, I should strongly advise that the greyhound should not be entered until he is at least 18 months old. These greyhounds do not come to maturity nearly so soon as the public kinds, and they should not, consequently, be entered so soon. Besides, there are not the same reasons for the early entering, since it matters little whether these puppies are shown a hare in November or December, and, consequently, they may just as well wait till their frames are well knit before they are tested so severely as the hare tries their bones and sinews. This postponement is particularly needful, because the private greyhound is seldom quite fit to run when slipped at the hare, and is also often slipped several times in the day; so that in every way he is more tried than the public one, and should be older before he is brought out. Many good private coursers take great pains to ensure good exercise and general management for their dogs, and they almost always beat all their neighbours by so doing; but few go to the length of training them, and are content to allow them to gallop themselves into wind, if they will. It is wonderful what condition will sometimes be obtained in this way; but, generally speaking, after a short time the dog becomes lazy, and refuses to exercise himself sufficiently to remove his superfluous fat, or to get himself in wind; if, therefore, it is desired that he shall be able to course his hares without distress, he must be trained in some way or other, and horse-exercise is the easiest mode of obtaining this. Most greyhound-owners are also horse-keepers, and if they send out their horses to exercise, they may just as well let their greyhounds accompany them. This, if done daily, will produce a tolerable degree of condition, but the greyhound will often be terribly distressed in a long course if only treated in this way. Unless, therefore, the courser is in the habit of running his dogs once or twice a-week, he should cer-

tainly give them a few slips to improve their wind. To do this all that is necessary is to take them up in couples, then send on their feeder half a mile or so, up a moderately-steep hill, if possible, and have them held by a stranger till he whistles to them, when they should be let go. This improves the wind if repeated once or twice, and by its adoption the greyhound may be got into pretty good condition. An occasional dose of physic should also be given, consisting of a dose of castor-oil, or an ounce of Epsom salts dissolved in cold water. Attention should of course be paid to health as in ordinary dogs. For private purposes clothing is not requisite, nor do I think it desirable, except when standing about the fields in coursing in very cold weather. Here a cloth is indispensable, and the dog without it is chilled, and rendered unfit for exertion on that day, and generally for some time afterwards.

390. THE FEEDING OF GREYHOUNDS for private running should be principally on Indian-corn meal and oatmeal, either plain boiled or made into bread; if the latter, the flour of the Indian-corn must be finely ground; but if only boiled, hominy answers perhaps better than meal. It requires several hours to boil it, and it should be done at least two hours longer than the oatmeal. It is, however, a very good and cheap meal for all dogs, and answers particularly well for greyhounds. This should be the staple, with milk or buttermilk. On two or three days in the week they ought to have from ½lb. to ¾lb. of meat well boiled; and on the alternate days, if they have not got the buttermilk, they should have a few greaves. Once a-week they ought to have a few greens, or potatoes, or carrots, boiled up with their meal. Greyhounds kept in this way are not quite so hard and fit to run as if fed on stronger food; but they keep in better health longer together, and will generally be fit for what the private courser wants, viz., a course or two whenever the opportunity offers. With these few remarks I shall pass on to other matters, reminding the private courser, that if he wishes to go to the full length of which the subject is capable, he has only to study the chapters on "Public Coursing," and then he will obtain the information. My object here is to place before the private courser the usual mode in which private greyhounds are managed, and the amount of trouble to which he must go in order to be on a level with his neighbours and rivals.

SECT. 3.—THE GROUND.

391. It is unnecessary for me to remark, that greyhounds are of no use unless there is ground to try them upon; if, therefore,

the proprietor has none of his own fit for the purpose, he must obtain leave from those who have. In most coursing districts there are certain estates which are thrown open on certain days to the public, for the benefit of the keepers, or of some landlord of an inn, generally an old servant of the proprietor of the land. But, supposing the land belongs to the courser, he will find that in all cases hares must be driven out before they will sit, and he will shoot the coverts the day before he intends to course, or have them driven expressly for the purpose. If he has the farm in his own occupation, he will of course choose such times when the fallows have been quiet for some little time—that is to say, if these are the fields which he intends to course over. It is seldom that private coursers have much choice of ground, and they content themselves with what they can get.

SECT. 4.—THE BEATERS.

392. Wherever it is determined to course, beaters are requisite, unless five or six gentlemen on horseback are present. But whatever is the mode adopted, a line should be formed, placing one beater at every thirty yards; and proceeding abreast of one another from one extremity of the field to another. Much art and experience are necessary to ensure the best management of the ground, for often a hare may be sent the right way by careful beating which would otherwise have been at once lost to sight. When a field lies near a covert, it should be regularly beaten *from* the covert, and not *towards* it; and after taking a breadth of land away from the covert, the beaters should take what is called "a dead beat" back—that is to say, they should return to the covert over the beaten ground, and should not attempt to beat the ground *towards* the covert. By these means hares are often driven the right way; but the worst of the plan is, that they generally wheel short round after the first turn and come back to the same covert, which they have been already prevented reaching by the "dead beat." When a beat is taken along a hedge-side, the beater nearest the hedge should be at least 10 or 15 yards in advance, in order to prevent the hare running at once to it and escaping altogether. If a hedge is being beaten, the horsemen should all range themselves on the side opposite to that where the greyhounds are; and the foot beaters should be a little in advance of the dogs. The slipper and dogs should be the only party on the side which the hare is wished to face. Sometimes a small field of turnips or potatoes, &c., borders on a good large open field; in such a case it answers best for the slipper to remain in the latter,

quietly concealing himself as much as possible at a short distance from the meuse, and waiting till the hare is driven through it. If now the beaters form a half-circle, they may drive the hare or hares to the greyhounds; and will thus obtain what would otherwise be impossible, a good course. In driving small plantations, &c., the slipper should remain just outside, if possible, concealed from the hare's view as she comes out by a tree. Hares driven out of covert, however, seldom run straight or well; and the plan should not be followed if it is possible to avoid it. In the early part of the season it is the only mode of getting a run; but for private coursing there is no great object in beginning so very early.

SECT. 5.—THE SLIPPER.

393. A very important functionary in private as well as public coursing. He should be taught to run well with his dogs, and not to stop running till after he has slipped them. Practice, however, is necessary for perfection, and few obtain it with that amount which private coursing usually affords. The great object is to slip without a jerk, and not to deliver the dogs unless they are both sighted, and equally strong at the time. He should walk about five or six yards a-head of the beaters, and should never be behind them. If, therefore, he is not able to keep up with the horsemen, they must slacken their pace; for no plan is so bad as to distress the slipper, or put up hares so wild as to be beyond his reach. If the slipper is distressed, he cannot run forward, and the consequence is, that the dogs are badly slipped; and if the hares get up too wild he has not time to get his dogs sighted and straight on their hare before she is out of their reach. In all cases the slipper should have some one to give him his orders to slip, and he should, on receiving the word "go," slip his dogs as quickly as possible.

394. There is a great variety in the make of slips, every one fancying that particular form which suits his own ideas of perfection. The essential feature is the delivery of both dogs at the same moment, with smoothness, and with as little jerk as possible. No slips answer better than the old crane-billed make; but they take a long time to put together. An improvement is made upon this principle in Scotland, called the Caledonian slips, and they are used with good effect by Mr. White. My own slips also, I believe, deliver the dogs with perfect fairness and smoothness; but they are not so well suited to uncouth puppies.

SECT. 6.—THE JUDGE.

395. All coursing, whether public or pri-

vate, is in the nature of a competition, and that cannot possibly be settled without a judge; one should, therefore, be appointed for the day, and this precaution will often save a disagreeable squabble as to the various merits of dogs. It is very seldom that the two owners see the course with the same eyes, and the aid of a third and impartial party is required to set them right upon disputed points. Even, therefore, if no person perfectly *au fait* can be found, it is better to nominate a judge of some kind whose decision shall be final, than to go on quarrelling about the merits of each other's dogs to the end of time.

SECT. 7.—THE COURSE.

396. No reason can be assigned why a series of courses in private may not be as good and as interesting as a similar number in public. If the ground is as good, and the hares equally so, and if the greyhounds are well matched, and of good quality, no reasonable man can contend that the course may not be identical with those exhibited in public; nevertheless, it is an admitted fact that, generally speaking, it is not so; and that private coursing is very inferior to what we sometimes see in public. It is true that the best ground is generally reserved for public coursing, and that when hares are not preserved for the purpose, they are seldom thick enough for the amusement of the spectators; but independently of these considerations, there is seldom sufficiently good management to ensure good sport. I have seen, on some occasions, private coursing conducted with as much good order as is often observed at any public meeting; but these cases are exceptional, and must not be taken as the rule. When the hare gets up, either after a "Soho!" or when getting up wild, the dogs should be held till she is from 50 to 80 yards off, when they should be slipped as directed above. Sometimes when a hedge is very close, and the hare is making straight for it, it is better to slip at 30 or 40 yards than to lose all chance of a course; but it should seldom be allowed under 50 or 60 yards. After the course the dogs should be taken up, and another brace put in the slips. It is very common in private coursing to run the same dog four or five courses in the day, if they are not very severe; but more than these should seldom be allowed, as they only serve to exhaust the dog, and to make him run cunning much sooner than he otherwise would do. It is a good plan to take a little boiled mutton into the field, and give the dog about an ounce after each course, if he is intended to run again. If he is much exhausted, he will of course not be allowed again to go into slips.

SECT. 8.—RULES FOR PRIVATE COURSING.

397. It is usual to judge the course in private exactly under the same rules as in public; and I shall therefore here refer to the rules which will be found at length under "Public Coursing." It is not a little remarkable, that all that I have described as the usual mode of conducting this sport in the present day, was practised in the time of Arrian, A.D. 150, who wrote a long treatise on coursing, containing all that is now known on the subject, and describing the course with as much exactitude as could now be done by the most ardent votary of private coursing.

CHAP. II.

PUBLIC COURSING.

SECT. 1.—ITS RECENT DATE AND IMPORTANCE.

398. In the chapter devoted to private coursing, I made the remark that the sport known by that name was fully known in the time of Arrian, and described by him A.D. 150. Public coursing, however, only dates back to the time of Charles I., when several matches are recorded to have been publicly decided; but since that time the number and frequency of public coursing meetings have so much increased, that there are now more than 600 stakes annually run for in the three kingdoms. The average number of dogs running in each of these stakes would probably be about twelve; the entrance-money may be estimated at about 4 guineas, which will give 600 multiplied by 48, equal to 28,800 guineas. This appears a very large sum to be invested every year in so useless a sport; but, when it is remembered that it is spread over a very large extent of country, among, perhaps, 4,000 coursers, it will only average an outlay for each individual of 7 guineas in stakes alone. This does not, then, seem too large a sum for the year's amusement, and the improvement of the health of so many people; and no one would, I think, contend that they are

dearly bought at that price, even if to it be added the outlay on a brace or two of greyhounds for keep and training. It must be borne in mind, that this sport is essentially confined and proper to the middle classes of society; for though some noblemen and gentlemen still condescend to partake of its allurements, they are the exceptions to the rule, and the great bulk of its supporters are those gentlemen in middle life who are neither noblemen nor even men of large landed property.' It is therefore fortunate for them that so many liberal land-proprietors throw open their preserves once or twice a-year to the use of their neighbours, for without such an assistance the sport could not possibly go on. But, with this kind and considerate help, the man of moderate means can enjoy the amusement with even greater zest than the proprietors of those large kennels, which formerly used to sweep everything before them. At a very recent date, and long within my memory, Lord Rivers, Mr. Goodlake, Lord Stradbroke, and Lord Eglinton, were so strong, that no ordinary individual had courage to pit himself against them; and though some few members of the various clubs continued to contend against them year after year, it was a hopeless and vain struggle, and was persisted in more from a desire to be seen grimly struggling to the last, than with any hope of victory. But all this is now changed, and the tenant-farmer or the professional man has as good a chance, or even a better one, than the most wealthy and large-acred nobleman. "If a thing is to be well done, it should be done by oneself," is a very common adage, and well exemplified in the case of the courser; for he is the most successful who, understanding the whole *arcana* of the business, sees himself that they are practically carried out. This, few of those in high places will do, and then, in consequence, they have "a pull" against them. Again, they are tempted into keeping great numbers of dogs, which it will hereafter be shown is a great cause of failure; so that altogether it is no wonder if they are sometimes less successful than the money and talent they bestow on the subject ought to insure. The sport, however, from many of these causes combined, has become a popular one with the middle classes; and they ought to be grateful for the facilities which are afforded them by such owners of preserves as Lord Craven, Lord Londesborough, Sir Edmund Antrobus, and Mr. Whitbread, whose examples are followed in numberless instances on a smaller scale; but the above-mentioned noblemen and gentlemen, not being themselves coursers, are doubly entitled to the thanks of those who are.

Sect. 2.—Difference from Private Coursing.

399. Between these two sports there are important points of distinction, which are not so evident to the cursory glance of the unlearned as might be imagined by those who are fully initiated into the mysteries of coursing. In private coursing, I have already observed that everything *may* be conducted on the same principles as in the public field; but this is the exception, and the rule is, that most men in private go out for the sake of killing hares, and not for the purpose of competing with their neighbours and friends. Those who do this are only intent upon the death of the hare, and accomplish their object often by mobbing her, or by starting her again with spaniels from her retreat in the covert which she has gained. This I have known done by old coursers, to such an extent as to course the same hare three or four times in one day, driving her out of her covert, and after losing her, putting spaniels on her scent, and again and again coursing her, till at length she succumbs. This of course would only be practicable in enclosed districts where there is a series of small coverts, and where hares easily beat greyhounds, unassisted by other dogs; but I confess that the sport, if worthy of that name at all, has no charms for me, and that I should despise myself for partaking in such a bastard kind of hunting, for it certainly cannot be called coursing. In any case, private coursing is too often converted into a "pot-hunting" kind of business, in which the hare is the great object of the pursuit. On the other hand, in public coursing the hare is only a means of trying the powers of the dogs, which are pitted against one another, and her capture or escape is not immediately connected with the success or failure of the sport. It often happens that the best course of the day is a bloodless one, and no good courser measures its beauty, or the goodness of the greyhounds engaged, by the same criterion which the private "pot-hunter" employs. The public courser's whole study is to excel and outrun all his competitors; and for this purpose only does he breed and keep his greyhounds. Many good coursers never see their dogs run in private, and will never attempt to form an opinion of their respective merits, for fear of condemning a good greyhound on insufficient grounds. Certainly this is, in my opinion, a weakness on their parts, though a very amiable one; for I can scarcely understand any one being afraid to judge amongst his own dogs, though it is very clear that few are capable of estimating their performance as compared with those

of strange, and, perhaps, superior kennels. This, however, does not alter the bearings of public towards private coursing, but it makes very clear the distinction between the two varieties. The one is the pursuit of the hare for sport; the other is a trial between greyhounds, using the hare only as a means of developing their powers, but quite ready to dispense with her if the trial could be efficiently made in any other way. Thus the one is a sport which undoubtedly comes within the present department of British Rural Sports, viz., the pursuit of wild animals for sport, whilst the other would perhaps more properly be considered as a branch of racing. But with this double difficulty before me, I preferred adhering to the old definition, and have consequently retained both descriptions of coursing under this head.

SECT. 3.—THE PUBLIC GREYHOUND.

400. Since there is but one object in keeping the greyhound for public competition, and that object is only attained by success, it is quite clear that by success must the greyhound be tested, and for success must he be bred. I do not mean to say that you can measure his value by his money-winnings, because luck is a most important element in public coursing; but I assert that by his success, or *his fitness to obtain it*, must the greyhound be estimated. Many greyhounds have had a series of misfortunes, and yet have been first-rate dogs, and have been considered such, though never victorious over good and large fields. There are so many elements necessary to this achievement, that it is no wonder that many fail without deserving their failure. A dog may get one or two undecided courses from hares dividing, or from a variety of causes, and this may put out his chance of a stake; or he may, in his excess of courage, lame himself, and yet be the more admired in his failure than the steadier runner that has won the stake. But in spite of all these exceptions to the rule, it is nevertheless a true one, that success in the long-run is the best guide to the selection of the best dog. This, therefore, is my test; and upon that test as a definition, I shall proceed to consider the points and merits of the greyhound for public running. In any other point of view there is an endless scope for controversy. One party may say, "Oh! we do not want speed, we want bottom;" another may care less for bottom than for speed; whilst a third may disregard both, and stick to working properties as the test of the true greyhound. All this is a mere matter of taste, except as tested by success in public contests; but with that criterion in view,

all these private opinions sink into the shade, and the result is that we all direct our efforts to produce what will ensure its being grasped. It must be remembered, that this success is obtained under certain rules, and that the greyhound is not pronounced the winner according to the particular fancy of any man, or set of men, but he is tested in such a way as (theoretically) shall decide upon his doing certain things in accordance with known and recognised rules; so that, after all, we have only to consider what greyhound is best calculated to effect those purposes; and this is the sum and substance of the present section. It will hereafter appear that, according to those rules, the properties of the greyhound are estimated in the following proportions :— first, speed; secondly, working and killing powers; thirdly, stoutness or bottom; and fourthly, courage.

401. SPEED is a quality which is very easily understood in the abstract; but it should be examined more closely, when considered in reference to the greyhound. It may be divided into speed from the slips, and speed from the turns. SPEED FROM THE SLIPS is variously displayed, according to the quickness of the particular greyhound. Thus, he may be slow immediately from the slips, yet soon increasing in pace, and going on to a perfect torrent in velocity. With some judges this is a very great point, since it scores four to begin with; for they count this feat as a "go-by," though on what principle I cannot imagine. A dog which goes quickly out of slips, and reaches the hare first by thirty lengths, is only allowed two points, while another which suffers his antagonist to get the start for a few yards, and then goes by him, and only reaches the hare first by a couple of lengths, is allowed to score four. Can this be justified on any grounds? I think not. Speed is the only foundation for the decision in both cases; yet the one which is thirty lengths faster than his antagonist counts only half as good as the one which is two lengths faster. I much admire that kind of speed which goes on smoothly, increasing in pace from the slip to the turn; but I think that the dog who thus runs is sufficiently rewarded by his after-power of working; for I am satisfied that the very courageous dog which starts from slips as if ready to burst himself, really does injure his chance materially by so doing, independently of his being robbed of the due reward for his superior pace. But so long as speed is the only criterion for judging of the first turn, I cannot consent to this mode of estimating it. If it were possible to do so, I would always breed so as to ensure the increasing speed, for the reasons I have given above;

but I would not punish the contrary, and make the most praiseworthy effort of the greyhound to reach his hare a double means of ensuring his defeat. Hundreds of dogs burst themselves by their excess of courage, and must fairly suffer the penalty; but they should not certainly be deprived of that which they have earned; and if more than one point is ever to be allowed for speed to the hare, over and above the turn, it should be given to that very superior speed which either ensures a long lead of twenty or thirty lengths, or a lead on outside ground; but no trumpery lead of one or two lengths, wherever gained, ought to give more than the one point for speed in addition to the turn; in all, two points for the cote, or first turn. It is this outgoing speed which characterises the public greyhound; he is the thorough-bred racer among dogs, and the points which give the faculty are easily recognised by the eye, though all dogs which have them are not necessarily fast. These points are—first, length from the hip-joint to the hock, *when extended*; and secondly, powerful and flexible shoulders. SPEED FROM THE TURNS is a somewhat different quality to the above; but it is generally met with in the greyhound which starts well from the slips, if he is clever, and of good bottom. A dog may be able to get well away at first, yet so soft that he tires himself in his first effort, or so slack that his courage is already exhausted. He therefore seldom does much after the first turn, but subsides into a second place, and is easily beaten by a much slower animal. He may get a turn now and then in the course; but if the hare is a good one he generally succumbs without a fight. On the other hand, the stout and yet fast dog, which is a rare combination, not only gets first from the slips, but also, after turning his hare, he is first away from his turn, and is at her again, that is to say if he can stop himself so as to start "even with his fellow." This point shows the perfect greyhound, and it is one which catches the eye of a good public judge sooner than any other. It should, therefore, as the cause of success, be carefully prized, and the blood which produces it should be diligently sought for. Next to these comes the speed which produces the "go-by," which is not necessarily connected with working power, but may be possessed without that attri-bute. In this kind of speed there may be no control over the exertions at all; but after the first turn there may be little or no power of stopping, and in the interval the other dog may get on the line of the hare and obtain a considerable lead. Being, however, a slow dog, the fast but bad worker, if the hare also is a fast one, is

enabled to go by him and score two points, even if he cannot turn the hare from his deficiency of working power, or from its being too fast even for him. Of these three kinds of speed, that one is the most valuable which leads off and maintains the lead, and which also is accompanied with stoutness sufficient to enable the dog to get away from the subsequent turns. In shape this is characterised, in addition to the two points already specified, by the possession of a muscular back, without which it is seldom attained; but, over and above all, there must be a good heart.

402. GOOD WORKING AND KILLING POWERS are generally co-existent, though not al-ways so; for some of the best workers are, and always continue, bad killers. But in most cases the power which gives the capability of turning the hare, *and of keeping her line afterwards*, also gives the capacity to kill. Sometimes, however, there is not the will; and this is very common in the puppy, who often does not attain the ten-dency to kill until the end of the first season. Of this late-killing *tendency* the celebrated Mocking-bird was an extraordinary ex-ample; whilst Figaro, her sire, never had the *power*, and ran a great number of hares before he ever tasted their blood. His progeny, however, have been generally good killers rather than otherwise. Many other examples might be given, but it will suffice for me to assert, as an undoubted maxim, that both these powers are of the highest importance—first, as scoring quickly and thereby gaining the course; and secondly, as quickly ending it, and thereby enabling the winner to meet his next antagonist on favourable terms. The work-ing of the greyhound is very different in different breeds, and even in varieties of the same breed. There is sometimes the bold, vigorous, and determined rush at the hare with the desire to kill; this produces a turn, and generally a full turn; and it is varied according as the rush is made straight at the hind-leg, or at the side, or at the shoulder. If the rush is made at the hind-leg, well on the line of the hare, and with a good command at the turn, it is very beautiful; and when united with good bottom and speed, is, in my opinion, the perfection of running for most countries. In the last case the line of the hare is left, more or less, and she is attacked on a line slightly varying from her's, but still parallel with it. This is called "not running the line of the hare," and is considered a fault for many reasons. Next, there is the steady line-running worker, who goes fast to his hare—running to her scut, and yet not rushing at her for fear of bringing her round, and thus losing ground at the turn.

If this is executed with sufficient speed so as to press the hare well and forcibly, it is a most winning style; especially in such countries as Wiltshire or Berkshire, because the hare does not come round, and the competing dog cannot, or does not, get in for many wrenches in succession. But too often the dog which works in this style does nothing really with his hare; he merely turns as she turns, and, instead of commanding her, is only commanded by her. He, therefore, is easily beaten by a more courageous dog, although with an inferior one he looks, to a common observer, a very formidable antagonist. Such an animal is just the one which leads on the young courser till he is put out by a good dog; as, from his apparent power of working, he thinks he is a very superior performer. Nevertheless, such dogs often win courses, though they do not deserve them; because, though they do nothing with a fresh and fast hare, yet when a hare has been well-knocked about by a fast greyhound, and reduced in pace (to the great reduction also of the powers and speed of the greyhound which has effected this alteration), the slow and good worker, as he is called, comes out to great advantage; and after turning *behind his hare* ten or a dozen times, is enabled to pick her up. Such is the conclusion of many courses in every public meeting; and by the inevitable decision, the *coup de grace* is given to a comparatively good greyhound by an animal which never would have turned his hare at all, but for the early assistance of his discomfitted antagonist. Besides these varied styles of going at the hare, there are variations also in the dog's coming round when she turns; thus, he may stop short and wheel round on his hind-legs by the power of his shoulders; or he may run a segment of a circle without attempting to stop himself, but rather to contract his circle. Many degrees of these styles are seen, but all kinds of coming round resolve themselves into one or other of these two. The former is *generally* the mode adopted by slow dogs, the latter by fast ones. Though many very fast dogs have the power of stopping themselves very suddenly, and some dogs display each mode at different times; sometimes adopting the one style, and sometimes the other. Indeed, it is wonderful to see the power which some dogs possess of accommodating themselves to circumstances, and more especially to the nature of their hare. Some must have a "good hare;" some want a short-running but stout hare; and some like a decidedly bad hare: but others can display their powers with any hare, and seem different dogs altogether with fast and slow hares. Again, in killing great difference exists,

some dogs seeming to be able to run into their hares without a turn; while others, as fast from the slips, never dream of killing till they have tried the effect of half-a-dozen turns. There must be some power of fascination like that of the rattlesnake in some dogs, or they never could run into their hares one after another as they do. No attempt seems made to escape from their jaws, but the hare succumbs without trying a turn. The external conformation which usually accompanies this power of turning and killing is not very well-marked; indeed, it may be said, that it is impossible to foretel by the form what working power the possessor may exhibit. Large dogs are often said to be bad workers, but many examples to the contrary might be adduced. Again, speed is thought to be incompatible with working power; but here again many examples to the contrary are well known; though it is manifest that, *cœteris paribus*, a slow dog can turn closer than a fast one. Still, though he may be able to turn more closely, he does not work better; because he does not really do so much with his hare, and though he turns on less ground, he does not knock his hare about, and reduce her speed in the same way as the faster dog. I am quite satisfied that working power is inherent in the breed; and its seat is the nervous system. This will be made clear in examining the various breeds, in some of which you see the same good style of working pervade every make and shape; whilst in others you see bad workers with forms which you would fancy the models of perfection. The fact is, that for perfect working a considerable degree of mental activity and quickness is required, which shall enable the dog to do enough to distress the hare, without distressing himself. A good greyhound is never a fool, whatever may be said by some old-fashioned coursers. Depend upon it, that a greyhound soon learns to know all the motions of the hare, and is prepared to defeat them; and this tact he learns often before he has ever seen a hare, by chasing his companions in their play. Cunning is often acquired in this way, but sufficient knowledge must be somehow obtained, and, I believe, this is the best mode. There is a great difference in the ways of starting off in the play; some go off straight a-head, without trying to throw out their pursuers, whilst others spirt here, there, and everywhere, and are generally good workers themselves, and also the means of making their play-fellows equally good. All this, however, is mental and not bodily, and no clue can be gained to its possession by any guide of which I am aware. Remember that too much knowledge or cleverness soon leads to lurching; and that in proportion to its rapid development will in general be its speedy decay by that dire malady. The extent of the killing propensity, I believe, in most cases to depend upon a proper development of the posterior part of the brain, occasioning a width across the ears, which accompanies the dog of high courage in most cases. But so little is known of the nervous system, that further than this I can give no clue to its mysteries.

403. STOUTNESS depends partly upon general muscular development, without which it can scarcely exist; but chiefly upon the state of the heart. This is well known in all animals, and the phrase is founded in truth which says that such a horse or dog "has got a bad heart." By this is meant that he succumbs to fatigue without a struggle, and that he does not use all his efforts when tested. Now this may arise from two causes—first, from a want of tone, so that the muscles cease to act, and become powerless, which is, in fact, a want of what is called *stoutness*; and secondly, from a want of *courage* to bear difficulties, fatigues, and punishments. The first is that which I am now considering, and is not confined to the brain, as far as I believe, but to the whole nervous system. Thus a man may be intellectually of a very low grade, and yet very stout, and able to bear fatigues and punishments of all kinds well, as we see in the prize-fighter well exemplified. He is often a mere machine, incapable of acting on the offensive to any brilliant degree, but able to bear such an amount of punishment as would annihilate a frame composed of more highly endowed and sensitive materials. So with the lower animals: the weasel, the polecat, and even the common cat will bear with impunity such injuries as would destroy half-a-dozen lives in some of the more highly developed animals, such as the dog or the monkey. All this shows that there is a vast disparity in the power of endurance displayed in different animals, and that it is a negative quality altogether, resembling in its attributes the characteristics of the true bulldog. This animal is not so remarkable for courage as for obstinate perseverance in his purpose, so that he will suffer himself to be cut to pieces before he will let go his hold. Many dogs will attack a bull, or even a tiger, just as boldly as the bulldog; but they will not bear their injuries without flinching, nor will they continue the attack regardless of all resistance like the high-bred bulldog. These attributes, then, are said to reside in the nervous system, because we do not know where else to locate them; and the ordinary name by which they are recognised, is stoutness, pluck, or bottom—the former being that which is usually applied to the greyhound.

404. COURAGE in the greyhound is the climax to all his other qualities, and without it, though ever so good in form, he is disinclined to use his powers, and is utterly worthless. What advantage is it to possess a dog as fast as the wind and as clever as a Solon, if he will not exert his powers, or if he succumbs in a severe struggle, or provided he has a fall or a broken nail? On the contrary, it leads to a loss instead of a gain, because stakes are paid, and expenses incurred, in the hope of success, which is marred by a want of that essential point whose properties I am describing. It is the quality which imparts vigour to act and courage to bear, whatever may befal the dog; and it is the one which puts the final touch to the general properties, which, without it, are useless, because they are not put into operation. The greyhound is unlike the racehorse, in that he has no persuaders at his side, or whip over his neck; but his own spirit is his only motive, and therefore without that stimulus in full perfection, he is a dull and useless cub. But beyond the formation of brain already alluded to, I know of no external mark of its development; and here, again, breed is the only probable guide to its existence. Some of those whose courage is of the highest class, look dull and sleepy till they are animated by the game before them; while, again, many lively and apparently high-couraged dogs quickly give up under the slightest punishment or distress. Hence it may be said that no rule can be laid down on the subject of either stoutness or courage, founded upon the appearance or form of the greyhound.

405. EXTERNAL FORM.—Such being the general qualities which must be possessed by the greyhound that is to be successful in public contests, let us now examine into the external form most likely to ensure that success. This can only be done by comparing the shapes, size, weight, and colours of the winning greyhounds with their defeated antagonists, and endeavouring to deduce certain rules from the facts which come out in the inquiry. I shall, therefore, begin by investigating the shapes most likely to ensure success; though, at the same time, there can be no doubt that the greyhound, like the horse, can run and win in all forms.

406. THE HEAD, I have already remarked should be wide behind, and should be considerably larger in circumference, if measured over the ears, than over the eyebrows. For dogs of good size, I believe the measure over the ears should be about 15 inches, and for bitches from 14 to 14½ inches, according

to the general size of the head, which is sometimes very small and neat in them without injury. The jaw should be very lean, with a good muscular development on the cheek, which gives a strong hold, and enables the dog to bear his hare in striking at her. The head of the greyhound is compared to that of the snake, but it is a very far-fetched comparison, save in the flatness of the top, and the width, which certainly are points of resemblance; but the nose is so very different that the likeness is a very poor one. The teeth should be good, and in young dogs white and free from tartar; indeed, in a well-reared dog, the whiteness is of such a kind as to excel the finest ivory. This is a strong mark of good rearing, and indicates the habitual use of bones, the gnawing of which not only cleans the teeth, but aids in their formation, and also increases the general health of the whole system. The eye should be bright and tolerably full, though I have never been able to satisfy myself as to the general possession of any one kind of eye by good public greyhounds. I have seen, I think, as many of any one colour which can be mentioned, as of others common in the greyhound. So with the ears; different breeds are so very variously furnished with this appendage, that nothing can be made of it as a sign of good or bad qualities. Some good ones are possessed of falling, soft, and broad ears; others of sharp and screwed-up ears; and others, again, of foxy pricked ears; and these are very remarkable in the descendants of Heather-jock, belonging to Dr. Brown, in Scotland, who often inherit this peculiarity to the third and fourth generation.

407. THE NECK is a very beautiful part of the high-bred greyhound, and is very properly compared with that of the drake, though not quite coming up to the elegance of that bird. In many breeds, however, the neck is very long and swan-like; and this point gives great power of reaching the hare without losing the stride, which would be a fatal drawback in the fast dog. Some of our best breeds are very remarkable for good heads and necks; as, for instance, those of the blood of Sir James Boswell's Jason, which possess these organs in great perfection, and are very remarkable in most instances for killing powers. In a well-formed dog, the junction of the head with the neck ought to be midway between the point of the nose and the front of the shoulder-blades.

408. THE CHEST AND BACK together constitute the body or trunk. The CHEST is a conical cavity adapted to contain the lungs, heart, and great vessels, to protect them from injury, and to inflate the lungs by enlarging the capacity of the chamber which contains them. Such a cavity must, therefore, be of sufficient volume for the first purpose, of sufficient strength for the second, and of sufficiently varying capacity for the third; and all these offices the chest of the greyhound efficiently performs. But, not only must it be thus formed, but it must also be so flattened on the sides that the shoulder-blades shall lie smoothly upon them, and have free play to extend themselves. In order to meet all these requirements, the chest of the greyhound is deeper than in most animals, so as to give increase of volume without separating the shoulders too much, or placing their blades upon too convex a surface. But if the chest is prolonged too far downwards, it strikes the ground in the efforts made to stop the speed at the turns, and in that way is prejudicial to the going of the dog. Thus, a happy medium is required in this department, and the chest must be wide but not too round, and deep, without being so much so as to interfere with the working powers. Besides these two points, it is important that the ribs shall be well separated from each other, so that they may expand the cavity properly, or otherwise respiration is not performed with sufficient power and velocity. This width of the spaces is known to exist by the comparative length between the breast and the last rib at the loin; but, again, this must not be too great, or the back is rendered weak, and incapable of those vigorous and quick efforts which the gallop requires. By a reference to the anatomy of the dog, it will be seen that the chest is composed of various bones, together making this framework, and moved by muscles which are attached to them, so as to expand and contract in the actions of respiration. To the upper and hinder part of the chest the BACK is firmly attached, the muscles of that important part in the greyhound being inserted into the necks of the posterior ribs. It may be said to connect the fore-quarter with the hind, and to be one of the chief means of producing those extraordinary strides peculiar to fast gallopers. It is composed of a flexible, bony centre, part of which runs up between the ribs, and is also a component part of the chest; while the remainder is free in its middle course (constituting the true loin), and attached behind to the pelvis. But it is more especially in the *muscles* of the back that the powers of the greyhound reside, though these again are partly indebted for their capabilities to the bones upon which they lie. It is quite clear, that unless the angles of the ribs are wide apart, and unless the hips (or couples, as they are commonly called) are also wide and free, there cannot

be a full development of the muscular structure, for want of framework to lie upon and contract. Therefore, though a good frame is necessary to form a good back, it does not always follow that it shall be accompanied by that greatly to be desired point. The old coursers desired "a back like a beam;" that is to say, with square edges, and as if chopped out of a block. This I have never seen fully displayed, except in one or two dogs, which were by no means good performers; and I attach more importance to depth and volume of muscle, than to squareness of the edge. The back ought to be well let into the shoulders; that is to say, the muscles which compose it ought to run well forward towards the shoulder-blades, and should leave a strong ridge of muscle standing up above the ribs, on each side of the spine. This is a very important point, and one which almost every good greyhound exhibits. Its absence betokens great weakness, and a want of endurance; for though the dog may be fast without it, he is seldom capable of continuing his speed. Another very important shape in the back, is the due development of the muscles *under* the spine. The back itself consists of four bundles of muscles, separated from one another by the spinous processes which project upwards, and also by the transverse processes which project out sideways. Now these transverse processes divide the upper muscles which straighten the back from the lower ones which arch it, and the latter are the main agents in bringing the hindquarters forward after the stride is taken. It is, therefore, upon them that this action depends, and without their proper development the hind legs do not sufficiently come forward to enable the dog to arrive at high speed. The essential points, therefore, are—first, sufficient volume of muscle; secondly, its being well carried forward to the shoulders; thirdly, its due development below as well as above; and fourthly, its not being weak in any part, for without this, a back, large in volume, may be rendered useless by being nipped at some particular part, often being so just at the junction with the back-ribs, or with the couples. The neck is attached to the front of the chest, and the tail to the back of the pelvis; so that altogether these parts form one continuous bony chain. It is supposed by many that the tail should be very fine and thin, and I am inclined to believe that the terminal bones should be, in order to show good breeding; but the root may be as strong and powerful as possible.

409. THE HIND-QUARTER is the main element of progression, and upon it in a great measure depend the speed and power of the greyhound. As in all other cases, size is power, and the greater the length and size of the hind-quarter, so will be the power of propulsion. This length is variously displayed, sometimes the hind-leg being long but straight; whilst in others it is more or less bent at two places—the stifle and hock. It will generally be observed that when the part of the leg below the hock is comparatively short, the bones above that part are bent at the stifle, and the whole hind-quarter is long, without raising the back from the ground; as would be the case with the same length of limb in a more straight form. As far as my observation goes, the bent hind-quarter is the more favourable form, but I have seen many good dogs with very straight stifles; and there can be no reason why these should not serve the purpose of propulsion as well as the bent ones. But, though they can propel as well, and perhaps even better under some circumstances, they are quite useless unless they are accompanied by a low fore-quarter; for if otherwise, the fore-leg is too long in proportion, and the power of working and killing is at a very low ebb. Two essentials are required, as I have already shown—viz., speed and working power. Now, speed may be given from length of hind-quarter, whether that length is usually in an extended, or in a bent form; because when in action they both assume the same condition, and are then precisely similar the one to the other. But the working power is deficient, if there is the *usual* accompaniment of the straight hind-quarter—viz., a long fore-leg. It will be evident that if the hind-quarter is straight, and the fore-leg is properly proportioned—that is to say, short enough for the working powers, the fore-quarter will appear very low, and the hips will stand up far above the shoulder. Now, if this formation co-exists with the straight hind-leg, all may be in good proportion; but if not, it seldom happens that the dog can stoop to reach his hare without spoiling his stride. Nevertheless, a remarkable exception is sometimes seen, in which there is great working and killing power displayed, with a high shoulder and long fore-legs. This, however, is contrary to rule, and in selecting a good shape, no experienced courser would take such a formation without a practical proof of its efficiency in that particular instance. Next to the length of limb, the due development of the joints is of great importance; the stifle joints ought to be strong and broad, and the bony processes powerful and large. The hocks, also, should be long and powerful, and well separated from the leg bone, by that thin double layer of skin, which may be felt and almost seen through. The muscles

are divided into two large masses, the upper thigh, which is scarcely to be made out without the touch, being, as it were, buried in the body and flank; and the lower thigh, which is much more distinct, and of very great importance to the powers of gallopping. This lower thigh is a very desirable point, if well developed; and in making a selection for breeding, its large size should be especially insisted upon. Good hind-feet again are necessary, but I do not like them too round and cat-like; at the same time, a long flat foot is opposed to high speed, and also prevents a due hold being taken of the ground. Wherever there is this long, flat, and broken-down foot, I should not look either for high speed, or for the power of continuing the efforts of the greyhound. There is a want of that elasticity and springiness which characterise the movements of this graceful animal; and he goes dull and dead instead of being animated and ready for any exertion.

410. THE FORE-QUARTER is the complement to the hind-quarter, and can do nothing until set in motion by that part of the animal economy; but, in spite of this secondary part in the locomotive department, it is not less important than the primary cause of motion, because though not originating it, it can and does neutralize the efforts of the hind-quarter, if not calculated to carry them out. The great purpose of the fore-quarter is to enable the animal to take advantage of the propulsion given by the vigorous contraction of the hind one, and thus to carry the animal on in the intervals of the strokes. If, therefore, the fore-quarter is dull, heavy, and incapable of extension, the stroke is broken and suspended, and the pace is reduced accordingly. But besides this purpose, in which the fore-quarter of the racehorse bears a similar part, that of the greyhound is also used in stopping the speed, and turning the body to the right or left, when the hare makes one of those turns which she delights in. Here the shoulder requires to be pliable yet strong, and there must be considerable play in all its parts, or it will give way in the violent effort made to change the direction of the speed. The outward formation for these purposes is well known and recognised by all in its general principles, though there may be a difference of opinion as to its details. Every one is agreed that the line through the shoulder-blade should be oblique, because that gives, in the first place, greater absolute length of blade; and, in the second, it gives greater power over the arm, so that it may be protruded further, and with greater force, than is the case with a short and upright blade. This will be made clear in the chapter treating of the structure of the dog; but it is acknowledged as a fact, that such oblique shoulders conduce to that conjunction of speed and working power which is desired. At the same time, I think I have seen so many cases of upright shoulders united with great pace and cleverness, that the rule is by no means an absolute one. But one rule is, I think, of that nature—viz., that where there are confined shoulders not acting with any liberty, but glued in their places, then the speed is not good, and the working power absolutely null. With good sloping shoulder-blades there is almost always combined a formation which is of the greatest consequence, and that is a long upper arm—that is to say, a long bone intervening between the shoulder-blade and the elbow. This length of arm generally coincides with good length from the hip to the hock; and when that quarter is bent, as I have already described, the oblique shoulder-blade, long upper arm, and low elbow, usually accompany it; in most cases, also, there is a knee close to the ground, and thus the fore and hind-quarters agree in formation, and will assuredly act together. When these points are combined, they make a perfect fore-quarter, and only want a strong useful foot, with a thick horny sole, to complete the requisites. As with the hind-foot, so with this; I am not fond of the very upright, small, and round foot; such are always drawing their nails, though they are certainly well suited for fine turf; but on fallows, or rough ground of any kind, the strong and moderately-flat foot is the more useful kind. The knuckles ought to be strong and well up, but the dog should not be too much on his toes; a spreading foot, however, with a thin sole devoid of horn, will never stand work, and should on that account be avoided.

411. THE COLOUR is one of those points in the greyhound which has been most disputed by different judges of his merits; one party considering it of the greatest importance, while the other decides that "a good dog, like a good horse, cannot be of a bad colour." With most people there is more or less of prejudice in this matter, and I am not perhaps exempt from this failing, when I own my leaning is to blacks and reds. This leaning, however, is not entirely guided by the eye; because it will be found that a large proportion of the winners in "Thacker" are of one or other of those colours. Indeed, my belief is, that all the colours exhibited by the greyhound are to be traced to them, and that when united with white (the result of domestication) they will produce any of the many other shades which appear in the lists

Thus, by ringing the changes of black, red, and white, every shade will be produced, as shown in the following table :—

THE MIXTURE OF	RESULT.
Black and red, No. 1	Red, with black muzzle.
Do. do. No. 2	Red-brindle.
Do. do. No. 3	Black and tan.
Black and white	Blue.
Red and white	Fawn.
Black, red, & white, No. 1	Blue-fawn.
Do. do. do. No. 2	Fawn-brindle.
Do. do. do. No. 3	Blue-brindle.

These colours only result when they are mixed together in the coat generally; for when that is not the case the dog is patched with these colours in blotches, either of colour on a white ground, or of white on a coloured ground; and I am quite satisfied that these several hues result from an admixture of the blood of those greyhounds which have these colours in their pedigree-tables. Wherever the colour is confined to one only for some generations, the progeny will almost always be the same, and the whole litter will resemble one another in that respect; but when all colours of the rainbow are met with, it is impossible to guess at the probable colours of the expected offspring. From the above table it may be gathered, that wherever black is the pre-vailing colour, you will generally have blue also, if combined with any blood containing much white; and the same may be said of fawn, as a result of breeding from red united with white; also of brindle, as occurring in a mixture of the various principal colours. This last is often thought to be *sui generis;* but it is nothing more than the consequence of the mixture of colours, and is seen in all the domestic animals but the horse, where there is a variety of colour, as in the cow, the pig, the dog, and the cat. In the horse the mixture of colours is shown in the roan shade, and not in a brindle; though in some breeds there is a near approach to it, as in the Norman cream-coloured horse, which has a black stripe down the back, and some bars generally over the shoulder and down the arm. Still the true brindle never appears in the horse, but piebald, skewbald, and spotted horses, in every other shape, are not uncommon. No reason for this exception can be given; but that such is the fact cannot be disputed. We may, from the above examination as to the causes of the varieties of colour, therefore, conclude that black and red are the original shades, and that all others are caused by their mixture, or by the mingling of one or both with white, which is the type and badge of domesticity. Now as this badge is not advantageous to the greyhound, we may, I think, reasonably discard it when possible, or, at all events, when it is easy to do so, and accept the pure colours in preference. By many experienced breeders it is thought that shape and performances follow the colour; and that, in picking a puppy, it ought to be selected by its near approach to that colour which its best ancestor showed. Thus, supposing a litter of whelps to be black, red, and brindled, if the dam or sire, or any one of their progenitors was par-ticularly celebrated, then that puppy should be selected which most nearly resembled him or her *in colour.* This rule I have seen tried in numberless instances, but I never saw that it led to any good results; on the contrary, as with most other rules in the choice of whelps, I believe it only leads to dependence on a rotten reed.

412. THE COAT is the last point in the conformation of the greyhound which will be here considered; and I believe it to be one of no consequence whatever. There is, however, one kind of coat which is radically bad; and that is a woolly fur, rather than hair, which, though short, has no gloss on it, and which gets wet on the slightest amount of rain. This is a very bad defence against the weather, and is a mark of weak-ness of constitution, which would always make me reject its wearer. In all other respects I am careless of the coat; and I regard coarse hair and thin hair as alike indicative only of particular breeds, equally good for all purposes. Many of our best breeds are very coarse in the hair, and often show a goodly brush in the tail, which however should, if hairy, be only fan-like, and not like the fox's brush, hairy all round. Some of the best Scotch blood have a cross of the old rough greyhound, but they seldom show the rough hair, which soon disappears in crossing with the smooth greyhound; though again it occasionally peeps out in a single puppy or two in a litter, far removed from the original strain. It is, I fancy, rather desirable than other-wise; but my experience of this cross is too slight to warrant a decided opinion. Most of the best modern greyhounds are well covered with hair; and the fancy for bare thighs and cheeks is well nigh out of date.

SECT. 4.—BEST MODE OF PROCURING GREYHOUNDS.

413. There are two ways of obtaining a kennel of greyhounds; one of which consists in purchasing, the other in setting to work to breed one. To the former mode there are many objections, not the least of which is, that few people sell what they believe to be good; and as they have better oppor-tunities of trial than the purchaser, they are

more likely to know than he is. It is very seldom that a *good* kennel of greyhounds is to be disposed of entire; few coursers are disgusted with the sport while success attends them; and even if they sell while in the heyday of their prosperity, a change in the management upsets all calculation, and the previously good runner turns out a loser instead. Of this many examples might be cited, not the least remarkable of which might be found in the last season in Lancashire, where a very celebrated and victorious kennel changed hands, and the cracks, although given into the management of a very successful trainer, were put down without difficulty at the Waterloo meeting. On the other hand, this change is sometimes advantageous, as in the case of Mortality, which changed hands four times before she could come out with anything like credit, and then beat one of her former kennel companions, supposed to be vastly superior to her. But, generally, it may be said that purchase is a bad speculation; and even when the whole kennel is *bonâ fide* to be disposed of, the young courser is generally supplanted by the old hand, who is possessed of information obtained from good quarters, and therefore to be relied on. In such a sale only the external form can be studied, and this is seldom to be depended on as a certain guide; action is the main reliance for choice at the puppy-age, and in a loose box, or in an auctioneer's yard, none can be seen. Some good purchases have been made in this way; as, for instance, Mocking-bird and Movement, into and out of a celebrated kennel; and, lately, Mr. Randell's celebrated bitch, Rival, purchased at Sir H. G. Gore's sale for about £15. At that sale also occurred a curious instance of the little value to be put upon information as to the relative value of puppies. Before the sale, a person who had had good opportunities of judging of the respective merits of the puppies, was asked for his opinion by Mr. Randell, and he advised him by all means to buy one by Magician out of Shade; and, acting upon that advice, he did buy her at about the same price as Rival, which bitch he selected on his own judgment. Here, then, was a bitch by a Waterloo-cup winner out of a Waterloo-cup winner, and recommended by a good judge, who had seen her in her play at various times, yet she proved utterly useless, while the comparatively disregarded companion turned out certainly one of the best, if not the very best, greyhound of her year. Such is the lottery in purchasing; and the same may perhaps be said of breeding; but then the outlay is not so great, and the annoyance also is relieved by the absence of any specific sum as spent upon a worthless brute. But in case of the necessity for a purchase, it is much better to buy a brace or two of whelps at weaning-time, than to buy puppies of the age of 10 or 12 months, for the choice is not worth much at the early period I have named, and the good judge will often allow the best puppies in a litter to pass into strange hands without intending it. Before three months there is very little choice; and if only the legs and feet are good, and there is no rupture or other malformation, I should care little as to the pick of the litter at weaning-time. There are, of course, some which are unhealthy and half-starved, but I do not speak of the last pick, but of the difference between the two or three best in the litter. Let the young courser, therefore, if he must buy, determine upon the blood he requires, and then let him purchase a brace or two of whelps of that blood, getting some friend to pick them for him out of the litter, but contenting himself with the second or third pick as quite equal to the first, in all human probability. These whelps he may proceed to rear upon the principles which will be found hereafter detailed. In the meantime, and while they are coming on, there will be a season to spare, and during that season the tyro should experimentalize on a brace of greyhounds of average goodness, which he may buy for £5 a-piece, or often obtain as a gift. With these he may appear in the private coursing-field, or on those semi-public days which are so common in every coursing neighbourhood, and where he may pit them against equally inferior dogs as often as he likes. Let him bestow every pains upon them, and try all he knows, or his trainer, if he has one, for it will require plenty of good management to make them do more in his hands than they did before in the hands of their previous master. But they will serve to give him an insight into the peculiarities of the animal, and he will learn to know what to avoid in his treatment, and what is injurious to them, if not always what is the most successful kind of management. In this way I have known gifts turned into winning dogs; and low-priced ones, after being discarded from large kennels, have been able to do wonders, comparatively speaking, when treated in a different way in a smaller and more limited stud. My advice, therefore, would be to all young coursers, not to attempt to do too much at first, but to purchase or beg a brace or two of inferior greyhounds, and make the most of them for the first season; and, in the meantime, to breed or purchase a few whelps, which, by the beginning of the second season, when practice has fitted the trainer for their management, will be ready to take the field with some prospect of success.

M

414. KENNELS for greyhounds should be constructed on a very different plan to those already described for foxhounds or harriers. For the more delicate greyhound, which is clothed on exposure to the cold, and otherwise protected, a covered court is always desirable; and without it, he will not leave his lodging-room in bad weather to empty himself, but will soil that apartment in a way which is certainly not conducive to his health. Besides this, more than four or five greyhounds should never be in one division, as they are so highly fed that they are always fighting and laming one another; and they are also less healthy than when in smaller numbers. The annexed plans and elevation will be found to be all that is required for from 12 to 16 running dogs, which is quite as great a number as ought to be kept together at any one time. These kennels should be from 25 to 35 feet long, by 24 or 25 feet wide; and the whole parallelogram should be roofed-in either with slate, or boarding, or felt; but whatever material is used should be white-washed, or painted of a light colour, on account of the heat absorbed by the natural colour of the slates, or by the dark colour of pitch, as usually applied to felt. This area should be subdivided longitudinally into three kennels, each 8 feet wide; and these again should be divided off into an inner sleeping-room, and an outer yard, with a door (*figs.* 1 and 3, *b*) and window (*figs* 1, 4, and 5, *a a a*) between, and a ventilator in the ceiling and outer-wall, as shown in the plan at *e e*. A bed (*d*) should be raised about 1 foot 6 inches from the floor, and the sides, back, and front should be lined with boarding about 9 inches high. If the dogs are quarrelsome, each should have a separate compartment boarded off, about 18 inches high, as shown at *ffff, fig.* 3, and at *d, fig.* 1. This will enable any one of four dogs to have a compartment to himself, even if he is continually chased about, because he will always have an empty one to fly to; and this is sometimes of great consequence, as it frequently happens that a cowardly dog is driven off the bed, and obliged to lie on the floor, to the imminent danger of producing rheumatism in some one of its multifarious forms. This is the way in which kennel-lameness is often produced, and also many other varieties of chronic rheumatism. *Fig.* 1 gives a perspective view of the interior of one division of the kennel, adapted for four quarrelsome dogs or bitches. It shows the outer-yard on the left, with its doors (*c* and *b*), and the sleeping-room on the right, with its ventilating window (*a*), also shown enlarged in *figs.* 4 and 5, and its ventilators in the ceiling and end-wall (*e e*). The beds, partitioned off, are shown at *d*. *Fig.* 2 shows the elevation of the end of the whole kennels, and *fig.* 3 the ground-plan with the course of the drains. If a greater number of greyhounds are kept than this kennel will accommodate, it is better to provide for them elsewhere in a similar way, or to put them for the time in loose boxes or outbuildings of any form. The walls should be of good hard-burnt bricks—not porous, so as to absorb the secretions; and are better covered with a layer of cement. The floor should be laid in glazed tiles, imbedded in a layer of cement, upon concrete composed of cinders, or clinkers, mixed with gravel and lime in equal proportions. This sets very hard, but it should have on it a layer of cement, just thick enough to hold the tiles securely in their places, and prevent the water from insinuating itself into the crevices between them.

415. THE KENNEL MANAGEMENT is mainly dependent upon cleanliness and regularity for success. Every kennel should be scrupulously clean, and should be washed down and carefully mopped dry once a day. This should be done while the inmates are at exercise, and it will be nearly dry when they return. A layer of sawdust should always be on the floor in cold weather, but in the summer it is cleaner and better without it. Some use straw, but I think sawdust better and more easily renewed and removed. For the beds, good straw is the best, and nothing in the heat of summer at all. Greyhounds will then far rather sleep upon bare boards than upon the straw; and will, if their beds are full of it, sleep upon the floor in preference. Deal shavings are said to be obnoxious to fleas, but I never found them of much use. The feeding need not be here described, as it will be given more in detail at the proper time. Water should always be kept in iron vessels, fixed at about a foot from the ground to prevent its being soiled; and it should be regularly boiled when the dogs are in training, to prevent the change from producing injurious consequences. In all ordinary weather the door between the yard and the sleeping-room (*figs.* 1 and 3, *b b b b*) may be left ajar, for which purpose a couple of loose tiles are very useful, one inside and the other out; but in severe weather it must be closed. Some cut a hole in the door, and hang a piece of carpet against it; but this is not a good plan, because, in severe weather, it allows the wind to penetrate to too great a degree for the health of the greyhound.

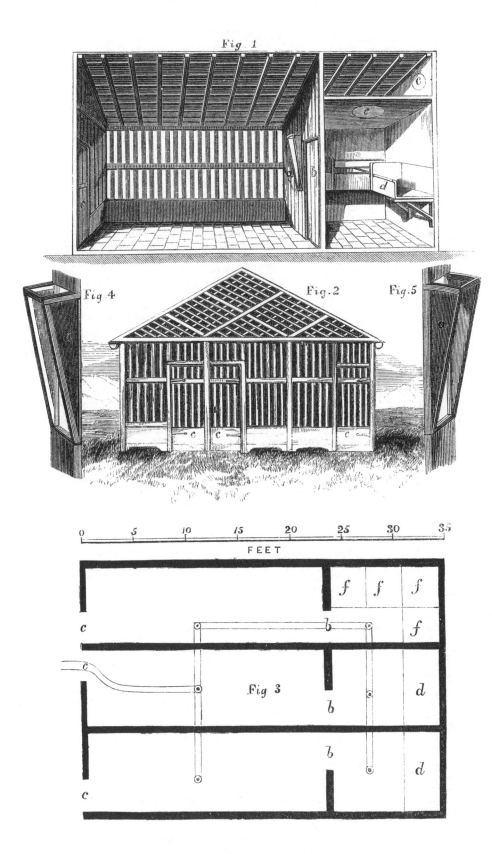

Fig. 1

Fig. 4   Fig. 2   Fig. 5

0   5   10   15   20   25   30   35

FEET

Fig. 3

VARIETIES OF THE MODERN GREYHOUND.

SECT. 1.—THE NEWMARKET GREYHOUND.

416. This variety stands at the head of the list as the probable root of all our modern subdivisions. It is well known that the greyhound has been used in public at Newmarket longer than elsewhere, and that the greyhounds running there, being considered as of superior quality, have been eagerly sought after throughout the length and breadth of the land. Pedigrees almost always end in some dog or bitch said to have come from a kennel celebrated at Newmarket; showing either that this breed was superior to all others, or else that it was supposed to be so. The characteristics, therefore, of this dog are really those which are generally most highly prized, as shown by the avidity which has always been displayed to obtain the breed, which, until lately, was very difficult to procure. In the days of Lord Orford and Lord Rivers, no money could procure the best blood of their kennels, and their inferior drafts only were obtained, and often these were not to be had without great difficulty and favouritism. Since the time, however, of Lord Rivers' final sale, when his blood became generally dispersed, Captain Daintree first began the system of throwing open his best blood to the public at a fixed price; and his King Cob, with Mr. Fyson's Fantail, were advertised at £5 5s., as is now so commonly done. The consequence has been, that any person who can procure a bitch, and has the command of five or ten guineas, is enabled to obtain as good blood as the highest nobleman in the land, and can compete on favourable terms in any company of coursers, at least as far as his breed of greyhounds is concerned. The characteristics of the true Newmarket greyhound are, therefore, those of the most racing-like dog, and are the result of a long selection from successful parents for many years past, over ground which is not so severe as to hold pace in abeyance, nor yet so confined as to make pace the only criterion. This was formerly more true of the ground at Newmarket than at present, as its character has been much altered by the encroachments of the railway upon the best part of it. The Newmarket greyhound, then, is a racing-like, speedy animal, yet possessed of, as much stoutness as possible, in combination with high speed. His head and neck are of the most approved form, but perhaps a little too elegant and light to be thoroughly efficient—that is to say, that, according to my ideas, there is scarcely sufficient room

for a brain of volume enough to form a good centre of the nervous system. The chest is very deep, and of good volume, though often rather flat-sided; back scarcely so stout as it should be; thighs and hocks extremely well bent, and strong; shoulders very slanting, light, yet muscular, and very moveable; fore-legs straight, and feet good. In action these dogs are very light and fast gallopers; and being generally of good size, they are able to beat most others to the hare. They are seldom very first-rate workers, being too large and fast to compete with slower and smaller dogs; but many of them have extraordinary powers of coming round with their hares, considering their speed and size. In effecting this purpose, most fast dogs of this breed turn by running a segment of a circle, without stopping themselves and starting afresh; and in doing this, they maintain their high speed in a wonderful manner; but this mode of working requires a very fast and racing hare to show itself; for with a short-running or weak hare, these round-turning dogs are all abroad, and seem unable and even unwilling to exert themselves. But with a fast hare they show themselves to great perfection; and if they let in a closer worker, they go by him in the stretches again and again. In moderately-short courses, therefore, with fast hares, they beat everything not so fast as themselves; but in severe courses with hares which will not allow themselves to be killed, they exhaust their powers by their efforts, and then often suffer defeat by a dog which would perhaps never have reached the hare in question but for them. This is one of the lotteries of coursing which makes the certainty of success so much more difficult in that pursuit than in any other; for as you can never tell beforehand either the length of the course or the nature of the hare, it is quite impossible to be always prepared to meet the exact difficulties which will have to be surmounted. The only thing therefore to be done, is to select the dog which will succeed in the greatest proportion of events out of a given number; and then, I think, the Newmarket variety, as above described, will always bear the prize. I do not mean that dogs such as now are used at Newmarket, but such as are descended from the best blood of those kennels which were victorious in the palmy days of that celebrated locality. The most successful of these, as sires, have been of late years Captain Daintree's King Cob, Mr. Fyson's Foremost and Figaro, both sons of his celebrated bitch, Frederica; Sir B. Smyth's

Sherwood, Lord Stradbroke's Mariner, and Mr. Dobede's Defiance and Doron. From one or other of these celebrated dogs most of our present fast greyhounds in the south are descended, and many also in the north; and though in speed their stock are certainly rivalled, and perhaps even excelled in cleverness by some of the Yorkshire greyhounds, yet they are, in my opinion, stouter than those dogs, and on the whole superior to them. They have been so intermixed with extraneous blood, that in the present day few pure Newmarket greyhounds are open to the public; the following being, as far as I know, the only advertised stallions of that breed, namely: Field-Marshal, Desperate, Damson, and Forerunner, by Figaro, out of Defiance bitches—Mirage, another of his sons (brother to Mockingbird)—Bourdeaux, also by Figaro, out of Cloak — Foremost, Jun., by Foremost — Esquire, Exchequer, and Jester, out of a Fantail-bitch — and Kentish Fire, out of Knab, by King Cob—Barrister and Dunkeld, by Doron—Steam Engine and Electric in Essex—and Mr. Harris' Baron, by Lincolnshire Marquis, but of blood bred purposely for Newmarket. The variously-crossed public stallions are so numerous as almost to prevent their enumeration; but they will more properly come under consideration after the examination of the breeds with which they are amalgamated. The Newmarket greyhounds are used in the counties of Essex, Surrey, Cambridgeshire, Suffolk, Norfolk, Bedfordshire, Huntingdonshire, and Lincolnshire.

SECT. 2.—THE LANCASHIRE GREYHOUND.

417. The flats of Lancashire which are used for coursing are nearly all reclaimed land composed of perfectly level plains intersected by ditches; the soil is peaty, and the greater part of it is cultivated by the plough; hence, the greyhounds for this country must be large and strong; and as the ditches which intersect the fields, for the purpose of draining them, are rather numerous, they must be possessed of sufficient tact and cleverness to avoid mistakes at those impediments to the course. The soil is very dead and non-elastic, from the presence of the peat either at the surface or close beneath it; and the gallop, which is the most telling on it, is rather a longer one than that which is the best suited to sound turf or a sandy soil. From the absence of hills, also, the faculty of climbing them is not called into play, and consequently there is no necessity for that formation which enables the greyhound to surmount them. Speed, therefore, is the chief element of success, and in the soft soil of the reclaimed land many a dog is able to

stop himself, who would be a very wide runner on the downs of Wiltshire, the sound land of Yorkshire, or the lowlands of Scotland. It must not, however, be supposed that stoutness is not required on this kind of ground, for, on the contrary, it will be seen by those who attend the Lytham and Altcar meetings, that many of the courses are of great length and severity; and, on account of the want of elasticity in the soil, they are of a most distressing character. Indeed, when a good Lytham hare is able to get away from a brace of greyhounds, she leads them such a dance as is seldom witnessed elsewhere, because, having often no home, she is obliged to persevere till she shakes them entirely off by running them to a stand-still. Nevertheless, greyhounds run through more seasons in that country than elsewhere, because they are seldom lamed, there being no flints or fences to do any damage; and as nothing makes a dog cunning so soon as the running him when in pain, so the absence of this condition ensures his going on without the appearance of any lurching propensity. With all these advantages in his favour, it has resulted that the Lancashire greyhound has not been improved to the same extent as his Newmarket rival; just as we often see the best natural soils in the worst state of artificial cultivation, so the greyhound which has the easiest task, and is the least tried by adverse circumstances, is really a worse animal in the long run than his more hardly-used antagonist. In shape and make the Lancashire greyhound very nearly resembles the Newmarket dog, but does not show such high breeding in any of those points which are considered signs of that quality; the head is not so lean, and the jaw is coarser; there is even less development of brain than in the Newmarket greyhound, and the neck is shorter and thicker, though still long enough for the purposes to which it is applied. In general size he is, perhaps, a little above the standard of Newmarket, some of the most celebrated dogs having been 28 inches high and 70 lbs. in weight; as, for instance, Tyrant, Emperor, Earwig, Priam, and Sandy. Most of the Lancashire dogs have a very long stride, and I am inclined to believe that this is a very important feature in their conformation, since, from the nature of the soil, it is not well adapted for those quick short strokes which are often successful on sound and short turf. Nevertheless, a good Newmarket greyhound, *when used to the ditches*, has generally succeeded in carrying off the Lancashire prizes, and that blood has latterly been extensively introduced by the Altcar and Lytham coursers. When, however, a really good specimen of the old

Lancashire greyhound has made an appearance there, nothing has been able to come near it; and the wonderful performances of Cerito will long be remembered in that neighbourhood. This bitch was entirely of Lancashire blood, and was exactly suited to the ground she won her triumphs on. Her stride was enormous, and consequently she was not successful upon hard ground like that of Amesbury and Market Weighton. But, putting her exceptional case on one side, during the last 12 years in which the Newmarket blood has been so much tried at the Waterloo-cup meeting, greyhounds of the true Lancashire breed have been victorious four times, whilst the true Newmarket have succeeded twice. Again, a cross of that breed with the Scotch has won the much-coveted prize once, in the person of Hughie Graham; against the same feat on the part of the combination of Newmarket and Lancashire in Sackcloth, and the Lancashire and Scotch in Judge; so that it stands thus — Lancashire, 7; Newmarket, 2; Lancashire and Scotch, 1; Lancashire and Newmarket, 1; and Newmarket and Scotch, 1: total, 12. In the runners-up during the same period, there were however only four Lancashire dogs and one Newmarket, the remaining seven being made up of five single specimens of the various crosses and two Scotch greyhounds, Larriston and Scotland Yet. It will thus be seen that the former great superiority of this breed on its own ground has not been maintained of late, and that others have had, with the single exception of Cerito, quite as good a chance during the last eight years. Still, the Lancashire blood is more fitted for its own plains than for other and more hilly countries, and consequently it is not often that its votaries are tempted to try their luck elsewhere. Sometimes, however, a good dog of this breed is successful on other ground, and the running of Sackcloth in Wiltshire will not soon be forgotten. It may be said that he is partly Newmarket, and certainly such is the case; but Lancashire can lay claim to three-fourths of the honour, he being only one-fourth Newmarket blood. Most of the Lancashire greyhounds are descended from very old blood, that is to say, blood which has been bred in-and-in, though not too closely, yet in the same families; and the consequence is that it tells very much in those dogs of which it composes a part. In this respect it resembles the Newmarket, and when the two are combined it is difficult to say which will predominate, though, as far as my observation goes, I am inclined to think that the Lancashire has the superiority in persistence. The chief public Lancashire stallions are now—Sefton, by Scythian, out of Syren; Syntax, by Marquis, out of Synecdoche; Port, brother to Mr. Borron's Bluelight, a very successful stallion, but only used in private by that gentleman; Pirate; Marquis, son of Marquis and Syren; Leander, Juggler, and Columbus. Many good dogs of part Lancashire blood are in existence, and some are used for stud purposes. Those crossed with the Newmarket are—Sackcloth, already described; Ranter, uniting the blood of Figaro, Bugle, and Marquis, with the Nottingham Violet; War Eagle and Wrestler; Jingo, brother to Staymaker; Haymaker, by the last-named dog; Clown, by Emperor, out of Mistley; and last, though not least, Mr. Brown's Bedlamite, which unites the Newmarket with the Nottingham blood; for, as this last is more nearly allied to Lancashire than any other, it may be considered as identical with it.

SECT. 3.—THE YORKSHIRE GREYHOUND.

418. The scene of the struggles of this greyhound is different, again, from either of those already described, being of a most varied character; sometimes the fine turf of Malton or Huggate is the ground selected; next, perhaps, the flinty and sandy hills of Market Weighton will be run over; and, finally, the rougher and stronger soil of Burneston. The length of course is not often very great, because the hares are most of them covert-bred, and are only driven out for the occasion of the meeting; they, therefore, lie near their homes, and seldom afford too long a contest. From these causes it results, that while speed is still the most sought after, cleverness is the next in importance to the Yorkshire courser, and stoutness is less thought of than is the case where the courses are more severe. The Yorkshire greyhound, therefore, is characterized by speed as great as that of Newmarket or Lancashire, coupled with a degree of cleverness rarely seen elsewhere; but, at the same time, sullied by a softness and tendency to lurch greater than is often met with further south. They are also of great size, but are rather coarse in their shapes, seldom having any appearance of blood, but looking ragged-hipped and useful, rather than level or elegant. No greyhound can beat them when in the humour, and the performances of Charles XII. and his descendants, among which are his nephew and grand-nephews, Velox, Rattler, and Assault, will make this blood remarkable for pace and cleverness. This breed may be said to extend to the borders of Scotland, where it becomes intermixed with that blood. The chief public stallions are—Velox now very old, and his sons Assault,

Rattler, and Wellington, in which there is a cross of the bulldog, through Raimes' Rattler; Croton Oil, Admiral, Beverlac, and Young Cedric, which are not quite pure, but as much so as most greyhounds; and Dutchman and his son Black Cap, brother to Restless. The cross with the Lancashire is shown in Juggler, by Worcester Marquis, and that with the Newmarket in Mr. Bagge's Trafalgar, who unites the blood of King Cob, Minerva, and Defiance, with that of Charles XII. and the Lincolnshire Marquis strain; also, in Sam and Tout, showing nearly the same combinations.

SECT. 4.—THE SMOOTH SCOTCH GREYHOUND.

419. This variety is composed of more varied strains than either of those I have already described, and is really now generally more English than Scotch. Thus, if we examine the pedigrees of its most successful stallions it will be found that they almost all go back to a denizen of one or other of the English kennels. Mr. Sharpe's Monarch, the most remarkable perhaps of their stud-dogs, is almost wholly English; and Lord Eglinton's Waterloo was half English, being a son of Mr. De Burgh's Exotic, an importation from the south. Lord Eglinton's Rufus, also, was in great measure of Lancashire blood, being a grandson of Ball's Bugle. But Dr. Brown's dogs, Sport and Chance, were, I believe, of pure Scotch blood; and Mr. A. Graham's rough breed, though much crossed with the blood of Bugle, were otherwise entirely Scotch. All these various sorts differ with one another in many most essential particulars, and certainly they might be split up into sections quite as easily as the Newmarket, Lancashire, and Yorkshire greyhound, which resemble one another quite as much as the descendants of Mr. A. Sharpe's Monarch, Mr. A. Graham's rough breed, or Dr. Brown's Sport. But still, though differing in some points, they all partake of some characteristics in common, not the least of, which is their early maturity. Puppy stakes have long been a prominent feature in the Scotch courser's card, and consequently he has bred a good deal for that purpose. Now, to ensure early maturity, there must be not only a frame which is rapidly set and furnished, but there should be a disposition to acquire tact and cleverness without much practice; of which there cannot be any great amount in the case of puppies engaged to appear in those public stakes that are run in October and November. From these causes it has resulted, that speed coming first, as it ought always to do in the estimate, early maturity and tact have next been considered in the scale; and the sire whose puppies have

come out victorious in the produce-stakes, has been overwhelmed with applications for his services. These peculiarities have been very apparent in the Jason's, the Heather-jock's, and Mr. A. Graham's blood; while the descendants of Waterloo and Sport, with many others of the old Scotch blood, have not stood that test so well, and have consequently been rejected. The Jasons are particularly remarkable for early maturity in working power, often seeming to run their second or third hares as cleverly as they ever do after long experience. This is also the case with the Heather-jocks, as shown in Rufus and his sister Blackbird, and in Haphazard and his son the Nutman. Quickness and cleverness is their *forte*, together with a great degree of hardihood of constitution and power of bearing punishment, though often coupled with an uncertainty of temper, for which there is no accounting. Their power of stopping themselves, and getting away from their turns, is quite distinct from the Newmarket sweep; and though they are nearly, if not quite as fast as those dogs, they are greatly their superiors with a short-running or bad hare. With a very fast one they do not seem to me to be able to sustain so well the prolonged racing pace, either from a want of courage or of wind, or both perhaps; but when it comes to a continuance of severe work, few dogs can come up to them. The stock of Sport more nearly resembles the Yorkshire strains in every respect; while the rough breed of Mr. A. Graham must have a separate consideration. There are now few public stallions of pure Scotch blood; but the following, I believe, strictly come within that designation, viz.—Wigan, Stanley, Larriston, Ecclefechan (of doubtful blood, but said to be a grandson of Waterloo), Jamie Forest, and Blue Baron. Hughie Graham and Bonnie Scotland combine the Scotch and Newmarket, as do also Vraye Foy and the Curler, Puzzle'em, and the Nipper—all four sons of Sir Jas. Boswell's Jason. Motley and Martinet, again, combine the Scotch, Yorkshire, and Newmarket; and Japhet and Fugleman unite the two former with the Emperor and Bugle blood, which has been so successful on all kinds of ground.

SECT. 5.—THE ROUGH SCOTCH GREYHOUND.

420. Of this breed, in its pristine purity, I know nothing; but I have seen some of the greyhounds largely crossed with the blood, and exhibiting all the roughness of the original strain. Their speed seems great, but, as far as I have seen, not quite first class. It is, therefore, chiefly as a means of improving the southern breeds that it has

been used, and with a considerable degree of success. All those which I have met with of this blood have been light in the loin, and apparently deficient in power there. This, however, is said to be accidental, and that the best specimens were remarkably good in that point. The characteristics of this breed are great size and good speed, with considerable working power, but some little deficiency of quickness. They are not very fast from their turns, but with a straight-backed hare they show well, and are able to lie well down, running the line of the hare, and bending with her without much apparent distress or trouble at the turns. They resemble the deerhound in external form, but differ in their power of stooping; the latter always carrying their heads high, whilst the former drop it well between their fore-legs. They are very hardy, and capable of sustaining any amount of punishment, and on that account are well calculated for crossing with the more delicate south-country breeds; but, as these are now much more accustomed to bear cold and hardships than they formerly were, the use of the rough greyhound has been a good deal superseded, and it is consequently neglected by most of the Scotch breeders. Mr. A. Graham, however, still adheres to this cross; and an opportunity will soon be afforded again of testing its value. Mr. Ridgway has also used it lately with success, having bred a very good litter of puppies by Motley out of Holyrood, one of Mr. A. Graham's blood. In addition to these, many of the Lancashire and Cheshire breeders have adopted a somewhat similar strain in Mr. Moore's Derwentwater, who is descended from Mr. A. Graham's Gilbertfield; and in the south the celebrated Mocking-bird has been put to Mathematics, a grandson of Mr. A. Graham's rough bitch Mavourneen. The result of this cross is a very beautiful litter of large racing-like greyhounds, and if their performances are equal to their looks, they will do much for the reputation of this much neglected variety of the animal we are now considering.

Sect. 6.—The Wiltshire Greyhound.

421. Lastly, as the most distinct variety, I shall describe the Wiltshire greyhound, which is intended for a peculiar hare, and a down-country; and, when well marked and of pure old blood, he is a very different animal from the five already described. The downs of Berkshire and Wiltshire are well known to most coursers, but to those who have never seen them I must observe, that they are composed of an undulating plain of fine turf mixed with light arable land, which is, however, cultivated without fences of any description. There is, consequently, no let or hindrance to hare, dogs, or horses; and not only do the greyhounds run their courses without risk of being thrown out by any kind of fence, but the judge is able to see the whole of the work from end to end. Hence, stoutness here has full play, and many a course is won by the slow and small, but lasting dog, who has never made a point of merit in the first half of the course. But as long as the judge is called upon to decide by estimating the value of points according to the present fixed rules, so long must this be the case; and, as the lesser of two evils, the principle must be carefully supported. Stoutness is no doubt a very fine quality, but without pace it is, in my opinion, of little value; and though I despise the soft brute which shuts up in three or four hundred yards, I have no greater affection for the slow one which could not come near him during the time he was at work. Neither is to my taste, though each will often win a stake in consequence of a run of luck favouring his particular efforts. The pure old Wiltshire greyhound was formerly bred exclusively for the extraordinary hares which are generally met with at Amesbury and the Marlborough Downs, or sometimes, though not so often, at Ashdown Park. These hares are generally fast, but they also have the power of throwing out even the best worker in a style quite different to the Lancashire and Yorkshire variety. Hence, the Wiltshire dog has been bred especially strong and stout-hearted, to cope with them, and with as much speed in addition as could be obtained. Stoutness, however, was the grand characteristic, and true running also, as essential to a continuance of those exertions after punishment which all coursers desire. It is well known that those greyhounds which do not naturally run the line of the hare much sooner take to "cheek" her than those which adhere to her line, and run only at her scut; and hence it was found by experience that a true runner lasted much longer over the Wiltshire Downs, where he often is severely punished, both by excessive length of courses, and also by the sharp flints so common there. Such is the general style of the true Wiltshire greyhound; and when examined more closely, it will be seen that he is not of very great speed, but that his power of stopping himself and getting away from his turns is the remarkable feature in his characteristics. These dogs, when once they get to a short-running hare, are glued to her scut, and no ordinary dog can put them out again; hence they often, after losing a turn or two, get in and make a dozen wrenches before they allow another

point to be made. In the meantime the faster dog is becoming savage; and when he has a chance he cuts his own throat by picking up his hare with a rush—thus deciding the course against himself. The Wiltshire greyhound is very often a small, stout, and terrier-like dog; but many of the best old Wiltshire breed were of larger size; as, for instance, Billy-go-by-'em, who, if not bred from Wiltshire strains, was used entirely for that country, and has left some good descendants to carry on the peculiarly true style in which he excelled. Wiltshire Marquis himself was a small dog, and so were most of his stock; but some were of good size, and when crossed with the New-market blood in Royalist and Figheldean, they showed good size and pace, together with the same true and close running already described. As far as I know, there are no true Wiltshire greyhound stallions, for the breed has become nearly extinct as public performers; but numerous crosses are open to selection, as with the New-market in Forward, the Czar, Factotum, Lablache, and Fire-office; and with the Lancashire also in Neville, though his Wiltshire blood was that of Mr. Goodlake's Gracchus, who was more calculated and intended for Newmarket than for Amesbury or Ashdown; and also with the Scotch in Lopez and Egypt.

422 Such are the varieties of the grey-hound. The next thing to consider is the selection from them of the individuals to form the foundation of the breeding-stud.

CHAP. IV.

BREEDING THE GREYHOUND.

SECT. 1.—SELECTION OF BROOD-BITCH.

423. Upon the proper choice of this primary and most important foundation of the stud, will in great measure depend the after-success of her progeny. Now, on what principles should the selection be made? Or, are there any such reliable principles known? To the second question I may answer decidedly, yes; and to the first I will endeavour to afford what answer I can, in the following remarks. If the returns of coursing meetings throughout England and Scotland are carefully analysed, it will be found that in very few instances will what is called private blood be successful, and that a large proportion of winners are allied to certain well-known families. Occasionally a greyhound of a pedigree unknown to fame appears as a winner, but rarely of a large stake; and if, by a great chance, such an event occurs, it will often be found that although the sire and dam may be unknown, yet their more remote progenitors are usually of winning public blood. Some remarkable exceptions to this rule might be adduced, but they are so rare as to make them exceptions of that character which prove rather than disprove a rule. Thus, rule the first may be laid down, viz., that it is desirable to select a brood-bitch of good winning blood. Next, it will be found, that throughout England and Scotland certain breeds are more successful than others; and Mr Welsh has published returns which show that the proportion of winners to losers varies in a very remarkable manner.

This part of his labours is of great use to the breeder, and I have great pleasure in thanking him for the trouble he has taken to simplify the calculation to all lovers of the greyhound. I prefer taking his list to any calculation of my own, because it might otherwise be said that I had "cooked the account" to suit my particular view. In his Synopsis for 1852-3, the performances of the progeny of 38 stallions are analysed, from which I shall reject all those where there are not at least 10 dogs, because a smaller number than that would scarcely form a reliable ground of selection or rejection. Thus, the courses won by the stock of Buzzard are 50, to their losses of 57; Columbus, 18 to 23; Croton Oil, 47 to 39; Figaro, 189 to 101; Figheldean, 50 to 43; Foremost, 142 to 76; Kentish Fire, 32 to 11; Sam, 99 to 68; Curler, 97 to 63; Czar, 89 to 66; Vraye Foy, 110 to 70; War Eagle, 73 to 60. Here then we find, after drawing out all those which have only produced 10 runners, that the largest proportion of winners to losers rests with Kentish Fire first, at nearly 3 to 1; next with Foremost, at nearly 2 to 1; then with Figaro, at not quite so great a proportion, being about 7½ to 4; Vraye Foy stands next, at rather more than 1½ to 1; then Sam, at rather less than that proportion; whilst Curler and Czar do not quite come up to his standard even; and Croton Oil, Figheldean, and War Eagle, are barely in the proportion of 5 to 4. On the other hand, the successes of the stock of Buzzard and Columbus are less than their failures, and judged by that test, they should at once be rejected; but, judged by another test, a slightly different result will come out, for if we compare the number of winners with the number of dogs beaten, it will stand as follows:—Curler heads the list, with an average of 19 5-7 dogs beaten in each victory; then Kentish Fire, 18 1-3; Buzzard, 16; Figaro, 14 1-3; Vraye Foy, 12¾; Columbus, 12 2-3; Sam, 12; Croton Oil, 11 2-3; Czar, 11; Foremost, 9¼; Figheldean, 8; and War Eagle, 7½. But, taking either mode of calculation, one breed stands out prominently, viz., the descendants of King Cob, for out of these two lists, Kentish Fire, his son, is first in the one case and second in the other, whilst Figaro is third in one and fourth in the other, and Sam takes a good place in both. Buzzard, also, is high in the second list, though when examined by the first mode of calculation, he will be reduced in value, from the fact that the defeats of his stock were more numerous than their winnings. Next to the blood of King Cob stands that of Jason, for his two sons, Curler and Vraye Foy, stand high in each; Curler heading the second list, and Vraye Foy being fifth, whilst in the first list they are fourth and sixth. After him come Foremost and his son, Czar, which stand high in the first list, though not so well up in the second. In the following season (1853-4) a rather different result will appear from the same mode of calculation, though here, again, Kentish Fire heads the list with 18 victories to 9 defeats, and with one 64-dog-stake won, and another run up for out of the number. Next to him comes Egypt, with 103 victories to 67 defeats. After him, with about the same proportion, viz., 194 to 125, is Figaro; then Neville, 95 to 64—Croton Oil, 71 to 47—Field-Marshal, 118 to 85—Buzzard, 35 to 26—Eden, 67 to 44—Lopez, 31 to 20—War Eagle, 90 to 53—Esquire, 37 to 25—Czar, 67 to 48—Vraye Foy, 83 to 66—whilst Foremost, with 29 to 27, scarcely balances the account—and Mercury, with 82 to 88—Columbus, 23 to 26—and Sam, 35 to 43, are quite on the wrong side, having lost more than they have gained. On the whole, therefore, King Cob stands first as the progenitor of Kentish Fire, Figaro, Buzzard, Field-Marshal, Esquire, and Sam. Next comes Jason, through Vraye Foy, the Curler, Egypt, and Lopez; and lastly, Foremost and his sons, the Czar and War Eagle, claim our notice during these two seasons. We may, therefore, draw the following deduction as a second rule, viz., that the stock of King Cob, Jason, and Foremost have latterly been more victorious than any other in Great Britain; and consequently, on the principle that "like begets like," the blood of one or the other, if selected in a brood-bitch, is most likely to succeed in producing winning puppies. This selection, then, is founded upon a kind of statistical calculation, and one which will, I believe, be more likely to lead to success than any other. But the young breeder may say that this information is not sufficient, since he cannot procure either of these breeds unmixed with other blood; and this is quite true; and therefore I shall proceed to show the best mode of arriving at correct conclusions as to further operations. By a more rigid examination of the returns in "Thacker," it will be seen that these breeds have not been much or often intermixed, and that, consequently, there will not be many brood-bitches to be had combining any two of these three strains. Two instances may, however, be adduced in which the Jason blood has been thus united—once with King Cob's stock, in the cross between Egypt and Mocking-bird, and again with that of Foremost in the union of Cobea Scandens with Egypt. It would, therefore, be reasonable to select either of these crosses for a brood-bitch; and I believe they will turn out very useful in that capacity. Beyond these few doubly-advantageous crosses for breeding purposes, it may be supposed that the next best plan would be to select a descendant of one or other of these dogs united with some other breed that may be best suited to the particular country which the breeder intends them for, or which may be fancied by him. Thus, he would have to select from the Newmarket, Lancashire, Yorkshire Scotch or Wiltshire breeds for this purpose, and with perhaps very little further guide than his own fancy or prejudice. During the last season there have been one or two very remarkable facts elicited in the field which may assist us in the present inquiry. In the first place there have been a great number of superior puppies descended from Ball's Bugle. Two litters belonging to Mr. Borron have signalized themselves, both having his blood; one combined with that of Streamer and Waterloo, the other containing a double cross of Bugle combined with the blood of Foremost and Heather-jock. The celebrated Bedlamite-litter, consisting of Ranter, Riot, and Rant, with Gipsy Royal, Gipsy Prince, and Gipsy Queen, are also out of a bitch combining the Bugle and Streamer blood; and, in addition, Habnab and Heroine are out of a bitch by Wrestler, who was of the same strain as the dam of this litter. Ptarmigan and Pantomime, again, in the north, are, by Japhet, also descended from Heather-jock and Bugle, mixed with the old Carron blood of the Duke of Gordon; and lastly, though not a puppy of this season, the winner of the Waterloo Cup is descended from Emperor and a sister to Bugle, also united with the above-mentioned Carron blood. Going back a little further, many more winners might be adduced, descended from Ball's Bugle; but the above illustrations are quite sufficient to adduce from one season's winners—Judge, Black Cloud, Bright Idea, Bonfire, Beacon, Bit of Tartan, Breast-knot, Ranter, Riot, Gipsy Royal, Gipsy Queen and Gipsy Prince, Habnab and Heroine, Ptarmigan and Pantomime—truly an array well worth the consideration of the breeder. Again, this Carron blood seems to have been of great use, and, equally with that of Streamer, to have added what was wanting to the blood of Bugle. It appears to me that though Bugle has got many winning descendants, yet, in all cases, they have only been so when united with very fast blood, as in the above instances, Streamer and Carron both having possessed that quality in a high degree, as well as Heather-jock, Foremost, King Cob, and Waterloo, which are also associated with him in the pedigrees of the above celebrated dogs. I should, therefore, anxiously look out for a combination of King Cob or Foremost (already fixed upon) with Bugle, and should expect it to answer all the better in proportion as it is free from an admixture with other inferior strains. My reasons for this would be, that these two are already shown to be in themselves highly desirable; and so also is Bugle proved to be when united with a fast strain. Now, both King Cob and Foremost were fast as well as their descendants, and therefore I should prefer relying upon their giving pace to the cross with Bugle, rather than risk any other admixture, if I could help it. But unfortunately the time which has elapsed since Bugle lived is too great to expect such a bitch to be available; and consequently one must be accepted not entirely of his blood. But, besides these two strains, the Yorkshire breed has been prominently brought forward, Restless and her brother Black Cap having signalized themselves by winning good stakes in this as well as the last season; and Lola Montes, with a combination of the Waterloo blood and the Yorkshire, having likewise caught my fancy, if not that of all those who have seen her run. Japhet I have already alluded to, and I shall now conclude by mentioning Wigan, the sire of Scotland Yet, a very promising descendant of Mr. Sharpe's Monarch, on both sides of her parentage. Lablache, the sire of Lydia Languish, and consequently grandsire of her daughter, Lizzie Lindsay, two first-rate Wiltshire bitches, displaying the peculiarly true running of the Billy-go-by-'em breed, from which they are descended; and lastly, Neville, sire of Sophy and Mixture, two very excellent greyhounds, as well as of others of fair average performance, but not equal to the two last-mentioned superior animals. Thus, I have first brought forward certain indications, founded upon statistical data, for the guidance of the breeder in the search for a brood-bitch, and to these I have added some few hints of my own, founded upon personal observation. With these helps, I trust that he may be able to fix upon the blood which will turn out triumphant; and, to prevent misconception, I now repeat the list of desirable breeds for the purpose under consideration, founding the choice on the above rules and fancies : 1st, Jason—2nd, King Cob—3rd, Foremost—4th, a cross of any two of these—5th, a cross with either of the two last and Ball's Bugle—6th, the Scotch blood of Heather-jock, Waterloo, or Sport—7th, the Billy-go-by-'em or Chieftain blood, both remarkable for true running and stoutness—8th, The Bugle and Emperor, which seems always to have "hit" when united with fast blood, as in Judge—9th, Mr. Sharpe's Monarch, especially through Lord Douglas's Driver—10th, Mr. Gregson's Neville, as a cross for very stout and honest bitches—11th, the Yorkshire blood, including that of Velox, Spanker, Cedric, Lambton, and some others.

424. CHOICE OF THE INDIVIDUAL.—Having thus given, as far as I can, some few useful guides to the young courser as to the choice of the breed which he shall fix upon, let me now say a few words upon the particular animal which is likely to be useful to him. At first sight, he may think that a great winner is necessary for his purpose, and may wait a long time in the hope of procuring such an animal. Here he would, no doubt, find great difficulty, for most people refuse to part with their pets, and retain them in their possession, even if they do not breed from them; but, fortunately for the young breeder, it happens that the successful runner is not always the mother of winners; and, indeed, I much doubt whether she is as likely to become celebrated in this way as another and less fortunate scion of the same stock. Again let us have recourse to statistics, and let us see how many of the dams of our best greyhounds are, or have been, great public winners. In this way, by taking our best litters for some years back, it will be seen that they are generally out of average bitches, and often not coming up to that degree; as, for instance, Lord Eglinton's Frolic, dam of Black-cloud, &c.; Fudge, dam of Judge; Black-fly, dam of Ranter, Riot, &c.; Lucy, dam of Brighton, Cromwell, &c.; Cobea

Scandens, dam of Barabbas, Banoo, &c.; Tollwife, dam of Motley, Miss Hannah, &c.; all however of winning blood, though not themselves victorious in any high degree. Again, we have seen many extraordinary public winners produce litter after litter of inferior or middling greyhounds; and even the illustrious Mocking-bird has as yet produced no very remarkable exception to that rule. It is true that some departures from this dictum may be adduced; as, for instance, Sackcloth, out of Cinderella; Staymaker, out of Dressmaker; Lurlie, out of Landgravine, &c. &c.; but, still, by far the greater number of good winners are out of bitches comparatively unknown to fame. The young courser may, therefore, be satisfied with a bitch of the blood he approves of, even if she is not a winner, or at all events not to any great extent. Again, it is unnecessary that she should be in size exactly what he requires, nor even that her shape should coincide in every particular with his ideas of excellence; but by all means let him be satisfied that she is individually healthy, and likely to transmit that indispensable condition to her offspring. By a reference to the principles of breeding hereafter given, it will be found that the rule is not exactly that "like begets like," but that "like begets the likeness of itself or of one of its family;" and, consequently, unless the whole family is good, there is no certainty as to the result. Thus, in addition to health, it is only necessary to take care that the family is such as you wish to perpetuate, and then to disregard the individual to a certain extent; at least to place the value of her particular good qualities, excepting health, below those of her immediate relations. Many reasons may be given why great winners are less likely to produce good offspring than their more unlucky rivals; as, for instance, the following:—First, they must have been severely tested and strained, bodily and mentally, in order to arrive at success, and consequently their bodies have been rendered less fit for breeding purposes; and their mental faculties have been so highly educated as generally to lead to a degree of lurching which is too apt to be transmitted to the offspring. I am quite satisfied that the dam and sire of greyhounds ought not only to be honest, but they ought, if possible, to possess their original fire of puppyhood in an undiminished state. This, it is true, is seldom the case; but the nearer it is carried to the desired state, the more likely will the produce be to run in a true, honest, and game style. This is especially necessary in those breeds which come early to maturity, for, as they are necessarily clever by nature,

they do not bear with impunity any great addition due to practice. If, therefore, the young courser can effect the purchase of a discarded little bitch of good strong frame and constitution, and belonging to a winning family of greyhounds, especially if she is of the same litter with two or three good public winners, he may content himself with the reflection that he has procured, at little cost, a brood-bitch as likely to suit his purpose as it is possible to select; and having made this choice, the next thing to be done is to decide upon the best stallion to cross her with, in order to remove her defects, and improve her excellencies or beauties.

SECT. 2.—CHOICE OF THE STALLION.

425. Next in importance to the choice of the brood-bitch is that of the stallion to cross her with. For many reasons the bitch is first to be considered, one being that she cannot so easily be changed every year; and another, that she really impresses her nature upon the whelps more than the sire does. This is a disputed point, and I myself doubt whether in shape the sire has not more effect than the dam; but in point of nervous temperament, as evinced by what is called stoutness and courage, I am satisfied that the preponderance is in favour of the bitch. Again, I think it is pretty clear that the whelps go back more to the blood of the grand-dam on the dam's side, than to the same ancestress on the side of the sire. So that not only is the immediate litter more affected by their dam than their sire, but their offspring also will show the same result. This, however, is very difficult of proof, and I offer it rather as an opinion, founded on general observation, than as proved by any facts capable of analysis. But, however, all this is foreign to the present subject, which is that of choosing the stallion for the brood-bitch already selected. Again I shall ask, are there any fixed and known principles upon which this selection should be made? I would that I could answer in the affirmative, with any strong belief in the truth of the opinion; but, alas, I am compelled to say that the more I see of breeding, the more I am convinced that we are in the dark on the subject of its mysteries. Some few guides, however, we have, but let us not delude ourselves with the idea that we have more knowledge than we can really lay claim to. The following will be found to embody all that we know on this abstruse subject which will interest the breeder:—

1.—The male and female each furnish their quota towards the original germ of the offspring; but the female over and above this nourishes it till it is born, and, consequently, may be supposed to have more influence upon its formation than the male.

2.—Natural conformation is transmitted by both parents as a general law, and likewise any acquired or accidental variation.

3.—In proportion to the purity of the breed will it be transmitted unchanged to the offspring. Thus, a pure Newmarket greyhound, if put to a bitch composed of Lancashire and Scotch blood, will get stock showing much more Newmarket blood than either Lancashire or Scotch.

4.—Breeding in-and-in is not injurious to the greyhound, as may be proved both from theory and practice; indeed it appears, on the contrary, to be very advantageous in many well-marked instances which have of late years appeared in public.

5.—As every greyhound is a compound animal, made up of a sire and dam, and also their sires and dams, so, unless there is much breeding in-and-in, the result is such that it is impossible to foretel with absolute certainty what particular result will be elicited.

6.—The first impregnation appears to produce some effect upon the next and subsequent ones. It is therefore necessary to take care that the effect of the cross in question is not neutralized by a prior and bad impregnation.

With these few rules, then, let us proceed to consider what particular cross will suit any of the above twelve selections. It must be mentioned, however, that in the choice of a sire it is necessary to avoid any great and sudden change; that is to say, that it seldom answers to put a little, compact, short-working bitch to a great, loose, fast, and wide-running dog, *unless she is of a much-crossed breed, and he is the reverse,* when the result will be that the progeny will follow his mould, and very few of them will resemble the dam. If, however, they are equally cross-bred, or equally purely-bred, the progeny will be made up of incongruous materials; and instead of taking the happy medium between the two, will be made up perhaps of large, loose, and racing hind-quarters, with strong, confined, muscular, and short fore-quarters. The consequence of this is, that the stride is a failure, and the animal is always over-reaching himself and falling, as is so constantly seen in the coursing field. The principle, therefore, should be to avoid too great a difference between the two, which can seldom be necessary if the bitch is well selected, and of a family as near perfection as I have pointed out to be desirable. When this is the case, a great contrast can never be necessary; and as there are many disadvantages attending upon it, it should be carefully avoided. Now, then, supposing

the breeder to possess a bitch of the Jason breed, and he is desirous to perpetuate the kind of running peculiar to that family, I should avoid any further in-breeding, because it has already been carried to a very great extent in that blood, and I should therefore advise the selection of a stallion partaking of the same quick, fast, and merry style of working, as seen in the stock of Lablache and Motley, and more particularly in Bedlamite, who has this year been put to that splendid great-grand-daughter of Jason, Mr. Laurence's Lurlie, and will next season show the result of the cross. Many other untried stallions are also suited to this breed, and among them may be named that brilliant dog Judge. With a King Cob bitch, or one got by either of his sons, I should, if possible, combine a Jason stallion; or if not, then I should select one of the following Scotch dogs—viz., Japhet or Wigan, believing that they would "hit" well with the King Cob blood. With a Foremost bitch I should be much puzzled, since I believe that in most cases—though the immediate influence of that dog was exceedingly great—that influence is not permanent; and his daughters do not throw puppies which follow him in shape or style of running. It would, therefore, depend more upon the dam's blood than upon the sire as to my choice of a stallion. Supposing the bitch to be composed of a cross with Jason and King Cob, or Foremost, as seen in Barbara and Banoo, and in the Mockingbird litter, I should return to some dog of the King Cob or Foremost blood—knowing from experience that in-and-in breeding will bring out their excellencies; and that this blood will bear it to a very great extent, as shown in Rival, Miss Hannah, Marqueterie, and many others. With a bitch of the Bugle, Carron, and Heatherjock breed, I should have recourse to Mr. Randell's Ranter, where the Bugle cross is in existence, but in a degree sufficiently remote to avoid all chance of too great a proximity of blood. The lines are also, with that exception, all fast, and there must, of necessity, be good pace as the result, if there be any truth in the principles we are going upon. The same dog, and for the same reasons, would suit the Bugle and Streamer cross. The descendants of Mr. Sharpe's Monarch, through Driver, are particularly well suited for Lablache, whose descent from a sister of Billy-go-by-'em causes him to get stock of that smooth yet close style of running so exactly suited to unite with the Wigan bitches. Lastly, the Yorkshire blood ought to be united with some of the stoutest and fastest blood of Wiltshire or Scotland. Barabbas, Lablache, or Lopez, would, I should say, best rectify the soft and slack tendency which, as far as I have seen, is so rife among them.

426. MANY OTHER STALLIONS besides those I have enumerated may be mentioned, and the following may be considered as an imperfect list of those most known, some being confined to private studs, but most of them being open to the public:—

Assault, by Velox, out of Alice.
Barabbas, by Egypt, out of Cobea Scandens.
Barrister, by Doron, out of Hebe.
Baron, by Lincolnshire Marquis, out of Highland Lassie.
Baron, by Kentish Fire, out of Linnet.
Bedlam Tom, by Field-Marshal, out of Bessy Bedlam.
Bedlamite, by Figaro, out of Bessy Bedlam.
Beehunter, by Eden, out of Fair Helen.
Beverlac, by Vagrant, out of Toast.
Black Cap, by Dutchman, out of Alice.
Blue Baron, by Waterloo, out of Mahratta.
Bluelight, by Monsoon, out of Stave.
Bonnie Scotland, by Liddesdale, out of Queen of the May.
Bordeaux, by Figaro, out of Cloak.
British Tar, by British Lion, out of Ringdove.
Butcher Boy, by Liddesdale, out of Hannah.
Buzzard, by Figaro, out of Fairy.
Clown, by Emperor, out of Mistley.
Columbus, by Frisk, out of Nettle.
Croton Oil, by Case-is-altered, out of Waterwitch.
Czar, by Foremost, out of Catch-'em.
Damson, by Figaro, out of Daisy.
Derwentwater, by Lanarkshire, out of Phantom.
Desperate, by Figaro, out of Duchess.
Dunkeld, by Doron, out of Destiny.
Ecclefechan, by Tam Raeburn, out of a Waterloo bitch.
Eden, by Winspiel, out of Brenda.
Egypt, by Vraye Foy, out of Elf.
Ernest Jones, by Fire Office, out of Tiny Trip.
Esquire, by King Cob, out of Edith.
Factotum, by Czar, out of Sister to Feathers.
Figheldean, by Wiltshire Marquis, out of Spotless.
Fire Office, by Cecrops, out of Perfection.
Figaro, by King Cob, out of Frederica.
Field-Marshal, by Figaro, out of Duchess.
Foremost, Junior, by Foremost, out of Cruiskeen.
Forester, by Eden, out of Hannah.
Forward, by Foremost, out of Catch'-em.
Frolic, by Oliver Twist, out of Fairy.
Fugleman, by John Bull, out of Fudge.
Gipsy Royal, by Bedlamite, out of Black-fly.

Guy Mannering, by John o' Badenyon, out of Gay Lass.
Haymaker, by Staymaker, out of Syren.
Highflyer, by Hermitage, out of Heresy.
High Aim, by Senate, out of Tiny Trip.
Hotspur, by Hotspur, out of Tippet.
Hughie Graham, by Liddesdale, out of Queen of the May.
Imitator, by Motley, out of Mocking-bird.
Jamie Forest, by Happy-go lucky, out of Beauty.
Japhet, by Rufus, out of Reform.
Jingo, by Foremost, out of Dressmaker.
Juggler, by Worcester Marquis, out of Empress.
Junta, by Senate, out of Tiny Trip.
Kentish Fire, by King Cob, out of Knab.
Lablache, by Figaro, out of Sister to Billy-go-by-'em.
Lansdown, by Hotspur (late Maccaroni), out of Theon.
Lariston, by Liddesdale, out of Hannah.
Launchaway, by Vraye Foy, out of Leeway.
Layman, by Hotspur, out of Lightning.
Leander, by Crofton, out of Phantom.
Lopez, by Vraye Foy, out of Elf.
Lucio, by Vraye Foy, out of Lucilla.
Mandarin, by Motley, out of Holyrood.
Mansoor, by Egypt, out of Mocking-bird.
Mathematics, by Juggler, out of Vote of Thanks.
Marquis (late Sergeant Snap), by Worcester Marquis, out of Syren.
Martinet, by Sam, out of Tollwife.
Mazzini, by Fire office, out of Tiny Trip.
Mirage, by Figaro, out of Malvina.
Merryman, by Foremost, out of Mischief.
Motley, by Sam, out of Tollwife.
Neville, by Scott, out of Grace.
Pilot, by Old Pilot, out of Gazelle.
Pirate, by Rector, out of Bess.
Port (Brother to Bluelight), by Monsoon, out of Stave.
Ranter, by Bedlamite, out of Black-fly.
Rattler, by Velox, out of Alice.
Sackcloth, by Senate, out of Cinderella.
Sam, by Traveller, out of Tippitywitchet.
Sampson, by War Eagle, out of Kitchenmaid.
Sefton, by Scythian, out of Syren.
Stanley, by Spring, out of Shepherdess.
Stephenson, by Figaro, out of Shuttle.
Sylvan, by Lightning, out of Secret.
Syntax, by Marquis, out of Synecdoche.
The Cardinal, by Kentish Fire, out of Linnet.
Tout, by Traveller, out of Tippitywitchet.
Tom Thumb, by Tom, out of Sister to Scott.
Trafalgar, by Miles, out of Twilight.
War Eagle, by Foremost, out of Flirt.
Wellington, by Velox, out of Alice.
Wigan, by Drift, out of Cutty Sark.

World's-fair, by Figheldean, out of Elite. Wrestler, by Foremost, out of Flirt.

427. BEST CROSS FOR OTHER BREEDS.— In the previous remarks I have been supposing that the brood-bitch is of one or other of the twelve various breeds which I have selected; but it may so happen that she is of blood foreign to them all, and my observations would not then in any way apply. But it must be recollected that I have selected the Newmarket and Yorkshire blood as possessed of the most speed, which quality they share on nearly even terms with the Scotch and Lancashire, but sullied in the last case with a want of stoutness, and in the Scotch and Yorkshire with rather too great a degree of cleverness. Hence, if speed is required, I should select these breeds in the order I have named. viz. : 1st, Newmarket—2nd, Scotch—3rd, Yorkshire—and 4th, Lancashire; always excepting from the last the descendants of Ball's Bugle, which certainly seem to differ from any other of their countrymen in possessing great stoutness and honesty, and in communicating these qualities to other breeds when mixed with them. But supposing speed and stoutness, together with working power, were wanted, then I should take a combination of the Newmarket and Wiltshire, or Newmarket, Wiltshire, and Scotch; as, for instance, Lablache, Lopez, or Barabbas. For a south-country bitch, I fancy Wigan, Japhet, or Stanley will afford the best cross; and for those Scotch dogs which require a south-country stallion, there is none, in my opinion, so likely to suit their purpose as Bedlamite, or his son Ranter, or very probably that very fast dog, Trafalgar. Field-Marshal has got a considerable number of moderately-good dogs, and some almost reaching the front rank, but none quite coming up to that standard; they do not generally run the line of their hares well, and they are rather inclined to rush without maintaining that even rate of fast speed which one likes to see. No dog can be doing his best all through, if he is able to put the steam on occasionally to the extent they display; and though perhaps a dog with good tact is never thoroughly extended to the utmost, yet he ought to be doing all he can without excessive distress, and especially when at work. I have thus designated a few which may suit the owners of general bitches, without reference to the blood suiting, but solely founded on their qualities. One point, however, must be attended to, and that is, that if the bitch, whether of private or public blood, is very much in-bred, she will not receive the full benefit of a cross unless put to a dog of equally pure blood with herself. It is an established fact, that the purest-bred parent tells the most in the offspring, whether that blood be good or bad; and consequently an inferior bitch of unmixed blood will throw whelps resembling herself to a very great extent, even if put to a very superior dog, composed of blood derived from variously-crossed sources.

428. BULLDOG CROSS. — Breeders are greatly at variance as to the value of this cross, some supposing that it is of great service, and others, that it mars the utility of the greyhound in various ways. One thing is quite clear, viz., that it does not diminish the speed; for some of our fastest dogs of late years have been thus descended; as, for instance, Czar, Assault, Rattler, Westwind, Fancy-boy, all the Jasons, &c. &c. My belief is, that it does not really increase this valuable quality, but that the courage being increased, there is a greater tendency to display the utmost speed of which the dog is capable. The dogs, also, are more high-couraged generally, and stand training better, which is a very important item; and they also bear the many accidents of the coursing-field with comparative disregard of their effects. But as there is seldom gold without an alloy, so these advantages are counterbalanced by a greater degree of mental cleverness than is always desirable; and as the puppy comes earlier to maturity, so he sooner becomes cunning and unfit for public contests. This cross, therefore, is unsuited for private running, or for those who do not care for puppy stakes, but reserve themselves for contests which only occasionally come off, such as the Waterloo Cup, or other peculiarly-constituted exhibitions.

SECT. 3.—THE BEST AGE FOR BREEDING.

429. The bitch is, I think, at her best for breeding purposes in the third year, but many bitches have produced good litters as early as the second, and some as late as the tenth and eleventh. Mr. A. Graham's Screw, the Wiltshire bitches Seidlitz and Magic, and the dogs of the same district, Lopez and Egypt, were all out of two-year-old bitches; but the great bulk of our best dogs have been out of bitches three, four, or five years of age. In the sire, another year is perhaps required to bring him to his prime, though many of our best runners have been got by two-year-old sires, and some even at one year; as, for instance, Mr. Garrad's Locomotive; and the best litter, by far, ever got by Wiltshire Marquis, were by him when only two years old. At three years old a great number of stallions have got good stock; but most of our best running dogs have been the offspring of

four, five, and six-year-old stallions. It will, therefore, be more safe to select dogs of that age; though sometimes there are reasons for advocating the selection of a younger one, as in the case of a very old bitch; here a young dog is thought to invigorate the worn-out properties of the dam, but I know not with what effect. For myself, even in that case I should prefer a dog in his full prime, to a younger and not yet fully-developed stallion.

SECT. 4.—BREEDING IN-AND-IN.

430. I have already made some few remarks upon this practice; but perhaps it will be desirable to return to the subject, as it is one which is of great importance. Like many other good practices, it has been shamefully abused, and carried to an extent which would and must assuredly end in failure. Lord Rivers was defeated in this way, and so have many other of our most prominent and at one time successful coursers. Mr. A. Graham's rule of twice in and once out is perhaps as strong an infusion of the same blood as can be safely tried; and most breeders think too strong by far. Latterly, however, the leaning has been towards this plan; and the successes of Auchinleck, Vraye Foy, and the Curler, and their stock, followed by those of Motley, Miss Hannah, and Rival, have recalled the wonderful exploits of Harriet Wilson, Hourglass, Screw, Wonder, Sparrowhawk, and Streamer. One thing is quite clear, namely, that this practice of in-breeding does not *necessarily* injure either the external form, or the stoutness, or the speed; for all the examples above quoted have a good share of those qualities. There can be no reason in nature why in-breeding should be prejudicial to the stock, because we find in many species of animals the rule usually followed, especially among gregarious animals, where the father often takes his own daughters, and even his daughters' daughters, to his harem. We know that it is a plan which succeeds well in some of the pigeons, and, therefore, while these examples can be cited in opposition to that of man, his exceptional case should be outweighed by them. At the same time, when all that is desired can be obtained in a dog of more distant blood, I confess that I should prefer him to one too closely allied to the bitch in question. This, however, is frequently not the case, and then I should boldly adopt the plan of in-breeding two consecutive crosses; but after that it becomes a ticklish operation, as I know of no recent instance in which good has resulted from carrying the plan to any greater extent.

SECT. 5. — BEST TIME OF THE YEAR FOR BREEDING.

431. The practice of breeding for produce or puppy-stakes has become so general, that a great deal is sacrificed to that end; and as they are run early in the autumn, it becomes of importance to obtain the puppies of good age at that time. Greyhounds take their age from the 1st of January, and therefore it is desirable to get the bitch to produce her whelps as soon after that time as possible, provided you have good dry and warm accommodation for them. Without this last precaution it is useless to attempt early rearing, as the whelps will be spoiled by the cold and wet of the winter and spring months. It is better in such a case to wait till April or May, as a well-reared late puppy is far better than a stunted and chilled early one. Bitches at 18 months old run almost as well as at a later age, and therefore if your litter is a late one, you should choose them in preference to dogs for puppy-stakes. Puppies whelped after May, or the early part of June, can scarcely be old enough for the purpose; but they may be brought out in the spring following with good effect, though still to some disadvantage. I should therefore advise, that bitches whelping early in the year should in all cases be selected when they can be procured, and that great attention should be paid to keeping them and their whelps warm and dry; thus the latter will be able to bear the exposure to the weather to the full extent which they require during the summer months, and when the winter comes on they are of good growth and strength, and may be kennelled like the other dogs. Besides these advantages, there is also this attending upon early litters, namely, that they may be entered to their game with impunity in the spring of their first year, so as to avoid the risk of doing this in the September following, at a time when the ground is hard, the weather hot, and the hares difficult to come at. It should be known that the bitch sometimes goes a few days less than her full time, and consequently it is not safe to put her to the dog before the end of the first week in November.

SECT. 6.—MANAGEMENT OF THE BROOD-BITCH.

432. PUTTING TO THE DOG.—As soon as that most difficult point is decided on, which has been discussed in the last section and those preceding it, it must be followed up by putting the theoretical notions of the breeder into practice. In order to accomplish this, the bitch must be sent to the dog,

if, as is generally the case, he is not in the same kennel with her. Now, there are two modes of sending bitches across the country, one of which is much easier and cheaper than the other, and often answers just as well. The easier plan is to procure an ordinary three-dozen wine-hamper (this size will do for any bitch under 52 lbs. in weight), and after lining the bottom with straw, to put the bitch in and fasten down the lid. An ordinary direction then completes all that is necessary to transport the package to any part of the kingdom which is reached by a railroad. In the summer, the night (being the coolest part of the 24 hours) is the best for this purpose, as the bitch will not then suffer so much from thirst, and she will easily bear the journey without food, if it does not last more than from 12 to 18 hours, which time is quite sufficient to reach any part of her Majesty's dominions. The hamper should be strong and sound, for fear of her escaping and choosing a mate for herself. After she has been served, she should wait a few days, and then be returned to her owner in the same way. The usual plan is to send a man with the bitch, who sees that every thing is quite right, and brings her back again after the performance is over. There are some cases when one of these plans is more suitable than the other—as, for instance, when a dog has such a very high character, as to be in great demand; here sometimes it happens that two or more bitches are sent together, and the man in charge, rather than refuse one of them, is very apt to pass off another dog of the same blood instead of the one intended; of course, in this case, the "hampered" bitch has the worst chance, and therefore when a very popular dog is the selection it is better to send a man upon whom dependance can be placed with her, for fear of such a result; and if it does not really happen, and the puppies do not come exactly of the expected colour, there is always a suspicion of its occurrence. I was once inclined to suspect such an unworthy deception, not from the above cause, but from a different reason altogether, the whelps being of a colour which I had little reason to expect. I therefore persuaded the owner of the bitch to see her himself put to the same dog again in the autumn for the sake of satisfying himself and me; and the result was that the puppies were exactly like the former ones, and all doubt was at an end. Coursers certainly are a most suspicious race of mortals, and are constantly fancying their rivals in the race are contriving schemes, which they would never suspect them of in any of the ordinary affairs of life. In this respect coursing is like horse-dealing,

no one seems to trust his own best friend; and often, perhaps, with as much foundation for his want of confidence as in that pursuit, which every one admits is not conducive to the honourable feelings of those who indulge in it. But let the suspicion be causeless or not, there it is; and for the purpose of avoiding all occasion for doubt, it is better to adopt every precaution. There are, however, some cases where no motive can be assigned for any substitution of one dog for another; as, for instance, when a young unfashionable dog is chosen, and where the owner of the bitch is satisfied, from personal knowledge, that she will have every care taken of her. In such a case the extra expense and trouble of sending the man is so much time and money thrown away. The kennel-man of the dog will see to every-thing being done, *secundum artem;* but if the bitch is accompanied by your man, he should satisfy himself that the act is fully performed. Greyhounds are, many of them, quite incapable of procreation, either from being improperly managed by over-stimulating, or from being long kept in kennel and away from bitches, so as to force them into an unnatural state of continence. But, whatever is the cause, there is no doubt of the fact, that many dogs are nearly or quite impotent; and therefore the above caution is not so unnecessary as it might at first sight appear to be. Many men use all sorts of stimulating drugs to increase this power in their dogs, but it is a most dangerous and improper plan, and one which ought never to be adopted under any circumstances.

433. There is a great difference of opinion as to the number of bitches which a dog is able to serve in the season, and I have often been asked the question; but I know of no mode of settling the exact line beyond which the dog should not be allowed to afford his services. As far as my own opinion goes, I do not think that a dog recovers himself *thoroughly* under three or four days, which would give two bitches a week as the *maximum* allowance. Now, as the season lasts from the 1st of November to the month of May, this would allow of 50 bitches being properly attended to; but, unfortunately, the bitches do not come "in season" in this regular way, but, on the contrary, they all come together, or in groups of two or three at one time. Besides, when a dog is likely to have a large number of bitches, he is generally priced so highly as to make him chiefly in demand during the early part of the season, for few breeders like to bestow 10 guineas upon a bitch in May or June, with the full knowledge that her puppies will be too late for the produce-stakes the next year. Hence, if a dog has more than 20 bitches in the season, he is sure

to have at least three or four a-week occasionally, and in this way, I am satisfied, that many of these fashionable dogs are rendered unfit for their arduous duties. It is not that they do not get stock while in this high demand, for I know that large litters of puppies have been got on consecutive days, but I have seldom known a good litter thus obtained; and Mr. Gibson is distinctly of opinion that a bitch lined soon after a previous act is likely to have only a small litter. Now, if small in numbers, how much more likely are they to be puny in strength, and deficient in activity of nervous system. From all this, therefore, I should advise, wherever the choice can be made, that a dog which is not likely to have more than a dozen or fifteen bitches should be selected in preference to one more in demand, unless the bitch requiring his services comes "in season" in November or December. At that time few are likely to be sent, or to have previously weakened the dog, and of course you are not the worse for what may be hereafter done.

434. DURATION OF THE PERIOD OF HEAT.—The bitch is fully three weeks "in season" altogether, and is generally said to be nine days coming on, nine days fully on, and nine days going off. This is rather a longer time than my experience would allow as the usual period, and I should fix seven or eight days as the full term of each division. The best time for the admission of the dog is towards the end of the middle period, when the bleeding which usually appears in the *vulva* of the female is beginning to subside. Sometimes this period is a very short one, and by waiting too long the bitch refuses altogether to submit, and is rendered useless for that season. It is better, therefore, to put her to the dog as soon as she will take him, for fear of this unfortunate result; and I believe that it is of very little consequence when the act takes place, so long as the bitch is fully consenting thereto, and no force is applied.

435. THE MANAGEMENT OF THE BITCH after her return should be of such a nature as to keep her in good health, without allowing her either to get too fat or too thin. As soon as she can safely be allowed to run at large, she should be taken out to exercise regularly every day, and until that time she should be led out for an hour daily. When a bitch can have a good run at liberty she is perhaps all the better for it; but I am quite sure that full health may be maintained by a couple of hours' exercise every day; and for the first six or seven weeks this may be with the other dogs, so as to occasion no needless trouble; after that time, however, she ought to be taken out by herself, for fear of her being knocked over or otherwise injured, or of her being tempted to jump over high gates, &c., by the example of the other dogs. She should, however, have her liberty in her exercise every day till quite the last, for if not tempted by others she will only take as much as comports with her matronly dignity. Great care should be taken as to her condition in point of flesh, for the two extremes are almost equally prejudicial. On the one hand, too high a state of flesh is mechanically adverse to parturition, and also tends to produce milk-fever after the process is completed; and on the other, too low a state of flesh is inimical to that full suckling of the whelps which ensures their growth to a good size. The only guide which I can give is this—viz., that the ribs should be easily felt, loosely rolling under the hand, without being clearly visible to the eye; beyond this the condition is too high, and if the ribs are very apparent to the eye it is too low. About once a-week a little castor oil should be given, unless the bowels are quite loose; but, at all events, I like a dose given a few days before the end of the nine weeks—say about the 60th day. This cools the bitch, and prevents any bones or other lumpy matter accumulating in the bowels and mechanically interrupting the birth of the whelps. During the last week or ten days—that is, after the 50th day—the bitch should be separated from the other dogs, and placed in the box which she is intended to occupy during her parturition; and she should be made quite at home there, at once preventing all occasion for fright, and keeping her perfectly quiet. A boarded floor should be raised for her a few inches from the ground, and this should be protected from the wall by a boarded partition, at least 6 or 8 inches high. If this flooring can not easily be procured, spread a good layer of straw on the ground, and place a piece of old carpet upon that, then more straw on the top of that, which will form a good bed for the bitch. The reason of the necessity for the carpet is, that the whelps in their struggles to get at the teats of the bitch scratch all the straw away, and if the carpet is not there they lie on the bare ground, and are often seriously injured or killed by the damp and cold. But with this protection they only scratch till they get down to it, when they are unable to do more, and lie upon the warm carpet with the thick layer of straw under it. These little points may seem of no consequence, but it is by attention to them that disease is prevented; and that is a much more easy matter than removing it after it is once developed, especially in the whelp. Towards the last few days more sloppy food than usual should be given, in order to cool the body,

N

and also to promote the secretion of milk; but it should be very gradually changed, so as not to disorder the system by too sudden an alteration from the usual diet. If, therefore, the bitch has been fed upon flesh and meal, it is only necessary to substitute a larger quantity of broth for some of the flesh, and to mix it up with the meal into a sloppy state. Where greaves and meal have been used, the addition of a little milk is the best plan, or if not, then some broth must be added, as the greaves do not mix well with slop.

436. MANAGEMENT DURING WHELPING.— It is seldom that the bitch requires any interference at this time, for the puppy is so small in proportion to the size of the bony passage, that nature generally effects her purpose very easily. Unless, therefore, the mother is suffering from disease, little assistance is required. The process generally lasts some hours, and there is, on the average, nearly half-an-hour between each two whelps. The bitch should not be interfered with till all is over, unless she seems very much exhausted, when a little warm brandy and water may be given; but as nature leads her to swallow a large quantity of animal matter, consisting of the secundines of each whelp, and also to digest them, food is not now required. When, however, all is over, a little luke-warm gruel made with milk, or mild broth, should be given her, and repeated after two or three hours. Nothing else but this kind of food should be allowed till the milk is fully come, which by nature would be as soon as the whelps are born, or very nearly so. Sometimes, however, in very young or very old bitches, it does not come on so very readily; while, again, in very fat and over-fed ones, milk-fever sets in, and the secretion is postponed, or entirely prevented. It is in these cases that over-feeding must be guarded against; but here prevention is much easier than cure; only take care not to have the bitch over-fed beforehand, and she will give no trouble from milk-fever, unless exposed to cold or wet. The opposite extreme of low-feeding is not felt so soon, but it leads to much more unmanageable results at the second or third week after whelping, when fits are apt to occur, accompanied with excessive emaciation, weakness, and loss of milk. Strong broths, flesh, jellies, bread and milk thickened with eggs, &c., may be tried, with even the addition of stimulants, in the shape of brandy and water, or gruel with ale in it, or sherry and eggs. A teaspoonful of aromatic spirit of ammonia may be given with the same quantity of Huxham's tincture of bark twice-a-day. In spite of all that can be done, it sometimes happens that these bitches continue to have fits, and to lose strength and flesh; they must in this case be taken from their puppies, and their place supplied by either hand-feeding or a foster-nurse. After this they generally rapidly recover; but unless they are very valuable, they should scarcely be tried again for the same purpose. For the first two or three days the food should be luke-warm, and the bitch should be compelled to come out for the purpose of emptying herself at least twice a-day, as many mothers are so proud of their newly-acquired wealth, that they neglect themselves in their care for their whelps. More than this is not necessary, as exercise may be dispensed with for the first week; but after that time she should be led out for an hour a-day. During the whole of her suckling the bitch should be well fed upon milk, if procurable, thickened with oatmeal or flour, and at least a pound of flesh with the broth, also thickened with meal, each day. Without this quantity and quality of food the milk is not sufficiently strong and good for the whelps, and they do not reach the size which is desirable, and which indeed is necessary, in order that they may go on afterwards to that perfection of frame which is the object of the courser. A few shillings will therefore be now well disposed of in milk and other good and nutritious kinds of diet.

SECT. 7.—MANAGEMENT OF THE WHELPS IN THE NEST.

437. The kennel-man should watch the whelps from the time they are born till they are two or three days old, as they often require a little assistance up to that time, especially in large litters. If it is desired that more than five or six should be kept, a foster-nurse should be obtained; but for a few days a good bitch will suckle eight or ten puppies very well. When one or two are very weakly—as often is the case with large litters—they are shouldered out by the stronger ones, and would, if left to their own efforts, speedily die of starvation; but by occasionally taking the strong ones away for a time, and leaving the others to suck, they soon are able to take their own parts, and often overtake their originally-larger and stronger brothers and sisters. At this time whelps are very readily chilled, and when they are thus seized they become purged, and soon die, emaciated to the highest degree. Six, eight, or ten drops of laudanum may be given in a little milk, two or three times a-day, which generally stops the diarrhœa, or the laudanum may be united with a few grains of chalk and two grains of aromatic confection. No bitch should be allowed to suckle more

than five, or, at the outside, six whelps, after the first week; and if a foster-nurse cannot be procured, it is better either to destroy all above that number, or to try and bring them up by hand.

438. THE FOSTER-NURSE may be of any breed, but the bull-terrier, or any smooth bitch of good size, will answer the purpose best; a rough bitch will do quite as well if her coat is healthy, and her skin free from disease. It may generally be reckoned, that for every seven or eight pounds in weight of bitch she will rear one puppy, and thus a 21 lb. bitch will do three whelps very well. She should have a muzzle on, except when fed, till she is quite accustomed to the new whelps; and to effect this, the best plan is to take away her own whelps, and place them with the young greyhounds in a basket for a few minutes; then return all to her, and when she has become in some measure accustomed to them, take away her own progeny one by one. This deprivation, however, should not be attempted for twenty-four hours at least. Many people fancy that puppies reared by terriers, &c., are not so good as those suckled by their own dams, but I have had and known so many examples to the contrary, that I cannot for an instant doubt the propriety of adopting this foster-nurse. Mr. Borron's Black Cloud litter are good examples of this plan, having all been reared by bull-bitches, in consequence of the death of their mother in whelping. On the other hand, I have known some good specimens of rearing by hand; as, for instance, Mr. Webb's Flirt and Havoc. At the expiration of about 10 or 12 days (seldom sooner), the whelps begin to open their eyes; and after this they may be fed as soon as they will take cow's milk. When it is desired to assist the bitch in this way very early, the whelp must be taught to lap, by dipping his nose in the milk, upon which he soon takes to it, and licks his lips, if he does not lap directly from the saucer. At three weeks, unless the bitch is very full of milk, they will require feeding two or three times a-day, and the food at first should be milk only, then milk slightly thickened with fine wheat-flour, and towards the fifth week this food with thickened broth alternately. To make this broth, a sheep's head should be boiled to rags, then the bones picked carefully out, and the pieces of flesh broken up into very small fragments, and the whole thickened to the consistence of cream with fine white flour. Up to weaning, one of these heads will last one litter of whelps two or three days; but after that time a head is used in a single day. As soon as the whelps are able to run, they must be assisted up and down from their wooden-

floored stage, if they have one, by lowering the front edge, and making it an inclined plane from the ground; the box also must be littered down with straw, and cleaned out every other day, as the whelps soon make it very dirty by their constant evacuations.

439. DEW-CLAWS are sometimes left on, at others cut off, and again by some coursers the nails only are pulled out with the teeth or a pair of pincers. The last is far the best plan, and it should be done at about the time of the whelp first seeing, before which the nails are hardly strong enough to draw well. There seems to be very little pain given, as the whelp scarcely whimpers.

SECT. 8.—WEANING AND CHOOSING WHELPS.

440. THE WEANING OF THE WHELP is the great test of the skill of the kennel-man, and very few understand it to such an extent as to avoid loss of flesh at that time. Some, however, will manage almost invariably to take them away, and keep them as fat as they should be for an indefinite period, afterwards depending of course upon accidental circumstances, but extending long beyond the effects of weaning. Generally, however, whelps become very thin, and many are irretrievably spoilt at this period. Whelps which have been very well suckled are the most difficult to wean without loss of fat; and indeed sometimes they are so unwieldy as to require some little diminution in order to bring them to a state fit for exercise. I am quite satisfied, that beyond five weeks the mother's milk is prejudicial rather than otherwise; and many whelps become thin and out of health from that cause alone. I have always found that by removing her entirely they take their food more regularly, and are not constantly on the fret for what after all is only a drop in the ocean among so many and such voracious swallows. There are three grand principles needful to successful weaning—first, warm and dry lodging; secondly, suitable quality and quantity of food; and thirdly, regularity in feeding.

441. THE LODGING should be warm in proportion to the season, and if the weather is very severe, a stove is essential to success, not only at weaning-time, but before and afterwards. I am quite satisfied that from January to April, in frosty weather, the stove-system is of vital importance to the rearing of young whelps, and is even better than the heat of a warm stable full of horses. The fire should be lighted in the morning, and kept in all day, with good ventilation; then by damping it down at night, and closing the ventilators, sufficient heat is retained to last till next morning, when, on entering the box for the purpose of feeding

and cleaning, &c., the stove may again be lighted. I have not found that young greyhounds reared in this way were afterwards more delicate and susceptible of cold; but from being more strong and well developed, they were actually more capable of resisting atmospheric changes. It is for the first two months that this artificial aid is required, after which time they generate heat enough when lying together to keep themselves warm, and by leaving the stove off they soon are prepared for facing the weather, either in their walks or elsewhere. Up to three months all puppies should be kept in a loose box, and should not be suffered to be at full liberty, as they are scarcely fit to take care of themselves till after that time. They do not get out of the wet if a storm of rain comes on, and are consequently, if exposed to the weather, at all times liable to chill. A loose box, with the upper half of the door open, especially if it admits the sun, is the best place for them; but the door should be closed in cold, windy weather, and at night in all cases.

442. THE QUALITY AND QUANTITY OF FOOD are the grand essentials in rearing the greyhound, especially at weaning time, when all the experience and tact of the kennel-man will barely enable him to avoid errors. At this time the whelps require feeding four times a day, and their food should be composed of milk and broth, alternately, thickened with meal. Up to two months fine flour only must be used, with a little oatmeal if the bowels are at all confined; but after that time a coarser meal may be substituted; the change, however, must be very gradually made, by mixing a little more each day of the coarse with the fine flour. A sheep's head will now be required every day among five or six whelps, and from a quart to three pints of good milk, which quantities will serve them till nine or ten weeks old.

443. REGULARITY OF FEEDING is also of the utmost importance to all young animals, and especially to the greyhound-whelp. The first meal should be at dawn, or as soon after as possible, and the last always about dusk; though in January the whelps must be fed a little later, or they will have to fast too long during the night. It is also of great consequence not to allow any one of them to overload the stomach; and if they are gross feeders, and very ravenous, those which are so should not be suffered to take more than the feeder thinks sufficient. Indeed I am strongly of opinion that whelps should *never* be allowed quite to satiate their appetites, unless they are out of health, and require a little extra nursing; but, as a rule, they should always leave off with a readiness for more if it were given.

SECT. 9.—CHOOSING THE WHELPS.

444. THE WEANING TIME is selected for this purpose, because up to that period they must remain with the mother; and while sucking her, the changes are often so great as to make what was at first the best, often now the worst of the litter. Most people would prefer waiting to make their selection till after the whelps are weaned, as they show their shapes better when comparatively thin, than they do when loaded with milk-fat. This, however, seldom suits the purpose of the breeder, who wishes to get rid of the trouble and responsibility as soon as he can. Unless, therefore, the breeder has the pick, he will generally insist upon the choice being now made; that is, as soon as the whelps are five or six weeks old. It is quite true that the age is just as good as a later one, in all but one particular, and that consists in *the strength of constitution*, which has not yet been tested by weaning. Many delicate breeds get very fat while with their mothers, but when weaned with all the care in the world some of them will become thin, and refuse to grow and thrive. These, of course, would be rejected after weaning; and yet before that process is accomplished, they are the most likely perhaps to catch the chooser's eye. In picking at weaning time, I should therefore by no means always choose the fattest, but the one which looks most hardy and firm, without, on the other hand, being wasted and thin. At this time the legs and feet are generally already sufficiently developed to enable the good judge to see what they are likely to be; and if the whelp bends his knees so far back as to stand upon nearly or quite the whole of the parts below the knee, I should certainly reject him, as he is always likely to be long and flat-toed, with weak knees. A spreading foot also shows itself by this time, and should be examined into, and rejected in favour of a close round foot. Examine also as to ruptures, which are now very evident; and though many good bitches as well as dogs have had them, they are by no means to be admired. Next, as to general shapes and sizes—many select by colour only, taking those which follow any particular ancestor in colour or marks. I cannot say that I have ever seen this guide of any use, but it is a very common practice, and certainly I have known it abused, by leading to the selection of a badly-grown whelp in preference to a much better shaped one, of a despised colour. The chooser should take the whelp up by the tail close to the root, when the shape will be well shown, as the fore-legs are then sure to be extended, and if they are well raised in front towards the

ears, they show a well-formed shoulder. The length of the stifles is also now beginning to be shown, and the general frame is visible, especially when held as above recommended. But nothing is more difficult and more dependent upon luck than this choice, and I have constantly known even the best judges make bad selections. When the choice is to be made after weaning, weight and size, with apparent health, ought to be very strong guides in selection; and I would never take a puny, half-starved whelp if I could get one well weaned and healthy-looking, with at all the same frame; that is, if free from any obvious and persistent defects. At three months the choice may be made with a very good chance of selecting the one which shall turn out the *best looking* at last; but, after all, this may very likely not be the best greyhound; so that even here the affair is a perfect lottery. Still, in the long-run, the best looking are the best greyhounds; and therefore they should be chosen at all ages till a trial can be had. But at three months the whelps begin to move as well as to show their forms, and this test should also be used, as well as those already described. By the end of the third month the style of gallop becomes apparent, and though some short and stumpy gallopers at that time become subsequently good goers, still I should always back the free and smooth-actioned puppy at that age to turn out the best goer at a subsequent period. It is astonishing how whelps of three or four months old will gallop, and what a pace they will go; and unless the one which is examined goes in a good form between the third and fourth month, I should certainly reject him, if I had the choice of another going in a different and superior style.

SECT. 10.—REARING THE WHELPS.

445. HOME-REARING AND WALKS.—Much difference of opinion exists as to the comparative merits of these two systems; and to this day there has never been any positive series of experiments made on the two modes. Most people adopt one or the other, and then argue in support of that which they have used; but the only way to settle the question, is to divide several litters, and rear part in one way and part in the other. This I have known done in some few cases, but never to such an extent as to lead to a satisfactory result. Of one thing there can be no doubt—viz., *that good dogs have been reared in each way.* If, therefore, I were asked my opinion, I should say, that it will depend upon the degree of perfection in which either plan can be carried out. If the "walk" is a good one, the food good, and the farm free from hares and rabbits, there can be no reason why puppies may not be reared there as well as elsewhere. Again, if at home you have good accommodation and a good servant, with plenty of opportunity for exercise, then there can be no objection to your using those advantages. My own opinion is, that the home-plan, when well carried out, is free from every disadvantage, and has all the recommendations of the other in addition; whilst the constant liberty leads the puppy to be lazy, and disinclined to exercise himself as he ought to do. This, however, *may* be a disadvantage for aught I know to the contrary; as it may really not be desirable that the puppy should gallop so much while he is growing. It will not therefore do to argue upon this point as a positive good, because, as I before remarked, it may really be a positive evil. But a home-reared puppy, if neglected, is a most deplorable object; being too fat or too thin, with long toes spreading like a duck's foot, and in every way unfitted for his task. Such a dog is a standing argument against this mode of rearing, and very many such are produced every year. I have known thirty saplings and more reared together in a large building, and scarcely ever let out of it; with the only result which could be expected, of producing all bad ones. Unless, therefore, proper care is likely to be taken, by all means run the chance of the "walking" system. In this latter mode the puppy is sure of air and exercise; food, therefore, is the only essential and desirable point in which he is likely to be deficient. But in most farms the puppies are able to get to the pigs' food, and that alone, with air and exercise, is better than the best food in the world without those essentials to health. But if a good "walk" can be obtained by a little extra pay, by all means should the money be bestowed, as a shilling a week extra only makes a pound or two's difference in the cost, while it often trebles the value of the puppy. My advice, therefore, is to keep your puppies at home if you can properly do so; and failing that plan, to select as many good walks for them, of not more than two in one place; being guided in the selection by the probability of good food, good lodging, and good treatment, for nothing spoils a puppy more than harsh words and severe floggings.

446. HOME-REARING, from three months of age till they are old enough to be kennelled, which they may be considered to be at nine or ten months, should be effected in the following manner; indeed, if they are at "walk" they should be fed in the same way, or as near to it as possible; but they then have their full liberty, and require no

one to look after them during their hours of exercise. It will be remembered that up to this age they have been fed four times a-day, alternately on thickened milk and broth, the latter with the meat of the sheep's head broken up in it, and that I have advised the gradual substitution of coarse wheat-flour for the fine quality necessary in early puppyhood. By these precautions the dog-whelps ought, if of a large breed, and also of *tolerably early maturity*, to weigh at this age about 20 to 24 lbs., and the bitches 18 to 22 lbs. The after weights are as follows; though much will depend upon the quality of food, and the amount of exercise allowed, as some puppies gallop of themselves till they are as thin as red herrings :—

	Dogs.		Bitches.	
	Small.	Large.	Small.	Large.
At three months .	20 to 24 lbs.		18 to 22 lbs.	
„ four months .	28	„ 32 „	24 „ 28	„
„ five months .	36	„ 40 „	30 „ 34	„
„ six months . .	40	„ 50 „	34 „ 40	„
„ seven months .	45	„ 53 „	38 „ 44	„
„ eight months .	50	„ 58 „	40 „ 48	„
„ nine months .	52	„ 62 „	42 „ 51	„
„ ten months . .	54	„ 65 „	44 „ 54	„

I have inserted in each column the weights of small and large dogs at each month, but even these vary a good deal, according to the condition and mode of rearing in each case. Thus a very fat puppy of five months will weigh more than the same dog at six or seven months of age, if he then happens to be thin from teething or any accidental cause. But, supposing the puppy to be well reared and in good condition, not over fat, and to be weighed at any of the above ages, then, according to his approach to the high or low weight there named, he will reach the highest or lowest weight given at any of the subsequent months; that is to say, as an ordinary rule liable to the usual exceptions met with in all such attempts at generalization.

447. THE KIND OF FOOD most proper for rearing puppies is, I believe, a mixed diet of meal and flesh, with an occasional change to green vegetables, and even greaves. Undoubtedly the best meal is a mixture of oatmeal and coarse wheat-flour; the former of the coarse Scotch kind, and the latter made from red-wheat, and ground simply without dressing. Indian-meal answers very well indeed, instead of wheat-flour; but, theoretically, it is not quite so full of strong muscle-making material. As far as my experience goes, it is quite as good practically, and I have used it very extensively, on account of the high price of wheat. The usual cost of Indian-meal is about that of barley, and consequently it is little more than half the price of wheat. The flesh should be good sound horse-flesh, selected from horses dying from accident or from short illnesses, and not full of drugs. It will keep a long time, even during the summer, if hung up in the thick part of a shady tree; and none answers the purpose so well as a hawthorn. It should be brushed over with quick-lime and water every five or six days. Besides these articles, butter-milk and potatoes, milk and flour, paunches with and without their contents, and barley or oatmeal with greaves, are all used by different rearers, and especially at the "walks" of the puppies. Many are never allowed to taste meat till they are trained, and then only for a few days, on the supposition that a long continuance of meat makes their flesh too hard, and their pace too slow. This opinion I am satisfied is not founded on fact, and that the puppy reared as nearly as possible on the same kind of food as will best suit a child, will be most likely to exhibit pace as well as the other *desiderata* in the greyhound. In order to prepare the flesh and meal a boiler is required, and if for more than one or two dogs it should be set as a furnace. The best plan is to get a Papin's Digester, untinned, which materially diminishes the expense, and order a small pipe to be fixed on to the side near the top, so as to carry off the steam, when in ordinary use, into the nearest drain. The pipe must be of iron for a few inches, after which it may be of lead, for the convenience of bending it into the required angles. This digester may be set in brickwork, like an ordinary boiler, and may be either used for boiling flesh, when the steam may be allowed to escape down the pipe into the drain, by which all annoyance to the nose is avoided; or, when boiling bones, the side-pipe may be stopped by turning a cock fixed in it, and then the usual valve of the digester comes into play. These digesters are made of all sizes, but they are generally sold tinned, and therefore they must be specially ordered, if the extra price of the tinning is objected to. In plain iron—which is also far better for the health of the dogs—they cost from 30s. to £2 10s., or thereabouts, according to the distance from the manufactory. When the flesh has been boiled till it is quite ready to leave the bones, which requires some hours' gentle simmering, it should be taken out of the broth, and the Indian or wheat-meal added by stirring it gradually in with a stick. Indian-meal requires nearly an hour's boiling; wheaten-meal fifteen minutes; and oatmeal ten only. Enough of the mixed flour should be stirred in to make the stirabout when cold so thick as to be

divisible with a knife without much sticking to it. In reference to the proportion of each, the rule is to give as much oatmeal as the dog will bear without becoming too loose in his motions. Some naturally costive dogs thrive on oatmeal alone, and others again will scarcely bear the smallest proportion of it, so that no rule can be given; but I have found about one-third oatmeal will generally agree with the greyhound. Some people make the meal up into balls with a little water, and boil them in the broth at the same time as the flesh; but I have never seen any advantage in this plan, and it is certainly more troublesome. As soon as the meal has boiled the proper time the fire should be withdrawn, and the whole either suffered to cool in the boiler or, which is better, it should be ladled out and cooled in thin layers, on flat tins or boards for the purpose. This, with the flesh cut up into small pieces and mixed with it, forms the ordinary diet of the puppies, according to this plan; and it is called "stirabout" and boiled flesh. The paunches are either cleaned and boiled with the meal to make stirabout (being used in the same way as the flesh in the above mode), or they are given raw and with their contents mixed with them. The latter plan answers very well, especially when the cow's paunch is obtained, and kept till tolerably dry, with the use of quick-lime rubbed over it to absorb the moisture and prevent decomposition. It may then be given to the greyhounds entire, and they quickly tear it to pieces and eat it greedily, with a considerable quantity of the green half-digested food of the cow mixed with the paunch itself. Barley, or oatmeal, mixed with greaves is prepared by boiling the latter quite soft in water, after breaking them up into lumps of the size of the fist. The meal is then added as in making the stirabout.

448. THE RELATIVE VALUE of these various kinds of food is shown by the following table, extracted from Leibig's Chemistry—

	Materials used for making muscle, bone, &c.	Materials used in respiration, or in forming fat.
	Parts.	Parts.
Cow's milk contains	10	30
Fat mutton . . . ,,	10	27 to 45
Lean mutton ,,	10	19
Lean Beef. . . . ,,	10	17
Lean Horse-flesh ,,	10	15
Hare & Rabbit . ,,	10	2 to 5
Wheat-flour . . ,,	10	46
Oatmeal . . . . . ,,	10	50
Barley-meal . . ,,	10	57
Potatoes . . . . . ,,	10	86 to 115
Rice . . . . ,,	10	153

It will appear from this table, that the flesh of the hare and rabbit contains an enormous proportion of muscle-making materials, and from this cause they have been used for training purposes, but not, as far as I know, with any good result. Next stands horse-flesh; and I am quite sure that when it can be procured of a healthy nature, and free from drugs, that it suits the dog's stomach remarkably well, even in training. The difference, however, is so slight between it and beef or mutton, that either will do; and certainly mutton is the mildest of the three, and can be given in the largest quantity without overheating or disordering the dog's stomach. Cow's milk comes next in this quality, and is used very generally in Scotland even as an ordinary food. As far as my experience goes, it promotes flatulence and dyspepsia, and though nutritious enough, it fills and loads the stomach, and causes the wind to be thick, and the power of endurance very slight. As an article for *rearing* puppies, it is good enough, but not equal in producing a good frame to meal and flesh, as I have proved, by direct experiment. It also unfits the dog for the subsequent use of flesh for training purposes, and the change from one to the other requires a very long and careful preparation. For this reason milk-fed dogs ought not to be fed more than a week upon mutton when in training, for when reared upon milk and kept upon it afterwards, they soon fall off when put upon flesh, and their motions show by their black character how much the bilious system has been disturbed. I do not, therefore, wonder at those who pursue this plan of feeding being averse to the use of flesh. One of the best kinds of food for dogs at all times, but especially for puppies, is the sheep's trotter, or cow-heel; the former should by rights be scalded, and the hair and hoofs removed, before boiling, which requires a good many hours; but I have known so many give them the whole mass of hair, hoofs, and bones, without injury, that I believe there is no harm in them. Puppies are the better for occasional changes of food, and thrive badly if kept upon one unvarying diet. If, therefore, the meal and flesh plan is adopted, they should once or twice a week have cabbages, or carrots, or turnips, boiled with the meal, or potatoes with the broth, instead of meal. Even an occasional change to greaves is better than always keeping to flesh of one kind; but mutton and horse-flesh, with that of young lambs or calves, will be sufficient changes, without having recourse to chandler's refuse, except in default of flesh.

449. THE WEIGHT OF FOOD required from three months to five, is greater than would be supposed; but the growth is so rapid,

that the puppy absolutely demands large supplies of nourishment. Nearly a pound of meal a-day will not be too much, and in some cases fully that quantity will be used, mixed, of course, with the broth, and with a small allowance, at first, of flesh, cut up and added to it. The feeder should begin with about one-quarter of a pound daily, increasing it to half-a-pound by the fifth month, at which weight it should remain till after the teething is accomplished, when three-quarters of a pound will not be too much. This quantity may be continued till the puppies have been entered and tried.

450. BONES MUST BE SUPPLIED daily for two purposes, one of which consists in mechanically cleaning the teeth, the other in affording a supply of lime for the nutrition of the young bones of the dog, and also in stimulating the secretion of saliva, which is necessary for perfect digestion. The larger the bones are the better, and a little dirt is no injury to them. The kennel-man should give them on the dry grass, while he is sweeping out the kennel, and should always be at hand with the whip, to prevent quarrelling.

451. THE HOURS OF FEEDING should be as follows—viz., an early and a late meal, and two others during the day, till the end of the fourth month; after which, to the end of the eighth, the two middle meals may be thrown into one; and at the expiration of the eighth month, except in very large and growing dogs, two meals a-day will be quite sufficient, taking care to give free access to water at all times, and to prevent the greedy dogs from taking more than their proper shares of the food.

452. THE FORM OF KENNEL for home-rearing is, I think, a mere shed with a raised bench, for the whelps to run into, and for sleeping in; and, in addition, a run of 40 or 50 feet in length, and 8 or 10 in breadth, fenced off for them from a field or garden—if possible, shaded by trees. I do not like a brick-floor, such as is put in the regular kennel described at page 100, because it does not wear away the nails sufficiently; and, also, it does not harden the pads of the foot. Besides, the earth is a healthy anti-acid for the whelps to get into their stomachs, which they obtain by licking it off their coats in cleaning themselves with their tongues. I have found that common sheep-hurdles, lined with the wire-net, and having that kind of fence raised a yard above them by straining it from post to post, fixed at the end of each hurdle, answers the purpose best, as no greyhound can clear it, and by leaning it inwards they cannot jump upon it. It is the most effectual and the cheapest fence which can be put up, as no mere wooden railing will hold the puppies, their teeth

soon cutting through the strongest bar, if any interstice is permitted. When grass is selected for the run, it is soon worn away; and a little gravel or sand should be laid down, to avoid mud.

453. THE AMOUNT OF EXERCISE required by home-reared puppies is not much more than they will take in their yard or enclosures, where they gallop up and down and play with each other for hours together. But, in addition, they should always be let out into a large field for a quarter of an hour before each meal, as the gallop which they then take causes the bowels to relieve themselves, and they are thus kept in a healthy state. The gallop should never be allowed on a full stomach; but when empty, I am satisfied that it does great good, and hardens and braces all their joints as they are formed. A puppy reared in confinement grows perhaps into a fine-looking dog, but being composed of soft materials which have never been strained, he lames himself the very first time he is let out, and is a long time recovering himself from its effects. Besides this, he must again be rested, to allow time for the restoration of the inflamed joint; and thus he never can be suffered to acquire that tone of ligament and hardness of bone which are necessary to enable him to stand the shock of the course with impunity. This therefore is the principal object in permitting these daily gallops, which often occasion slight temporary lamenesses, but not of such a degree as to lead to permanent mischief. If puppies are reared in this way, with the daily use of a large field, and the run of a yard or strip of natural soil, especially if it is gravelled, they do not want any other exercise until they are kennelled, which should be commenced at nine or ten months, or earlier, according to the season of the year. It must be remarked here, that this open-yard system does not answer after October or the beginning of November, and then only in fine seasons; for in a cold and wet one it must be stopped as soon as weather of that kind is thoroughly established.

454. GENERAL TREATMENT.—During this time no brushing should be used, and the dog's natural cleanser, the tongue, is the best adapted for the purpose of keeping his body free from dirt. In all but the very hot months, plenty of clean straw should be allowed; but in the height of summer the boards must be left bare, as the dog will lie on the ground in preference to a straw-bed. At this time fleas, ticks, and other vermin, are very apt to infest the dog, and may be removed by the use of soft-soap and soda, as I shall presently explain. If the tick is the kind present, some white precipitate must be rubbed into the skin, and after a few days

brushed out again; but the muzzle must be kept on for some days, and the dog must not be suffered to get wet. Brimstone may be occasionally rubbed into the coats with advantage, though it does not kill any kind of vermin in a dry state, but it is licked off by the tongue and thus forms a cooling kind of medicine for the puppy. At this time the occasional use of a dose of castor-oil and syrup of buckthorne, in equal quantities, when the puppies are a little "off their feed," will serve to restore them to their appetites and prevent further loss of health. If they are otherwise ill, they must be treated according to the directions given under the head of "Diseases of the Dog."

455. EVERY PUPPY SHOULD HAVE A KEN-NEL-NAME given him before he is many months old; and he should be accustomed to it as soon as possible, so that he may be able to know when he is rated or called back, and may come when called, &c. This is very important in saving the young greyhound from unnecessary correction, which he might otherwise incur from ignorance rather than vice.

CHAP. V.

BREAKING, KENNELLING, AND ENTERING.

SECT. 1.—BREAKING TO LEAD, KENNELS, &c.

456. LEADING is necessary for various purposes, and should be taught the puppy either during the progress of his rearing, if this is effected at home, or, if not, as soon as he is brought from his walk. Of course in bringing him, he must have had a collar on; but it is not only necessary that the dog shall come along by force, but that he shall follow cheerfully and handily. One of the most common causes of failure arises from the awkwardness of the greyhound in the slips, and this has its origin in imperfect breaking to the leading-strap. I have seen the chance of many dogs utterly destroyed by their pulling in the slips, and therefore I would strongly caution the young courser to be careful that the whole process is thoroughly effected by which handiness in the slips will be effectually secured. Now, as I before remarked, steady leading is the first part of the education, and it should be taught as follows:—The neck-strap should be the ordinary wide one, at least 2 inches in breadth, with the common swivel, by which it is attached to a leading-rein about 5 feet long; this should be buckled on tightly in a field of soft turf, and the man should then call the dog by name in an encouraging manner. Generally he begins to pull against the strap at once, and fights most resolutely, by attempting to throw himself into all sorts of forms, and biting at the strap. He should be suffered to exhaust his efforts for a few minutes, and then the man should pat him and endeavour to make him follow, which, if he still refuses, he must be steadily dragged along by the leading-strap. After a few yards he almost always gives up all resistance for a time, and follows at the heel, but soon tries another bout, and this is often followed by a fit of the sulks. The only remedy is a patient pull upon the collar, and generally in half-an-hour the dog follows pretty quietly; but in some cases there is a much longer and more troublesome resistance. After the dog has followed his master about the field for a short time, the collar may be removed with a few encouraging words, and another dog taken in hand; but it generally requires several lessons before the young puppy is quite perfect in leading. Indeed, he seldom is so until he has been led about for hours in the coursing field, which should always be the last lesson before he is himself entered to his game. At first when the hare is seen the greyhound seldom takes much notice, but when other dogs are heard whimpering, and their anxiety is witnessed, the contagion is soon conveyed to the young one, and he begins to pull at his collar and to enter keenly into the nature of the sport. This is the critical period when the good manager makes his dog handy, and the bad one confirms him in the foolish habit of pulling. All young dogs naturally pull against their straps when they see anything going on in which they are interested: and the unskilled leader pulls again; upon which the dog, in his eagerness, keeps up the strain, and leans upon his collar in a steady, dull, continued pull, which tires him a good deal, but without being of much consequence at that time. When, however, he is put in the slips, he is all anxiety to be doing, and pulls away as he has been used to do with his awkward leader; and, more-

over, he tires himself at a time when it is of such consequence that he should be fresh and vigorous. In order to avoid this habit, as soon as the young dog is felt to pull, the leader should give him a sharp check, and hit him lightly on the nose, if the first is not sufficient; but by continually checking him when he begins to pull he soon leaves it off; and however eager he may be he never ventures to run the risk of the disagreeable sensation produced by checking him severely, unless a hare crosses so closely to him as to overcome his prudential feelings; and, in this case, the leader should let him pull, and run with him as the slipper does, and thus teach him to *pull steadily when the hare is actually before him, but at no other time.* This is the essential feature of the well-broken dog, and it is a point which ought never to be overlooked.

457. A MUZZLE should also be put on occasionally, of the following form :—

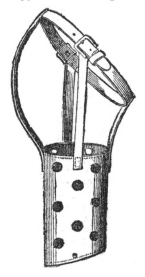

and should be left on even in the kennel for some hours. The reasons for this necessity are the following :—First, it may very probably be required in the kennel before training, in case any accident occurs, or any poisonous dressing is to be applied, and then it is a bad time to begin the use of it. Secondly, many young dogs are such savage fighters or biters, as to require the muzzle always on at exercise; and, when well made, they can gallop and play with it on just as freely as without it. Thirdly, in leaving the dog in a strange kennel during the week of running, a muzzle must always be left

on; and also in his exercise on the day of the running, for fear of accidents, &c. The earlier the dog is accustomed to it the better.

458. THE AMOUNT OF EXERCISE necessary to keep young dogs in health, after they are brought into the kennel, is very considerable; and if well fed, they must have from two to three hours a-day at the least. It is much better to be on foot than on horseback with young puppies, as they are very rebellious, and inclined to chase everything which will run away from them; unless, therefore, they are taken out on the open downs, and the horse is very handy, they are apt to get into enclosures and there set the horseman at defiance. The whip should be used as sparingly as possible, but still the dog must be kept in some degree of subjection, or he will get kicked to death by running at horses, or perhaps be gored by bullocks. Cats, fowls, sheep, pigs, &c., will each in their turn be chased, and the man in charge will have his hands full, in saving the lives of the cats and fowls. If cat-killing did not lead to other mischief, it would no doubt be beneficial, but as it leads to wilful and malignant injuries from the owners of the cats and fowls—and very naturally so—it must be avoided by every possible means. There are some breeds which are very averse to cats, and can scarcely be broken from killing them, while others never take any notice of the feline species, and give no trouble in this way at all. The muzzle is the best remedy in confirmed cases; but it sometimes leads to the loss of an eye, from the cat scratching the dog when he attacks her without the power of killing her. Sheep are the most important, as the expense of one killed is serious; and when once the greyhound takes to this kind of amusement he can never be depended on afterwards; he must, therefore, never be allowed to chase sheep for a moment longer than can be avoided. Many people lead their greyhounds on the road as a regular practice, and loose them only when they arrive at the fields; it is, perhaps, the safest plan; but they take a great deal of good exercise on the roads when at liberty, and harden their feet thereby very considerably. Couples are dangerous things on dogs without leading them, as they often start off together; and in passing posts, &c., if they each take opposite sides at a racing pace, they damage themselves very considerably; if, therefore, *any straps* are put on, they should be all led by single leading-reins.

459. BATHING OR SWIMMING GREYHOUNDS I believe to be a very healthy and useful practice in the summer, as it induces them to gallop at a season of the year when

otherwise they would not be much inclined that way. In hot weather greyhounds are very lazy, except in the early morning and in the cool of the evening; but after going into the water they almost always gallop about till they dry themselves, and in this way avoid the ill consequences which might otherwise ensue. On this account therefore the plan may be encouraged, and I believe it will never lead to rheumatism in the greyhound if care is taken to keep them on the move till they are thoroughly dry. Some greyhounds can never be kept out of the water, even in the depth of winter, and they are generally very hardy; but it is not a thing to be then encouraged, as they are apt to get in when you least wish it, as for instance, just before reaching home. For the last two months before training is to commence, an occasional hour or two of horse-exercise should be given, as it accustoms the dogs to that kind of work, and hardens the feet by wearing them down on the road. This should be given about once a-week or three times in a fortnight; and the distance may be gradually increased from 6 miles to 12 or 15.

460. NO CLOTHING is necessary before training commences, except in standing about in the coursing-field for the purpose already described at paragraph 456, when a good warm cloth is required in cold weather.

461. THE FOOD, from the tenth month to the commencement of training, should be of such a nature as to keep the dog in high health, without over-stimulating him, or making him fat and unwieldy. After the growth is completed, and the spring-trials are over (which may be fixed at the month of March) it is not desirable to keep up quite so stimulating a diet as I have advised for the last four or five months of rearing. From a third to a half-pound of flesh daily is amply sufficient, and one day in the week the dog should have nothing but a pint of thin slop. The same *kind* of food should be given as before, but in such *quantities* only as to keep his ribs just covered, and it should not be of quite so rich a *quality*. Oatmeal may be given in larger quantities than before, and a slight occasional looseness is of no consequence if there is no actual purging accompanied with an appearance of mucus. It is very important to avoid all food which shall lead to eruption of the skin, and to give only such an amount of nourishment as will sustain the health, without doing more. A certain amount of flesh is beneficial, because it must be given in training, and if the change is suddenly made it disagrees frightfully with the stomach and bowels; but when a portion is given as a regular article of diet,

it may be used for many months together without leading to any bad result. From March to July inclusive, I should advise the puppies to be fed twice a-day upon stirabout and a small quantity of flesh, varied as much as possible by getting horse-flesh, inferior beef, paunches, dead sheep, "slink-calves," &c., &c., at different times. These may be used four days in the week; then one day with potatoes, instead of meal; one day with greens, carrots, or turnips, mixed with the stirabout; and one day of starvation on the pint of slop will complete the round. This last banyan-day is necessary for health in all the tribe to which the dog belongs, and it will greatly add to his stock of that valuable commodity. It is better to use this diet on the Sunday, when most people give their dogs a day of rest, to which the starvation is more applicable than the fuller kinds of diet.

462. THE KENNEL for the public greyhound should be constructed in two portions, both of which should be under cover. One of these is the lodging or sleeping-room, and should have a raised bench or bed for the dogs to sleep upon. Each kennel should be made to accommodate 4 or 5 dogs, which is the very utmost number that should ever be put together. The plan already described at page 170 as suited to the private greyhound, is equally adapted for the public performer; it is intended to accommodate 12 dogs in the regular way, or 18 at a pinch. It is divided into three compartments, which will each do for from 4 to 6 dogs. Each of them is a fac-simile of the others, and therefore a description of one will suffice.

The floor should be laid in glazed-tiles well set in cement, upon a foundation of concrete. There should be a trapped-drain in the middle of each compartment; and it is a very good plan to have a pole suspended over this for the dogs to lift their legs against. A fixed pole is often injurious, by occasioning 'sprains against it in play. The bed should be raised from the level of the floor about 18 inches, as by this means all chance of damp is avoided, and the greyhound likes to be high and dry. Sometimes there is a very tyrannical dog in the kennel, and he will not allow any other to rest in peace near him, but drives him off the bed. When this is the case, the beds are better made in separate compartments, and on different sides even. Ventilation is of great consequence; and a window of the following form answers the double purpose of giving light and air. It is made to open with a hinge at the bottom, and when closed, as in *fig.* 1, it has two boarded V-shaped sides projecting into the open air at *a*. When open (*fig.* 5) it carries these sides with it into the sleeping-room, and the air is admitted at the top without any draft at the sides, which are closed by the V-shaped flaps already described. A door is required between the court and the sleeping-room, and an iron trough for water in each. Of course there must be a gate into the outer-court, and the whole of the lower part of the wooden rails must be guarded with wire-netting, or wire-work in some shape. Stoves are not wanted in these kennels, because it is never desirable to use more warmth at home than can be obtained abroad; and as it is impossible to get such luxuries supplied in the boxes of inns where greyhounds are usually located, it would never do to lodge them more warmly at home than abroad. Indeed, without stoves the difference is sufficiently great, and a cloth or two will be required to equalise the difference even then. Many dogs catch cold at the meetings, from insufficient warmth; and therefore it would not be desirable to increase the risk.

463. KENNEL MANAGEMENT.—The man in charge should clean out the kennels daily in the most thorough manner; and in the summer-time should wash them down every morning In the cold weather I do not like water, but prefer sawdust, which may be kept constantly fresh, and swept out quite clean every morning. An occasional wash-down must be had recourse to, in order to make all sweet; but the greyhounds should be kept out of the kennel till it is quite dry. No bones should be suffered to remain in the kennel, or they will assuredly lead to fights, often of such a savage nature as to cause serious injury at the very time when the services of the dogs are particularly wanted; but they should be given regularly every day for half-an-hour or an hour, and, in fine weather, the green turf is the best place for this. At other times all but one dog may be shut in the lodging-room, and that one may be left outside by himself with his bone; and after a time another one may be let out, and the first one shut up inside. By these precautions, the needful amount of bones may be given without risk of injury.

464. No PHYSIC during this time will be required, if plenty of green vegetables are given, and the dogs have access to grass; but an occasional dose of oil will do no harm. Of course all deviations from a state of health must be watched and rectified, upon principles to be hereafter described under the head of "Diseases of the Dog."

SECT 2.—ENTERING.

465. The greyhound requires very little teaching, or "entering," as it is called, to his game, but readily takes to it, partly by instinct and partly by imitation. Some dogs, however, are very late in acquiring the savage desire for blood which is essential to good running, and often go through their puppy-season without caring to kill, as was the case with the celebrated Mocking-bird, who would hardly run into her hare till the end of her first season. Many others have the same kind of good-tempered style for a time; but generally the taste for blood comes sooner or later, and the greyhound often becomes doubly savage in proportion to his late acquirement of it. It is, however, desirable that the young dog should know what he is allowed to chase, as soon as his bones and sinews are sufficiently set for the purpose. Besides, if he is to be used in puppy-stakes, he will be wanting experience more or less according to his natural abilities, before he is fit to compete in them; and as the ground is hard in the autumn, and the weather hot, he must be spared at that time as much as possible. Spring-entries, therefore, are preferred by most people, if the age of the puppies will allow of them; and I believe that ten months in the bitch, and twelve in the dog, will enable them to bear the shocks of the course with impunity. A large, loose and overgrown animal should of course be husbanded; but most dogs and bitches of those ages will, if well-reared, be fit to be entered.

466. THE CONDITION AT THE TIME OF ENTERING TO HIS GAME should be carefully attended to, for a very fat puppy will do himself, or herself, great injury in a severe course. A little gentle physic and light feeding will however, with plenty of exercise, get the puppy fit for his trial; and I should never advise more severe training than this. All puppies gallop a good deal if they are properly reared and exercised; and if attention is paid that they are not grossly fat their wind will be good enough for a single course. They should be fed very lightly on the previous day, but not so much so as to weaken them—say, to about two-thirds of their usual feed. They may also be fed a little earlier than usual, but still in the evening—say, at five o'clock.

467. OLD ASSISTANTS v. YOUNG ONES.—This is another point of dispute, some people preferring to put their puppies down with old companions, while others dispute the propriety of this plan. My own opinion is in favour of the young greyhounds having the work all to themselves, as I am quite sure they are more discouraged at being beaten by their old assistant, than when they fail to kill their hare without one. I much doubt the utility of blood to

the greyhound as an encouragement, unless he himself effects the kill; and I have never seen any good done by allowing an old dog to kill a hare for a young one. But if it so happens that the young one kills, after the old one has knocked the hare about for him, much good may result; and therefore instead of selecting a *good* killer to put down with a puppy, I should, on the contrary, choose a fast dog which had not the faculty of killing, but which would reduce the hare to the pace and powers of the puppy. This is the kind of dog wanted, and when such a one can be procured, I should certainly prefer him to any young puppy as an assistant, if one which is highly prized is intended to be orought forward, so as to be ready early in the next season. But if this kind of old dog cannot be obtained, then it is much better to put down two puppies together, taking care that both have seen enough to lead them to give chase as soon as the hare is a-foot. If the dog has never been slipped at all, it is better to let him have an old assistant, as he may otherwise, when put down with one his own age, refuse to leave the slips and leave his fellow in the lurch. When a puppy sees another dog run forward in pursuit of the hare, he generally follows suit; and if he does not do anything else, he acquires a zest for the sport. But after this is once acquired, the entering should be conducted upon the above principles. Many saplings of modern breeds will run very smartly and cleverly when 11 or 12 months old, and this is especially the case with bitches, some of which run into their hares at that age with great certainty. It must be remembered, however, that March hares vary very much in their running; and therefore if a puppy commands his hare well at that time, it does not follow in all cases that the dog is good, as it may so happen that the hare is of an inferior kind, rather than that the dog is a superior animal. This mistake has often led to a bad greyhound being nursed during the summer as something very wonderful; and on the advent of October the bubble has burst by the discovery of his possessing very opposite qualities. The young courser, therefore, should never calculate upon the goodness of his sapling upon the ground that he worked and killed his hare in good style; but if he or she ran well with a known good greyhound, he may depend upon having something likely to turn out a flyer in the next autumn—barring the usual accidents to which this frail animal is subject. As soon as the sapling knows his business, and has seen three or four hares, and especially if he has made a good kill, no more should be done till the next autumn. The grand point is not so much to give the dog practice, as to instil into him the zest for the sport, and to save the trouble of finding two or three extra hares in the following autumn, when they are very difficult to come at. Besides, if the greyhound is now encouraged after running his hare, he is prepared for rating in case of his chasing sheep, poultry, &c., and thus distinguishes between the proper object of his pursuit and the forbidden subjects, for chasing which he is constantly being scolded and punished.

SECT. 3.—REMOVAL OF TICKS, FLEAS, &c.

468. FLEAS, TICKS, &c.—Prior to commencing training in earnest, it is necessary to remove all parasitical animals, which disturb the rest of the greyhound if permitted to continue to infest his skin. Fleas may be destroyed by soft soap and soda rubbed into the skin in a state of solution. Equal quantities of the two should be boiled gently in enough water to make a solution of the consistence of syrup, and when this is lukewarm it should be well rubbed into the skins of the dogs with the hand, and suffered to remain on for a day, if the weather is not very cold; and taking care to keep the dogs moving till they are quite dry. After the expiration of 24 hours it should be well washed off with plenty of warm water, and the dogs well dried with a cloth, and then taken out to exercise. This not only kills the fleas and lice, if there are any, but it also cleans the skin, and is not injurious to the dog if he licks himself. It does not, however, kill the ticks, and they must have plenty of white precipitate, mixed with sulphur, rubbed in dry; using the muzzle carefully while it is applied, and keeping them out of all contact with water. After 36 hours the powder should be brushed out with a dandy-brush, and the above soft-soap solution may then be applied with advantage.

469. WORMS.—During the whole of the rearing, a constant watch should be kept for worms; and if present, they should be eradicated with the medicines prescribed under the head of *Worms*, in the "Diseases of the Dog." But at this time, before going into training, so constantly are they present, that I should never rest satisfied without giving the dogs a dose of worm medicine to clear them, in case any are in existence. I believe that 19 dogs out of 20, at 18 months old, have some of these parasites infesting their bowels; and as it is too late to give them strong medicines when in training, I prefer the precautionary treatment in all cases. I have known so many instances in which a dog has been obliged to be thrown by in the middle of his work for this purpose, that I am satisfied

the above is the best plan. I should therefore give him half a drachm of stinking hellebore first, and if it brings away any worms, I should repeat it, or give the Indian-pink, as hereafter advised, or the remedies for tape-worm if it is present. The hellebore is the best for this purpose, as it always brings some away if there are any, but does not clear the greyhound; and it is not so injurious to the constitution as the other kinds of vermifuge. It will almost always show the presence of tape-worm, and is sufficiently to be depended on for that purpose; but it brings the joints away alive, and therefore it is only as an index to the state of the intestines that I advise its use. It should be given with a little jalap mixed up in a ball. Whilst under these remedies the dog must be kept separate, in order that his motions may be watched, though if the others are quite firm in their *fœces*, the kennel-man will always know, if only one is in physic, what is the result of its operation. When at exercise also the dog in physic must be watched, as it is then that he is most likely to pass the worms, from the effect of his play. Whenever he has passed this ordeal satisfactorily, or if otherwise, and he has been cleansed by a regular course of worm medicines, he may be considered fit to begin his preparatory training.

CHAP. VI.

TRAINING, AND GENERAL MANAGEMENT IN RUNNING.

SECT. 1.—GENERAL REMARKS ON TRAINING.

470. Up to this time the *good breeder* has been chiefly in requisition; but now another official comes into play; and it does not always happen that the same person unites the qualifications for both these functions in equal proportions. Many men can breed good greyhounds without knowing anything of their treatment while in training; and, again, the reverse holds good in a still greater proportion of cases. Nothing is so simple as the rearing of the puppy, excepting during illness, if due attention is paid to his food and exercise; but few things are more difficult than the bringing out a kennel of greyhounds, of various breeds, in a high state of perfection. The fact is that in a dozen running dogs, even of the same blood, no two will take the same amount of work; and when of divers strains they must all be studied separately, and each must be fed and trained without any reference to his kennel-companions. It is a well-known fact, that one dog will run best while as fat as a dog *can* run, while another must be reduced to the condition of a scarecrow before his racing qualities are developed. No rule therefore can be laid down as to weight or work in all cases; and all that the trainer can do is to study the various constitutions which he has to treat; and, in addition, to make himself fully acquainted with the peculiar characteristics of their several breeds; that is to say, as to carrying flesh with advantage or the reverse, as to the amount of work and practice required, &c. Then when he has once satisfied himself as to the form in which each will best appear, either by the above analogical process, or by direct experience in former instances, he will set to work to prepare his dog so as to bring him up to that standard on the day of running. Thus I will suppose, for example, that A has a dog (No. 1), 25 inches high, and weighing at 10 months, when in good condition, 60 pounds. He knows that most dogs will run at about the same weight as they were at that age, when in good order, and therefore he would expect that his dog, under ordinary circumstances, would do so too; but, on the other hand, he also is aware, from a knowledge of the breed, that they require to be drawn very fine, and stand a vast deal of work before they are at their best; and that if they are at all fleshy they are pursy and thick-winded, having a tendency to lay on fat inside and out. This dog, therefore, he will work much more severely, and feed more lightly (with extra physic, &c.), than the rest of his kennel. Again, he has another (No. 2), of about the same size and weight, but belonging to a breed which he knows is shy of work, runs well if in flesh, requires very little practice, and is soon spoilt by over-training. This dog, therefore, he will prepare very differently to No. 1, and will, most probably, leave alone to his ordinary exercise till the second or third week before running. Some dogs of the sort similar to No. 2 will bear very little work, and if they are taken out for a few miles with a horse they loiter behind, and when forced to work become dull, heavy, and unfit, as well as unwilling, to exert themselves. Such animals are my abhor-

rence, as they often run a single course, or even two, most brilliantly, and in private lead their owners to fancy them perfection itself; but when they come to stand the ordeal of two or three severe courses they die away, and are utterly useless. But there is a third kind which the trainer often meets with, which we will call (No. 3.) These are capable of being trained, doing good work in a cheerful manner, and being of good constitutions, and apparently all that is desired. They make their first appearance in high feather, and perhaps run and win their courses in an extraordinary style. Hope is on tiptoe, and they are considered safe to win their stakes; but on their return from their second or third courses a nail is discovered to be drawn, or a stopper slightly cut, or some other mechanical injury done, as so often happens in the coursing-field. This in No. 1 would most probably be of no importance, as, even if he went lame into slips, the first sight of the hare would take all the starch out of him; but in No. 3 the leg is held up in the air, and very often is scarcely put down when the hare goes away, but the dog gallops on three legs behind his antagonist without making an effort. This kind of dog, therefore, the trainer will know must be drawn whenever he meets with an injury; and the good judge always does so in case of his having any of that kind which will not bear punishment, either in the nature of severe courses or mechanical injuries. It is astonishing what a difference there is in this respect. One kind will be tired to death by either training-work or coursing, and yet will come out the next day as gay as larks. These are the animals which should be prized and bred from; and if they can be obtained of good pace and working-powers, they are the sort to pull through good stakes.

471. Dogs to be Classed.—Every trainer, therefore, should consider each of his dogs, and class them under one or other of the above three sets according to their capabilities: first, of carrying flesh; secondly, of bearing continued work; thirdly, of standing punishment, both in the shape of sharp work and also in that of accidents; and fourthly, as to the amount of practice required. Then let him make up his mind what each will require to bring him to his best. I shall therefore consider each of the above three classes separately, and describe the kind and amount of work suited to each. The only and the great difficulty is to decide upon the class to which any particular greyhound belongs.

472. Individual Distinctions.—But besides the difference in the breeds, there is also great variation in the tempers, dispositions, and habits of the individuals composed of those bloods, though these points will generally correspond with the breed of dog in a remarkable degree. Thus, some are almost invariably savage and surly with one another, but fondling on man, and always anxious for his approbation; others, again, are sulky brutes, and even refuse to follow their feeder with any degree of alacrity; they are always poking into queer places, and lagging behind, and do not come when called by the whistle or voice. These dogs are seldom certain runners, as they turn sulky if they cannot at once command their hares, or if they sustain any fall or other accident. On the other hand, many greyhounds are merry and good-tempered on all occasions, and give no trouble either in kennel or out. In general it will be found that dogs bear that kind of treatment to which their ancestors have been accustomed; and therefore, if your greyhounds are from a kennel where horse exercise has been largely adopted, you will find that they train well with it, and follow a horse without trouble. On the other hand, Lancashire greyhounds, where horses are not much used, seldom follow well, and do not stand that kind of work with impunity. I have always found that these particular dogs must be treated differently in this respect from either the Wiltshire or Newmarket, or most of the Scotch breeds, where horses have been used to train them for many years. Hence, no rule can be laid down in all cases, and no surprise need be felt that one man trains without the aid of a horse, while another requires two, if he can get them, to bring his charge to perfection. Again, there is a great difference in the desire for play in different breeds, and in the various individuals also; some dogs will run themselves into most excellent condition, if only suffered to play as much as they like; but, again, others are either so lazy as to refuse altogether to gallop without necessity, or else so savage as to stop the play of all (including themselves) by rushing upon the leading dog, and biting him severely. It is seldom that a playful dog can be found which will lead off in spite of these attacks, as, if fast enough to escape them for a time, he must be caught at last, and is then severely punished for his long defiance of his pursuers. The very best dogs are often thus savagely inclined; but they are very difficult to manage, as they seldom lead off, knowing that their victims on former occasions are sure to retaliate upon them. Whenever there is this tendency to bite and rip one another in play, a muzzle should be constantly worn, of the pattern

described at page 186, and as with it on the dog can drink water out of a pond or brook, by thrusting in his muzzle, and can also put his tongue out and open his mouth, it is no impediment to free exercise.

473. WEIGHING.—It is in my opinion a good plan to weigh all dogs before beginning to train them, which may easily be done by using a pair of steelyards and a couple of horse-girths, one of which, with a knot in it to make it shorter, is passed under the flank, and the other between the fore-legs and over the shoulder on each side; the four buckles may then be tied together, and the dog suspended from the steelyard by them. By thus weighing the dog, the food and work may be much more exactly proportioned, for it is much easier to tell by this test how fast a dog is losing or gaining flesh, than by the eye, which is not capable of any nice distinction from day to day.

474. WATER should still be supplied in the kennel, but it should now be boiled, in order to accustom the dog to the same kind of drink when at his quarters at the meeting, where the variations of this liquid require boiling, in order to make all as nearly alike as possible.

475. After his feeding, the dog may be left quiet till next morning; and I do not even like the kennel to be disturbed for any purpose. If the dog is brought out, he will generally empty himself, but he is far better with his food in him, than that it should pass on before he has fully extracted the nourishment from it. I am satisfied that the dog, if fed once a-day, should never be disturbed after his meal till the next morning; but if fed twice a-day, as is the practice in some kennels, he may of course be brought out, to prepare him for the reception of his second meal.

476. CLOTHING AT EXERCISE is used by some people, in order to reduce the weight of the dog, and I am bound to admit that I have lately seen a fast kennel of dogs trained in this way. Their condition was not perfection, certainly, as they seemed deficient in stoutness, but they were not rendered slow by the clothing which they carried, as is generally supposed to be the result of that practice. On the other hand, I have certainly seen it attended by "the slows" in other hands, and I cannot fancy that the practice is a good one. The dog does not sweat by his skin, and the only way in which the clothing acts is by its weight increasing the work he has to do, and by its warmth causing the tongue to throw off its fluid by evaporation somewhat more rapidly than usual. In the kennel I speak of, the dogs are accustomed to be slipped a distance of nearly a mile with one,

two, or three cloths on, according to the desired effect to be produced. Their training is very short, and they are seldom at work more than a fortnight or three weeks. This plan is said to supersede the necessity to a great extent of physic and starvation; but, as I never tried it, I cannot speak from actual observation.

SECT. 2.—VARIETY No. 1.

477. DOGS OF THE SAME CHARACTER AS No. 1, should have at least five or six weeks' preparation before they are fit to run; that is, if they are to be tried in private before they are exhibited in public. Most people like to know which are their best dogs, and to do this they must get them fit at least three weeks before the public contest. Now I am quite satisfied that it is impossible to do justice to a dog of this character, and to get him into anything like his best form in less than three weeks; and in order that this time shall suffice, he must already have been regularly exercised two or three hours a-day, with an occasional journey, following a horse. Under this treatment he will be half fit to run, and with many dogs like No. 2, it is nearly all that can be done; but No. 1, and such as he, can be brought out in a much better form, by attending to the following directions, which, I again repeat, are utterly injurious to No. 2. The dog thus prepared by regular exercise on foot, and also following a horse, and having had his doses of worm medicine, should have, as a final dose, a ball composed of the following ingredients:—Take of

Powdered jalap, ten grains.
Barbadoes aloes, one drachm.
Ginger, five grains.
Oil of aniseed, three drops.

Mix, and make into a ball. This is the dose for a large, strong dog, and will clear him out, and render him cool and yet lively, and fit for anything.

478. THE FIRST DAY'S WORK should begin the day after this ball has worked itself off, with the aid of good slops, &c., when the dog may be taken out with an assistant, who should be a stranger to him, for the purpose of holding him while the trainer gets to a distance from him. Before this is done the dogs should be allowed to play about for an hour and a half; keeping them on the move by walking, in order to prevent the idle ones from lying down. After the expiration of this time the assistant should take up all the dogs to be slipped, or as many as he can hold, and running the loops of their leading reins through a stirrup-leather he should buckle it round his waist. Here, again, a muzzle is often required, as I have known dogs fall upon the boy holding

them and bite him severely; whilst he could not release himself from them, on account of their refusing to let him unbuckle their neck-straps. When the trainer has left them a sufficient distance behind, the assistant should, as soon as he hears the whistle, begin to loose one after another, in the order already fixed by the trainer; who directs the one he thinks most likely to run quickly to him to be first loosed, and the others, according to their degrees of perfection, in this very useful particular. Some dogs are very careless and independent, especially farm-reared dogs which have been accustomed to their liberty; while, on the other hand, kennel-reared dogs are uneasy unless they are with their breeder and rearer. An interval of a few seconds should intervene between each liberation, as the first dog ought scarcely to be overtaken by the second till he reaches his master, and the same with the others. The hindmost dogs exert themselves more than the leaders, because they have a double stimulus; and hence the most free should be first loosed, and the lazy ones kept back; indeed, an idle dog will hardly train in this way without one of another disposition to lead him; and even then, if he has the chance, he will stop his leader by biting him or knocking him over. The best place for a slip of this kind is an open valley, with a gradual descent on the one side and rise on the other. Here the assistant should remain on the hill on one side, and the trainer pass over to the other, where he is conspicuously seen and his whistle easily heard. When the trainer is anxious to give a long slip, and his space is rather limited, it answers very well for him to be on a horse or pony, and to gallop off still further as soon as he has given the whistle, and the leading dog is in good view. Sometimes half or three-quarters of a mile can thus be made available for training purposes, especially on open downs of an undulating character. One or two slips of this length will generally suffice for the first day, then walk them about for another hour and take them home. This kind of training should always be upon the same kind of ground as that over which the public courses will take place. Thus for down-courses the slips should be over hilly turf; for enclosed arable land, over fields of the same character; and for marshy land with ditches, over that species of ground.

479. DRESSING AND FRICTION. — After arriving at the kennel, the feet and legs should be washed and dried if dirty, and also the under parts of the body if they require it; but if this is done, the greyhound should be rubbed till dry with a cloth. After this the whole body should be well-frictioned with the horse-hair glove, of a coarser and cheaper kind than Dinneford's, now made at 2s. 6d. per pair. Laurence's glove, which is made on the same principle as a brush, that is to say, with the ends of the hair cut and turned outwards, is better than either, and is to be purchased at prices varying from 5s. to 7s. 6d. per glove. This rubbing should be chiefly over the muscles of the thighs, *sides* of the back, shoulders, and fore-legs, avoiding the upper surface of the back very carefully, which should never be strongly rubbed. In doing this kind of work the trainer should stride over the dog, and first face his hind-quarter while that part is being rubbed, and then turn round and look towards his head, using his two hands on corresponding parts of the animal's body at the same time.

480. FEEDING.—When all have had their dressing, they may have a bone a-piece, which will amuse them for a while, and at about three or four o'clock they should be fed. Most trainers feed at one o'clock, because that is the usual hour of feeding when the dogs are to run the next day; but I think a somewhat later period is more convenient for all purposes, and the dogs rest better during the night in the usual way. The slight acceleration of their feeding time on the day before running is of no consequence, especially as the meal is generally lighter than usual. For dogs of the kind I am now considering (No. 1), the feeding must be lighter than for more delicate sorts; and I think that the only rule is to take off from a quarter to half-a-pound of their usual allowance, making the alteration chiefly in the meal, but partly in the flesh. Most people give their dogs in training bread instead of stirabout, and jelly made from cow-heel and sheep's trotters, the mode of making each of which I shall give hereafter in this chapter. But whatever the diet, it must be scanty in quantity, but good in quality, and of such an amount as gradually, in conjunction with the work, to get the dog to the weight which the trainer has fixed upon as his object to be attained.

481. HORSE-EXERCISE.—On the next day a horse should be provided, and the trainer should take the dogs out for at least two-and-a-half to three hours, keeping on the turf as much as possible, and never going beyond a gentle trot on the roads, if he can any how obtain sufficient turf. I should not give more than half-a-mile twice over of galloping on this day, but should keep up a succession of trots and walks of two or three miles each during the time. This will give eight miles of walking, occupying two hours; six miles trotting, three-quarters of an hour; and one mile at twice of galloping, making up nearly three hours altogether, and fifteen miles in distance.

O

This distance is not too much at this pace, to begin with; and after the return home, the dogs may be cleaned, dressed, and fed, as on the previous day. At this time the feet often are rather sore, and if so, they should be bathed in warm alum-water, then carefully dried, and afterwards rubbed over with pitch-ointment. The trainer should be very careful not to wear the soles of the pads too thin, as it takes some time to restore their soundness, if the horny matter is actually removed by the formation of a blister.

482. ON THE THIRD DAY, instead of one or two slips, three or four may be given, according to circumstances, and the amount of work which the trainer thinks each particular dog will bear; but, whether he has them slipped once, twice, or thrice, he should at all events keep them out for three hours, and walk them steadily, and as much as possible upon turf, where they may play as they go along as much as they please. Some dogs are playful whether at work or not, but in the majority, when they are in good work, they cease to be very playful among themselves, though still ready for mischief, and full of life and animation on returning to kennel. On all occasions after the day's work, the frictioning must be had recourse to, and the feeding as usual.

483. ON THE FOURTH DAY the horse may be again put into requisition, increasing the pace a little, but not yet venturing upon a greater distance.

484. SUBSEQUENT PROGRESS.—Thus alternately using the slipping system and the norse-exercise, at the end of the first week the dogs must be carefully weighed, and the trainer must then conclude whether he is doing enough to get them to their proper weight and condition by the time upon which he has fixed. It will generally be found that half-a-pound a day is the utmost which can safely be got off without physic, that is to say, in a hardy dog of the class now under consideration. If, therefore, at the end of this week a reduction of 3 lbs. has not been made, it will be necessary to give physic of a more reducing nature than the jalap and aloes; Epsom salts will generally answer the purpose with least injury; and they may be given in doses varying from half-an-ounce to an ounce, dissolved in a teacup of warm water, with a little cream of tartar and grated-ginger. This dose may be given every third morning fasting, during the second week of training, but very few dogs require more than one dose a-week. It is far better to *diminish* the supplies, than to *remove* them by this severe kind of purgation. If the dose is given, the day of rest is chosen, and it is worked off with slops. A very small

quantity of food, about 5 or 6 ounces, is to be given at night, as the dog, if left quite empty after his clearing out, will be too weak on the next day to stand his usual work. He must now go through a repetition of the same kind of alternate horse exercise and slipping which I before described, and it will generally be found that he will bear his work during this week better than on the previous one, though he will perhaps lose quite as much flesh; but he will be more ready to follow the trainer, and less sore-footed and stiff than he was before. During this time, and towards the end of the second week of training, many dogs will bear cheerfully and well an amount of exercise which to some is quite incredible, and from 20 to 25 miles are often run over on the horse-exercise days without the least fatigue more than sufficient to make the dogs enjoy their beds. For dogs of stout blood, I should say the average is nearly 20 miles, with from two to three spirts of a mile or two on the gallop during that distance. The great difficulty is to get all the dogs to follow well, and some, though capable of bearing a great deal of work, are so lazy as to require to be led. The trainer should always take a leading-string of common broad tape, and when he finds any dog obstinately lag behind, he should dismount and put a collar on him to which the tape is attached. In this way a dog may be compelled to move himself at whatever pace the trainer proposes, and even at a fast gallop he soon learns to follow handily and without pulling. This is preferable to using the whip in the hands of a man who is to follow behind, as the dogs naturally cower with the lash at their backs, and will not go on cheerfully in the way which they ought to do. When the dogs have thus, by steady and long-continued work, varied by occasional gallops and slips, been brought at the end of the second week to a high state of efficiency, in point of wind and capability of bearing fatigue, they may be weighed again, and should be a little under the weight at which they are supposed to be the best capable of running. If this is the case no physic need be given on the second Sunday, but a rest-day, with slops only, will answer all the purpose. On the Monday, Tuesday, and Wednesday, the exercise should be nearly but not quite so severe as on the previous week; and on the three last days of the third week they may be kept to walking exercise on the turf, with a single short slip each day, of only a quarter of a mile, feeding, frictioning, &c., the same as before; and on the first day of the fourth week the dogs are fit for their trials, and may indeed be considered fit to run.

SECT. 3.—VARIETY No. 2.

485. THE DOG No. 2, and those of the same character, will require a very different treatment from the above, for, as I before remarked, they are incapable of bearing the same amount of work, and become dull and heavy, instead of continuing lively and fit for anything. Such dogs are often very fast for a short distance, and sometimes are so clever with it as to run little risk with ordinary hares of being distressed. But with such hares as we sometimes see in Wiltshire, Berkshire, and Scotland, they are so punished and distressed as to lose all chance of the stake for which they are entered. Nevertheless, some coursers adhere to this style of dog, and as he is often a merry, playful, and good-tempered animal, he will thus run himself into as good condition, or nearly so, as the art of man can effect. Horse-exercise to any extent is very injurious; and as he is generally fond of his trainer, and inclined to follow him, he will be more likely to be over-trained, with his small amount of exercise, than the more lazy dog No. 1 would be with double or treble the work. I need scarcely say that there are various shades and degrees intervening between these two types, and that the treatment in consequence must be modified accordingly.

486. THE AMOUNT OF WORK necessary for this class will be very little more than that which they themselves take, if at all playful. The weight must seldom be reduced by this means, but by physic and reduction of food. In most cases they lose flesh rapidly, and I have known six pounds got off a small bitch in four days, without destroying her form. This was done by strong physic and very little more than walking exercise. Two hours and a half of walking exercise should be given these dogs, and they should be suffered to play during that time, which if they do fully, very little more will be necessary. Three times a week they should be slipped about half a mile from their trainer, as described in paragraph 478; but not more than once or twice at farthest. This will amply suffice for the worst and softest of these dogs; but, as I said before, according to the degree of this bad quality must the two kinds of training be combined. The trainer should always recollect that *courage* and *stoutness* are quite separate and distinct from one another, and that a very high-couraged dog may be very deficient in stoutness, and in that wiriness of frame and tenacity of life which enables some to bear injuries with impunity. The high-couraged dog will bear them, as far as the pain is concerned, but on the next day he will be completely *hors de combat*, in consequence

of the inflammation following them, and its effect upon his nervous system. All this must be considered by the trainer, as upon his dog's possession or otherwise of these qualities must his treatment, both in training and in running, be founded.

487. THE QUANTITY OF PHYSIC necessary for No. 2 will vary very considerably, in accordance with the degree of flesh which he carries. Some of these dogs, if drawn fine, will not run a yard, and require very little to be got off from their usual weight. A dose or two of aloes and jalap must almost always be given, as dogs are so naturally inclined to take purgatives, that they are never long in their highest form without one. These dogs may therefore generally have a ball, as prescribed at paragraph 477, once a-week; but they should have nothing but walking exercise on the following day.

488. Their food should be in larger quantity than the amount ordered for No. 1, and it should be about four-fifths of their usual allowance, if they are not very high in flesh when training is commenced. About a fortnight is ample, with two balls, for the purpose of preparing them for their private trials, and no more need be done with them than I have already advised, as to work, food, and physic.

489. THE FRICTIONING, WATER, &c., for these dogs should be as advised for No. 1. The feet will seldom require attention to prevent chafing or blistering; but sometimes their claws are too long, and then they should be reduced by the nail-nippers.

SECT. 4.—VARIETY No. 3.

490. THE THIRD KIND OF DOG which has been alluded to must be trained according to one or other of the above modifications, according as he is able to bear work, or otherwise; and his peculiarities do not come into play until he is exhibited in public, in describing which I shall again return to his mode of treatment.

SECT. 5.—MANAGEMENT OF THE BITCH "IN SEASON."

491. Her treatment, if intended to run again, should be either the natural one of allowing her to breed, without reference to the puppies, or the artificial plan of bleeding and physicking her. It appears to me that there is a great deal of risk in both modes; as, on the one hand, the treatment in the latter case is calculated to reduce the strength of the bitch; and on the other, the breeding system often fails, from the large number of whelps which the bitch sometimes brings forth. If it was possible to limit the number of these to four or five, I believe that it would be by far the better

plan to allow the bitch to indulge her natural propensity; but as this is not practicable, I think perhaps the balance is in favour of the bleeding and physicking. Many bitches have run well after breeding, and some only a few months subsequently; as, for instance, Mr. Temple's Titania, and in the last season, Mr. Laurence's Lufra; but, nevertheless, it has ruined others, who have never recovered their maiden form. By bleeding and physicking, the change which would otherwise take place in the constitution appears to be checked; there is not the same tendency to form fat, and the spirits and general health are more rapidly recruited. In this way I have known a bitch run well within eight or ten weeks of her being in season; whereas, either by simply putting her by, or by breeding from her, at least fourteen weeks must elapse before she is fit to run.

SECT. 6.—PRIVATE TRIALS.

492. The immediate preparation for the private trial should be, as nearly as may be, the same as for running in public, to which I beg my readers to refer. No mistake is greater than to try the greyhound in a different form to that which he will appear in hereafter, for it by no means follows that because he runs badly when fat, he will do the same when prepared. On the other hand, if he runs badly in private, after a severe preparation, and it is still determined to start him, the only plan is to try what rest and light work will effect. Sometimes a dog may be tried when drawn fine, and be found to run very badly; after a week's comparative rest, he may show a very different form; and if he pleases his master in every respect, the trainer should endeavour to bring him out at that weight, and in every way in the same state of condition as to work, food, &c., &c. If not quite satisfactory, another week may be suffered to elapse, and if there is such an improvement as to lead to the idea that he is quite up to his highest point, then that particular state should be fixed upon. All these delicate shades require a master-hand to decide, as it is often very difficult in private to test a dog's running very satisfactorily, on account of the difficulty of procuring good hares on ground good enough without being too severe. When this can be procured, it often leads to the other extreme; and the courser is never satisfied till he has taken all the running out of his dogs.

493. THE NUMBER OF COURSES which a puppy should have, by way of learning his business, depends so much upon his form and breed, that no rule can be given. The courser will naturally select the small and early dogs and the bitches in preference to large and awkward and over-grown dogs. Generally, with these forward dogs and bitches, a very few courses will make them handy enough with their game; but so much depends upon breed, that no rule can be given. Much also depends upon what has been done in the spring; but no dog should be suffered to appear in public till he is quite *au fait*; that is to say, he should have had practice enough to know what he is about, and to be aware of the various devices of the hare, in the shape of short turns, wrenches, &c. Sometimes a puppy has been accustomed to short-running hares, which come back in almost all cases, and he will be sadly puzzled with a strong hare which refuses to be brought back by all the exertions he can make. Such a dog often resigns his task after two or three efforts, while the one which is accustomed to that variety of hare perseveres as long as he has any wind or strength left. On the other hand, a puppy accustomed to fast hares is all abroad with a short-running and bad hare, and will over-run himself at his turns, without attempting to come round, because he is wholly unprepared for their peculiarity of style. But, over and above this education of the puppy, there is the trial with another of the same age, or more often with a known good greyhound of the previous year. This should be merely a test of speed and of comparative working power, as the practised greyhound almost always outworks the puppy at this time of the year. But the experienced hand can draw a line, and will probably remember how that particular greyhound ran at the same age in her trial with an older competitor. All these calculations must be made on the supposition that both dogs are fit to run, for it will not do to try the puppy with an unprepared aged dog, even if he was ever so good during the previous season. Here no line could be drawn, as the unwieldy old one could or ought to be easily beaten by his more fit competitor. Not more than two courses a day should often be run in private, unless they are very short and inconclusive. If the first is ot moderate length, it is better to wait for another day, than to risk injury by a second course.

494. THE RESULTS OF THE PRIVATE TRIAL are often very melancholy, from the breeder being disappointed in his expectations. Nothing is so trying as to see a high-bred greyhound exhibit want of pace, or want of courage; or of any other of the essential qualities of the first-class dog. Such, however, is too often the case, and therefore the young courser must not be discouraged if such a lot falls upon him in common with his older and more experienced rivals.

When we see coursers of good judgment, and of forty years' standing, fail in their attempts, and often for a series of years, it leads one to suppose that luck has a great deal to do with success. Nevertheless, in the long run, care and judgment will be served; and though it cannot with certainty be predicted that any particular litter shall turn out well, yet it is very remarkable that some men who only rear one litter a-year will almost always produce some good dogs out of each litter. If the puppy shows awkwardness, there is great hope of his still turning out well, and even if he runs a little slack, he may *perhaps* come off thus; but lurching is a trick which ought to condemn him at once, as the cunning puppy in private is sure to exhibit this propensity still more strongly when running his third or fourth course in a stake. Such, therefore, should be at once condemned to a watery grave. Wild and headstrong running is often the precursor of the best style; but such dogs require a good deal of practice, and should even see a hare within a few days of their public performance. When the kennel is large enough to admit of running the risk, I think a trial on the third or fourth day before the stake is commenced will always do good, especially in Wiltshire or any other severe country, as it is impossible to extend the greyhound to the same wiry degree by any other means. His wind therefore is perfected, and he is also practised in turning, which brings very different muscles into play to those which are used in straightforward gallopping.

But if the kennel is only composed of such a number of dogs as are wanted in public, it is dangerous to put them down to run a course nearer than 10 days from the time of the meeting in which they are to be engaged. The annexed sketch of the private trial between Mr. Randell's Rival and Ranter, shows the awkwardness of the puppy, which afterwards turned out to be "a clipper," and the difficulty of getting a satisfactory slip in the early part of the season. The scene is Croome Park, near his own house.

SECT. 7.—TREATMENT AFTER THE TRIAL.

495. This should be of a quieting and cooling description. A ball of the aloes, &c., should be given, or, if the dog is very lusty, the salts, &c., as advised in paragraph 484. After this has operated, but not till the following day, give a meal of potatoes mixed with the bread, or a very few greens, in order to freshen up the stomach, and prepare it for its final effort. If the dog has not been long accustomed to flesh, he will often train-off at this time, if that kind of food is continued, and therefore he should be fed for some four or five days without it, using only jelly, with a little broth to flavour the meals; but if he has been reared upon the principles advocated by myself he will bear its continuance well, by using the precaution to give the vegetable diet above-mentioned. With these remarks, I shall proceed in the next chapter to the final preparation for running, and to that ordeal itself.

CHAP. VII.

TRAINING, FINAL PREPARATION, AND RUNNING.

SECT. 1.—FINAL PREPARATION.

496. THE TWO FIRST CLASSES I have already alluded to as requiring very different training; and the third will hereafter be found to demand greater care than usual at the time of running. There are also various states of constitution which interfere with training, such as the effects of the "heat" of the bitch, excessive grossness of constitution, aggravated by long rest, &c., &c., which must be met by appropriate treatment; but the ordinary greyhound, irrespective of these accidental complications, must be treated on some modification of the two types described in the last chapter, and by that mode will have been brought up to such a mark as

to enable his master to try him with some chance of judging of his powers. I have already remarked, that at this time the trainer not only comes to a conclusion as to his actual capabilities when quite fit, but also as to his present "form;" that is to say, he judges whether he is too much or too little worked, and also whether he is too light or too heavy. Having, however, settled all this to his satisfaction, and finished his trials, he has let his dog down for a few days, as shown in paragraph 495; and the next thing is to bring his recently-gained experience as to all the capacities of the dog to a practical result, by concluding his training during the interval of a fortnight or three weeks before the meeting at which he is to run, and till then he may alter his plans according to his experience gained.

497. BOTH THE DOGS NOS. 1 AND 2 will again require exactly the same routine of exercise, feeding, frictioning, &c., as before, unless the trainer, from the running in these trials, sees reason to vary it. He should give them severe work, and proportionally light food during the first week, and then gradually diminish the former, and increase the latter, up to the fourth day before the day of running. During this time the dogs should have been kept almost entirely off the road, so that the horny covering of the sole of the foot may have had time to grow, and thus often save it from the sharp edges of flints which abound in some countries, and easily penetrate a thin, worn-out sole. On the fourth night before running, I should advise a mild aperient, believing that it does not weaken the dog, but, on the other hand, it freshens his stomach, improves his wind, and makes him lively and full of energy. Some coursers at this time give an emetic, and I have known very good results follow its use, where the liver is sluggish, or the dog is what is called "bilious;" but otherwise, I think the simple aperient ball (paragraph 477), or a dose of castor-oil, will answer the purpose better. From this time the same management will suit both kinds of dogs, to which, on the third day before running, walking exercise only should be given for at least four hours, feeding as before. On the second day, the same amount of walking exercise, with one or two slips of half-a-mile each. At this time the dogs similar to No. 1 are generally recovering fast from their severe work, and are, or ought to be, as well as No. 2, very fresh and full of play, which they should all be indulged in, using the muzzle if they are inclined to be spiteful. On the day before the final struggle, the dogs should be walked out for three hours, with a single slip of half-a-mile, to open their pipes; then home and well frictioned; and afterwards fed at one o'clock, on not more than three-quarters of a pound of mutton toasted before the fire, and, after being cut up, mixed with the same quantity of bread, soaked in melted jelly. The dogs may then rest till the next morning, though many trainers take them out for a short walk in the evening; but I do not believe it is a good plan, unless they are intended to be lightly fed before running the next day. The following receipts and rules will conclude this part of the subject.

498. FOR MAKING BREAD WITHOUT BARM, which sometimes agrees with the stomach better than bread made with it—take of

Flour, 12 lbs.
Bicarbonate of soda, 2 oz.

Mix them well together with the hands; then take of

Muriatic acid, 2 oz.
Water, 8 pints.

Mix well together, and then stir the acidulated water quickly into the flour with a large wooden spoon. The dough thus formed should be quickly put into common earthen flour-pots, filling them about two-thirds full, and baked without delay, in a quick oven, *rather hotter than for common bread.* The flour may be of wheat alone, or mixed with oatmeal, according to the habit of the dog.

499. TO MAKE JELLY FOR TRAINING.— Procure four cow-heels, *unboiled,* and two-score of sheep's-trotters, scald them, and scrape off the hair and hoofs. Then put them in a digester, and boil gently till they tumble to pieces, covering them with such a quantity of water as will just serve to float them. After they are quite tender, let the whole cool, then pull them to pieces and take out the bones, after which they should be again gently simmered for an hour, adding a little more water. The whole is then put by, and forms a thick jelly, which in the winter will keep four or five days; but in October and March will often become sour in 36 or 48 hours.

500. VARIOUS MODES OF DRESSING THE MEAT:

1.—HORSE-FLESH is usually boiled, but if sound and of good quality, it makes good steaks, even in training, and should be toasted before the fire, or fried in the ordinary way, or grilled on a gridiron.

2.—BEEF is best toasted, or fried, or broiled, and it should be well beaten with a rolling-pin before being dressed, in order to ensure its tenderness. Horse-flesh is usually much more short and tender, and when good, is superior to beef in all respects. The fat should be removed from both.

3.—MUTTON is certainly the best kind of animal food for training purposes. The part used should be the leg, which is the only joint from which a solid mass can be obtained free from fat. It may be broiled or toasted in the usual way. The reason for the preference of these modes to boiling is, that as dogs are seldom indulged in them, from their being more troublesome, they are relished better, and appear to give tone to the stomach. Boiled meat, with the broth, is quite as nourishing as when broiled or toasted, but it is not convenient to give the broth in the latter days of training, as the bread is soaked in jelly instead; and, as the boiled flesh alone is not good, the above modes are to be preferred.

4.—Either of the above should be chopped into fine pieces, and put into a saucepan, with sufficient *boiling*-water to cover them.

Then set on the fire and just boil up, carefully stirring, to prevent burning.

501. SHORT RULES FOR TRAINING :—

1.—Give no more physic than just enough to freshen the stomach, unless it is wanted as a means of reduction.

2.—When used in this way try mild physic before giving stronger.

3.—Give as little bread as will suffice for health. The quantity may be known by the colour of the fæces, which ought to continue of a good gingerbread colour, and which become black, or nearly so, when the flesh is overdone.

4.—Reduce the dog more by increase of work and reduction of food, than by physic.

5.—Give as much horse-exercise as the stoutness of the dog will enable him to bear, without over-doing him.

6.—Use plenty of friction.

SECT. 2.—TRAVELLING.

502. RAILWAYS afford great facilities to the courser, and the dogs may now be conveyed two hundred miles more easily than they could be travelled forty on the road before the present system came into vogue. If possible, the trainer should have his greyhounds with him in the railway carriage, as they are much more nervous and excited when removed from his presence. In most cases a second or third-class compartment may be obtained for the trainer and dogs, but if not, the luggage-van is better than the boxes in which dogs are ordered to be placed in most of the lines. A horse-box may generally be procured by giving notice, if there are enough dogs to occupy it, and nothing can be better than this. It is astonishing what a difference is made by attention to these trifling particulars. Most people prefer arriving at the place of meeting some-time before the day of running—that is, ten days or a fortnight; and I think, if it is a healthy place, and there is good training-ground near, that is the best plan; but if ten days can not be given up, it is better to allow only one clear day's rest, as dogs often get more unsettled after a week than they are at the end of two days, and consequently they begin their contest at the worst, instead of being at their best. If they can be slowly travelled with a dog-cart, and exercised as they go along, a clear day is scarcely necessary, if the dogs are hardy; and it is quite time enough to get into the new quarters by twelve o'clock on the day before running, so as to feed at one. But as the average of dogs seldom sleep quite so well in a strange place, this is perhaps not to be recommended as the ordinary rule.

SECT. 3.—MANAGEMENT AT THE MEETING.

503. THE AMOUNT OF EXERCISE required during the progress of the meeting is not very great, as the courses run will generally be sufficient. About an hour or an hour-and-a-half will be required to give time for the dogs to empty themselves. They should be led out with their clothing on, and when the trainer can find a quiet field where there is no chance of a hare getting up, they may be loosened for a few minutes' play. Those dogs which are going to run on that day should have muzzles on, for fear of picking up bones or refuse of any kind; which precaution also serves to guard against wilful poisoning. After this they may be walked home, and well frictioned and dressed for half-an-hour each dog.

504. NO FOOD should be given, if the course is likely to take place by twelve or one o'clock; but if later than that, about one or two ounces of mutton and one of bread or toast will serve to keep up the tone of the system, which is lowered by excessive starvation. If more than one course is run, and the first is a severe one, a ball of mutton, spiced according to the following formula, or a simple spiced ball, should be given about a quarter of an hour before the course, with a mouthful of weak whisky-and-water, or brandy-and-water :—

SPICED-MEAT BALL.

Take of Carraway seeds, 10 grains.
Cardamoms, 10 grains.
Grains of Paradise, 5 grains.
Ginger, 5 grains.
Lean boiled knuckle of mutton, ½ oz.
Bruise the seeds in a mortar, and then mix with the mutton, and form it into a ball.

COMMON CORDIAL-BALL.

Take of Cummin seeds, 10 grains.
Coriander seeds, 10 grains.
Carraway seeds, 10 grains.
Grains of Paradise, 10 grains.
Saffron, 1 drachm.
Syrup, enough to form a ball.
Bruise in a mortar, and mix well together, then make up into a ball.

EGGED-WINE is a very common remedy, but I believe it is very inferior to brandy-and-water alone, and certainly not equal to the spiced-meat ball, which I have seen effect wonders in many cases. As soon as the dog can be taken to his kennel after his course he should be fed, in preparation for the morrow, on the same quantity and quality of food as before.

505. A DOG-CART, if possible, should be used on the ground; but if the distance is not more than two or three miles, and the weather is fine, the dogs are much better kept out till after they have run. But it is

after the course that the cart is so useful, as the dogs may then rest quietly till they are taken home; and if they are detained very late, they may be fed on the ground, if the trainer has taken the precaution to bring the food out with him. Hardy dogs bear this well, but delicate ones sometimes are made sick by riding in a cart on a full stomach. The annexed plan of a dog-cart, given at the end of this chapter, will be found to be very useful, and will accommodate eight or nine dogs very well, viz., four in the compartment A, three in B, and one or two in C: the dotted lines show the divisions between the three compartments. The head may be made to let down partially, for convenience of seeing on the ground; and the compartment A ought to have a door opening into the interior, so that the trainer may take out or put in a dog, without subjecting him to the weather. By this plan he may strip and rub him, &c.,

under cover, and keep him there till he is ready to take him to the slips. Such a dog-cart ought to weigh nearly 7 cwt., and cost about from £25 to £45, according to the materials and finish.

506. WHEN THE TRAINER, who has his card in hand, finds that he shall soon be wanted, he should get his dog ready, and give him a good frictioning. If he has already run, he should treat him according to the rules laid down in paragraph 504; and when his turn comes he should take him to the slips, keeping him walking about for about a quarter of an hour, if the weather is not very unfavourable. When the dog is put in the slips, the trainer should take care that he is on his right side, and, if necessary, that he has his collar on. If the weather is cold, or wet, the cloth should be kept on as long as possible, and for that purpose it should button across the breast. These particular patterns are called " slip cloths :"

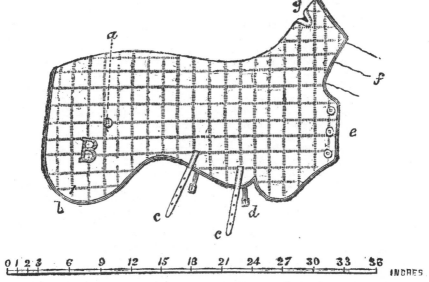

a b, button and hole, to loop up the cloth when the roads are very dirty; *c c*, belly straps; *d*, a slit, to allow of the cloth hanging smoothly down over the arm; *e e e*, three buttons for closing the front over the breast; *f f f*, three strings for closing the throat; *g*, a slit, guarded by leather, for allowing the leading rein to appear. If the dog is young and uneasy, the trainer should walk by his side, and stop his pulling if inclined that way; or if he is inclined to hang back, he should be ready to prevent his getting twisted, or to put him right, if such an event happens. He should have an assistant mounted, if in an open country, to pick his dog up, or if enclosed, he should have one, two, or three, posted at the most likely coverts, which the hares make for. By

these precautions the dog is prevented from getting a second course, which often destroys the chance of a good dog, after he has won his first.

507. THE ACCESSORIES which should be taken in the dog-cart are: Spiced-meat balls, brandy or whisky, waterproof clothing, and spare cloths for dogs, muzzles in case they fight, leading straps, sponge, cold water, food in tin cases, bluestone, Canada balsam spread on leather for wounds, needles and thread, bandages, lancet, and Friar's balsam.

508. EXTERNAL RESTORATIONS are of two kinds—those which can be used in the field, and those which may be applied in kennel. Of the former, friction with whisky is the best. The hand should be applied well for

some little time in the ordinary way, then a little whisky should be rubbed in, and finally a good deal should be rubbed rapidly on, taking care to choose a perfectly sheltered place, and clothing the dog warmly at once before the spirit has had time to evaporate. When the dog is much distressed by his work, and is panting severely, with blueness of the mouth, and the eyes red, take about four to eight ounces of blood, and use the whisky as above. After a short time, when the blueness abates, give the spiced-meat ball and a little brandy-and-water. If the dog's work has been very severe, a warm-bath at 98 degrees of Fahrenheit is the best restorative. He should be immersed in it up to the neck for fifteen minutes, then take him out, dry him well before a good fire, and afterwards rub him over all the body with hot whisky. He should be clothed before the latter is quite dry, and left to take his rest. The best time for the warm-bath is about three hours after the feeding-time.

509. THE WATER given at the meeting should all be boiled and cooled, as in this way the effect on the stomach of a change in the fluid is greatly diminished.

SECT. 4.—TREATMENT OF INJURIES, &c.

510. When the dog No. 1 (Chapter vi.) is punished, either by work or injuries, he may be suffered to try his best, and will often pull through. The dog No. 2 will also often bear injuries for one day, but will generally feel their effect very acutely on the following one, and must then be drawn, if he is ever to be of use hereafter, as he does not often try his best after being thus severely tested. The dog No. 3 had better, in any case, be drawn at once, if he is either severely worked, or bruised by a fall, or cut, or his nails broken or stripped. By nursing him in this way, he may at some time do good; but if liberties are taken with him, he will neither win on that day nor on any future one. By attention to these various indications, and carefully studying the powers, constitutions, temperaments, and habits of his dogs, the trainer is enabled to call out all the good, and prevent the appearance of the bad, qualities of his charge. Herein the really-useful man is shown; and by this careful study, many middling kennels have been made "to do the right thing at the right time." On the other hand, by a neglect of them, many a good dog in some countries has been taken to others for which he was unfit, and sacrificed to the ignorance or infatuation of his trainer or master.

511. CUTS ON THE LEGS are best managed by fixing on the adjacent skin a piece of white kid leather, spread with Canada balsam by means of a warm knife. This answers better than anything I have ever seen tried, and it agrees well with the dog's flesh. The balsam is very adhesive, and even the dog's tongue fails to remove it. It must be heated first before applying.

512. WHERE A LARGE PIECE OF SKIN is loosely hanging, as is often the case in enclosed countries, the flap must be held in its place by a suture. The plan is, to pass a needle, armed with a strong thread, through the corresponding sides of the wound, at intervals of half an inch, then to tie each stitch separately, and cut the ends of the thread off, but not too closely. The Canada balsam over this makes it very secure, if the cut is on the head or the ribs; but it cannot well be applied without a firm foundation, such as those parts afford.

513. IF A STOPPER is detached from the leg, so as to be quite loose, it is far better to remove the hanging portion with the knife, and apply a bandage, with some Friar's balsam. Just before running, the raw surface must be rubbed with bluestone, which deadens the soreness, and prevents the dog from feeling the contact of the ground. Over the whole cut-surface a piece of leather, spread with the Canada balsam, may be strained, and made to meet in front, so as to encircle the leg.

514. WHEN A CLAW is broken, the ragged bits should be carefully removed with nail-scissors, and a little Friar's balsam applied. On the day of running, about an hour or two before going to slips, take a piece of blue-stone, and rub well over the quick which is exposed. A piece of lunar caustic answers better; but it requires great care in its use.

515. CUTS IN THE SOLE of the foot are best treated by a small patch of leather spread with the Canada balsam, which adheres very closely, if properly applied. A little blue-stone, previously rubbed in, dries up the surface, and renders it less sensible to pain.

516. BRUISES OF THE LEGS, or elsewhere, are relieved by warm fomentations, followed by a lotion composed of a teaspoonful of tincture of arnica in half-a-pint of water, with which they should be kept constantly wet.

517. AFTER THE MEETING is over, the dog should be given a dose of physic, and a few potatoes or greens, according to his health.

518. EXPENSES OF REARING AND TRAINING.

	£	s.	d.
Cost of brood-bitch, per year . . .	£5	0	0
Stallion, and travelling	8	8	0
Tax on bitch	0	12	0
Keep of ditto	2	12	0
Keep of 6 puppies, at 1s. 6d. per week till 18 months old	35	2	0
Tax on do. after 6 months	3	12	0
6)	55	6	0
Cost of each puppy	£9	4	4

Thus, reckoning the brood-bitch to cost £20, and to last four years, and calculating on six puppies from each litter, the mere keep of greyhound-puppies, without extra charge for kennels or attendance, will make them cost £9 4s. 4d. each, at 18 months of age. Add to this the wages of trainer and travelling expenses, with stakes, &c., and it will be clear that our large kennels cost no inconsiderable sum.

CHAP. VIII.

MANAGEMENT OF COURSING-MEETINGS.

SECT. 1.—ORIGIN OF MEETINGS.

519. COURSING-CLUBS form one source of coursing-meetings, and were, until lately, the sole causes of public contests between greyhounds. For many years coursing-clubs have existed, and some time before the present century the oldest of them, held at Swaffham, was instituted. At that time the sport was confined to those who could gain admittance to this and some one or two other select clubs, and the day of open champion-meetings had not yet dawned. The chief clubs now in existence are the Everleigh, the Deptford Inn, the Cardington, the Baldock, the Amicable, and the Spelthorn, in the south; the Altcar, the Ridgway, the Market Weighton, the Coquetdale, and the Newcastle clubs, in the north of England; and in Scotland, the Caledonian,

the Biggar, the Aberdeenshire, the North Berwick and Dirleton, and the Nithsdale and Galloway. These clubs have all of them more or less ground to course over, which they hold either by a rental, or by the favour of the owners of the property. In some cases, as at Cardington and Amesbury, the proprietors of the property over whose land the coursing takes place, not only permit the club to hold regular meetings, but pay all the expenses of preserving; whilst in others the club has to pay for preserving, as well as to give a rent for the manor. The latter is the usual plan in Scotland; and but for the existence of clubs, few large meetings could be held in that country.

520. OPEN MEETINGS are often originated by clubs which are anxious to try their strength in competition with their neigh-

bours; in which case they throw their ground open to all coursers, instead of limiting their entries to members of their own body. More frequently, however, they are held for the benefit of some particular innkeeper, who is the tenant or an old servant of the lord of the manor, and who has permission to use the lands of his patron for the purposes of an open meeting. In the former case the meeting is under the control of the members of the club, but in the latter it is generally managed by the innkeeper himself—as at the Waterloo meeting—or by some person who is constituted a secretary by general accord, or by the consent of the patron, and who arranges all the proceedings, without any control but that of public opinion. Here, however, it is found that this control is sufficient, because if he does not give satisfaction his entries will not fill. The chief open meetings are the Amesbury, the Ashdown, the Newmarket, and the Cardington, in the south; the Waterloo, the Southport, the Kenilworth, the Sundorne, the Wolverhampton, the Burneston, the Huggate, and the Malton, in the north ; and the Caledonian, the Biggar, and the Dirleton, in Scotland.

521. A COMMITTEE OF MANAGEMENT should be formed in any case, who should meet and decide upon the election of the judge and slipper, the stakes to be run for, and their apportionment, and the rules which shall guide the meeting.

522. THE COMMITTEE to consist of a flag-steward, a field-steward, and the secretary. Sometimes a slip-steward is added, in which case there should be two field-stewards, in order to keep the number an uneven one. All disputed questions to be decided by vote, and the chairman, in case of an even number, to have the casting-vote.

523. THE ELECTION OF JUDGE, either to rest with the committee, in which case it should be published with the advertisements giving notice of the meeting, or else it should be vested in the general subscribers to the stakes, each of whom should have one vote.

524. The secretary to draw up, with the approbation of the committee, a programme of the meeting, which should be advertised, and should specify—

1st—The date of the meeting.
2nd—The names of the stakes.
3rd—The qualification for ditto.
4th—The entries for ditto.
5th—The apportionment of ditto.
6th—The expenses to be deducted.
7th—To whom applications are to be made for entries.
8th—The time and place of entry and drawing.
9th—The rules to regulate the meeting.

10th—The judge, if named, or, if not, the mode of election to be stated.
11th—Names of stewards.
12th—The secretary's signature.

525. THE DRAW should be conducted on the following plan : first, the money for each stake should be paid to the secretary by the subscribers; second, after this is completed, small squares of paper, exactly like each other, should be handed round, and each subscriber should, either himself or by his deputy, write the name of his dog, with the pedigree, colour, and age, upon one of them; after which they are folded up. The secretary then collects these for each stake in succession, placing them at once in a hat, from which they are to be drawn in regular order, and entered as they are drawn. Nothing can be more simple than this plan, and it does away with all necessity for numbered cards, &c., which are the source of constant confusion and mistakes. It also facilitates guarding, and prevents all hanging back to see what dogs are entered, which is not conducive to fair and large entries. It was introduced in the "Directions for the Management of Meetings," published by Mr. Welsh, in his 8th vol., but it has not been commonly acted on, and I was not aware of its existence until reminded by that gentleman.

526. THE DUTIES OF THE FLAG-STEWARD are to receive the fiat of the judge, and see that the flagman hoists the right flag (red or white for the left or right side of the card respectively, and *both* for undecided courses).

527. THE SLIP-STEWARD, if there is one, regulates the proceedings of the dogs at the slips, and sees that the next brace is ready.

528. THE FIELD-STEWARDS regulate the beating and the general proceedings of the field. They should have one or two flagmen, with blue flags, who should always be in sight of the beaters, and should restrain the progress of the crowd beyond their own boundary. The field-stewards should also see to the beaters, with the assistance of the secretary, who is usually one of their number.

529. THE RULES FOR THE GUIDANCE of meetings are of great importance to their success. Mr. Welsh's rules were usually acted on until the National Coursing Club, on its establishment in 1858, determined to draw up a new code. Under the presidency of the celebrated courser known as "Mr. C. Jardine," a set of new rules was drawn up by that gentleman, with the aid of a small committee, and received the sanction of the club at the next meeting, and of the whole coursing world since. In the following Pages they are given at length, together with Mr. Thacker's rules for the decision of courses, which have been affirmed by the National Club.

MEMBERS

NATIONAL COURSING CLUB.

THE EARL OF SEFTON, President for 1860.

THE EARL OF CRAVEN.

VISCOUNT GREY DE WILTON

HON. ADMIRAL ROUS.

C. JARDINE, Esq.

J. ALLISON, Esq.

G. BLANSHARD, Esq.

J. S. BOWLES, Esq

COL. CONYNGHAM.

R. ETWALL, Esq.

A. GRAHAM, Esq.

J. GORDON, Esq.

B. H. JONES. Esq.

H. F. MILLER, Esq

CHARLES RANDELL, Esq.

J. SPAIGHT, Esq.

J. H. WALSH, Esq.

J SMYTH, Esq.

THE EARL OF HADDINGTON.

THE EARL OF STRADBROKE

THE LORD LURGAN.

COL. ARCHDALL, M.P

JAMES BAKE, Esq.

W. G. BORRON, Esq.

H BROUGHAM, Esq.

G. F. COOKE, Esq.

J. GIBSON, Esq.

G. GREGSON, Esq.

J. D. HORNBY, Esq.

G. A. POLLOCK, Esq.

N SLATER, Esq.

CAPT. SPENCER

R. A. WELSH, Esq.

W H. LANGLEY, Esq.

All communications to be addressed to

JAMES BAKE, Esq.,

Secretary of the National Coursing Club,

MANCHESTER.

FUNDAMENTAL LAWS.

COMPOSITION OF CLUB.

The National Coursing Club shall consist of not more than thirty-five members, of whom five shall be a quorum.

ELECTION OF MEMBERS.

At the Waterloo Meeting, in each year, five members shall go out by lot, and at the same time five new members shall be elected *viva voce* by the members of any recognised coursing club present.

OBJECTS.

All complaints, of whatever description, or any matter in dispute connected with coursing, can be referred to the National Coursing Club for arbitration and adjustment.

MEETINGS.

Meetings for the despatch of business, and for the revision or alteration of rules, shall be held at noon, in London, on the Saturday of the Epsom Derby meeting, and at three o'clock p.m. at Liverpool on the day of entry for the Waterloo Cup. But the secretary, upon a requisition addressed to him in writing by any three of the stewards of a meeting or by six public coursers who may happen to be present, shall summon a special meeting at the earliest convenient opportunity

CODE OF LAWS.

The National Coursing Club recommends that the following code of laws shall be adopted universally; clubs merely adding such special or local regulations as may be required to adapt the National code to their own peculiar use

SUBSCRIPTIONS.

It may be necessary to make some provision to meet the printing, advertising, and other incidental expenses incurred by the National Coursing Club; all regularly constituted coursing clubs are therefore asked to subscribe an annual sum, and those approving of the object could be assessed in proportion to the number of their members or otherwise.

RULES

1. *Decision of courses.*—Every course shall be decided according to the judge's estimate of the balance of points in favour of either greyhound. The value of the points in a course, viz., the cote, go-bye, wrench, turn, trip, or kill, as well as allowances or penalties, to be for the present considered as settled by Thacker's rules.

2. *Disputed decisions.*—The judge shall deliver his decision aloud immediately the course is ended, and shall render an explanation of such decision (if required by the nominator or his representative before the third succeeding course is run) to the stewards of a meeting, who shall express their opinions in writing on the same evening, whether such explanation is satisfactory or not; but his decisions once given shall not be reversed.

3. *Allowance for being unsighted.*—If a greyhound be unsighted in going from the slips, or afterwards, it shall be at the discretion of the judge to decide what allowance, *if any*, is to be made under the circumstances.

4. *Dogs dividing.*—If a second hare be started during a course, and one of the dogs follow her, the course to end there.

5. *Definition of courses.*—A "no course" is where sufficient has not been done to show superiority in either greyhound, and must be run again; but where both dogs have a single-handed course, and one is agreed to be drawn, the judge shall decide whether enough has been done for the other dog to remain in without running an additional bye; and it shall be at the option of the owners either to run again immediately or at the expiration of two courses, the latter being fixed if they do not agree. An "undecided course" is when the judge considers the merits of the dogs so equal that he cannot decide, and the dogs shall be put in again after two courses, unless one be drawn, but the owners must at the time declare to the flag steward which dog remains in. If it is the last course of the day, fifteen minutes shall be allowed after both dogs are taken up.

6. *Slipping.*—The control of all matters connected with slipping the greyhounds shall rest with the stewards of a meeting. Owners or servants on delivering their dogs into the hands of the slipper may follow close after them, but not so as to inconvenience the slipper, or in any way interfere with the dogs, hallooing them on when running, or otherwise, under a penalty of £1.

7. *Collars.*—When two greyhounds drawn together are of the same colour, they shall each wear a collar, and their owners shall be subject to a penalty of 10s. for non-observance of this rule; the colour of the collar to be red for the left-hand side, and white for the right-hand side of the slips. After the first round, the upper dog on the card for the day will be placed upon the left hand, and the lower dog on the right hand in the slips.

8. *Accidents in slips.*—If through accident one greyhound gets out of slips, the slipper shall not let the other go. If the slips break and the dogs get away coupled together, the judge shall decide whether it is to be a no-course, or whether enough has been done to constitute it an undecided course. In any case of slips breaking, and either or both dogs getting away in consequence, the slipper may be fined not exceeding £1, at the discretion of the stewards.

9. *Riding over, &c.*—If any subscriber or his servant shall ride over his opponent's greyhound while running a course, the owner of the dog so ridden over shall, although the course be given against him, be deemed the winner of it, or shall have the option of allowing the other dog to remain in and run out the stake, and in such case shall be entitled to half his winnings, if any.

10. *Dog getting loose.*—Any person allowing a greyhound to get loose, and join in a course which is being run, shall forfeit £1. If the loose greyhound belongs to either of the owners of the dogs engaged in the particular course, such owner shall forfeit his chance of the stake with the dog then running; unless it can be proved to the satisfaction of the stewards that the loose greyhound had not been able to be taken up after running his own course. The course not to be considered as necessarily ending when the third dog joins in.

11. *Impugning decision.*—If any subscriber openly impugns the decision of the judge on the ground, except by a complaint to the stewards according to Rule 2, he shall forfeit not more than five nor less than two sovereigns, at the discretion of the stewards.

12. *Committee and stewards.*—The secretary of any proposed open meeting shall associate with himself a committee of not less than three members to settle preliminaries. The management of the meeting shall be intrusted to stewards and field stewards (in conjunction with this committee), who shall be elected by the subscribers present the first evening of a meeting. No steward to have a right to vote, as such, during a meeting, in any case where his own dogs are interested. The secretary shall declare, as soon as possible, how the prizes are to be divided; and a statement of expenses may be called for by subscribers after a meeting, if they think proper.

13. *Election of judge.*—The judge may either be elected by the secretary and committee appointed under Rule 12, in which case his name shall be announced simultaneously with the meeting; or his appointment shall be determined by the votes of the subscribers taking nominations, but each subscriber shall have only one vote, whatever the number of his nominations. The appointment of the judge to be published at least two weeks before the meeting, and the number of votes, as well as the names of the voters, to be recorded in a book which shall be open to the inspection of the stewards, who shall declare the number of votes for each judge if called upon to do so by any of the subscribers. A fortnight's notice shall also be given of the day of voting, which shall be duly announced in the public papers. When a judge, from ill health, or any other unexpected cause, is prevented attending a meeting, or during a meeting, leaving it, the stewards of the meeting shall have the power of deciding who is to be one.

14. *Postponement of meeting*—If a meeting, appointed to take place upon a certain day, be interfered with by frost, the committee shall have power to postpone it, but not beyond the week. If, through a continuance of frost, the meeting be void, the subscribers shall be liable to their quota of expenses. This rule not to apply to produce meetings, which must take place as soon as the weather will permit.

15. *Penalty for absence from slips.*—Immediately before the greyhounds are drawn at any open meeting, the place and time of putting the first brace of dogs into the slips on the following morning shall be declared, and the owner of any dog which shall not be ready to be put into the slips st such appointed time and place, or in proper rotation afterwards, shall be fined 1*l.*; if not ready within ten minutes from such time, the absent greyhound shall be adjudged to have lost its course, and the opponent shall run a bye. If both dogs be absent at the expira-

tion of ten minutes, the stewards shall have power to disqualify both dogs, or to fine their owners any sum not exceeding 5*l.* each. No dog to be put into the slips for a deciding course until thirty minutes after its previous course, without the consent of its owner.

16. *Entry and draw.*—No entry by a subscriber shall be valid unless the amount of stake be paid in full, when a card or counter, bearing a corresponding number, shall be assigned to each entry. These numbered cards or counters shall then be placed together in a bowl, and drawn out indiscriminately. This classification once made shall not be disturbed throughout a meeting, except for the purpose of guarding, or on account of byes. Dogs whose position on the card has been altered in consequence of guarding must return to their original position in next class, if guarding does not prevent it.

17. *Guarding.*—When more than one nomination is taken by one person, the greyhounds, provided they are *bona fide* his own property, or the property of one person, shall be guarded—if more than 8, two dogs; if more than 16, three; if more than 24, four; if more than 32, five; if more than 48, six. In Produce Stakes any number may be guarded. This guarding is not, however, to deprive any dog of a natural-bye to which he may. in running through a stake, be entitled.

18. *Byes.*—No greyhound shall run more than one natural bye in any stake, and this bye shall be given to the lowest available dog on the list in each round. In Puppy Stakes each bye must be run with a puppy or single handed; but if it is proved to the satisfaction of the stewards that no puppy can be found on the field or otherwise in time to run an unexpected bye in the first class, the owner shall have the power of substituting an old dog.

19. *Change of name.*—If any subscriber shall enter a greyhound by a different name from that in which it shall last have run for any stake or piece of plate, without giving notice to the secretary at the time of entry, of the alteration, such greyhound shall be disqualified.

20. *Penalty for not prefixing "names."*— Any subscriber taking an entry in a stake, and not prefixing the word "names" to a greyhound which is not his own property, shall forfeit that dog's chance of the stake. He shall likewise be compelled to deliver in writing, to the secretary of the meeting, the name of the *bona fide* owner of the greyhound named by him if called upon, and this communication to be produced should any dispute arise in the matter.

21. *Pedigree and marks of puppies.*—For Produce Stakes, the names, ages, colours,

and distinguishing marks of the puppies shall be detailed in writing to the secretary at the time of entering them. The subscriber must also state in writing the names of the sire or sires, the dam, and their owners, together with the names and addresses of the parties who bred and reared the puppies, and where they are kept at the time of entry; and any puppy whose marks and pedigree shall not correspond with the entry as thus given shall be disqualified, and the whole of its stakes forfeited. No greyhound shall be allowed to run in any puppy stake whose description is not properly given as above, and it must be capable of being proved, if required by the secretary or committee. No greyhound to be considered a puppy which was whelped before the 1st Jan. of the year preceding the season of running.

22. *Objections.*—An objection may be made at any time before the stakes are paid over, upon the objector lodging a sum of not less than 5*l.*, as may be required, in the hands of the secretary, which shall be forfeited if the objection prove frivolous; and the owner of the greyhound objected to shall be compelled to deposit a like amount, and to prove the correctness of his entry. The cost of the expenses incurred in consequence of the objection to fall upon the party against whom the decision is given.

23. *Where objection cannot be substantiated at the time.*—Should an objection be made which cannot at the time be substantiated or disproved, the greyhound may be allowed to run under protest, and should the objection be afterwards substantiated, and if the winnings have been paid over to the owner of a greyhound, who will thus be disqualified, he shall return the money or prize, or be declared a defaulter. The money returned shall be divided equally among the greyhounds beaten by the dog thus disqualified, but if a piece of plate has been added, it must be run for by them.

24. *Stakes divided when one dog is drawn.*— If two greyhounds belonging to the same owner or to confederates remain in for the deciding course, the stake shall be considered divided, as also if the owner of one dog induce the owner of the other dog to draw him for any payment or consideration; but if one greyhound be drawn from lameness, or from any cause clearly affecting his chance of winning, the other may be declared the winner, the facts of the case being proved to the satisfaction of the stewards.

25. *Third and fourth prizes.*—When more than two prizes are given, the greyhound beaten by the winner in the last class but one shall have precedence of that beaten by the runner-up. When only three dogs run in this class, then the greyhound first beaten of these three shall have the third prize, and the fourth prize shall be given to the greyhound beaten by the winner in the previous class, unless the winner had a bye in that class, in which case the fourth prize shall be awarded to the dog beaten by the runner-up in that class.

26. *When two winners meet on unequal terms.*—If two greyhounds shall each win a stake, and have to run together for a final prize or challenge cup, should they not have run an equal number of ties in their respective stakes, the greyhound not having run the sufficient number of courses must run a bye or byes to put itself upon an equality in this respect with its opponent.

27. *Defaulters.*—No person shall be allowed to enter or run a greyhound in his own or any other person's name who is a defaulter for stakes or bets.

28. *Judge or slipper interested.*—If a judge or slipper be in any way interested in the winnings of a greyhound or greyhounds, the nominator of these dogs, unless he can prove satisfactorily that such interest was without his cognizance, shall forfeit all claim to the winnings.

29. *Bets.*—All bets upon an undecided course to stand, unless one of the greyhounds be drawn. All bets upon a dog running farther than another in the stake, or upon the event, to be p.p., whatever accident may happen.

30. *Bets where dogs divide.*—Where money has been laid against a dog winning a stake, and he divides it, the two sums must be put together and divided in the same proportion as the stakes.

MR. THACKER'S RULES FOR THE DECISION OF COURSES.

Rules 1, 2, 3, 4, 5, and 6 are repealed by the above rules.

7. *Score for the cote.*—A cote to be reckoned two points; and a cote is when two dogs start even together, and one outruns the other, and gives the hare a turn or wrench; but if the hare take a circuitous route, and the dog which runs the outer circle gives the turn, to be reckoned three points.

8. *The turn and wrench.*—A turn to be reckoned one point; but if the hare turns not as it were round, she only wrenches; and two wrenches are equal to one turn. A wrench is when she strikes off to the right or left, at about a right angle. Anything short of that in a forward direction is only a rick or whiff, for which nothing ought to be allowed. [This rule is sometimes connected with the 7th and 12th rules, namely, a cote and a fall; and but for the contingencies, and their confusing the matter, those three rules might be condensed into one rule, as thus:—Turn about, if gained without that superior speed which constitutes a cote, one point; if with that superior speed, two points; or if the turn about is given when a dog falls in giving it, two points without superior speed, or three points with superior speed; if he only wrench the hare when he falls it ought to be taken into account the same as a wrench under other circumstances. Those contingencies render it necessary that the three rules should be distinctly and separately understood and acted upon, and the points will be as easily counted under the three rules as under one. They must not be counted under both or all three heads; nor, on the contrary, must the fall be counted and omit the turn, which I have known to be done. With respect to a wrench being originally meant as I have here defined it, the hare striking off to the right or left at about a right angle, which has been suggested to me as being only my own interpretation of the meaning, and would be better backed by some other authority, I have applied to the only work I know capable of illustrating the question, and that in very few hands, the Noble Art of "Venery, or Hunting," by Tuberville, from which the translator of Arrian has favoured me with the following copy, and which bears me out in having interpreted the meaning properly:—"A cote serveth for two turnes, and two strypping or jerkinnes (as some call them) stand for a cote; also many times a hare doth but wrench and not turne; for it is not called a turne

unless the hare be set and do turne (as it were) round about; two such wrenchys stand for a turne."—*Note by Mr. Thacker.*]

9. *For the go-by.*—A go-by to be reckoned two points; but one dog being behind the other, and then getting first, by the hare running in a curve, or any way but in a straightforward stretch, or by superior speed, when both are fairly on their legs after a turn, is no go-by; if a dog give half go-by, to be allowed one point for it, unless that half a go-by forms part of a cote, in which case it should be reckoned in the cote.

10. *The kill.*—Killing or bearing the hare to be reckoned two points, if it be a kill of merit; but if one dog turn the hare into the other dog's mouth, or the hare being taken by other casual circumstances wherein there is no merit in the dog, to reckon nothing; but there may be a kill which has not the first degree of merit in the dog, yet not without merit, wherein the judge shall use his discretion in allowing one point for it.

11. *For the trip.*—A tripping or jerking the hare to be reckoned one point. A jerk is when a greyhound catches hold of a hare, but again loses his hold; and a trip is when he misses his catch, but throws her up with his nose, or other hindrance of that kind. It has been said when a hare is tripped or jerked that the dog ought to have held her, and that it is a clumsy trick in letting her go again; it may sometimes be the case, but whether it is or not it contributes towards the main object, as it distresses the hare, and delays her so that his fellow-dog has the bettter chance of taking her; a dog giving either tripping or jerking generally effects quite as much as by giving a complete turn.

12. *Allowance for a fall.*—If a dog take a fall in a course whilst performing his duty, to be allowed one point for it; if he falls from pressing the hare closely, or flinging himself to take her, and causes her to turn about, he is entitled to two points, one for the fall and one for the turn; or if the turn were by superior speed, he gains three points, one for the fall, and two for the cote. This rule is connected with the 7th and 8th rules.

13. *For being unslipped.*—If one dog see not the hare when slipped by any accidental occurrence not his own fault, to be deemed no course; but if owing to his own untract-

P

ableness or infirmity of sight, or the fault of his owner or servants, the dog that follows the hare to win, and the judge to decide whether his not seeing the hare was accidental or the fault of the dog. If he afterwards join in the course, it must be in the discretion of the judge, if he deem it no fault in the dog his not seeing the hare when slipped, to give it no course; or decide it according to the merits of the dogs when running together, allowing for the distance or number of turns given by one while the other was absent from it, and comparatively not so much at work. But if his not seeing the hare when slipped was his own fault, or that of his owner or servant, the course to be given against him.

14. *Speed to count where no turn is made.* —If there be no turn or other point gained, an equal start, and the hare run in a straight direction the dog leading first to the covert to win. If one dog lose ground at the start and afterwards evidently gain upon the other by superior speed, though he does not pass or get even with him, yet if there be no turn or other point gained between them he ought to be deemed the winner; either dog leading first to the covert by an unequal start, an inside turn, or other occurrence where there is no superiority of speed shown, the course to be adjudged dead; but if the unequal start were the fault of that dog which lost ground by it, and who does not regain that loss by superior speed, he ought to forfeit the course for his own untractableness. But if a dog lose his start by the slipper standing still instead of running forwards for the dogs to press against the collar, and in his natural struggling to get to the hare when he sees her has his eyes in a contrary direction when loosed, it ought not to be deemed his untractableness but the slipper's awkwardness.

15. *If a dog lose ground in the start* by any untoward circumstances not his own fault, and yet maintain equal speed with the other, if that other give the hare a turn, or gain any other point, but the course ends immediately by the hare gaining covert, sough, squatting in turnips or other brush, except killing her, that turn or point not to be allowed for, but the course to be adjudged dead. If that turn were gained by the advantage of an inside turn, the hare running in a curve, without any superiority of speed being shown, to be adjudged dead. If the course continue longer, and other points are gained, that first turn or point to be taken into the account; and if that unequal start were owing to the dog's untractableness, or otherwise his own fault, the turn or point gained by the other dog to entitle him to win.

16. *Penalty for standing still.*—If a dog wilfully stand still in a course, or depart from directly pursuing the hare, or to meet her, the points he has gained to be reckoned only to the time he stood still, or left the course, though he may afterwards join in it. If the points he has gained up to the time he stood still or departed from the ordinary course should equal what the other gained in the whole course, his standing still or leaving the course, to give the casting point against him. If both dogs wilfully stop with the hare in view, to be decided by the number each gained; and if they are equal, to be decided by a toss up, though one run longer than the other. If one or both dogs should stop with the hare in view, and relinquish the pursuit through utter inability to continue it, the course to be decided according to the number of points each dog gained in the whole course, and not to that dog which ran the longest, though he continued the pursuit to the covert.

17. *For refusing to fence.*—If a dog refuse to fence where the other fences, his points to be reckoned only up to that time, though he may afterwards join in the course. If he do his best endeavour to fence, and is foiled by sticking in the meuse, or the fence being too high to top it, whereby he cannot join in the rest of the course, such course to be deemed to end at that fence. Should the points be equal between them, to be undecided; but if one be thrown out by being a bad fencer, and yet the points be equal, a good fencer to have a casting point over a bad one.

18. *If a fence intervene* in a course that the judge cannot get over, and thereby lose view of the remainder of the course, the course to end at that fence.

19 and 20. Repealed.

21. *Superiority of speed over other qualities.*—If the points are even between two dogs, and one evidently show most speed, that extra speed to entitle him to win; but where a dog has a balance of one point, and the speed of the other is only a trifle more, the point to win. If very few turns or wrenches are given, and one dog has a balance of only one point and the other a great degree of superior speed, that speed to win. If the points be equal, and one has most speed at the first part of the course, and the other at the last part, if in equal proportion up to the last turn, or kill, the course to be adjudged dead; but if the points are equal, and speed also up to the last turn, and one shows more speed than the other in the run up to cover, that extra speed to win. If two dogs are slipped even, the course straight, without a turn, and one shows most speed at first and the other at the last part, so as just to get even with his fellow, *and no more,* the course to be ad-

judged dead. [The last section of this rule is just like a race with horses, and it is immaterial whether a dog loses ground at first from waiting or deficiency of speed, or whether he gains at last from having waited or being stouter than his fellow; whether he begins to gain exactly half way, or either before or after ; then, if they come even at last, it is to all intents and purposes a dead heat. There is no distress from turns, or any other by dependencies, but the same ground run over in the same time. —*Note by Mr. Thacker.*]

PEDIGREES OF CELEBRATED DOGS.

The following pedigrees are inserted partly for the information of the courser, but chiefly to serve as a comparison between those of the thoroughbred horse and the greyhound. The breeding of this latter animal has not been carefully attended to for so many generations as in the horse; and, consequently, his descent cannot be traced nearly so far back. Mr. Randell's celebrated *Riot* and her brother *Ranter* can be traced back as far as probably any other dog, but even his pedigree, as will be seen, breaks down in the fifth generation. The lines of Mr. Reed's *Mechanic* and Mr. West's *War Office* have been searched with great diligence by their respective owners, but the result shows, as in the case of Mr. Randell's dog, the great difference between the horse and the greyhound.

RANTER, Brother to Riot, Gipsy Prince, Gipsy Royal, &c.	Bedlamite (*Brown*)	Figaro (*Fyson*)	King Cob (*Daintree*)	Ion (*Inskip*)	Stumps	Old Pilot
						Bliss
					Ida	
				Kate (*Daintree*)	Deptford	
					Sister to Fanny	
			Frederica (*Fyson*)	Damon (*Dobede*)		
				Daffodil	What Not	
					Nonpareil	
		Bessy Bedlam (*Brown*)	King Cob (*Helmsley*)	Smoker (*Helmsley*)		
				Lady		
			Lively (*Woodroffe*)	Brother to Brigand	Rubens	Rocket
						Violet (*Nottingham*)
					Eve	
				Lady (*Nixon*)	Tinker	Brutus
						Sister to Nun
					Fan (*Parr*)	
Black Fly (*Pridmore*)	Marquis (*Webb*)	Rocket (*Bennett*)	Streamer	Colwick		
				Sister to Herdsman		
			Fly			
		Stella	Sambo	Duke		
				Countess		
			Rose			
	Kirtles (*Kershaw*) (*sister to Coquette*)	Kouli Khan (*Kershaw*)	Topper (*Calvert*)	Hercules (*Hassall*)	Nelson	
					Madam	
				Laura (*his*)	Stretcher	
					Fly	
			Hannah (*Hassall*)	Harold	Grasper (*Derby*)	
					Fly	
				May-Fly		
		Knavery (*sister to Ball's Bugle*)	Bachelor (*Hill*)	Merlin	Merlin	
					Transit	
				Spider		
			Nimble (*Jackson*)	Lunardi		
				Fairy		

CHAP. IX.

DEER AND RABBIT-COURSING.

SECT. 1.—DEER-COURSING.

530. The deer which is coursed in the island of Jura, the only locality where this sport is now practised, is the red deer already alluded to at page 82. The hound used has also been fully described in the same chapter.

531. THE MODE OF CONDUCTING THE SPORT is as follows:—The deer is first stalked in the usual way, just as in deer-stalking; to the chapter on which the reader must refer for the particulars. Two deer-hounds are then slipped, and either succeed in pulling down their quarry, or are foiled by his speed and lasting powers. Mr. Scrope's description of one of these courses will give some idea of its exciting nature, but its length must preclude my giving it insertion. Suffice it to remark, that after the dogs were slipped, a long and severe course ensued, in which various casualties took place, incidental to such rough and rocky ground. At the termination of the course, when the party arrived at the spot where the deer lay, "Buskar was perfectly exhausted, and had lain down, shaking from head to foot like a broken-down horse; but on our approaching the deer, he rose, walked round him with a determined growl, and would scarcely permit us to come near him. He had not, however, received any cut or injury, while Bran showed several bruises, nearly a square inch having been taken off the front of his fore-leg, so that the bone was visible, and a piece of burnt heather had passed quite through his foot. Nothing could exceed the determined courage displayed by both dogs, particularly by Buskar, throughout the chase, and especially in preserving his hold, though dragged by the deer in the most violent manner. This, however, is but one of the many feats of this fine dog. He was pupped in autumn, 1832, and before he was a year old killed a full-grown hind single-handed." Mr. Scrope goes on to remark, that "the speed of a deer may be estimated as nearly equal to that of a hare, though in coursing the latter, from its turnings and windings, more speed is probably required than in coursing the former; but, on the other hand, if a dog is in any degree blown when he reaches a deer he cannot preserve his hold, nor recover it if it is once lost; and, as it is only from his superior speed and bottom that a dog can continue to preserve his hold, and thus by degrees to exhaust the deer, till at length he is enabled to pull him down, this great power of endurance is only to be found in a thorough-bred greyhound of the original sort; for, even though a cross-bred dog might succeed in fastening on a deer, he seldom has the speed or endurance necessary for preserving his hold; and should he receive a fall will, in all probability, suffer much more than a greyhound whose elasticity of form is better able to resist such shocks. Perhaps the greatest advantage possessed by superiority of speed is that the dog runs less risk of injury; for so long as the deer has the power of movement, he will not turn round or attempt to defend himself with his horns, but endeavours to fly from his pursuers until they have fastened on him, and are enabled, by seizing on some vital part, to pull him down; whereas a cross-bred dog who has not sufficient speed for a deer, and succeeds only in running him down by the nose (and that after a long chase), at length finds the deer at bay with his back against some rock. In this situation no dog can possibly attack a deer with the slightest chance of success. In fact, so skilfully does he use his horns in defence, and with such fury does he rush upon the dogs, that none can get to close quarters with him without the certainty of instant death. In this position, indeed, he could without difficulty destroy a whole pack. When running obliquely down a hill (which is a deer's *forte*), no dog can equal him, particularly if the ground is rough and strong; and in such a situation a dog without great roughness of feet is perfectly useless. It is, therefore, advisable not to let loose a dog at a deer in a lofty situation, as the ground is generally most rugged near the tops of the hills, and the dogs run a great risk of being injured. On the other hand, in low and level grounds, a dog is an over-match for a deer in speed; and as the deer generally attempts to make for the high grounds for security, and is a bad runner up hill, the dog has a decided advantage when slipped at a deer in such a situation."—Page 363.

It would be idle for me to add any remarks upon a sport which it has never fallen to my lot to be engaged in; indeed, it is so limited in extent, and so rare even in Jura, that very few individuals are enabled to participate in it. Mr. Scrope seems to set great store by it, but, saving its rarity and the wildness of the accompanying scenery, there does not seem to be very much to recommend it in preference to the coursing of the hare. The dogs must have more courage perhaps, but they require little besides that quality and stoutness; whilst the ordinary greyhound requires working power and speed in addition. The one is more straightforward and bold, the other more scientific and full of the delicate points of distinction which give the chief interest to the coursing of the hare. I cannot but think, as I have stated at page 86, that the modern smooth greyhound, of good, stout, and hardy blood, would soon enter to this sport with great zest and spirit, and would pull down the best deer which ever ran.

Sect. 2.—Rabbit-Coursing.

532. The Rabbits used for this purpose are usually caught in warrens, or elsewhere, and they are let out of a trap similar to the pigeon-trap, but of larger dimensions, by pulling a string. They require to be turned into an enclosed ground two or three times, and driven about, or they are apt to squat, and suffer themselves to be killed at once.

533. The Dogs are a cross of the terrier and greyhound, and are usually limited in weight, 25 lbs. being that which is generally adopted. They are very fast for their size, but would of course be beaten by even an inferior thorough-bred greyhound; hence, the stipulation is generally made as to breed and weight. They have great power of turning and stopping themselves, which is required by the short running and quick turning of the rabbits, which spirt about even more sharply than hares. Many of these dogs are very nearly, if not quite, of the pure old Wiltshire breed of greyhounds, and would kill many a hare in that locality, though not fast enough for some of the flyers found there.

534. The Mode of Conducting the Sport in rabbit-coursing is the same as in coursing the hare, except that the rabbit is let out of a box by pulling a string, instead of being found in the natural way. Slips are used, and a brace of dogs only are let loose. Generally the contest is confined to matches, in which the winner must gain two courses out of three; but sometimes sweepstakes are run for as in hare-coursing.

535. The Rules are precisely analogous to those given at page 219, some of which however are not wanted in this species of sport, where there are no fences, and where dogs are seldom run to a stand-still.

536. The Chief Localities where this sport is carried on are the suburban gardens of our large manufacturing towns; as, for instance, the Pomona Gardens, Manchester. Here the mechanic is enabled to amuse himself by trying his dog's powers in competition with others belonging to his companions. It may be open to the charge of cruelty, but so is every sport depending upon the death of its victims for its existence; and certainly in this respect rabbit-coursing is not to be compared with shooting, in any of its multifarious forms. It may not be very interesting to those who can obtain more expensive and more exciting amusement, but to those who are confined in the murky air of our manufacturing towns, it affords an incitement to comparatively fresh air and out-door recreation of the body.

PART I.

THE PURSUIT OF WILD ANIMALS FOR SPORT.

BOOK IV.—ANGLING.

CHAP. I.
VARIETIES OF LAKE AND RIVER FISH.

586. THE COMMON SALMON (*Salmo Salar*) stands at the head of British fish, as affording the best sport to the angler, and the greatest treat to the *gourmand*, its flesh being rich in flavour, and of a beautiful red colour. It is a fish of large size, sometimes attaining to the weight of 50 or even 60 pounds, and of beautiful proportions. The head is small; upper jaw longer than the lower; vomer furnished with teeth; body slightly arched on the back, which ought to be broad and muscular, and gradually tapering to the tail, which is broad, and ends in a crescentic curve. The colour of the salmon when in season is a purplish-black on the back, softening into a silvery-grey on the sides, and ending in a pure white on the belly. When out of season, these colours are represented by a dull brown on the back, reddish or pale-brown on the sides, and reddish-white on the belly. The male has several small, irregular, and copper-coloured spots on his sides. These in the female are larger, darker, and generally round or lunated. The male is also more slender. The scales are middle-sized, and are easily detached. The average length is from two and a half to three feet. Salmon feed freely on fish and mollusca, but digest their food so rapidly, that when opened their stomachs are generally found empty. Their growth is proportionate to the quantity of food which they can procure; and hence when they reach the sea they increase in size in a marvellous manner, during a very short period. The successive stages of development of this fish are now supposed to be as follows:— The fry are hatched chiefly in the spring and early summer, and grow very slowly till they are about a year old, up to which time they are called *salmon fry*, and have several transverse bars on their sides. When these disappear, and the fish becomes uniformly silvery in colour, it is about to commence its first migration to the sea, and is called a *smoult*. After the smoult has remained in the sea a few months, it returns to its native river, if possible, and is then greatly increased in size, generally weighing two or three pounds, or even considerably more. They are now called *grilse*; and after a second time descending to the sea, where they again rapidly add to their size and weight, they attain the full dignity and name of salmon. The female salmon deposits her ova in the gravelly beds of mountain streams, where she ploughs a groove with her nose, and is assisted by the male in the whole operation. The size of the salmon does not entirely depend upon the age, but on the nature of the river in which it is bred; some rivers never produce large salmon, whilst others are remarkable for fish of great size. These points have all been recently discussed with great care and ability by Messrs. Shaw and Young, in Scotland, and by Mr. Yarrell and "Ephemera," in England; but the above conclusions may be considered to embody the present general opinions on the subject, embracing those of all the above authorities but Mr. Shaw, who still adheres to the belief that the salmon is two years old before he seeks the sea. The *fence months*, when it is illegal to take salmon, vary in the different rivers; but in most of them that time extends from the 10th of September to the 25th of January.

587. SALMON, OR SEA-TROUT (*Salmo Trutta*).—According to Mr. Yarrell, this fish is distinguished from the common salmon by the gill-cover, which differs in the following points:—The line of union of the operculum with the sub-operculum and the inferior margin of the sub-operculum is oblique, forming a considerable angle with the axis of the body of the first. The posterior edge of the pre-operculum is rounded, not sinuous. The teeth are also more slender and numerous. The flesh of this fish is very similar in flavour and colour to that of the common salmon, with which it is very generally confounded; and the two are sold indiscriminately by the fishmongers as ordinary salmon. In habits, haunts, &c., they are also alike.

588. THE BULL-TROUT, SEWEN, OR WHITLING (*Salmo Eriox*), is known from the two preceding varieties or species, according, again, to our chief authority, Mr. Yarrell, by the gill-cover, which in the bull-trout presents the line of union of the sub-operculum oblique, forming a considerable angle with the axis of the body of the fish.

The teeth are longer and stronger than those of the salmon and sea-trout, and the tail is square. This variety is found in the Tweed, in several of the rivers of Wales, and in Devonshire and Cornwall. Its weight is usually from 12 to 16 pounds. It is a bold fish, affording good sport to the angler. Its flesh is much paler than the two first described, and not of such high flavour.

589. The Parr (*Salmo Salmulus*) is decidedly considered by Mr. Young to be a distinct variety of the *Salmonidæ*, and not, as was at one time supposed, the young of the common salmon, or sea-trout. Mr. Young says that this is clear, because parr are very commonly met with at a time when the young fry of the salmon are all gone off to the sea; but the other side of the argument is supported by the assertion, that as salmon spawn at very late as well as early periods of the year, so *all* their fry are not at any one time at sea. The arguments, however, in favour of Mr. Young's side of the question appear to preponderate, as there seems to be a considerable difference in the shape of the head of the two fish; and in some cases parr are found in rivers which are never frequented by salmon. The parr is a lively little fish, and will take the fly with great eagerness. Except in the form of the head, the parr closely resembles the fry of the salmon.

590. The Common Trout (*Salmo Fario*) is distinguished by the length of the lower jaw being greater than that of the upper. It weighs from half a pound to four or five, or even, in rare cases, up to eight pounds; and its ordinary length is from 10 to 18 or 20 inches. In shape it is not quite so elegant as the salmon, but it is, nevertheless, a very beautiful fish. The snout is more blunt, and the jaws are thickly supplied with teeth inclining inwards, and very sharp. In colour it is of a pale yellowish-grey, darker on the back, and nearly white on the belly. It is marked on the sides with several distinct round spots of a bright red colour, each surrounded by a halo of pale grey; occasionally a black spot occurs, especially on the fins. These are of a purplish-brown colour, except the ventrals, which have a reddish tinge. Trout vary so much in different rivers, that no one description will minutely apply to all, but the above will give the general characteristics of the species. The trout feeds like the salmon, and in habits resembles that fish in all respects but the migration to the sea. He is generally found in swift and gravelly streams, and rejects those of an opposite character, though he is occasionally to be met with there, in consequence of the artificial and compulsory interference of man. The spawn is deposited in the same way as that of the salmon, but as the young do not migrate, their successive changes and growth cannot be so clearly made out. The spawning time begins in September, in some few cases, but it is not commonly in full operation till October or November, after which it may be said to be completed. The trout is in full season from March to July, but the time varies in different rivers so much, that it is impossible to lay down any decided rule. When in high perfection, its spots are peculiarly brilliant and distinct; the head is small, the body being plump and thick, and the belly silvery.

591. The Great Lake-Trout (*Salmo Ferox*).—Mr. Yarrell defines this magnificent fish by its proportions, which he says are as follows:—The head is to the body as 1 to 4½, depth of body to length as 1 to 4; teeth large, strong, and numerous, and in five lines; it reaches nearly the same proportions as the salmon, from which it differs in not migrating to the sea. The flesh is less highly flavoured, and of a much paler colour.

592. The Char (*Salmo Umbla*) is only found in a few of our northern lakes, and in those of Ireland. Several varieties are known, as the *silver char*, the *gelt char*, the *red char*, and the *case char*, according to the peculiar shade of the colour. It is a beautiful fish, but it is not clearly described, and authors vary as to the peculiarities of its colour and formation.

593. The Grayling (*Thymallus Vulgaris*) is found only in certain streams, and particularly those descending from granite mountains. It is a very elegant fish, of middle size, seldom exceeding 15 or 16 inches, and slender in proportion. The head is small; upper jaw the longer of the two; teeth small, and spread over the roof of the mouth; the colour of the back varies from a blackish-green to blue, gradually shading into a silvery grey towards the belly. When first taken, there are several black spots on the back, and some irridescent patches of gold colour on the sides; this appearance rapidly fades, and the general colours soon sober down. The scales are proportionally large. Sometimes, though rarely, the weight is greater than that given above, and in some few cases graylings have been taken of four or five pounds weight. This is a very bold fish after the fly, but it does not afford such good play when hooked as the salmon tribe. The season is from September to March, after which they begin to spawn.

594. The Gwiniad (*Coregonus Pennantii*) found in the lakes of Scotland and Ireland, and in those of Cumberland, the Powan (*Coregonus Clupeoides*), found only in Loch

Lomond and one or two other Scotch lakes, the VENDACE (*Coregonus Albula*), found also in the Scotch lakes, and the POLLAN (*Coregonus Pollan*), found in Lough Neagh, in Ireland, are four closely-allied lake-fish which somewhat resemble the *Salmonidæ*, but have prolonged snouts resembling the herring. Hence, the first has been called the fresh-water herring. They none of them afford sport for the angler, and are only taken with the net.

595. THE PIKE, OR JACK (*Esox Lucius*).— This voracious fish is met with in the gently-flowing rivers and ponds of Great Britain, and is called a pike when above four or five pounds in weight, and a jack if of less than that size. It is a very ugly-looking fish, the head being large, the jaws long and savage-looking, and armed with several hundred teeth; the tail is lunated; the colour is a pale olive-grey, becoming deeper on the back, and marked on the sides with several yellowish spots or patches. Sometimes the pike reaches an enormous size, instances having been known in which it was taken more than three feet in length. The food of the pike consists of fish, frogs, rats, the young of water-fowl, or, in fact, anything in the shape of animal food. They spawn in March and April, among the weeds of their favourite haunts. Like all other fish, they are only in high season for the few months before this process is commenced; the flesh is white, and of a good flavour, resembling the haddock.

596. THE BREAM (*Abramis Brama*) is more like a flat-fish than any other of the fresh-water fish, except the flounder. It is very narrow across the back, which, as well as the belly, is much arched, forming altogether almost an oval. It frequents still-water like the pike, and is often found in the same rivers and ponds as that shark in miniature. The head is very small, with a pointed snout, small mouth, and no teeth. The colour is a blueish iron-grey on the back, inclining to white on the belly. The bream is rarely above one pound and a half in weight, and is not highly prized for the table, though, when stuffed and roasted like a pike, it is not to be despised.

597. THE CHUB (*Leuciscus Cephalus*).— This fish has various names in the different counties of England, where it is also called the *chevin* and *skelly*. It is a powerful fish, but very timid in its nature, and retreats to the deepest holes of the river when there is the slightest appearance of motion in the neighbourhood of its own body. In weight it is from one to four pounds. It is a short, thick, and high-backed fish, with large scales; head and back of a greenish-brown; sides, silvery-brown, approaching to yellow

in the summer; belly, white; pectoral fins, yellow; anal, red; tail, forked, and of a brownish colour. The chub spawns in April, and is very soon recovered from that process, being again in season in June. It frequents deep rivers running through alluvial districts, and lives chiefly upon worms.

598. THE ROACH, OR BRAISE (*Leuciscus Rutilus*), inhabits the same kind of rivers as the chub, and is a gregarious fish. It has a small, round, leathery mouth, and is provided with a circle of teeth placed in the throat. The roach is as deep, but not so thick as the chub; scales large, and of a pale golden tinge approaching to brown on the back; fins red, as is also the iris.

599. THE DACE, OR DARE (*Leuciscus Leuciscus*) is also a gregarious fish. The head is small; body slender; tail forked; colour dusky on the back, varied with patches of pale olive-green; sides and belly, silvery; fins reddish, but not so much so as the roach. It is about nine or ten inches long. Its haunts are unlike those of the roach and chub, inasmuch as it prefers swift, gravelly streams, but selects those which are thickly infested with weeds. It is a fish very generally spread over England, but is not highly esteemed either by the angler or for the table.

600. THE GRAINING (*Leuciscus Lancastriensis*) occurs only in the Mersey. It is merely a variety of the common dace.

601. THE RUDD, OR RED-EYE (*Leuciscus Erythrophthalmus*), is a very rare fish, occasionally found in the Thames and the sea, and in some of the ornamental waters of our southern parks. There is a great dispute among naturalists as to its characteristics. It is a middle-sized fish, rather more than a foot in length, with a deep and thick body; head small; iris, yellow; large scales; colour somewhat like the dace, but the sides and belly are of a more golden hue.

602. THE AZURINE (*Leuciscus Cœruleus*) is another fish only found in Lancashire; it resembles the roach in shape, but is of a dull-blue colour, and is called the blue-roach in the county where it is found.

603. THE BLEAK, OR BLICK (*Leuciscus Alburnus*).—This little lively fish is constantly seen in large shoals near the surface of every still-flowing river. It is seldom more than four or five inches long. Head small and neat; eyes prominent, with a patch of blood-colour below; back, olive-green; sides and belly, silvery; scales large; fins colourless, and very transparent; tail forked.

604. THE MINNOW (*Leuciscus Phoxinus*).— This fish, likewise called the *pink* and *mennow*, is to be met with in most of our clear brooks, which it prefers to larger and stiller

rivers. It is gregarious, and is in the habit of retreating to the mud and weeds in the winter months. The colour varies much in different localities, from blue to green on the back, and from white to red on the belly. Sometimes it is of a pearly-white, which is a colour much prized when the fish is wanted as a bait, and sometimes of a yellow cast. It is chiefly sought after for the purpose of using it as a lure for the trout, salmon, and pike.

605. The LOACH, OR GROUNDLING (*Cobitis Barbatula*), is unlike the last described fish in being nearly of the same size throughout its length. It has a compressed head, furnished with a well-marked beard composed of six tufts. It is about three or four inches in length, of a dusky-brown colour. It also is only used as a bait; but for this purpose it is not equal to the minnow, bleak, or gudgeon.

606. The COMMON CARP (*Cyprinus Carpio*), is the type of a family which have all a small mouth without teeth, but possessing a bony apparatus in the throat as a substitute. They have only one dorsal fin. The common carp is not a native of Great Britain, but was introduced by the monks to serve the purposes of the table during their fasts. In length it is usually from one foot to one foot six inches. The back is arched and thick; colour yellowish, approaching to brown over the back, and to white under the belly. The mouth has a short beard on each side, both above and below; on the sides are some blackish specks; fins, brown; tail, brown, and forked. Carp feed on worms and insects, and are very prolific, living also to a great age. They are a very wary and cautious fish, and very uncertain in appetite, being sometimes ready to take a bait, and at others obstinately refusing every temptation. The *crucian* appears to be only a variety of the common carp.

607. The BARBEL (*Barbus Barbus*), like the carp, has a beard, which has given its name to this fish. This beard consists of four distinct prolongations; two on each side of a very prominent upper lip. The colour of the fish is a silvery-grey, becoming darker on the back, and white on the belly. Scales middle-sized, and rounded; dorsal fin, small, and of a blueish-brown; other fins, brown, tipped with yellow; tail, forked, and of a purplish-brown. They frequent deep but rapid rivers, and are gregarious, feeding on insects and worms. They are not so wary as the carp, and afford good sport to the bottom-fisher.

608. The TENCH (*Tinca Vulgaris*), like the carp, has been introduced from abroad, for the purpose of supplying the tables of the Roman Catholic population of Great Britain. It thrives in stagnant or slowly-changing ponds, especially those made in loamy or rich soils. It is a thick fish, resembling the carp in shape, and having a small thin beard at each corner of its mouth. Like the carp, it has no teeth. Gill-covers, bright-yellow; colour of the body, deep-olive, with a tint of gold; scales small, thin, and covered with a thick viscid slime; fins of a dark brownish-purple; tail, square. Tench spawn in the spring among the weeds, and the young grow rapidly, so that a pond is soon stocked with these fish, which are of a very superior flavour to the carp.

609. The GUDGEON (*Gobio Fluviatilis*), though small, is highly prized from its good flavour, and affording sport to the young angler. It is gregarious, and is taken in immense numbers in the neighbourhood of London. Gudgeon rarely come to the surface, but frequent the bottoms of rapid rivers and brooks, preferring moderately-shallow water with a gravelly bottom. This fish has a small beard on the upper lip. It is about five or six inches in length, with a round body and a thick head. Colour, pale-brown on the back, and reddish-white on the belly; fins slightly tinged with reddish-yellow; the dorsal fin and tail are spotted with black.

610. The PERCH (*Perca Fluviatilis*) is a very handsome fish, of medium size. Body deep, with high-arched back; head small, with sharp teeth in the jaws and the roof of the mouth. The edges of the gill-covers are serrated, with a spine on the lower part. Colours as follows:—Back, deep olive-green, with broad black bars, gradually becoming white towards the belly; ventril and anal fins of a rich scarlet, as also is the tail, though not so distinctly of that colour. The dorsal fin is furnished with spinous prolongations, so sharp that it can scarcely be handled with impunity by the angler. It thrives best in large tidal rivers, where it seeks the point at which the water is usually brackish, and grows there to an extent never seen elsewhere. In stagnant ponds it will live, but does not thrive. It is a slow-growing fish, requiring many years to arrive at its full size. The perch spawns in the months of March and April. It is a gregarious fish, and is very tenacious of life.

611. The RUFFE, OR POPE (*Gymnocephalus Cernua*), is generally considered as a variety of the perch, which it differs from in colour, being of a dusky olive, with black spots. In its generic and anatomical arrangements, however, it varies so much as to be classed under a different subdivision of the fishes found in Great Britain. It is very abundant in the Thames.

612. THE STICKLEBACK (*Gasterosteus Aculeatus, G. Spinulosus, and G. Pungitius*).— These three varieties of the smallest fish known in Great Britain differ from one another only in size, and in the number of the spines which are attached to the scales of the sides, but which are more or less excitable at pleasure. The largest of them, which heads the above list, is two inches and a half long, whilst the smallest is not much more than an inch and a half. They are great devourers of the young fry of all fish, and are therefore destroyed as far as possible by the guardians of the best rivers. Without their spines they form good baits for trout and pike.

613. THE BULLHEAD (*Cottus Gobio*) is known by the enormous size of its head, which is out of all proportion to its body. It is a small fish, and conceals itself under stones, waiting there for its prey, and at the same time saving itself from the attacks of larger fish.

614. THE FLOUNDER (*Platessa Flesus*) is met with in the Thames in great numbers, and affords pretty good sport to the angler in that river, as well as most others near their mouths. It is a flat-fish of moderate size, seldom reaching to more than two pounds in weight. The upper part is of a dirty brown, with a few dusky-yellow spots; belly, white. It has a row of sharp small spines surrounding the body, and between it and the fins, by which it may be distinguished from other flat-fish.

615. THE SHARP-NOSED EEL (*Anguilla Acutirostris*), the BROAD-NOSED EEL (*A. Latirostris*), and the SNIG-EEL (*A. Mediorostris*) are the three varieties of the common eel known in Great Britain. They vary only as their distinctive names imply, in the shape of their noses. In length they are from 1 to 3 feet; colour, on the back sometimes a dark-olive brown, at others light-brown; belly, always white and silvery, especially in the silver-eel, a variety peculiar to some rivers. Head flat, and jaws more or less oblongated, but the lower jaw always the longer; eyes very near the mouth, and small, with a reddish iris; gill-opening set far back, and close to the temporal fin. The eel is now ascertained to spawn in the sea, for which purpose it descends from its usual haunts and visits the ocean. It has the power of overcoming all obstacles, because it can leave the water, and, by its serpent-like form, travel over or round any flood-gate or mill-dam in its course, whether up or down stream. It generally chooses dark stormy nights for this purpose; and its migration downwards takes place in the months of August, September, and October, during which time eels are taken in large numbers by the millers throughout the kingdom, who set their nets at the chief water-courses. Eels are generally considered to be viviparous, but they seem, like many other animals, sometimes to produce their *ova* already hatched, and at others to eject them with their contents still in an embryo state. The young first appear on the coasts in March and April, and are then seen in enormous quantities. They soon ascend the rivers, and by various devices they surmount the flood-gates, &c., which impede the progress of other fish; sometimes the millers put straw-ropes for this purpose, up which the young eels swarm in myriads. While ascending the larger rivers they may be seen in a double column, one close to each bank, swimming with great power and speed. These young eels are from half an inch to an inch in length. The eel is a very voracious fish, and will feed upon all kinds of garbage, and upon small fish, frogs, rats, &c.; it may be said to be the great scavenger of our rivers. Eels feed chiefly by night, and they lie chiefly by day in the deep pools of rivers, or under stones or stumps of trees, or among the weeds, or other impediments to the current of water, which they seem in all cases to dislike.

616. THE LAMPREY AND LAMPERN (*Lampetra Fluviatilis and L. Planeri*) are entirely unfitted for giving sport of any kind, and are taken with traps for the purposes of the table only.

APPARATUS USED IN FISHING.

SECT. 1.—THE LINE, REEL, AND HOOK.

617.—This, which is the essential part of all fishing-tackle, consists of a reel-line, varying in length, strength, and size, according to the nature of the fish which is sought after; of a reel to wind this upon, also varying in accordance with the line; and of a smaller and finer foot-length attached to the line, which is usually composed of silkworm-gut, hair, or gimp, and is armed with one or more hooks, variously baited.

618. REEL-LINES are made of horse-hair (from the tail), of silk, or silk and hair mixed, of Indian-weed, and of silkworm-gut. It is usual for the amateur fisherman to purchase these lines which are made by a small machine, but sometimes the angler prefers making them himself, and if at all handy, he may do this with great advantage by the following mode, which is much superior to the twisting-machine, because it admits of the introduction of fresh hair with much greater facility.

619. IN MAKING the horse-hair line, first procure a quantity of good hair, which may be bought at the shops; but if it can be obtained from a good *young* chestnut horse with a flaxen-tail so much the better. When such a horse is docked, a considerable portion of his tail with the hair attached is removed, and that is the very best for the present purpose. A grey horse with a silver mane will give white hair, which requires staining, but the colour of the flaxen mane is as good as any art can give. Young hair is twice as strong as the milk-white hair, which is peculiar to old horses. Next procure three pieces of strong goose-quill, each about half an inch long, and fit loosely into them three pieces of deal three or four inches long; then divide your hair intended for your line into three equal portions; thus, if your line is to be of eighteen hairs altogether, then let each of your quills receive six, leaving about four inches projecting; then push in the sticks gently, and tie the loose ends together, as shown in the annexed woodcut (*fig.* 1). The knot formed by the union of the three divisions is to be attached to some fixed object by a pin; then take out each stick, one after the other, and pass the quill up to within an inch of the knot, replace the stick, and take two of them in the left hand. The remaining stick is to be gently twisted from right to left, and when sufficiently so, passed over the other two also from right to left, when it should be grasped by the left hand, gently keeping up a slight strain upon the knot. At this time the three are in the position shown in the woodcut; then let the angler take hold of *a d*, draw it towards him about a quarter of an inch, allowing the hair to slip through the space between quill and wood; twist it as before, and pass it over to the left. Repeat this with *b e*, and then with *c f*, when *a b* will again occupy the same position as at first. By carrying on this process a line may soon be turned out of great strength, and of any degree of tightness of twist; but if too tight, it will be liable to be entangled, or to *kink*, as it is generally called. As soon as the angler has mastered this part of the process, and has twisted a few inches of line, he must divide the remaining length of his hair into the same number of portions as he has hairs in his line, and cut off one hair at each of these lengths, so that he may splice his line regularly throughout its whole length. As soon as one of these cut ends appears loose above the head of the quill, the stick must be removed, and another hair of full length inserted and twisted in with the rest, and so on with every succeeding break. In this way the line appears, when finished, to be furnished with a series of projecting hairs, but these may be removed without danger with a knife, or scissors, or a taper, previously soaking the whole line for twenty-four hours in water. The line may also be gradually reduced in size at the pleasure of the maker, by omitting to insert fresh hairs. By this mode all links and joints are avoided, and the line is everywhere within one hair of the full strength with which it would be furnished if joined in links in the ordinary way.

620. SILK AND HAIR MIXED LINES are those usually sold, and they are the best for all purposes, because they wind so well on the reel, and are strong and durable. They are made of all lengths, and may be purchased at any of the tackle-makers. INDIAN-WEED OR GRASS LINES are also sometimes used, but they do not stand sudden jars, being inclined to snap. A PLAITED SILK LINE is now made without hair, and is very generally adopted. It is much more free from kinking or ravelling than the other lines.

621. THE REEL is generally used by the angler, partly for the convenience of carrying the line safely, but chiefly in order to allow of rapid extension or drawing in of the line which is wound upon it. Multiplying-reels, in which, by the introduction of machinery, the barrel is made to travel several times to the single revolution of the

handle, were formerly much used, but they are now in great measure replaced by the more simple plan of having a large barrel or drum on which to wind the line, instead of a small central spindle. The difference will be seen at once by reference to the wood-cut, in which a view of both reels is given (*fig.* 2); *a* being the multiplying reel, and *b* the simple one with a large spindle. By the use of this large drum even a salmon line may be taken in as rapidly as can be desired, and the line lies much more evenly and free from any kind of hitch, with the great advantage that it will give off the line readily to the end.

622. THE FOOT-LENGTH, or the extreme portion of the line, is composed of finer materials than the reel-line, in order to escape the eye of the fish. It is generally made of pieces of gut, knotted together, and altogether comprising a length of from three to eight feet. Sometimes it is of single gut throughout, but generally of two or three thicknesses of twisted-gut at the end next the line, then of two, and finally of one piece of gut. This material is the produce of the silkworm, and is the unspun substance intended for silk, but made into gut instead by the art of man. The silkworm, just before spinning, is broken in two by the hands of the gut-maker, who, by drawing the pieces apart, obtains gut of any firmness, according to the length to which he pulls it. Considerable knack is required to make it uniformly round and free from weak places, which should be searched for carefully in selecting gut for the single lengths. Horse-hair is sometimes used for this purpose, and in some instances gimp, consisting of silk protected by wire. All these various sorts will be treated of under the respective kinds of fishing in which they are employed.

623. HOOKS are pieces of bent steel-wire, barbed at the point, and of various sizes and forms. They are made according to the respective patterns which are fancied by the English, Scotch, and Irish makers. The round-bend hook is that which is most used in England, the Limerick pattern being chiefly in vogue in Ireland, and the Scotch anglers using some of them, the former and others the latter; while many Scotchmen use what is called the sneckbend, differing slightly from both of the above, in being made of a more square shape. The round-bend hook is numbered from 1, the largest salmon size, to 14, the smallest midge. The best Irish hooks, made by Philips of Dublin, are classed in a different way: F E is intended for the smallest trouting-fly; F, the next; then F F; then, again, F F F. After this come C and C C; then B and B B. The C's and B's have intermediate or half-numbers, and above B B the hooks for salmon are known by numbers, beginning with B B, which corresponds with 9, and going on regularly up to No. 1.

624. Various articles are required for uniting these portions of the line—viz., silk of different degrees of strength, cobbler's wax, spirit varnish, and small scissors, &c.

625. THE JOINTS used are—first, *whipping*; second, *knotting*. Whipping consists in drawing successive circles of silk, well waxed, tightly around the two objects laid in apposition; as, for instance, two portions of the line, or the line and hook. This is finished off by slipping the end of the silk through the last circle and drawing tight, and, if necessary, repeating the operation again and again; this is called the half-hitch. Knotting is effected by several modes, the most common of which is the water-knot, which is managed as follows:— Lay the two pieces of gut or hair together, one overlapping the other three inches or more, then hold one end in the left hand and form a simple slip-knot upon it, turn the other end to the right and do the same thing, then draw the two together and the knot is complete; by whipping with fine waxed silk this knot is made still more firm. The advantage of this knot is that it will never give way to a direct pull, and yet may always be undone without difficulty.

626. THE ACCESSORIES to the line are the float and the shot or leads. These are used in bottom-fishing only, and are intended to keep the hook at a certain distance from the bottom. The float is either of quill or cork, and is fixed upon the line by a ring at one end and a sliding-quill at the other. The shot are partially split and then brought together again upon the line. In this way, by plumbing the depth of the water, and adjusting the float so as to keep the bait at a certain depth, the object of the bottom-fisher is attained.

627. BOX-SWIVELS AND HOOK-SWIVELS may be readily understood from their name, and are used in spinning tackle, in order to prevent the line from twisting.

628. GIMP is composed of silk or other material strong enough to resist any straining force applied to it, and protected from the teeth of the fish, or from sharp stones, by fine brass wire neatly wound round. It is made of various sizes and strength.

SECT. 2.—THE ROD.

629. THE ROD is the machine with which the line is conveyed to the place where the fish is the most likely to take it, and with which the various manœuvres prior to his capture are effected. It is made of several pieces united by joints, and these are of varying size, length, and materials, according

to the kind of fishing to which it is to be applied. It is also sold to suit all purposes in one by changing the top joints, and it is then called a general rod; but though this may suit the pedestrian tourist who wishes to avoid carrying more than one rod, yet it interferes a good deal with the efficiency of both, and especially does it fail as a fly-rod. It is, however, well enough suited to the beginner. The extra pieces are contained in the butt, which is 'hollowed out to receive them. The specific varieties of rods will come under consideration in each chapter devoted to the particular sport for which they are intended, but I may enumerate them here as the general rod, the trolling rod, the trout fly-fishing rod, and the salmon fly-fishing rod. The materials of which these are composed are ash, hickory, lancewood, and cane, which are united together by brass ferules. Whalebone is also sometimes used in the top joints of fly-rods, but these are made so much better by the tackle-maker than by the amateur, that it is useless to go into the description of their manufacture. Mr. Blacker, of Dean Street, Soho, or Mr. Farlow of the Strand, will serve the young angler with rods in every variety, and of the very best quality; and if he finds that he cannot afford their prices, which are as low as a good rod can be made for, he can procure plenty at the cheap shops which will answer his purpose much better than any of home manufacture.

SECT. 3.—NATURAL AND GROUND-BAITS.

630. THE EARTH-WORM is the most primitive and simple of all baits, and is that which is generally first used by the juvenile angler, because it is easily obtained, and applied without difficulty. There are several varieties of these worms, known to anglers as the *dew-worm*, or *lob-worm*, the *marsh-worm*, the *tagtail*, the *brandling*, and the *red-worm*.

631. THE DEW-WORM, or large garden-worm, is of considerable size, varying from 6 to 12 inches in length when extended. The tail tapers somewhat, but in the squirrel-tailed variety it is flattened. In colour this worm is of a dull brick-red, approaching to a crimson towards the head. These worms are obtained either by digging, or by searching for them quietly at night with a candle and lantern on the lawns or paths of the garden. In dry weather they are always out when the dew is falling.

632. THE MARSH-WORM, OR BLUE-HEAD, is found in moist and undrained localities, where they may be obtained with a candle and lantern in large numbers during the fine summer nights. In colour they are of a light dirty or brownish-purple. These worms should be kept in damp moss with a little earth mixed with it. A variety of this worm found in land only partially marshy, is called in Scotland the BLACK-HEAD or BUTTON-WORM, and is more tough, and therefore better calculated for standing the rough treatment which it must undergo in swift and wide streams. It is an excellent bait for trout.

633. THE TAGTAIL is common in good strong clays, which are well manured for turnips, mangold-wurzel, &c. It is a small worm of about 2 or 3 inches in length. Head larger, and of a deeper blue than the body, which is a dingy-red; tail, yellowish.

634. THE BRANDLING is a small worm found in artificial composts, and in rotten tan, or other decaying vegetable matter, of a dirty-red colour, approaching to brown.

635. THE RED-WORM is about the same size as the brandling, which it resembles in all respects but colour, that being in the red-worm exactly what its name implies. It is found in the banks of ditches and sewers. The *gilt-tail* is a variety of this worm, but larger, and of a paler colour towards the tail.

636. ALL THESE WORMS SHOULD BE SCOURED, a process which consists in starving them, by placing them in damp moss, neither too wet nor too dry. The worms here are not only deprived of their usual food, but in their efforts to escape they mechanically compress their bodies between the fibres of the moss, and in that way completely empty themselves of their fœcal contents. Before putting them in the moss, Mr. Stoddart recommends that worms should be placed in water for a few minutes, after which they should be suffered to crawl over a dry board, in order still further to cleanse their skins. They may then be transferred to the moss, as described above. The worms should be examined from day to day, and those which are unhealthy or injured should be removed. When the worms are quite sufficiently scoured, they should be stored for use. Three or four days is the average time required for scouring.

637. WORMS ARE PRESERVED in the following manner:—Procure some fresh mutton suet, cut it fine, and boil it in a quart of water till dissolved; then dip in this two or three pieces of coarse new wrapper large enough to supply each variety of worm, which should not be mixed together. When these are cold, put them into separate earthen jars, with some damp earth and the worms which are to be kept, and tie over all a piece of open and coarse muslin.

638. SHRIMPS are used for angling in docks and canals, and are good baits for perch, if used alive.

639. The Cockchafer is a common bait, but is not of much value in angling, except for chub.

640. Dung-Beetles, of various kinds, are also employed, and some anglers use thém after removing their wing-cases. They should be placed crosswise on the hook.

641. Grasshoppers form good baits for some fish, and are much used for chub in particular. They are met with after the beginning of June till the end of September. The greener and larger they are, the better they take.

642. Butterflies and Moths are also sometimes efficient baits, but their artificial representations are more commonly used.

643. The Ephemera, or Natural May-Fly, is used as a bait during the period when it comes forth in countless myriads. By baiting with this fly in May and June success is often attained, putting two flies on the hook at the same time.

644. Caddis-Flies are also used in the same way as the ephemera.

645. Humble-Bees, Blue-Bottle Flies, Gnats, and Ant-Flies are held in estimation by many anglers, as well as the Harry-long-legs, and the Common House-Fly.

646. Many Larvæ or Grubs are used in bottom-fishing, and are of great service in that department. Of these the principal are—1st, *flesh maggots*; 2nd, *beetle larvæ*; 3rd, *caddies*; and 4th, *caterpillars*.

647. Flesh Maggots, or Gentles, are obtained and scoured in the following manner:—Procure any kind of flesh, or the body of any small animal. If there is any difficulty about this, the liver of a horse or cow answers remarkably well. With a knife cut some deep gashes in the substance of the liver or flesh, and hang it up in a shady place, but near the haunts of the blow-fly. In a few days the maggots will attain a lively state of existence; but they require about a week to reach their full development to the green or soft state, and another week to reach their maturity, when they are large and fat, with black heads. The various stages are adapted for different fish. Blow-flies are abroad from May to the end of November, or even to the middle of December in mild seasons. The scouring of these gentles is effected by placing them for a few days in a mixture of bran and fine sand, slightly damp. By this process they are emptied of their contents, and rendered tough in their skins. When the object is to preserve them in this state for many days, they must be kept in a very cool place, such as a cellar, or they even should be buried in the earth. Without attention to this precaution they are almost sure to assume the chrysalis condition, in which stage they are useless as baits. A low temperature and exclusion from air and light retard this development; and by burying the carcase of a small animal (after the larvæ are a day old) in a cool place, and confined in a box containing a mixture of dry cow-dung and fine earth, the gentles may be preserved in their larva state during the whole winter. The place selected should be protected from severe frosts, which would kill the gentles, and therefore an outhouse is well suited for this purpose, or any space in the garden well sheltered by a thick shrub, such as the lauristinus.

648. The Larvæ of the various beetles are called by anglers, the *white-worm grub*, the *cow-dung grub*, the *cabbage grub*, and the *meal-worm*. The first is the larva of the cock-chafer, and is found in loose loamy soils, especially near the horse-chestnut. It may be easily found by following the plough. The second, as its name implies, is found in cow-dung, and is the larva of several of the beetle tribe. The third is found in the stalks of old cabbages, and often about their roots, and is the larva of two or three varieties of the beetle. The last is found in the meal-tub, is much smaller than the three first mentioned varieties of grubs, and is not so good for angling purposes as the gentle.

649. These Grubs may all be Preserved by simply placing them with some of the earth in which they are found, in any receptacle, keeping them afterwards in a cool situation.

650. Caddies are the larvæ of the ephemera, or May-fly, as well as the stone-fly and the caddis-fly. They are easily found beneath the stones, weeds, &c., of shallow brooks, and may be stored by putting them in water, with some sand, in a cool place. By placing them in a perforated box, they may be suffered to remain in a running stream, where they continue to grow and thrive as well as in their native haunts. They are not, however, much prized as angling baits.

651. Caterpillars, or the larvæ of the butterfly, are either smooth or rough. The former are not much used, and the latter are so thoroughly imitated by the artificial fly called the palmer that they are scarcely ever employed. There is no doubt that in angling natural products are better than artificial, if they are equally capable of enduring the rough usage required to drag them through the water. In this respect it is that the artificial palmer beats the hairy caterpillar, its original; and hence the latter is almost wholly driven out of the angler's list of baits.

652. Salmon-Roe is a very favourite and killing bait for trout, and is found to be so

destructive that its use is often considered to be a species of poaching. I cannot understand on what principle this odious stigma should be cast upon its adoption, because it may be employed, like any other bait, in open day; and the only objection to it which can be urged is its very great success. No one would call an unerring shot a poacher, simply because he kills more than his neighbours; then why should the bait which is more successful than any other labour under this imputation? It appears to me that every one is straining to effect a certain purpose, viz., the killing of the greatest number of fish, and yet when a certain mode of attaining this object is at hand, its adoption is forbidden because it will ensure what all are aiming at, and by open means too. However, as I cannot discover any real foundation for this crusade against the salmon-roe, I shall include it in the list of baits, and describe its preparation and mode of application to the hook. The roe itself should be collected as near the time of spawning as possible, and should either be preserved whole, or be made into a paste at once. If the former, the best way is to keep it in a jar, with alternate layers of wool. The roe should be carefully separated from its enveloping membrane, and should be sprinkled with salt, as also should the wool. When the jar is filled, it should be tied down with a bladder, and kept in a cool and rather moist place, such as a cellar.

653. SALMON-ROE PASTE is made by boiling the roe without its envelope for 20 minutes, then bruising it in a marble mortar until it forms a uniform mass. After this add to each pound of the roe one ounce of common salt and a quarter of an ounce of saltpetre; beat them all up together, and keep in a jar tied down with bladder.

654. SHRIMP PASTE is made exactly in the same way, after removing the shells.

655. BREAD PASTE is also used as a means of taking fish, and is made from new bread, well kneaded, and with or without the addition of honey. It is either used in the white state, or it is coloured with vermilion, lake, or turmeric. Sometimes stale bread is used, but it requires more kneading, and the addition of gum water, or soaked greaves, or some more adhesive material. It is often flavoured with the roe of salmon, or other fish; the size of the portion used must vary with the fish angled for. Cheese is also sometimes made the foundation of paste, either by itself or mixed with bread; by constant kneading it becomes perfectly tough, and withstands the action of the water for a long time. A peculiar kind of paste, called *patent paste*, is made by washing away all but the pure gluten. A paste of flour is first to be made in the usual way, then by successive washings in cold water, by degrees the process is completed, care being taken not to dissolve the gluten itself by mixing it up with the water; and to avoid this, after each successive washing, let the paste drain for a few minutes. This paste will keep for any length of time, if protected from the action of the air by wrapping it in sheet-lead.

656. GROUND-BAIT.—The object of this very general accessory to the angler's art is to collect an unusual number of fish to a given spot, and at the same time to do this by offering them a quantity of bait of the same kind as that which is afterwards to be used on the hook, but of an inferior quality to it. Thus if intending to fish with earthworms, bait with unscoured worms, and fish with them well scoured. Worms in clay-balls are a good ground-bait, because they are not all at once presented to the fish, but appear gradually as the clay dissolves. Mr. Salter, who is a good authority in bottom-fishing, recommends the crumb of a quartern-loaf to be cut in slices 2 inches thick, and soaked in water till thoroughly saturated, then squeeze it tolerably dry, and add bran and pollard, kneading all together till a firm mass is the result as tough as clay. *Soaked greaves* mixed with tenacious clay are a very useful ground-bait; and may be made into large masses, and thrown into the water in lumps of two or three pounds weight. *Gentles* mixed with sand are also used, but they should be unscoured, and coarse old carrion gentles for this purpose are the best, as the fish will be attracted by them, but will take the scoured gentle on the hook in preference.

657. DEAD FISH AS BAITS are usually so arranged on the hooks as to spin or rotate on their axis rapidly, by the action of the current, or by drawing them through the water. This is an unnatural motion, and unlike any movement of any known inhabitant of the river; nevertheless, it takes well with many fish; and, judged by that unerring criterion, it may safely be approved of and adopted. Minnows, parr-tails, gudgeon, sticklebacks, and other small fish, are thus used; but the preference is always given to the two first when they can be procured. There are various modes of baiting with minnows and these small fish, and almost every fisherman has his particular whims and oddities here as well as in other matters connected with fishing. Nothing could more completely disprove the necessity for the adoption of any peculiar mode of baiting than the immense variety in the plans of the most successful

anglers. Some use one hook, some two, some three, and others even four. Some—as, for instance, Mr. Stoddart—bait tail-foremost, after removing the head; others always take care to present the head to the trout or pike. The great thing to be attended to is to make the bait spin well, which can only be done by producing a slight curve in its body, and by making the line draw it on one side more than the other. In this way, with one or two swivels, which prevent the line throwing any impediment in the way, the bait rotates rapidly if well applied, and the fish is deceived to his ruin. When two hooks only are used, the extreme one is larger than the other (usually Nos. 3 and 5, English sizes), and they are whipped on the same piece of gut or gimp, at an interval of about half an inch clear between them. A baiting-needle is required for most of these hooks, but here it is not necessary, as the larger hook is passed through the mouth and out at the root of the tail, so as to leave the barb free. When this has been done nicely the min-now assumes a bent form, corresponding with that of the hook, and if properly put on, it will spin or rotate when rapidly drawn through the water. But for this purpose its mouth must be closed mechanically, and this is effected either by a leaden cap which slips down over the line, or by the second hook being passed through both lips, and thus holding them shut; or sometimes, in addition, by a few stitches with a fine needle and thread. Colonel Hawker recommends a hook or two to be allowed to float loosely and openly by the side, on a stout piece of gut, but I cannot advise their adoption. The usual mode of employing the third hook is to whip it on to a piece of gut about an inch long, and then to include this gut in the whipping of the second or smaller hook, which it should also match in size. This third hook then lies closely adapted to the side of the bait, but not floating loosely, as advised by Colonel Hawker. The two first are applied exactly in the same way as when two hooks only are used, when the third will lie flat against the side of the bait, and retains its position there by the stiffness of the gut or gimp. This last form is used for the application of the celebrated parr-tail as a bait, which is much used in Scotland; and is strongly recommended by Mr. Stoddart, one of the highest authorities on the subject. He advises all the fins and tails to be cut off, and the head and shoulders to be then obliquely sliced off with a sharp knife. When this is done, the tail-end is to be used forward—that is, nearest the rod, and is then made to appear as the head of a fish. In this mode the gudgeon, dace, or other small fish may be prepared, when the

parr is not to be found; and they answer well for large trout or pike. But nothing takes so completely and generally as a good minnow of the proper size, requiring no paring, and fitting the hooks exactly so as to allow the one to project slightly through the tail, while the other closes the mouth. Some other modes are described as useful variations in adapting dead fish-baits, but I believe the double or treble-hook, as above, will suit all purposes where the bait is required to spin rapidly, whether it be the entire fish or part, as already mentioned. The gudgeon, loach, or dace may be divided in the same way as the parr, and will spin remarkably well when used as he recommends that little fish to be employed; as will also the perch itself when deprived of its back fin, or any of the smaller fish which are attractive to the pike. All these various hooks require swivel-traces, single or double, which will be found described under the head of Pike-fishing.

658. MINNOWS ARE ALSO MOUNTED ON GORGE-HOOKS : see woodcut, in which *a* represents the hook itself, and *b* the fish and hook

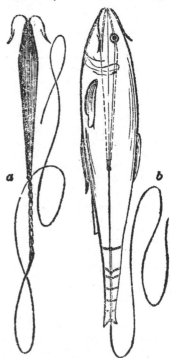

ready for use. Gorge-hooks are either single or double, the latter being represented in the annexed woodcut. In baiting this hook, after it has been whipped to a piece of strong gut looped at the other end, take a needle used for the purpose, and by its means draw the gut and hook through the mouth and body of the fish, bringing the needle out at the root of the tail, and leaving the hook buried in the body of the minnow, with the bend and barb of the hook on each side of its mouth. After the needle has been brought out, re-enter it on the other side, so as to include a piece of the flesh of the tail in a loop of the gut. If this is neatly done it will be found, after drawing the gut tight, that there is no disposition in the fish to slip off the hook, unless very flabby, in which case a single turn of light silk tied tightly round the root of the tail is sure to make all safe. Besides these modes some others are used in pike-fishing, but as they are peculiar to that department, they will be treated of under the head of Pike-fishing.

659. DEAD MINNOWS MAY BE PRESERVED for use, as well as other small fish, by keeping them in salt and water, or pyroligneous acid and water; but the latter I believe gives them a flavour which fish do not like. Sugar also will answer the purpose, or any kind of spirit—as whisky or gin; but by far the best material is oil, which will keep them sweet, and also stiff, for a great length of time, if they are just raised to the boiling temperature, by immersing the vessel containing the oil and fish in boiling water for a few minutes. More than this renders them tender and liable to break. All fish-bait should be killed by a blow on the head as soon as taken.

660. LIVE FISH form a very common lure for the larger kinds of fish, and they are used by inserting the hook in some part of the body not necessarily vital. This is called ROVING, and is practised with any of the smaller fish, such as minnows, bleak, gudgeon, &c., in capturing trout, perch, pike, &c. The hook is merely entered in the back close to the fin, and the barb is suffered to protrude above that appendage, and with the point of the hook directed towards the tail of the fish. The line must be shotted so as to sink the fish to the required depth, and it may be used with or without a float. Some other methods of fixing the hooks have been recommended, by which the hook is entered in one part, then made to traverse the fish under the skin, and finally brought out at the mouth; but they are so abominably cruel that I must decline having anything to do with their description. All field sports are too much mixed up with an undercurrent of cruelty; but where there is a choice, no man of any ordinary feeling will hesitate in selecting the least severe modes of taking game.

661. FROGS AND NEWTS may be used exactly in the same way as the minnow, by passing the hook through the skin of the back. They must be well shotted, to keep them down, and must be raised to the surface every four or five minutes, to allow them to respire.

662. MINNOWS ARE PROCURED for the purpose of using them as baits, either by angling for them, and carefully removing them from the hook, and then placing them at once in a vessel of water, or by taking them with a large hoop-net or fine casting-net. The last plan is that usually adopted, but it requires some little practice for its use, and nothing but an ocular demonstration will give any idea of the mode of employment. Any fisherman will, however, initiate the tyro for a trifling consideration. With the hoop-net they may be taken, by sinking it by means of weights to the bottom of the brook; then, after enticing the minnows by means of small pieces of worms dropped over it, the string is suddenly raised, and the minnows are caught in its meshes.

663. MINNOWS MAY BE PRESERVED ALIVE by placing them in a perforated tin or wooden case, and sinking them in any running stream, in which mode they retain their health and liveliness for an indefinite period. They may also be kept alive for a long time in any clean vessel by changing their water frequently; but in this way they are not so healthy as in the above plan. When wanted for use, a small bait-kettle is used with a perforated lid, and capable of containing from one to two quarts of water. This should be kept under the shade of a tree or hedge while the fishing is going on, as the heat of the sun soon raises the temperature of the water to such a height as to destroy the life of the fish, or so nearly so as to cause their death soon after putting them on the hook.

SECT. 4.—ARTIFICIAL BAITS AND FLIES.

664. MINNOWS are now manufactured so as closely to resemble the real fish in appearance, but most of them fail in imitating the consistence and softness of the original, and consequently do not take nearly so well as their appearance would lead one to expect. The Archimedian minnow spins beautifully, and so do some others constructed on similar principles, and all will take good fish, but certainly not so well as the real minnow. In many localities, however, these are very scarce, and there the substitute is certainly useful. Mr. Flinn's flexible minnows are far the best, as they are soft and yielding to the grasp of the fish; they are made of gutta percha, painted very closely in imitation of the minnow, gudgeon, &c., and are of sizes suited to all fish, from the trout to the salmon. The Archimedian, on the other hand, is hard and inflexible, and though it spins well, and is to the eye all that can be

desired, yet from its hardness to the touch it is very apt to deter fish from a close approach, and is not so successful as Mr. Flinn's imitation. Mr. Blacker, also, has recently introduced a modification of the "devil-bait," with the addition of a pair of Archimedian fins; this is said to spin well, and to take good fish, but I know nothing personally of its properties.

666. ARTIFICIAL FLIES are so numerous, and their importance is so great, that a great part of the angler's time is generally occupied in mastering a knowledge of their various forms, and the mode of tying them. All of them are composed of three essential parts: first, the hook; second, the gut or loop to attach the hook to the line; and third, the various articles tied on the hook for the purpose of imitating the natural fly. The angler will have no difficulty in procuring his hooks and gut, both of which however he ought to select with great care; but he will experience some little vexation and disappointment when he attempts to tie an artificial fly, especially without the practical instruction of some older craftsman. Mr. Blacker, of Dean-street, Soho, has endeavoured to supply this *desideratum*, by publishing a small 8vo. volume in explanation of the whole process of making artificial trout and salmon-flies. His illustrations are most beautifully executed, being engraved on steel, and coloured by hand in the most elaborate manner; and every young fly-fisher who aspires to any degree of proficiency in this elegant art ought to possess himself of this volume. His great practice as a fly-fisher, and also as a manufacturer of flies, renders him perhaps more capable than any other man in the kingdom of performing the task which he has attempted.

666. THE MATERIALS are first to be collected, and if they are not at once bought in the mass from the fishing-tackle maker, they require some little time to get them together. They should be kept in a case expressly for them; the best form for which is somewhat like that of the common travelling writing-case. In this the body of the case contains the solid articles, such as wax, hooks, scissors, &c., and the lid may be converted into a series of large pockets, for feathers, silks, wools, &c.

FLY-MAKING MATERIALS.

1st—Hooks of all sizes.
2nd—Gut, plain and dyed, fine and stout.
3rd—Fine, curved, and common scissors.
4th—Nippers and pliers.
5th—Silks of all kinds and colours.
6th—Wax, spirit—varnish, and brush.
7th—Wing-picker or pointer.
8th—Pair of fine spring-forceps.

9th—Dubbings, viz.: pig's wool, mohair, coloured wools, hare's ear-fur, white seal's or white rabbit's fur, water-rat's fur, cowhair, squirrel's fur, mole's fur, black spaniel's ear-fur, black bear's hair, &c.
10th—Tinsels, viz.: gold and silver, flat wire, twisted and fretted cords, &c.
11th—Feathers for trout-flies, viz.: wing-feathers of snipe, woodcock, partridge, landrail, thrush, lark, starling, blackbird, wren, waterhen, coot, and redwing. Body feathers of grouse, pheasant, mallard, teal, and golden plover. Hackles of barn-door fowl in all colours. Neck-feathers of partridge, starling, lapwing, wren, to be used as hackles. Peacock-herls and ostrich-herls of all colours, dyed.
12th—Feathers for salmon-flies: including those of the turkey in all shades, golden pheasant neck and body-feathers, silver pheasant, common pheasant, and argus pheasant, peacock, jungle-cock. Blue feathers of the lowrie and mackaw, and of the jay's wing. Green feathers of the mackaw. Besides the natural colours, there should be dyed cock's hackles of larger size than for trout, of the following shades, viz.: purple, blue, crimson, scarlet, orange, yellow, green, and brown. Feathers of the kingfisher, swan's feathers for dyeing. Guinea-fowl, bittern, heron (pendant and breast feathers), ostrich, and raven. Few collections comprehend the whole of the above, but the angler may endeavour to obtain as many of them as possible; still he may rest satisfied even if he is not able to fill up every link in so extensive an assortment.

667. DYEING is required when the natural feathers, &c., are not sufficiently varied. It is an art exceedingly simple in principle, though not always so easy in practice, if the colours are required to be very delicate or brilliant. All the light and transparent shades require for their perfect development either a white material, or one of a shade somewhat resembling the intended one. Thus, the pale or bright yellows can only succeed with a white ground; reds will take on brown or yellow; greens on any light colour, but not well on deep brown or red; purple on light brown or red, &c., &c. The chief materials required to be dyed for the purposes of the angler are silk, feathers, and wool, or hair. The first is usually to be bought of the required colour and shade, and it may therefore be dismissed from consideration. The second and third require to be well scoured before they will take the dye, and for this purpose a solution of carbonate of potash (one drachm to a pint of water) is to be employed, or putrid urine, the material being well soaked, and then washed in it, and finally thoroughly rinsed

in clean water. All dyes, or nearly all, are effected upon the same principle; namely, to saturate the substance with the colouring matter while in a soluble state and dissolved in water, and then to add some substance that will convert the soluble dye into an insoluble one, by which process it is retained within the substance of the material, and is rendered permanent, or incapable of being washed out. This latter substance is called a *mordant*. Thus in almost every case the art of dyeing requires the dye-stuff and the mordant to be separately applied; sometimes the mordant being first introduced, and then the dye-stuff, whilst at others the opposite mode is adopted. In some cases, however, the two are applied together, and in others no mordant whatever is required.

668. THE MORDANTS used in dyeing are numerous; but for our purposes a few only need be employed. These are—first, alum and acetate of alumine; secondly, muriate of tin; thirdly, nutgalls; fourthly, acetate of iron. Alum is most generally used, with the addition of a little cream of tartar, which is added in order to engage the *excess* of acid when decomposed by the oily matter contained in the material. Half an ounce of alum and half a drachm of cream of tartar are dissolved in boiling water in an earthen pipkin, and the materials are then boiled for two hours in the solution, which is called "a bath." They are then taken out, drained, and washed, and are ready for the dye. For dyeing feathers, purified alum should be used, as the common sort is impregnated with sulphate of iron. The other mordants are used in the same way, in quantities which will be specified when required.

669. THE DYE-STUFFS are either soluble or insoluble in water. When the former is the case, as it generally is, they are dissolved in it at a boiling temperature in an earthen pipkin. Into this the material, after receiving the mordant, as described in the preceding paragraph, is plunged, and allowed to remain a specified time, varying according to circumstances. When the colouring matter is by nature insoluble in water, as in the case of indigo, its solution is effected by means of some other fluid, with which the article to be coloured is imbued; after which, by the addition of some third body, it is again rendered insoluble, and thus retained in the meshes of the material.

670. To DYE BLACK.—Make a mordant-bath of one drachm of acetate of iron dissolved in half a pint of water; boil the materials in this for two hours, then rinse, and boil gently for one or two hours, according to the shade required, in the following dye-bath:—Madder and logwood, of each two ounces; water, half a pint.

671. PURPLE is dyed by using the above mordant-bath and half the quantity of dye-stuff. If a crimson-purple is required, the mordant must be composed of equal quantities of acetate of iron and acetate of alumine.

672. CRIMSON OR CLARET.—The mordant must be composed of one part of acetate of iron and three of acetate of alumine; then use the madder and logwood as before. If required to be very bright, use the alumine without the iron. Another mode consists in using the alum-bath as a mordant, and cochineal as the dye-stuff; but there is not so rich a result as with the first receipt.

673. RED.—Mordant of acetate of alumine alone. Dye-stuff, madder or cochineal.

674. SCARLET is dyed by making a mordant-bath of muriate of tin, two drachms to the half-pint, with the same quantity of cream of tartar. Then make a dye-bath of three or four drachms of cochineal, and boil till dissolved, after which the materials must be gently simmered in it for an hour or two, and then dipped in the mordant-bath, examining carefully to see when the full colour desired is obtained.

675. ORANGE.—First use the mordant-bath of acetate of alumine, then boil in a dye-bath of madder, and afterwards one of quercitron. The exact shade must be obtained by repeated trials.

676. YELLOW.—Very strong mordant-bath of acetate of alumine, then dip in a dye-bath of quercitron or turmeric, varying the quantity according to the shade required.

677. A GOLDEN COLOUR is obtained by alternately using two baths, one of copperas and the other of lime-water (one drachm of the copperas to half a pint of water). By the absorption of oxygen, the protoxide of iron soon passes into the golden-coloured deutoxide.

678. A BUFF is obtained by a diluted bath of each of the last materials.

679. BLUE is produced by rendering indigo soluble, either by dissolving it in three times its weight of sulphuric acid, which, however, to a certain extent destroys the toughness of the feathers, or by adding to it equal quantities of potash and orpiment, which make it of a greenish-yellow for a time, from which it recovers its colour by exposure to the air; or by adding to the indigo a solution of copperas in lime-water. Both of these last processes, however, require some time and exposure to the air to produce the full blue colour. The proportions are one of indigo to two of the copperas and lime, respectively.

680. GREEN is produced by dyeing first the yellow colour, and then dipping in the

indigo till a proper shade is produced. It must always be remembered that the blue becomes more fully developed by time, and consequently the colour should be at first of a more yellow shade than is required.

681. The following shades are not so permanent as those already given, but they are sufficiently so to suit the purposes of the angler:—

682. A PALE GREEN, as required for the green-drake, is obtained by using the muriate of tin mordant, and then immersing in a dye-bath composed of prussian-blue and tincture of turmeric, both being used very sparingly.

683. LAVENDER OR SLATE is obtained by bruised nut-galls and copperas, with more or less logwood according to the shade required.

684. BROWNS may be procured either by boiling walnut-shells down to a strong solution, or, when required of a more chestnut hue, it may be made of that colour by boiling in a bath composed of a small handful each of sumach and alder-bark boiled in half a pint of water with half a drachm of copperas.

685. OLIVE is obtained by adding to the green, as above described, a portion of the walnut-dye, more or less according to the colour required. Brown-olive requires the foundation to be of the walnut decoction, and only a little green to be added, while green-olive must be fast dyed in the usual way of a green colour, and then submitted to the walnut decoction.

686. WAX is used either in the shape of the common "cobbler's-wax," or in a transparent form, composed of—white-wax half an ounce, Burgundy-pitch half a drachm, lard half a drachm; melt all together, then cool, and when nearly cold work and draw it well out till it becomes white, opaque, and ductile.

687. SPIRIT-VARNISH is sold in all the shops of good quality; and, also, good TURPENTINE-VARNISH, which should be obtained of the best coachmaker's quality. It cannot be made in small quantities nearly so well as by the varnish-makers.

688. Such are all the materials which are necessary for artificial fly-making. We will now proceed to consider the best mode of tying them on the hook.

689. GENERAL PRINCIPLES OF FLY-MAKING. In all cases the gut and hook should first be selected of such size and strength as will serve to hold the fish which they are intended to capture; then whip the hook on one end of this piece of gut, after flattening it with the teeth, using for the whipping a piece of strong silk well waxed with cobbler's-wax. Sometimes the continuation

of this same silk is used for the purpose of tying on the feathers, wool, &c., but usually a finer kind is employed, and especially where great neatness is required, as in the smaller sized-flies. Some fly-makers begin their whipping at the bend, and others at the end of the shank, but this is very immaterial, and is almost always a matter of choice. The most simple fly is made up of a head, body, and legs; the next stage of complication gives a pair of simple wings, then a tail, and finally in the salmon-fly, the compound bodies which separate joints and legs, and the wings and tails, composed of various-coloured feathers.

690. THE BODY is made of one or other of the following materials: first, coloured floss-silk wound round the shank regularly, and giving a uniform, smooth, and shining surface, as in the caperer; secondly, of wool, fur, or mohair called dubbings, attached to the tying-silk by the adhesive power of the wax with which it is covered, and forming with it a rough hairy line, which is then wound round the shank from the end to the bend, or *vice versâ*—this forms a rough hairy-looking body, as in the hare-lug and numerous other flies; thirdly, of peacock or ostrich herl, either of which is wound singly or in double layers round the shank, and forms the body of several of the most killing flies—as, for instance, the black-gnat and peacock-hackle; fourthly, of a foundation composed of either of the above materials ribbed with silk, or gold, or silver-twist wound spirally round, or sometimes in a circular manner at intervals in the body, or as a terminal joint at the lowest part.

691. THE LEGS OR FEELERS are generally made of feathers wound spirally round the shank of the hook, but sometimes dependance is placed on the dubbing, which, after it is wound round, is pulled out by means of the picker, and made to take the form of the legs, as in the hare-lug and brown-rail. This, however, answers badly, except in very small flies, as all the dubbings lie close in the water, and do not serve to conceal the bend and barb of the hook like the hackles or any other kind of feather. Generally speaking, the legs are imitated by some of the many-coloured cock's hackles, which the fly-fisher ought to possess, either of the natural colours of the cock, or dyed by one of the receipts given above. These are first tied at the point to the shank, beginning always from the side next the bend and ending at the shoulder, and thus keeping the longest fibres of the hackle outwards. Sometimes the whole body is invested with two or more hackles, after first making it up full with dubbing

R

of some kind. This is seen in the single and double palmers.

692. THE HEAD is generally made by a few turns of silk, or by the black herl of the ostrich, or that of the peacock's feather.

693. THE TAIL, when used, is composed in the trout-fly of two or three fibres of some feather, as in the grey-drake; or of two fine hairs, as in the stone-fly. In the salmon-fly it is often much more complicated, and is then generally composed of a part of the crest-feather of the golden pheasant, with or without the addition of a tag of coloured silk or other gaudy material.

694. THE WINGS in the trout-fly are generally composed of two pieces of the web of some of the feathers enumerated in the list already given. They are sometimes tied on at the shoulder, in the direction which they finally assume, but the best plan, and that which gives the best appearance in the water, is to tie them on first the reverse way to that which they must take when finished, and then turn them back again, and retain them in that position with a couple of turns of the silk. In the salmon-fly the wings are often made up of six different feathers, each called a topping.

695. A LITTLE VARNISH added with a fine brush to the head, and also at the lower end next the tail, but with great care, prevents those parts from coming to pieces, and greatly adds to the lasting properties of the fly.

696. HACKLES AND PALMERS.—The mode of tying the peacock-hackle (fig. 1), which is one of the simplest of all flies, is as follows:—Begin by whipping the hook on the gut, leaving a loose end of the silk hanging from the shoulder where the whipping is to be commenced. When the whipping has proceeded to within two or three turns of the bend, include within its folds the ends of two or three peacock-herls, which are to be left projecting beyond the bend, and after making these turns fasten off. Then take a red cock's hackle, and smooth the fibres of it well; with a pair of scissors trim these off at the point, leaving the shank bare for about an eighth of an inch; next include this within two or three turns of the silk left at the shoulder, directing the hackle towards the gut and fastening off the silk. Then taking the bend of the hook between the finger and thumb of the left hand, lay hold of the herls with the right, and wind them carefully round the shank of the hook up to the point where the hackle is tied, where they are to be included in the silk which is still left there and then cut off. The body is now complete, but the legs are still to be imitated by the hackle, which should be carefully wound round the hook

above the herl; arranging the fibres, as it is wound, by means of the picker, and fastening off at last by means of the silk which is still projecting, and left for the purpose. Now cut off the silk at both ends lay on carefully a very little varnish at each end, and the fly is complete. All palmers and hackles (figs. 2, 3, and 4) are made on this principle, substituting various feathers for the cock's hackle, and various dubbings for the peacock-herl.

697. SIMPLE WINGED-FLIES.—Sometimes a pair of wings are tied on at the same time as the hackle-point, and afterwards the hackle is wound round the shank, and thus serves to keep the wings from lying flat against the hook when in the water. (See the black gnat, hare-lug, yellow sally, oak-fly, caperer, &c.)

THE BLACK GNAT (fig. 5) is tied in the same way as the peacock-hackle, using a smaller hook (No. 13), and fine black silk. A small black ostrich-herl forms the body, and a piece of the starling's wing-feather the wings. A very fine black cock's hackle is used for the legs.

THE HARE-LUG (fig. 6) is composed of a body consisting of a dubbing from the back of the hare's ear, making it thin and neat towards the tail, and pretty stout near the shoulder. The hook is of the same size as in the black gnat, and the wings are the same. After these are tied, pick out a little of the dubbing to make the legs.

THE YELLOW SALLY (fig. 7), is tied exactly like the hare-lug, with the substitution of yellow or buff mohair or fur for that of the hare, and the addition of a fine yellow cock's hackle for legs; wings from a feather from the inside of the thrush's wing. Hook No. 12.

THE OAK-FLY (fig. 8). — The body is made of brown mohair and a little hare's ear-fur towards the tail. Legs of a bittern's hackle, or partridge feather, or a furnace-cock's hackle; wings of a woodcock's wing-feather. Hook No. 8.

THE CAPERER (fig. 9) is made up as follows:—Body of rich brown floss-silk; legs of a fine red or brown hackle; wings of a woodcock's feather. Hook No. 9.

THE WINGED-PALMER (fig. 10), a good common autumn fly, is made on the same plan as the peacock-hackle, but of a smaller size, and with the addition of a pair of wings made from the outside-feather of the thrush's wing. The end of the body is finished with a few turns of orange silk. Hook No. 9 or 10. It is the cock-y-bondhu of Wales.

698. WINGED AND TAILED-FLIES.—These are made like the last set of flies, except that at the time of whipping on the hook the fibres are included which are to

constitute the tail. The body is then formed by the dubbing, floss-silk, or herl, and the wings tied as before. This set includes, among a vast variety of flies, the May-fly, green drake, stone-fly, March-brown, red spinner, &c.

699. THE GREEN DRAKE OR MAY-FLY (*fig.* 11).—Body made of yellow floss-silk or mohair, dyed a pale yellowish-green, and ribbed with bright yellow silk; tail of two or three hairs of the sable or fitchet, or of fine horse-hair from the mane; legs of a grey cock's hackle, dyed the same colour as the mohair, or of a ginger pile undyed; wings from the mallard's back-feather, dyed of the same yellowish-green. Hook No. 6 or 7.

700. THE GREY DRAKE (*fig.* 12) is made as follows:—Body of pale dun-coloured mohair; tail of two fibres from the feather of the mallard's back; legs of a brown or ginger cock's hackle; wings from the grey feather of the mallard's back, undyed. Hook No. 6.

701. THE STONE-FLY (*fig.* 13).—Body of red mohair, ribbed with gold or yellow silk; tail of two long fibres from a coarse red cock's hackle; legs a red cock's hackle, carried down over all the body; wings of the hen-pheasant's tail-feather, or of the grey goose wing-feather. Hook No. 6.

THE MARCH-BROWN (*fig.* 14).—This fly is made of two sizes; one on hook No. 7, the other on No. 11 or 12. The body is of brown floss-silk; tail of two long fibres of the red cock's hackle; legs of brown cock's hackle; wings of a woodcock's feather.

THE RED SPINNER (*fig.* 15) is tied on hook No. 7. Body of red mohair, sometimes ribbed with gold; tail of two fibres of a red cock's-hackle; legs of the same hackle; wings of a brown mallard's feather.

THE WINGED-LARVA of Mr. Blacker (*fig.* 16) resembles the green drake in all but the body, which is prolonged separately from the hook by means of a couple of hog's bristles, which are tied in with it and the tail-hairs, and extend about a quarter of an inch beyond the bend. The silk or dubbing is then carried from the shank to the bristles; and thus the fly has the appearance of a long body. The legs are often made with a dyed feather of the mallard's back, used as a hackle.

702. EXTRA TROUT-FLIES.—Those given in the preceding paragraphs will suffice for all common purposes; but they may be varied *ad infinitum* by the angler, to suit particular localities. If, however, he makes himself perfect in the manufacture and use of these, and has the stock of materials which I have enumerated in paragraph 666, it will be at all times easy for him to extend his list, either by imitating the prevalent natural fly, or that which is successfully employed by the anglers familiar with the district. Mr. Stoddart is of opinion that for the trout the red, brown, and black hackles, with or without wings, and the hare-lug are sufficient for all ordinary purposes. This is perhaps carrying simplicity to an extreme length; but there can be no doubt that the young angler is often overwhelmed with useless flies, as well as other complicated forms of fishing-tackle, in order to suit the trading propensities of the tackle-makers. No doubt in Mr. Stoddart's case the above flies would be more successful than others attached to the line of a beginner; but even the above celebrated *piscator* does not maintain that no others will be more successful at times than the three he has selected, but that there is no absolute necessity for them. This certainly is in accordance with my own experience, as I have known a very successful angler who never possessed any fly but the red and black palmer and the black gnat. Still I have no doubt that at least as great a variety as I have enumerated will at certain times be useful, though some of them will only suit particular months. The following list will perhaps be some little aid to the young angler who is anxious to try a greater variety.

THE WREN'S TAIL.—Body of sable-fur and gold-coloured mohair mixed. No wings; legs of a wren's tail-feather, used as a hackle. Hook No. 8.

THE GROUSE-HACKLE.—Body of gold-coloured mohair mixed with the dark fur from the hare's ear. No wings; legs made with a reddish-brown grouse feather, used as a hackle. Hook No. 7.

THE DARK CLARET.—Body of claret mohair, fine towards the tail, and full towards the shank. Wings four, two below from the starling's wing, and the upper two from the partridge's tail.

THE SPIDER-FLY.—Body of lead-coloured floss-silk; legs of a small black cock's hackle below and above, with a hackle made from the woodcock's feather taken from near the butt-end of the wing. Hook No. 7.

THE LITTLE IRON-BLUE.—Body of slate-coloured mohair; tail of two fine hairs from a dark sable; legs of a fine dun cock's hackle; wings of the coot's or starling's wing-feather. Hook No. 9 or 10.

THE BLUE-BLOW.—Body of mole's fur; wings of the tomtit's tail-feather. Hook No. 14.

THE HARE'S EAR AND YELLOW.—Body the dark fur of a hare's ear, mixed with a little yellow mohair; wings of a starling's feather. Hook No. 8.

THE ANT-FLIES are of four kinds—the

large and small red, and the large and small black. The red are tied on Nos. 7 and 12. Body of amber-mohair, made large towards the tail; legs of a red cock's hackle; wings of a starling's feather. The black have a body of black ostrich herl, with a black hackle for legs; wings of the blue feather of the jay's wing.

THE MEALY-WHITE NIGHT-FLY.—Body white rabbit-fur, made fully as large as a straw on a No. 5 hook; legs of a downy white hackle; wings of the soft mealy feathers of the white-owl.

THE MEALY-BROWN NIGHT-FLY.—Body of the same size as the preceding, made of the fur of a tabby-rabbit; legs of a bittern's hackle, or a grey cock's; wings the brown-feathers of a white-owl. Hook No. 5 or 6.

703. SALMON-FLIES are made on the same principle as the trout-flies, but as they are larger, so they are capable of being tied with greater exactness and finish. They are generally of much more gaudy materials than the trout-flies; and in this respect they have latterly been used still more richly coloured than was formerly the case, even in Ireland. Until lately, very sober salmon flies were ordinarily used in Scotland, the prevailing colours being grey, brown, buff, and brick-dust; but now it is found that a much more brilliant set of colours will answer far better, and the Irish favourites, viz., scarlet, bright yellow, blue, and green, are the fashion, united with less bright toppings—as, for instance, the tail-feather of the pheasant, or the back or breast of the bittern or turkey. In Wales more sober flies are still in vogue; straw colours, natural mottles, and pheasant or turkey feathers being considered the most killing. Tinsels are however approved of in all three localities, and are used more or less in almost every salmon-fly. In nearly all cases this fly consists of a body, a head, legs, and tail, and wings of a very compound nature; but the mode of tying is very similar to that adopted in trout fly-making. Most salmon-flies are tied with a small loop of gut attached to the shank, instead of, as in the trout-fly, a full length of that material; sometimes a bristle or a piece of wire is bent for the purpose, and again in some cases the gut, either plain or twisted, is tied on as in the trout-fly. Whichever mode is adopted, the end or ends of the gut or bristle must be shaved off, and moulded with the teeth into slight ridges, so as neither to present an abrupt and unsightly edge where they leave off, nor to be so smooth as to be liable to slip from the hook. This eye or length of gut is to be first whipped on to the hook in the usual way with strong waxed-silk, which is then to be fastened off and removed; and for the subsequent tying, a finer and generally a bright-coloured silk adapted to the particular fly is to be employed. We will now enter upon the construction of six salmon-flies, which are given in the plates annexed, of the exact size. Nos. 1 and 2 are well suited for either Scotland or Wales, and for comparatively clear waters; the remainder are calculated for more turbid water in Ireland or Scotland.

THE SALMON-FLY, No. 1.—After tying on the loop of gut, take a piece of crimson silk about half a yard long, and fasten it on at the bend, leaving an end to reach beyond the shoulder; next take a part of a golden-pheasant's crest-feather for tail, and tie it on the upper side of the bend, also including a flat piece of gold tinsel; then dub the silk, after waxing it, with crimson mohair, and lap it round the shank for about one-third of the length; when arrived at this stage, tie in the point of a long and coarse cock's hackle, dyed crimson, then proceed with the rest of the silk and dubbing to complete the body. As soon as this part is finished, the dubbing must be removed from the remainder of the silk, which must be fastened off; now take a piece of the tail of the pheasant of the requisite length and substance for the wing, and a single herl of the peacock for the head, and tie them on firmly one above and the other below the shoulder of the hook, using the other piece of the silk left projecting at the shank-end, and laying the feathers for the wings either at once where they ought to go, or else tying them first the reverse way and then turning them over, and keeping them down with an extra turn or two of the silk over the root of the wing; fasten this off, and proceed to finish the body, for which purpose the hackle is first rolled round till it comes close under the wings, where it is fastened off, and then the gold tinsel is wound several times round the bare hook under the tail, then once over it, and afterwards spirally round the shank, following the hackle till it arrives at the shoulder, where it also must be fastened off, and neatly cut off with the hackle. The fly is now complete, with the exception of the head, which is made with the peacock's herl wound round the part of the shank left projecting beyond the wing, and is fastened with the same piece of silk as the wing, which fastening receives a touch of varnish with the brush kept for the purpose. This is one of the most simple of all salmon-flies, and is well adapted for the practice of the young fly-maker. (See fig. 1.)

SMALL SALMON OR GRILSE-FLY, No. 2.—This is tied almost exactly on the same principle as the last, but the mate-

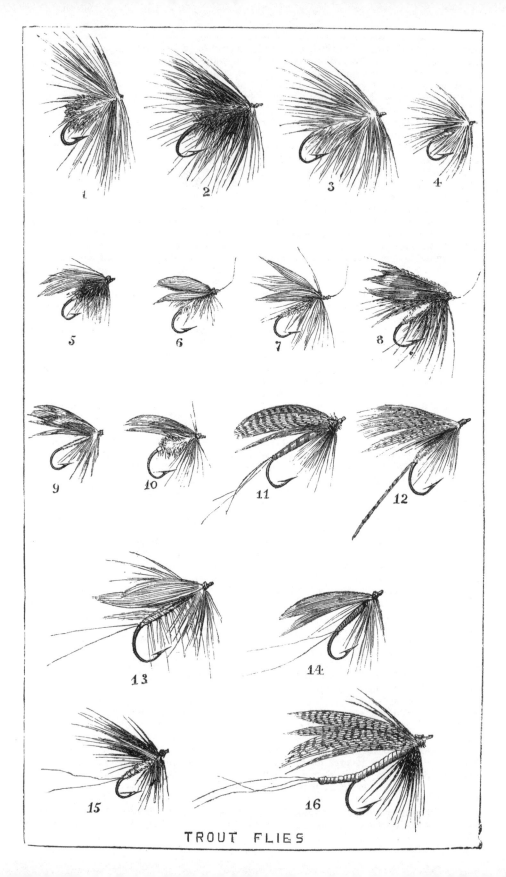

TROUT FLIES

rials, &c., being different, it presents when finished a lighter and somewhat brighter aspect. The body is of brown mohair or weasel's fur, the last joint being of bright yellow floss-silk, finished off with a single turn of gold tinsel; tail of six or seven fibres of the golden-pheasant's crest-feather; wings of two portions, the outer part being of the grey feather of the mallard, the inner, of the yellow part of the web of the hen pheasant's tail; a reddish-brown coarse cock's hackle is rolled over the whole of the mohair forming the body, and with it a piece of silver twist. The head is composed of a few turns of the tying silk only, without any other materials. (See *fig.* 2.)

GAUDY SALMON-FLY, No. 3.—After whipping on the loop, a portion of golden-pheasant's tail and a piece of silver twist are fastened on to the bend of the hook; after which the silk used in the process is dubbed with blood-red mohair, with which one-third of the shank is covered, then another third with orange, and finally, the remaining third with deep green-dyed wool, Corresponding with each division, and before proceeding to the next, a cock's hackle of the same colour as the body is tied on, and wound spirally round, finishing it off and tying it down with the silk used for the dubbing of each division. After completing the last division, the point of a bottle-green or purple cock's hackle is to be tied in, together with a pair of wings composed of two full golden-pheasant's crest feathers, with two toppings of the yellow crest of the mackaw under; and in addition, a black ostrich herl for the head. After the wings are partly tied on, and before they are reversed, the silver twist is wound round, the purple hackle is then turned round and finished off; after which, the wing is reversed and tied down, and the herl formed into the head in the usual way. It is a very light and taking fly in the water. (See *fig.* 3.)

GAUDY SALMON-FLY, No. 4.—Tail of two slips of brown mallard's feather, with a thin topping of golden-pheasant's crest. This is tied on *after* making a short joint at the bend of the hook of gold tinsel and orange floss-silk. The tinsel is carried on under the latter, and is left for further use. Next tie in a black ostrich-herl, and turn it round three times closely together, finish off and remove the end; then dub the silk with crimson mohair or wool, and make up one-quarter of the shank with it for body; tie in a black cock's hackle, and make up another quarter by dubbing the silk with scarlet wool; then another quarter with the crimson, and tie in when finishing this part a bright-red coarse cock's hackle. Now wind the black hackle up to the last quarter

of the body, following it up with the gold tinsel, and fasten and remove the ends of both. Next take a pair of wings composed as follows, placing one of every sort of topping on each side in a corresponding manner: first, two long fibres of red mackaw; secondly, two portions of reddish-black mottled turkey's feather, not quite so long; thirdly, two portions of the back feather of the golden-pheasant; fourthly, two short feathers of the blue lowrie or mackaw. These are to be tied on above the shoulder, and a piece of dark guinea-fowl's back feather below; also a black ostrich herl for head. In tying on wing-feathers of this compound sort, pinch them flat between the finger and thumb, and do not attempt to tie them on the reverse way. After the wings are secure, and also the guinea-fowl's feathers for feelers, wind the last red hackle as a support to them, and then finish off with the herl for the head. (See *fig.* 4.)

MEDIUM SALMON-FLY, No. 5.—First whip on the loop as usual, then commence by fastening a piece of silver plait or braid, which is to make one turn at the bend of the hook, and is to be afterwards concealed by some turns of purple floss-silk for about the eighth of an inch; next tie in for the tail a fine pointed red cock's hackle and a golden-pheasant's crest feather projecting beyond it; then a black ostrich herl, which is to conceal their root by making a raised ring of black above the silver braid, which is now allowed to hang over ready for use. The body is then made up of three equal portions of floss-silk, orange, yellow, and lilac, over which the silver braid is to be spirally wound. Next tie at the shoulder a blue jay's wing-feather, to be used as a hackle, and then a compound wing of the following dubbings: first, a large piece of brown mallard's feather; secondly, a fibre on each side of the green or blue mackaw; thirdly, a dyed crimson cock's hackle on each side; fourthly, two slips of bustard's feather. Below this is to be tied a long tag of the short herls at the root of the ostrich feather, and surrounding the shoulders of both the wing and the feelers a portion of reddish mohair is tied on, and afterwards picked out so as to shade off gradually over both. Finally, a head is formed with a few turns of well waxed silk. This is a very good and useful fly, and will take in a medium state of water, being neither very gaudy nor quite plain. (See *fig.* 5.)

A VERY GAUDY SALMON-FLY, No. 6.—Begin as usual, then fasten on at the bend a piece of tying silk, half a yard long; well wax it, and then lay on, first of all, at the bend two or three turns of flat gold tinsel, which fasten off with the silk; next include in the silk the tail, consisting of a golden-pheasant's crest feather, a small bright crimson cock's hackle, dyed, and three or four fibres of a pale-green mackaw's feather. Now tie in a short tuft of crimson wool, surrounding the hook, and do this either by using it as a dubbing or otherwise at discretion. In fastening this off, include a piece of twisted gold cord, and then dub the silk with snuff-coloured wool, mohair, or pig's wool, with which the lower half of the body is to be made up; finishing the upper half with crimson wool as a dubbing. In the interval between the two dubbings, tie the point of a large and coarse crimson-dyed cock's hackle, and, before finishing off the crimson dubbing, tie on first the feather of a cormorant's neck as a hackle; a dark guinea-fowl's feather will do, in the absence of the cormorant's feather. Next wind the gold cord spirally round the whole body, then lay down the crimson hackle, and finally the cormorant's neck hackle, tying each down *seriatim*. A very large and handsome compound wing is now tied on, and with it a black ostrich-herl for the head. The wing is composed of the following toppings: first, two from the golden-pheasant's or bustard's tail feathers; secondly, two fibres of the red mackaw; thirdly, two of the blue mackaw; fourthly, two of the bustard or brown wood-duck's feather. Under this lies the cormorant's neck feather, which being used as a hackle, appears above and below the shoulder of the hook. This is a good spring-fly, and is the largest ordinary size suited for Scotland or Ireland.

704. SEA-TROUT FLIES may be made of sizes and colours intermediate between the trout and salmon flies. They are tied of all colours, and with or without the addition of a gaudy tail of golden pheasant fibres, and tinsel wound round the body. The following size and form, however, will suit the trout in lochs, and the average size of the sea-trout when ascending from the sea. The body is of brown mohair; legs of a black cock's hackle; wings of a brown mallard's feather; head of plain waxed silk. Hook No. 5 or 6. A good variation consists in using purple or scarlet dubbing for the body; red or lilac-dyed hackle, and the green-dyed feather generally used for the May-fly for the wings; with a tail of a few fibres of the common pheasant's tail feather. Numberless variations of these flies are made and sold, but the whole of them are fanciful creations of the maker's brain, and not imitations of any living insect. The fisherman therefore may please his own fancy, and try his skill in any way that strikes him, and perhaps the more novel the fly the better it may succeed, though there is still a considerable section of good anglers who adhere to the old-fashioned flies called the butcher, the doctor, &c.; but I fully believe that any slight variation or alteration from the annexed models, according to the contents of the angler's stock of materials, will be just as likely to succeed as the celebrated "ondine" of Ephemera, or the new "spirit flies" of Mr. Blacker. The whole of the above set are tied after the models of the last-mentioned maker's flies, but differ considerably from those published in his very beautiful series of plates. The change, however, is in favour of the fisherman, as I believe the flies will be found to be equally killing, and not near so expensive or difficult to tie as those published by him; nevertheless, I should strongly advise every fisherman to procure his book, and study his models for himself; they are so beautifully engraved, and coloured by hand, that the fly-maker can scarcely fail in detecting their mode of tying; but he must not expect to equal them in beauty, for even Mr. Blacker himself cannot by any possible degree of neatness come up to the delicacy of finish with which he has endowed his painted imitations. This caution I have added, fearing lest the tyro should give up his task in disgust, and without the slightest wish to detract from the merits of a performance the utility of which, with the above caution, I am ready most fully to allow.

SECT. 5.—THE LANDING-NET, GAFF, BASKET, &c.

705. THE LANDING-NET (see *fig.*) is merely a hoop with a handle to it, and

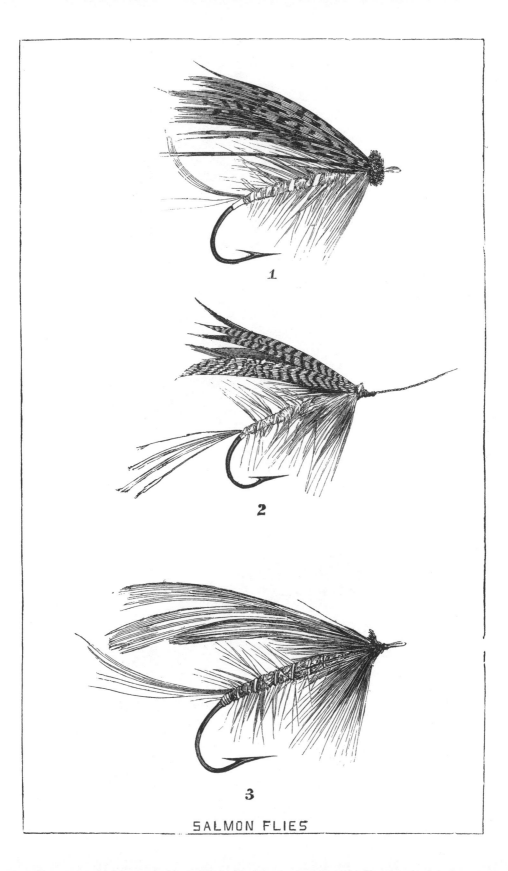

1

2

3

SALMON FLIES

SALMON FLIES

armed with a net for the purpose of taking the hooked-fish out of the water, without danger to the tackle or of losing the fish. It is generally now made with a hollow handle, to take the top joints of the rod, and this handle screws off the ring, which is also jointed, for the convenience of carriage.

706. THE GAFF AND LANDING-HOOK are constructed for the same purpose. The simple hook now used, attached to a firm handle, inflicts the least severe wound, and is more manageable than the gaff.

707. THE BASKET OR CREEL is slung over the shoulder by a belt, and is made of various sizes to suit the probable amount or weight of fish expected by the angler.

708. FISH-BAIT-KETTLES are made of tin, with a perforated lid, and a handle to carry them by.

709. THE DRAG-HOOK is a long line of strong whipcord wound on a thumb-reel, and armed with a three-hooked blunt drag weighted with lead, so that when a hook is caught in weeds or other impediment, the drag may be thrown on to the same spot,

and the weed dragged away with the hook, or at all events the greater portion of the line may be saved.

710. THE CLEARING-RING is intended for the same purpose, and is a jointed-ring of heavy metal which opens and closes again with a catch. It is attached to a long line like the last, and is passed upon the end of the rod open, and when closed is slipped down the reel-line as low as possible, and then drawn to land, bringing sometimes the hook and obstacle with it, but generally breaking the casting-line near the hook or about the shot. This does not act so well as the drag-hook when a float is used.

711. THE BAIT-BOX is merely a flat box perforated with small holes in the lid, for containing worms, or gentles, or dead minnows, in bran.

712. THE DISGORGER is an instrument for removing the hook from the throat of those fish which swallow their bait, and is made of various forms. One end should be forked, and the other perforated with a hole, and ending with a sharp-cutting round surface like a spatula.

CHAP. III.
BOTTOM-FISHING AND TROLLING.

SECT. 1.—THE FISH ANGLED FOR IN THIS WAY.

713. Every fish enumerated in the first chapter may be taken by this mode of angling; even the noble salmon and the wary trout may thus be captured. But almost all require some slight modification of the apparatus or bait employed, and of the mode of using them; and therefore each must form a subject to be studied by itself. Commencing with the smaller varieties of fish, and those most easily caught, I shall take all in the order of their usual presentation to the young angler. With each variety it will be my purpose to specify—first, the kind of rod, hook, and line to be used; secondly, the best bait; thirdly, the time and place best suited for each kind of fish; and fourthly, the mode of fishing.

SECT. 2.—FISHING FOR MINNOWS, AND SIMILAR SMALL FISH.

714. THE ROD, LINE, AND HOOKS for the minnow should all be fine and delicate, especially the last, which must be of the smallest size. Three or four hooks should be whipped on fine gut or strong horse-

hair, and attached to a short line of horsehair or silk, leaving the hooks each about three or four inches longer than the one next above it. This is better than the paternoster line, which will be described in section 3. A crow-quill float, and any light

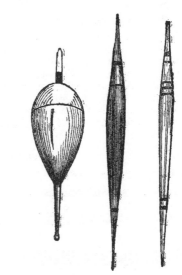

but stiff rod, will complete the angling requisites for this fish. A plummet may be wanted to obtain the exact depth of water, but the eye is generally a sufficient guide.

715. THE BAIT should be of very small red worms, or pieces of them.

716. MINNOWS ARE FOUND from March till Michaelmas in small gravelly brooks, and sometimes in large rivers. They take the worm freely all day, especially in warm still weather.

717. THE LOWEST HOOK AND BAIT SHOULD BE SUFFERED to float tolerably near the ground, and the highest at mid-water, above which these fish seldom feed. At the slightest indication of a bite the rod should be rapidly raised, as by this means many minnows which would otherwise be lost will be taken, while the worm is only partially in the mouth. In this way it is that the juvenile angler, with his crooked pin, succeeds in catching this little fish.

718. THE STICKLEBACK may be taken exactly in the same way. They form an excellent bait for the larger kinds of fish, with their spines removed.

719. THE BULLHEAD lies under stones, and it is therefore to be angled for with a single small hook, and the bait must be suffered to float along very near the bed of the river. These fish are very voracious, and rush out with great greediness upon the bait as it passes by their place of retreat.

720. THE LOACH also may be taken with the same kind of tackle and bait; but as it is neither a good fish for the table nor suited to the palates of larger fish, it is seldom sought after. None of these fish require ground-baits, as they are so plentiful when they exist as to be easily obtained in large numbers.

SECT. 3.—BLEAK-FISHING.

721. THE ROD, LINE, AND HOOK.—Two kinds of line are used for this fish—one similar to that described under Minnow-fishing at paragraph 714; the other, usually called *a paternoster line*, which is made as follows:—A bullet is attached to a strong line, and is dragged along the bottom of the river by it. A few inches above the bullet a strong and long bristle is whipped at right angles to the line, forming a cross with it (hence its name). To the ends of this bristle fine hooks are whipped in the ordinary way; and at intervals of seven, eight, or nine inches up the line other bristles are attached in a similar manner. In this mode four, six, or eight baited hooks are dragged along at intervals above the bed of the river, each hook being kept from entanglement by the stiffness of the bristles.

722. THE BAITS for the bleak are gentles, red-worms, caddis, paste, &c. GROUND-BAIT should be used when it is intended to take any quantity of these fish; but as they are not considered very good eating, it is seldom that this amount of trouble is taken.

723. THE HAUNTS OF THE BLEAK are exceedingly extensive, it being found in almost every British river. Mid-water is the best general depth to angle for them; but in warm weather they swim very near the surface, and in cold, quite on the bed of the river. In the former case they prefer the fly, and may then be taken in large numbers by whipping with a small black gnat, which forms a very good introduction to the young fly-fisher, as I shall hereafter show. They spawn from the middle of March to the end of April.

724. IN FISHING FOR BLEAK there is no great art; all that is required is to pull them out at once, but not so rapidly as with the minnow, as they do not adhere to the worm with the same pertinacity as that little fish does.

SECT. 4.—FISHING FOR DACE AND ROACH.

725. THE TACKLE for these fish is the same for both, and they may be taken precisely in the same way in every respect. THE ROD should be very light, but yet stiff and long. It is generally of bamboo or cane, about 17 or 18 feet long, or even a foot longer, as it is a most essential point in this kind of fishing to command a great extent of water without showing the person, and yet to drop the bait very gently into it. A light GENERAL ROD answers the purpose pretty well, and the spare tops for fly-fishing will avail for common purposes in that depart-

ment. Such a rod should be about 17 feet long, and made of hickory or split-cane; and will suit either for trolling, spinning, or barbel-fishing with the lob-worm. (See woodcut, which gives a good idea of the common general rod in its cheapest form, with a spare top for fly-fishing.) The LINE should be very fine down to the FLOAT, which should be of swan-quill. Below the float it should be either of single hair or fine gut, with the knots unwhipped with silk in order to be more invisible. The lengths of hair being longer than those of gut, the knots are not so frequent; but as the hair is not so strong as the gut, more dexterity is required in landing a large fish. The HOOK should be No. 10 or 12; and enough split-shot should be attached to the line, beginning about a foot above the hook, to immerse the float three-fourths of its length. The shot should be No. 1 to 4. A plummet is required to ascertain the depth of the water, of either of the forms given in the annexed woodcut, one of which is of solid lead, the other of sheet-lead rolled upon the line.

726. THE BAITS FOR ROACH AND DACE are any of the following:—Gentles, paste coloured with vermilion, worms well scoured, and grubs or salmon-roe; the two first being almost exclusively used in the neighbourhood of London. GROUND-BAITS are very generally used, and should be composed of some of the above baits, used on the principles described in paragraph 656.

727. THE LOCALITIES best suited for dace and roach-fishing are moderately rapid and deep streams. Dace are fond of mill-streams, but are also to be found in more sluggish parts of the rivers. Both are chiefly to be found at the bottom. THE TIME when roach are in season is from August to the following spring. Dace spawn in March and April, but soon come in season again, and may be taken from June to December.

728. THESE FISH MAY BE ANGLED FOR in the following manner:—First, plumb the depth and allow your bait to float very near the bottom, by adjusting your line to the required length. Then keep your eye on the float, and when you see it move downwards from the biting of the fish, strike smartly, but gently. The rod, line, float, and bait ought to be perpendicular to one another, and no more line should be used than necessary, so as to lose no time in striking; which evolution should be from the wrist only, the arm being nearly motionless the while. When the fish is securely hooked great care must be used in landing him, as he will break the line inevitably if he is jerked, or if not carefully humoured, especially if hair is used in lieu of gut.

729. GRAINING, RUD, AND AZURINE may be taken in the same way as the above. Rud require a rather larger hook, and a coarser line will not interfere with their capture.

SECT. 5.—CHUB-FISHING.

730. THE CHUB is a larger fish than the dace, but otherwise very similar in habits and appearance, so that a young chub is often taken for an old and mature dace, and *vice versâ*. Several modes of taking this fish are practised, one of which is similar to that already described for roach and dace, but requiring a larger hook and stronger tackle. Being a very violent fish when first hooked, although soon giving in, it is very apt to break fine lines. It also frequents weedy places and stumps of trees.

731. SINKING AND DRAWING is therefore practised, because by this mode the line is not so likely to be entangled as with the ordinary line and float. A strong rod and line are used for this purpose, without a float, and the line is shotted so as just to sink it. When the hook, which should be about No. 6, is baited, drop it gently in some clear place and suffer it to sink to the bottom, then immediately draw it up again as obliquely as the weeds, &c., will allow, and with a quivering or gently jerking motion to imitate the actions of aquatic insects. Chub are also taken in large numbers by dipping with the natural fly or humble-bee, or with a very good imitation of the latter which is sold by the tackle-makers.

SECT. 6—GUDGEON-FISHING.

732. THE TACKLE FOR THE GUDGEON should be as fine as that for the minnow, and the hook or hooks No. 8 or 9. Very fine shot also must be used, and a light quill-float.

733. THE BAIT which is the most killing for gudgeon is the red-worm, next to which is the gentle or caddis-worm, and then come the various pastes. Instead of ground-baiting, raking the bottom with a long rake is practised, which has the same effect in attracting the fish, and in which alone gudgeon-fishing differs from that described in the first section of this chapter.

734. In the Thames gudgeon are taken in great numbers from the punt, but in smaller rivers there is no necessity for this accessory. Gudgeon spawn in April, and by the 1st of June are in good season, after which they may be taken in almost all our rivers.

735. THE HOOK must always trail on the ground, as this fish invariably feeds there. It should be steadily drawn along, or suffered to remain quiescent, some fishermen using several rods at once. The moment a bite is seen, the wrist should be raised and the fish landed, as it is too small to endanger the tackle, however light and frail.

SECT. 7.—FISHING FOR BARBEL.

736. THE LEDGER-LINE is that most commonly used for taking this fish, and may be described as follows:—The line should be of single gut, three or four feet long, with a No. 5 hook tied on it, and a single large shot firmly fixed about a foot from the hook. Upon the part of the gut above this shot a bullet with a hole in it should freely play, and the ledger-line, after the bullet is dropped on it, may be attached to a long silk or hair-line in the usual way. If the punt is used the ROD should be short and stiff, but if the fishing is from the bank of the river, one at least 16 feet long will be required, but still stiff and free from play. The LINE should be 30 or 40 yards in length, and of good strength; and a winch will of course be required.

737. FLOAT-ANGLING is also practised for the barbel, and in roach-fishing it is very common to hook this fish, but as they plunge very desperately when hooked, they often break away with the fine tackle used in roach-fishing. When the barbel is the chief object in float-fishing, the line must be of very strong gut, and a cork-float should be used. (See woodcut of floats at paragraph 714.) The rod may be the general rod already described, or the light one adapted for roach and dace-fishing. A long line and winch are doubly necessary in this kind of fishing.

738. GROUND-BAITING for barbel is always practised, and without it there is very little chance of good sport in any given locality. If, therefore, the fishing is to be from a punt, the ground-baits should have been diligently used over-night, and repeated at intervals till the end of the fishing, or it will be in vain. The BEST BAITS are—for clear water, red-worms well-scoured, gentles, and greaves; in muddy water, lob-worms or marsh-worms, cheese or paste may be used; but whatever bait is fixed on should completely cover the hook; thus, one, two, or three gentles will be required; two red-worms, or a lump of greaves. If lob-worms are employed, one will generally conceal the hook; but as these fish gradually suck in their bait into their small mouths, it is important to conceal the hook not only from the eye, but from their sense of touch.

739. THE SEASON FOR BARBEL-FISHING is from March to the end of October, and the most likely time is quite late in the evening; but though they do not bite freely till then, they may be taken during the whole of the afternoon; in the early morning, also, they take a bait as freely as in the evening, and especially after rainy weather. The most likely spots where they may be found are the deeps of rapid rivers, where they lie in small shoals; under bridges they are very apt to lie, and round piles, or at the foot of flood-gates clear of the rapids, they often remain quite stationary for hours, and are then sometimes taken by unfair means—such as eel-spears, or landing-hooks, &c.; or by means of a large treble-hook dragged over their backs with some little knack, however unfair it may be.

740. THE MODE OF FISHING FOR BARBEL with the ledger-line and punt is as follows: The punt should be moored across the space already ground-baited over-night; the short rod is then to be held over the stream, and the bait gently dropped into the water, keeping the line moderately "taut," but not so much so as to prevent the fish pulling the bait slightly through the bullet, but still enough to show when he is actually sucking it in. When the point of the rod indicates this action strike smartly, and the hook is sure to get secure hold of his mouth, when, unless he is a very large fish, he is quite safe; but if very large, his struggles with his tail will be likely to break the line, and even sometimes to carry away the top joint of the rod. In this case—that is, if he is a strong fish, the line must be suffered to run out as far as the weeds, &c., will allow; but it must always be managed so that the fish is kept in clear water, as he fights most energetically among piles or weeds. A landing-net or hook should always be at hand in such a case, and an assistant will then save all trouble by bringing him to shore; but if this can be avoided without danger of losing the fish, and the sport is desired to be prolonged, he may be played till exhausted, and then brought out without risk by the landing-net used in the punt. The same mode may be adopted in fishing from the shore, but here, as the angler can run with his fish if the weeds are not very rife, he may play him to greater advantage. Some anglers consider the sport afforded by this fish almost equal to that of the trout, and superior to the grayling.

734. In the Thames gudgeon are taken in great numbers from the punt, but in smaller rivers there is no necessity for this accessory. Gudgeon spawn in April, and by the 1st of June are in good season, after which they may be taken in almost all our rivers.

735. THE HOOK must always trail on the ground, as this fish invariably feeds there. It should be steadily drawn along, or suffered to remain quiescent, some fishermen using several rods at once. The moment a bite is seen, the wrist should be raised and the fish landed, as it is too small to endanger the tackle, however light and frail.

SECT. 7.—FISHING FOR BARBEL.

736. THE LEDGER-LINE is that most commonly used for taking this fish, and may be described as follows:—The line should be of single gut, three or four feet long, with a No. 5 hook tied on it, and a single large shot firmly fixed about a foot from the hook. Upon the part of the gut above this shot a bullet with a hole in it should freely play, and the ledger-line, after the bullet is dropped on it, may be attached to a long silk or hair-line in the usual way. If the punt is used the ROD should be short and stiff, but if the fishing is from the bank of the river, one at least 16 feet long will be required, but still stiff and free from play. The LINE should be 30 or 40 yards in length, and of good strength; and a winch will of course be required.

737. FLOAT-ANGLING is also practised for the barbel, and in roach-fishing it is very common to hook this fish, but as they plunge very desperately when hooked, they often break away with the fine tackle used in roach-fishing. When the barbel is the chief object in float-fishing, the line must be of very strong gut, and a cork-float should be used. (See woodcut of floats at paragraph 714.) The rod may be the general rod already described, or the light one adapted for roach and dace-fishing. A long line and winch are doubly necessary in this kind of fishing.

738. GROUND-BAITING for barbel is always practised, and without it there is very little chance of good sport in any given locality. If, therefore, the fishing is to be from a punt, the ground-baits should have been diligently used over-night, and repeated at intervals till the end of the fishing, or it will be in vain. The BEST BAITS are—for clear water, red-worms well-scoured, gentles, and greaves; in muddy water, lob-worms or marsh-worms, cheese or paste may be used; but whatever bait is fixed on should completely cover the hook; thus, one, two, or three gentles will be required; two red-worms, or a lump of greaves. If lob-worms are employed, one will generally conceal the hook; but as these fish gradually suck in their bait into their small mouths, it is important to conceal the hook not only from the eye, but from their sense of touch.

739. THE SEASON FOR BARBEL-FISHING is from March to the end of October, and the most likely time is quite late in the evening; but though they do not bite freely till then, they may be taken during the whole of the afternoon; in the early morning, also, they take a bait as freely as in the evening, and especially after rainy weather. The most likely spots where they may be found are the deeps of rapid rivers, where they lie in small shoals; under bridges they are very apt to lie, and round piles, or at the foot of flood-gates clear of the rapids, they often remain quite stationary for hours, and are then sometimes taken by unfair means—such as eel-spears, or landing-hooks, &c.; or by means of a large treble-hook dragged over their backs with some little knack, however unfair it may be.

740. THE MODE OF FISHING FOR BARBEL with the ledger-line and punt is as follows: The punt should be moored across the space already ground-baited over-night; the short rod is then to be held over the stream, and the bait gently dropped into the water, keeping the line moderately "taut," but not so much so as to prevent the fish pulling the bait slightly through the bullet, but still enough to show when he is actually sucking it in. When the point of the rod indicates this action strike smartly, and the hook is sure to get secure hold of his mouth, when, unless he is a very large fish, he is quite safe; but if very large, his struggles with his tail will be likely to break the line, and even sometimes to carry away the top joint of the rod. In this case—that is, if he is a strong fish, the line must be suffered to run out as far as the weeds, &c., will allow; but it must always be managed so that the fish is kept in clear water, as he fights most energetically among piles or weeds. A landing-net or hook should always be at hand in such a case, and an assistant will then save all trouble by bringing him to shore; but if this can be avoided without danger of losing the fish, and the sport is desired to be prolonged, he may be played till exhausted, and then brought out without risk by the landing-net used in the punt. The same mode may be adopted in fishing from the shore, but here, as the angler can run with his fish if the weeds are not very rife, he may play him to greater advantage. Some anglers consider the sport afforded by this fish almost equal to that of the trout, and superior to the grayling.

however, is not the result of my own experience, as I have always found a marked difference in perch as well as other fish in connection with strong winds, and also with the time of day. Young anglers, therefore, should take this *dictum* with some caution.

751. LITTLE DIFFERENCE IN THE MODE OF USING THE BAIT need be made from those recommended for roach and dace, if the perch sought for are small; but in localities where large perch may be expected, and where the live or dead fish-bait is used, some considerable variation must be practised. Hitherto I have not had occasion to describe the mode of using THE LIVE AND DEAD FISH-BAITS; but as we now are considering their adoption in taking perch, it will be proper here to enter upon the subject. I have already (paragraph 660) alluded to the mode of applying the live minnow to the hook, or rather of inserting the latter in the back of the fish close to its fin. When this has been done, and the gut is properly shotted with about two or three No. 1 shot, quietly enter the fish at some distance from the shore, and let it take its own course, swimming where it chooses. A float is only a hindrance to the live bait; and as it is dragged about on the surface of the water, it serves to attract the attention of the perch, and is very apt to scare them away. As soon as the perch is seen or felt to take the bait, strike pretty firmly, though not with much force. Live frogs may be used in the same way, as well as newts.

752. SPINNING for perch is practised as follows:—The bait being applied according to either of the methods described at paragraph 657, the angler should use the general rod with the short-top; a reel and reel-line of plaited-silk or twisted hair and silk will be necessary, and a good length of strong gut (or, when pike are likely to be met with, of gimp), armed with one or two box-swivels. With this apparatus the angler proceeds as follows:— He first casts or throws the minnow down the stream, if there is any, or, if in still water, as far out as he can; then, pulling the bait gently yet firmly to him for a yard or so, it revolves rapidly on its axis, and must be allowed to sink for a few inches at the end of that distance by his ceasing to draw in. The angler then repeats the operation till he brings the bait out of the water, when a cast in a fresh direction must be made, but exactly as before in principle. It is obvious that for this purpose a long rod is required to command a greater extent of water, and a more numerous series of spins, and that running water materially assists the spinning; still, in dead water a well mounted minnow or gudgeon may be spun with great effect, and will kill there in preference to any other bait, except perhaps a live one of the same species.

753. THE GORGE-HOOK is used with the full-sized trolling-rod and a long line, a yard or two of which is pulled out in a loop clear of the reel, and held loose in the left hand. Cast as gently as possible the minnow from you down-stream, or out into the water, if it is still. In thus casting, the loose portion of line is expended, and the bait is thrown considerably further than it otherwise would be. Then begin to wind-up a little at a time, stop, and wind again; thus imitating the actions of the living small fish represented by the dead bait. When the length of line is reduced to a manageable amount, the action may be varied a little, and the fish may be eased downwards or upwards, or among piles or other likely places; but in all cases proceeding by slight jerks, and at the same time not too rapidly. When the bait is thus brought to hand again, repeat as before, and try all likely spots—first casting and drawing over and through the nearest places, and then extending the reach to the most distant ones. The expert angler will always study the actions of living fish, and endeavour to imitate them, which example is far better than any precept that can be given in print.

SECT. 10.—PIKE-FISHING.

754. As these fish are strong and often of good size, and are furnished with sharp teeth, the tackle must be in proportion. The rod is necessarily longer and stronger than that known as "the general rod," and must be of the kind known as a "trolling rod," which may be described as follows:— It should be here mentioned that pike are taken with the minnow or gudgeon in three different ways—first, with live bait; secondly, with dead bait, in a way called "snap-fishing;" and thirdly, with the gorge-hook, on principles similar to those already described. The first and last of these modes require a long and tolerably stiff rod, while snap-fishing must be practised with the top joints of the rod reduced in length, and of greater stiffness. This will serve to make the following account more intelligible. The angler who is very *exigeant* in his desires for the most perfect implements of his craft, will perhaps require two separate rods of varying sizes for each purpose, so as to suit broad and narrow rivers, as well as large and small fish; but the more easily satisfied fisherman will make one rod of the following dimensions serve every purpose:—A bamboo rod is the lightest, and is yet strong and stiff enough

for any practised fisherman; it will not however bear very rough usage, and for very large pike the butt and second joint should be of some light yet tough wood, such as holly, which may be bored for the sake of diminishing its weight, and also to accommodate within its cavity, as in a place of security, the small top joints. Of these it should have three—one short and stiff, and two others similar to one another, longer and more elastic than the first. The short one is made entirely of whalebone, and is not more than 12 or 18 inches long; the longer tops are made two-thirds of hickory or lancewood, and the remainder of whalebone. These rods are generally made in five joints of nearly equal length; the first, second, and last as above described, and the intermediate two joints of bamboo. They are united by the ordinary brass ferules in the usual way, but sometimes other methods are practised; but there is so little occasion for any alteration, that it is unnecessary to take up the reader's time by any further description of them. Almost all trolling-rods used in the south are furnished with rings which are made to stand up from the rod, in order to allow the line to traverse their openings with greater facility. These are usually made of broad brass ferules encircling the rod, and having lesser rings of wire rivetted into them; but a much lighter and cheaper plan answers perfectly well, and may be described as follows:—Take a piece of wire of sufficient strength, and bend it into a ring of the usual size, leaving a short tail on each side; turn these tails to a right angle each way, and flatten the ends so that they will lie along the side of the rod, when they may be whipped in the usual way. They thus form stand-up rings, easily removeable by cutting the whipping-silk, and very capable of being restored, if by any accident they are injured. One of these to the head of each joint, and a second to the middle of the last, are about the proper number. Some northern anglers, including that high authority, Mr. Stoddart, approve of the same kind of ring as is used in ordinary rods, and which is only attached by a piece of quill, or other similar material; but I confess that though I have the highest opinion of Mr. Stoddart's judgment in general, yet in this instance I cannot agree with him, as there can be no doubt in my mind that the fixed and upright ring allows the line to run much more freely than the ordinary one such as he recommends. A large reel is wanted, capable of holding from 35 to 70 yards of line, according to the nature of the fish and extent of water intended to be fished. This reel should have a simple large barrel without multi-

pliers. FLOATS may or may not be used, but if used they should be of cork. The REEL-LINE must be strong, and the plaited silk is that form now usually adopted, as it is found to be more free from "kinking" than any other. An essential accessory to pike-fishing is the swivel, which may be either the box-swivel or the hook-swivel; the latter differing from the former only in having a small hook at one end. These are attached to lengths of *gut*, or more usually *gimp*, forming with their help what are called double or single swivel-traces.

755. THE SINGLE SWIVEL-TRACE consists of about 12 inches of gut or gimp, with a hook-swivel at one end and a loop of its own substance at the other, which attaches it to the reel-line by the usual draw bow-knot. THE DOUBLE SWIVEL-TRACE has, in addition, an extra length of gut or gimp, ending also in a loop, and between the two a box-swivel by which the tendency to twist in spinning is still further diminished. In both cases the hook-swivel receives the loop of the hook-length of gut or gimp *after it is baited*; and in both instances, also, swan-shot or lead, in some form, is required to sink the bait; and it is attached in greater or less weight, according to circumstances, to the gimp close to the hook-swivel.

756. THE HOOKS will be more particularly described under each mode of fishing; and for their application to the bait a needle, called a BAITING-NEEDLE, is required.

757. A LANDING-NET, OR HOOK, will be required, as pike are sometimes of such a size as to demand their assistance. The former is merely a circle of iron, either plain or jointed, with a handle which may be made to take on and off for the sake of convenience; and armed with a deep net, which receives the fish. The hook is intended to supply the place of the net, but is a clumsy substitute. (See paragraph 705, and accompanying woodcut.)

758. THE BAITS used for pike are exceedingly various, reaching from the common lob-worm and ordinary hook, which will often take jack—*alias* small pike—through all the degrees of live minnows and other fish, as well as frogs and newts, dead minnows and gudgeons, artificial minnows and gudgeons, and even the artificial fly. These various baits are used also in almost as many different ways, of which three have been already described in the list of baits, under the heads of "The live Minnow-bait," "The Spinning-minnow," and "The Gorge-hook-bait." But besides these, the snap-hook bait is employed at those times when pike are shy of gorging, and inclined to eject the bait, or *blow* it out, as the angler denominates this act. The snap-hook is either the plain

or the spring snap-hook, and they are both used for live as well as dead fish baits; though the spring snap-hook is very apt to destroy the life of the fish very rapidly, and is a very cruel mode of baiting. The plain snap is made in several ways, as follows : first plan—two hooks (No. 4.) should be tied back to back, then to these tie another smaller hook (No. 8.) together with a piece of wire ending in an eye (see snap-hooks, *fig*. 1). To the eye is whipped a piece of gimp, and the other end of this has a loop by which it is attached to the hook-swivel in the usual way. In fixing on the bait proceed as follows : take a good sized gudgeon, or small roach, or a perch with the back fin removed, arm the gimp with a baiting-needle and insert it behind the back fin, bringing it out again at the mouth and drawing the gimp after it, so that the short hook stands with the point rising out of the back, and the others are one on each side the belly; this bait ought to spin well. Second plan— exactly similar to the mode recommended by Mr. Stoddart of applying three hooks to the parr-tail, only that in England it is used with a whole fish, and the hooks point towards the head. Mr. Stoddart's plan is no doubt the best, and with a tail of the roach, dace, or perch, is admirably adapted to pike-fishing. Third plan—in this mode four hooks are used, which are separately whipped on to two pieces of gimp, looped at the other ends ; one about three-quarters of an inch in length, the other about three times as long. After arming them with the baiting-needle, they are each passed through the fish, the short one at the shoulder, the other near the tail, and both the loops being brought out at the mouth are attached to a hook-swivel, after which the mouth is sewn up and the bait is finished and ready for use; though sometimes, in addition, a leaden weight is sewn up in the mouth to sink the bait. THE SPRING SNAP-BAIT is a more complicated machine, and is composed of a case which connects and keeps in place the shanks of the hooks, which, when in the case, resemble the common snap-hook (*fig*. 1.), but which, when drawn out, expand by their own elasticity, and assume the form indicated in *fig*. 2. This is sometimes applied to a live fish, but usually to a dead roach or gudgeon, or to a small bream. The bait should be about six ounces in weight, for a smaller one will not effectually conceal the hooks. In baiting the hooks insert the small hook in the back of the fish, near the back fin, taking a good hold of the flesh and allowing the point to project a little way out of the skin, and the other two hooks to lie one on each side of the belly. The mode in which this acts is as follows : as soon as the pike seizes the fish in its mouth he pulls slightly on the line, which causes the angler to strike, and this action draws the case from the shanks of the hooks and allows them to expand themselves, and thus prevent the pike from blowing the bait out of his mouth.

759. LEDGER-BAITS, OR BANK-RUNNERS, are often adopted in pike-fishing, and are merely used as a mode of dispensing with the rod. The bait is a live minnow or frog, attached to a long line wound on a reel at the top of a strong pointed staff which is driven into the bank, and the line suspended over the water by a forked stick ; a cork float is used, and the fish or frog-bait is suffered to swim about ; the angler visiting his ledger-baits every half-hour or so. This, like the following, is a poaching kind of fishing, more adapted for filling the fish-kettle than for showing sport. Its worthy companion is The TRIMMER, which is a floating reel, allowed full liberty on the lake which is to be fished, and of which several are thus set afloat at one time. This also is baited with a live fish, and its action is similar to the bank-runner, except that as the trimmer follows the hooked fish it does not require so long a line. The hook is sometimes a single one inserted in the back, and at others a double snap-hook passed obliquely through the body. Two sorts of trimmer are described by Mr. Daniel—the first is made of flat cork, or light wood, painted, seven or eight inches in diameter, circular in shape, with a groove in the edge deep enough to receive a fine whipcord or silk line 12 yards long (the proper rule is five yards longer than the depth of the water). A small stick, two inches long, stands up from the water, with a slit in the end. In setting this the bait is attached with a double hook, which is passed obliquely beneath the skin only, and the line, at about three feet from the bait, is gently dropped into the slit, so that when the pike is hooked he tilts up the cork and disengages the line from the slit, which only serves to keep the bait at a proper depth, and near enough to the floating cork. The second kind instead of being circular is made in the form of a wedge; and the line in place of being coiled round the edge, is wound in the form of a cross over the float, like the cotton over an old-fashioned card. It answers better for weedy places perhaps, but on the whole is scarcely to be preferred to the common plan.

760. PIKE ARE IN SEASON from May to February, but the best time for the sport of taking them with the hook is the period immediately before the weeds shoot, and again in October when they have rotted. The latter is the true pike season, as they

are then firm and fleshy, and also voracious, so as to afford good sport. This fish is usually taken of good size in artificial waters, or in deep alluvial rivers. In these situations there are almost always great quantities of weeds, and when they exist in full vigour it is almost impossible to land large pike, even if they are hooked. The bait also can scarcely, at such times and situations, be properly manœuvred, and hence, it is by common consent considered that pike, though perfectly edible, should not be angled for till after Michaelmas, from which time till February the water is in good order for their capture.

761. THE MODE OF FISHING for pike varies with the particular hook and bait employed. If the LIVE BAIT is used with the ordinary hook, it can only be successful at times when the fish are voracious and ready for any bait, which, indeed, they often are. If this happens to be the case, the bait must be gently passed into the water, and will be more easily managed with a float, as with the length of line required in pike-fishing it is impossible otherwise to maintain a proper depth for the bait, which should as far as possible be made to swim at mid-water. This is effected by the float keeping the bait up, and the shotted line preventing its rising to the surface. If the bait seeks the weeds or other shelter it must be stopped, and if dull and sluggish it must be stimulated by a gentle shaking of the rod. When removing the bait for a fresh throw, great care should be taken to do this gently, as a very little extra force will make a great difference in the duration of the life of the fish; and not only so, but the gentle mode will give the bait less pain than any other. The use of live baits is always more or less cruel, and surely every unnecessary degree of pain should be avoided. When the bait is seized by the pike, which may be known by the float disappearing under the water, be very careful to allow him to carry it off without restraint, and for this purpose draw off the line with the hand and let it run loosely through the rings. If the slightest impediment occurs he will be sure to blow it out, and your hopes are blasted. After a short time, during which he has been quietly gorging the bait, he will again move off, and then is the time to strike, which you may do sharply, but not roughly. If this is cleverly done the fish is firmly attached to the line, which, if of good materials and the hooks equally efficient, will land your fish for you with the aid of a little skilful management. Pike may be played with great advantage, and a considerable increase to the interest of the sport. The principle consists in yielding to him for a time, by letting out the line as far as is prudent and the absence of weeds, &c., will allow; and when otherwise, making the elastic power of the rod withstand his progress by advancing the butt. In this way he will at last be tired out, and may then be landed with safety by means of the landing-net.

762. THE SNAP-BAIT is employed only when the fish are wary and inclined to eject the ordinary kind, and it is used as follows:—I have already (paragraph 758) described the mode of arming the hook with the bait, and also the peculiarly short and stiff top to the rod which is required. This last is necessary in order to give increased quickness to the stroke. The chief difference in this mode from that last described consists in the striking, which should be done the moment the pike seizes the bait, when, if successful, he may be landed or played according to circumstances, as before described, or if not too large, pulled out at once over the shoulder. TROLLING, however, by means of the gorge-hook, is the most common mode of taking pike, and is also the most sportsmanlike, inasmuch as it is deprived of the stain of cruelty which attends upon live-bait fishing. It requires, as I have already observed, the full-sized trolling-rod, with long and strong line, a good-sized reel free from multipliers, and all the apparatus peculiar to the gorge-hook—viz, cork-float, swivel-traces, gorge-hooks, and bait. When these are all artistically adjusted, the bait must be manœuvred in the manner already described at paragraph 753 for perch, and it will generally be successful where good fish abound, and the fishing for them is attempted at the proper season. The butt of the rod should be rested against the thigh or groin, and it should be grasped by the hand about 18 inches higher up, which will give the angler great power over his rod, and also leave the left hand at liberty to manage the line, a loop or two of which should be held in that hand, ready to "pay out," as the sailors say, when the bait is cast. When a pike has seized the bait, wait patiently, as already recommended, and the average time necessary for this exercise of patience will be about six minutes; then strike and play, or not, as before mentioned.

763. IN REMOVING THE BAIT FROM THE MOUTH of the pike after landing him, be careful of his jaws and teeth, which sometimes inflict severe wounds. The first thing to be done is to knock him on the head, which will enable you to recover your hooks and gimp at your leisure, whereas by attempting, by means of the disgorger, to remove them while he is alive, great risk is incurred not only to them, but to your own fingers. After he is quite dead, open the

mouth, and if the bait is still there, after propping the mouth open, liberate the hooks with the knife, and remove the bait; but if this has been swallowed, make an incision into the stomach, and remove them through it. Very often the process is a delicate and tedious one, and many fish will require to be slit open from the mouth to the stomach before the hooks, if well fixed, can be so cleared as to allow the bait to be removed without injury to them or to the gimp.

Sect. 11.—Eel-Fishing.

764. The Apparatus which is used for taking eels is exceedingly various, inasmuch as almost every kind of hook is occasionally adopted. Some of the different modes and tackle have been already described, such as the ledger-line (under Barbel-fishing), the ordinary float-angling, &c. These may be used with eel-hooks and strong tackle; and the eel should be landed as quickly as possible after he is hooked, for the reason that he is otherwise sure to coil himself round some weed or pile, or other fixed object, and so set at defiance the efforts of the angler. Usually, however, these fish are taken at night, and the ledger-line answers very well for that purpose, the hook being mounted on strong whipcord or on gimp. The regular Night Line consists of a long and tolerably stout cord, to each end of which a brick or stone is attached weighing three or four pounds. At intervals of two or three feet a piece of whipcord or gimp 18 inches long should be firmly tied, and armed with an ordinary eel-hook. When all are baited, drop one brick or stone gently into the water, then with a long pole or a boat drop the other at the full length of the line, and leave the whole apparatus sunk till the next morning, when at early dawn they may be taken up again with a boat-hook, and the eels, if caught, removed. They should be set the last thing at night, that the bait may be fresh, and taken up at very early dawn.

765. Bobbing for Eels is practised with a common darning-needle and worsted, several lengths of which are strung with worms, and then, after being gathered into loops, they are united by a strong line to a piece of lead weighing nearly a pound, and pierced with a hole for the purpose of attachment to the line. The eels are taken by their teeth catching in the worsted.

766. Trimmers are set for eels exactly as for pike, except that the hooks should be eel-hooks.

767. Sniggling is another mode of taking eels, which is carried on during the day, and the apparatus consists in a strong needle about two inches long, a stout whip-

cord-line, which is whipped to the needle from the eye to the middle, from which part it is suspended, and a short rod with a notch at the end, and capable of being set at any angle or curve, for which purpose it is either made of flexible wire or with hinged-joints. The needle is baited with the worm, which is drawn over both needle and line, and when the angler strikes he fixes the needle across the eel's throat.

768. The Eel-Spear is the most common of all the implements used in taking eels; but as it requires very little art, it is scarcely fitted for the sportsman's use, and is solely intended to be employed by those who take fish for profit. But the great bulk of the eels caught in this country are taken in traps set in the weirs of the rivers, when they run in the floods which are so constantly occurring.

769. The Best Baits for Eels are either live fish or lob-worms. Dead bait are not so readily taken, as there is no means during the night of simulating the motions of the living fish, as can be done with perch, trout, and pike, which take their food by day. Lob-worms, therefore, as being the most readily procured, and remaining alive on the hook for a considerable time, are the most common bait. The lampern is used in those rivers where it is met with, and is a very deadly bait. It requires care in its application not to injure the nine-eyes or gills, for if they are destroyed the fish soon dies, and lies motionless and unattractive. The hook, therefore, should be entered below them, leaving the head and these openings hanging free. It is too large a bait for any but full-sized eels, as the small ones pull off the pendant portions without hooking themselves.

770. Eels may be taken during the spring, summer, and autumn. They haunt the recesses of the banks, or lie in the mud and weeds during the day, leaving these places only at night for food. Ponds, canals, and alluvial rivers are the chief localities for this fish, but few rivers are totally free from them. In some, however, they absolutely swarm, and even in small brooks they may be taken in quantities amounting to many hundredweight during their runs or migrations.

- 771. The Modes of taking these Fish vary with the apparatus employed. During the day, sniggling, bobbing, or ledger-line-fishing will be the most successful. The first is practised as follows :— Take the needle, armed and suspended as already described, and draw on it a large lob-worm in the following manner. Enter the eye of the needle at the head of the worm, and run it down till the whole needle is covered except the point, which is inserted in the notch or slit at the end of the rod, leaving the head of the worm free. In this way the head of the worm is presented to the eel, and is conducted into his hole or haunt by the bent end of the rod. As this end can be set at any angle, it may be guided round stumps or stones, and when it is gently insinuated as far as it will go, it is quietly left there. The line attached to the hook is held in the left hand, and as soon as the fish seizes the bait and has drawn it out of the cleft stick, slacken the line, and gently withdraw the stick; give a little time for the eel to swallow the bait, and then strike, when the needle will cross his throat, and hold him securely. Do not attempt at once to draw him out, but let him tire himself first, and when he is exhausted, pull him out. BOBBING is practised with the worms strung on worsted, as already described, and gathered up in links, which are to be attached to a line of whipcord about two yards long, having a knot on it eight or ten inches from the worms, and the lead slipped down to that point. When the eels bite, their teeth stick in the worsted, and they may be gently pulled out before they disentangle them. This mode I have never seen practised, and I have great doubts of its efficiency with any but small eels. LEDGER-LINE-FISHING for eels is similar to that for barbel, described at paragraph 738. For the purpose of taking eels by night, the trimmers may be set as for pike, or the night-line, as described at paragraph 764.

SECT. 12.—BOTTOM-FISHING FOR COMMON-TROUT, LAKE-TROUT, AND SEA-TROUT.

772. THE BOTTOM-ROD for trouting should be at least 17 feet long, and should be in fact similar to that described as the trolling-rod for pike (see paragraph 754). An ordinary TROUTING REEL and REEL LINE are sufficient for the purpose; and the casting line should have six lengths of good single-gut slightly stained with brown or brownish-green by means of common black or green tea. No silk should be used at the knots, but the simple angler's knot should be employed. THE HOOK for trout best adapted for the worm is No. 3 or 4, and for the minnow according to the kind of fishing adopted. When the hook is intended for the worm it ought to be whipped on to the gut with crimson silk, as the dark silk usually employed alters the colour of the transparent worm, and deters the trout from taking the bait. SHOT or lead, in some form, is required in order to sink the bait, and its weight should depend upon the strength of the current. Swan-shot answers best for this purpose, and, more or less, must be applied at the discretion of the

angler when by the water-side he ascertains the rate of the current. A FLOAT will sometimes, though not always, be needful, and may be either of cork or swan-quill, the latter being to be preferred. THE HOOKS FOR SPINNING-TACKLE are similar to those described at page 657; and the GORGE-HOOK will be found treated of at page 236.

773. THE BAITS FOR TROUT used in bottom-fishing are chiefly worms and minnows, the latter either natural or artificial. Caddies, however, and caterpillars, with gentles and salmon-roe, are in some localities much prized. The worms which are the best for trout-fishing are the marsh-worm, the button-worm, and the brandling; the last being chiefly adapted to the smaller sizes of fish. They should be well scoured, and applied as follows:—Six or eight dozen worms will in all probability be required in a good day's fishing, and should be carried in some damp moss in an appropriate bait-box, or canvas-bag. In putting the worms on the hook, take the latter in the right hand, between the finger and thumb, then taking a worm in the left finger and thumb, insert the point of the hook near the head of the worm and run it along its body until the whole of the hook is concealed, and also a very short portion of the gut; in doing this great care should be taken not to expose any part of the hook, and especially the barb, which should not on any account penetrate the side of the worm. If the worm is too small to conceal this quantity of the hook and line, and also to leave a portion, at least an inch long, hanging free from the end, two may be applied; and if on the other hand it is too long, the barbed-end may be brought through and re-entered an inch or so lower down, so as to pucker up a coil of the worm's length, which adds to its allurement, and at the same time prevents too long a free portion from hanging from the end. The worm is thus injured as little as possible, and will live a considerable time if not roughly used in the water. It should be examined every now and then to see that it is not broken. Grubs, caterpillars, and gentles are applied two or three at a time on the hooks—first one lengthwise, then one obliquely so as to leave each end free, and finally one lengthwise to conceal the barb. The mode of applying the dead minnow and parr-tail has been described under the head of "Baits," as well as the other ordinary methods of baiting the gorge-hook and the live minnow-tackle.

774. THE ARTIFICIAL MINNOW, in all its varieties, may be tried, and in some rivers and states of water will do great execution. In none, however, will it take equally well with a good and well-baited real minnow; and if these can be obtained, it is useless to

S

attempt to take fish with an inferior article. The DEVIL-BAIT is also sometimes successful; indeed trout are so capricious, that it is difficult at all times to say beforehand what they will take, and what refuse. I have already mentioned and described Mr. Blacker's modification of this bait.

775. THE COMMON TROUT is found in almost all the clear, gravelly, and quick-running streams throughout the three kingdoms, and sometimes, though not in the same perfection, in streams of an opposite character. They spawn in the autumn, the exact time varying in different localities; and they come into season in the spring, when also their time of perfection will be early or late, in accordance with the nature of their *habitat*. A low temperature seems rather to accelerate than retard their condition; and many of the Scotch streams are much earlier than those in the southern and western parts of the island. After August trout are not fit for the sport, being full of roe, or else spent from the operation of spawning. For bottom-fishing, the deeper and stiller parts of the stream answer better than the very rough freshes, though even for this kind of fishing perfectly still water is not so well calculated as that rate of stream which will move the bait without destroying its form or texture. The great lake-trout is met with in a few of the large lakes in Scotland, while the sea-trout are common in all the Scotch salmon-rivers. Under this term, so well known to anglers, are comprehended the bull-trout, the salmon-trout, and the finnoch or herling.

776. THE VARIOUS MODES OF TAKING TROUT will be now entered upon. First, fishing with the worm is practised by obtaining all the apparatus and bait described at paragraphs 772-3; the angler then, with his wading-boots on, if he uses them, quietly wades into a part of the river which will command an extensive sweep of likely water; or, if preferring *terra firma*, he keeps as much as possible out of sight of the fish upon a part of the bank suitable for his purpose, and below the water to be fished. It must be known, that the worm should in all cases be cast up-stream, and suffered to float down again, for reasons which will be clear enough when explained as follows :— first, the trout always lie head up-stream, and therefore do not see the angler so well below them as above; secondly, the bait floats gently down without injury, which must be done to it if dragged against stream; thirdly, in hooking the fish, the barb is much more likely to lay hold in this way than if he is struck in the line of the axis of his body; and fourthly, the water is not disturbed by the wader till it has been already fished. The angler swings or casts

his worm gently as far up-stream as he can, using as long a line as he can easily manage, and no more, and suffering it to float down with the stream till within a short distance of the place where he is standing, when it should be lifted and recast. When a fish is felt to bite or lay hold of the worm, wait a few seconds till he has done nibbling, and the moment he is running off with it strike smartly but tenderly with the wrist, not with the whole power of the arm, and proceed to land your fish with as little delay as possible.'

777. GRUBS, CATERPILLARS, GENTLES, &c., are all used in the same way, and will serve the angler well in many localities, but as a general bait for trout they are not equal to the worm. Fishing with the salmon-roe will be found more particularly described at the end of this section.

778. IN USING THE LIVE MINNOW, the hook (of size No. 3) should be entered at the back-fin, and the barb should stand up a little above the surface; the line then being shotted, and a swan-quill float applied at about three feet from the hook, the bait is suffered to swim about in any direction but that of weeds, or other dangerous spots in the bed of the river. As, however, trout are chiefly found in strong running streams, and as in such situations some force must be exerted upon the minnow in keeping it from running with the stream, its life is soon destroyed, and therefore the live minnow is not so well adapted for trout-fishing as for perch or pike; but in those rivers whose current is comparatively slow, and which are nevertheless the haunts of large trout—as, for instance, the Thames, the Severn, the Warwickshire Avon, &c., the minnow may be used alive with advantage, keeping it out of the rough water which is always at the foot of weirs and waterfalls, where dead or artificial minnows are much more useful.

779. THE DEAD MINNOW USED WITH SPINNING TACKLE, according to one or other of the modes recommended at page 238, is most suited for taking large trout; and the precise style of fishing with these baits is as follows; but the angler should understand that the principle on which he conducts his operations is not that of a slavish imitation of the motions of the natural live minnow, such as will answer to a certain extent with the pike and perch, which are less wary than the trout, but rather to produce such a quick and constant spin of the bait as shall conceal the hooks from the fish to be caught. The principal point, therefore, is to fix the bait on the hooks so as to spin well, and to last in this state a long time; and thus to avoid as much as possible the renewing of the bait.

by which time is lost, and generally just at the most valuable period of the day. No bait comes so near perfection in these several points as the parr-tail, and it will, I am persuaded, as far as a limited trial will allow of an opinion, be found to be better suited than any other to spinning for trout, in all streams where the current is strong. I have already remarked that gudgeon, or other fish of the same size, in the absence of the parr, will be large enough for this purpose. When the bait is properly applied, according to the mode recommended at page 236, the line should be cast as gently as possible by means of the trolling-rod, taking care not to injure the texture of the fish-bait by jerking it violently, and therefore avoiding too long a line and too forcible a throw. Underhand casting does less damage than when the bait is thrown overhand, and by its adoption the splash in its fall into the water is also much less considerable. In working the bait everything depends upon the strength of the stream; but the rule always is to make the minnow spin as fast as possible without injury to its texture. Thus when it is drawn against the stream, it may be steadily brought towards the hand, and made to revolve, chiefly by the action of the current. If, however, it is drawn down stream, a series of jerks must be given, or it will not spin sufficiently fast; and yet if the pull is maintained so as to keep up the spinning at the same rate throughout, the casting-line itself makes a very prominent ripple, and by the overdoing of the attempt serves to scare away the fish. The line should always be well shotted, as the minnow will otherwise rise too near the surface, and no float will be required, inasmuch as the bait is always at the end of a "taut" line. Mr. Stoddart also recommends the adoption of a plain hook, baited with a minnow as when using a worm, running it in at the tail and bringing it out at the mouth; after which he hitches the gut over the tail to suit the bait in its proper position. With this he fishes as with a worm in low and clear states of the water; but as I have never seen this bait used I cannot speak as to its efficiency. It is exactly the reverse of Izaak Walton's mode of entering the hook, and according to Mr. Stoddart's practice and theory, is much to be preferred to it. Colonel Hawker's mode of baiting the hook with the addition of side hooks, is used in the same way as ordinary spinning tackle, and the minnow baited as he recommends will be found tolerably serviceable. It is merely the addition of the side hooks to Izaak Walton's method of applying the hook, which has the objection of offering the wrong end to the trout, having the barb at the tail instead of the head. It is therefore no wonder that trout so often are missed when rushing at it, since they almost invariably endeavour to seize the head. This is the case with most predacious animals, which are instinctively made aware that this part is the most vital organ, and they almost always begin by eating the brain where such an organ exists. When fishing with the minnow well leaded and in deep water, the angler seldom sees the trout rush at his bait, but is warned by the sense of touch, rather than by his eyes that the trout is at it. At this moment the angler slackens his line gently for a couple of seconds, and then strikes with his wrist, using only a slight jerk. The trout is now either hooked or alarmed, but generally the former is the case, unless he is a very shy, wary old fox; in which case he is not likely to be again tempted on that day. If, however, the trout is seen approaching the minnow, the angler ought to endeavour, as far as his nerves will allow him, to continue the precise kind of motion which attracted the fish, until he not only *sees* him at the bait, but *feels* his pull, when he should proceed exactly as if all was out of sight. This, however, is a difficult task, and few young fishermen have sufficient command over themselves to avoid the mistake to which their attention is here directed. Every one who has hooked fish of any size with fine tackle must be aware how difficult it is when commencing trout-fishing, to carry out in practice the theory which he has been endeavouring to realise for some time past; and each, in his turn, must have been made painfully conscious of the danger not only of striking too soon and too hard, but of attempting to land a large fish with fine gut before he is tired. My own early recollections satisfy me on this point; and I remember on one occasion losing a trout of at least five pounds weight, through excess of anxiety to land him rapidly and triumphantly; although, theoretically, I was fully aware of the folly of my proceedings. All of us, I have no doubt, could tell the same tale; and so it must ever be. Nothing but practice can give that steadiness of nerve and presence of mind which will enable the fisherman, or any other sportsman, to do the right thing at the right time. In bringing the minnow home, if the angler is on the bank, he should be very careful to lift it from the water slowly and quietly, as it is very often at that moment that the trout seizes it. Whether he fancies that the bait is a live minnow leaping out of the water, or whether the value of the thing is increased by the prospect of losing it, cannot of course be surely known, but it is certain that at this moment many large trout which have cautiously followed the bait all through the cast, are at last tempted to rush at it, and may then be taken if the above precaution is adopted; whilst, on the other hand, they are assuredly scared if the bait is carelessly drawn out of the water.

780. TROLLING FOR THE GREAT LAKE-TROUT is often practised in the Scotch lakes. For this purpose two strong and long trolling-rods are required, with lines of at least 80 yards of strong twisted silk, or good hand-made hair-line. This kind of fishing must be carried on from a boat suited to the state of the lake, which, if liable to strong currents or winds, will require it to be of full size and seaworthy. This is rowed out into the lake by a couple of men, who manage it and impel it in the direction and at the rate of speed indicated by the angler, or by some experienced hand, if he is young or a stranger to the locality. Very strong swivel-traces will be required with the double swivels, and either strong gimp or treble-gut must be used for the hook-length; but if the latter, it also must be guarded with brass wire, as these fish are very apt to bite through anything which is capable of being easily cut or divided. The parr-tail form of hooks may be used with one of the rods, and baited with a small trout or smoult; on the other may be used, by way of variety, any of the ordinary forms of hooks, or the following, which, as being equally simple and efficacious, may be strongly relied on:—Two hooks of No. 3 size are tied together at a considerable angle with a third of No. 5 size, whose shank comes quite close to the point of junction of the two hooks. This form of hook is used with a large smoult or small trout, and will generally succeed, though not I think so good as Mr. Stoddart's parr-tail. The traces should be heavily leaded with rolled lead or swan-shot. In using these baits the angler is rowed out into deep water, and then drops one of his baits from the stern of the boat whilst slowly progressing under the oars, and allows the line to run out about 30 yards, when it is stopped by some kind of hitch, such as a slip-knot or any other device, and the rod is fixed over the side of the stern at an angle of 30 or 40 degrees. The other rod is then set in the same way, and the boat steadily kept going at about two miles an hour. If the boat nears the shore, or rows along it in a circular direction, the line on the shore-side ought to be shorter than the other by at least 10 yards. The line ought to be free, or so nearly so as to barely withstand the force of the boat moving through the water; if therefore a slip-not is used, see that it is a very free one. A stone is some-

times employed, placed in the bottom of the boat, or a piece of cobbler's-wax on the butt-end of the rod to which the line is attached by the thumb, and from which it is easily torn by the pull of the fish. When a large trout is hooked, the boat should be rowed to the shore, and the fish landed with the landing-net or gaff. ARTIFICIAL MINNOWS, or other fish, are used for the common trout, or lake-trout, exactly as in fishing with their originals for which they are substituted, except that the striking must be quicker, so as to prevent the trout from detecting his error, and thus leaving the bait before he is hooked. There is one other bait to which I have alluded, the description of the mode of using which must now be given; it is a very deadly bait, and will so generally take trout, that it is by many considered to be closely allied to poaching—this is the SALMON-ROE, the mode of using which is as follows:—The directions for curing the roe and making the paste have been already given, but the *ova*, or beads, must be removed from the jar before use, and placed in flannel in a warm place, and under slight pressure, so as to toughen the skin. In fishing with this bait, the refuse particles are used as ground-bait, and then the hook is strung with the beads or baited with the paste, and the trout taken as fast as this attractive food will tempt them to their fate. Mr. Stoddart recommends two hooks to be tied back to back, and then brought half round so that their bends stand at right angles to one another, in which state they hold the paste very well. He is of opinion that this bait is too murderous in ordinary rivers, and only suited to such localities as are frequented by trout in search of salmon-roe, when it may be desirable, for the sake of the salmon, either to get rid of the trout or to scare them away, and disgust them with this particular food. His mode of fishing with salmon-roe is the following:—"Let the angler, provided with a stiffish single-handed rod and the tackle already described, sally forth either alone or consorted, at most, with one companion in arms. He may either betake himself to one of the accustomed beats, if not previously occupied by another party, or pitch upon some untried piece of water which, although of limited range, possesses the same qualities of depth, speed, and bottom. Near the head of this he ought to select his stand, or post, on a dry and unexposed portion of the bank. There is no necessity, on commencing operations, that he should bait the spot. This in the course of a few throws will be done quite sufficiently without occasioning, as the other practice does, the gorging and repletion of a portion of the fish further down. In throwing, the angler should generally employ a short line, not much exceeding his rod in length, and occasionally a good deal shorter. He can always in that highly discoloured state of water in which the salmon-roe is most effective as a bait, entice his sport to within a yard's distance of the margin. Accordingly he loses no advantage by employing the description of line I have recommended, and in the matter of striking acquires a very important one. Sometimes, however, in certain localities, and where bull-trout or whitlings are observed moving in his vicinity, it may be expedient to increase the length of his cast, or throw; also, in brown or fine waters it is essential to do so. In baiting with the paste, let the angler extract a small portion, equal in size to a horse-bean, from the pot or jar. He requires then to insert it between the projecting barbs of his hooks, in the angle formed by their junction. A slight pressure of the finger will assist in attaching it, but it is not necessary to conceal every portion of the hook as in worm-fishing. When casting, the angler ought to be extremely cautious, lest, by excess of force, he should occasion his bait to drop off . . . . In the mode of fishing recommended, the angler ought to restrict his operations to a single spot in the range or beat occupied by him, when he will effectually concentrate the feeding trout, and render available a great proportion of his casts. He should always keep his line *taut*, sounding, as it were, the bottom with the leads attached to it; and holding himself on the alert in case of any sudden stoppage by the seizure of the fish." Such is Mr. Stoddart's account of his mode of fishing with the salmon-roe; there seems to be one objection only to its use, namely, that it is too successful; but that is a ground of rejection the force of which the young angler will be little inclined to admit.

SECT. 13.—SALMON-FISHING WITH THE WORM OR FISH-BAIT.

781. The most simple kind of tackle used in bottom-fishing for the salmon, is that employed when the worm is used. For this purpose a single hook (Nos. 1 or 2) is whipped to a length of strong single salmon-gut, which should extend at least five or six feet, and then be joined through the intervention of a swivel-hook to the casting-line. The reel-line should be about 45 yards long, made of good plaited line, or hand-twisted hair-line; and the reel should be of full size, simple, and with the large barrel instead of the multiplier. About two feet from the hook five or six swan-shot are to be applied, or a piece of roll-lead if the stream is very strong and powerful; since the tendency in such cases always is to cast *up* all objects

thrown into the water, and therefore the increased weight is required to counteract this power. Sometimes two hooks are used in worm-fishing for salmon (Nos. 1 and 4); the first is tied on below, and the latter a little above its shank. The rod for this kind of fishing is the ordinary trolling-rod, with the substitution of a more elastic top for that which is required to manœuvre the bait in minnow-spinning.

782. THE SPINNING-TACKLE for salmon is exactly similar to that used for the *Salmo Ferox*, or great lake-trout; the only difference being that it requires a greater weight of lead to sink it to the bottom, where the salmon always feed when in search of fish or worms.

783. THE MODE OF BAITING the single hook with the worm, is to take two or three lob-worms, or marsh-worms, and run the point of the hook through an inch of one of them near the head, then omit about an inch and a quarter, and insert the hook again through another inch; after which a second worm is to be served in the same way, and if they are not of good size a third, always finishing by leaving the point and barb within the body of the lowest worm, and about two inches from the point of its tail. In this way the worms lie in four or six loops on the hook, with their heads and tails free, and they are killing in proportion as they are constantly moving in their struggles to free themselves from the hook. In baiting the double-hook, the lower one is entered at the head of the worm and brought out at the tail; the worm is then drawn over the point of the upper hook by bending the gut, and it is stretched up to the shank as well as partially over the gut, in which process the point appears projecting from the middle of the worm. Next, transfix another worm with the lower hook, and then impale one half of it upon the upper hook so as to conceal it, leaving the lower half of the worm free; finally, conceal the bend and barb of the lower hook with a third worm.

784. MINNOWS, PARR, SMOULTS, TROUT, &c., are applied to the hook exactly in the same way as in trout-fishing, remembering always that the bait should be of a larger size, in order to tempt the salmon, and that as the baits are larger so the hooks must correspond in dimensions, in order to carry them properly. ARTIFICIAL FISH-BAITS are used also for salmon similar to those for trout, but larger.

785. SALMON ARE CHIEFLY TAKEN with the worm or minnow from the beginning of March to the middle of June, but sometimes even in the autumn they may be tempted with the worm or fish-bait. Still water—that is to say, water comparatively still—is

the best fitted for bottom-fishing; and in such situations they often take the fish-bait or worm in preference to the fly. It often happens in severe spring frosts when the water is clear, but of a cold uninviting green colour, that the salmon will take the parr-tail freely, and yet refuse the fly *in toto*. But all further rules on this subject are useless, as so much depends upon the variations of the season, that what will suit in one year will fail in an exactly similar condition of water in the following season. The safe plan, when the salmon are shy, is either to try all baits in succession until the killing one is pitched upon, or to watch others doing the same thing, and then to profit by their experience. If, however, the angler is himself trying the various experiments necessary to the final selection, he ought to have a thorough knowledge of the locality, and be able to judge *at a glance*, from the condition of the river, what humour the salmon are likely to be in. It must be known, that a pertinacious use of an unseasonable bait not only destroys all chance of sport with other bait on that day, but disgusts the fish with that particular kind of lure for many days, or even weeks to come. Hence, this practice is a dangerous weapon in the hands of the tyro, and, though very successful with the experienced hand, is capable of doing great mischief if abused. This is more especially the case with the worm, which requires the water to be exactly in one particular state for its successful employment; and if used at any other time will disgust the fish for a long period. Hence, it is essential to its use that the water shall be just low and clear enough to allow the bait to be seen, and yet that the stream shall be sufficient to carry the worm down at a certain distance from the bed. The fly may have been used to any extent, and will not interfere with bottom-fishing; but if the worm has been often exhibited to the salmon, it is useless to repeat the offer for some time to come.

786. THE MODE OF FISHING for the salmon with the worm is the following:—Let out about 20 feet of line, and attach the worm in one or other of the modes described in paragraph 783. Then let the fisher take his stand on the bank, and draw out a yard and a half of the line from the reel, letting it hang loosely from the butt-end of the rod, so as to offer no impediment to the salmon when he seizes the bait. He then casts his worm well across the water, directing it slightly downwards; the current immediately seizes hold of it, and sweeps it onwards with a tendency towards his own side, and in this sweep the salmon takes it, if so inclined. When it reaches the side of the river on which the angler

stands, he must lift it gradually from the water, but without jerking it, and repeat his cast, slightly varying the direction. If during this proceeding the fisher experiences any pull, whether decidedly from a fish or from any other cause, he should give out line until he finds some very decided pull upon it, such as to leave no doubt upon his mind that the salmon has bolted the bait, when a very slight elevation of the wrist will strike the hook or hooks into the throat of the salmon, and the angler has only to proceed according to the size of the fish in order to effect his capture. Of course with the strong tackle used in worm-fishing less danger of losing him is incurred than with the fly; but still with large and vigorous fish some care is necessary, and the butt-end of the rod must be advanced pretty constantly, and for some little time, before the gaff or landing-net can be safely called into requisition. IN USING THE SPINNING-TACKLE with the parr-tail or troutling as a bait, it is spun exactly as for trout; but as the leads are heavier there is more danger of its fouling the bottom; and if so, the angler must proceed as the coachman does with his whip when it is fast in a buckle or trace—that is to say, he must by a rapid throw of the rod suddenly slacken his line and thrust the bait away from him. This often succeeds; but if it fails, recourse must be had to a long forked-stick, or the clearing-ring, or drag-hook (see paragraphs 709 and 710), by which a great part, if not all of the line may be saved; and as the loss of a part is better than the whole, so the loss of the hook will be borne better than that of the whole of the tackle.

SECT. 14.—GRAYLING BOTTOM-FISHING.

787. THE TACKLE FOR GRAYLING must be of the finest description; and most grayling-fishers prefer a single hair casting-line on that account. This or a single-gut length of six or seven feet, with a swan-quill float and a fine hook of No. 6, 7, or 8, will complete the equipment for this species of sport—that is to say, in conjunction with a rod of 16 or 17 feet in length, and a reel and reel-line of such dimensions as to afford about 25 or 30 yards of available line. Three or four No. 2 shot will generally be wanted, or if gentles are used, No. 4 or 5 will be heavy enough.

788. THE BEST BAITS for graylings are the gentle (well-scoured), the caddis-worm, and the brandling, or the red-worm. The various grubs are also employed with success in grayling-fishing; indeed all the small larvæ will take this fish, but none are better than the gentle and the caddis-worm. GROUND-BAITING should always be practised, but not too profusely, as this fish

is more easily satiated than some others in which ground-baiting is employed; and it is also less discriminating, so that it will take unscoured bait as readily as the well-scoured bait on the hook. Still, without the temptation afforded by a few unbaited gentles, it will be less likely to take the armed ones with avidity, and will consequently refuse to be charmed out of its gravelly bed. The minnow is not often taken by the grayling, but occasionally it has been used with success; still, the grayling-fisher will waste his time by endeavouring to capture this fish with any bottom-lure but those which I have specified above.

789. GRAYLING ARE IN SEASON in the autumn, coming in just as the trout go out. They spawn in April and May, and come round so as to be edible by the end of July; but they are not in high season till the 1st of September. They are found in clear gravelly streams, as well as those which are loaded with mud, such as the Wye in the lower part of its course; but in the latter kind of river they are not so fine and beautifully coloured as in the pellucid and gravelly bed of the Teme, and the upper course of the Severn, as well as in the Wye above Hereford. Unlike the trout, they are not spread over the three kingdoms, but are confined to about 12 or 18 rivers, including, chiefly, the Wye, Usk, Lug, Teme, Severn, Dove, Trent, and Humber. From this circumstance, they have been supposed to have been introduced into this country by the monks, and the theory is very probably correct, though wholly incapable of proof.

790. THE GRAYLING is taken either by simple float-angling (the angler striking pretty quickly, but gently) or by dipping (see par. 794) or sinking and drawing. The depth at which the bait is to lie varies much, but in general, during the first part of the season, these fish feed near the surface, and later on nearer the bottom. All sorts of natural flies and grasshoppers may be used successfully as dippers, and the artificial fly also; but as this will be here-after treated of under the head of Fly-fishing, it will be unnecessary to allude more fully to this mode in the present chapter. Grayling play pretty freely at first, but do not fight nearly so strongly as the trout of the same size; hence, even with the single hair, they may generally be landed in twenty minutes, or even less; and the instances in which tackle is broken by this fish, in the hands of a skilful angler, are rare indeed.

CHAP. IV.
NATURAL AND ARTIFICIAL FLY-FISHING.

SECT. 1.—THE FISH WHICH WILL TAKE THE FLY.

791. In the chapter on Bottom-fishing I have remarked, that all fish may be taken by that mode; but now it must be explained that the circle from which the victims of the fly-fisher's art are to be selected is much more limited. He may, however, flatter himself that all, or nearly so, of the most prized varieties are included in his list, and this is the case not only in the British islands but in almost all countries. In India fly-fishing is practised to a great extent, and indeed wherever the *salmonidæ* are found it may be freely indulged in. The following list includes all those fish which will take the fly so freely as to be worth the angler's notice; and I shall describe the particular mode of fishing for them in the order of their value, not only as edible fish, but as affording sport to the angler, beginning with the little playful bleak, and ending with the lordly salmon. They are— first, bleak; secondly, dace; thirdly, roach; fourthly, chub; fifthly, grayling, sixthly, trout in all its varieties; seventhly salmon.

SECT. 2.—VARIETIES OF FLY-FISHING.

792. NATURAL FLY-FISHING consists in the use of the various living flies, grass-hoppers, &c., which are found on the banks of rivers and lakes. It is practised by a process which is called DIPPING, but chiefly in such situations as are so much overhung with bushes as to preclude the use of the artificial fly. In these spots the water is generally still, and there is no possibility of offering the lure in any other position than a state of almost entire quiescence. Hence all imitations are easily discoverable; and the real fly and grasshopper, &c., are the only surface-baits which the fish will take.

793. ARTIFICIAL FLY-FISHING, on the other hand, consists in the use of imitations of these flies, and also of other fancy flies, by means of an elastic rod and fine tackle, and by a process which is called whipping. All fish which will take the one will take the other kind of lure, but not always with an

equal degree of avidity, as we shall hereafter find; but as the principle is the same in both cases, they are better treated together, rather than to go over the same ground a second time.

794. THE TACKLE FOR DIPPING is much more simple than that employed in whipping, and it consists of a moderately-short and stiff rod (the spinning or trolling-rod, *minus* its butt-joint, answers this purpose well)—of a short but strong reel-line of hand-twisted hair—of a single length—or two at most of gut—and of a fine hook suited in size to the bait and fish. In dipping, it is usual to lengthen or shorten the line, which is used from a foot in length to two or three yards, by coiling it round the end of the top joint, and uncoiling it as the line is wished to be extended, and after the rod has been insinuated through the trees or bushes growing on the banks. Some anglers use a reel fixed upon the lower part of the second joint, and with a hair-line it acts pretty well; but with a plaited one it is difficult to protrude the line from the end of the rod without so great a degree of disturbance as to alarm the fish. The uncoiling from the end of the rod is not unattended with this disadvantage; but it is less objectionable than doing so entirely from the reel, though I think, for the sake of convenience, that appendage may be added, taking care to have the lowest joint free, so as to be able to shorten the rod by that amount at pleasure.

795. FOR WHIPPING, OR FLY-FISHING as it is generally called—that is, for the use of the artificial fly, a rod, either single or two-handed, according to circumstances, is required, with a fine reel-line and large barrelled-reel; and, also, a long casting-line, with one, two, or three droppers, each armed with a fly.

796. THE FLY-ROD is either a single-handed one, or, when used for the larger varieties of the trout or for salmon, the two-handed rod. Both of these rods are usually made of the same materials, and they differ only in size, the single-handed varying from 11 to 13 feet in length, while the two-handed extends from 14 to 20 feet. They are both usually made in four or five lengths, but in Scotland they are, I-believe, seldom in more than three pieces. The butt-end is generally an ash-sapling, sometimes solid, and at others hollowed out to receive the small joints. The middle joints are almost always made of hickory, and the top joint either of lancewood alone, or of that wood spliced with the bamboo and strengthened with silk. Many of the best and lightest fly-rods are now made, except the butt-end, of rent and glued bamboo; and none are more beautiful and efficient than these if properly used; but they are very fragile in careless hands, and therefore scarcely fitted for the young angler. Mr. Blacker's rods are of the most beautiful construction, and may be obtained at a price varying from two guineas upwards. They are far superior to any of home manufacture, or to those obtained at inferior and cheaper shops. Nothing in the whole range of the manufacture of fishing-tackle requires greater skill than the putting together of a good fly-rod; for it must possess great pliancy and strength, and yet it must balance exactly in the hand, and *yield equally in every part.* This last quality is essential to the due management of the fly, for without it it is impossible, except by long use of the same rod, to do full justice to the art which is under consideration. These various materials are generally brought up in colour to that of the red hickory, by means of the application of a mineral acid, aided sometimes by logwood if the colour is desired to be very dark. Finally the whole rod is varnished, and this process should be repeated at the end of each season before the rod is put by. The portions of the rod are united together in the same way as the bottom-fishing rod, by means of brass ferules; but, in addition, a small pin, or a flat hook of doubled and bent wire, is usually fixed close to the socket and head of each piece, and after the latter is passed into the former these pins are united by a few turns of waxed silk, in the form of a figure of 8, so as to prevent the force exacted in throwing the fly from separating the rod into two or more portions. On finishing the day's fishing these may be cut away or retained at the discretion of the fisher, who will sometimes prefer keeping his rod together from day to day, to the trouble of repeating this operation on each visit to the river. About from 10 to 14 good sized rings should be fixed on that side of the rod on which the reel is used, whichever that may be; and they may be applied by means of a piece of quill and a few turns of waxed silk above and below the ring. At the butt-end a SPIKE, which is capable of being withdrawn like a toothpick into its case, is exceedingly useful; and as its weight serves to balance the outward length of the rod, it is rather advantageous than otherwise. It is moreover so useful in fixing the rod while recovering the fly when entangled, that I should strongly advise the young angler to adopt it, or to have with him a screw-spike capable of being attached whenever that unpleasant occurrence takes place. THE REEL is either simple, with a large drum or

central barrel, or otherwise. The multiplier is made with a series of wheels, which are intended to give out and take in the line more rapidly than the simple machine. In this desirable point I am satisfied that the object is attained much more completely by the simple large drum; for though the multiplier is very pretty in theory, yet in practice it is constantly failing in its powers when tested by a strong fish. Besides this, the large drum actually gives out line much faster than the multiplier, and has therefore that point in its favour; while in taking it in, he must be a bungler indeed who cannot wind the winch or handle rapidly enough to do all which he wishes to effect; and it is quite certain, that what is done is better and more smoothly done in this way than by the aid of wheels and cogs, which are liable to jerks and interruptions. Upon this reel is wound from 30 to 80 yards of line, varying with the rod and the fish for which it is to be used; thus, the smaller fish, including the ordinary run of common trout and the grayling, will require only 30 or 35 yards, while the larger varieties of trout and the salmon should always have from 60 to 80 yards ready for their capture. The HAIR-LINE, as made by the hand, I have already described at paragraph 619, and I believe this, if well-made by a careful yet handy man, will be superior to those usually sold in the shops, and made by the machine. It should be regularly tapered, and should vary in strength from 24 hairs down to 14 for salmon, and from 18 down to 10 or 12 for trout. The tapering portion, however, should only extend, in the trout-line, as far as it is clear of the reel, which may be estimated at about half the length of the line; and in the salmon-line only for about 20 yards from the end. Plaited silk lines are now much used, especially for salmon, but I confess I have never seen any line which could be thrown with as much certainty as the hand-made horse-hair line. It has just sufficient stiffness to carry itself smoothly through the air, with pliancy enough to adapt itself to all the varying evolutions of the angler's wrists and arms. Nevertheless, I am aware that many good anglers give the preference to the plaited line, and it is no doubt very superior to the old machine-twisted article, which was constantly "kinking," and from that circumstance liable to break. The CASTING-LINE is composed of two, and sometimes of three portions; the first, or extreme portion, consisting, in all cases, of several lengths of single-gut carefully knotted together, with or without silk "lapping;" the next portion is usually of treble-gut, twisted by the machine, or by the quills and

bobbins which I have described at paragraph 619. To these some anglers add a third portion of twisted hair, which however is unnecessary if the reel-line is properly tapered, and is of hair also. The great principle to be carried out is to taper the line from the point of the rod to the end, so that in working it through the air it shall play smoothly, and obey the hand to the greatest nicety. In this respect it should imitate the four-in-hand whip, which is so graduated that it tapers all the way, and is hence capable of taking a fly off the leader's ear. The gut varies in strength and size, from that required for the salmon to the finer sizes used in grayling or small trout-fishing. The single-gut portion is generally about two yards long, and terminates in a fly which is called the stretcher, and which is either dressed on a length of gut, or has a fine loop left at its head by which it may be attached to any fresh length of gut. About three or four feet from this stretcher another fly, called a dropper, is attached by means of a short length of gut, usually about three or four inches long; and at the junction of the single-gut with the twisted portion there is another dropper, with a somewhat longer length of gut. If more than two droppers are used, the single-gut length is increased to eight feet, and the third dropper is then introduced midway between the two already described, with a length of gut of about six inches, while that of the highest is increased to eight; by which gradual increase of length the stretcher and the droppers all ought to touch the water at the same time, while the foot-length of the casting-line extends in a gentle sweep from the stretcher to the point of the rod. The mode of attaching these droppers to the casting-line is by opening the water-knots, and then introducing the dropper-gut between their two portions, after having previously knotted its end. This should be done as neatly as possible, to avoid making an unsightly projection. Most anglers whip the ends of the water-knots with white silk waxed with white wax, and also take a few turns round the dropper-gut to make all secure. The ARTIFICIAL FLIES have been already fully described in the second chapter.

SECT. 4. — BLEAK-FISHING, AND GENERAL DIRECTIONS FOR THROWING THE FLY.

797. WHIPPING FOR BLEAK forms the best introduction to the use of the fly-rod, especially as these little fish may be met with on almost all our canals and rivers, and often in situations where there are no trees to interfere with the use of the line. Almost any small midge or gnat will take the bleak, and the tackle throughout should

be of the finest description, with a light single-handed rod of about 11 or 12 feet in length. The young angler should now take as much pains in throwing his fly as if he were intent upon the capture of the finest salmon. In watching the evolutions of the general run of fishermen, it is common enough to see two or three feet of line touching the water before the fly, whereas the contrary ought to be the case, and the fly should alight on the water as airily and gently as its natural prototype, with scarcely any portion of the line following its example by coming into contact with the water at all. If the angler will only endeavour to avoid jerking his line, and will coax his fly rather than force it forwards, he will soon see the difference. The cast or throw is effected as follows, when the rod is light and there is plenty of elbow-room. I am now supposing that the angler has a rod of 11 feet in length, and a line, altogether, of about 18, with either a single stretcher, or in addition one or two droppers, all very minute; he takes the casting-line in his left hand, at such a distance from the fly that it is quite clear of the ground, and with the rod pointing forward and to the left; then at the moment when he looses the line, he, with a half side and half backward movement of the arm, sweeps the line in a gentle curve till it is well behind and above him. It is at this point that the first mistake is likely to occur, as here the awkward hand generally jerks his fly (which is sometimes even whipped off with a snap), and after this jerk he can never regain that even and smooth flow which would otherwise follow its alteration from the backward to the forward direction. When this movement is elegantly and effectively carried out, the line, without any abrupt change, is brought round the head from the backward to the forward movement without passing directly overhead, but in a line considerably above the level of the head of the angler; when it has passed before the body, it is thrown forwards *at the full length of the arm*, and, without the slightest hurry, to the point which it is intended the fly shall alight upon. If this is badly executed, and with any jerk, the line is doubled upon itself, and the loop thus made touches the water whilst the fly is two or three feet from its destination, and finally descends with a whole series of convolutions of gut or hair, enough to alarm all the fish within sight. This is called throwing from the left shoulder, from which mode throwing from the right shoulder, or back-casting, differs in bringing the rod and arm (after they have achieved the backward movement) forwards again by the side of the head, delivering the fly over the right shoulder

without making the complete circular sweep behind the body. Sometimes when it is desirable to throw the fly with great delicacy, it is dried by waving the line from right to left over the head, in the form of a figure of 8; but this can only be effectively done with a single fly, as the droppers interfere with the manœuvre too much to allow of its being tried when they are used. The young angler should practise both methods, and should never consider that he has mastered the first great difficulty until he has acquired the power of dropping his fly upon the water tolerably near a given spot by both the above methods, and without its being preceded by any portion of the line, or followed by more than a few inches of it. As soon as he has thus dropped his fly he begins to draw it more or less directly to him, and with a series of jerks, varying a good deal according to the fly and the fish to be taken. In whipping for bleak, very little more need be done than to bring the fly gently and steadily towards the bank, and then repeat the cast in a fresh direction. When hooked, they may be landed at once, even with a single hair-line. DIPPING may be practised with the bleak, using the natural house-fly, or in fact any small fly; but it requires very little art, and I shall therefore postpone the description of this species of fishing until the section treating of Chub-fishing.

SECT. 5.—ROACH AND DACE.

798. DACE may be taken with the artificial fly, and afford even better practice than the bleak, since they will take a coarser fly, and the tackle may be somewhat larger in proportion. The line, therefore, having more substance is more easily handled, and the fly may be manœuvred to a much greater nicety. Black and red palmers, or gnats, will generally take dace; and two droppers may be added in almost all cases to the stretcher, the angler varying the fly upon each,

799. ROACH may also be taken with the same flies and tackle, but they do not rise to the fly nearly so well as the dace and bleak.

800. DIPPING may also be used with both of these fish, but they will in general take the artificial fly quite as readily, even in still water.

SECT. 6.—MODE OF TAKING CHUB WITH THE ARTIFICIAL AND NATURAL FLY.

801. THESE FISH generally lie under the shade of willows or other trees, and very often are difficult to get at with the artificial fly, which, moreover, they do not at any time take so readily as the natural one. Sometimes, however, good chub may be taken in the middle of the day, while

basking on the surface of the water, by means of fine tackle and an artificial humble-bee, or a small red hackle, or an ant-fly, on a No. 6 or 7 hook; but their best time is in the mornings and evenings. When they do take the fly on this fine tackle, they require great care at first, as they fight very hard for a short time; and are, on that account, excellent practice for the embryo salmon-fisher.

802. IN DIPPING FOR CHUB, which is the best and most certain mode of bringing them to the basket, the following flies, &c., will be found most useful :—First, the blue-bottle fly (two of which may be put on one hook) is a most killing bait for chub; secondly, hairy caterpillars; thirdly, beetles of all kinds, including cockchafers; fourthly, grasshoppers and humble-bees also are among these most destructive lures; and lastly, the May-fly is a certain killer. All these various natural baits must be used very cautiously, and the angler should make as little noise as possible, and should hide himself behind as large a tree as he can find. The beetle, or other bait, having been applied on the hook so that the barb lies under the division between the wing-cases, the quantity of line necessary, which seldom exceeds two yards, is coiled around the end of the rod, so as to be capable in this state of being portruded quietly through an opening in the overhanging branches of the trees, whose shade the chub chiefly affects. When the trolling-rod, thus armed, has insinuated itself, and is clear of all obstruction, it may be very gently turned round so as to lengthen the line by unrolling it, and the bait in the most imperceptible manner is suffered to reach the water. If there are water-lilies or other flat leaves floating on the water, a good plan is to drop the beetle on one of them, and then gently draw it off the side into the water, when, if there is a chub near, he generally seizes upon it. But in all cases avoid a splash, and let the armed hook reach the water so gently as to cause scarcely a ripple. When there it may be very gently jerked in all directions, a few inches at a time; avoiding all contact of the line with the water, and imitating the movements on the water of the insects which frequent it. In this way good fish may generally be tempted to their fate, and when hooked, may be played and landed in the same way as with the artificial fly; but as the rod is not so suited to this purpose, owing to its stiffness, and as the line is shorter, the chub must be mastered and landed with the net as soon as possible.

SECT. 7.—GRAYLING-FISHING.

803. WITH THE ARTIFICIAL-FLY the gray-ling affords good sport; and as this fish is in season at a time when salmon and trout are going or gone out, it is highly prized on that account, if not owing to its intrinsic sport-giving powers.

804. THE FLIES FOR GRAYLING are similar to those for trout, and especially to those used in the autumn. Nos. 1, 2, 3, and 5, of the trouting-flies, at page 268, may be used early in the season; and later on, Nos. 7, 8, and 9. Sometimes the May-fly will take these fish, but not very commonly, except at a time when they are not considered so fit for the table as in the later months of the year. The winged larva, No. 16 in the preceding list, will also take the grayling; and it may be used with advantage on a stretcher with droppers of Nos. 7 and 8. The trout casting-line should be used with a rod of about 11 or 12 feet in length, and a reel and reel-line of 30 yards will suffice, as the grayling very rarely exceeds two pounds in weight, and the average in most rivers is not much above one pound.

805. IN FISHING for grayling with the artificial fly, there is not much occasion for concealment, as this fish is very bold and fearless of the presence of man. When hooked there is little necessity for striking, as the hold on the mouth is not in any case good, and the attempt to improve it by striking often ends in breaking the hook away from its hold. At first plenty of liberty should be given, short however of a slack line; but in a very few minutes the attempt may be made to wind-up, and this will seldom be resisted. Grayling do not fight very severely, and are not nearly so violent as the chub; they sometimes, however, are strong enough to break away, because their mouths are so tender and the hooks used so small, on account of the limited size of their jaws, as compared with the trout. But the line is seldom in danger, and if the hook is only securely fixed, the landing of its victim is safe enough.

806. DIPPING FOR GRAYLING may be practised as for chub, but with flies only, avoiding beetles and grasshoppers. It is not, however, a plan often adopted, since the grayling will generally take either the artificial fly or some kind of bottom-bait better than any natural fly, by the dipping process.

SECT. 8.—TROUT-FISHING.

807. THE TACKLE REQUIRED for this most beautiful and exciting sport is described in the third section of this chapter, paragraph 796.

808. THE MODE OF USING IT has also been to a certain extent explained in the next section, at page 241. Some few peculiarities,

however, must be alluded to in the following account of fly-fishing for trout, which differs in many respects from all other kinds of sport practised on the waters of this country with the rod and line. Unlike the mere whipping for bleak, which I have dilated upon as forming an excellent introduction to trout-fishing, the latter requires great caution not to scare the fish, either by the too near presence of the angler, or by the awkward manipulation of his line and flies. The management of the two-handed rod will more properly come under salmon and lake-trout fishing, for although it is sometimes employed in fishing for common trout in large and wide rivers, yet it can scarcely even then be needed, and it certainly loses in delicacy of manipulation much more than it gains in its power of controlling a larger extent of water. Different men adopt various plans of throwing the fly, but it is of little consequence which mode of many is followed, so that the angler has only entire command of his rod and line, *and can do what he likes with his flies.* When this perfection of casting is arrived at, the angler may choose whether he will fish up-stream or down, but he will soon find out by experience that the wind in his back is advantageous to him, and that he will scarcely succeed in any case in casting his fly in the face of a strong breeze. Beyond this no rule will in all cases apply, and the fly-fisher must use his own discretion, founded in great measure upon practical observation, as to the precise mode in which he will reach and fish particular parts of the water that he believes to be the resort of good trout. Indeed it is useless to attempt instructing the tyro by theoretical lessons in the details of an art in which it is certain that nothing but practice can give any degree of proficiency. This is constantly shown even in the professed fly-fisher of two or three seasons' experience, who throws his fly with all the most approved motions, and is beforehand fully convinced that he is the equal of any angler, from John o' Groat's to the Land's-end; but, when he sees fish after fish hooked and landed by some older hand following in his wake, and using the very same fly, with perhaps an inferior rod, is obliged to confess that theory must succumb to delicacy of handling, and that fly-fishing is a practical art, rather than a science attainable in the closet. The various degrees of success mark the difference between the master and the scholar, and show that a life-time may be spent in acquiring the power of deceiving this wary fish, and yet there may be room for improvement; hence it is that so many men of talent have been devotees to the fly-rod, and while they have enjoyed the beauties of nature displayed to them during the prosecution of their sport, they have nevertheless been much more deeply engaged in acquiring the art of fascinating a fish seldom of more than 20 ounces in weight. No one of these men would care for taking trout in any way unaccompanied by difficulty, and attainable without dexterity; but when it is found that by long practice and careful observation a feat can be accomplished which no other means will give, then the man who has mastered the power congratulates himself upon its possession, and is not unnaturally pleased in being enabled to display it by showing what may be done after another's failure. Rivalry is the great zest in sport of all kinds, and the trout taken by an artist, in water which has been well flogged by his inferiors, are thought much more of than those landed where they rise to any bungler's throw. But to proceed to such a general description as may be of some little use to the tyro, I must first observe, that he should confine himself to a single-handed rod with a moderately long line—say, of from 15 to 18 feet, which he should at once draw off the reel, and of which he should hold the gut in his hand near the fly. With this he may proceed to fish the river which is the seat of his intended sport, and may walk quietly along its bank, throwing successively over every yard of likely water; but always fishing first the water nearest to him, and lengthening or shortening his line according to circumstances, such as the breadth of water, the freedom from trees, &c. He will find that he must not throw straight across the river, neither must he allow the fly or flies to be drawn too near his own bank, or he will not be able to lift them cleverly from the water, so as to get such a clear sweep as will enable him to re-cast them with precision and delicacy. Hence, instead of fishing the water under his feet, he will throw his flies so as to take the edge next his own bank at the length of his line; and will thus successively throw over all on his side long before his person is seen; and when he brings his flies up to within 10 or 12 feet of where he is standing, he may lift them, because he has already well tried that portion of the water. But besides the excellence in throwing the fly, there is also a great art in STRIKING AND HOOKING the fish exactly at the right time, and with the proper degree of force. When the trout rises at the fly, which may always be seen by the angler, the rod should be raised with a motion upwards of the wrist only, avoiding, as far as the excitement of the moment will permit, all shoulder or elbow-work, and using just such a degree of wrist-action as may be judged will fasten so sharp an implement as the hook in so soft a substance as the mouth of the trout. Theoretically this may easily be estimated, but practically it will be found that the tyro generally jerks hard enough to strike a blunt hook deep into the jaws of a shark or dolphin. The object of striking at all is to prevent the fish from having time to discover his mistake, the natural consequence of which would be to "blow-out" the fly from his mouth. The fly-fisher, therefore, waits till the moment when the fly is actually within the lips of his victim, and then, with a gentle yet rapid wrist-action, he fixes the hook there. This is much more easily done with a light single-handed rod than with one used by both hands, and hence it is advisable for this reason, as well as on account of the greater facilities in casting with it, to limit the young trout-fisher to its use. IN PLAYING trout when hooked, much depends upon their size; if small, they may be landed immediately; but if above half or three-quarters of a pound, according to the fineness of the tackle, and the gameness of the fish of that locality, it is necessary to yield to his powers for a time, and to give him line for running; always taking care not to give him so much liberty as to enable him to reach adjacent weeds, or to rub his nose against the ground, and thus, in either way, get rid of his hook. When tolerably exhausted, by advancing the butt of the rod and so using its flexibility as a safety-spring, the reel may be gradually wound up until the fish is brought near enough to be dropped quietly into the landing-net, after which it may be considered secure. But whoever has charge of the net must keep well out of sight of the hooked fish until he is effectually exhausted, or he will be sure to make fresh struggles, and often to such an extent as to cause his loss. The fly may easily be cut out of the lip with the penknife, and is generally none the worse for the service it has performed.

809. GOOD TROUT are found in almost all the gravelly and quick-running rivers of Great Britain and Ireland, but they vary much in size and gameness, without which latter quality they are little valued by the fly-fisher. In Scotland they are highly prized, since they afford excellent sport, and are also of good size and flavour.

810. SEA AND LAKE-TROUT, when they take the fly, are to be managed in the same way as salmon, whose size and strength they approach much more nearly than those of the common trout.

SECT. 9.—SALMON-FISHING.

811. FOR THE SALMON, tackle must be employed of a description much stronger than that used for trout; in principle, however, it is nearly similar; and a salmon-rod with its line may be compared, in all respects, to a trout-rod magnified with a slight power of the microscope.

812. THE SALMON-ROD should be from 14 to 20 feet in length, and should be made of three or four lengths, at the discretion of the fisher. The butt is always of ash, the middle piece or pieces of hickory, perfectly free from flaw, and the top-piece of the best bamboo, either rent and glued up or spliced in lengths, which of course only extend from joint to joint; this is better than lancewood, which is apt to make the rod topheavy. Anglers of note differ as to the nature of the joints, which are sometimes made to screw together; at others, with the bare wood of one joint dropping into the brazed ferule terminating its next neighbour; and at others again, by having both ends brazed, so as to oppose brass to brass. In both the latter cases the double-pin, or bent-wire, and silk fastening, as described at page 254, are used, in order to prevent their becoming loose and unattached in the ardour of fishing. The rod should balance pretty evenly at the part where the upper hand grasps it above the reel, which is usually fixed at 18 or 20 inches from the butt-end. These essential characteristics, coupled with those already given at page 266, will suffice for the description of the salmon-rod. The REEL-LINE has also been there described, and is of 80 to 100 yards in length, with the last 20 only tapered down to little more than half its regular size. To this is appended a casting-line made on the same plan as the trout-line, but one-third longer in all its parts, and entirely of gut, which should be of the size called salmon-gut. The FLIES for salmon are described at page 246. When a dropper is used, it is generally appended at about four feet from the end.

813. THESE IMPLEMENTS ARE USED on a scale very different to trout-fishing, and, generally speaking, with less delicacy in proportion to the increase of sweep, and the coarseness of the tackle; but in salmon-fishing so much depends upon the extent of water covered in throwing the fly, that no pains should be spared to acquire this power as fully as possible. It must be remembered that in salmon-fishing, unlike trout-fishing, the river is often too broad for any line to reach nearly over all the good casts, and success is here often obtained solely by the power which some men have of sending their fly into parts which their weaker or less expert rivals cannot possibly cover. With the young angler, the first thing to be done is to

secure the assistance of some resident guide well acquainted with the haunts of the fish, who will give him confidence, if he does nothing else. Without his aid the angler, if unsuccessful, will wander from point to point, and will be unable to do justice to himself, because he has no confidence that there are fish where he is trying for them. Indeed, even the experienced salmon-fisher is all the better for this assistance, if he is on strange water, as though he may give a shrewd general guess as to the most probable casts for fish, he will often pass over good ones, and select those which are much inferior to his rejected localities. He will also get some information as to the probability of his flies suiting the particular river and time, and generally as to the fitness of his arrangements for that precise spot. This knowledge, once obtained, will serve as long as the river continues in the same state; but if rain, or the reverse, should alter the condition of the water, making it either much lower or much higher than before, the tyro will require additional aid from his *quondam* friend. This is known to all salmon-fishers, inasmuch as these fish frequent very different parts of the same river in a low and, again, in a high state of the water; and the flies also will require considerable modification, according to these changing elements. There are, however, some general rules which may be of service, though they by no means apply in all cases. Thus, large rivers usually require larger flies than small streams, which latter will more often be successfully fished with a gaudy but comparatively small fly—that is, if the water is not too clear. The fish, generally lying at the bottom, will scarcely be attracted from the depth of a large river by a small fly, whilst if it is too gaudy, they are scared by its colours when they rise near the surface. Again, in small streams salmon seldom take any fly, except when the water is rather discoloured, and in that state a dusky or dull one is not sufficiently attractive; and when the same condition of water exists in the large rivers a gaudy colour will also be preferred. The size of the fly is of course an index to that of the hook, which is its foundation. Beyond these imperfect hints little aid can be given to the tyro, and he must learn by experience in his own person, or from that of others, the peculiar rules applicable to each locality.

814. THE CASTING is generally from the left shoulder, backwards; after which the line is steadily and rather slowly brought over the right shoulder, with the rod held in both hands, and its point directed upwards and backwards. It is then brought forwards with an increase in speed and force, when, still accelerating the speed, the angler delivers his fly at the spot upon which he wishes it to alight. This throwing from the left shoulder is chiefly useful where there are low bushes or other impediments near the ground behind the angler, under which circumstances the fly must be kept aloft; but sometimes the reverse is the case, and with impending trees and a bare background, the right shoulder or back-casting will avail much better than the rival mode above alluded to; but it is not so manageable with the two-handed rod as with the light single-handed trout-rod, which may be used with as much certainty and facility as the four-in-hand whip. Mr. Stoddart lays it down as a rule that no man can manage properly, without the aid of the wind, a line more than four times the length of his rod, measuring from the fly to its point, and not including that part within the rings. This is certainly much within what is generally considered the extreme length of the salmon-line, and many professed fishers maintain that they can throw nearly twice as far as that length will command. But there is a vast difference between simply throwing a fly and throwing it cleverly and effectually; still I cannot help thinking that Mr. Stoddart has a little understated the power of the salmon-rod and line in good hands, when he limits the range to 35 yards from the spot where the angler stands. This I should say is about the average length of good fly-fishers, but I should think that some few tall and muscular men, who are also adepts, can command nearly 10 yards more, when the air is perfectly still and the situation is favourable to the display of their power and skill. Much must depend upon the tackle, which should be very nicely graduated, and if the cast is intended to be very extensive, one fly only should be used; indeed in salmon-fishing it is seldom that much good is derived from a dropper in addition to the stretcher. When the fly is to be thrown in a wide river of rather sluggish current, it may be directed nearly straight across, especially if the opposite bank can be reached, and the fly, after it has touched the water, may be brought back with a circular sweep, keeping the rod low until it is absolutely necessary to raise it in order to bring home the fly, and working it by gentle fits and starts so as to imitate the movements of a living insect. When, however, there is a considerable stream, the fly may be thrown obliquely downwards, as in trout-fishing, and is then brought back against the stream, and often without that attempt at jerking which must be made in comparatively still water. In all cases the salmon-fisher should keep as

much as possible out of sight; and when he has recourse to wading, he should only enter the water which he has already effectually tried; and when there, he should make as little disturbance in it as he can possibly avoid. In this respect, however, salmon are duller and less wary than common trout, or even than sea-trout; but still they are easily scared, and no one should incautiously run risks which are not absolutely required. The fly is worked very differently to the trout-fly, which must always be on the top of the water to be effectual; whereas the salmon-fly should always be sufficiently under the water to avoid making any ripple as it is drawn towards the thrower, and yet not so deep as to be wholly out of sight. The young angler should not however follow his lure too closely with his eye, or he will be apt to strike when the fish rises at it; whereas, he should always depend upon the sense of touch before he raises his rod, which is the only motion to be adopted. Sharp striking, as in trout-fishing, is wholly reprehensible; and all that is required is the instinctive stand which it is impossible to avoid making against the fish as he seizes the fly to run away with it. Sometimes, however, it is found difficult, or even impossible, to tempt the salmon into actually seizing the fly; they will rise at it again and again, but from some cause or other refuse to take it into their jaws. In this case it must be changed until one is found to suit their fancy, but the change need not be made until the same fly has been tried two or three times unsuccessfully. Patience and perseverance, with skill and science, will here be required, and will always be served in the long-run.

815. In PLAYING the salmon, greater art is required than in the corresponding department of trout-fishing; and, in consequence, nearly one-third of all the fish hooked escape before they are landed. This arises generally from imperfect hooking, but often also from defect in the tackle, which has escaped the notice of the angler. Besides these causes of danger, there are others depending upon the direction taken by the fish, which cannot always be followed by the angler; either from the depth of the water in large rivers, or from mechanical causes in the shape of rocks, woods, &c., where the stream is smaller. When hooked, the first thing to be done is to raise the point of the rod, commonly called "giving the fish the butt," which motion must be carried out with as much power as the fisher considers his tackle will bear; always remembering to give way by releasing the line when the strain is too great for it to bear, and when the fish is resolutely bent upon running. But this exact calculation as to restraining or giving way is sometimes very difficult, especially as the size of the fish is no certain index to his power; nor can the size always be correctly estimated at the first commencement of the struggle, especially by the tyro at this kind of sport. A lively and fresh run fish will appear twice as big as he really is, whilst a large but dull one will sometimes deceive his pursuer into the belief that he is weak and powerless, and then in a fit of desperation he will show his real size and capabilities by breaking away with a long line towing astern. Mr. Stoddart's directions for playing the salmon are so good, that I am tempted to quote them in his own words:—
"Always in running a fish, keep well up to, or, if possible, at right angles with its head. In the event of its taking across the current, instead of stemming or descending it, give the butt without reserve. In the case of a plunge or somerset, slacken line as quickly as possible, but lose no time in recovering it when the danger is over. When fish are plentiful and in the humour to take the fly, it is better to risk the loss of an indifferent-sized individual which you happen to have hooked, than to allow a long range of unfished water to become disturbed through its capricious movements. In this case stint the line and hold on obdurately, but not beyond the presumed strength of your tackle. During the grilse season there are many portions of water, on Tweed especially, where it would be absolute folly in the angler were he to humour the fish to its heart's content. A lively nervous grilse may occasion more alarm among its kind than one is aware of, especially if the water be of the transparent hue it generally bears during the summer and autumnal months. In event, however, of the salmon being few or rising shyly, I would advise that some degree of care and ceremony be taken with what fortune brings to the hook; and that on such occasions more regard be paid to the management of the fish under control than to the non-disturbance of a few yards of stream, where the chances of adding to one's success are at the least extremely doubtful. In these circumstances avoid using undue violence. Should the fish escape, the consciousness of your having done so will only add to the disappointment. There is one precaution particularly to be attended to in respect to a newly run fish, and that is, immediately on hooking it to use a moderate degree of pressure. The salmon will then brave or stem the current, and direct its course upwards; whereas, on tightening the reins, it will frequently do the reverse, and thus not only may a portion of the water in prospect become disturbed, but there is considerable chance, and in some places an

absolute certainty, of the fish, if a large one, making its escape." Baggits generally descend the stream, as a rule, when hooked, and no management will make them leave the current; but as they fight sluggishly, and as their loss is of little consequence, provided they do not run away with a good line, the butt may be shown them pretty early, and with a considerable degree of power.

816. THE GAFF is to be used in the following manner:—When the salmon has been thoroughly exhausted by his efforts to free himself from the hook, in which he has been opposed by the elastic resistance offered by the rod, he is brought near the bank, still keeping the butt-end of the rod well advanced, and the assistant then proceeds to strike the gaff into the shoulder of the fish, or if he uses the single hook, to insert it into the gill-cover. The latter plan is the least injurious to the beauty of the fish, and in skilful hands will answer every purpose. In all cases, however, the assistant should keep out of sight until the angler is satisfied, by the yielding of the fish, that it is safe for him to approach, for a neglect of this precaution leads to the loss of many a fish. The assistant, or gillie, attempting to strike him before he is spent only makes him desperate; and the efforts to escape, which before this were within bounds and under the control of the angler, are now rendered madly violent. This tries even good tackle too far, and either the hook itself or the gut gives way, or else the hold on the fish actually tears away. Tact and experience are the only safe guides in this delicate point, and without them apparent victory often ends in defeat. Instead of the gaff or hook the landing-net is much used; and in the south, as well as in Wales, is perhaps more in vogue than the gaff. The only objection is its size; but as both must be carried by a gillie, since neither can be well managed by the angler himself, this is really of little consequence. If, however, the angler is either unable or unwilling to obtain an assistant, the hook with sliding-stick is the best instrument for the purpose; but even with its aid he must wait until the fish is nearly spent, and must then draw near a low and shelving shore before he can venture to hook him under the gills. Most rivers, however, present these convenient spots at intervals, and the angler should play his fish until he reaches one, let the distance be what it may, if he wishes to run no unnecessary risk. In all cases when landed, the salmon should at once be knocked on the head, and the hook carefully removed with a penknife.

<hr>

CHAP. V.

THE CHIEF RIVERS OF GREAT BRITAIN, AND THE FISH FOUND IN THEM.

SECT. 1.—SALMON RIVERS.

817. SALMON AND SEA-TROUT are found in all the four divisions of the three kingdoms, but chiefly in Scotland and Ireland In Wales there are still some pretty good rivers; and in England they are taken in small numbers in the Wye, the Severn, and the Tamar. The two first of these are however partly Welch; and either of them can be recommended as affording pretty good sport to the angler. The Wye is no doubt the best; the Severn is in progress to become a tolerably good river; but the Tamar is, I believe, becoming daily less and less frequented by this noble fish. For many years past a salmon taken with the fly in the Severn was a rarity, but lately the feat has been tolerably often witnessed, and hopes are held out of making it the headquarters of the southern salmon-fishers.

818. IN WALES, the Conway, the Usk, the Wye, the Dovey, and the Tivey are the salmon-haunts; and are preserved with great care for the lovers of the sport.

819. IN IRELAND, the Shannon is the chief seat of the sport, and affords perhaps more facilities than any other river in the British Isles. Next to it come the Moy and the Erne, the Ban and the Bush, together with the rivers Blackwater and Lee, and the numberless lakes of Killarney, Connamara, &c. Every year, however, these rivers are more cautiously reserved for netting, and the angler, without good introductions, has not the facilities which were formerly at his disposal.

820. IN SCOTLAND, the Tweed almost equals the Shannon in size and opportunities for sport. It however is so much fished as to be to a certain extent spoiled as a salmon river; and it is obliged to hide its naturally higher head before its more northerly rivals, the Shin, the Thurso, and the Esk. The Tay and its tributaries also are first rate salmon rivers, 50,000 fish being taken on the average in each year by the net. The Findhorn comes next, but is more remarkable for trout than for salmon, which are not so plentiful in that river as they

formerly were. The Clyde also has the same repute as a trouting river, but is not much frequented by the salmon. There are numberless smaller rivers throughout Scotland in which salmon are occasionally taken, and in which trout abound; but the above are, I believe, the principal seats of this exciting sport; yet as my experience of their qualities is very limited, I cannot pretend to offer any observations on their comparative merits or demerits.

Sect. 2.—Common Trout and Grayling Rivers.

821. In Scotland, Ireland, and Wales every river swarms with trout in some shape or form, varying from the fine, well-formed fish of the best rivers, down to the small half-starved ones found in the small rivers which descend from the barren sides of the northern granite mountains. It is, however, quite useless to particularise those which afford the best sport, since their name is legion; and I shall pass on to the English scenes of the rod and fly. These are chiefly the following, commencing with those near London, and proceeding more and more in all directions:—The nearest trouting-river to the metropolis is now the Wandle, since the Thames near London has been almost extinguished as a haunt of this fish; the Colne is also close upon London, and both are well stocked with trout of middling-size, but they are strictly preserved, and good fishing is difficult to obtain, except by interest with the proprietors. Buckinghamshire and Oxfordshire afford the higher parts of the Thames, the Ouse, the Colne, and the Wick; Berkshire, Hampshire, and Wiltshire present the Kennet, the Lambourn, the Test, the Itchin, and the Avon; Dorsetshire and Devon are remarkable for the Frome, the Axe, the Charr, the Tamar, the Dart, the Ex, the Tyd, the Teign, and the Tarridge—all of them good trouting rivers; whilst the borders of Wales afford the Teme, the Wye, the Lugg, the Usk, the Froome, and some others remarkable for fine trout and grayling. Proceeding towards the north, we find good trouting-rivers in Derbyshire, Yorkshire, and the adjacent counties of Durham, Cumberland, Westmoreland, and Northumberland, where the Trent, the Erewash, the Dee, the Dove, the Derwent, the Ribble, the Swale, the Wharfe, the Tees, and the Wear employ numberless rods in each succeeding season. To these must be added, as part of the same district, the Coquet, the Tyne, the Aln, and the various lakes of Westmoreland, with their tributaries, all of which are full of fine trout, and may be expected to please the taste of the most fastidious angler, as well as to gratify the eye of the admirers of the beauties of nature.

Sect. 3.—Bottom-Fishing Rivers.

822. The Thames, the Lee, the Medway, and the New River, near London, the Kentish and Dorsetshire Stours, the Ouse, the Cam, the Humber, the Severn, the Warwickshire Avon, and the Isis, are the chief seats of bottom-fishing; together with the preserved artificial waters sprinkled throughout England in the ornamental grounds of our nobility and gentry. They are however so numerous, that an extended list would occupy too great a space, and the limits which can be assigned to the present subject forbid my going further into the scenes of the angler's passion, which is so strongly developed in the votaries of the art as to be only described with propriety by that word. Those who desire more minute information upon this, as well as other points connected with the rod, I must refer to the practical works of Messrs. Stoddart, Blacker, Ephemera, and Salter, who, together, will enlighten him upon all the branches of the subject.

CHAP. VI.

EXPENSES OF FISHING, AND LAWS RELATING TO INLAND FISHERIES.

Sect. 1.—Expenses of Fishing.

823. The chief expense of fishing is the tackle, which may be made to cost any sum from three pounds to almost any amount. The average cost, however, of a complete outfit will not be more than twenty pounds, if due economy is used in procuring fly-making materials. If, however, the angler is extravagant, he may easily spend from £50 to £100 in rods and tackle. Beyond this the expense is only in procuring tickets for fishing, and travelling expenses. The tickets vary from ten pounds to ten shillings per month, according to the nature of the sport and the locality.

T

SECT. 2.—LAWS RELATING TO INLAND FISHERIES.

824. FOR DESTROYING or killing fish in enclosed ground, being private property, a penalty of five pounds, or imprisonment in the House of Correction for a time not exceeding six months.

825. FOR BREAKING INTO an enclosed or private ground, and stealing or destroying the fish, transportation for seven years, and receivers the like punishment.

826. NO PERSONS MAY HAVE IN POSSESSION, or keep, any net, angle piche, or other engine for taking fish, but the makers and sellers thereof, and the owner or renter of a river fishery, except fishermen and their apprentices, legally authorised in navigable rivers; and the owner or occupier of the said river may seize, and keep, and convert to his own use, every net, &c., which he shall discover laid or used, or in the possession of any person thus fishing without his consent.

827. ANY PERSON DAMAGING or intruding, by using nettrices, fish-hooks, or other engines to catch fish, without consent of the owner or occupier, must pay any amount the magistrate or justice orders, provided it exceeds not treble the damages, and be fined, not exceeding ten shillings, for the use of the poor of the parish, or imprisonment in the House of Correction, not exceeding one calendar month, unless he enters into a bond, with one surety, in a sum not exceeding ten pounds not to offend again, and the justice may cut or destroy the nets, &c.

828. IF ANY PERSON UNLAWFULLY OR MALICIOUSLY CUT, break down, or destroy any head or dam of a fish-pond, or unlawfully fish therein, he shall, at the prosecution of the queen, or the owner, be imprisoned three months, or pay treble damages, and after such imprisonment, shall find sureties for seven years for his good behaviour, or remain in prison till he doth.

829. LIMITS OF SIZE OF MESH.—To prevent the fish in the Thames from being improperly destroyed, the 30th of George the Second enacts, that no person shall fish, or endeavour to take fish, in the said river, between London-bridge and Richmond-bridge, with other than lawful nets. For salmon, not less than six inches in the mesh. For pike, jack, perch, roach, chub, and barbel, with a flew or stream net, of not less than three inches in the mesh throughout, with a facing of seven inches, and not more than sixteen fathom long. For shads, not less than two inches and a half in the mesh. For flounders, not less than two inches and a half in the mesh, and not more than sixteen fathom long. For dace, with a single blay-net, of not less than two inches in the mesh, and not more than thirteen fathom long, to be worked by floating only, with a boat and a buoy. For smelts, with a net of not less than one inch and a quarter in the mesh, and not of greater length than sixteen fathom, to be worked by floating only, with a boat and a buoy. Under the penalty of paying and forfeiting the sum of five pounds for every such offence.

830. LIMITS OF SIZE OF FISH.—No fish of any of the sort hereinafter mentioned may be caught in the Thames or Medway, or sold, or exposed to or for sale, if caught in the Thames or Medway:—No salmon of less weight than six pounds. No trout of less weight than one pound. No pike or jack under twelve inches long, from the eye to the length of the tail. No perch under eight inches long. No flounder under seven inches long. No sole under seven inches long. No plaice or dab under seven inches long. No roach under eight inches long. No dace under six inches long. No smelt under six inches long. No gudgeon under five inches long. No whiting under eight inches long. No barbel under twelve inches long. No chub under nine inches long. Under pain to forfeit five pounds for every such offence.

831. LIMITS OF TIME OF TAKING FISH.—Salmon and trout may be taken only from January 25th to September 10th. Pike, jack, perch, roach, dace, chub, barbel, and gudgeon, may be taken between July 1st and March 1st. Bottom-fishing is prohibited in the river Thames, as far as the Corporation of London has jurisdiction, from the 1st of March to the 1st of June. The right of fishing in the sea, and in all rivers where the tide ebbs and flows, is a right common to all the king's subjects.

832. RIGHT OF APPEAL.—Any person or persons considering themselves wronged or aggrieved by any decision against them by the magistrate or justice, may appeal against it at the quarter sessions.

833. PROTECTION OF PRESERVES.—"That no person shall fish with any sort of net, weel, night-hook, or any other device, except by angling; or make use of any net, engine, or device to drive the fish out of any place which shall be staked by order of the Lord Mayor of the City of London for the time being, as conservator aforesaid; and that no person shall take up or remove any stake, burr, boat, or any other thing which shall have been driven down or sunk in any such place as aforesaid, upon pain to forfeit and pay, from time to time, the sum of five pounds for every offence or breach of any part of this order."—City Ordinances, Item 44.